T0329164

PUBLIC-PRIVATE PARTNERSHIPS FOR INFRASTRUCTURE

SECOND EDITION

By the same authors:

Yescombe, E.R., *Public-Private Partnerships: Principles of Policy & Finance* (Oxford: Butterworth-Heinemann 2007); translated into Chinese, Croatian, Polish and Russian.
- 'Public-Private Partnerships' in John R. Bartle, W. Bartley Hildreth & Justin Marlowe (eds.), *Management Policies in Local Government Finance* (ICMA Green Book Series, International City/County Management Association, 6th edition 2012).
- 'PPPs and Project Finance' in Piet de Vries & Etienne B. Yehoue (eds.), *The Routledge Companion to PPPs* (Oxford: Routledge 2013).
- *Principles of Project Finance* (San Diego CA: Academic Press, 1st edition 2002, 2nd edition 2014); translated into Chinese, Farsi, Japanese, Hungarian, Polish and Russian.
- *Public-Private Partnerships in Sub-Saharan Africa: Case Studies for Policymakers* (Dar-es-Salaam: Uongozi Institute 2017).

Farquharson, Edward, Clemencia Torres de Mästle, & E.R. Yescombe with Javier Encinas, *Public-Private Partnerships in Emerging Markets: How to Engage With the Private Sector* (Washington DC: World Bank/PPIAF 2011); translated into Chinese and French.

E.R. Yescombe is an independent consultant on project finance and public-private partnerships, advising investors on financing for PPP projects, as well as public-sector entities on PPP policy issues, project procurement, contracting and PPP contract management. He was formerly head of project finance for Bank of Tokyo-Mitsubishi in London. See www.yescombe.com for further information.

Edward Farquharson is an adviser in the European PPP Expertise Centre (a division of the European Investment Bank) with a background in the public and private sectors in financing and developing PPP projects and policies world-wide.

PUBLIC-PRIVATE PARTNERSHIPS FOR INFRASTRUCTURE

PRINCIPLES OF POLICY AND FINANCE

SECOND EDITION

E. R. YESCOMBE

EDWARD FARQUHARSON

Butterworth-Heinemann
An imprint of Elsevier

Butterworth-Heinemann is an imprint of Elsevier
The Boulevard, Langford Lane, Kidlington, Oxford OX5 1GB, United Kingdom
50 Hampshire Street, 5th Floor, Cambridge, MA 02139, United States

Notices
Knowledge and best practice in this field are constantly changing. As new research and experience broaden our
understanding, changes in research methods, professional practices, or medical treatment may become necessary.

Practitioners and researchers must always rely on their own experience and knowledge in evaluating and using
any information, methods, compounds, or experiments described herein. In using such information or methods
they should be mindful of their own safety and the safety of others, including parties for whom they have a
professional responsibility.

To the fullest extent of the law, neither the Publisher nor the authors, contributors, or editors, assume any liability
for any injury and/or damage to persons or property as a matter of products liability, negligence or otherwise,
or from any use or operation of any methods, products, instructions, or ideas contained in the material herein.

British Library Cataloguing-in-Publication Data
A catalogue record for this book is available from the British Library

Library of Congress Cataloging-in-Publication Data
A catalog record for this book is available from the Library of Congress

ISBN: 978-0-08-100766-2

For Information on all Butterworth-Heinemann publications
visit our website at https://www.elsevier.com/books-and-journals

www.elsevier.com • www.bookaid.org

Publisher: Candice Janco
Acquisition Editor: Scott Bentley
Editorial Project Manager: Susan Ikeda
Production Project Manager: Anusha Sambamoorthy
Cover Designer: Matthew Limbert

Typeset by MPS Limited, Chennai, India

Contents

I
INTRODUCTION

1. Overview

2. What Are Public-Private Partnerships?

3. Cash Flow and Investment Analysis

II

THE PUBLIC-SECTOR PERSPECTIVE

9. The PPP Decision—Affordability, Budgeting and Reporting

10. PPP Procurement

III

PPP RISK ANALYSIS AND ALLOCATION

11. Risk Analysis—Theory and Methodologies

12. Risk Allocation—Construction Phase

13. Risk Allocation—Operation Phase

14. The Rôle of Insurance

IV

THE PPP CONTRACT

15. Service-Fee Payment Mechanism

V

THE PRIVATE-SECTOR PERSPECTIVE

20. Sponsors and Other Investors

21. Project Finance and PPPs

22. Project-Finance Debt—Sources and Procedures

23. Financial Structuring

24. Macroeconomic Risks and Hedging

25. Lenders' Cash-Flow Controls, Security and Enforcement

26. Debt Refinancing and Equity Sale

VI

ALTERNATIVE MODELS—SUMMING UP

27. Alternative Models

28. PPPs—For and Against

List of Figures

List of Tables

PART I

INTRODUCTION

CHAPTER

1

Overview

Public-private partnerships (PPPs) have become increasingly popular as a way of procuring and maintaining public-sector infrastructure, in sectors that include transport (such as roads, bridges, tunnels, railways, ports and airports), social infrastructure (such as hospitals, schools, prisons and social housing), public utilities (such as water supply, wastewater treatment and waste disposal), government offices and other accommodation, and specialised services such as communication networks or defence equipment.

This book reviews the general policy issues that arise for the public sector in considering whether to adopt the PPP procurement route, and the specific application of this policy approach in PPP contracts. This book also offers a systematic and integrated approach to financing PPPs within this public-policy framework. Policy and finance are inextricably entangled in PPPs, so the public sector must develop PPP policies taking account of financing constraints, and be careful to avoid entering into PPP arrangements whose financial implications are misunderstood, or not understood at all, thus undermining the benefit of the PPP. Similarly, the policy background and drivers for public-sector decisions are also often quite unclear to private-sector investors and lenders.

Structuring PPPs is complex because of the need to reconcile the aims of the large number of parties involved—on the private-sector side, there are investors, lenders and companies providing construction and operational services; on the public-sector side, there are public-sector entities creating, implementing and overseeing PPP policies as well as those actually procuring and managing the PPP contract, not forgetting the general public who use the facilities that a PPP provides. Most of these parties need to have a basic understanding of policy and finance issues, and how their part of the project is linked to, and affected by, such issues.

Reflecting the authors' own practical experience while sitting on the public- and private-sector sides of the table, this book is intended to provide a guide to both the general policy principles and the related financing issues that can cause the most difficulty in PPP negotiations and in the long-term management of PPP contracts. It serves both as an introduction for those who are new to the subject, whether in the academic, public-sector, investment and finance or contracting fields, and as an aide-mémoire for those developing PPP policies and negotiating and managing PPPs. No prior knowledge of PPPs or financing is assumed or required. The views expressed by the authors are their own and do not reflect those of any institution for whom they work.

This book is divided into six parts.

PART 1: INTRODUCTION

- Chapter 2 defines PPPs and reviews their place in the provision of public infrastructure as a whole.
- Chapter 3 provides a basic introduction to cash-flow and investment analysis, which are at the heart of understanding the financial benefits, costs and structuring of PPPs for both the public- and private-sector parties.

PART 2: THE PUBLIC-SECTOR PERSPECTIVE

This part covers the process of selecting, appraising and procuring PPP projects from the public-sector point of view:

- Chapter 4 sets out the policy, legal and institutional frameworks behind a PPP programme.
- Chapter 5 provides an initial summary of the PPP project cycle.
- Chapter 6 discusses public-sector project management up to the end of the procurement process.
- Chapter 7 deals with the initial needs assessment, project definition and selection; logically, these processes come before the decision to procure a particular project as a PPP, the processes for which are set out in the following chapters.
- Chapter 8 explains the issues that arise when considering whether a PPP project provides value for money.
- Chapter 9 looks at the further key issues of a PPP project's affordability, budgeting for PPPs and financial/statistical reporting requirements.
- Chapter 10 describes the procurement process for a PPP.

PART 3: RISK ANALYSIS AND ALLOCATION

Risk allocation between the public and private sectors lies at the heart of the PPP process.

- Chapter 11 summarises the theory behind risk allocation in PPPs, and the main risk categories.

- Chapter 12 covers risk allocation during the construction phase, and Chapter 13 during the operation phase of a PPP project.
- Chapter 14 explains how insurance is used to mitigate risks in both the construction and the operation phases.

PART 4: THE PPP CONTRACT

This part covers the main elements of a PPP contract, the support that the public sector may provide for such contracts and public-sector management of a PPP contract.

- Chapter 15 describes the payment mechanisms and performance incentives usually found in a PPP contract.
- Chapter 16 explains how changes in the original assumptions behind the PPP can be accommodated.
- Chapter 17 covers termination of a PPP contract, either during or at the end of its term, and the hand-back of the asset to the public sector.
- Chapter 18 describes the different forms of public-sector support for PPP contracts.
- Chapter 19 sets out good practice for public-sector contract management during the life of a PPP.

PART 5: THE PRIVATE-SECTOR PERSPECTIVE

This part moves to the other side of the table and covers PPPs from the private-sector point of view.

- Chapter 20 sets out the different categories of equity investors (*i.e.* shareholders) in PPP projects, how they organise themselves to bid for, develop and manage such projects.
- Chapter 21 describes project-financing techniques, and why these are used to raise debt for PPPs.
- Chapter 22 looks at the sources of, and procedures for, raising project finance.
- Chapter 23 explains how the different elements of the financial jigsaw are fitted together to create a financing plan.
- Chapter 24 deals with the important topic of financial hedging, and the effect of interest-rate movements, inflation and changes in currency exchange rates on a PPP project and its financing.
- Chapter 25 describes how lenders control and take security over a PPP project.
- Chapter 26 considers ways of sharing the benefits of financial 'windfalls', derived from debt refinancing or sale of the equity investment, between the public and private sectors.

Part 6: Alternative Models—Summing Up

- Chapter 27 reviews various alternative models for public-sector infrastructure procurement, compared to the 'standard' PPP models considered elsewhere in this book.
- Finally, Chapter 28 reviews the complex arguments for and against using PPPs as one method of delivering public infrastructure investment.

In addition to details of references in the text, the References and Further Reading provide some further background reading, both about aspects of PPPs generally, and specific countries' PPP programmes.

Financial and other terms used in this book are defined and cross-referenced in the Glossary and Abbreviations. Dynamic spreadsheets that were used to construct a number of the tables in this book can be downloaded from www.yescombe.com.

Although this book is entirely self-contained, it can be usefully read in conjunction with E.R. Yescombe's *Principles of Project Finance* (San Diego, CA: Academic Press, 2nd edition, 2014), which deals in more detail with some of the topics only covered briefly here, in particular process-plant projects (such as power stations), project-finance loan negotiation and the use of project finance in emerging markets.

In conclusion, it might be thought that this book concentrates too much on detailed process rather than broad policy. But in the real world, it is all too easy for the potential benefits of a PPP programme to be eroded by failures of detailed implementation. Similarly, the credibility of some academic and political discussion on PPPs is eroded by a lack of understanding of how policy translates into practice. The old aphorism, quoted in *Principles of Project Finance*—'the devil is in the detail'—is equally applicable to the PPP field.

What Are Public-Private Partnerships?

§2.1 INTRODUCTION

This chapter examines the reasons for private involvement in public infrastructure (§2.2), defines what is meant by a PPP (§2.3) and traces PPPs' historical development and current structures (§2.4). The place of PPPs in the provision of public infrastructure is considered (§2.5). Finally, some statistics on the scale of the worldwide market for PPPs are provided (§2.6).

§2.2 PUBLIC INFRASTRUCTURE AND THE PRIVATE SECTOR

Public infrastructure can be defined as facilities that are necessary for the functioning of the economy and society. These are thus not an end in themselves, but a means of supporting a nation's economic and social activity, including facilities that are ancillary to these functions, such as public-sector offices or other accommodation. Broadly speaking, public infrastructure can be divided into:

- 'economic' infrastructure, such as transport facilities and utility networks (for water, sewage, electricity, etc.), *i.e.* infrastructure considered essential for day-to-day economic activity; and
- 'social' infrastructure, such as schools, hospitals, libraries and prisons, *i.e.* infrastructure considered essential for the structure of society.

7

A distinction can also be made between 'hard' infrastructure, whether economic or social, primarily involving provision of buildings or other physical facilities, and 'soft' infrastructure, involving the provision of services, either for economic infrastructure (*e.g.* street cleaning) or for social infrastructure (*e.g.* education and training, social services).

There is probably universal agreement that the state has to play a rôle in the provision of public infrastructure, on the grounds that:

- The private sector cannot take account of 'externalities'—*i.e.* general economic and social benefits—and therefore public-sector intervention is required.
- Without such intervention, infrastructure that has to be freely available to all ('public goods') will not be built, especially where this involves networks, such as roads, or services, such as street lighting.
- Competitive provision of infrastructure may not be efficient, but at the same time monopoly provision requires some form of public control.
- Even where competition is possible, the public sector should still provide 'merit goods', *i.e.* those that would otherwise be underprovided (such as schools, as the rich could pay for private schools but the poor would get no education).
- Infrastructure requires a high initial investment on which only a very long-term return can be expected. It may be difficult to raise private capital for this investment without some public-sector support.
- Some of the risks in the delivery of infrastructure are more efficiently managed by the state or may simply not be investible by the private sector.

It could thus be argued that infrastructure should be provided by the public sector if competitive market pricing would distort behaviour or lead to loss of socio-economic benefits. But history suggests that there are two ways for the state to do this—either by direct provision or by the facilitation of private-sector provision (whether through regulation, tax subsidy or similar incentives, or by contract). As discussed below, the use of private capital to finance economic infrastructure (*e.g.* for transport) is of long standing. Equally, it was generally only during the 19th and 20th centuries that the state took over responsibility, mainly from religious or private charity, for the provision of much social infrastructure (*e.g.* for schools and hospitals). Indeed, it may be said that private provision of a large proportion of public infrastructure was the historical norm until recently—but the definition of 'necessary' public infrastructure has clearly widened over the last couple of centuries. PPPs may therefore be considered a modern way of facilitating private provision to help meet an increased demand for public infrastructure.

§2.3 PUBLIC-PRIVATE PARTNERSHIPS

The term 'public-private partnership' appears to have originated in the United States in the early 20th century, initially relating to joint public- and private-sector delivery of educational programmes, and then in the 1950s in connection with similar approaches in the utilities sector (*cf.* §27.5.3). By the 1960s the term came into wider use in reference to public-private joint ventures for urban renewal. It is also used in the United States to refer to publicly-funded provision of social services by non-public-sector bodies, often from the voluntary (not-for-profit) sector, as well as public funding of private-sector research and development in fields such as technology. In the international-development field the term is used when referring to joint government, aid agency and private-sector initiatives to combat diseases such as AIDS and malaria, introduce improvements in farming methods or promote economic development generally. Most of these can be described as 'policy-based' or 'programme-based' PPPs.

However, the subject of this book is what may be called 'project-based' or 'contract-based' PPPs, a more recent development. (Although some urban-renewal PPPs are also project-specific, they do not involve the same long-term relationship.) PPPs as defined here have the following key elements:

- a long-term contract (a 'PPP contract') between a public-sector party and a private-sector party;
- the design, construction and operation of public infrastructure (the 'facility') by the private-sector party;
- the use of private-sector capital to finance all or a substantial part of the facility's construction;
- payments over the life of the PPP contract to the private-sector party for the use of the facility, made either by the public-sector party or by the general public as users of the facility or both;
- the facility remaining in public-sector ownership, or reverting to public-sector ownership at the end of the PPP contract;
- some form of risk sharing between the public- and private-sector parties; and
- the provision of a public service.

(In some cases, a PPP contract may involve major upgrading of existing infrastructure rather than a 'green-field' construction.)

Private-sector acquisition or management of existing public infrastructure without any major new capital investment or upgrading is not considered to be a PPP as defined here. Similarly, private-sector provision of services that involves no significant investment in fixed assets (and hence no need for private-sector financing) falls into the category of 'outsourcing' rather than PPPs, although obviously the boundary is not precise as a variety of services are often associated with the provision of infrastructure (*cf.* §15.2). Nor is a PPP a simple joint-venture investment between the public and private sectors, unless this is also linked to a PPP contract (*cf.* §27.4). Also, this book does not deal in detail with smaller PPPs, usually at a municipal level, in sectors such as parking garages; this smaller end of the market follows the same general principles, but is usually less elaborate in contract form and financing (*cf.* §21.6), unless projects can be bundled together (*cf.* §7.5.1).

The public-sector party to a PPP contract (the 'contracting authority')[1] may be a central-government department, a state or regional government, a local (county/municipal) government, a public agency or other public-sector entity.

---

[1] Also known by a variety of other terms, such as the 'public entity', 'public party', 'government procuring entity', 'institution', 'grantor', 'procuring authority', 'public authority' or just the 'authority'.

The private-sector party is usually a special-purpose company (the 'project company'),[2] created by private-sector investors specifically to undertake the PPP contract.

The entities (usually companies) on the private-sector side that put the PPP bid together and, if successful, become the key investors in the project company, are known as the 'sponsors'.[3]

It should be noted that the relationship between the public and private parties in the types of PPP covered in this book is not a partnership in the legal sense, but is contractual, being based on the terms of a PPP contract. 'Partnership' is largely a political slogan in this context.

An important terminological distinction needs to be made between what it being *built* (i.e. the physical public-infrastructure assets or 'facility', as mentioned above), what is being *procured* (i.e. the infrastructure asset and the services it provides) and *how* this bundle of assets and services is procured and delivered. For the purposes of this book, the bundle of assets and services is referred to as the 'project' and its procurement using a PPP arrangement as a 'PPP' or 'PPP project'. This is important because the decision about how a project is best procured is distinct from the decision about what project to procure.

There are a number of alternative names for PPPs:

- P3, used in North America;
- Private Finance Initiative (PFI), a term originating in Britain, but also used in Japan and Malaysia;
- Private Participation in Infrastructure (PPI), used in Korea[4];
- P-P Partnership (to avoid confusion with PPP meaning 'purchasing power parity', a method of comparing currency exchange rates to reflect the real costs of goods and services in different countries);
- Public-Private Partnerships for Infrastructure (PPPI), the term used in this book's title, which helps to avoid the ambiguity of the term PPP as discussed above.

But over time, the term PPP has become more universally accepted. Governments may use other terms to label particular parts of their own PPP programmes or types of PPP. AFP (Alternative Financing and Procurement) in Ontario is one such example and, more recently, the British Treasury has modified and relabelled its PFI policy as 'PF2'[5] to signify a break from, and changes to, its previous PFI programme.

In some countries, 'PPP' is more narrowly defined as those arrangements where the public-sector party is the entity that mainly pays for the service and 'concession' is used to

---

[2] Again known by a variety of names, including the 'private party', 'contractor' or 'SPV'. (SPV = special-purpose vehicle; *cf.* §20.6.1.)

[3] The term sponsor is sometimes, confusingly, used to refer to the contracting authority because it is 'sponsoring' the project, but it is not so used in this book.

[4] The term PPI is also used by the World Bank, but includes both PPPs and privatised or private-sector owned infrastructure. This is the basis for the World Bank's PPI database (see References and Further Reading).

[5] This is the full name of the programme, not an abbreviation.

describe those PPP-type arrangements where the general public as users pay for the service. This is often a product of history and of the laws that may govern these different arrangements (such as in Brazil and France). However, in this book, 'PPP' will be used for the general concepts covering both models. These models are discussed in more detail in the following section.

PPPs are often confused with privatisations. Perhaps the two most fundamental differences are firstly that, unlike a privatisation, the ownership of the asset is not transferred to the private sector and secondly that the contracting authority remains ultimately responsible for the public provision of the service provided by the PPP. Governments launching a PPP programme should communicate this difference clearly, as not doing so may lead to confusion and opposition later on (*cf.* §4.4, §28.2, §28.13).

§2.4 DEVELOPMENT AND STRUCTURES

There are a number of different approaches to the introduction of private financing into the provision of public infrastructure. Concessions have a long history (§2.4.1), as do their subtype, franchises (§2.4.2). Power-purchase agreements (PPAs) (§2.4.3) provided the modern contractual (§2.4.4) and financing (§2.4.5) framework for PPPs—both for concessions (§2.4.6) and availability PPPs (§2.4.7).

§2.4.1 Concessions

Although the term PPP is a new one (at least in the current context), the concept of using private capital to provide public infrastructure is very old. In France, the construction of canals with private-sector capital began in the 17th century. In 18th- and early 19th-century Britain, groups of local magnates formed turnpike trusts which borrowed money from private investors to repair the roads, and repaid this debt by charging tolls. Most of London's bridges were also financed by similar bridge trusts until the mid-19th century, and in the late 19th century, the Brooklyn Bridge in New York was also built with private-sector capital.

This type of PPP is known as a 'concession': that is, a 'user pays' model in which a private-sector entity (the 'project company'[6]) is allowed to charge the general public 'service fees'[7] for using the facility. These service fees may also be referred to as 'user charges' or, in the case of a road concession, 'tolls'. User charges reimburse the concessionaire for the cost of building and operating the facility, which usually reverts to public-sector control at the end of the concession period. Apart from roads and related facilities, concessions were used in many countries in the 19th and early 20th centuries to construct facilities such as water supply and wastewater treatment networks.

[6] Also known as the 'concessionaire' in this context.

[7] The term 'service fees' is used in this book to mean payments to the project company for the use of the facility either by users or a contracting authority.

The rôle of the public sector in concessions is:

- to establish the framework within which the concessionaire operates, usually under a general concession law or legislation specific to the particular concession;
- to choose a concessionaire; and
- to regulate the detailed requirements for the construction and operation of the facility, usually through a concession agreement signed between the contracting authority and the concessionaire.

Although the use of concessions for constructing new infrastructure faded away in many countries after the 19th century, as the rôle of the state expanded, franchises (see below) continued to be important in France and a number of countries in Africa and Latin America. The use of concessions began to increase again towards the end of the 20th century, as interest started to grow in this and other types of PPP as an alternative funding model.

§2.4.2 Franchises and *Affermage*

A variant of concessions is the franchise, or to use the less-ambiguous French term, *affermage*. A franchise is the right to exploit an already-constructed facility, *i.e.* it is similar to a concession but without the initial construction phase. The franchisee (equivalent to a concessionaire) makes a lump-sum payment to the contracting authority in return for this right, or pays a share of the revenues. 'Farming', in its older English meaning (*e.g.* 'tax farming') means the same as the French term but has largely gone out of use in this sense. 'Lease' is also used, but this is misleading given its other meanings. In European Union terminology a franchise is known as a 'service concession', while a concession as defined in this book—*i.e.* involving the construction of new infrastructure—is known as a 'works concession'.

A franchise is not considered to be a PPP as previously defined, because it does not involve the provision or upgrade of infrastructure, but only its operation.[8] However, the contractual and financial basis is similar in some respects (and hence is covered in this book). New types of franchise have also evolved, such as in the British railway sector.

§2.4.3 Power-Purchase Agreements

PPAs, developed in the United States in the 1980s, provided the template for modern PPP contracts. PPAs began after the 1978 Private Utility Regulatory Policies Act (PURPA), which encouraged the construction of cogeneration plants, whose electricity could be sold to the regulated power utilities. These utilities' long-term commitment under a PPA to purchase the power enabled the finance to be raised for the cogeneration plant, using the PPAs as security. PPAs arrived in Europe in the early 1990s, with the privatisation of the British electricity industry; this encouraged a separation between private-sector companies involved in power generation and those involved in distribution, and the development of

---

[8] Although *affermage* contracts may include an obligation to make some capital investments from the facility's cash flow.

'independent power projects' selling their power output to the distribution companies so increasing competition in power generation. Under a PPA, the investors are paid a 'tariff' split between:

- an *availability charge* (also known as a 'capacity charge') for making their power station available to provide power to the utility: this covers the capital expenditure involved in building the power station and its fixed operating expenditure; and
- a *usage charge* (also known as a 'variable charge') for the marginal cost of generating power as and when required by the electricity utility: this mainly covers the cost of the fuel used to generate the electricity (*e.g.* natural gas).

A key aspect of a PPA is therefore that the project company that builds and operates the power station does not take any risk on whether the electricity which it has the capacity to generate is actually needed: this 'despatch' risk remains with the utility, which pays the availability charge whether it uses any power or not. The project company is, however, responsible for completing the power station on time and to budget, and thereafter for the operating performance of the power station. If for any reason it is not capable of generating the level of power committed, the availability charge will be reduced accordingly. This is obviously unlike the position of a concessionaire, who is only paid if people use the facility. PPAs are now widely used in many parts of the world for both conventional and renewable power projects.

§2.4.4 BOO—BOT—BTO—DBFO

The PPA as first developed was a 'build-own-operate' (BOO) contract between private-sector parties, whereby the ownership of the power facility remains with its investors at the end of the contract term. However, it soon became apparent that a similar structure could be used for developing public-sector projects. The concept of the 'build-operate-transfer' (BOT) contract was first developed in Turkey; this was also intended for power generation, but with the key differences that the off-taker (purchaser) of the power would be a public-sector entity (the state power utility), and that at the end of the contract, ownership of the power station could pass from its investors to the off-taker (usually for a nominal or zero cost) and hence to the public sector.

It was but a short step from the BOT model to the 'build-transfer-operate' (BTO) contract, where ownership is transferred to the contracting authority on completion of construction, and the 'design-build-finance-operate' (DBFO) contract, under which legal ownership of the facility remains with the contracting authority throughout the contract; the private-sector's interest in the project is based solely on the contractual rights to operate the facility and to receive revenues from the off-taker for doing so, rather than on ownership of the physical assets.

In developing countries, BOT, BTO and DBFO contracts provided a means for cash-constrained state power utilities to finance investment in more efficient plant, without relinquishing control over either the generation of the power (since the off-taker decides when the power from the facility is to be despatched, *i.e.* when the facility is brought into use to generate power), the delivery of power to the consumer, or the cost of power to the consumer—in other words, the private sector delivers the service on behalf of the public sector, but under public-sector control.

§2.4.5 Project Finance

The other vital factor that enabled the PPA model to be developed was the financing technique known as 'project finance', which provides the high ratio of long-term debt financing required for such projects (*cf.* §21.5). Although such techniques had existed previously in the natural-resources sector, the particular project-finance structures used to finance PPAs provided the basis for financing all types of PPPs.

An important aspect of project finance is lack of recourse to the project sponsors (*i.e.* they do not usually guarantee the debt raised by the project company), as well as the transfer of the risks mentioned above from the project company to subcontractors. Figure 2.1 shows how this risk transfer fits within the main building blocks for a

FIGURE 2.1   Project finance for a power-purchase agreement

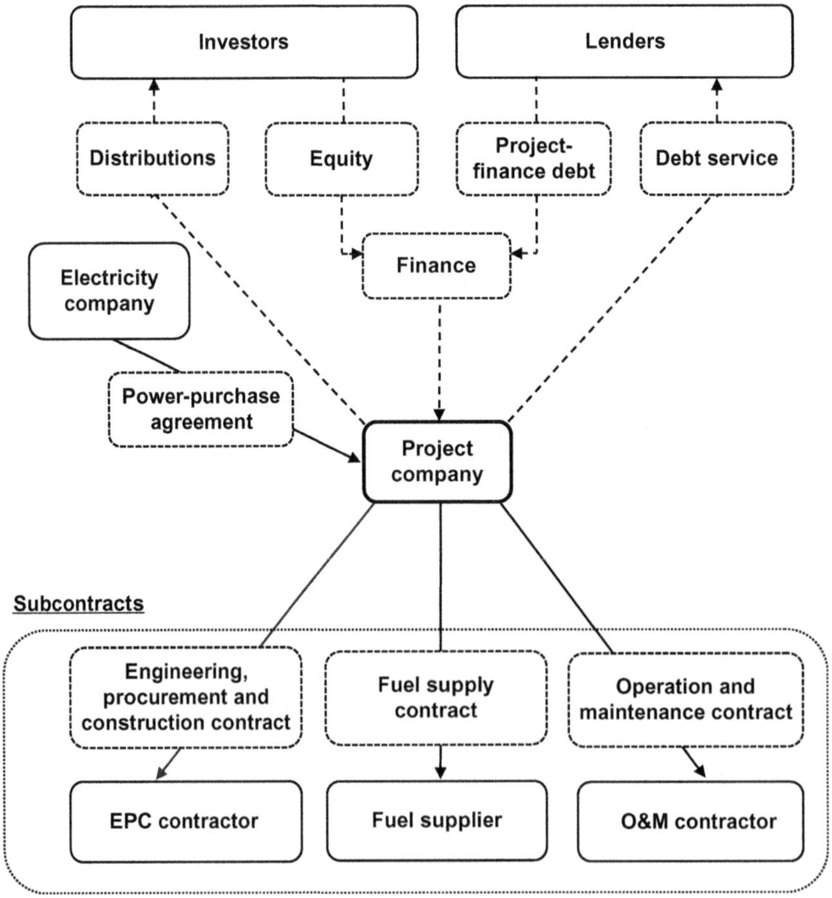

power-generation project. (The arrows show the direction of cash flows—contract cash flows are shown with solid lines and financing cash flows with dotted lines.) The main components in the structure are:

- a project company, owned by private-sector investors;
- a PPA with an electricity-distribution company (which may be a public- or private-sector entity), with payments based on availability and usage charges as discussed above;
- financing for the project's capital costs ('capex') through shareholder equity investment and project-finance debt;
- an 'engineering, procurement and construction' (EPC) subcontract, under which the EPC subcontractor agrees to deliver a completed and fully-equipped power facility to the project company to the required specification, at a fixed price and schedule; this type of contract to provide a complete facility at a fixed price is known as a 'turnkey' contract;
- where relevant, a fuel-supply subcontract, under which, say, natural gas is provided to the project company to fuel the power facility's turbines;
- an operation and maintenance (O&M) subcontract, under which an O&M contractor agrees to operate and maintain the facility on behalf of the project company; and
- surplus cash flow after payment of fuel and operating costs ('opex') is used, firstly, for payments of interest and repayments of loan principal ('debt service') to the lenders, and then to give a return on investment to the equity investors ('distributions').

The subcontractors have thus taken over many of the key risks that the contracting authority had passed to the project company, *e.g.* as to the outturn capital cost of the power station and its operating costs (other than fuel costs).

§2.4.6 Project Finance for Concessions

The modern use of project-financing techniques for concessions, influenced by the BOT model, began with a number of transport projects in the 1980s including Eurotunnel—the Channel Tunnel project between Britain and France—in 1987 (albeit in the event this was a financially disastrous project), and the Dartford Bridge (across the Thames Estuary east of London) around the same time. It has to be said that neither of these were 'typical' projects, but the lessons learned from them have been widely applied to financing concessions since then, most commonly in toll-road projects.

Figure 2.2 shows the main contractual and financing building blocks for a toll-road concession. The resemblance to the 'spider diagram' as in Figure 2.1 for the power project is evident, the most important difference being the source of revenues (from tolls). Here the key elements in the structure are:

- a project company, owned by private-sector investors;
- a 'concession agreement' (a standard name for this type of PPP contract) with the contracting authority that allows the collection of tolls from road users;

FIGURE 2.2   Project finance for a toll-road concession

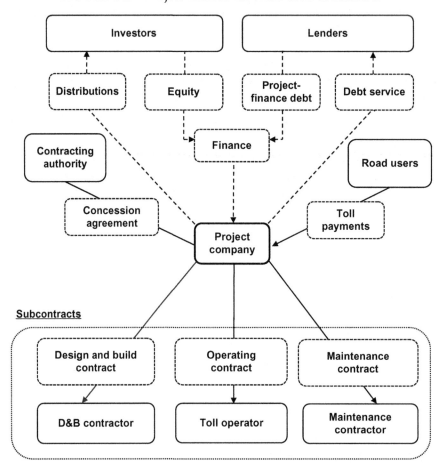

- financing for the project's capex through shareholder equity and project-finance debt;
- a 'design and build' (D&B) subcontract, under which the D&B subcontractor agrees to design and construct the completed road and related works (*e.g.* toll booths) to the required specification, at a fixed price and schedule;
- an operating subcontract, under which a toll operation company provides services, such as manning the toll booths, minor repairs and accident management, to the project company;
- a maintenance subcontract, under which a maintenance company provides road-maintenance services to the project company; and
- surplus cash flow after opex (consisting mainly of payments to the toll operator and maintenance contractor, being used by the project company, firstly, for debt service, and then to pay distributions to the investors).

§2.4.7 Availability PPPs

In 1992 the British government launched the PFI programme, with the aim of bringing private finance into the provision of public infrastructure. This really began from the rediscovery of concessions in the 1980s, as mentioned above. The first wave of projects, in 1994, therefore involved construction and operation of new roads. But since the scope for toll roads in Britain was limited, instead of the 'user pays' principle of a concession, the PFI model introduced the concept of payment by the contracting authority instead. Initially, however, payments from the contracting authority were still based on usage by drivers, through so-called shadow tolls, *i.e.* a fixed schedule of payments by the contracting authority per driver/km (*cf.* §15.5.4).

The next stage in the development of the PFI model was the use of PFI contracts for the provision of infrastructure where usage risk inherently cannot be transferred to the private sectors, such as prisons, schools and hospitals. In these cases, the structure of the contract is still based on the PPA, in that the private-sector investor is paid by the contracting authority for 'availability', *i.e.* constructing the facility to the required specification and making it available for the period of the PFI contract, as well as for provision of services such as maintenance, cleaning and catering. The service fee in this instance is often referred to as a 'unitary charge' (or 'unitary payment'). This underlines an important feature in that the payment cannot be split into different parts to pay for the different costs of the project such as the financing or maintenance costs, sometimes referred to as the concept of 'separability'. If an element of the service fee was always paid to cover the financing costs irrespective of (*i.e.* separable from) the availability of the service, then the important mechanism of having private capital at risk to performance would be lost. For the purposes if this book, this model of PPP is referred to as an 'availability PPP'.[9]

Figure 2.3 shows the main building blocks for a school project in an availability PPP. The resemblance to a PPA is evident. Here the key elements in the structure are:

- a project company, owned by private-sector investors;
- a 'project agreement' (a standard name for an availability PPP contract) with the contracting authority, under which the project company is paid for the provision of the school building and associated services;
- financing of the project's capex through shareholder equity and project-finance debt;
- a D&B subcontract, under which the D&B subcontractor agrees to design and construct the school to the required specification, at a fixed price and to a fixed schedule;
- a 'soft' facilities-management (FM) subcontract, under which a service company provides services such as security, cleaning and catering for the school ('soft FM');
- a 'hard' FM subcontract, under which a maintenance company (or the original D&B contractor) provides building-maintenance services ('hard FM'); and
- cash flow after opex—mainly payments on the FM subcontracts—is used, firstly, for debt service, and then to pay distributions to the investors.

---

[9] Also known as the 'PFI model', 'build-transfer-lease' (BTL) in Korea, or just as a PPP in countries where this term relates only to availability PPPs, distinguishing from concessions that are not referred to as PPPs (*cf.* §2.3).

FIGURE 2.3   Project finance for a PPP school project

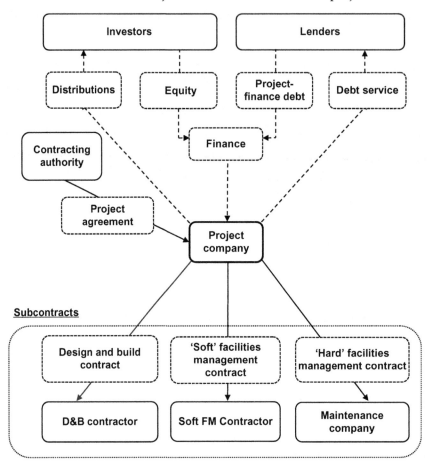

An availability PPP (like a concession) is thus an alternative to procurement of the facility by the public sector ('public-sector procurement'[10]), using funding from tax revenues or public borrowing. In a typical public-sector procurement (known as 'design-bid-build'), the contracting authority sets out the specifications and design of the facility, calls for bids on the basis of this detailed design and pays for construction of the facility by a private-sector contractor. The contracting authority has to fund the full cost of construction, including any cost overruns. The contracting authority may undertake FM itself, or engage a private-sector company to do so under a separate contract.

On the other hand, as with PPPs generally, an availability PPP is based on the delivery of a service: the contracting authority specifies its requirements in terms of 'outputs', which set out the public services that the facility is intended to provide, but does not specify how these are to be provided. It is then left to the private sector to design, finance,

---

[10] The term 'public procurement' will be used for procurement of a PPP by a contracting authority.

build and operate the facility to meet these long-term output specifications. The project company receives service fees over the life of the PPP contract (perhaps 25 years on average) on a pre-agreed basis, which are intended to repay the financing costs and give a return to investors. The service fees are subject to deductions for failure to meet the output specifications, and there is generally no extra allowance for cost overruns that occur during construction or in operation of the facility.

The result of this PPP approach is that significant risks relating to

- the costs of design and construction of the facility;
- service provided by the facility (including its availability for use); and
- the facility's operation and maintenance costs

are transferred from the contracting authority to the project company.

Availability PPPs comprise three main sub-categories: accommodation; equipment, systems or networks, and process plant.

— Accommodation

Accommodation-based projects are those such as hospitals, schools and prisons, where the contracting authority pays for the availability of a building (typically in the social infrastructure field). In addition to the provision of the use of the building to an agreed standard, and hard FM services, the private-sector partner may also provide soft FM services such as cleaning, catering, maintenance or even custodial services in a prison. However, this provision of soft services is secondary in importance to the construction and maintenance of the building and its availability to the contracting authority (*cf.* §15.6.2).

— Equipment, systems or networks

For equipment, systems or network-based PPPs, payments by the contracting authority are based on a form of availability. For example in a road project, instead of payments being dependent on usage, they are dependent on the road being 'available', availability being judged by measures such as whether any traffic lanes are closed, the speed at which traffic is able to move on the road and the rate at which accidents or spillages are cleared from the road. Similarly, payment for rail projects can be made on the basis of how well the system (*e.g.* signalling or the train sets) works rather than the volume of passengers. Projects can also involve systems like street lighting or information technology, and another important sector is that of defence equipment.

— Process plant

The original BOT model for power generation of course falls into this category. Outside of power, important types of PPP-related process plant are water and wastewater treatment plants, and municipal waste incinerators. The key difference between these and other types of projects set out above is that they all involve a clearly-measurable process. Water-treatment projects can be undertaken either under as a concession or an availability PPP, but in either case payments are primarily made for the ability to produce an end product, *e.g.* treated water or wastewater, rather than on the actual volume processed or produced. Similarly, in a waste-incineration project, the contracting authority pays for processing the waste, and if this requirement cannot be fulfilled, payments will not be made. The principles in such projects are the same as those set out above for a PPA, but payments based on usage are comparatively less important; hence, availability is again the main criterion.[11] This book focusses mainly on concession and availability PPPs, excluding PPAs. While the power sector shares many similar characteristics with concessions and availability PPPs, this is a large sector in its own right, with a number of specific contractual and financing issues that are better dealt with elsewhere.[12]

§2.5 PPPs in the Spectrum of Public Infrastructure

Figure 2.4 shows where PPPs lie on the spectrum from wholly public-sector projects (and risk) to wholly private-sector projects. It is important to note that:

- Ownership of the facility has little or nothing to do with which particular PPP model is applied, and hence concessions or availability PPPs can be used whether the contractual basis is DBFO, BTO or BOT (*cf.* §2.4.4).
- Terminology for the various types of contract is not used consistently, but the most common usage has been followed.
- Figure 2.4 does not purport to show all possible structural variations, but does set out the most important models.

The same public infrastructure may be placed at different points on this spectrum in different countries. Using water treatment and supply services as an example, there is a range of possibilities in this respect[13]:

- Public-sector ownership and operation: common in many countries.
- Public-sector ownership and private-sector management: for example, *affermage* contracts in France, where the franchisee takes over facilities that are owned by the contracting authority under a long-term management contract (typically for 10-12 years).
- Availability PPP: in Turkey and China, for example, BOT/BTO contracts, transferring usage risk and payment to the public sector (*i.e.* with payments by a contracting authority rather than end users), have been used for the development of new water-services projects (in these cases, water distribution may be carried out separately by the contracting authority).

[11] For waste-processing projects, the payment is usually on a per ton basis, *i.e.* usage, but there may be either a minimum tonnage of waste, or the contracting authority agrees that it will send all its waste to the project, meaning the project company takes the risk on the quantity of waste. Also, the waste delivered has to have certain characteristics, such as calorific value within an agreed range.

[12] PPAs and similar 'process-plant' off-take contracts are discussed in detail in Yescombe 2014.

[13] Treatment and supply can also be provided separately, *e.g.* treatment under a PPP and supply (distribution) by the public sector.

FIGURE 2.4   Public and Private Provision of Infrastructure

Contract Type	Public project ←— —→ Private project					
			←— — Public-Private Partnership — — — — — — — — — — — — — —·······························→			
	Public-sector procurement	Franchise (*Affermage*)	Design-Build Finance-Operate (DBFO) *	Build-Transfer-Operate (BTO) **	Build-Operate-Transfer (BOT) ***	Build-Own-Operate (BOO)
Construction	Public sector [2]	Public sector [2]	Private sector	Private sector	Private sector	Private sector
Operation	Public sector [3]	Private sector	Private sector	Private sector	Private sector	Private sector
Ownership [1]	Public sector [4]	Public sector	Public sector	Private sector during construction, then public sector	Private sector during contract period, then public sector	Private sector
Who pays?	Public sector	Users	Public sector or users	Public sector or users	Public sector or users	Private-sector off-taker, public sector, or users [5]
Who is paid?	n/a	Private sector	Private sector	Private sector	Private sector	Private sector

*   Also known as Design-Construct-Manage-Finance (DCMF) or Design-Build-Finance-Maintain (DBFM)
**   Also known as Build-Transfer-Lease (BTL), Build-Lease-Operate-Transfer (BLOT) or Build-Lease-Transfer (BLT)
*** Also known as Build-Own-Operate-Transfer (BOOT)
[1]   In some cases, ownership may be in the form of a joint venture between the public and private sectors (*cf.* §27.4).
[2]   Public sector normally designs the facility and engages private-sector contractors to carry out construction on its behalf (design-bid-build).
[3]   Public sector may enter into service (outsourcing) contracts (for operation and maintenance) with private-sector contractors.
[4]   Ownership may be through an independent publicly-owned project company, *i.e.* a 'Public-Public Partnership' (*cf.* §27.2.2).
[5]   The BOO contract form applies to PPPs in the minority of cases where ownership of the facility does not revert to the contracting authority at the end of the PPP contract (*cf.* §17.8).

- Concessions: here the project company builds a new treatment or distribution system or upgrades an existing one, collects service fees (tariffs) from users—prices being regulated under the concession agreement, takes the demand risk and has to meet output specifications such as water quality and availability; at the end of the concession, the facility reverts to the contracting authority.
- Privatisation (BOO): in some parts of Britain, the state-owned water boards have been converted into private-sector regional water companies that own the water supply and sewage networks; the public-sector involvement is through a Water Services Regulator that monitors the service provided, fixes maximum costs for water based on a reasonable rate of return on the project company's investment and ensures a degree of competition in water supply; a similar system can be found in Chile (*cf.* §27.6).

So, can it be said that one type of public infrastructure is inherently more suitable for a PPP than another? There is some public infrastructure that it would be generally agreed cannot be privatised, such as roads, and for which PPPs (either concessions or availability PPPs) are therefore the only way of bringing in private finance and the efficiencies of private-sector management. These tend to be types of infrastructure that are parts of a network and therefore where privatising different components is less practical. For other types of infrastructure such as water supply, there are clearly differing views on whether state ownership, privatisation or the PPP approach is appropriate. In other cases, such as building mobile-phone networks, there is little disagreement in most countries that this is best done on the basis of licences to the private sector, *i.e.* in a competitive private-sector market rather than via a PPP. There is probably an irreducible core of public-sector activity which has to be provided by the state without any delegation to the private sector—private armies were used in the Middle Ages but are rarely to be found now (although the private sector may well provide PPP-based accommodation, equipment and services to the armed forces).

§2.6 PPP Markets Worldwide

Figure 2.5 shows the development of PPPs from 2000 to 2016. As can be seen, Europe and to some extent Latin America were the most active regions initially. However, in more recent years, PPP activity has become more evenly distributed throughout the world. Europe's relative decline in activity is probably a result of lower levels of public-sector investment when compared with other parts of the world, particularly after the financial and then fiscal crises in 2007-11.

Many countries around the world have been developing their PPP programmes for a number of years and now have well-developed processes and experience over the project

FIGURE 2.5 PPPs worldwide by region, 2000-16. Source: *ProjectWare, Inframation, EPEC*

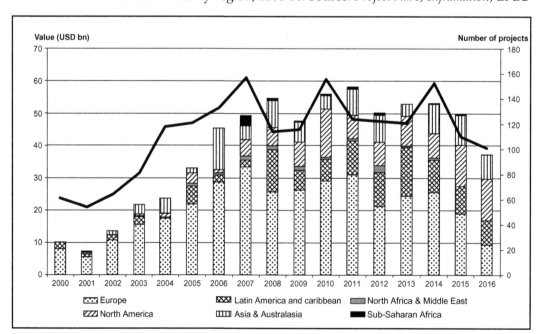

FIGURE 2.6 PPPs worldwide by sector, 2000-16. Sources: *ProjectWare, Inframation, EPEC*

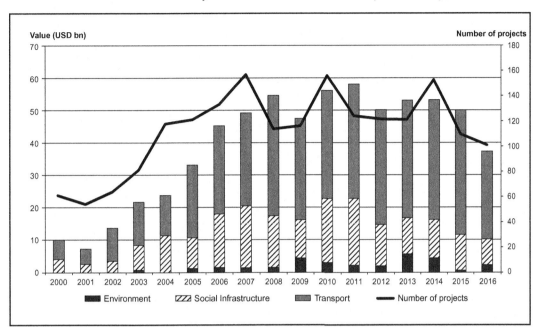

life-cycle. These include Australia, Britain, Canada, Chile, France, India, Japan, Mexico, South Africa and South Korea. Countries such as Colombia, Peru, Philippines, the Netherlands and New Zealand have more recently increased their use of PPPs and developed a number of sophisticated approaches. And there are signs of increasing activity in the United States.

Figure 2.6 shows the levels of activity by sector for the same period. As can be seen, transport consistently dominates, reflecting the long use of concessions in this sector and the relatively large size of projects.[14] However, PPPs have also been consistently used to deliver social infrastructure projects, particularly in health and education, since the early 2000s. Projects in this sector are generally smaller than in transport (with some notable exceptions such as the health sector in Turkey), so that in terms of numbers of projects, social infrastructure is more active than the total value of projects in this sector might otherwise suggest.

Information on PPP project pipelines is greater interest for the market. A number of attempts have been made over the years to try to capture this information. However, wide variations in the level of preparedness and maturity of different projects make this a challenging exercise. Nevertheless, initiatives such as the Sustainable Infrastructure Foundation's 'Source' and the Global Infrastructure Hub's 'Project Pipeline' have recently developed more sophisticated approaches to this problem, seeking to ensure greater

---

[14] Transport projects are also procured as availability PPPs.

standardisation and integrity of project information and more active tracking of the development of projects.

Some caution needs to be exercised with PPP statistics due to the varying definitions of PPPs and the way their values are calculated and as further discussed in §22.2.1. The data in Figure 2.5 have been compiled from a range of publicly-available sources and cross-checked to the extent possible for a degree of consistency, as different sources classify financing activities in different ways. Also, the values are based on the level of private-sector project-finance debt and equity finance in sectors assumed to be dominated by PPPs, as a proxy for PPP activity.[15] Equally, the cost of PPPs with capex funded in part with government resources (*cf.* Chapter 18, §22.9) will be understated. The figures may also include privatisations and refinancings, although these have been eliminated as far as possible. Also, some projects are cancelled after financial close or revert to public-sector funding which may not always be captured in the data sets.

---

[15] However, projects in some countries in some sectors are nevertheless probably fully private-sector, *i.e.* not involving a PPP contract between the public and private sectors.

Cash Flow and Investment Analysis

§3.1 INTRODUCTION

The question of whether the costs of investing today are justified by the expected future benefits is fundamental to both public- and private-sector investment decisions. A widely-used approach is to express the costs and benefits in numerical, usually money, terms.

A large part of this book deals with the financial, and to some extent the economic, aspects of PPPs and their effect on policy issues. It is therefore necessary for the reader to have a basic understanding of certain key concepts used in financial and economic analysis that are used in this book. This chapter is therefore aimed mainly at those not familiar with these concepts—those who are may omit the chapter.

A PPP deals with cash flows over long periods of time, and the value of money is affected by the time that this money is received or paid. It is evident that a dollar today is worth more than a dollar in a year's time, but is a dollar today worth more than two dollars in a year's time? Two interlinked types of calculation are normally used to make this decision:

- a discounted cash flow (DCF) calculation, which gives a value today, or 'present value' (PV), for a future cash flow (§3.2); and
- an internal rate of return (IRR) calculation, which determines the overall rate of return on an investment based on its future cash flow (§3.3).

Although both of these methods of calculation have some problems (§3.4), they are widely used in PPP projects in a variety of contexts (§3.5).

§3.2 PRESENT VALUE / DISCOUNTED CASH FLOW

§3.2.1 Present Value

The PV is the value today of a sum of money due in the future, discounted at the cost of money, *i.e.* a relevant interest rate.[1] The formula for a PV calculation is

$$PV = \frac{FV}{(1+i)^n},$$

where

PV = present value, *i.e.* the 'money of today',
FV = future value, *i.e.* the 'money of the future',
i = the discount rate, and
n = the number of periods (*e.g.* annual or semi-annual with the discount rate adjusted accordingly) until FV is paid.

Thus if the discount rate is 10% *p.a.*, and a sum of $1,000 is due in a year's time, the PV of that sum is $1,000 \div (1 + 0.10)$, or $909.1. To turn the calculation the other way around, if $909.1 is invested for a year at 10%, $1,000 (*i.e.* 909.1x1.10) will be repaid at the end of the year. Similarly the PV of a sum of $1,000 due in 2 years' time at a discount rate of 10% *p.a.* calculated semi-annually (*i.e.* 5% per half year) is $1,000 \div (1 + 0.05)^4$, or $822.7.

§3.2.2 Discounted Cash Flow

A DCF calculation is the PV of a series of future cash sums, the purpose of the calculation being to find what this stream of future cash flows is worth in money of today. It is calculated as the sum of the cash flow for each future period (usually semi-annually in PPP cash-flow calculations), each period's cash flow being discounted to its PV as set out above.

Typically the cash flow in a DCF calculation offsets, or 'nets off', the costs (such as investment and running costs) in a project against the stream of future revenues which the project produces. When this happens, the result is called the *net* present value (NPV). The term 'net present cost' (NPC) may be used when looking at the DCF from a contracting authority's perspective (because the future cash flows are a series of payments by the contracting authority or users), but the calculation is the same as an NPV.

Although DCF calculations can easily be done using the relevant spread-sheet software function, it is useful to understand the underlying formulæ and calculations as a way of checking and understanding the final result.

The choice of discount rate is obviously crucial in determining the NPV of a project's cash flow, and hence the value of the project as an investment: the higher the rate the lower the NPV, and *vice versa*. The discount rate used also depends on the context in which the DCF calculation is being performed, and by whom, as discussed at the end of this chapter.

---

[1] This chapter looks at cashflows from an investment or financing perspective and hence the use of cost of money or interest rates as a discount rate. From an economic perspective, however, the discount rate may be based on different factors, such as a social time preference rate (*cf.* §8.6.2), but the principles of discounting are the same as described here.

§3.2.3 Using Discounted Cash-Flow Calculations

The use of DCF calculations can be illustrated by the two contrasting investment cash flows set out in Table 3.1. Both involve an initial investment of $1,000, and cash flows over five years of $1,350, producing a surplus (net of the initial investment) of $350. The cash flow for each annual period has been discounted to its NPV at 10% *p.a.* Year 0 is the first day of the project, when the investment is made (the investment being shown as a negative figure in the cash flow); the remaining cash flows are received at annual intervals thereafter.

Table 3.1   DCF calculation

(a) Year	(b) Discount factor $((1 + 0.1)^{(a)})$	Investment A ($)		Investment B ($)	
		(c) Cash flow	NPV $((c) \div (b))$	(d) Cash flow	NPV $((d) \div (b))$
0	1.0000	−1,000	−1,000	−1,000	−1,000
1	1.1000	340	309	200	182
2	1.2100	305	252	235	194
3	1.3310	270	203	270	203
4	1.4641	235	161	305	208
5	1.6105	200	124	340	211
Total		350	49	350	−2

It will be seen that although the undiscounted cash flows produce the same net result over the five-year period, the NPV of Investment A is $49 (*i.e.* DCFs from years 1 to 5 of $1,049, less the original investment of $1,000), whereas that of Investment B is −$2. Investment A is thus the better project. These differences in the DCF calculations illustrate the importance to investors of the *timing* of cash flows.

The discount rate is often used as a 'hurdle rate', meaning that if the NPV is positive using this rate the investment is acceptable, whereas if it is negative the return is too low and therefore the investment is not acceptable. Thus if the same cash flows are discounted at 5% *p.a.*, the NPV of Investment A is $184 and that of Investment B is $154; so, changing the hurdle rate does not affect the decision that Investment A is the better one, but it also turns Investment B from a doubtful into an attractive investment. If Investment B were the only choice, changing the hurdle rate from 10% to 5% would affect the decision whether to go ahead with it or not, which illustrates the importance of the choice of discount rate.

A DCF calculation also provides a means of valuing an investment that is already held (in which case there is no initial investment cost outflow). If a PPP contract is expected to provide a stream of revenues of $1,000 a year for the next 20 years, the financial value of this business is determined by discounting this stream of revenues to its value today, *i.e.* its PV. The choice of discount rate again makes a substantial difference to the result: if this stream is discounted at 15% *p.a.*, its value today is $6,259, but if discounted at 8% *p.a.*, its value is $9,818. As will be seen, investors have different views about the value of a stream of future revenues, and so use different discount rates—thus the same PPP project may have a different value for different investors.

§3.3 Internal Rate of Return

The IRR measures the return on the investment over its life. It is the discount rate at which the NPV of the cash flow (adding up both the outflows and the inflows) is zero. Thus using the examples in Table 3.1 as set out in Table 3.2, the IRR of Investment A is 12.08% and Investment B is 9.94%, so again showing that Investment A is the better of the two; the calculation can be checked by discounting the two cash flows at these respective rates. Again a minimum IRR can be used as a hurdle rate, so if the investor has an IRR hurdle rate of say 12%, Investment A will be acceptable but Investment B will not.

Table 3.2   IRR calculation

End year	Investment A ($)		Investment B ($)	
	Cash flow	NPV@12.08%	Cash flow	NPV@9.94%
0	−1,000	−1,000	−1,000	−1,000
1	340	303	200	182
2	305	243	235	194
3	270	192	270	203
4	235	149	305	209
5	200	113	340	212
Total	350	0	350	0

§3.4 Problems with Discounted Cash Flow and Internal Rate of Return Calculations

Some caution must be exercised with DCF and IRR calculations, as both have defects or weaknesses which need to be understood.

§3.4.1 Single Discount Rate

The use of a single discount rate or IRR to assess investments suggests that the risks involved in a project are the same throughout its life. In reality, of course this is not the case (cf. §20.3.1).

Similarly, in a typical PPP, there is a construction period lasting several years, during which the project's cash flow is of course negative, generally followed by positive cash flows for the rest of the project life, unlike the cash flows in the tables above, where all the investment is assumed to take place on day one of the project. If a high discount rate is used to calculate the NPV of the project, which is usually the conservative approach because a higher discount rate gives a lower NPV, the negative cash flows over an extended construction period are also being discounted at this high rate, which is not conservative: where future cash flows are negative, the conservative approach is to use a low discount rate. Arguably two different discount rates should be used for the initial negative and subsequent positive cash flows although this is not generally the case in the PPP market.

§3.4.2 Discounted Cash-Flow Calculations and Different-Sized Projects

When comparing two different projects, account has to be taken of their relative sizes. This is illustrated in Table 3.3.

Table 3.3   DCF calculations and different-sized projects

	Investment C ($)	Investment D ($)
(a) Original investment	−1,000	−2,000
(b) Cash flow 1 year later	1,400	2,600
NPV@10%	273	364
IRR	40%	30%
Cost-Benefit Analysis		
(c) PV of benefits (=PV of (b))	1,273	2,364
(d) PV of costs (=(a))	1,000	2,000
Benefit to cost ratio ((c)÷(d))	1.27x	1.18x

Investment D has a higher NPV than Investment C, but this is merely because of its larger size. As is apparent from the IRR calculation, Investment C is the better investment; the incremental $1,000 invested in Investment D compared to Investment C gives a much poorer return.

To better compare these investments the NPV comparison can be broken down into a comparison of the PV of the costs and the PV of the benefits, as shown in the second half of Table 3.3. This suggests that Investment C gives a better return, *i.e.* the value of benefits in relation to the amount of the investment, a point confirmed by the IRR calculation. The approach here is that any project with a benefit to cost ratio (BCR) over 1x is a sound one, but the project with the highest BCR is the one which should be chosen. On the other hand, if availability of funding is not a problem, and if there is no other use for the funds, it could be argued that Investment D is still worthwhile because it produces a greater absolute net benefit.

§3.4.3 Internal Rate of Return and Cash Reinvestment

A fundamental problem with IRR is the assumption in the calculation on what happens to interim cash flows. This is illustrated by Table 3.4.

Table 3.4   IRR and interim cash flows

Year	Investment E ($) Cash flow	Investment F ($) Cash flow	Annual cash flow reinvested @15% to year 5
0	−1,000	−1,000	
1	0	298	522
2	0	298	454
3	0	298	395
4	0	298	343
5	2,011	298	298
Total	1,011	492	2,011
NPV@12%	141	75	
IRR	15%	15%	

It is evident that Investment E gives a better return, and the DCF calculation supports this, but the IRRs of the two investments are the same. This is because the standard IRR calculation assumes that cash taken out of the project is reinvested at the IRR rate until the end of the calculation period. Thus as shown in the last column of Table 3.4, if the Investment F cash flow in years 1-4 is reinvested at 15% *p.a.* compounded, the total amounts to $2,011 at the end of year 5, the same as Investment E. Clearly, some account should be taken of Investment F generating cash more quickly, but the assumption that this cash can be reinvested at 15% is not correct unless this is the investor's cost of capital (*cf.* §20.3.1), and so may double-count the return on another investment at that rate. The effect of an IRR calculation can be clearly seen in Table 3.4; it overvalues early cash flow—the longer the cash-flow period, the more the IRR is exaggerated by using a high reinvestment rate—and conversely undervalues cash flows further into the future. This is of particular relevance to PPP projects, which have very long cash flows.

There are two ways of dealing with this type of distortion:

- Modified IRR (MIRR)

   The MIRR calculation assumes a lower reinvestment rate (*e.g.* the investor's cost of capital, as assumed for the discount rate in a DCF calculation, instead of the IRR rate) for cash taken out of the project. This is a better representation of the real world. If we take the examples in Table 3.4, but the reinvestment rate is taken as 12% (*i.e.* the cost of capital used for the DCF calculation) as shown in Table 3.5, the MIRR of Investment F is 13.6%, while that of Investment E of course remains at 15% (as there is no interim cash flow to invest). This then makes it clear that Investment E is the better one. Surprisingly the use of MIRR by PPP investors is not widespread.

Table 3.5   IRR and MIRR

Year	Investment E ($) Cash flow	Investment F ($) Cash flow	Investment F ($) Annual cash flow reinvested @12% to year 5
0	−1,000	−1,000	−1,000
1	0	298	469
2	0	298	419
3	0	298	374
4	0	298	334
5	2,011	298	298
Total	1,011	492	105
NPV@12%	141	75	
IRR	15.0%	15.0%	
MIRR	15.0%		13.6%

— Payback period

An alternative (or at least supplementary) approach is to ignore the reinvestment issue in looking at IRR calculations but require that any investment also has a maximum payback period (*i.e.* the length of time that it takes to recover the original cash investment). This to a certain extent balances the exaggerating effect of IRR calculations on longer term cash flows, but it is a crude measure—in particular it does not take account of returns after the end of the payback period. Nonetheless, it may still provide a useful check. Thus besides requiring a minimum IRR level, a maximum payback period of not more than a certain number of years may be required as one of the criteria for making a new investment. The payback period for Investment F in Table 3.4 is 3-4 years, and that for Investment E is the full 5 years.

§3.4.4 Internal Rate of Return and Different Project Lives

Another consequence of the over-valuation of early cash flow in the IRR calculation is that projects with different lives cannot be compared using their IRRs. This is illustrated in

Table 3.6, which shows the cash flow from two projects which have identical IRRs—but it is evident, and confirmed by the DCF calculation, that the longer Investment J is better than the shorter Investment G (assuming there is no greater risk in Investment J).

Table 3.6   IRR and different project lives

Year	Investment G($)	Investment J($)
0	−1,000	−1,000
1	200	145
2	200	145
3	200	145
4	200	145
5	200	145
6	200	145
7	200	145
8	200	145
9		145
10		145
11		145
12		145
13		145
14		145
15		145
IRR	11.8%	11.8%
NPV@10%	67	106

§3.4.5 Internal Rate of Return and Positive / Negative Cash Flows

More esoterically, IRR calculations may not be suitable where a cash-flow flips between negative and positive and back again in different periods (*e.g.* where an investment takes places in phases, with revenues building up between each phase of investment, or where there is a final cost to an investment, such as cleaning up a quarry after it is exhausted), as the same calculation may then give more than one answer. This is illustrated in Table 3.7, in which it can be seen that the same cash flow, in which amounts are negative at the beginning, then positive in year 1, then negative in year 2, can be discounted at both 10% and 20% to produce an NPV (*i.e.* adding up all the positive and negative PVs) of zero, *i.e.* the IRR can be either 10% or 20%.

Table 3.7   IRR and negative / positive cash flows

Year	Cash flow($)	10% discount rate		20% discount rate	
		Discount factor	PV($)	Discount factor	PV($)
0	−50,000	1.00000	−50,000	1.00000	−50,000
1	115,000	0.90909	104,545	0.83333	95,833
2	−66,000	0.82645	−54,545	0.69444	−45,833
	NPV		0		0

It should be noted that standard spread-sheet software will probably only give one of these answers, with no obvious indication that different answers are possible.[2]

§3.4.6 Cash Investment *vs* Risk

DCF and IRR calculations are based only on investment of cash; they take no account of the risk involved in making a commitment to invest cash in the future (*cf.* §20.3.6), nor of the need (and hence the cost) of setting aside resources to make this future investment. This is of particular relevance in PPPs, where construction and hence investment may take place over several years, or where there may be investments of cash in later stages of a project.

§3.5 USES IN PUBLIC-PRIVATE PARTNERSHIPS

DCF and IRR calculations are used in a variety of different ways by the different parties to a PPP project. The following just summarises these and provides cross-references to the context in which they are used elsewhere in this book. However, one general point should be made—all these calculations involve estimates of future cash flows, and the calculations are thus only as good as the data used for these estimates. Financial models (*cf.* §23.8) often work to a spurious level of accuracy down to fine decimal points—such calculations may be correct arithmetically, but have limited use since the underlying data cannot be that accurate.

§3.5.1 By the Public Sector

A DCF calculation may be used by the contracting authority:

- when deciding whether to proceed or not with a project (*cf.* §7.4.2)—an 'economic rate of return' calculation (a form of IRR) may also be used in this case (*cf.* §7.4.4);
- in a quantitative 'value for money' (VfM) assessment (*cf.* §8.3); and
- to evaluate private-sector bids for a PPP project (*cf.* §10.6.5).

[2] Excel can be forced to give one answer or the other, depending on the 'guess rate' entered into the formula.

§3.5.2 By Private-Sector Investors

The project IRR—*i.e.* the IRR of the cash flow before debt service or equity returns—may be used by investors to assess the general financial viability of a project without taking account of its financial structure (*cf.* §20.3.2).

However, the main measure for investors is the equity IRR—*i.e.* the IRR of the equity cash flow *versus* the original equity investment (*cf.* §20.3.3). This is commonly used as a hurdle rate for PPP investments—*i.e.* in order for an investment to be justified the equity IRR must be $x\%$ or above.

Investors also use an NPV calculation as a method of valuing the project company (*cf.* §26.3).

§3.5.3 In PPP Contracts

The equity IRR may be used to calculate

- the initial service fees (*cf.* §23.9.5);
- revisions to service fees, or compensation for changes in circumstances during the life of the PPP contract (*cf.* §16.2.2);
- refinancing-gain calculations (*cf.* §26.2.6); and
- compensation to investors for early termination of the PPP contract, for which a DCF calculation may also be used (§17.3);

and the project IRR may be used as a discount rate to calculate the payment due on termination for a default by the project company (*cf.* §17.2.4).

§3.5.4 By Lenders

Lenders use the project IRR to calculate their loan-life cover ratio (*cf.* §23.3.3).

PART II

THE PUBLIC-SECTOR PERSPECTIVE

Policy, Legal and Institutional Frameworks

§4.1 INTRODUCTION

This chapter deals with some of the general requirements for developing a PPP programme (§4.2) including legal (§4.3) and policy (§4.4) frameworks and PPP guidance manuals (§4.5). The benefits of programme approaches (§4.6) and the rôle of PPP units (§4.7) are considered. The increasing interest in the use of national infrastructure plans is also discussed (§4.8).

§4.2 DEVELOPING PPP PROGRAMMES

A fairly similar pattern can be seen in the way in which PPP programmes are developed in different countries. These generally begin with toll-road concessions (or tolled road bridges or tunnels): the concept is a familiar one to most users, even if it is new to the country concerned, and the 'self-financing' nature of such projects (at least from the public-budget point of view) makes them immediately attractive. But the scope for toll projects tends to be limited, and many countries move to a next stage, adding availability PPPs and thus widening the application to other areas of public infrastructure such as schools and hospitals (social infrastructure). The PPP programme then becomes much more diverse, and tends to require closer management, *e.g.* through central-government PPP units, PPP laws or standardised forms of PPP contract, as discussed below.

The characteristics of a successful PPP programme can be summed up as:

- political will (*cf.* §4.4, §28.13);
- an adequate legal framework (*cf.* §4.3);
- adequate public-sector institutional capacity, both to handle the PPP programme as a whole and to deal with individual projects (*cf.* §4.7);
- an underlying pipeline of projects that are economically justified (*cf.* §7.4) and affordable (*cf.* §9.2), and that meet the suitability criteria to be procured as PPPs (*cf.* §8.8); and
- a consistent and predictable flow of such PPP projects, making it worthwhile for the private sector to build up the technical, investment and financing capacities required.

§4.3 LEGAL FRAMEWORKS

The legal framework for PPPs varies between countries depending on the nature of the underlying legal system. However, concessions always require a specific law relating to the project, or a 'framework' law relating to concessions in general. This is necessary to allow a private-sector company to charge and collect revenues from users for providing a public service. In some countries, especially common-law countries (*i.e.* those whose legal systems originate from the English common law), availability PPPs are treated as a variety of government procurement for which no special legal arrangements are usually needed; in others, primarily civil-law countries (*i.e.* those whose legal system originates from the French *Code Civile*), specific PPP laws may be needed to provide a framework for this type of contract, in a similar way to concession laws. (Civil-law countries also often have separate legal frameworks and courts for public administrative law, which includes PPPs.) Thus it was necessary for France, for example, to pass a specific administrative law to overcome legal obstacles to availability PPPs (which are quite understandable in the standard public-sector procurement context), such as:

- the requirement to conduct separate bids for construction and long-term operation and maintenance works, rather than combining them as in a PPP;
- prohibition of deferred payments for public works (on the grounds that these are obligations against future budgets, which legally have to be agreed on an annual basis, and not be committed in advance), which obviously makes it impossible to pay service fees for a PPP over many years;
- limitations on transfer of control of public-sector infrastructure; and
- lenders' security requirements (*cf.* §25.3).

Depending on the structure of government, PPP laws may be at national or subnational levels. A large number of US states[1] have passed or amended legislation on highway concessions and other forms of PPP.

There are benefits in framework legislation, whether for concessions or availability PPPs (even if not legally necessary for the latter). It provides an opportunity for the government:

---

[1] Thirty-five US states at the time of writing.

- to confirm its political commitment through explicit legislation;
- to define the scope of PPPs in terms of contractual arrangements, sectoral limitations and other parameters (*e.g.* project size, length of contract);
- to set out the rôles and powers of the different arms of government, including control and approval of individual PPP projects;
- to provide clarity on procurement procedures (*cf.* Chapter 10);
- to set out the basis on which a contracting authority may provide support for various project risks, *e.g.* revenue guarantees (*cf.* Chapter 18);
- to give lenders the ability to take security over the PPP contract (which the law might not otherwise allow), as well as 'step-in' rights (*cf.* §25.3.3); and
- if appropriate, to allow for provision of investment incentives such as special tax treatment, *etc.*

The PPP legal framework may comprise a mixture of an enabling law and secondary or administrative legislation, with the latter dealing with more detailed requirements such as the administrative preparation and approval requirements for a PPP. As secondary legislation can be more easily amended, this allows for changes to be made in detailed areas in response to policy and market changes while the enabling law remains unchanged and continues to provide the necessary stability and certainty.

In common-law countries, where availability PPPs generally do not need specific legislation, there is greater flexibility to make changes in the PPP programme in the light of experience gained from previous PPP contracts.

Unfortunately, some PPP laws and regulations are poorly written or even unnecessary. Sometimes they can create more confusion adding layers to existing legislation or contradicting other laws. If creating a new PPP law, it is a good idea to ask first what is strictly required and then use a mixture of experienced PPP practitioners and local legal expertise to develop it so that it is clear, appropriate and unambiguous, and does not go into excessive detail instead of leaving this to secondary legislation as discussed above.

§4.3.1 Other Laws

In addition to any specific legislation, PPP projects are subject to other laws and regulations such as environmental, tax, employment and procurement laws. Taxation is one example where special arrangements may be required to deal with issues such as value-added tax (VAT) increasing the cost of the project at the contracting authority level, even if the overall impact for government as a whole is much less (*cf.* §23.6.3). A number of countries around the world have also passed special tax provisions for PPPs (but often as part of a wider set of investment incentive activities) that may reduce the rate of tax for the private sector, such as tax holidays, reduced tax rates, accelerated depreciation and investment allowances, and additional deductions for qualifying expenses.

§4.3.2 Contract Standardisation

A PPP law may set the overall legal framework including some of the general obligations and rights of the parties, but since many aspects of a PPP contract are common to all projects, much can also be achieved by standardisation of the PPP contracts themselves. This can significantly improve the quality and consistency of contracts, create greater certainty for bidders and lenders on contract terms to expect and speed up the procurement process. (The end result of contract standardisation may be quite similar to framework legislation in prescribing how certain risks and obligations should be allocated and dealt with.) Examples of countries that have developed standardised contracts include Britain, France, India, the Netherlands, New Zealand, the Philippines and South Africa.

However, if a standard contract is developed too soon in the development of a PPP programme, there may not yet be enough experience to structure it properly, and if left too late then the benefits are reduced and the public is left with a mixture of different contract forms up to that point (as happened in Britain by the late 1990s). Clearly, there has to be a reasonable pipeline of PPP projects to justify standardisation in the first place.

The phrase 'standard contract', however, can be a bit misleading. At a minimum, contract standardisation may establish certain core principles such as the performance-based nature of payment (*cf.* Chapter 15), public-sector ownership of the asset and the requirement for clear processes to deal with contract changes (*cf.* §16.2.2). It usually goes further, establishing a number of standard contractual provisions such as:

- the requirement to complete the facility to the agreed specification by a certain date (*cf.* §15.4.1);
- the ability of the contracting authority to monitor design and construction (*cf.* §19.3.1, §19.3.3);
- the obligations of the contracting authority in relation to construction (*cf.* §16.2.4);
- provisions for the contracting authority to vary its requirements (*cf.* §16.2.2);
- restrictions on changes in ownership of the project company (*cf.* §20.6.4), or in the terms of the debt financing (*cf.* §26.2.3);
- provisions on insurance, and application of insurance proceeds to reinstate of the facility (*cf.* Chapter 14);
- provisions for the contracting authority to intervene and take over running of the facility (*cf.* §17.6.1);
- long-term maintenance obligations, including provisions for return of the facility to the contracting authority at the end of the PPP contract (*cf.* §17.8);
- provisions for early termination of the PPP contract, including compensation payments to the project company (*cf.* Chapter 17); and
- hand-back provisions (*cf.* §17.8).

But there will still be specific issues that vary between different PPP structures (*i.e.* a concession or availability PPP) and sectors (*e.g.* schools or roads). Therefore, the standard contract document may act more as a guide, highlighting the factors for a contracting authority to consider when drafting the relevant clauses such as for the service-fee mechanism and service requirements (*cf.* Chapter 15). However, if the pipeline of PPP projects is long enough for a particular sector, governments can draw up sector-specific standard-form contracts.

Contract standardisation also requires the capacity to develop the contracts in the first place and modify them over time as the market evolves, as well as the capacity in central government to enforce the use of standard provisions and process justifiable exceptions ('derogations') when contracting authorities request them. This ability to enforce the use of centrally-developed standard contracts by different line ministries and contracting authorities may not be possible if these are highly autonomous.

Various industry bodies have from time to time put forward the case for taking standardisation of PPP agreements even further to a global or regional set of standards, in a similar way to the development of FIDIC standards for construction contracts.[2] However, differences in legal systems and the variety in forms of PPPs suggest that this is not straightforward. Nevertheless, institutions such as the World Bank have and continue to develop guidance on recommended standard PPP contractual provisions (World Bank Group 2017), and the similar contractual provisions recommended by international legal advisers as they work on different projects have made the provisions of PPP contracts increasingly consistent around the world.

§4.4 POLICY FRAMEWORKS

Successful PPP programmes are usually underpinned by clear and strong political commitment. PPPs require change and reform to the way the public sector goes about its business. They also require the confidence of the private sector, not only to risk resources in bidding for projects but also to make substantial up-front investments, recoverable over long periods of time, in the projects themselves.

A PPP law is clearly a statement of government support for a PPP programme, but governments also sometimes publish policy documents setting out their commitment to, and their rationale for, using PPPs and explaining the core benefits using a PPP approach (*cf.* Chapter 28) to wider government, the market and citizens. PPPs are complex and confusion around what they are and why they are used can be widespread. The rationales or drivers for PPPs typically include reference to VfM, whole-of-life asset management, performance-based payment, a focus on service outputs rather than inputs, mobilisation of private-sector resources or innovation and/or a commitment to wider reforms to public investment and services. These drivers usually underpin the criteria that are used when it comes to assessing individual projects for their suitability as PPPs (*cf.* §8.8). Policies may also specifically rule out reasons for doing PPPs based purely on lack of public funding or balance-sheet treatment. The policy document may also set out the broad scope of the PPP approach such as limiting its application to projects over a certain minimum investment size, or the exclusion of certain sectors or a maximum length of PPP contracts. It may set out in summary form what the PPP process involves in terms of what has to be done by whom and when. Such documents should be short, clearly-worded and avoid technical and legal detail—they are after all communication tools. Examples of countries that have published such documents include Australia, Britain, Poland and New Zealand.

This raises the issue of communications more generally. Because PPPs can be new, controversial and part of a reform agenda, in a well-run programme close attention also needs to be paid to communications. In addition to using tools such as a policy document, the PPP unit (*cf.* §4.7) may have specialist staff (or use those of its parent ministry) to deal with enquiries from parliament and citizens, develop 'lines to take' for ministers, provide

---

[2] International Federation of Consulting Engineers; www.fidic.org

information on projects and their progress, give visibility to success and handle media comments to ensure accurate reporting.

§4.4.1 Positive PPP Tests

A number of countries specifically require a PPP option to be considered or tested on all projects above a certain size at an early stage in the project cycle. This is sometimes referred to as a 'positive PPP test'. The aim of this is to ensure that the PPP option is always considered and to encourage contracting authorities to consider PPPs as an alternative to traditional procurement approaches, especially in the early stages of developing a PPP programme when there might be reluctance on the part of a contracting authority to try something new. In some countries, the 'positive test' may be softer in that the PPP option needs to be considered *if appropriate.*[3] In due course, the whole public-investment process may move on to requiring that a wider range of procurement options has to be considered as part of the normal public-investment process, such as in Australia.

§4.5 PPP GUIDANCE

PPP policies, laws and standardised contracts address the issue of what is needed and why, but they often do not address in the detail required *how* to go about preparing and procuring a project as a PPP. Many governments have developed handbooks and guidance for their programmes addressing issues such as how to conduct a VfM assessment (*cf.* §8.9.2) or run a competitive-dialogue procurement (*cf.* §10.6.4).

Guidance is usually linked to quality-control or 'gateway' processes. These check that the PPP is being prepared in a prescribed way (*cf.* §5.4). National audit offices that either have to approve PPPs before they are signed (as in Greece, for example) or review them later when they conduct *ex-post* evaluations (as in Britain and France), often check to see if agreed processes and guidance have been followed (*cf.* §19.9). Guidance also protects public officials if projects go wrong. If processes have been followed correctly but there are still problems, then the public official can point to the guidance. But woe betide the public official who, when questioned by a parliamentary committee about the difficulties faced in his or her project, admits that she or he decided not to follow guidance!

Guidance is particularly important where contracting authorities are expected to prepare and procure their own PPP projects. This helps to address the knowledge gap that inevitably exists for this complex form of procurement (many contracting authorities may only ever procure one PPP project) as well as develop greater consistency of approach across government (which is important so that potential investors and lenders are not faced with a new approach for each project). For smaller programmes, especially where many processes may be conducted in-house by a specialist team, or where programme approaches are used (*cf.* §4.6), it may appear less necessary to have detailed guidelines.

---

[3] The harsher alternative is to require that all public-investment projects above a certain size should be procured as PPPs unless confirmed otherwise, known as a 'negative PPP test' but this is rare and may be too constraining.

But these still serve a useful purpose in preserving institutional memory, preparing for external scrutiny and ensuring greater consistency and transparency in decision-making.

A positive feature of such guidance is that most of it is publicly available. But it has to be understood in the context for which it is written as it reflects specific policies of the relevant government and the administrative systems it applies to. Sometimes the guidance material can also be over-complex and fail to distinguish between the requirements of large and complex projects and much smaller ones. Faced with several hundred pages of detailed instructions (and formulæ), a small local government is likely to be very reluctant to pursue a PPP approach for its project.

Development of guidance can be one of the main rôles of a specialist PPP unit, discussed below.

§4.6 PROGRAMME APPROACHES

If groups of similar projects have been identified (*e.g.* within a sector such as roads or schools), governments can often benefit from delivering these projects in a programmed way. This is distinct from an overall national programme of PPPs or packaging smaller projects into a single PPP contract (*cf.* §7.5.1). A programme approach can bring a number of advantages such as:

- focused and strengthened sector-specific public-sector expertise for the preparation, procurement, negotiation and even contract management of the projects in the programme;
- reduced need for externally-sourced transaction advisory support for each individual project and better management of advisers where they are used;
- standardised sector-specific contract terms, processes and guidance;
- strengthened market interest through coordination and management of a pipeline of projects for the market (especially where individually the projects may be too small to elicit market interest—*cf.* §20.4);
- improved understanding of the affordability of the programme as a whole;
- strengthened stakeholder management and communication;
- collection and sharing of data, such as construction and operating costs;
- ability to capture experience from preceding projects to improve subsequent procurement and management of projects; and
- reduced transaction costs.

Programme approaches, however, do not work as well if individual contracting authorities (*e.g.* at the local-government level) are concerned about losing control of their projects. One approach is to share control of the programme between these the contracting authorities and a central ministry responsible for the sector, such as education. Funding the management of the programme and the powers of the programme body need to be agreed from the start—these may also cut across existing approval processes. Programmes sometimes take a while to deliver the flow of projects, as standardised documentation and processes are worked up, so expectations on timing need to be managed. Programme approaches can either involve the programme team providing extensive technical support to the relevant contracting authorities or they may, in addition, provide, or act as controllers of, any central-government funding to pay for the projects. If so, the programme team may assess eligibility for projects to enter the programme and access the funding available and require projects to be developed in line with the programme's processes. Programme approaches have been used in a number of sectors including schools, waste processing and street lighting (EPEC 2015).

The programme itself may be delivered by a joint venture between the public[4] and private sectors (a form of institutional PPP—*cf.* §27.4). Projects within the programme are then procured as PPP projects or using more traditional approaches such as D&B, whichever is best suited to the facility being procured. The private-sector joint venture partner, which is selected under a competitive process at the start of the programme, is required to deliver the projects within an agreed cost and performance framework (this also obviates the requirement for a separate public-procurement process for each individual small project) using template contracts. At the same time, the individual projects are not necessarily identified or committed to by the public partner upfront. Examples of this approach include sectoral programmes in primary healthcare and schools in Britain, and regional programmes for a mix of social-infrastructure facilities, as in the Scottish regional government's 'hub model'.

§4.7 PPP UNITS

One of the main difficulties for the public sector in delivering PPPs is a lack of expertise in specialist areas such as finance, law, project management, engineering, planning, PPP public policy, *etc.* Therefore, an important building block in PPP programmes is the creation of a specialised PPP unit, usually within the National Treasury or Ministry of Finance or Economy, which provides a centre of expertise and technical support to government ministries and other contracting authorities developing PPPs. There are three main areas where governments can benefit from specialist PPP input:

- PPP policy support. This can involve a wide range of activities including:
  - developing the legal framework (*cf.* §4.3);
  - developing the policy framework (*cf.* §4.4);
  - publishing guidance materials on preparing, procuring and managing PPP (*cf.* §4.5);
  - training;
  - communicating PPP policy to the rest of government, the market and citizens;
  - handling enquiries on PPP policies, programmes and projects, such as dealing with parliamentary enquiries and requests for information (*cf.* §19.10);
  - reporting on PPP financial activity for financial and statistical reporting (*cf.* §9.4);
  - collecting data on PPP activity for market-development purposes; and
  - ensuring a consistent strategy and policy approach by the public sector as a whole.

[4] The public sector in turn may involve both local governments and the central PPP unit (*cf.* §4.7).

This is one of the most common activities found in PPP units and one of the reasons they tend to be based in, or report to, a National Treasury or Ministry of Finance or Economy.

− PPP project review/approval

Most PPP programmes require some form of approval or quality-control process, not least because most PPP projects involve long-term government obligations (*cf.* §5.4). The approval body, which may comprise senior officials, needs to be well-informed to make decisions that can be very technical in nature. A PPP unit may have some approval powers itself or carry out reviews and make recommendations to such a separate approval body.

− PPP programme and project support

Due to the specialist skills required to prepare, procure and manage PPPs, a PPP unit is an efficient way to bring public-sector and commercial expertise together and make it available to individual contracting authorities. Of particular importance is a good understanding of how the private sector works. Such skills are typically in short supply in the public sector (*cf.* §6.2) and are relevant for:

* developing initial pilot projects to test PPP models;
* providing continuing technical and commercial advice and support to contracting authorities on specific projects (*cf.* §6.3);
* coordinating public-sector 'buying power' to obtain the best terms;
* coordinating the PPP programme and thus avoiding 'bunching' of too many projects approaching the markets at the same time; and
* developing and communicating lessons from *ex-ante* and *ex-post* project evaluation.

In providing project support, PPP units generally complement rather than substitute for the contracting authority's external professional advisers (*cf.* §6.4). It is important to ensure that appropriate sector expertise from the line ministry is not swept aside by an overbearing Ministry of Finance-based PPP unit.

There is no model rôle for a PPP unit, given the different capacity needs of governments and the ways different administrations operate. PPP units can carry out some or all of these different functions. These rôles are mutually reinforcing, so the quality of policy work is reinforced by practical experience in the delivery of projects. There may be potential conflicts between approval and project-support rôles, but these are often managed quite successfully. In larger PPP programmes, there may also be specialist units operating in line ministries with active PPP programmes but these still follow policies and approaches established at the central unit, not least to help ensure a consistency of approach to PPPs across government. The depth of PPP unit support must be dictated by the needs of the PPP project pipeline—there is little point in building up a significant PPP skills base if the flow of projects is only likely to be modest (which is a problem for smaller PPP programmes) or if the political commitment to PPP is missing.

It is important that the PPP unit has a strong mandate that cuts across divisions between different branches of the public sector, and also has short reporting lines to senior government ministers. This sends a powerful signal to the market and across the public sector of the government's commitment to the PPP programme. In practice, much rests on the shoulders of the head of the PPP unit as it is a job that involves commanding the respect and trust of ministers and senior decision-makers (who may not always appreciate or have the time to understand the complexities of the PPP process), persuading and cajoling contracting authorities to do something that is new and complex for them, and presenting a competent public-sector face to the private sector.

Recognising that many of the disciplines of PPPs (such as the requirement for thorough project preparation or a good understanding of commercial principals) may apply to other forms of procurement and that PPPs are but one of a range of delivery modes for infrastructure, a number of countries have developed their PPP units into infrastructure units with a broader scope over public investment and infrastructure delivery. This can reduce the difference between what may sometimes appear to be an onerous PPP process compared with other types of public procurement. At the same time, it is important to ensure that the processes for making the economic case for the underlying investment (*cf.* Chapter 7) are independent of those delivering it as a PPP, otherwise there is the risk that the PPP drives the rationale for the project and not the other way around.

§4.8 INFRASTRUCTURE PLANS

Just as the PPP dimensions of a project may be defined in accordance with a legal and policy framework, projects themselves should also originate from within a larger government investment framework. The framework may be in the form of a long-term infrastructure plan. These plans are often regional, urban (or spatial) or sectoral but increasingly use is being made of national-level plans. Such plans provide an overall direction and framework to guide the selection and priority of projects in the country over the medium to long term.

The focus of the plans, particularly long-term national infrastructure plans, is not necessarily just to list what projects to invest in over the future, but rather to set out recommendations for changes to the way things are done, such as change to how public assets are managed, procured or regulated, or for future reforms in different sectors. Equally, addressing infrastructure needs does not necessarily mean building large new facilities. It can be more effective and efficient to make smaller targeted investments or refurbishments, or use demand-led initiatives, such as congestion charging, to improve utilisation of existing infrastructure.

A long-term national-infrastructure plan therefore provides direction for investment activity across government within an agreed set of high-level objectives. It also helps the market to set itself up to respond in advance to future infrastructure investment needs as well as indicating to investors the ambitions of the country and preparing wider society for change. Another advantage of long-term planning, particularly national plans that are cross-sectoral, is better recognition of the inter-dependency of projects, improving their resilience: a new electric railway line depends on reliable power sources and may have an impact on the location and dimension of other transport alternatives, housing, education and health facilities. Yet planning of infrastructure often takes place within sector-focused line ministries that ignore some of these issues.

Developing a national infrastructure plan usually involves agreeing a vision and a setting out of long-term goals or needs. Multiple objectives, such as economic growth, health benefits, environmental outcomes, national *versus* local concerns and regional fairness, might require trade-offs but at least the plan recognises these and seeks to address them. The plan usually involves an assessment of the current situation, such as the state of existing infrastructure, government policies and laws, and market capacity. The gap between the current situation and the agreed long-term needs then identifies what needs to be done in terms of new policies, reform and investment.

Methodologies for selecting projects and prioritising them in a rational way usually involve some form of options appraisal and an assessment of benefits and costs to rank them (*cf.* Chapter 7). Equally the planning exercise should consider how new projects will be paid for. This may require agreeing policies as to whether tax-payers, direct users or both should pay for a particular project (*cf.* §9.2). It may also need to take account of how public funds are allocated in the budget process (annual as opposed to medium-term budgets can lead to sub-optimal projects being chosen—*cf.* §9.3). Stakeholder consultation (*cf.* §6.5) is also another feature of a well-run process to help ensure that all relevant interests have been considered and that there is wide support for the eventual plan. Any projects identified may each require further more-detailed assessment, and issues such as land use and planning approvals also need to be dealt with in due course (but their origin in the plan helps).

One of the issues with long-term national-infrastructure plans is ensuring the stability of the plan as the political environment changes, policies and supply-side issues such as technology evolve and demand-side issues change (such as users' willingness and ability to pay for services). To help ensure long-term stable political support, a separate independent national-infrastructure commission or agency that, although publicly funded, is apart from any ministry and has a degree of independence enshrined in its statutes is helpful. The work of developing the shorter-term investment project pipeline within the agreed long-term framework, however, may be led by a unit based in a cross-sectoral ministry such as an economy or finance ministry.

Other tools to help ensure stability of the plan include explicitly setting out the processes for project assessment and selection, ensuring cross-party political support, and having wide acceptance and publicity for the recommendations of the planning body. However, investment decisions ultimately need political ownership so the process is more about giving the right recommendations for decision-makers, rather than removing the decision-making from them.

At the same time, such long-term plans must not be too rigid. Thus, within the national plan that sets out the agreed overall direction and goals, the project-specific plans are usually developed on a medium-term rolling basis and periodically updated. The independent long-term planning body may also track and report on the performance of actual project delivery against the agreed plans.

To address the other issue of uncertainty about future requirements, planners might identify different versions of the future or 'scenarios'. Projects are then chosen on the basis of their robustness to deliver the agreed needs under various scenarios rather than the best one for one scenario only. Of course, this can make the process quite complex and communicating the results of the assessment a challenge.

PPPs are usually only a small part of an infrastructure plan, but they are increasingly recognised as one of the standard tools to be considered. Of course, the decision on using a PPP is one that should only be taken later on once the case for the project investment itself is made, but projects or groups of projects may be initially flagged as PPPs. On the other hand, infrastructure plans may be extremely relevant to PPP development as they may be one of the principal sources of PPP projects.

CHAPTER

5

The Project Cycle

§5.1 INTRODUCTION

This chapter provides an outline of the 'project cycle'—*i.e.* the various phases through which a PPP project passes. There are some important general themes that run through the cycle, especially in the earlier phases (§5.2). The different phases of the project cycle are summarised in this chapter (§5.3), while subsequent chapters identify the various activities and the issues associated with these in more detail.

At various points in the process, approval checkpoints may need to be passed to move to a next phase such as launching the procurement of the project (§5.4). Such checkpoints are also important sources of quality control, especially given the size and long-term nature of the commitments that PPPs may involve for the public sector. Various frameworks have also been developed by governments to help guide the overall project preparation process, such as the 'Five-Case Model' (§5.5).

§5.2 THE PROJECT CYCLE

Project development, especially in the early stages, is an evolving and iterative process. But there is a broad sequence of events and it is possible to identify a series of phases:

1. Needs Assessment (§5.3.1);
2. Project Definition and Options Appraisal (§5.3.2);
3. Project Economic Assessment and Selection (§5.3.3);
4. Procurement Review (§5.3.4);
5. Procurement Preparation (§5.3.5);

Public-Private Partnerships for Infrastructure
DOI: https://doi.org/10.1016/B978-0-08-100766-2.00005-X

6. Procurement (§5.3.6);
7. Construction (§5.3.7);
8. Operation (§5.3.8) and
9. Hand Back (§5.3.9).

Experience shows that the more thoroughly the earlier phases are carried out, the less risk there will be of the contracting authority procuring the wrong project, or of procuring it in the wrong way. The early stages of the life of a project have (or at least should have) less to do with PPP issues but if these stages are not dealt with properly, the PPP is less likely to succeed if the underlying project is poorly conceived. Public officials may be under political pressure to rush or skip parts of this process. But, rather like the foundations to a building, if these earlier often less-visible activities are neglected, the success of the project is likely to be undermined. Thus, PPP-related activities are part of a larger continuum in the development of a project from its initial conception to its final delivery.

The contracting authority is almost exclusively involved over the first five phases of the project cycle. With the exception of unsolicited proposals (*cf.* §10.7.5), these phases do not involve potential private-sector investors and lenders (other than in a consultative or advisory role).

While these early phases are presented as a series of separate steps, in reality there are a number of basic issues concerning the project and the way it should be delivered that have an impact on each other, and need to be re-examined as the project is developed. The difference between the phases is therefore more one of emphasis on a particular issue—phases 1 and 2 focus heavily on establishing the requirement for the project and its nature and scope, while phases 3-5 look at the best way to procure it and to prepare it for the chosen procurement approach.

This iterative or circular approach during the early phases helps to ensure that all the different components that will affect the success of the project as a PPP (or other chosen delivery route) have been properly considered before taking the decision to launch the public procurement. Any changes can then be assessed and made before they all become a part of the proposal that is put to the market in phase 6.

In addition to the change of focus over the early phases, the other characteristic of the earlier phases is that the contracting authority commits resources increasingly more intensively and more narrowly as the work converges on a particular project and procurement option.

The phased approach also links in with decision points within the contracting authority and in the wider public sector (*e.g.* the Ministry of Finance). These are usually linked to points in time when increased resources need to be committed for further work or the contracting authority commits itself to a formal process (such as procurement) or the long-term obligations of a PPP contract (*cf.* §5.4).

The later phases 6-9 reflect the more obvious phases in the project's life, namely procurement, construction of the facility, its operation (the longest phase) and hand back at the end of the PPP contract. The rôle of the contracting authority thus changes significantly in these phases from one of managing the preparation and procurement of the PPP project (*cf.* Chapter 6) to that of managing the PPP contract itself (*cf.* Chapter 19).

§5.3 PHASES IN THE PROJECT CYCLE

§5.3.1 Phase 1: Needs Assessment

This is the period during which the contracting authority:

- identifies the need for the project (for example to provide greater, safer and faster transport capacity between two cities);
- ensures that the needs fit with the wider government goals in terms of required objectives and strategies (for example as identified in a national infrastructure plan—*cf.* §4.8), other investment projects or programmes and any wider impact on government policies and strategies; and
- sets down the needs clearly as a benchmark to measure success later on in the project cycle (*cf.* §19.9).

This process should be the starting point of any project, whether eventually procured as a PPP or through conventional public-sector procurement, even if the need for the project may have been initially identified in a wider plan. An outline of the approach to needs assessment is described in §7.2.

§5.3.2 Phase 2: Project Definition and Options Appraisal

This is the period during which the contracting authority starts to identify potential different project options (*cf.* §7.3.2) to deliver the required needs (for example as a road, railway or airport)—by identifying an initial long list and shortlisting these project options towards the end of the phase, to be considered in the next phase for more-detailed economic assessment.

Even if procurement as a PPP may appear early on to be the only realistic way forward (*e.g.* due to public-sector budget constraints), the underlying need and economic rationale for the project should always be firmly established. So, any initial identification of the project as a potential PPP is just indicative at this stage. This avoids procuring the 'wrong' project.

Phases 1 and 2 are usually carried out by a small team within the contracting authority with limited expenditure on external advisers or detailed studies. At the end of this phase, the contracting authority decides whether or not to invest more time and resources on assessing the project further, usually based on a narrower list of options. As this involves a significant step-up in time and resources, the contracting authority may need to consider setting up a more formal project-management structure to oversee a wider team across the contracting authority (*cf.* §6.2) as well as the appointment and management of external advisers (*cf.* §6.4) for the next phases.

§5.3.3 Phase 3: Project Economic Assessment and Selection

In this phase, the contracting authority assesses in more detail the economic viability of the shortlist of project options identified in the previous phase and selects a preferred project option. The scope of the project is more closely defined and detailed demand, social and environmental, and other studies are carried out.

The focus of this phase is to assess which of the shortlisted project options is best able to deliver the identified needs in terms of benefits and costs. There may be a prescribed methodology for carrying out such an analysis (*cf.* §7.4). The key difference between this phase and the previous phase is the more detailed focus of the assessment on a narrower range of options.

During this phase, there may also be an initial scan of the suitability of the project as a PPP (*cf.* §8.9.1), the affordability of the project option will start to be assessed (*cf.* §9.2.2), early market sounding of the project options may take place (*cf.* §10.4) and the risks associated with the project start to be determined (*cf.* §11.2, §11.6), all in the context of identifying the option that maximises public value. The choice of PPP may sometimes be a strategic decision that has already been taken on how the service is to be delivered. This may be due, for example, to the absence of any realistic alternative or evidence of previous similar projects in a programme delivering VfM as PPPs (*cf.* §8.8.4). However, the underlying need for the project and the benefits of the project compared with its costs delivered as a PPP still need to be justified. In many other cases though, the VfM of the PPP as a potential mode of delivery for the underlying project compared to other modes is assessed in more detail, which is one of the key tasks of the next phase.

§5.3.4 Phase 4: Procurement Review

Unless the decision to use a PPP has already been taken at a policy or programme level, this is the phase during which the contracting authority assesses a PPP in more detail as a potential procurement approach for the project option selected in the previous phase by looking at:

- the scope of the PPP (*cf.* §7.5);
- whether PPP procurement will provide 'value for money' (VfM—*cf.* Chapter 8);[1]
- whether the PPP project is affordable (*cf.* §9.2) and how it is to be budgeted for (*cf.* §9.3);
- if relevant, the expected impact of the of the PPP project on the government's balance sheet (*cf.* §9.4);[2]
- the nature and level of commercial interest in bidding for the project as a PPP (*cf.* §10.4); and
- how the project risks are expected to be allocated between the public and private sector and the associated potential PPP contract terms (*cf.* Chapter 12).

---

[1] This may include the preparation of a 'public-sector comparator (PSC) to compare the cost as a PPP with conventional public procurement (*cf.* §8.3).

[2] In some countries, such as Australia, the balance-sheet impact is not assessed as this stage: all projects are assumed to be fully government funded; this also helps to remove the incentive to engineer the project to be off the government balance sheet when a PPP may not be the right choice for other reasons, such as value for money (*cf.* Chapter 8).

The final decision whether to launch the procurement of the project as a PPP may not be taken until the end of phase 5, when the proposed detailed terms of the PPP contract will be clear. Furthermore, arriving at these terms will involve assessing their impact on a range of areas including VfM and affordability. So in reality, phases 4 and 5 take place more in parallel than in sequence as they are usually dependent on each other. This book emphasises the importance of ensuring that the underlying project is sound before the procurement route (such as a PPP) is considered in any detail. However, consideration of the different procurement options can also take place in parallel with assessment of the underlying project if this is part of a disciplined options analysis where all aspects of the project are considered in a sequence of increasing detail (as in the Five-Case Model—*cf.* §5.5). The key point is to be careful if the decision 'to do a PPP' precedes and drives all future decisions of the project.

§5.3.5 Phase 5: Procurement Preparation

This is the period during which the contracting authority:

- prepares the project for PPP procurement including the bidding documents (*cf.* §10.6), and in particular the draft PPP contract and its key components such as:
  - the proposed risk allocation (*cf.* Chapters 11-14);
  - the service-fee mechanism (*cf.* Chapter 15);
  - other key PPP contract terms (*cf.* Chapters 16 and 17); and
- starts to clear all necessary permits and consents it is responsible for (*cf.* §12.2.3, §12.2.4), so that these are in place ideally prior to launching the public procurement and certainly before financial close (see below). This may include land acquisitions needed for the project, often one of the most significant causes of delay (*cf.* §12.2.1).

Phases 1 to 5 lead up to the critical point when the PPP project is ready to be launched on the market. These phases could be envisaged schematically as in Figure 5.1.

§5.3.6 Phase 6: Procurement

This is the period during which:

- the contracting authority requests and receives bids and chooses a bidder (*cf.* §10.6);
- the winning bidder establishes a special-purpose project company (*cf.* §20.6) in whose name the PPP contract and the various subcontracts for construction, service delivery, operation and maintenance, *etc.* (all of which are known collectively as the 'project contracts') are negotiated;
- the contracting authority's due-diligence process is completed (*cf.* §10.8); and
- the investors' equity investment (*cf.* Chapter 20) and the lenders' debt financing (*cf.* Chapter 22) are put in place.

The end of the Procurement Phase is known as 'financial close' (or the 'effective date'), *i.e.* the point at which all the interlinked conditions precedent for the project contracts and the financing are met (*cf.* §10.8.4), and construction of the facility can begin.

FIGURE 5.1 PPP project-development phases 1-5

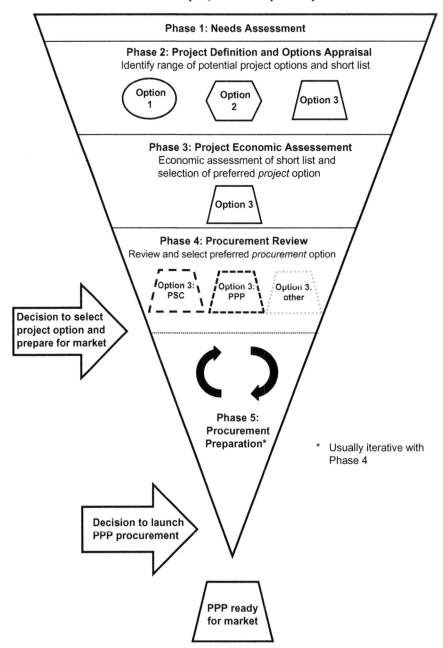

§5.3.7 Phase 7: Construction

Once a PPP project has reached financial close, the contracting authority's relationship with the project company (and through the project company with the investors, lenders and subcontractors) is one of contract management (*cf.* Chapter 19).

During the construction phase, the project's debt and equity investment are drawn down, and these funds are used to build the facility—the end of this process, when the facility is formally accepted as being available for use as specified in the PPP contract, is known as the 'service(s) availability date' (or the 'service(s) commencement date'); it is also commonly referred to as just 'completion'.

§5.3.8 Phase 8: Operation

This is the period during which the facility provides the services required by the PPP contract and produces cash flow to pay the lenders' debt service and the investors' equity return. The contracting authority's contract-management rôle continues (*cf.* §19.4).

§5.3.9 Phase 9: Hand Back

This is the period when the facility is handed back to the contracting authority at the end of the PPP contract (*cf.* §17.8, §19.5). The contracting authority may launch a new procurement to contract another private-sector entity to operate and provide the service using the existing facility.

§5.4 QUALITY-CONTROL REVIEWS AND APPROVALS

The latest form and status of the project are often reflected in a 'business case'. This is a document that evolves through each phase of the project cycle, becoming increasingly detailed and focussed on the particular recommended way forward. It is presented for political approval within the contracting authority (or to regional or central government) at the various approval points, such as before the decision to launch the procurement phase for the project.

Quality-control reviews and approvals are often used to manage the progression through phases 1-6 so ensuring that time and resources (such as engaging advisers) are not wasted in developing up the wrong projects or those unsuited for PPP procurement for reasons that can be identified earlier on. This usually involves reviewing successive updates of the business case.

Approvals are normally given by a regional or central government committee in the sponsoring line ministry or by a ministry of economy or finance depending on how, say, spending authority is delegated. In some cases, the approval committee-members may have wider PPP experience, including in other economic sectors. In other cases, where the committee members may not themselves have the necessary technical expertise to assess the project, the PPP unit (*cf.* §4.7) may review the project on its behalf and make a recommendation. The latter is typically the case where the approval committee is comprised of senior government officials or even ministers. (The seniority of the decision-makers can be an important signal of government commitment to the project.)

Reviews may be carried out by officials in the contracting authority not directly involved in the project—in this case the purpose of the review is not for approval but as a tool for the project team (*cf.* §6.2) to help it determine if the project is ready to move on to the next stage and so profit from the experience of colleagues who may have been involved in similar projects, a process sometimes referred to as 'assurance'. As the conclusions are for the benefit of the project team, review discussions are usually more technical and open. This 'peer-review' approach can also help spread best practice across the public sector.[3] Of course, there will still be a separate and independent approval process.

Clearly a balance has to be struck between numerous reviews and approvals and good quality control. Key approval points are usually:

- at the end of phase 2, before the decision to spend more resources on the project selection and its assessment and preparation as a potential PPP;
- at the end of phase 5, before launching the procurement; and
- prior to appointing the preferred bidder (*cf.* §10.5), or just prior to signing the PPP contract towards the end of procurement phase (*i.e.* towards the end of phase 6).

However, it is important to allow the project team and the project board (*cf.* §6.2.1, §6.2.2) to make key decisions as far as possible—this focuses attention on ensuring that the quality of the project board and project team is strong from the beginning.

Of course, quality-control reviews and approvals can be applied more widely across public-sector investment activities, but they are particularly useful for PPPs given (i) the costs involved in preparing and procuring projects, (ii) the complexity of the procurement documents involved and (iii) the long-term nature and value of the PPP commitment that the contracting authority is entering into.

Some countries, however, have found that if the PPP process appears more onerous in terms of reviews and approvals than other procurement options, it will simply be avoided for that reason (even if over the longer term the benefit of a strong review process means the PPP project gets to the finishing line sooner than one that is conventionally procured). This raises the question whether more needs to be done to improve quality control for other forms of procurement and create a common system across the whole of a government's public-investment decision and project-delivery process. This has been reflected in a number of countries that have extended the scope of their PPP units into infrastructure investment units (*cf.* §4.7).

§5.5 THE FIVE-CASE MODEL

Various management tools and approaches are available to guide contracting authorities, particularly over the earlier phases of the project cycle. Britain's 'Five-Case Model' (British Treasury 2015) provides a 'thinking framework' based on the approach that there are five core 'cases' that need parallel continuous development and assessment on the road to the eventual choice of project and the way it is procured, whether as a PPP or otherwise. Each 'case' is developed and reviewed throughout the process to ensure that the eventual project choice and the way it is procured:

---

[3] The 'gateway process' developed in Britain is an example of this (HM Treasury 2016).

1. Does the project meets the contracting authority's clearly-identified needs and fits its strategy and objectives—the 'strategic case';
2. Does it maximise public value, based on the identification of options and selection of the one that best meets the required needs (both for the project option itself and the way it will be procured, such as through a PPP)—the 'economic case';
3. Is it realistic and credible to the market place, can be procured and is commercially viable based on an identified service delivery structure, risk allocation and time-line—the 'commercial case';
4. Is it affordable to the public sector—the 'financial case'; and
5. Can the project actually be managed and delivered by the contracting authority involved based on identified governance arrangements and required resources—the 'management case'.

One of the benefits of the Five-Case Model approach is the recognition that each phase in the project cycle, as described earlier, is not in reality a single type of activity but a collection of different activities (*e.g.* phase 3 may be dominated by the economic assessment of project options but at this stage analysing affordability, risks and commercial viability through market sounding and even early stage assessment of PPP viability may also take place).

The Five-Case Model process is split into three main stages (somewhat confusingly also referred to as 'Cases'). These are represented by the document that is developed for each stage containing all the relevant project information for review at each stage, namely the 'Strategic Outline (or Initial) Case' (SOC)—up to around the end of phase 2 (Project Definition and Options Appraisal) as described in §5.3.2, the 'Outline (or Intermediate) Business Case' (OBC)—up to around the end of phase 5 (Procurement Preparation) as described in §5.3.5 and the 'Full' or 'Final Business Case' (FBC)—the end of phase 6 (Procurement) as described in §5.3.6. Quality-control/approval check-points (*cf.* §5.4) are applied to move from one stage to the next. The development of the business case however is the key issue rather than the precise number of stages as this is this a continuous process.

Over the different stages, the relative importance of each of the five cases may change as the questions in relation to them evolve, but the basic approach is to ensure that each of the five cases continues to support the project and the approach to procuring it and that they complement and do not conflict with each other. This model thus recognises that the public-sector choice of a project and the way it is procured is a multi-dimensional decision, and aims to reduce the risk, for example, that the eventual project that is delivered no longer meets the required needs (the Strategic Case) as a result of having to address issues around procurement (the Commercial Case) or affordability (the Financial Case). For example, the project might be identified as a 500-bed hospital to meet the identified health-care need. But later, further analysis reveals this to be too expensive or difficult for the market to deliver, suggesting it should be a smaller 300-bed hospital. This size of facility might be much less appropriate to meet the healthcare needs than, say, a much smaller central hospital and a range of primary healthcare facilities for the same overall cost. Thus, at each quality-control point or gateway, all five cases have to be in balance. The argument to procure the project as a PPP (or not) is built up over the course of the process alongside the other dimensions of the project and is based on the outcome of the different cases.

Public-Sector Project Management

§6.1 INTRODUCTION

Getting the project-management arrangements right from the start is one of the main drivers to a successful project. This is not a book about how the public sector manages its wider public-investment activities. However, focusing more narrowly on PPPs, this chapter briefly considers some of the organisational and management issues for a contracting authority once the underlying project rationale has been established, *i.e.* managing the process of taking a PPP project through Phases 4-6 (Procurement Review, Procurement Preparation and Procurement—*cf.* §5.3.4-§5.3.6). The contracting authority's rôle in the management of the subsequent phases is covered in Chapter 19.

A specific team is usually put in place for a project once it has reached a certain level of development, with appropriate arrangements to deal with reporting, decision-making and oversight (§6.2). PPP units can be important sources of support to the project team, particularly in the early years of a PPP programme or if the contracting authority is new to the PPP process (§6.3). Even in mature PPP programmes, project teams also make use of specialist advisers but care needs to be taken to select and manage these well (§6.4). Another key activity throughout the project cycle, and particularly as the PPP project is being prepared, is stakeholder management (§6.5).

§6.2 PROJECT GOVERNANCE

The PPP preparation and procurement process is very demanding for a contracting authority. It may have limited experience of preparing and procuring major projects, and even less with PPPs, since such projects are typically scattered across a variety of different public-sector bodies within a country. If this is the case, it may not make economic sense for the contracting authority to maintain staff with PPP procurement skills, so PPP procurement seldom forms part of the regular career path for a public official. Furthermore, it is often difficult for expertise gained in a PPP by one contracting authority to be transferred to others. For these reasons, although it can be argued that PPPs improve public-sector procurement skills (*cf.* §28.10), in reality the experience may be wasted. The importance of an organisational structure linked to public-sector centres of expertise, *i.e.* PPP units with a project-support rôle (*cf.* §4.7), is therefore evident.

Private-sector bidders also pay close attention to the way the contracting authority organises itself before deciding whether or not to risk the substantial time and costs in bidding for a PPP project. The key elements of such an organisational structure are set out below.

§6.2.1 Project Board

An *ad hoc* project board (or steering committee) is usually established, comprising senior officers from the contracting authority, and possibly politicians as well, depending on the contracting authority's general organisation. The project board has two main functions:

- *Oversight and decision-making*: This includes approving the overall plan and resources for the process, the parameters for any negotiation and the monitoring of progress against targets.
- *High-level support*: The project board provides the necessary high-level support to the project team (§6.2.2) to enable it to get its job done. In this respect, the rôle of chairman of the project board is vital in ensuring that there is strong senior 'ownership' of the project by the contracting authority. This needs to be visible across the rest of government and to potential private-sector bidders. The seniority of the chairman of the project board may also help the project team obtain the necessary approvals from other parts of the public sector and ensure that wider political support for the PPP is not lost (*cf.* §13.9, §28.13).

The project board typically meets monthly, sometimes more frequently, when key decisions and approvals (*e.g.* during the evaluation of proposals in the procurement phase) are required.

It is tempting to use the project board as a means to co-opt a wide range of stakeholders (*cf.* §6.5). This may lead to large boards that are difficult to operate—the project board needs to be able to meet regularly and have the ability and skills to take decisions, provide support to, and properly oversee the activities of the project team. Stakeholders are often better managed through separate arrangements whose activities are reported to the project board (*cf.* §6.5).

§6.2.2 Project Director and Project Team

A full-time project director (or manager) is needed—this is not a job that is easily combined with other official work. The project director should have strong project-management skills and be able to draw in expertise from the contracting authority's other departments, *e.g.* technical, finance and legal, to put together the project team. As discussed in §6.4, external advisers provide support, but should not be put in the position of running the project because of a vacuum within the contracting authority's project team.

One of the most regular criticisms of public procurement of PPPs is a lack of clarity about the decision chain. To the extent possible, it is obviously important for the project director to have delegated authority to negotiate matters of detail with the private-sector side of the table rather than constantly having to refer back to the project board. In turn, the project board will probably need to obtain approvals from the contracting authority's political masters and perhaps also other government bodies for key decisions such as approval of the final contract. The project board and team should therefore have a clear plan as to what is required to be reviewed and approved, by whom and when, and a realistic timetable for this. An established project-management methodology may also be used.

In addition to managing the day-to-day activities of the project team, the project director's rôle is also likely to involve management of the stakeholder engagement process (cf. §6.5). If important stakeholder groups are not properly involved, this is likely to mean either that outright opposition to the project develops, or that late and expensive alterations have to be made to the plans when stakeholders start raising objections.

§6.3 Rôle of the PPP Unit

A central or departmental PPP unit (cf. §4.7) is an important source of advisory or consultancy support to the project team.[1] For example, a PPP unit should know what internal and external resources are actually needed to prepare the PPP project, how much these will cost and how to procure and manage them. Similarly, if the contracting authority has had little previous experience of the PPP process, the PPP unit can help the project team to prepare the terms of reference for specialist external advisers (cf. §6.4).

In some cases, experts from the PPP unit may actually be members of the project board and/or the project team, sharing the tasks with colleagues from the contracting authority. This may even be mandatory as, for example, in Portugal (for all central-government PPP projects).

Sometimes the PPP unit may even take over the management of Phases 4-6, handing the project back to the contracting authority at some point after financial close. This approach is taken in Ireland (through National Development Finance Agency—NDFA) and the Canadian province of Ontario (through Infrastructure Ontario). A permanent specialised team within government thus manages the process. However, this requires a reasonable pipeline of projects, as well as willingness by the contracting authority to transfer, and the PPP unit to assume, full responsibility for the project from preparation to early operation.

§6.4 External Advisers

Contracting authorities normally use external advisers throughout Phases 4 (Procurement Review), 5 (Procurement Preparation), 6 (Procurement) and (to a lesser extent) 7 (Construction) and 8 (Operation) as laid out in §5.3. Failure to use advisers, or the wrong

[1] Consultancy support in this context means carrying out certain tasks as part of the required activities, whereas advisory support means providing guidance on how to do a task but not carrying out the task itself.

advisers, is likely to cause the PPP project to perform poorly, with consequent costs to the contracting authority well exceeding the costs of using advisers. Advisers help to ensure not only the feasibility and VfM of the PPP project, but also that the contracting authority fully understands the obligations into which it is entering. An inexperienced contracting authority, however, may understandably not always be aware of the type of advice needed and what it would have to pay for good-quality advice. This is another important area where support from a PPP unit can be valuable.

The costs of these advisers—along with those of the bidders (*cf.* §20.7) and the lenders (*cf.* §22.2.7)—make up a significant part of the initial project costs. While advisers are usually necessary to give the contracting authority objective advice, a wider commercial perspective and the benefit of experience in similar projects, they also need to be well-managed. Broadly speaking, the rôle of the contracting authority's advisers is to provide support in:

- the assessment of VfM (*cf.* Chapter 8) and affordability (*cf.* §9.2) of the project as a PPP;
- preparing the project for procurement (*cf.* §10.3, §10.4);
- negotiating with bidders (*cf.* §10.6.3);
- evaluating bids (*cf.* §10.6.5); and
- monitoring the activities of the project company, especially during the construction phase (*cf.* §19.3).

But advisers must advise, not run the project, or costs will never be kept under control. Unfortunately, it is quite common for the contracting authority's own staffing to be seriously under-resourced, or lack the necessary project-management skills. Far too much reliance is then placed on the advisers (*e.g.* advisers are left to make policy decisions on the contracting authority's behalf). If there is no command and control from within the contracting authority, this is usually a recipe for a project to drift on much more slowly and expensively (in advisory costs at least) than necessary. It also misses an opportunity to develop capacity in the contracting authority by its officials being actively involved in all the steps. It is important therefore to understand that PPP advisory work is different from some forms of technical assistance work that the contracting authority may be more used to, where the contracting authority's rôle is to review from time to time and finally accept a deliverable, such as a report. While PPP advisory work may involve some report preparation, it is 'active' with the advisers working closely with the contracting authority's project team throughout the preparation and procurement process. Thus the project team needs to be available and closely involved throughout if the advisers are to be effective in their work.

Advisers should generally be selected on a competitive basis, and should demonstrate that they have the skills relevant to the scope of their work. For example, a legal adviser who is experienced in public administrative law but has never worked on a privately-financed PPP project will only be able to provide limited support. Advisers should also not be allowed to learn about PPPs at the expense of the contracting authority. A pre-qualification process, including references from other contracting authorities for whom other work has been carried out, is therefore important. If procurement rules allow, interviews of those who will be providing the advice (not the 'sales' team) can be very valuable in ascertaining the adviser's approach to the task, the technical competence and availability of those who will actually be providing the advice and their understanding of the contracting authority's requirements.

The appointment of a 'big-name' adviser will not necessarily be efficient and effective if the advisory work is then delegated to a junior member of staff—therefore when advisers are appointed, the contracting authority must ensure that named individuals with appropriate experience are committed to working on the project, rather than the adviser's senior director turning up to make the initial presentation and then never being seen again until the signing dinner.

Typical external advisers are:

- financial (§6.4.1);
- legal (§6.4.2);
- technical (§6.4.3); and
- insurance, social, environmental and other specialist areas (§6.4.4).

Sometimes a lead transaction adviser is appointed to coordinate all the advisers (§6.4.5).

In all these cases, a method of payment for services needs to be agreed which keeps the contracting authority's development costs under control (§6.4.6). It need hardly be said that lowest cost should not be the sole criterion for selecting advisers (although a high cost is no guarantee of quality either).

§6.4.1 Financial Adviser

The financial adviser's scope of activities may include advice or assistance with:

- initial feasibility and structuring of the PPP, including advice on its financeability;
- risk analysis (*cf.* Chapters 11-14);
- preparation of the initial VfM appraisal (*cf.* Chapter 8);
- affordability assessment (*cf.* §9.2);
- soundings in the PPP market (*cf.* §10.4);
- preparation of bid documentation (*cf.* §10.6.2);
- support with dialogue or negotiation with bidders (*cf.* §10.6.4);
- financial evaluation of the bids (*cf.* §10.6.5);
- involvement in any equity or funding competition (*cf.* §26.4, §22.6); and
- specialised advice, *e.g.* on taxation (*cf.* §23.6).

Financial-advisory services can be provided to the public sector by the same banks that also advise bidders in the private sector (*cf.* §20.7.1), but the most active players in this market are the major firms of accountants. Project-finance work is people-intensive and financial-advisory work even more so as it requires more resources for a longer period of time. This is unattractive to banks because they have a limited number of people available, whereas accountants work on a different staffing model. In general, banks prefer to lend money rather than acting as pure financial advisers (*cf.* §22.2.5). Public-sector advisory work is also inherently less attractive to banks because the public sector tends to pay less, and there is less repeat business than from private-sector bidders that are pursuing world-wide PPP business.

However, accountants' staff are predominantly trained as accountants and may not always have direct lending experience behind them; also, accounting firms rely on a very broad-based pyramid of staff, so although they have more staff available for this work than banks, they are predominantly relatively junior staff. This means that there may be a lack of financial creativity in the advice given to the authority. Consequently, the financial-advisory 'firepower' on the public-sector side of the table may at times match up rather poorly with the support that lenders offer to the bidders on the other side of the negotiating table.

Some project-management and technical advisory firms, whose normal rôle is discussed below, have added financial advice to their overall service, either by sub-contracting this work to smaller advisory boutiques, or recruiting their own staff for this purpose.

§6.4.2 Legal Adviser

The contracting authority may have an in-house legal department, but handling of the work for a PPP will probably be beyond its capacity and experience, especially when it comes to detailed issues of PPP contracts and project finance. However, the legal department should be closely involved in the process, and in particular should manage and control the work to be undertaken by external legal advisers, as well as its costs. External legal advisers' scope of work may include advice on:

- general legislative background (for a new PPP programme) (*cf.* §4.3);
- drafting the PPP contract (*cf.* Chapters 15-17), making use of standard forms, where these exist (*cf.* §4.3.2), and the experience of PPP contracts in other countries;
- other specialised legal aspects of the project such as site-related issues (*cf.* §12.2), staff transfers (*cf.* §28.13), tax (if not covered by the financial adviser) and possibly the impact of contract clauses on balance-sheet treatment (*cf.* §9.4.5);
- preparing bid documentation (*cf.* §10.6.2), and ensuring that the bidding procedure fits with relevant procurement legislation (*cf.* §10.5);
- support with dialogue (*cf.* §10.6.4) with bidders; and
- handling the formal legal procedures and documentation including any changes proposed by bidders to the draft PPP contract.

The competition for legal-advisory services to the public-sector for a PPP is probably greater than that for financial-advisory services, and although law firms also work on a pyramid structure, this is less broad at the base than accountants. International law firms, especially the London-based ones, have played a major rôle in developing PPP programme documentation around the world, but clearly local legal expertise is also required.

§6.4.3 Technical Adviser

The scope of the technical adviser's work can be wider or narrower, depending on the contracting authority's in-house ability to take on rôles such as project management and technical or costing aspects of project design; the work may therefore include different aspects of the project such as:

- general project-management services throughout the procurement process;
- preparation of construction and operating costs estimates and assumptions to be used for the financial model, including for the affordability assessment (*cf.* §9.2);
- support in risk analysis (*cf.* Chapters 11-14) and drafting output specifications for the PPP contract (*cf.* §15.2);
- structuring the technical aspects of the bid documentation;
- evaluating the technical aspects of bids;
- support in dialogue on technical aspects of the bids with bidders (*cf.* §10.6.4);
- design review (*cf.* §10.8.1); and
- construction supervision (*cf.* §19.3).

In concessions, the technical adviser may also prepare the initial traffic or other demand studies (*cf.* §13.2). As mentioned above, the technical adviser's rôle may even be extended into financial-advisory work.

This work is generally undertaken by professional-services firms that provide consultancy in some or all of design, planning, engineering and project management. Depending on the scope of the work, parts of it, such as traffic studies, may be subcontracted to specialist firms. Alternatively, the contracting authority may split the work among two or more advisers.

Design review and construction supervision may be carried out by an independent 'checker'.[2] The checker's rôle is to be impartial between the project company and the contracting authority, and in due course to certify that the completed facility meets the initial output specifications. Costs are paid by the project company, but the appointment is a joint one with the contracting authority. Employment of a checker should not relieve the project company of its own obligations under the PPP contract to meet output specifications.

§6.4.4 Other Specialist Advisers

Insurance advice in the PPP context is provided by specialist advisory departments of major insurance brokers. Similar but separate advisers are appointed by the project company (*cf.* §20.7) and lenders (*cf.* §22.2.7). The rôle is a minor but important one, since the contracting authority's interests in the PPP project insurances have to be properly protected (*cf.* §14.7).

Social and environmental advisers may also play an important rôle, especially during the preparation stages of the project, to identify and assess potential risks in these fields and consider the mitigation of such risks in developing the scope and design of the project (*cf.* §12.2.4). Identifying adverse issues after bid award is likely to be devastating to the viability of the project or cause significant delays (*e.g.* delays and cost overruns experienced as a result of having to meet additional environmental requirements).

---

[2] Also known as the 'independent certifier' (or 'IC'), 'contract administrator' or '*maître d'œuvre*'.

§6.4.5 Lead Transaction Advisers

In a number of markets, a 'lead transaction adviser' may be appointed. This adviser covers one of the specialist areas, usually financing, as well as sub-contracting and managing the other advisers. The objective of this is to make the procurement and management of the various advisers easier for the contracting authority, especially if it has limited PPP transaction experience. However, it may also prevent access to the most appropriate advisers in each of the specialist areas. For this reason, lead transaction advisers are not commonly used in more mature PPP markets.

§6.4.6 Advisory Costs

While the first criterion for choosing an external adviser is certainly expertise, not cost, the contracting authority has to plan and control advisers' costs carefully or they will soon become a cash hæmorrhage. A clear and detailed brief should be agreed for the work, ideally split into stages such as initial feasibility, bid preparation, procurement and bid evaluation. Payment may be split to match these stages, with an option to terminate at the end of each stage.

Payment may be on a simple hourly- or daily-rate basis, but there is merit on considering other alternatives to limit the cost risk, *e.g.*:

- a fixed fee or cap for each stage of the work; or
- regressive fee arrangements, whereby the more the work the lower the hourly rates or
- payment of part of the fee on a success basis.

Fixed fees or capped fees are likely only to apply for a period of time, after which time-based fees will resume: this means that if the timetable is unrealistic, fixed or capped fees are of limited value. Care needs to be taken in negotiating success fees, so that the adviser is not given a perverse incentive to close the deal to earn the fee even if this is not in the contracting authority's best interests; on the other hand, a pure hourly-rate basis creates a reverse incentive to spin out discussions. Fees based on a percentage of project costs, rather than fixed amounts, are also best avoided.

Particular care needs to be taken to control legal costs if the legal advisers are paid for the time they spend working rather than by a fixed fee: their time needs to be used effectively. For example, lawyers should not be used as an expensive secretarial service, *e.g.* hosting and writing notes on meetings discussing commercial issues, rather than just being told the result of such meetings. However, this is not to say that lawyers should always be kept away from commercial issues, as their experience in other PPPs may be useful in this respect.

§6.5 STAKEHOLDER MANAGEMENT

An important activity in the development of any project (PPP or otherwise) is the identification and management of those who are likely to be affected, both positively and negatively, by the project. These are usually referred to as 'stakeholders' and range from immediate users, to those whose rights or property might be affected by the project, and to the various approval bodies across the public sector. Identifying stakeholders should take place in the initial phases of the project cycle and continue thereafter with a register of stakeholders updated and reviewed regularly, including over the contract-management phase (*cf.* Chapter 19).

Stakeholders are a vital source of information throughout the life of a project, be it in helping to develop the output requirements of the projects (such as teachers or clinicians), or in sounding the market (*cf.* §10.4) to assess costs and market appetite and identify risks and obstacles.

Not identifying and engaging with stakeholders, especially users, or those whose rights may be affected by the project, can lead to significant obstacles later on. Early engagement helps to ensure that the project team identifies objections to the project at a time when they may be able to take steps to redefine the project to avoid such obstacles. It also helps to generate support and enthusiasm for the project. The difference between a PPP and privatisation (*cf.* §2.3) should be clearly communicated as part of this engagement process.

To help manage the process, stakeholders are often classified into a grid along the lines of high and low influencers on one axis and high and low impacted on the other axis. This helps to prioritise engagement, *i.e.* to focus on the most highly impacted and most influential stakeholders but this may not always be appropriate either in terms of fairness or of accessing those whose views may be valuable for the project. Stakeholder communication is therefore not just about 'selling' the idea of the project, and 'winning people round', but of *listening* to stakeholders and ensuring that the project best meets the needs of those it affects.

7

Assessing Needs, Project Definition and Selection

§7.1 INTRODUCTION

This chapter outlines some of the main approaches used in Phases 1-3 and the start of Phase 4 in the project cycle, namely:

- assessing the underlying needs for the project (§7.2)—a Phase 1 activity;
- identifying the definition and scope of the potential project options (§7.3)—a Phase 2 activity;
- assessing economic viability in terms of its benefits and costs (§7.4)—a Phase 3 activity; and
- defining the scope of the potential PPP project (§7.5)—an early Phase 4 activity.

These activities logically precede and lead into the decision whether to pursue the project *as a PPP*, which is dealt with in Chapters 8 and 9.

This is not a book about project appraisal and assessing the economic viability of public investment, which are large topics in their own right. Indeed, those assessing projects for PPP procurement may not necessarily be directly involved in these earlier phases so the following only provides an overview of some of the main issues integral to the sound foundation of any project, whether or not procured as a PPP. Those responsible for delivering a PPP need to make sure that the underlying project is a sound one: as the often-repeated saying goes 'a PPP cannot turn a bad project into a good one'. There is much guidance available on this topic such as the European Commission's *Guide to Cost-Benefit Analysis of Investment Projects* (European Commission 2014), the planning tools available on the US Federal Highways Administration website (see References and Further Reading) or the British Treasury's *Green Book* (British Treasury 2003, 2006, 2013) and its supplementary guidance on the Five-Case Model (*cf.* §5.5), to name a few examples.

§7.2 Needs Assessment

The starting point in the life of a project requires identifying where it is one is trying to get to, *i.e.* clearly defining the objectives that are being sought. The gap between these objectives and existing arrangements defines the needs for the project, *i.e.* the problem or difficulty, which the public intervention[1] aims to meet sometimes referred to 'as the case for change'. This takes place in Phase 1 of the project cycle (*cf.* §5.3.1).

It is important to be able to measure later on if the actual outcomes of the project are in line with the originally identified objectives (*e.g.* faster, safer and greener transport links between *a* and *b*). Thus, objectives are often expressed in terms of measurable *outputs* that are easier to define and measure (such as provision of *x* km of road space of a defined quality between *a* and *b*) and that collectively deliver the outcome. However, in choosing a particular set of outputs, care must be taken not to exclude other solutions that may be better at achieving the required objectives. For example, provision of *x* km of road space presumes that the best way to meet a transport link is to build a road. But an air or sea link or a combination of the two may be better. This can be done by considering all options that could deliver the required outcomes, which should take place in Phase 2 (*cf.* §5.3.2, §7.3.1).

In defining its objectives, the contracting authority usually has to consider broader strategies or national, regional or sectoral investment plans or policies (*cf.* §4.8). A typical example is a hospital, which in almost all cases needs to be considered in the context of a wider health strategy. Or the objective may be to comply with a regulatory requirement (such reducing landfill waste disposal by *y*%). At this early stage, the contracting authority's focus is on being clear about what needs to be done and less on the detail of how to do it, which comes later. This phase aims to ensure that there is a strong link between the eventual shape of the project and the policy behind it.

Identifying the needs and objectives at the beginning of the process (and ensuring that there is political agreement on these) reduces the risk of the contracting authority changing its mind later and fundamentally affecting the rationale for the project. This is bad for any project but particularly for a PPP: a change in requirements during the procurement phase will cause delays, increased costs and reduce the credibility of the contracting authority. And once the PPP is under way it is expensive if major changes to a long-term PPP contract are required (*cf.* §16.2.2). Furthermore, the clearer the initial definition of the needs and objectives, the easier it is to define the actual project for the purpose of assessing all the relevant risks and developing the output requirements.

Another benefit of clearly identifying the needs and objectives is that this provides a benchmark against which success of the overall project can be measured by a national

---

[1] A public intervention can be analysed as 'a set of financial, organisational and human resources mobilised to achieve, in a given period of time, an objective or set of objectives, with the aim of solving or overcoming a problem' (European Court of Auditors 2013).

performance-audit body (*cf.* §19.9), may be several years later. Such bodies may use tools such as a 'logic model' (*cf.* EPEC 2018) in which needs, objectives, outcomes and outputs can have precise meanings. Failure to be clear about the needs and objectives risks the contracting authority being judged later against different objectives identified at the time of the review and not at the start of the project with the authority's involvement.

In defining the needs and objectives, a contracting authority assesses the expected levels and type of demand for the service and determines whose demands are being met (*i.e.* the beneficiaries of which there may be a core group for whom the benefits may be essential and a wider group for whom they are desirable). Estimating the nature and level of expected demand for the services may be difficult especially if this involves an assessment of users' willingness and ability to pay for the service (*cf.* §9.2.3, §15.5). The contracting authority must also identify those parties that are likely to be affected, positively and negatively, by the project through identifying and engaging with all the relevant stakeholders (*cf.* §6.5).

Of course, defining needs and objectives is not exclusive to the development of a PPP project and should apply to all public-investment decisions.

§7.3 PROJECT DEFINITION AND OPTIONS APPRAISAL

Once the needs and objectives are clear, the next step is to identify the best way to meet these. There are usually various different solutions or project options to do so. Thus, the task is to identify these different options, *i.e.* to identify the definition and scope of each option and chose the one that is best able to ensure that the needs, and ultimately the objectives, are met.

§7.3.1 Project Definition and Scope

The European Commission defines a project as 'a series of works, activities or services intended to accomplish an indivisible task of a precise economic and technical nature that has clearly identified goals' (European Commission 2014). A project therefore typically includes the following main components:

- the scope of works or activities;
- the services provided (the outputs);
- the timing of the works and services;
- costs; and
- the technology involved.

It is important to avoid the scope of the project being so wide as to be meaningless or too narrow that vital works or activities are missing. This is particularly relevant for a PPP project where great precision will be needed later on in defining who is responsible for what and the basis upon which the private partner is rewarded (or penalised) for providing the outputs.

Another way of looking at a project is as a bundle of different activities each with its associated risks. So, in defining the project, the main risks need to be identified early on including any constraints, such as government regulations, that may affect achieving the required needs. Any dependencies that the project has on other activities or related infrastructure also need to be identified. For example, a power project relies on the availability of a sub-station and grid connection, which may have to be included as a part of the project scope—otherwise the PPP project may become a 'stranded asset' (*cf.* §12.2.7, §28.12). It may also be necessary to include any future works or activities in the project scope to ensure continued delivery of the service.

§7.3.2 Options Appraisal

It is tempting immediately to pick one particular way or project to address the defined needs and objectives. But, as alluded to above, is it the best way? One of the major reasons for projects to fail is to choose the wrong project in the first place. This is often the result of ignoring a comprehensive assessment of options or, even if some options are considered, to start off selecting these from too narrow a field. A common approach to identifying the 'right' project is to identify an initial 'long list' of different project options likely to meet the identified needs and objectives, with each option defined at a fairly high level (*e.g.* an option for a single central hospital or for a number of smaller clinics to deliver a required health need), rejecting any options that are considered obviously unsuitable. This assessment of options also includes looking at how the required needs and objectives could be met through other means, such as a change of procedures or management, rather than simply more investment. Phase 2 of the project cycle therefore involves identifying the project options long list and then whittling this down to a shortlist of potential candidates, including 'a business as usual', 'a do minimum', a preferred and a more ambitious option. Phase 3 involves assessing the economic viability of the shortlist and identifying, usually, a single preferred option. The reason for conducting this process in two phases is to avoid wasting time and resources assessing too many project options in detail and recognising that a decision usually needs to be taken in order to focus more time and resources on the much more detailed analysis of the shortlisted project options. Thus, the activities in the two phases are quite similar, but it is the level of detail and analysis (and cost of doing so) that changes.

Options appraisal should always include a 'do-nothing' or 'business-as-usual' option. This serves as the basis against which the incremental costs and benefits of the other more comprehensive project options can be measured, as well as revealing the economic costs of *not* doing anything.[2]

A good options analysis seeks to be as comprehensive as possible, to disaggregate a problem into its constituent parts, to reveal and challenge implicit assumptions and to consult stakeholders in a structured and transparent way. The sequence to identify a particular option involves first identifying the different levels of the scope (essential, desirable, optional), then, for each particular scope, the range of potential solutions (*e.g.* use of

---

[2] If undertaking the project as a PPP is the only way forward, the most important comparison is with the 'do-minimum' option.

infrastructure), then the potential of ways to deliver this scope and solution (*e.g.* in-house), then the potential ways to implement this bundle of scope/solution/implementation (*e.g.* in phases) and finally the available ways to fund this (*e.g.* public or private resources, or a mix). For each of these 'layers' different alternatives would be matched against how well they achieve the objectives (or 'critical success factors') identified earlier. Options appraisal is, for example, a core part of the Five-Case Model approach (*cf.* §5.5).

Preliminary designs for each project option are unlikely to be available at the initial stage, so cost estimates are likely to be based on readily available unit costs, and many of the benefits are likely to be expressed in qualitative rather than in money terms. As the number of options is narrowed down, the benefit and cost estimates are examined in much greater detail (*cf.* §7.4).

In essence, the decision whether or not to include a particular project option focuses on two broad issues:

— Whether or not the project option *could* be realised.

This reviews the issues associated with the project components listed above in §7.3.1—for example is the technology involved proven or will it involve significant risks, are the costs likely to be so high as to fall well outside the funding capacity of the contracting authority or are there likely to be any legal barriers to a particular project option or issues around compliance with environmental and social standards or regulations due to the nature of the works or activities involved? This filter helps to rule out unrealistic project options.

— Whether the project option *should* be carried out in terms of benefits and costs to society.

This involves assessing the economic viability of the project option, the topic of the next section. (For the purposes of this discussion, 'economic' is assumed to include social as well as environmental costs and benefits, as may be required by a government's policy and regulations.) This process also helps to rank and therefore choose between possible more realistic project options.

§7.4 Assessing Project Economic Viability

When deciding if a project option is economically justifiable, a contracting authority:

- identifies the benefits and costs of the project option, including its indirect effects (§7.4.1);
- prepares a benefit-cost analysis (§7.4.2), a key element of which is the discount rate to be applied to future benefits and costs (§7.4.3);
- may adjust the analysis to take account of 'optimism bias' (*cf.* §8.3.3); and/or
- may calculate the 'economic rate of return' (ERR) of the project (§7.4.4).

This is mainly a Phase 3 activity although high level assessment of economic viability may also be used in Phase 2 during the process of shortlisting the project options.

§7.4.1 Identifying Benefits and Costs

Market prices may be available to reflect the value of benefits but care should be taken in case monopolies, taxes or subsidies distort these values. If market values do not exist, various techniques can be used to determine a value (such as willingness to pay, 'revealed preference',[3] or shadow prices,[4] in the case of costs). Determining the value of benefits may be one of the most difficult tasks in the economic assessment. The value of benefits and costs will also vary depending on the nature of the different people affected.

The evaluation of a public-sector project also has to take account of (and place a valuation on) its wider economic benefits or costs. These are referred to as 'externalities'.[5] Externalities, which are positive where they provide a benefit and negative where there is a cost, may include:

- economic development—*e.g.* increases in land values and general economic activity;
- effects on safety or public health—*e.g.* reductions in accident deaths once a new road has been built; and
- environmental impact—*e.g.* increases or decreases in noise or air pollution (*cf.* §12.2.4).

When it comes to a PPP, it is worth noting that the cost of externalities cannot easily be included in the service fees paid by users of a concession, which is why there is often a case for public-sector subsidy in such instances (*cf.* §18.1).

§7.4.2 Benefit-Cost Analysis

The benefits and the net externalities should be compared with the project costs. These are usually expressed in real terms (*cf.* §24.3.1) or constant prices, *i.e.* without adjusting for future inflation.

Funding or financing of these costs—whether from taxation, public-sector borrowing or as a PPP—is not relevant at this stage. Indeed, there is often confusion between the affordability analysis of a project, which focuses on whether and how a project can be paid for, which is obviously important (*cf.* §9.2) and the economic analysis of a project, which assesses its net benefit or cost to society. Thus, in addition to excluding the costs of capital, an economic analysis should not include such 'costs' as depreciation (*cf.* §23.6) or transfer payments within government (*e.g.* VAT—§23.6.3).

Because of the different timing of these benefits and costs, the contracting authority normally uses either a DCF (*cf.* §3.2.2) or an IRR (*cf.* §3.3) calculation to compare the benefits with the costs and to compare the *net* benefits or costs of one project with another (*cf.* §3.4.2). Using a DCF calculation, the benefit of a public-sector project can be assessed as:

---

[3] Revealed preference is a technique to reveal user preferences by analysing users' purchasing habits.

[4] A shadow price is the opportunity cost to society of participating in some form of economic activity, used when a market price is not available or where prices do not reflect the true scarcity value of a good.

[5] Also known as 'external economies or diseconomies'.

- the PV of project benefits; and
- the PV of positive externalities

and the costs can be assessed as:

- the PV of project costs; and
- the PV of negative externalities.

The NPV (*cf.* §3.2.1) of these figures is calculated using the public-sector discount rate (PSDR) (*cf.* §7.4.3, §8.6.2). As with any investment, if the total NPV is positive, the investment can be justified. However, as discussed in §3.4.1, the difficulty with a simple DCF approach is that if a choice of projects is being evaluated, the more expensive project may be favoured by the DCF approach, and therefore the *ratio* between the benefits and costs, as opposed to the absolute *difference* between the benefits and costs, is needed.

If benefits cannot easily be measured (or there are unlikely to be many different possible benefits), which may often be the case with social infrastructure, then just the costs of different solutions have to be compared—this is known as a 'cost-effectiveness analysis'. Of course, this approach is not much use for assessing if the underlying benefits themselves are economically justified.

There is a further issue with using DCF calculations to make public-sector investment decisions: the effect of discounting costs a long way in the future (*e.g.* the decommissioning costs for a nuclear power station, or the cost of repurchasing land). If, say, a project involves a cost for the public sector of $1 million in 30 years' time, discounting this at 6% gives a cost in today's terms of $174,110, which may be considered small in relation to the NPV of the project as a whole. But in 30 years' time, the $1 million will still have to be found, unless $174,000 is set aside today and saved up with interest at 6% for 30 years, which does not usually happen in reality. Thus, the generation of today may place an undervalued burden on future generations by using a DCF calculation to make investment decisions where there are large-scale costs towards the end of the life of a project (*cf.* §15.3.2). Moreover, the higher the discount rate, the more the effect of such costs in the future is disregarded in today's terms.

Of course not all benefits and costs can be captured in money terms and therefore the ranking of project options is also subjected to any relevant qualitative benefit, cost and risk factors. The ranking should also be assessed taking into account the sensitivity to changes in key assumptions, the impact of any policies relating to the social and geographic spread of benefits and costs or the impact on particular groups (such as age or sex).

§7.4.3 Public-Sector Discount Rate

The discount rate to be used is a key issue, not only in the economic-viability calculation where a DCF approach is being used, but also in any comparison between the PPP and public-sector procurement options. Because this involves a decision on how the public sector should deploy public resources, this is referred to as the public-sector discount rate (PSDR). The question of what rate should be taken as the PSDR is difficult to resolve, and the approach varies from country to country, as discussed in more detail in §8.6.2. The results of the calculation will vary greatly depending on the discount rate used.

§7.4.4 Economic Rate of Return

The alternative to a DCF-based calculation is to use the 'economic rate of return' (ERR), *i.e.* an IRR (*cf.* §3.3) calculation that uses the same economic data. This may be contrasted with the 'financial rate of return' (FIRR), *i.e.* the direct cash-flow return from the project, or project IRR (*cf.* §20.3.2). In the ERR calculation, the investment has to pass an IRR hurdle rate similar to the PSDR to be justifiable. But again, as discussed in §3.4, an IRR calculation has its defects in this respect—in particular, the undervaluation of benefits received in the long term. This measure too must therefore be treated with care, and ideally adjusted by changing the reinvestment rate to the PDSR *via* a MIRR calculation to better reflect reality (*cf.* §3.4.3). So, choosing the hurdle rate and dealing with risk adjustment is as difficult as an evaluation using a DCF calculation.

§7.5 SCOPE OF THE PPP

Identifying the project definition and scope and choosing the best project option are the initial stages of the process. But when it comes to deciding whether the project could or should be delivered as a PPP the immediate question arises as to the scope of the PPP itself, *i.e.* whether the PPP should cover all or only a part of the overall project. There is a fundamental difference between projects such as roads, where most if not all the services that are part of the project itself (such as accident recovery, repair and maintenance) are normally included within the scope of a PPP contract, and projects such as hospitals, where there is a considerable variation on the possible scope of services (for example it obviously makes a substantial difference to the PPP contract whether or not medical equipment or clinical services are included).[6]

So, the contracting authority needs to consider whether or not it is appropriate to include ancillary services in the long-term PPP contract if it would not be usual to do so in a non-PPP contract. For example:

- Clinical services in a hospital: it is probably inappropriate to sign a contract for such services for 15 years or more as it is difficult to take account of how the requirements for clinical services would change over that time.
- Soft FM services (*cf.* §13.6): again, such services are usually provided on comparatively short-term contracts and so there is a question of whether they should be 'hard wired' into a PPP (*cf.* §15.6.7).
- Waste processing: a PPP project for a waste incinerator can also involve the provision of waste-collection services, but it is questionable whether the latter should be for a long period of time, partly because requirements may change (*e.g.* as to frequency of collections, recycling requirements, *etc.*) and partly because if this is only an add-on service in the PPP contract, the ability to impose penalties for poor performance is

---

[6] Indeed, this may point to more than one PPP option to consider before coming to the preferred option.

limited; a contract for, say, five to seven years should ensure that the waste-collection contractor is incentivised to perform well or the contract may be lost at the next renewal.[7]

What all these ancillary services have in common is that they involve little capital investment,[8] and make the PPP contract 'service-heavy', which is not attractive to financial investors or lenders (*cf.* §15.6.4). In a similar vein, contractor capacity and interest may also be limited if too many project services are combined into the scope of the PPP. One of the purposes of market sounding (*cf.* §10.4) is to determine whether there would be any such market constraints to the scope of the PPP.

Limiting the number of activities to be included in the PPP component has to be balanced with the potential of increased interface risk (*cf.* §18.7, §28.9.3) if the project is split into different contracts (which may need to be of different lengths) potentially reducing the rationale for the PPP from the contracting authority's perspective. All this highlights the iteration that takes place between defining and refining the project scope during Phases 2 and 3 and assessing and preparing it as a PPP during the Procurement Review and Procurement Preparation phases (Phases 4 and 5). There is also the risk that such considerations in later phases may 'bend the project out of shape'. It is important to re-check at later stages in the project cycle that the project scope as defined at these stages is still able to deliver the originally defined needs and objectives.

§7.5.1 Packaging Smaller PPPs

PPPs usually involve significant upfront preparation and procurement costs. This makes them unsuitable for smaller projects. However, programme approaches that standardise the processes and documentation help to address this issue (*cf.* §4.6). And if the contracting authority is seeking to procure a batch of similar facilities, these may be packaged into a single contract. In fact, the history of Britain's schools PFI projects is broadly one that originated with a single school procurement, matured into packaging schools contracts and subsequently developed into various programme approaches.

Packaging projects into a single larger contract may also make the offer more interesting to the market and help improve competitive tension. However, packaging too many individual projects may make it difficult for the contracting authority to manage the overall PPP contract (especially if these are early projects in a country's PPP programme with limited contracting experience available), or including facilities that are geographically too dispersed may make it difficult for the private sector to deliver an effective service. Such packaging of projects across different local contracting authorities can also conflict with the autonomy that individual authorities usually seek to preserve. As with many of the issues surrounding the use of PPPs, a balance has to be struck and judgement exercised after considering a number of different factors.

---

[7] In some countries, there may be entrenched interests in waste collection that make it politically difficult to disturb existing arrangements and include the waste-collection services in a new PPP arrangement.

[8] In the case of waste collection, investment in refuse trucks is needed, but these have a fairly short life and so renewal of these is more like an operating cost.

The PPP Decision—Value for Money

§8.1 Introduction

Having decided that a new facility is economically justified (*cf.* §7.4) and the scope of a potential PPP might be (*cf.* §7.5), how can a contracting authority decide whether the PPP route is the 'right' one? This brings us to one of the key activities of the Procurement Review (Phase 4 of the project cycle)—assessment of value for money (VfM).

The concept of VfM can be confusing and it is helpful to understand the different contexts in which it is used (§8.2). Assessing VfM often involves determining the cost of a public-sector procurement option (§8.3) and the cost of a theoretical private-sector PPP option and/or actual tenders (§8.4) and comparing the two options (§8.5).

There are significant flaws and practical limitations in this methodology (§8.6). However, so long as the flaws and limitations are understood, the process still has value in providing the discipline to assess the long-term risks and costs of a PPP project (§8.7).

In view of the difficulties of measuring VfM in quantitative terms, an other approach involves comparing the characteristics of a particular PPP proposition against a set of criteria that indicate whether or not VfM is likely to be achieved. As evidence is built as to what these criteria are (such as minimum project size), this more qualitative approach (§8.8) is increasingly used, but usually still complimented by quantitative approaches. When and by whom these various VfM assessment tools are used over the project cycle is discussed in §8.9.

§8.2 The Concept of 'Value for Money'

When talking about VfM, it is helpful to distinguish between *assessing* VfM and *achieving* VfM:

- Governments need to *assess* VfM both in the context of *looking forward* to help in making and justifying a decision for something they are about to do and in *looking back* to measure if public resources have been deployed well, *i.e.* as part of the process of holding contracting authorities to account for what they do as well as learning from the past.
- *Achieving* VfM is about how well a contracting authority goes about the process of selecting, preparing, procuring and managing a PPP project (and this need not be limited only to those projects procured as PPPs).

Thus, just because a project is assessed as likely to deliver VfM does not mean that it will do so. On the other hand, what the contracting authority *does* to achieve VfM (such as running an efficient and competitive procurement process) is arguably more important than what it *measures*.

But what is meant by VfM? VfM was a term first used by government audit bodies as a framework to assess how well (or badly) government entities had deployed public resources based on the criteria of economy, efficiency and effectiveness (the '3 Es'— *cf.* §19.9). VfM therefore started life as an *ex-post* (retrospective) evaluation or assessment concept. It was only later that it came to be used in the context of making future PPP-procurement decisions, as an *ex-ante* (forward-looking) assessment tool to identify whether or not there was an opportunity for VfM and so help decision-making.

This chapter largely discusses VfM in this *ex-ante* assessment context (while much of this book is really about achieving VfM).

As an *ex-ante* decision tool, VfM compares possible options. VfM is therefore a relative concept. When we say '*x*' represents 'good VfM', we actually mean '*x*' represents better VfM than '*y*', *i.e.* a better combination of cost and quality than '*y*'.

VfM aims to take into account the balance between cost *and* quality, highlighting that *both* elements should be considered when making a spending decision. The British government, for example, defines VfM as 'the optimum combination of whole-of-life costs *and* quality to meet the user's requirement' (British Treasury 2006). The definition goes on to say that 'VfM is not the choice of goods and services based on the lowest cost bid.' (The point here is that quality should not be ignored.) Cheapest is not always best: a meal in a café may be cheaper than one in a five-star restaurant but poorer VfM because the quality of the food, service and ambience may be much lower. So, it is the combination of the cost and quality, not just the cost that makes for a better choice.[1]

The reference to 'whole-of-life costs' in the British Treasury's definition should be noted—implicit in the concept of VfM is the importance of the *long-term* nature of costs and quality: comparing the construction costs of different options to build a road is fairly meaningless unless one also compares the differing longer-term costs of its upkeep and associated benefits, depending on which option is chosen.

---

[1] In some countries, the term 'efficiency', rather than VfM, is used to describe the delivery of the quality of service for a given cost, as for example in Poland.

The other important element that VfM tries to take into account is that of *risk.* A project is essentially a collection of risks and managing these risks in the cheapest possible way ensures that public (and users') resources are used efficiently. VfM assessment helps to ensure that public-investment decisions take into account the important questions of who bears what risk and for what cost (*cf.* §11.4).

Assessing VfM for PPPs can be done in a variety of ways (and may need to be consistent with how costs and benefits are assessed in other public-spending decisions). It is better if governments set out the rules for how a VfM assessment is conducted, if contracting authorities are expected to do this, rather than leaving it to individual contracting authorities and their advisers to make up their own approach to assessing VfM on a project-by-project basis.[2] As shown below, the different ways to assess VfM reflect the context in which VfM is being measured. Sometimes the context is not so obvious or well understood when approaches are simply copied from one country to another.

If VfM is the framework for making the PPP-procurement decision, in many countries this now involves seeking the answers to two related but slightly different questions:

- Does a PPP offer VfM compared to other options to procure the project—*i.e.* some sort of *comparison* test (§8.3-8.7)?
- Is a PPP approach likely to be appropriate for the particular project when the project features and capacity available are compared against criteria that are conducive to achieving VfM—*i.e.* some sort of *suitability* test (§8.8)?

§8.3 QUANTITATIVE VfM ASSESSMENT AND THE PUBLIC-SECTOR COMPARATOR

The standard approach for a comparison test is to set out alternatives, usually just a public-sector procurement option and a PPP option, and compare the long-term risk-adjusted costs of the two options. This can take place:

- before launching the procurement, to help decide whether or not to launch the project as a PPP; and/or
- during the procurement, to compare actual bids with the public-sector procurement alternative (in which case the private-sector alternative is the actual bids received).

The calculation for the public-sector procurement option is referred to as the 'public-sector comparator' (PSC).[3] The calculation for the private-sector alternative ahead of the procurement phase is referred to as the 'PPP option'.[4] If the PPP option (or actual bid if the PSC is used after receiving bids) can deliver the same project services at a lower

---

[2] However, if a PPP unit (*cf.* §4.7) is responsible for this, it may prefer, particularly in the early stages of a programme, to develop its internal guidelines once it has had some experience of VfM assessments and any limitations on these, such as access to reliable information.

[3] Also known as the 'public-sector benchmark'. While the obvious meaning of PSC is a *comparison* between public procurement and the PPP route, *i.e.* it relates to *both* sides of the calculation, it is more often taken to mean just the public-sector side of the calculation. This is the sense in which it is used in this chapter.

[4] Also known as the 'PPP reference model' or 'shadow-bid model'.

long-term cost, after adjusting for the costs of the risks involved, then the PPP option (or bid) is deemed to deliver VfM.[5] Despite the practical difficulties of conducting a credible quantitative assessment (*cf.* §8.6), this approach is still widely used and therefore the following section describes the various ways this is done in more detail.

The main additional cost in a PPP compared to public-sector procurement is the greater cost of private-sector finance compared to the public-sector cost of financing. But the PPP option involves risks, and therefore costs, for the project company that the contracting authority no longer has to bear. Thus, the use of a PSC to determine if a PPP procurement is VfM involves determining whether the additional cost of private finance in a PPP (*cf.* §23.4) and other associated costs (such as transaction costs) are justified by the value of the expected risks that are no longer borne by the contracting authority (*cf.* Chapters 11-13) together with any private-sector cost efficiencies over the life of the project (*cf.* §8.3.2, §28.9.4).

The common criticism that PPPs cannot be VfM because the public sector can always borrow more cheaply (*cf.* §28.4) therefore misses the point that the costs of the risks no longer borne by the contracting authority also need to be taken into account. The costs of these risks may be more or less than the additional cost of private-sector finance. In this context, this is the basic VfM question.

As costs and revenues are estimated and compared in money terms, this is often referred to as the *quantitative* approach to assessing VfM. It usually involves trying to estimate the NPV of *risk-adjusted* estimates of long-term costs (and revenues) of a project if it were to be procured using 'conventional' public-sector procurement and subsequently managed and operated by the public sector, and comparing this (in the case of an availability PPP), with the estimated NPC of the service fees payable in the PPP alternative delivering the same quantity and quality of services over the same period.

Applying similar logic to a concession, the PSC is based on the risk-adjusted costs of building and operating the facility that would be incurred by the public sector. The 'cost' of the concession is the value of the user-charge payments foregone, *i.e.* paid by users to the project company and not the contracting authority. The concession option is VfM if the NPC of the public-sector costs is greater than the PV of the user-charge revenue foregone by the authority.

The PSC was largely developed in Australia and Britain in the 1980s and 1990s as an attempt to provide a more 'objective' numerical underpinning of the PPP decision. As a communication tool, this was also believed to help present the PPP decision in a simple, clear and 'scientific' way. For reasons mentioned below (§8.6), however, the credibility of this approach has been substantially undermined.

When comparing the PSC with the PPP option, the benefits of the two options should be considered to be the same in terms of service provision—this is a decision about which way to procure a project, not about the project itself.

---

[5] The comparison need not be a simple one between a public- and one private-sector option, but may involve a number of private-sector options (*cf.* §2.5), not just PPPs (as is the case, for example, in Virginia, the United States).

§8.3.1 The PSC Calculation—the 'Raw' PSC

After defining the need for and scope of the proposed project (Phases 1-3 in the project cycle—*cf.* §5.3.1-§5.3.3), and moving on to Phase 4 (Procurement Review), the first step in developing the PSC is to determine the PV of the cash flows associated with the estimated investment, *i.e.* construction, operation and maintenance costs, less any expected revenues, all expressed in nominal (*cf.* §24.3.1) cash terms.

The calculation is done for the 'lifetime' of the project, which usually means the expected tenor of the PPP contract, even though the facility usually has an economic life that is longer than the PPP contract. If the assets have a 'residual' value at the end of the PPP contract and the contracting authority pays the project company for these, then this needs to be reflected in the PSC, but in most cases, the project is structured on the basis that the asset is handed back at a zero or nominal value (*cf.* §17.8).

The costs (and revenues) of the PSC should be on the basis of the project being procured and operated as efficiently as possible by the contracting authority.

There is a danger of underestimating opex if these costs are derived from existing public projects whose efficiency or levels of service may be lower than those required in the new project, or reflect an historic underspend on necessary maintenance. It may therefore be difficult to estimate what the 'right' level of expenditure should be for the PSC. Nevertheless, it is important that the level and quality of service of the public- and private-sector options for the purposes of this comparative exercise are similar.

This bundle of costs (and revenues) is often called the 'raw' PSC, as the cost of any risks relating to costs (or revenues) has not yet been included.

§8.3.2 The PSC Calculation—Risk Adjustment

The next step in developing the PSC is to adjust the project costs (and any revenues) to reflect the risks associated with each cost (and any revenue) component. This is probably the most contentious aspect of constructing the PSC.

Identification of these risks (some of which may be shared between the public and private sectors), and what they are worth, is a complex exercise (*cf.* Chapters 11-13). Broadly speaking, these risks relate to construction, operation and maintenance costs, usage, and macroeconomic risks—*cf.* Table 11.1. Risk checklists and risk workshops (*cf.* §11.2) are often used to assist this process. Standardised contracts, if available (*cf.* §4.3.2), are also a good source of information on risk identification and allocation.

This separate stage for the risk adjustment is important because a number of risks may remain with the contracting authority even under the PPP alternative, *e.g.* the risk of additional costs resulting from delays in obtaining land for the project (*cf.* §12.2.1). This follows the principle of allocating risks to the party that is able to assess the likelihood, manage or absorb the particular risk for the lowest cost (*cf.* §11.4). These risks are referred to as 'retained risks' and must either be included in both the PSC and PPP options or excluded from the PSC/PPP comparison in the first place (for example in Ireland). However, the consequences and therefore cost to the contracting authority may be different—*e.g.* failure to acquire land or build a connecting piece of infrastructure may lead to delay for a public-procurement project, but in a PPP project they may lead to financial penalties for the contracting authority (*cf.* §16.2.4).

In some cases, the costs in the PSC may also be adjusted upwards relative to the PPP option to reflect assumed private-sector innovation or efficiencies in construction methods. Studies by Infrastructure Ontario and others suggest in their market that the cost savings of the PPP option may be as much as 15% (Infrastructure Ontario 2015). At the same time, to reflect traditionally lower spending on life-cycle costs by the public sector, these costs are lower in the PSC relative to the PPP option but the expected impact of reduced or deferred maintenance of the asset (*i.e.* greater costs later on, the longer maintenance is deferred) is then quantified adding to the overall cost of the PSC. But this adjustment for reduced public sector maintenance may not be the case in other markets (*cf.* §8.6.3).

§8.3.3 The PSC Calculation—Optimism Bias

Optimism bias is the observed tendency for the public sector to be over-optimistic about outcomes both in time and cost leading, for example, to substantial cost overruns compared to the original projections (*cf.* §28.6.1). (One reason for this 'optimism', other than poor project-management skills, is that when public-sector investment is constrained, politicians and public-sector officials—whose careers benefit from completing projects, and are not necessarily penalised if project costs overrun—have an incentive to understate likely costs to get their projects approved.) Studies were carried out in Britain in 2002 and 2004 (MacDonald 2002, Flyvbjerg et al. 2004) to establish a reasonable range of 'optimism bias' as a pragmatic basis for adjusting projected public-sector project outcomes for risk. The wide range of results, and thus the optimism-bias factors used, illustrates just how much uncertainty is there in this area. For example, the British Treasury's optimism-bias factors for capex for new (standard construction) buildings is between 2% and 24%, and for new roads is between 3% and 44% (British Treasury 2013).

Optimism-bias factors can be used to adjust expected costs to reflect risks for both the PSC and PPP options. As project costs become assessed in more detail and adjusted in the course of the project-preparation process, optimism-bias factors may be reduced, reflecting the greater levels of certainty around costs.

Using optimism-bias factors has the benefit of clarity, consistency and ease of use when it comes to estimating the cost impact of risks. However, the approach is open to criticism because of the small sample sizes that generated the adjustment factors in the first place and how up-to-date they are. There can also be problems in choosing the right factor to apply given that every project is a mix of different activities, as well as the stage during the project's preparation at which the factors are applied. In the case of VfM assessment, such adjustments can have a significant impact on the relative costs of the PSC and PPP options and so distort the assessment.

§8.3.4 The PSC Calculation—Competitive Neutrality

After arriving at the risk-adjusted costs (however imperfectly), final adjustments to the PSC may then be needed to ensure that the PSC and PPP options are compared on a 'level playing-field' basis, for example taking into account that the PPP may generate greater tax payments than the PSC, which is a benefit to the public sector as a whole. This step is usually referred to as adjusting the PSC for 'competitive neutrality'.

However, the theoretical and actual tax payments made by a PPP have a tendency to deviate from each other, being very dependent on the structure of the project company's actual ownership and how it and its investors deal with their tax affairs. For example, the use of shareholder subordinated debt instead of equity can almost eliminate tax payments by the project company (*cf.* §20.3.5). It is therefore very difficult to generalise about the extra tax benefit to be received from PPPs, or even to compare one bidder accurately with another in this respect. So, while this adjustment should be done, it may not be a straightforward calculation.

§8.3.5 Should the PSC be Updated?

If the PSC is being used to assess bids at the procurement stage, should the assumptions in the PSC be updated as new market information becomes available or the scope of the project changes?

The NPC of the PPP option should be recalculated regularly throughout the procurement process and compared with the PSC. Equally, the PSC should be updated over the preparation period to reflect the latest available information. But because the objective is to assess the efficiency and innovation of the private-sector relative to the public-sector alternative, further changes to the PSC are usually no longer permitted once the procurement is launched.[6] In some countries, however, the PSC may be revised for changes in project scope, service specifications or even assessment or allocation of risks as a result of dialogue with bidders, but care needs to be taken that the PSC still represents the public-sector approach to the project with these changes and not a private-sector solution.

§8.3.6 Should the PSC be Disclosed to Bidders?

Should the PSC be disclosed to bidders? Practice on this is varied: many countries take the view that it should not be disclosed because it may lead bidders to treat the PSC as a target price instead of submitting their best bids. The contracting authority may, however, disclose the raw PSC only, *i.e.* without the adjustments for risk (*cf.* §8.3.1).

The PSC can be used as an instrument for negotiating with bidders to push their prices down (Australia and the Netherlands are examples of this). Of course, in this case, the PSC is serving a different purpose and is no longer being used purely as an assessment tool.

---

[6] The PSC may be updated in line with a pre-agreed index such as for inflation, because such changes would affect the costs in both the PSC and PPP options.

§8.4 THE PPP OPTION

As mentioned above, the PSC then needs to be compared with the PPP option. If this exercise is being carried out before launching the procurement, *i.e.* its purpose is to help decide whether or not to launch the procurement of the project as a PPP, a cash-flow model of what the PPP option might look like has to be constructed. The cost of the PPP option is then the NPC of the estimated service fees that are required to ensure financial viability of the project and its costs to the contracting authority. Developing such a financial model is described in §22.8. However, the PPP option is also only as good as the assumptions involved—these need to include assumptions about the structure and cost of private financing (including how risks might be priced by the private sector—*cf.* §11.3), how much it will cost the private sector to construct and run the facility over the next 25-30 years and any efficiency improvements assumed (so increasing the PSC relative to the PPP option or reducing the cost of the PPP option compared to the PSC).

If the exercise is (also) being used to compare actual bids with the PSC during the procurement phase, then the comparator is the NPC of the actual bids. It is important in this case to ensure that the bids are compared with the PSC on similar bases, *e.g.* as to inflation assumptions (*cf.* §10.6.5).

As the quantitative VfM assessment compares the costs of the different options from the perspective of the contracting authority's cash flows, the PPP alternative also needs to include any additional risks and costs retained by the contracting authority that would not be required in the case of the PSC, such as procuring, negotiating and managing the PPP contract itself. These costs have to be added to the PPP to make the comparison a fair one.

§8.5 COMPARISON OF THE PSC AND PPP OPTIONS

When a PSC/PPP comparison is published, either by the contracting authority or by a government audit office, the end result may look something like Table 8.1.

Graphs can be used to show the range of values and the point at which the level of costs makes the PSC and PPP options the same (sometimes known as 'indifference'

Table 8.1   PSC/PPP comparison

($)	For reference	PSC	PPP
NPC of public-sector procurement (including capex and opex)	§8.3.1	900	
PV of risk adjustments	§8.3.2, §8.3.3	90	
PV of additional tax	§8.3.4	45	
NPC of service fees	§8.4		1,000
Risk-adjusted NPC		**1,035**	**1,000**

points). This focuses attention on the cost assumptions that are likely to have the most impact on the assessment, *i.e.* the key costs and risk components that are the main basis for the difference between the PSC and PPP options.

§8.6 PROBLEMS WITH QUANTITATIVE ANALYSIS

There are major problems in using quantitative analysis to assess VfM, in particular the credibility of the risk adjustments (§8.6.1), and the discount rate used to produce the NPV figures (§8.6.2).

§8.6.1 Credibility of Risk Adjustments

It is easy for those opposed to a PPP to challenge the risk adjustments, as the evidential basis for these is limited, may not apply in the same way between one project and another, and at best are only rough estimates.

Information on risks may be very incomplete, especially at the earlier stages of the quantitative analysis (see Chapters 11-13 for further discussion on risk assessment). Some *ex-post* evidence on the financial performance of PPPs (Makovšek and Moszoro 2016) suggests that lack of information to enable proper pricing of risks remains a problem, *e.g.* over-estimating the value of the construction risks that are transferred to the private sector under a PPP (*cf.* §12.3). On the other hand, it is possible that the opposite could be happening in undervaluing long-term operating and maintenance risks, but only time will tell if this is a systemic issue as more projects get to the end of their contract lives.

In addition to specific risks that are in effect 'measured uncertainties', there may also be defined but 'unmeasured uncertainties' around the costs estimates, *i.e.* risks that have yet to be identified. Experience of mature PPP projects in their operating phase suggests that the risks that really matter may often turn out to be those that were never identified at all (so-called 'black swans'). These may be particularly underestimated in the PSC if it is used to compare with bids, as bidders bid on the basis that all project risks, other than those specifically retained by the contracting authority, are transferred (*cf.* §11.4). This of course throws the whole risk analysis, and therefore the accuracy of quantitative VfM assessment, into question.

§8.6.2 Discount Rate

As with the choice of discount rate to assess the economic viability of the underlying project (*cf.* §7.4.3), the contracting authority applies a discount rate in comparing the PSC and PPP options in the VfM assessment. In both cases, the choice of discount rate used can have a profound effect on the result.

Any methodology that uses a relatively high discount rate can excessively favour the PPP option simply because of the very different cash-flow profiles of the PSC and the PPP—the PSC costs usually consist of a high level of initial capex and a lower level of long-term opex, whereas the costs of a PPP are all further into the future with no initial cost. So, the NPC of a PPP will reduce more than the NPC of a PSC as the discount rate is increased.

The choice of discount rate is open to debate. It reflects a particular underlying policy choice for government (which is one reason why the contracting authority should not just 'leave it to the advisers to work it out'). There are broadly four different approaches that governments take on this issue:

— Cost of government borrowing

The first, and mostly widely used, approach is to use a discount rate based on the cost to government of borrowing for a period equivalent to that of the PPP contract. In most cases, the same rate is applied to the cash flows of both the PSC and PPP options. Examples of this approach include France, Germany, Ireland, Ontario (Canada) and South Africa. If the cost of borrowing for the contracting authority is higher than the central-government cost of borrowing, a premium may be added. There is an implicit assumption in the use of a discount rate derived from the government-borrowing rate that the comparison is being made between the government cost of borrowing and the cost of private finance, so the use or not of a PPP is a *financing* decision (unless the government-borrowing rate is being used as the rate for making a public investment or *spending decision*, i.e. as a proxy for society's preference of current over future consumption—see below).

As with the PSC, the cost consequences of project risks are usually reflected in adjustments to the cash flows to which the discount rate is applied rather than increasing the discount rate to reflect these risks—from the contracting authority's perspective, it is comparing cost streams, not revenue streams, so discounting a future *cost* at a higher (riskier) rate, which makes it *lower* in NPC terms, seems somewhat counter-intuitive when making a *spending* decision. Still, where risks cannot be adequately covered by cash-flow adjustments, countries such as South Africa make a small upward adjustment to the discount rate.

One practical problem with this approach is if market rates for long-term government borrowing fluctuate significantly. To help smooth such variations, historical averages may sometimes be used instead of using the long-term borrowing rate at the time of the assessment. A related problem is if fiscal crises lead to temporary high costs of borrowing or if policies, such as quantitative easing, depress levels of borrowing rates, either of which, it could be argued, do not reflect 'true' long-term borrowing costs (or society's preference for current versus future consumption).

— Higher discount rate for the PPP option

In some countries, such as Australia, an upward adjustment is made to the discount rate[7] that is applied only to the PPP option. This is done to reflect the cost of those risks that are not covered by adjustments to projected cash flows and to the extent that they are allocated to the project company. These risks (often referred to as 'systematic risks') are generally market-wide, as opposed to project-specific (or 'endogenous') risks. An example of such a risk could be changes in demand as a result of changes in general economic activity.

---

[7] Based on the government cost of borrowing.

Some would argue (Boardman and Hellowell 2015) that the discount rate applied to the PPP option (as opposed to the PSC) should actually be *lower* because under the PSC, as market conditions improve and demand for public services increases, costs to government go up (*i.e.* the PSC option is more exposed to systematic risk).

— Social time preference rate

This approach assesses the PPP option from the perspective that government is making a *spending* decision based on overall costs and benefits to society, as opposed to a *financing* decision. On this basis, the discount rate is based on the social time preference rate (STPR) (*cf.* §7.4.3), *i.e.* the same PSDR that is applied across all public-sector investment decisions, not the cost of financing to the contracting authority (whatever that cost may be). This approach argues that as an individual contracting authority is likely to be funded from a mix of different sources (taxation, government borrowing and other sources), its actual cost of funding is the result of this mix of sources, usually decided by central government. The contracting authority is therefore not responsible for managing the overall *cost* of its funding, but it is responsible for *spending decisions* within the budget allocated to it from this mix of funds. In the context of quantitative VfM assessment, it is therefore a *spending decision* either to make availability payments under a PPP contract (or forgo revenue from a concession) or to make payments on the individual items of construction, maintenance and operation of an asset to deliver the same public service. It follows from this that if the STPR is used as a discount rate, the PSC should assume that the contracting authority pays for the project capex as and when incurred, rather than borrowing to pay these costs at a later date.

One practical benefit of using an STPR is that it is more consistent over time than a fluctuating financing rate and relatively easy for a contracting authority to apply: it does not have to make individual calculations of the discount rate on a project-by-project basis (which themselves might be open to debate).

However, the risks of the PPP option may look under-priced when financial market rates move substantially out of line with the STPR, particularly if the STPR is higher. This is because the pricing of the risks that are transferred under the PPP option is the (smaller) difference between the private sector's cost of capital and the STPR, as opposed to the (greater) difference between the private sector's cost of capital and the lower current government-borrowing rate. Maybe financial markets, for other reasons, are under-pricing future versus current consumption, but this still invites the criticism, e.g. from Britain's National Audit Office (National Audit Office 2013) that the costs of PPPs are being understated.

— Portfolio investment rate

The fourth approach is based on the perspective that when government is making a decision about *how* to procure an asset, it is in effect making a decision about whether or not to *invest* in an asset. This is a different decision to when deciding *what to procure* (*cf.* Chapter 7) which would merit using a discount rate more in line with an STPR. On this basis, the discount rate should be based on that which a portfolio investor (public or private) would use to invest in an asset, taking into account the asset's risk profile.

The discount rate should therefore be based on the returns that apply to the particular project (*cf.* §20.3), not the government's cost of money. Even though an availability PPP is a flow of payments from the contracting authority, as opposed to a flow of revenue to the contracting authority, the 'revenue' to the contracting authority of the public-sector procurement option is the service fee it would otherwise be paying to the private sector under the PPP contract. In the case of a concession, the returns would be those that the contracting authority would receive if it were not to concession out the asset. If the contracting authority can earn a higher return by investing directly in the asset, then it should do so rather than choosing the PPP. This is the approach used in, for example, British Columbia.

But again, this option may be criticised as favouring the PPP by using a high discount rate.

As can be seen, choosing a discount rate is not a straightforward matter. While the PSC was originally intended to provide 'political cover' through a clear rational analysis for the choice of the PPP-procurement route, issues such as the choice of discount rate can actually end up inviting more controversy and criticism.

The arbitrary nature of discount rates, in this case a fixed PSDR, is illustrated by changes made by the Norwegian government in 2005. Until then, the PSDR was 3.5% plus a sector-based risk mark-up in the range 0.5-4.5%. 4.5% was applied to road projects, considered to represent a high risk, making a total discount rate of 8%. Sweden, on the other hand, used a total rate of 3%. This meant that a particular bridge between Sweden and Norway was economically justified for Sweden but not for Norway, even though most of its users were Norwegian. In 2005 Norway changed the PSDR to 2% plus a general risk mark-up of 2%. An article on this change in *Nordic Road and Transport Research* (VTI Stockholm 2005) was entitled (presumably with tongue in cheek) 'Norwegian Road Projects are now Profitable—the Government Reduces the Discount Rate'.

Apart from being clear about the underlying policy perspective in the choice of discount rate, an overall prudent approach would be to use a discount rate that is on the low side, especially when large differences exist between government-borrowing rates, STPR and private-sector returns. The same can be said for the level of discount rate used to assess the benefits of different project options in the earlier assessment of economic viability, for the reasons discussed above.

§8.6.3 Comparing Like with Like

Another criticism of the quantitative approach is that the PSC may not always reflect the true costs of the public-procurement option. If the PSC assumes that the contracting authority will carry out the management of the project in a reasonably efficient way and ensure the asset is maintained to the same standard as it would be under a PPP over the same period, the reality of actual practice may be different with stop-start construction periods, annual budget pressures that affect required maintenance and other behaviours that the PSC does not adequately reflect.

§8.7 BENEFIT OF THE QUANTITATIVE APPROACH

Thus, estimating future costs, identifying and valuing risks, choosing and applying discount rates and the sheer complexity (and often 'black box' nature) of the calculation has led to charges of spurious accuracy for the PSC and PPP option calculations, particularly when the contracting authority and its advisers may be under strong pressure (*e.g.* for balance sheet reasons—*cf.* §9.4.4) to manipulate the process to achieve the 'right' result (*i.e.* the PPP option is best). This in turn makes it hard for a contracting authority to defend the PPP decision on this basis alone, however 'scientific' it may appear. And in many cases, the numerical difference between the PSC and the PPP is so small as to be within the margin of error in the underlying assumptions. It is even debatable whether the approach of weighting of risks for value and probability properly reflects the real world—lenders do not take this approach when considering their risk analysis (*cf.* §11.5, §23.9.7).

Consequently, it is now widely accepted that the quantitative VfM assessment, if it is used at all, should *assist* (alongside other factors such as qualitative considerations), but not exclusively *make* the PPP decision. However, there are probably still too many examples where a marginally-lower NPC of the PPP overrides all other considerations and the quantitative analysis is taken as absolute.

Nevertheless, the *process* of constructing a long-term financial picture of different procurement options along the lines of the PSC and PPP options, however approximate these are, helps the contracting authority to establish a better understanding of the project's long-term costs and risks. This should support better design of the PPP contract and prepare the contracting authority for any negotiation with the bidders (if a negotiated procurement process is being used). This financial picture can also help to 'sense check' the bids when they come and it may play an important rôle during competitive dialogue and in the separate exercise of helping to establish the affordability of the project (*cf.* §9.2).

This would suggest that the quantitative approach and the level of detail of the analysis should be proportionate to the importance of the PPP decision. For smaller projects, especially those that follow standard approaches and where the qualitative assessment discussed below point to a reasonably obvious choice, there is probably not much to be gained in carrying out a quantitative assessment. Here the focus should be mainly on achieving a good competition and effective project and subsequent contract management to secure VfM. If the decision on how a project is delivered is likely to have a larger impact on how national resources are deployed, or the project is unusual, then a quantitative assessment (both for the decision to launch a PPP and sense-check bids) may be justified albeit with the dedication of the appropriate level of analysis and resources and realism about the capacity and quality of the information available to conduct the assessment. So, for smaller but unusual projects, the depth of the analysis, for example on risks, can be kept at a fairly high level (*e.g.* by applying optimism bias factors to fairly broad risk categories).

In some countries, quantitative VfM assessment may be limited to decisions involving the use of availability PPPs, assuming that as far as concessions are concerned, user charges are seen as the most economically-efficient way to pay for infrastructure. In essence, the VfM decision is the same as the economic decision to use user charges in these cases. Chile and France are examples of this approach.

It is noticeable that in developing countries, where concessions are more prevalent than availability PPPs, quantitative VfM assessment is also less commonly used. It is often argued that real limits on public-sector resources mean that there is no public-sector alternative, so comparing a PSC with a PPP option is meaningless. Other countries with active concession programmes, however, assess all projects for VfM on the basis that user-charge funded projects can be delivered under either the availability PPP or concession structures, so there are still VfM questions to be answered irrespective of who is actually paying for the infrastructure.

§8.8 QUALITATIVE ANALYSIS

Because of these problems with the quantitative approach, the justification (or otherwise) for procuring a project as a PPP is often subject to a set of qualitative suitability checks, and in some cases only these suitability checks are used (*i.e.* with no quantitative analysis). These checks assess whether the project has characteristics or qualities that suggest that the PPP option has the potential to deliver VfM. Applying such suitability criteria is a relatively easier process, and also covers factors that are not easily captured in a quantitative assessment of VfM.

This qualitative approach therefore does not *measure* VfM, as in the comparative (quantitative) approach. Instead it *tests* the PPP against a series of criteria. To the extent that these criteria have been shown to help ensure VfM, it is evidence-based.

Countries such as Australia, Britain, Colombia, France, Germany, India and South Africa have developed qualitative VfM assessment checklists as part of their PPP guidance materials. The British qualitative VfM guidelines, for example, use around 50 questions split into the three themes of:

- *viability*: can the project be viably structured as a PPP (*e.g.* can requirements be clearly defined and measured in a PPP contract?)
- *desirability*: are the benefits of doing so likely to outweigh the costs? and
- *achievability*: are public- and private-sector skills available to deliver the project as a PPP and will there be strong competition from bidders to drive the best deal?

Another way of looking at this, and based on the criteria used in a number of countries, is to set out the qualitative questions in two main categories:

- the *motivations* to use a PPP, *i.e.*, the potential benefits or opportunities that the contracting authority is seeking from using a PPP-procurement approach to help achieve VfM (§8.8.1); and
- the *criteria* that need to be met to ensure that the PPP route works for the project to deliver VfM (§8.8.2).

§8.8.1 Motivations for Using a PPP

The contracting authority should first try to identify and prioritise its aims when considering which procurement route to use. While there may be no or few constraints to using a PPP (as identified later) and the PPP option may even be marginally better VfM on the quantitative assessment, if there are no other particular benefits for the contracting authority to get behind the PPP, then the PPP procurement is unlikely to deliver its full VfM potential. This is especially so if the PPP is likely to involve more or unfamiliar work for the authority.

Furthermore, there are usually a number of 'non-financial' benefits that are associated with a particular procurement option that are not captured by the quantitative assessment. In other words, there may be benefits intrinsic to the procurement route itself, not just the project, that need to be recognised.

Thus, possible benefits, and therefore *motivations*, to use a PPP could be to:

- improve long-term maintenance of the asset (*cf.* §28.8);
- improve service quality and consistency through better maintained facilities;
- improve long-term risk management (*cf.* §28.9.7);
- improve the understanding and certainty of whole-of-life costs (including capital costs) (*cf.* §28.8);
- improve certainty of on-time asset-delivery;
- enable innovation in the design and/or provision of the service (*cf.* §28.9.5);
- access skills not available within the public sector (*cf.* §28.9);
- enable the contracting authority to focus on its core activities, which may not include long-term asset management;
- enable third-party project scrutiny (*e.g.* from contractors and lenders—*cf.* §28.9.8);
- transfer interface risks to the private-sector through integration of design, construction and operation and create a single point of responsibility (*cf.* §28.9.3);
- drive reform in current public-sector practices (*cf.* §28.10);
- if relevant, enable more effective revenue generation by the project company through improved asset utilisation (*cf.* §28.9.6);
- mobilise private-sector capital to enable earlier/additional investment (*cf.* §9.2);
- enable off-balance sheet treatment of the investment (subject to the caveats as set out in Chapter 9); and
- better match the cost of infrastructure to those who use it or benefit from it over time (*cf.* §9.2.3, §28.2).

VfM policies may exclude some motivators, such as balance-sheet treatment, due to concerns that these could be the exclusive justification for a PPP or over-ride other factors that point to the PPP otherwise being poor VfM. The key point is that a particular motivator should not be the sole justification for the use of a PPP without considering other factors, such as the quantitative assessment and the constraints set out below.

While the motivations listed are project specific, these may be linked to wider benefits such as reduced accident costs on a well-maintained road as a result of better and more consistent life-cycle maintenance through a PPP, or the introduction of innovation in design more widely to a sector or the benefits of 'contestability' (*cf.* §28.10.4).

In some cases, benefits may be quantified separately. An example in some countries is to quantify the economic benefits of earlier delivery of the services provided by the project because the PPP enables the project to take place sooner than otherwise or delivers it faster (*cf.* §28.4).

§8.8.2 Criteria for Choosing the PPP Route

In addition to the motivations, there are criteria that need to be met to ensure that a PPP would work well and be likely to deliver VfM. These can be further grouped under a number of sub-headings, as set out below. In this case, failure to meet *any one* of the criteria should signal cause for concern about pursuing the project further as a PPP (or in risk terms, areas of high risk, to be logged in the risk register—*cf.* §11.6):

— Criteria related to the nature of what is being procured:

- There are no legal or regulatory restrictions to contracting with the private sector for the service expected to be delivered by the PPP (*cf.* §4.3).
- Long-term service requirements and quality can be clearly defined, objectively and independently measured and expressed and enforced in a contractual structure (*cf.* Chapter 15).
- Service requirements are not expected to change significantly over the medium to long term that would require significant changes over the expected term of the PPP contract (*cf.* §19.4.3).
- There are clear boundaries to the services that are required to be provided (*cf.* §7.3.1).
- There are limited operational interface risks between the project and outside interfaces and the project company is likely to have clear control over what it is expected to deliver (*cf.* §7.3.1).
- There are no obvious benefits/synergies to extending the contracting authority's existing management of operations.
- There no major stakeholder issues, including political opposition or impact on existing employment relationships, that cannot be resolved through effective stakeholder management (*cf.* §6.5).
- There is scope for innovation in design and/or provision of the service.

— Criteria related to private- and public-sector capacity:

- The private sector can provide access to skills/experience that are not readily available to the contracting authority in asset or service delivery to the required quantity and quality and in more effective management of the associated risks (*cf.* §28.9).
- Market interest of contractors and operators is expected to be strong, ensuring good competition for the PPP contract when it is tendered and this can be expected to continue over the operational phase (to ensure competition in case the original contractors need to be replaced) (*cf.* §10.4).
- Long-term debt and equity finance is expected to be available on acceptable terms (*cf.* Chapters 20 and 21).
- Skills in the contracting authority are available to manage the preparation and procurement of the project as a PPP (*cf.* Chapter 6) and to manage the long-term PPP contract (*cf.* Chapter 19).
- A project-development process exists in the contracting authority with effective and informed governance arrangements such as quality-control checkpoints during the course of the preparation, procurement and management of the PPP contract (*cf.* §5.4).
- The PPP preparation and procurement can take place within an acceptable timescale (*cf.* Chapter 10).

— Criteria related to the nature of the project itself:

- There is existing evidence of projects with similar characteristics successfully delivering VfM.
- It is possible to integrate design, construction and operation of the project (*cf.* §28.6, §28.9.3).
- The project risks can be identified and allocated between the public and private sectors and the private sector can be held accountable for the risks allocated to it (*cf.* §11.2, §11.4).
- The expected level of project risks is enough to merit transfer to the private sector and have an impact on VfM (*cf.* §11.3, §11.4).
- The technology and the technical means to deliver the project are unlikely to change significantly (*cf.* §28.12).
- It is reasonably possible to estimate the costs of maintaining the assets and providing the service over the long term (*cf.* §23.9.3).
- Any interfaces with other projects are clear and manageable (*cf.* §7.3.1, §18.7).
- Any constraints as a consequence of the PPP, such as restrictions on building competing facilities, are acceptable over the life of the PPP (*cf.* §13.3).
- The size of the investment required justifies the level of PPP transaction and monitoring costs (*cf.* §4.6, §7.5.1, §20.4, §28.7, §28.12).
- The level of investment financed by the private sector will ensure that sufficient private finance is at risk to long-term project performance (*cf.* §18.6, §28.9.7).
- Operating costs represent a meaningful share of whole-of-life costs (but *cf.* §15.6.4) including the tenor of the PPP contract being sufficiently long to ensure this.
- The overall improvement in expected benefits (risk transfer, quality of service, cost certainty, *etc.*) is expected to be justified in light of the higher finance and transaction costs of a PPP. (Further analysis including quantitative analysis may assess this in more detail.)

Elaborate approaches with scoresheets and weightings have been developed in some countries to apply these qualitative criteria to try to ensure more consistency and comprehensiveness of the assessment. Of more significance, however, is the recognition that the VfM procurement decision should not be a binary one between a PPP option and the 'traditional' procurement option. Instead it should involve a methodical assessment of a wider range of different project-delivery options in addition to PPP (such as design-construct-maintain, use of a construction manager or managing contractor, or alliancing). This is the approach used in Australia and increasingly in other countries.

§8.8.3 VfM of the PPP Process

Some suitability assessments also look at whether the PPP process itself is being conducted to ensure good VfM. An example would be using qualitative criteria to track that the project is being prepared in such a way as to ensure strong competitive interest from the market. This recognises the point that *achieving* VfM is a product of a well-run PPP preparation and procurement (and contract-management) process.

§8.8.4 Difficulties with the Qualitative Approach

A criticism of the qualitative approach is that it still relies on judgement and subjectivity. Answering some of the criteria may also require considerable analysis, raising similar problems to a quantitative assessment. The criteria should wherever possible be under-pinned by evidence from previous projects. This is one reason is why *ex-post* assessment of PPPs is important (*cf.* §19.9). The criteria should also be revisited at various stages over the project cycle (*cf.* §5.2) as information (and the willingness to spend money on getting the information) becomes available.

In some cases, the criterion could simply be one of determining if the project is similar to a previous one that has been already been shown to deliver good VfM. Some regional governments such as Scotland and Madhya Pradesh use this approach where possible. This works well for programmes of similar projects (*cf.* §4.6), dispensing with the need for 'bottom-up' VfM assessment each time.

In some countries, VfM qualitative criteria include tests of the ability to pay for the project, or a project's prospects to generate revenue. While these may be important criteria for the contracting authority, they are not strictly VfM issues and should be considered separately as part of the affordability analysis (*cf.* §9.2).

§8.9 INTEGRATING VfM ASSESSMENT IN THE PROCUREMENT PROCESS

Most countries now use a mix of the comparative (quantitative) and suitability (qualitative) approaches to assess VfM. But the frequency of such assessments, and the phases of the PPP project cycle (*cf.* §5.2) when they are used vary considerably. The following describes approaches in various more mature PPP markets where VfM guidance is made available.

§8.9.1 Stages in VfM Assessment

In a number of countries, a 'quick scan' suitability test is first applied. This takes place during the long- and short-list options appraisal in Phases 2 (Project Definition and Options Appraisal) and 3 (Project Economic Assessment and Selection) or at the beginning of Phase 4 (Procurement Review). This is to decide whether or not to spend time and money in assessing a PPP procurement in more detail at a later stage—at this point, the application of check-list criteria does not require a detailed analysis (when information on the project in any case is less precise). Britain, France, Germany and the Netherlands, for example, do this.

The mix of quantitative and qualitative VfM assessment varies more noticeably between countries over the subsequent stages of the project cycle. In Germany, the Netherlands and South Africa, the quantitative approach plays a major rôle in the decision on whether or not to launch the project as a PPP, *i.e.* during Phase 4 (Procurement Review) and then again during Phase 6 (Procurement). Other countries, such as Australia, use a largely qualitative approach in Phase 4, with the quantitative approach used in the Phase 6, where the PSC is used to compare and test the private-sector bids for their VfM.

Britain, like France, largely leaves the quantitative approach behind once the decision to launch the PPP procurement has been made, because of concerns about comparing a PSC (which is necessarily based on estimated rather than actual costs) with actual PPP bids (as opposed to estimated PPP costs). A mainly qualitative approach is then used at the end of the Phase 6 (Procurement) prior to financial close: as competitive tension between bidders is a strong driver of VfM, the assessment mainly reviews how well this has been achieved (as well as ensuring the other previously-applied criteria continue to be met). For example, this could involve simply ascertaining if at least three compliant and credible bids are received.

It could be argued that carrying out a quantitative VfM assessment before the procurement phase is too soon—detailed project information is incomplete and the PPP option is a purely hypothetical calculation. So, a qualitative assessment alone makes more sense before this phase. On the other hand, the problem with applying the quantitative VfM assessment at later stages, when the contracting authority is far advanced with the preparation of the project as a PPP, is that it may be difficult to abandon this route no matter what the quantitative VfM assessment indicates. And what if the earlier PSC assumptions turn out to be wrong? The answer is probably to use an incremental approach to VfM assessment, with quantitative and qualitative approaches both playing a rôle in testing for VfM at various stages and not relying on the quantitative VfM assessment as the sole criterion at any particular stage. In some countries, like Portugal, where the PSC is mainly used to confirm or otherwise the VfM of bids, failure of bids to 'beat' the PSC requires retendering the project. In other countries, such as Ireland, there is some scope to proceed even if the PSC is not beaten but this usually requires a ministerial decision (while also helping to avoid the incentive deliberately to inflate the PSC to reduce the risk of it not beating the bids).

§8.9.2 VfM Assessment Guidance

In a number of countries, such as Australia, Britain, Colombia, France, Ireland, the Netherlands and the United States, detailed VfM assessment guidelines, developed by PPP units (cf. §4.7), set out when and how the qualitative and quantitative VfM assessments should take place. For example, British VfM guidance is currently provided in such documents as the Five-Case Model guidance together with more general guidance on public spending and infrastructure assessment set out in the British Treasury's 'Green Book' (British Treasury 2018). A prescribed financial model to make the quantitative assessment was used for a while (to try to ensure greater consistency, simplicity and reduce manipulation of the result) but this ceased to be mandatory in 2012 (partly because the quantitative assessment was still seen as a pass/fail test, despite attempts by the Treasury to encourage a more balanced approach between quantitative and qualitative approaches).

While methodologies help to ensure some consistency and quality of process, they can lead to a 'tick box' mentality to the assessment. To help counter this, VfM guidance by the US Department of Transportation Federal Highway Administration (FHWA 2013), for example, takes an explanatory approach to VfM assessment: a variety of different approaches are set out for a contracting authority to consider. Other examples of this explanatory type of guidance can be found in Australia, Canada, and France and South Africa, to name a few examples (Department for Infrastructure and Regional Development, Australia 2008, 2013, Infrastructure Ontario, Canada 2015, Ministère de l'Économie et des Finances, France 2014, 2016, National Treasury South Africa 2004). This encourages the contracting authority to think about the VfM issues rather than mechanically applying a 'process' that may not be appropriate in the circumstances.

§8.9.3 Responsibility for VfM Assessment

VfM assessment is usually the responsibility of the contracting authority, often with the help of external advisers (*cf.* §6.4). A PPP unit may then review the contracting authority's assessments to ensure that they are completed in line with agreed policies often followed by making a recommendation to a separate project approval body. In some countries, VfM assessment may be carried out by the PPP unit (*cf.* §4.7): for smaller PPP programmes, this may help to ensure that the work is carried out consistently using specialist experience and expertise that may not be available within individual contracting authorities. This is the approach taken in Ireland by the NDFA (*cf.* §6.3) and in Portugal.

§8.9.4 Importance of Project Preparation and Competition to Ensure VfM

The use of qualitative criteria, especially if they are based on evidence and applied at multiple points over the PPP process, may often be a more practical tool to use in arriving at the PPP decision, especially where data for a quantitative assessment may be scarce or unreliable. At the same time, a focus on ensuring strong competition for the PPP contract and effective contract management by the contracting authority is likely to have as much, if not greater, impact on getting the best long-term VfM outcome. Thus, any VfM assessment needs to be part of a well-structured and disciplined project-preparation, procurement and contract-management process with effective quality assurance and approval mechanisms (*cf.* §5.4). As mentioned earlier, achieving VfM is more important than assessing it.

The PPP Decision—Affordability, Budgeting and Reporting

§9.1 INTRODUCTION

Having considered how the contracting authority assesses whether the underlying case for a project is economically sound and whether procuring it as a PPP represents VfM, this chapter deals firstly with one of the other main activities that takes place mainly during Phase 4 (Procurement Review) (*cf.* §5.3.4), namely how to determine whether the payments due under a PPP contract will be affordable to the contracting authority and/or users (§9.2).

Secondly, if service fees are paid by the contracting authority, they need to be reflected in its budgeting systems. PPP payment obligations present special problems, as their long-term nature usually falls well beyond the horizon of normal government budgets or appropriations. For concessions that do not involve direct government payment obligations, other obligations such as guarantees may still need to be recognised and accommodated as they could otherwise present unwelcome surprises for government at a later date. Some governments may also set specific caps on PPP payments to control long-term payment obligations (§9.3).

Thirdly, governments need to consider how to report the impact of PPPs in their financial and statistical reports. This is especially relevant for countries subject to limits on levels of deficit and debt as a result of international obligations that impose constraints on the type and number of PPPs undertaken. But determining how PPP project assets and associated liabilities should be reported and their impact on a government's financial statements is not straightforward (§9.4).

Managing these issues well helps governments better understand and plan for the impact of a PPP on its future funding obligations and avoid fiscal shocks. Managing them badly is the cause of some of the biggest problems with using PPPs. Indeed, the reporting and budgeting rules themselves can often create perverse incentives to use PPPs when they may not represent VfM. Not surprisingly, these topics create debate and controversy.

Of course, governments can publish supplementary information on the fiscal impact of PPPs where systems are not wholly adequate. The IMF has also developed tools to help with assessing and presenting this (§9.5). However, given the complex nature of PPPs and the nature of how government assets and liabilities are reported, there is still more to be done to enable reporting systems to give a clear picture of the impact of PPPs when it comes to presenting a government's fiscal position (§9.6).

§9.2 Affordability

§9.2.1 The Affordability Illusion

PPP projects may appear to be affordable because *financing* is available today to enable the project to be built. But financing only bridges the gap until the project has to be paid for, or in other words *funded* either by users (under a concession) or by the contracting authority (under an availability PPP), or both. Ignoring the difference between financing and funding can lead to the 'affordability illusion', *i.e.* the illusion that a PPP project can take place because the financing is there but forgetting that the project eventually has to be paid for and the financing paid back.

Apart from creating payment commitments for which there may be no money in the future, if a PPP project appears to be 'free' (because the funding constraints are not recognised), there is a danger that lower priority or less-needed projects are given preference. The construction of excessive motorway road space in Portugal (Abrantes de Sousa 2011) and surplus university accommodation in Hungary (Posner *et al.* 2009), both using PPPs, are past examples of this problem.

Assessing affordability is therefore about answering the *funding* question, *i.e.* determining how much the project will cost and whether it can eventually be paid for.

For availability PPPs, affordability focuses on the expected availability-based service-fee payments that will need to be made by the contracting authority over the life of the PPP contract (*cf.* §15.6). For concessions, affordability focuses mainly on the expected level of revenue from user charges and the willingness and ability of users to pay such charges (*cf.* §15.5). In both cases, funding the project may also involve other forms of payment or support from the contracting authority (*cf.* Chapter 18).

Affordability may also be affected by the way the contracting authority is funded by the rest of government and the proportion of its spending that the PPP project represents. A project may be affordable, but the proportion of the contracting authority's overall funding that is taken up by the long-term fixed-payment obligation of the PPP contract may be unacceptably large, limiting future flexibility in spending in other areas. This has been an issue for some contracting authorities for hospital PPP projects in Britain, especially where they are required to find further efficiency savings to pay for additional services. But this does not necessarily mean that the PPP is the wrong option; it is more about the priorities in committing future resources to today's projects.

§9.2.2 Affordability and Availability PPPs

An availability PPP changes the *timing* of when the project has to be paid for significantly, but if a contracting authority cannot afford to pay for the project using public funding, it will be equally unable to do so with a PPP and *vice versa*.

Of course, the payment-timing issue may be a significant advantage, for example for a government that faces resource constraints today but with the prospect of higher future revenues for itself and/or citizens—developing countries with high immediate growth prospects are examples of this. But clearly there are risks that these higher levels of revenue will not materialise.

Assessing affordability of an availability PPP project involves firstly estimating what the costs of the project, structured as a PPP, are likely to be over the life of the PPP contract period and from this determining what the expected service fees or other payments are expected to be. These are then compared with the sources of the contracting authority's funding available to make these payments. This involves the use of a financial model.

§23.8 sets out in more detail how a financial model of the project is constructed. The model is used by the different participants in the project to estimate their future obligations (and returns): in the case of the contracting authority the model is used, *inter alia*, to predict its long-term funding obligations. In summary, the steps in creating this model involve:

- Estimating project costs

  The contracting authority, using its technical advisers (*cf.* §6.4.3), builds up as complete a picture as it can of the expected construction, operating and maintenance costs (*cf.* §23.9.2, §23.9.3). Using financial advisers (*cf.* §6.4.1), it establishes its best estimate of the financing costs and structure expected to be required by equity investors and lenders (*cf.* §23.2, §23.4).

- Determining expected service fees

  Using the financial model, the service-fee payments that will be required to ensure a financially viable PPP project (*i.e.* a set of cash flows that enables costs to be covered, debt to be repaid and a fair return to investors) can be estimated. This is a complex and resource-intensive process, in which external advisers are again usually involved.

- Determining the types and sources of funding

  Depending on the nature of the project, the types of funding and their sources typically comprise some or a combination of the following:

  - the contracting authority's budget to pay for the service fees over the operating period;
  - initial capital grants (*cf.* §18.6) from the contracting authority, a central government or multilateral grant pool; and
  - third-party and secondary sources of revenue (*cf.* §15.8).

— Problems with affordability assessment

As can be seen, estimating the affordability of a PPP project relies on making estimates of future costs. If these turn out to be underestimates, the contracting authority is presented with a problem if the actual bids for the service fees come in higher than the initial assumptions. The contracting authority may already be working within a pre-determined budget so it is faced with having to cancel the procurement or, to the extent possible, adjusting the scope of the project (which may have an impact on the rationale and VfM for the project). The financial model should therefore be run with a range of sensitivities (*cf.* §23.9.7) around capital, maintenance, operating and financing costs to establish the 'affordability envelope' that leaves sufficient margin in case the bids from the market are higher than expected.

Typical causes of poor affordability assessments and subsequent affordability issues include:

- fixing the proportion of the service fee indexed for inflation greater than it needs to be, creating an affordability issue in the later stages of the PPP contract's life (*cf.* §24.3.5);
- unanticipated costs as a result of environmental issues (*cf.* §12.2.4);
- estimating maintenance and operating costs based on the costs of current levels of the public service rather than those actually required, which may be higher;
- over-estimating the levels of third-party revenue expected (*e.g.* from sale to the public of the use of school sports facilities outside school hours); and
- over-estimating the expected price and timing from the sale of public land that is expected to be used to fund a part of the project capex (*cf.* §12.2.9).

Service fees should not be manipulated so that they are abnormally low at the beginning of the PPP contract, as a way of making the PPP 'affordable' to begin with, and then rise steeply later on (*cf.* §15.3.2). This is a particular temptation when affordability is primarily measured by taking the service fee during the first full year of operation as a baseline to assess bids (*cf.* §10.6.5).

For projects where the contracting authority is paying in accordance with levels of use, as in the case of shadow tolls (*cf.* §15.5.3), estimates of future levels of demand are highly relevant, especially as contracting authority budgets are typically inflexible (although the shadow-toll payments are usually calibrated to limit payments above a certain volume of traffic).

Determining the affordability of a project is one the main activities that a contracting authority needs to carry out during Phase 3 (Project Economic Assessment and Selection, *cf.* §5.3.3) and this continues to be refined in the PPP context over the subsequent two phases before launching a PPP project on the market (*i.e.*, if and as the project is prepared as a PPP during Phases 4 and 5, assessing and re-checking the affordability of the service fee is an important task).

Apart from avoiding unexpected budgetary risks or longer-term fiscal problems, assessing affordability during the preparation phases of the project ensures that any adjustments to the scope of the project as a result of comparing expected costs and financing terms against the budgets available can be made and considered well ahead of the bidding stage. Market sounding (*cf.* §10.4) and the use of competent advisers to provide information on expected costs is therefore a particularly important part of the affordability exercise. Because of the affordability illusion, there is a risk that the PPP project is 'gold-plated' i.e. the service requirements are higher than can realistically be afforded. To help counter this, and where possible, the PPP equivalent of the 'do minimum' option is sometimes calculated. This underlines the importance of estimating the expected PPP project costs and their affordability.

During the procurement phase, bids then need to be assessed to ensure that the PPP project remains affordable. Assessing affordability also enables the contracting authority to have its own views on costs to check that the bidder's assumptions are realistic and that the project is unlikely to get into difficulties later on (even if this is a problem for the project company).

§9.2.3 Affordability and Concessions

One of the most common reasons why governments are attracted to the use of concessions is that they make projects affordable to government because users, not the contracting authority, pay for the assets over time. For a contracting authority facing immediate spending constraints, a concession may be the only option for a project to move forward. However, while this may be good news for government, a concession does not necessarily increase the overall level of resources over the longer term to fund the project. User charges paid to the project company could otherwise have been paid to the contracting authority or paid in taxes to government. There are also limits to what users can be expected to pay for new services.

Nevertheless, there are a number of other arguments why charging users may make sense (Engel *et al.* 2014):

- It can be argued that it is more efficient if users pay the service provider directly. This avoids the additional costs of using money from tax revenues to flow *via* the government for the project, with the associated overheads, inefficiencies and even leakage that can arise.
- It may improve the bankability of the project if there is low trust in the government's ability to pay promptly for the project's services on behalf of citizens.
- There may also be fairness reasons for charging users rather than taxpayers for the use of certain types of project, especially if the benefits are considered to accrue only to the users who can afford to pay for them, and not the wider population.
- Requiring the private sector to take the demand risk that often goes with user charges leads to stronger scrutiny of demand forecasts (*cf.* §13.2). This can help to avoid 'white elephant' projects. However, this is more an issue of who takes the usage risk than who pays. The two do not automatically go together (*cf.* §15.5.4).

The decision to charge users may be driven by what public services citizens normally expect to pay for directly and therefore what is politically acceptable. This varies considerably between countries: in Latin America, Asia and many parts of Europe, the idea of motorists paying tolls for use of a motorway, for example, is accepted. In other countries, this would be considered less politically feasible.

Finally, who pays will also depend on the nature of the project's services: in many cases, it is simply not practical to charge users, for example PPP projects in sectors such as prisons, streetlighting or defence. These are therefore usually structured as availability PPPs.

As with availability PPPs, the contracting authority needs to assess the expected levels of costs and revenues needed to ensure financial viability of the project. As concessions usually, though not necessarily (*e.g.* least present-value of revenues (LPVR) concessions—*cf.* §15.5.2), involve transfer of demand risk, this in turn requires estimating the likely levels of demand (*cf.* §13.2) and therefore the level of user charges that will be needed to ensure financial viability. In some cases, the user charge is set by government policy, in which case the expected level of demand will determine how much, if any, funding (direct or contingent) will be required from the contracting authority (*cf.* Chapter 18) to make the project financially viable. As can be seen, even though users pay for the service under a concession, assessing affordability for concessions is as important as for availability PPPs and in fact can be more difficult given the need to estimate future usage levels as well as users' ability and 'willingness to pay'.

Estimating users' ability and willingness to pay (*cf.* §15.5) depends on studies of user behaviour and on effective stakeholder consultation, communication and management (*cf.* §6.5). Concessions in a number of countries have suffered from demand and willingness to pay forecasts being carried out inadequately. An example is the M1/M15 concession in Hungary: local users refused to accept the level of tolls, complaining that these were some of the highest in Europe at the time; actual traffic volumes were around half those predicted (PPIAF 2009). The Lekki Expressway in Lagos, Nigeria, is another more recent example where difficulties arose, partly as a result of opposition to tolling levels (Yescombe 2017).

§9.2.4 Affordability and VfM

Assessing affordability is sometimes confused with assessing VfM: the PPP option financial model developed for the VfM assessment (*cf.* §8.4) includes many of the same components as the financial model used for assessing affordability. The main difference is that the VfM model may exclude those costs that are common to the public and private sector, such as prior acquisition of land (*cf.* §12.2.1), as the VfM calculation is about comparing the *relative* costs of two approaches, whereas as the affordability calculation is about measuring *all* the costs of the project to the authority.

To put it another way, assessing affordability addresses part of the question 'could a PPP project be carried out?', whereas assessing VfM addresses the question 'should a PPP project be carried out?'. A PPP project may be affordable but still represent poor VfM. Both are important but different questions.

§9.3 BUDGETING FOR PPPs

While affordability assesses what needs to be paid, and either provides information for budgeting purposes or compares the costs to the budgeted resources available, a budgeting assessment considers how government resources are made available to the contracting authority for the PPP project in the first place.

The public-sector budgeting process *prioritises* and *allocates* spending (because there are usually more projects to spend money on than is available). Budgeting also involves some form of approval, reporting and accountability process, *e.g.* to parliament.

For concessions, the affordability and therefore budgetary impact for government may seem much lower than for an availability PPP and therefore budgeting may be considered less relevant for concessions. Nevertheless, as seen with affordability issues (*cf.* §9.2.3), there may still be sizeable funding obligations arising from guarantees required of government (*cf.* §9.3.4).

§9.3.1 Long-Term PPP Spending Commitments

Government budgets usually have time horizons of one to three years. But most of the service-fees for a PPP usually fall due long after this. To address this issue, medium-term expenditure frameworks (MTEFs) are increasingly being used as a means to forecast budget commitments into the future, although even these are unlikely to cover the full term of a PPP contract. Some governments use a separate budget-approval process for all spending commitments that fall beyond one year. This also addresses the problem where a one year 'use it or lose it' budget approval forces a contracting authority to choose a sub-optimal project over a better project simply because the capital spending requirement for the poorer project falls within a year while the better project's capital spending requirement falls over several years.

An MTEF may be based on longer-term high-level public-investment plans and national-development strategies (*cf.* §4.8), although the links between these plans and MTEFs are sometimes quite weak. MTEFs also differ quite significantly from one country to another in their political commitment and how binding they are, as well as their planning horizons, coverage and level of detail.

§9.3.2 Dealing with Off-Balance-Sheet PPPs in the Budget System

If a government's accounting rules (*cf.* §9.4) lead to PPP projects being classified as government assets, they are usually included in the normal budgetary system and treated in the same way as conventionally-procured projects. Any incentive to use PPP schemes principally to avoid budgeting constraints is thus obviously reduced. In some countries (such as in Australia, Canada, Germany and New Zealand), many PPP projects are now classified as government assets and so are budgeted for in the normal way.

In addition to short-term horizons, problems for budgeting can arise if the PPP project is classified as off the government's balance sheet. This is because it may fall outside the budgeting process and so escape the normal disciplines that would apply for public-sector investment decision-making (*cf.* Chapter 7). This of course may make the PPP attractive to a contracting authority, but not always to the Ministry of Finance, which will be concerned about how the future payment obligations will be funded, what fiscal risks this may create and ensuring that sound public-investment decisions are made.

However, even if the project is not treated as a government asset, it is still possible to ensure that future obligations are subjected to investment decision-making processes and budgeted for. In Britain, for example, service-fee payment obligations are included in 'resource' (*i.e.* current rather than capital) spending budgets as and when they are expected to fall due.[1] In France, public-sector budgets also recognise the deferred payments of such committed costs (although this necessitated a change of law:), and PPP projects are subjected to the same underlying preparation and decision-making process as publicly-funded projects.

In fact, in some countries, PPP budgeting requirements may be *more* conservative than for traditional projects because the total lifetime costs of the project, not just the initial capital costs, all have to be appropriated up-front and not in the future. If the full lifetime costs of a public-procurement project do not have to be appropriated in the same way, this budgetary requirement actually creates a bias *against* the use of PPPs. Thus, budgeting rules may result in perverse decisions to use (or not to use) PPPs.

§9.3.3 Credibility of Future Budget Appropriations

As appropriations for government budgets, *i.e.* the budget amounts approved by the legislature on a periodic basis, usually only cover the immediate payment commitments under a PPP contract, private-sector investors and lenders need to take a view on the responsibility of future legislatures to ensure that budget appropriations are made to meet those payment commitments that fall beyond the term of the currently-approved budgets. This may be a particular problem for PPP projects with regional or local contracting authorities because their access to resources may be considered weaker than for central government (*cf.* §13.4), unless supported by a central-government commitment (but such a commitment may require the central government to seek the power to divert local-government resources or control the project in exchange for such support). If there is any doubt about the ability of the contracting authority to pay, it will be difficult to finance a PPP.

§9.3.4 Budgeting for Contingent-Payment Commitments

Budgeted PPP payment commitments fall into two broad categories—*direct* and *contingent*. Direct payments are obviously made under an availability PPP. In the case of a concession, direct payments would include any explicitly-agreed payments by government, such as a grant towards a part of the capital costs of the project or a fixed operating subsidy (*cf.* Chapter 18).

However, there may be additional payment commitments by a contracting authority that are *contingent* upon certain events that may or may not happen but are *explicitly* set out in the PPP contract. Examples include:

- guarantees, *e.g.* for minimum levels of usage or revenue (*cf.* §18.4);
- compensation events, *e.g.* for certain risks retained by the contracting authority, such as land-acquisition costs (*cf.* §16.2);
- variations, *e.g.* for contract changes requested by the contracting authority that would otherwise be a cost to the project company (*cf.* §16.2.2);

---

[1] There is still a risk that this creates an incentive to use PPPs if it means that the project costs can be met out of resource budgets if they are more accessible than capital budgets, rather than for VfM reasons.

- inflation-indexation provisions in the service fees that leave the contracting authority exposed to inflation risk (*cf.* §24.3); and
- termination payments, *e.g.* for losses to the project company arising from cancellation of the PPP contract by the contracting authority (*cf.* §17.3).

There may also be contingent commitments that are *not* explicitly set out in the PPP contract. These are *implicit* commitments usually as a result of a government's perceived responsibility to its citizens. Expenditure following a natural disaster or bailing out banks to avoid a worsening economic situation are wider examples of implicit payment commitments for a government. For the narrower field of PPPs, examples include a contracting authority rescuing a troubled project to ensure continuation of the public service even if it is not obliged to do so within the terms of the PPP contract (*cf.* §17.2.9, §17.6.1).

Budgeting for *contingent* commitments is especially difficult since, by definition, such commitments are not explicitly quantified and are uncertain. These are particularly common with concessions where the contracting authority is sharing demand risk, *e.g.* a minimum traffic or revenue guarantee (*cf.* §18.4). Payments can arise unexpectedly and, if existing budget appropriations are insufficient, may require a difficult and unwelcome approach to the legislature to authorise additional funding.

Estimating these future liabilities presents similar difficulties to valuing risk in the VfM assessment (*cf.* §8.3.2). Approaches to this problem (to the extent that countries have them) range from simply estimating costs that result from certain assumed future events, to using more detailed probability calculations to quantify the likelihood and costs of different future events. In Chile, for example, a standard model has been used for a number of years to calculate the expected costs of revenue and exchange-rate guarantees for each year of each concession to estimate cash flow at risk. For very significant projects, a government may commission a specific report on contingent liabilities—an example is the assessment of the contingent liabilities for the Gautrain project in the province of Gauteng in South Africa (Irwin and Mokdad 2010).

But many governments still only recognise a contingent commitment once it is triggered. The United States is one of the few countries that does budget for the costs of guarantees up-front. Some governments, while not reflecting contingent liabilities in budgets, do so in a statement of risk accompanying the budget. Some governments establish a budget line for contingent PPP payments (such as in Colombia for minimum revenue guarantees—*cf.* §18.4) or for those contingent payments that are considered particularly high risk. In other cases, a separate contingent liability fund may be set up, as in Indonesia, and in various central and state governments in Latin America. For the occasional smaller project, such contingent liabilities may not be a problem. The issue is if and when such liabilities start to accumulate and no-one has been keeping the score.

§9.3.5 PPP Affordability Caps

In addition to controlling fiscal exposure on a project-by-project or sector-programme basis, some countries set an overall cap (or ceiling) on direct PPP payment obligations over a defined period. This may enhance a government's commitment to managing the level of future PPP payment commitments and its credibility to do so in the eyes of creditors. It may also address concerns about not over-committing future resources and inter-generational fairness.

Another potential benefit of affordability caps is that they isolate a specific 'fiscal space' to pay for PPPs. PPP payment commitments may become politically unpopular if they are seen to limit other expenditure needs—for example, if there is less money to pay doctors because the hospital's PPP service fee has to be paid out of the same overall shrinking health budget (even if the overall cost of the PPP over its life is the same or even lower than the public-sector alternative would have been).

Caps should limit the expected total future service-fee payments, not just a current annual amount (to avoid over-committing in future years). The caps themselves should be unambiguous and easy to verify—the simplest being a total monetary amount for a defined period (other approaches include a fixed percentage of a capital expenditure budget or government revenues). If not, such a mechanism may just create another exercise of trying to get around fiscal rules. The level of the cap should be compatible with the MTEF (and possibly any national infrastructure plan—cf. §4.8) and with what is fiscally sustainable, also leaving budget space in case unexpected budgetary pressures arise.

A single body (such as a PPP unit) needs to be responsible for monitoring all commitments, assessing the overall status of the affordability cap and for looking across the whole forward programme for PPPs. It should also be able to delete projects that are logged potentially to use the cap which subsequently do not go forward. There should be a mechanism early on in the preparation of the project cycle to anticipate uses of the cap, monitor the quality of the affordability assessment and later on to record and approve any additional payment obligations as a result of subsequent changes to the project.

A cap can be set for a particular sector but ideally it should cover PPP payment commitments all across sectors and levels of government if it is to be truly effective (and include all PPP-related payment commitments, such as capital grants, as well as availability payments).

However, caps may fail to set an effective limit to indirect payment commitments such as those listed in §9.3.4, because the potential cost of such commitments is more difficult to determine. This may give rise to a false sense of security.

And clearly if the cap is reached, further good VfM PPPs may be excluded. This may adversely affect overall VfM in public investment (which is similar in effect to the Maastricht fiscal constraints applying to EU countries), especially if the earlier projects approved within the cap are not as good as those that come later but fall outside the cap (highlighting the importance of identifying pipelines of future projects). This also raises the issue as to whether such caps are substituting for the normal controls on the quality and level of public investment or work in parallel with these (preferably the latter).

There is no single methodology nor any single figure that indicates an 'optimum' level of future PPP liabilities. The rules around what is included in affordability caps and how they are monitored are highly country-specific, making it difficult to translate good practice to other countries. Brazil was one of the first countries to use a budget cap for availability PPPs, establishing a limit for annual PPP payment commitments of 5%[2] of the previous year's net revenues (and of 5%[3] of the projected net revenues over the next 10

---

[2] Initially it was 1%.

[3] Initially it was 1%.

years for the annual payments in those years). Other countries, such as Peru, set a limit based on the PV of PPP commitments (including contingent liabilities) of 7% of gross domestic product (GDP). More recently, Britain announced an overall absolute cap or 'control total' of £70 billion over the five years from 2015-16 onwards to limit central-government PPP payment commitments. Greece and Poland also use limits on various overall PPP payment commitments.

§9.4 FINANCIAL ACCOUNTING AND STATISTICAL REPORTING

When compiling national accounts, a government needs to know whether the PPP project assets and any associated financing liabilities are classified as belonging to government or the private party.

Governments often provide two sorts of financial information: *financial accounts* that are used to report on their financial performance, usually a legal requirement (§9.4.1-§9.4.3), and *statistical reports* used for measuring fiscal-policy decisions (§9.4.4, §9.4.5). Statistical reporting may also be required to measure compliance with levels of deficit and debt under regional agreements, such as in the EU, or to draw international comparisons of the health of a government's fiscal affairs. There are international efforts to bring these two forms of reporting more into line but there is still some way to go on this.

For both forms of reporting, the concept of *economic ownership* lies at the heart of determining whether the public or private party is assumed to own the PPP asset and associated liabilities. Behind this is the idea of substance over form, *i.e.* determining the *de facto* as opposed to nominal legal ownership of the PPP project. Economic ownership in turn is determined either on the basis of which party carries the majority of the *risks and rewards* (or benefits) from owning the asset or on who is deemed to *control* the asset. Reporting for the purposes of government financial accounts has now largely moved over to the control approach. For statistical reports, on the other hand, the risk/reward approach is generally still used.

Financial and statistical reporting are not only backward-looking exercises: they provide important information for decisions relevant to the future sustainability of government spending and on how to allocate spending between today and tomorrow.

§9.4.1 Financial-Accounting Standards

Governments are increasingly using financial-accounting standards consistent with International Financial Reporting Standards (IFRS). These standards are issued by the International Accounting Standards Board (IASB) and aim to bring a common set of accounting rules across the world in the way both businesses and governments report their financial affairs. This makes it easier to interpret and compare financial information between countries.

Because some of the issues faced by governments are different to businesses, specific standards based on IFRS have been developed for the public sector. These standards are referred to as International *Public-Sector* Accounting Standards (IPSAS). IFRS, and consequently IPSAS, have led governments to change from preparing their financial accounts on a more traditional cash-movement basis ('cash accounting') to reporting on an 'accruals basis'. The latter is similar to how businesses compile their accounts: revenue and spending are recorded when economic value rather than cash has changed hands. Thus, contracting authorities and the government as a whole must publish balance sheets that report financial assets and liabilities that are not only limited to traditionally-defined debt. The use of accrual accounting therefore raises the issue of where to record PPP assets and liabilities.

§9.4.2 Financial Accounting—The Control Principle

In 2006 the IFRS Interpretations Committee developed, and IASB published, an 'interpretation note' called IFRIC 12 (IFRS Interpretations Committee 2006). This required a private-sector business to recognise the PPP asset and associated liabilities in its balance sheet if it *controls* the asset. To mirror this, and to avoid assets falling outside both the private- and public-sector balance sheets, in 2011 the IPSAS board published a similar standard called IPSAS 32 for the purposes of public-sector financial accounting (IPSASB 2011). Both availability PPPs and concessions are covered by IPSAS 32.

Under the control principle in IPSAS 32, the contracting authority is deemed to have control (and therefore has economic ownership and is obliged to report the PPP asset on its balance sheet) if it:

- controls or regulates what services the project company must provide with the facility, to whom it must provide the services, and at what price; and
- controls any significant residual interest in the facility at the end of the term of the PPP arrangement.

What is meant by controlling the price is quite broadly determined and can take a variety of forms, from setting the price in the PPP contract, to the contracting authority controlling the framework in which the price is set. Furthermore, with regard to the second test, residual value, the contracting authority very often has a residual interest in the asset (*cf.* §15.5.2).

For an availability PPP, even if significant construction and operation risks have been transferred to the project company, the contracting authority does not relinquish control over the type of service it requires and the price it will pay for these. So, applying the control principle to availability PPPs is more likely to classify them as public-sector assets than a risk/reward approach would do. For concessions, the application of IPSAS 32 and the control principle is more controversial—this is because significant commercial risks may be transferred but the contracting authority may still control key issues such as the level of user charges.

Before IPSAS 32, countries such as Australia and Britain used a risk/reward approach to classify PPPs in their financial accounts, *i.e.* looking at the balance of risks and rewards from the project between the contracting authority and the project company. IPSAS 32 and the control principle resulted in changing most of their PPPs into assets and liabilities on the government balance sheet. Many governments now apply accounting standards that are broadly consistent with IPSAS (for example the United States and Canada) or are in the process of adopting or harmonising their standards with IPSAS.

§9.4.3 Financial Accounting for Guarantees

Government guarantees (*cf.* Chapter 18) also raise issues for financial accounting. This is particularly relevant for concessions. Under the different IPSAS 19 accounting standard (IPSAS 2002), if the guarantee is more likely than not to be called (i.e. an over 50% probability), a liability (or 'provision') is recorded on the government's balance sheet for the PV of the expected amount to be called, and government expenditure is recorded for the same amount. Changes in expectations are reflected in a change to the value of the liability and recorded as an expense (increase in liability) or revenue (decrease in liability).

Less likely (or 'contingent') liabilities should be disclosed as such. Where practicable, a description of the estimated PV of the liability, the level of uncertainty as to the amount, timing and possible reimbursement of the liability should also be disclosed.

§9.4.4 Statistical Reporting

The basic standards for macroeconomic statistical reporting are set out in the *System of National Accounts* (SNA) (European Commission *et al.* 2009) under the joint responsibility of the United Nations, the IMF and a number of other multilateral bodies. For non-EU governments, the key source of guidance for the format of statistical reporting, based on the SNA, is the IMF's *Government Finance Statistics (GFS) Manual* (IMF 2014). This is aimed at 'helping national authorities to strengthen their capacity to formulate fiscal policy and monitor fiscal developments'.

There is no worldwide agreement yet among statisticians on the treatment of PPPs and thus the SNA, and the GFS Manual based on this, are currently non-prescriptive. The IMF's GFS Manual generally takes a risk/reward approach to determining economic ownership but recognises that each case needs to be considered on its merits as the *relative importance* of each different risk/reward factor will have a bearing on the overall determination of economic ownership and therefore balance-sheet treatment. The factors involved are closely related to the conditions prescribed by IPSAS 32 for financial accounting. So, GFS rules and IPSAS 32 should usually lead to the same result.

If limits (*e.g.* imposed by the IMF) exist on levels of public deficit and public debt and a country is close to these limits, how a PPP project is classified for statistical-reporting purposes is particularly important. There may be an incentive to 'financially engineer' a structure to get the project classified as off balance sheet so that it does not contribute to the reported level of public debt. If risk transfer is the deciding factor, this may lead to paying the project company for a risk that it is not well-equipped to assume, resulting in poor VfM. It also puts pressure on the process of measuring risk and the integrity of the VfM assessment by creating an incentive to ensure the assessment 'proves' VfM, when this may not be the case.

However, the bias to use PPPs by the prospect of off-balance-sheet treatment can sometimes be overstated. A study of the impact of the requirement that all French local-government PPPs should be classified as on-balance sheet as of 2010 (Buso *et al.* 2016) showed that this did not lead to materially fewer PPPs. In other active PPP markets, such as Canada or Germany, PPP programmes have developed even though almost all projects have always been and continue to be classified as on the public-sector balance sheet.

§9.4.5 Eurostat

With the exception of the EU, detailed approaches to the statistical (as opposed to financial) reporting of PPPs in many countries are not yet available. Because of the importance of debt and deficit criteria under the Maastricht Treaty,[4] and the prevalence of PPPs in the region, the EU has developed a detailed approach to classifying PPPs as part of its wider rules on statistical reporting. This approach is in line with a variant of the SNA called the *European System of Accounts* (ESA). The version at the time of writing is called ESA 2010 (Eurostat 2013).

To implement ESA 2010, Eurostat, the EU Statistical Office, is charged with ensuring that statistics are provided from EU member countries on a harmonised basis and from time to time issues updated editions of its *Manual on Government Deficit and Debt* (MGDD) (Eurostat 2016). National statistical offices then compile the information in line with Eurostat's reporting rules.

Eurostat's approach to classifying economic ownership is based on the risk/reward principle. The broad principle is that if the majority of the risks of construction and either of demand or operation are transferred to the private party, then the PPP project is considered off balance sheet for statistical-reporting purposes. The principle of also including rewards (as opposed to just risks) was introduced in 2010 (causing some concern around issues such as the sharing of refinancing gains (*cf.* §26.2.5)).

Eurostat distinguishes between 'concessions' (which it defines as those PPPs where the majority of the revenue comes from users, such as a toll road) and availability PPPs (which it simply calls 'PPPs'), and has separate, but similar, rules for each. Concessions are generally more readily classified as off balance sheet primarily because the project company is considered to bear the majority of commercial (*i.e.* demand) risks.

The application of the Eurostat rules, written more for statisticians than PPP practitioners, has raised frequent concerns around the difficulty and consistency of interpretation. To help address this, Eurostat developed with the European Investment Bank's (EIB) European PPP Expertise Centre (EPEC) *A Guide to the Statistical Treatment of PPPs* in 2016 (Eurostat/EIB 2016). This identifies how the main terms in a typical PPP contract are considered to influence the statistical treatment (legal advisers may sometimes assist on this issue—*cf.* §6.4.2) and whether the influence of a particular issue, such as the level of public funding, is significant or not. The *Guide* then provides a basis to determine how the different issues, *when taken together*, determine the overall statistical-reporting classification of the PPP project. If the result is marginal, then Eurostat will look at the degree of the contracting authority's control over the facility to come to a final determination. The individual types of risk, and how they influence the statistical reporting classification of the project, are set out in detail in the MGDD and the *Guide*. It should be noted that if a PPP is classified as on balance sheet, then it is only the capital element of the PPP that is put on the balance sheet, recorded on an accrual basis as the works proceed.

Examples of how Eurostat accounting treatment may affect (or be affected by) the project structure can be found in §14.10, §15.5.2, §15.6.1, §16.4, §18.4, §18.13, §21.5.1 and §27.5.2.

---

[4] Signed in February 1992 by the then members of the European Community, the Maastricht Treaty led to the creation of the euro. One of the obligations of the Treaty is to keep sound fiscal policies, with debt limited to 60% of GDP and annual deficits no greater than 3% of GDP.

§9.5 OTHER FORMS OF REPORTING

Reporting on the fiscal impact of PPPs can be strengthened in a number of ways if current systems are not considered adequate, particularly for governments that use cash-based accounting systems. These include, irrespective of the financial reporting or statistical treatment of PPPs:

- publishing long-term forecasts of all government PPP spending and revenue commitments;
- publishing details of the main fiscal risks to government and details of the PPP contracts themselves;
- publishing supplementary fiscal indicators that include all PPPs (including PPPs that may lie outside the central-government coverage of public-sector fiscal indicators such as regional or local-government PPPs); and
- including planned spending and revenue forecasts for all PPPs in the MTEFs (as well as estimated contingent liabilities, where possible).

In Chile, for example, in addition to financial and statistical reporting, the government publishes annual reports on future availability payments, committed subsidies and revenue-sharing arrangements, and the expected cash flows under these arrangements. In Britain, the Office for Budget Responsibility includes the impact of PPP liabilities in its fiscal sustainability reports. The British and South African treasuries also publish information on all future service-fee commitments under availability PPPs, irrespective of their balance sheet treatment.

The IMF has developed a publicly-available downloadable tool to help governments assess the impact of future PPP payment commitments on their fiscal position called P-FRAM (the 'PPP-fiscal risk assessment model') (IMF/World Bank Group 2016). This tool provides a structured process for gathering information for a PPP project on an Excel-based spreadsheet using this to generate a set of calculated outcomes. These include: (i) project cash flows; (ii) fiscal tables and charts both on a cash and accrual basis; (iii) debt sustainability analyses with and without the PPP project; (iv) sensitivity analysis of the main fiscal aggregates to changes in macroeconomic and project-specific parameters and (v) a summary risk register of the project (*cf.* §11.6).

§9.6 FINAL OBSERVATIONS

PPPs are a complex mix of risks and rewards that somehow have to fit into the binary world of accounting (*i.e.* they are either on or off balance sheet for the public sector). This can sometimes lead to the perplexing situation where private-sector investment and lending, that is exposed to project risks *and paid for as such*, is still treated as government debt applying the rules set out above. This may even crowd out necessary public-sector borrowing and investment when fiscal constraints apply.

Perhaps more could be done to distinguish government borrowing used to fund current consumption and that which is used to fund long-term productive investment that delivers economic benefits for years to come. Yet a country's financial statements, and its consequential treatment by those who assess its costs and capacity to borrow, often fail to make this distinction: an economy that borrows to invest in its future is a very different prospect to one that borrows only to maintain its current levels of consumption.

CHAPTER

10

PPP Procurement

§10.1 INTRODUCTION

This chapter considers the activities in the procurement process for a PPP that take place over Phases 4-6 of the project cycle with preparation for procurement taking place over Phases 4 and 5 prior to the Procurement Phase itself (Phase 6—*cf.* §5.3.6). As with the chapters so far, this chapter takes the point of view of a contracting authority (sometimes known in this context as the 'promoter' of the project), and reviews:

- the objectives of the procurement process (§10.2);
- preparing for procurement (§10.3);
- market sounding (§10.4);
- procurement procedures (§10.5);
- the bidding process (§10.6);
- other procurement-related issues (§10.7); and
- due diligence of bids (§10.8).

§10.2 OBJECTIVES OF THE PROCUREMENT PROCESS

In preparing for and running a procurement process, the contracting authority aims to ensure a number of things:

- bids from highly-qualified suppliers;
- a strongly-competitive process, *i.e.* at least two bidders make it through the process until the final tendering stage;

Public-Private Partnerships for Infrastructure
DOI: https://doi.org/10.1016/B978-0-08-100766-2.00010-3

- bids that fit its requirements as closely as possible from bidders who fully understand these requirements;
- a process that is as efficient as possible—the costs for bidders and the time taken for the process can easily discourage good-quality bidders to fall away or not decide to take part in the first place;
- the quality of the process is not compromised—a well-developed procurement process can expect to take 18 months from launch to financial close; and
- a process run in strict adherence to the prescribed procurement rules—failure to do so will discourage bidders and can may lead to challenges from losing bidders, which may entail having to cancel the whole process and start again.

A competitive public-procurement process is a legal requirement in most countries where services are being provided to the public (as in a concession), or a public contract is involved (as in an availability PPP). In these cases, the bidding process has to follow a specific procurement procedure. It is also required if financing or guarantees are being provided by development-finance institutions (DFIs—*cf.* §22.9).

§10.3 PREPARING FOR PROCUREMENT

Much of the work necessary for the Procurement Phase takes place during Phases 4 and 5 (*cf.* §5.3.4, §5.3.5). The Procurement Phase itself is very demanding for the contracting authority, with fixed deadlines to meet under the relevant procurement regulations and decisions taking place as the interaction with bidders unfolds. This is not the time to be preparing project documents, for example. Where possible the draft PPP contract and all the other bid documents (*cf.* §10.6.2) should be ready in advance of the Procurement Phase. The contracting authority's project team (*cf.* §6.2.2) also needs to be briefed and in place, including the advisers (*cf.* §6.4), who may need to be reappointed for this phase.

Launching the project on the market when it is not fully prepared is a common mistake. This damages the credibility of the contracting authority and reduces bidder interest. In almost all cases it leads to delays later on, so the overall time saved often turns out to be an illusion. Nevertheless, political and other pressures on the contracting authority may push it to do so. To help avoid this, many governments have an approval point at this stage (*cf.* §5.4), assessing the readiness of the project to be launched on the market. Various PPP checklist tools are available such as the EPEC *PPP Project Preparation Status Tool* (EPEC 2016).

There are five basic questions that the contracting authority should ask before launching the Procurement Phase:

- Does the contracting authority have the capacity in terms of organisation and resources to manage the procurement and subsequent phases of the project (*cf.* Chapter 6)?
- Does the project itself still make sense in terms of need and economic viability (*cf.* Chapter 7)?
- Should the project be procured as a PPP (*cf.* Chapter 8)?
- Is the project likely to be financially viable and affordable as a PPP (*cf.* Chapter 9)?

- Does the private sector have the willingness and ability to deliver the project as a PPP (*cf.* §10.4)?

These questions are largely addressed during the Procurement Review Phase (Phase 4). Preparation of the bid documents including the draft PPP contract, obtaining permissions and consents required and acquiring any land needed should be concluded to the extent possible in the Procurement Preparation Phase (Phase 5). To some extent these two phases overlap each other: developing the contract terms may involve sounding out the market and adjustments to the proposed terms based on market feedback, as discussed below. And the advisers (*cf.* §6.4) are often appointed to assist the contracting authority with both Phase 4 and 5 activities (such as VfM assessment and contract preparation).

§10.4 Market Sounding and Commercial Assessment

When preparing the project for procurement it is important to check that the contracting authority's view of the basic viability of the project as a PPP (including its scope, costs, nature of services and allocation of risks) is shared by major private-sector participants in the market. This is also an important part of the process of developing the draft PPP contract as well as assessing affordability, VfM and identifying any barriers to competition. Unless the project is attractive to the market, it will attract few bidders, if any. Without competition for the project, VfM will be hard to achieve and demonstrate.

The process of interacting with the market is often referred to as market sounding. Those approached may be construction contractors, operators, lenders, investors or even other advisers. The initial objective of market sounding is to identify the capacity and quality of potential bidders. While some sounding of the market can take place early on in the process during the Project Economic Assessment and Selection (Phase 3—*cf.* §5.3.3), it mostly takes place during the Procurement Review (Phase 4—*cf.* §5.3.4) and Procurement Preparation (Phase 5—*cf.* §5.3.5). During Phases 4 and 5, the contracting authority also needs to determine the expected costs and terms of a potential PPP contract with more accuracy as a basis for the assessments of VfM (*cf.* Chapter 8) and affordability (*cf.* §9.2), as well as the risk allocation (*cf.* Chapters 11-14) and PPP contract preparation activities (*cf.* Chapters 15-17).

The key to successful market sounding is to be as precise as possible about what the contracting authority is seeking to get the market's view on (such as the allocation of a particular risk). This means ensuring those approached have a clear understanding of the concept behind the project and the nature of the issue. Accordingly, the contracting authority should generally not approach the market too early, when the issues will not be well enough defined, or too late, when market feedback may be difficult to incorporate in the design of the project. The contracting authority's external advisers (*cf.* §6.4) can play an important rôle in identifying the issues and interpreting the responses from the market, as well as using their networks to approach relevant parties.

Although this process is conducted prior to the procurement and therefore not subject to formal procurement rules, clearly the contracting authority needs to ensure that no party is given an advantage through having been involved in these soundings. The contracting authority should also be clear that market sounding is not part of the formal procurement process and avoid using terms such as 'bidders' in case it is misinterpreted as such.

Market sounding usually involves holding open public meetings and sending question-naires to, or requesting written submissions from, market players on specific topics. One-to-one discussions are also valuable but there should be governance arrangements in place (such as using more than one person from the contracting authority to attend these meet-ings, consistency in how the meetings are conducted, recording of meetings and clear audit trails). It is important to talk to a wide range of potential bidders and to keep an open mind to avoid the project being developed in a way that favours a particular bidder's solution—inevitably the contracting authority will be subject to 'sales pitches'. It is also worth bearing in mind that the process will start to raise market awareness of the project as well as expose the contracting authority's level of organisation and professionalism to potential bidders. For this reason, it is a good opportunity for the contracting authority to 'show its face', so this process should not be left wholly to the advisers.

§10.5 PROCUREMENT PROCEDURES

Procurement procedures may be considered no more than a technical matter of little general importance, but actually they are at the core of the PPP process. The major argu-ment in favour of using PPPs is that they create savings in long-term costs compared to public-sector funded projects (*cf.* §28.6), but a badly-run procurement can all too easily destroy any potential for such a saving. An effective competition—*i.e.* an efficient procurement procedure—is probably the strongest contributor to generating VfM for the contracting authority.

In preparing for the Procurement Phase, the contracting authority may need to consider which procurement procedure to use where alternatives are available, as is the case in the EU for example. The global framework for public-procurement procedures is provided by the *Agreement on Government Procurement* (GPA), administered by the World Trade Organisation (WTO 2014), to which many countries are now party. This was first signed in 1979 and last amended in 2014 (at the time of writing). Detailed rules, based on these provisions, are contained, for example, in EU public-procurement regulations.

The WTO GPA allows for three types of public-sector procurement:

- 'Open' procedure: This procedure allows anyone to submit a bid.
- 'Selective' procedure: This procedure allows the contracting authority to reduce the number of prospective bidders through a pre-qualification procedure (*cf.* §10.6.1).
- 'Limited' procedure: Under this procedure, the contracting authority approaches prospective bidders directly rather than calling for bids (with or without pre-qualification).

The open and limited procedures are unlikely to be appropriate for a PPP, and are therefore not considered further in this context. Most countries with PPP programmes usually use some form of procedure that involves pre-qualifying bidders, for reasons that are explained below. The key differences then relate to whether procedures prohibit or allow for interaction or 'dialogue' between pre-qualified bidders and the contracting authority before asking for final bids, after which the requirements and bids cannot generally be altered further.

By way of an example, one of the most detailed procurement regulations based on the GPA principles is the *EU Public Procurement Directive* (EU 2014) that covers, *inter alia*, availability PPPs.[1] Under the Public Procurement Directive, four types of bid procedure are prescribed:[2]

- Open procedure

    As under the GPA—not normally used for PPPs.

- 'Restricted' procedure

    Under this procedure, which involves proposals from pre-qualified bidders, bidders can be asked to supplement, clarify or complete the relevant information before making bids, but once the bids are received, that is the end of the process. The decision is made on the basis of the bids, and there should be no further negotiation with bidders, who are expected to sign the PPP contract on the basis set out in their bids. This approach has mainly been used for concessions, *e.g.* in Italy and Spain, and provides a relatively quick and hence potentially lower-cost procedure for bidders. However, it does require the contracting authority to be confident about all the terms of the PPP contract and the market's ability and willingness to understand and deliver them. Accordingly, it is less well-suited to more complex contracts where bidders may provide different solutions for the service concerned, and where the basis for bidding the overall pricing cannot be so easily specified in advance. Thus, the risk with this procedure is that the contracting authority does not get what it really wants and the bidders do not understand and deliver what is really needed. This may increase the risk of subsequent renegotiation of the PPP arrangements.

- 'Competitive-dialogue' procedure

    In many cases the approach to delivering the service is not ready-made and may benefit from more innovative solutions, the legal and financial structures may be complex or the technical specifications cannot be established with sufficient precision. The competitive-dialogue procedure[3] allows for greater interaction with bidders, which also pass through a pre-qualification process, while ensuring competition throughout the process. This helps to ensure that bids are better

---

[1] A contracting authority may choose to use a slightly less-prescriptive set of regulations if it procures a concession under the principles of the EU Concessions Directive (EU 2014).

[2] These include an 'innovation partnership procedure', which is more suited for research and technology projects where there is significant uncertainty the final shape of the solution allowing the contracting authority more freedom to explore possible solutions before deciding whether to go ahead with a particular one. This is not relevant to PPPs.

[3] An alternative to the competitive-dialogue procedure is the 'competitive procedure with negotiation' under which the contracting authority can choose to proceed with a bid without the need for dialogue if the bid closely meets its requirements, or if not it has the option to proceed with dialogue.

adapted to the specific needs of the contracting authority. It also prevents continuing negotiations on the final shape of the contract even after choosing a preferred bidder,[4] and therefore in the absence of competition (*cf.* §10.6.8).

Under the competitive-dialogue procedure, the contracting authority invites increasingly-detailed proposals from pre-qualified bidders in a series of stages or bidding rounds (the number of which is up to the contracting authority). When launching the process, key documents, such as the draft PPP contract, must be available to bidders, so it is not a process that starts with a blank sheet of paper. The objective of the dialogue is to identify and define the means best suited to satisfying the pre-defined needs and outcomes (*cf.* §15.2). At any stage, the contracting authority can narrow down the number of different solutions (and bidders): practice on this varies. During this process, the contracting authority discusses issues such as the detailed terms of the PPP contract and the technical specifications of the project. When the contracting authority believes that solutions have been arrived at, as a result of the dialogue, that meet its needs and that are potentially deliverable by the bidders, it invites the bidders to present their final bids (sometimes referred to as 'BAFOs'—best and final offers). These final bids may be 'clarified, specified and optimised', but 'essential aspects' of bids cannot subsequently change. The preferred bidder can be asked to confirm financial commitments or other terms contained in their bid.

A form of dialogue procedure is also used in other countries outside the EU such as Australia (there referred to as an 'interactive tender'), Egypt and South Africa.

However, many countries still use the restricted procedure, reflecting concerns about the perceived complexity and governance challenges of the competitive-dialogue process. In these cases, there may be a second round of bids, if the first round of bids is inconclusive. It is important, however, to avoid a situation where a bidder is selected and further negotiations proceed in the absence of competition, as discussed further in §10.6.8.

Given the long-term nature of the PPP contract or to put it another way, the limited opportunity to use competition to negotiate better terms after selection of the bidder, the choice of PPP-procurement procedure is very important. This was one reason why the 'negotiated procedure' was replaced in the EU procurement directives by other forms of procedure that prevent, or at least severely restrict, such post-selection negotiation.

§10.6 THE BIDDING PROCESS

§10.6.1 Pre-Qualification

In some cases, such as in the EU, a 'prior information notice' may be issued several months in advance of the bidding process itself, giving the market notice of the forthcoming procurement. This provides a brief description of what is to be procured and when.

---

[4] The term 'preferred' reflects the fact that although the bidder is its first choice, the authority is not yet committed until all the financing and other conditions are met and the PPP contract is signed.

The bidding process then begins with a 'pre-qualification questionnaire' (PQQ) from prospective bidders,[5] usually advertised in official publications and the financial and trade press.

At this stage, a bidder may be a group of contractors and investors that have agreed to come together for the purposes of putting forward a bid (*cf.* §20.2). This group is often referred to as a bidding consortium. In most cases, their relationship will be governed by a project-development agreement until the project company is established closer to financial close (*cf.* §20.4-§20.6).

The PQQ provides interested bidding groups with an outline of information on the project and its requirements, including details of how the bidding process will take place.

It is important to be careful about the information provided at this stage. Any departures from these details later on could invalidate the process—for example not stipulating that variant bids are allowed (*cf.* §10.7.1). The contracting authority's needs and requirements, award criteria (*cf.* §10.6.5) and an indicative timeframe for the procurement process must often be provided at this stage.

Bidders are then invited to set out their qualifications to undertake the project, demonstrating:

- relevant technical capacity to carry out the project (either directly or *via* specified major subcontractors);
- experience and performance with similar projects; and
- financial capacity to carry out the project (*cf.* §10.8.3, §20.2.1, §22.2.6).

Pre-qualification decisions are fairly subjective, since the criteria for pre-qualification are themselves subjective judgements, albeit set out at the start of the process. Nevertheless, it is important to be as clear as possible on the evidence that is required to demonstrate capability and capacity, as well as who is expected to provide the evidence— such as the relevant consortium members. The financial capacity of candidates is particularly important—PPP projects may fail because the sponsor simply cannot bear the costs when things go wrong (*cf.* §20.2.1). Lenders, for the same reason, may not find the risk of supporting the PPP project acceptable, making it unbankable. Common pitfalls that lead to disputes between the contracting authority and bidders or reduce interest from the right bidders include:

- undefined terms (*e.g.* requirement for experience of 'road construction in adverse weather conditions');
- unreasonably restrictive criteria (that could lead to unreasonable exclusivity such as the requirement to use specific brands or processes);
- too many minimum requirements (leading to the unintended exclusion of candidates);
- requiring too much information (which could put bidders off as well as overwhelm the authority).

As the objective at this stage is to encourage bidders to come forward, the information requested (and therefore the effort and expense involved at this stage) should be reasonably limited. Thus, bidders should not be asked to make proposals at this stage on how they would deliver the project.

---

[5] Also known as a call for 'expressions of interest' (EoI) or 'request for qualifications' (RfQ).

Bidders that do not meet these minimum criteria are then excluded under a pass/fail approach, or the contracting authority can stipulate a minimum and maximum number of candidates it will prequalify, which would involve scoring and ranking the prospective bidders. Practice varies on the numbers to prequalify: some countries leave it open to the contracting authority to decide, others prescribe a minimum number (usually three).[6] If one of the prequalified bidders drops out, it may be possible to invite the next highest-ranked bidder that did not pre-qualify initially to participate. The contracting authority may also be allowed to proceed even if the number of bidders seeking to prequalify is below the threshold, although this is not generally desirable.

Regulations may set a minimum period to allow sufficient time for bidders to submit the information to prequalify. In the EU, this period is 30 days but in practice contracting authorities typically allow for around six weeks (and even longer for larger and more complex tenders or where the criteria are unfamiliar or to allow for any queries on the criteria to be raised).

A pre-qualification and ranking procedure is usually preferable because if there are too many bidders for the project (*i.e.* too many get through the pass/fail test), the chances of winning the bid may be too small to make it worth the prospective bidders' while to spend the considerable time and cost involved in preparing and submitting good-quality bids. Of course, fewer bidders also make the managing the whole process easier for the contracting authority. One of the drawbacks, however, is that it may lead to the same small group of bidders each time, reducing growth in the market and possibly the risk of collusion.

§10.6.2 Bid Documents

There is a variety of names for the bid-document package, depending on the nature of the bidding procedure:

- Restricted procedure—'request for proposals' (RfP), 'invitation to tender' (ITT) or 'invitation to bid' (ITB).
- Competitive dialogue—'invitation to competitive dialogue' (ICD), 'invitation to participate in competitive dialogue'(ITPCD).

The basic content of all the bid documents is the same; it is mainly the interaction with bidders and procedures before and after the bid documents are issued, as discussed above, that differs. To the extent that many of the project details have not already been released when launching the pre-qualification stage,[7] the bid documents set out details of the project such as:

- general legislative and policy background;
- project *raison d'être*;

---

[6] Under EU procedures the minimum number of bidders has to be five for the restricted procedure and three for the competitive procedure with negotiation and for the competitive-dialogue procedure.

[7] For example, under EU procedures, the contracting authority is required to set out 'its needs and requirements' and 'where appropriate, particular conditions to which performance of the contract is subject' when launching the pre-qualification stage (EU *Public Procurement Directive* (EU 2014), Article 30, paragraph 2 and Annex V).

- service requirements;
- support to be provided by the contracting authority, either financial (*cf.* Chapter 18), or, *e.g.*, through building a connecting road (*cf.* §12.2.7);
- data on the market, *e.g.* traffic flows, for PPPs where demand risk is being transferred to the private sector;
- a draft PPP contract, including risk-transfer provisions, performance specifications and proposed service-fee mechanism (*cf.* Chapters 12-17);
- programme for site visits, bid meetings and procedure for clarifications;
- the form of bid required;
- bid deadline;
- bid-evaluation criteria (*cf.* §10.6.5); and
- overall project timetable.

The bidder's response is likely to be required to cover issues (insofar as these have not been clarified in advance) such as:

- technology and design;
- construction programme;
- service standards and delivery;
- details of subcontracts and subcontractors;
- management and reporting structures for both the construction and service delivery/operation phases;
- quality- and safety-assurance procedures;
- commercial viability (*e.g.* traffic or demand projections for a concession);
- insurance coverage;
- project costs (*cf.* §23.8);
- financing strategy and structure (*cf.* §22.2.6);
- qualifications or proposed amendments to the proposed draft PPP contract; and
- proposals for the service fees.

It is also a fairly standard practice for bidders to be required to provide a financial model based on their bids (*cf.* §23.8), including key results from the model, such as the service fees, set out in a common format prescribed by the contracting authority for all bidders.

It is important for the contracting authority to be very clear in its instructions with regard to the form and deadline for the submission of bids. For example, in the case of bids that are submitted electronically, if there are problems with the transmission of large quantities of documentation, disputes may arise if the time of receipt is significantly different to the time of transmission. To avoid the risk of exposing itself to a challenge by an unsuccessful bidder through departing from the bidding instructions (as mentioned above), the contracting authority should not set itself any unnecessary restrictions and allow for options that it may wish to use later on, such as the use of a funding competition (*cf.* §22.6).

§10.6.3 Communication With Bidders

Whatever the bid procedure, the same information should be made available to all bidders, *e.g.* by:

- holding bidder meetings and site visits which all attend, which are helpful to flush out any major issues which bidders may have with the project; and
- copying written answers to questions or issues raised by one bidder to all of them, without indicating who asked the original question.

Bidders should be given a specific point of contact within the contracting authority, and should not be allowed to make contacts elsewhere in the organisation.

Discussions with bidders (especially if competitive dialogue is used) may lead to modifications in the bid requirements: in such cases the bid schedule may have to be delayed to give bidders enough time to deal with these modifications. On the other hand, bidder confidentiality has to be respected, *e.g.* if they are offering several different solutions to executing the project.

Contracting authorities are usually too optimistic on the bidding timetable (or they may be under pressure to deliver a result quickly). It is important to ensure that bidders are given enough time to develop their bids—a minimum period may in any case be established in the procurement regulations. The time required by the contracting authority to evaluate responses should also not be underestimated, especially if there are different layers of authority inside the contracting authority's hierarchy that need to be involved.

§10.6.4 Running a Competitive-Dialogue Process

Conducting a competitive dialogue is demanding on the contracting authority and bidders alike, but is increasingly widely used and is feasible with good preparation. At the start of the process, the contracting authority should explain to bidders (those who have been invited to participate after the pre-qualification stage) the expected topics to be subject to dialogue. The contracting authority should also agree which particular part of each bidder's solution is specific to its proposals and should be protected from sharing with other bidders.

There is no limit to the number of dialogue phases or 'rounds' that can go on until the contracting authority has identified one or more solutions that it is confident will meet its needs. Clearly, however, it must be conscious of the time and costs involved for bidders or it will lose their interest. The process, however, should not be used as a way for the contracting authority to identify its own requirements—these should have been settled in the preparation stages prior to launching the procurement.

Submissions may be requested at the end of each dialogue stage and evaluated against pre-stated criteria, so reducing the number of bidders invited to the next dialogue stage (although reducing the number of bidders is not mandatory). The intention to ask for such submissions should be explained to participants at the start of the process.

The earlier dialogue rounds are likely to focus on more technical solutions, settling these before moving on to more detailed commercial and contractual issues. If there are concerns about affordability, bidders can be asked to submit outline costings at an early stage, on the understanding that these are not yet binding. Due to the restrictions on further changes after final bids are submitted, the contracting authority may request fully-developed draft proposals towards at the last stages of the process so it can assess if final tenders will meet its needs and be affordable. When the contracting authority is satisfied that it is likely to receive proposals that will meet its requirements, the dialogue is formally closed and BAFOs are requested from the remaining bidders.

Dialogue in each round is held with each bidder in sequence over a short period of time (the sequence of bidders during successive dialogue phases should be altered if possible). On the contracting authority side, a stable project team should be involved so that there is a consistent view of the proposals across the bidders. The project team should be well prepared and organised and able to make quick decisions: the process requires preparing for each dialogue, conducting the dialogue itself and feeding back the results of the dialogue to reassess requirements and identify and prepare for the next set of topics for dialogue. To help ensure momentum and keep the process moving quickly with the right people available on all sides, there has been some success in Britain in conducting the dialogue process using a 'boot camp' approach with the whole process taking place in a short highly concentrated effort involving all the relevant parties at a single location.

§10.6.5 Bid Evaluation

A method is needed to compare the bids with each other, and bidders need to understand clearly what they have to do to produce the best bid. There are various approaches for comparing the bids:

- Price comparison

  If the bids can be submitted on virtually-identical bases, the final decision may be a question of simply comparing the service fees, although it may be necessary to discount the amounts payable in future to their NPC to compare like with like. The choice of a discount rate for this purpose will obviously affect the result (*cf.* §8.6.2).

  This approach may be workable for a well-controlled restricted-bid procedure for a process plant or, say a concession where all other project-related issues have been clarified before the bid. However, it is unlikely to be the only basis for a decision in an availability PPP project that may be delivering a range of services or a concession where a number of technical solutions may apply. Furthermore, even when considering the cost of service fees alone, which appears simple in principle, one of the most difficult aspects of PPP bid evaluation is the trade-off between cost and long-term flexibility, especially where a low initial service fee is produced by financial structuring (*cf.* §15.3.2, §24.3.4).

  Furthermore, adjustments may still have to be made to a simple comparison, *e.g.* for the cost of exceptions to the proposed terms of the PPP contract, other differences in risk transfer, or bids that are considered to be over-ambitious in their projections of performance or financing plans.

- PPP contract tenor

  An alternative approach, especially for concessions, is to fix the service fees and then ask bidders to bid for whatever tenor of PPP contract they require—obviously, the shortest tenor wins (*cf.* §15.3.1). But this can lead to excessively high user-charges and low usage levels, ultimately making the PPPs untenable as happened with the Mexican roads concession programme in the early 1990s (Ruster 1997).

A variant on this approach is to leave the tenor open-ended (a long-stop date of say 50 years may apply), and terminate the PPP contract when the NPV of revenues required by bidders has been reached—here the bidder with the lowest required NPV of revenues wins the bid: this is known as 'least present-value of revenues' (LPVR)—*cf.* §15.5.2.

– Level of subsidy

Some bids are not based on the basis of the price to be charged for the service, but the level of subsidy to be provided by the contracting authority. This approach is relevant if the bid relates to a concession where it is expected that service fees will not produce sufficient revenue to cover the funding required for the project (*cf.* §18.4)— for example, the level of tolls charged to users has to be at a pre-determined level.

– Level of capital grant

Similarly, the bid may be evaluated by the level of capital grant required by bidders to make the project viable (*cf.* §18.6).

– Payments to the contracting authority

Conversely, bids may include payments by the project company instead of to it, such as payment of a concession fee (*cf.* §15.5.2), or making an initial capital payment (*cf.* §15.5.3).

– 'Most economically advantageous tender' ('MEAT')

The principle of MEAT gives the contracting authority the scope to choose the appropriate basis of bid award. This could include selecting on price alone but after meeting a minimum quality threshold—'qualifying tenders'—or the best price/quality ratio. This is important for VfM, as the lowest price may not necessarily be the best VfM (*cf.* §8.2). This more complex system is based on 'scoring' different aspects of the bid—giving points for design, speed of completion, reliability, quality of service, risk assumption by the bidder (*i.e.* transfer of risk away from the contracting authority) and any other characteristics that are important to the contracting authority as well as the price. Hence identifying the bid that is the 'most economically advantageous' to the project.

The weight to be given to different factors should be set out in the bid documents; there must inevitably be an element of subjectivity, both in how these factors are weighted against each other, and how different aspects of the same factors are compared when these are non-financial. Weightings are obviously quite project-specific: *e.g.* if bidders are likely to rely on the same design or technology solutions, the service fee proposed (*i.e.* the price) could be weighted 70%, but if there is much scope for innovative solutions, technical proposals could be weighted 70%. Under a competitive-dialogue procedure, price may have a greater weighting on selecting final bids than otherwise, as the dialogue process often moves bidders towards more comparable solutions. Because of concerns that lowest cost is not necessarily best value, the principle of MEAT is now core to some public-sector procurement approaches, such as in the EU.

The possible disadvantage of this approach is that bidders may 'game the system'. For example, if the weighting for the best service fee is 50%, and that for legal aspects of the bid (*e.g.* accepting the terms of risk transfer in the PPP contract) is 10%, a bidder may offer a poor risk transfer knowing it will lose on this aspect of the evaluation, but reduce its price thanks to this low risk transfer, knowing that it will score more points in the evaluation this way. A lower bid but with poor risk transfer may not be the best VfM.

The pre-qualification process should have already eliminated bidders for whom there are questions about financial capacity, technology or ability to undertake the project, so further fundamental qualitative comparisons of this nature should be limited in scope at this stage. However, the overall financing plan for the project does need to be examined (*cf.* §10.8.3), and bids must be submitted using common financial, and even modelling, assumptions where this is appropriate (*e.g.* as to base interest and inflation rates and calculations—see Chapter 24). Similarly, the detailed feasibility of the construction and operation arrangements, including subcontracts, needs to be reviewed (*cf.* §10.8.2).

§10.6.6 Affordability of Bids

If bids come in over expectation and the contracting authority's budget cannot be increased or the user charges are considered unaffordable, the contracting authority will have to redesign the project in some way, *e.g.* by reducing its scope, to reduce payments to an affordable level. There are two things to bear in mind in this situation:

- If the bids are found not to be affordable, a preferred bidder should not be appointed until there has been a further round of bidding on a reduced project scope (if the procurement regulations allow this). Entering into negotiations with a preferred bidder without a defined project scope (*cf.* §7.3.1) is certain to lose VfM.
- The service fees should not be manipulated so that they are abnormally low at the beginning of the PPP contract, as a way of making the PPP 'affordable' to begin with (*cf.* §9.2.2; §15.3.2).

As discussed in relation to the PSC (*cf.* §8.3.6), a contracting authority has to consider whether to let bidders know what the affordability limit is from the start. In British Columbia and Greece, for example, a firm 'affordability ceiling' is published. In other countries, the expected maximum capital cost may be indicated (but not the maximum service fee). Information on the relative importance of the different elements of the service requirement may also be published so that bidders can develop their bids within the ceiling and the required scope of the project. Later-stage disclosure of the affordability limit may also be used in some circumstances as a way of negotiating with bidders to bring their final bid prices down.

One of the benefits of competitive-dialogue procedures is that by the time final bids are requested, the requirements of the contracting authority should be well-known by bidders and the likely range of solutions narrowed. This may reduce the need to reveal the affordability limit as an indication of the level and scope of services being sought.

§10.6.7 Commercial Viability

When evaluating bids, it is always worth stepping back and considering whether the bidders' proposals make commercial sense—*i.e.* if the bid is accepted, would the facility be provided on viable terms for all parties—investors, lenders, subcontractors, the contracting authority and end users? Contracts that give a disproportionate advantage to one side are vulnerable, as an aggrieved party will obviously make use of any flaw in its contract to get out of an unduly onerous obligation.

If a bidder's pricing is much lower than the contracting authority's original estimates (*cf.* §8.3.1), or those of other bidders, this suggests that the bidder or a subcontractor may have made a mistake somewhere. The contracting authority may take the view that pricing mistakes are the bidder's problem, but the primary objective of the PPP is to deliver a public service, and it is highly likely that this delivery will be jeopardised if the project company or its subcontractors cannot earn enough to make the work worthwhile. If the project company fails to perform as required, the contracting authority can terminate the PPP contract (*cf.* §17.2), but this is likely to result in extra costs to sort the situation out, and unlikely to result in the service being provided in the way originally expected. The MEAT principle is a helpful safeguard in this respect as it provides the contracting authority with the option not necessarily to accept the lowest-cost bid. Similarly, in a toll-road project, the contracting authority may take steps to discourage traffic projections from bidders that are higher than its own and so avoid over-optimism over-traffic forecasts and subsequent problems with the project.

Where lowest cost is the only selection criterion, there is a danger that bidders will submit unrealistically low-cost bids ('low-ball bidding') on the basis that the contracting authority has no alternative other than to accept their bid. The winning bidder then uses the opportunity, once awarded, to renegotiate terms in the absence of competition.

§10.6.8 Post-Bid Negotiation

Negotiations after appointing the preferred bidder are undesirable and effectively prohibited under, for example, the EU procurement procedures (*cf.* §10.5). If they do take place, such negotiations sometimes drag on for long periods of time. Reasons for these delays (and the need for negotiations in the first place) include:

- lack of adequate preparation by the contracting authority before launching the bid process, often linked to political pressure to be seen to be moving the project forward; this results in incomplete project specifications or PPP-contract drafting, so forcing the contracting authority into substantial renegotiation of the bid under the guise of 'clarification';
- even worse, the contracting authority changing its mind about the requirements after the bid process has begun, perhaps because of affordability problems;
- poor contract management by the contracting authority and a failure to drive the project forward;
- tripartite negotiations with the lenders, if their commitment to provide funding has not been secured before the bid is presented (*cf.* §10.8.3, §22.2.6);

- environmental, planning or other site-related issues that were not dealt with before the bids are submitted (*cf.* §12.2); and
- issues arising from the due-diligence process on the part of the contracting authority (*cf.* §10.8), the lenders (*cf.* §22.2.7) or other parties such as subcontractors.

Any significant delay between appointment of a preferred bidder and financial close almost inevitably leads to rises in project costs, and hence in the service fees. The construction subcontract price, for example, will be based on starting work by a certain date, and will be subject to inflation indexing, or open to complete revision, if this date is not achieved. Worse than this, the issues set out above may be used as an excuse, as with low-ball bidding (*cf.* §10.6.7), to increase other aspects of the PPP contract pricing or to change risk transfer for the benefit of the preferred bidder (a process known as 'deal creep'), even though substantial changes to the final bid terms could be open to legal challenge by losing bidders (*cf.* §10.6.9).

On the other hand, restrictions on post-bid negotiations should not be such to prevent finalising financing issues—bond-financed bids may require adjustments to accommodate changes in conditions in the capital markets (*cf.* §22.4.2).

It is a fairly simple rule that the longer the post-bid negotiation period the worse the contracting authority's position becomes. Without any competitive tension between bidders, the preferred bidder effectively becomes a monopoly supplier. Even if theoretically the contracting authority could go back to the other bidders, this is seldom workable in practice, not least because the losing bidding team will have been redeployed elsewhere by their employers. The contracting authority, which by then will be heavily and publicly committed to the project, cannot easily walk away and start again without causing major political problems. The claim that PPP projects do not involve cost overruns (*cf.* §28.6.1) becomes dubious if deal creep causes increases in cost (or reductions in project scope, which comes to the same thing) between appointment of the preferred bidder and final signature of the PPP contract. Time and care spent on preparation before beginning the bidding process is seldom wasted. Therefore, there is a lot to be said for using procedures that encourage preparation and a thorough development of bids to avoid deal creep after the bids are submitted.

It is also true to say that even though long negotiations may be beneficial to private-sector bidders, a lengthy and complex procurement process is of concern to them because of the accumulated bid costs which they have at risk (*cf.* §20.4).

§10.6.9 Bid Award

Fairness and transparency in the bidding process are essential; if bidders do not understand or trust the process, or do not believe there is a genuine competition in which they have a good prospect of winning, it is evident that the best results will not be achieved. Thus, a full and detailed record should be kept of the bid comparisons, and why a particular bidder was chosen (indeed this is often a legal requirement). It is a common procedure for the losing bidders to be given a briefing on why the winner was chosen in preference.

In some countries, a mandatory 'standstill' period between notification of the award decision and contract signature is required. This provides the opportunity for an unsuccessful bidder to challenge the award decision before the contract is signed but it also protects the contracting authority from a losing bidder bringing a claim against it later to make the contract ineffective. It is important that the award decision notice is fully compliant with the procurement regulations in what it must contain by way of information.

Failure to follow procurement regulations and the contents of the bidding documents that set out how the bid will be conducted may make the award of the PPP contract open to legal attack; this may be a problem only for the contracting authority if the legal remedy is financial compensation to a disadvantaged bidder, but it may also be possible for the PPP contract to be declared invalid, which clearly has serious consequences for the investors and lenders, and the project itself. In some countries, bid challenges may be a serious problem simply because they are used a matter of course irrespective of the underlying justification. Some countries have specially established agencies to appeal to for these cases so that they are handled quickly and professionally. But this emphasises the importance of preparing well for the procurement phase and carrying out the bid process with scrupulous regard for the relevant procurement regulations.

§10.7 OTHER PROCUREMENT ISSUES

§10.7.1 Non-Conforming Bids

While the rules of the bidding process should be scrupulously adhered to, the requirements should not necessarily be such as to prevent bidders coming up with solutions that, although not previously considered, may actually be better for the contracting authority. This links to the 'private-sector innovation' argument for PPPs (cf. §28.9.5).

A standard procedure is that bidders must make at least one bid that conforms to the minimum requirements set out in the bid documents, but they may, if the bidding instructions so allow, also offer alternative ('non-conforming' or 'variant') bids that do not conform (perhaps within pre-defined parameters). The contracting authority then has the option to choose such a 'non-conforming' bid if it offers a better solution.

§10.7.2 Bid Consortium and Other Changes

After a particular bidding consortium has been pre-qualified, one of its members may decide not to proceed, and the consortium may wish to introduce a new member, perhaps a bidder in a consortium that previously did not pre-qualify. Other bidders may object to this, but it may be preferable not to exclude changes of this kind completely and to leave some discretion on the matter (e.g. if the new member can demonstrate, it is as well qualified as the one it is succeeding, and would not have caused the consortium to be ruled out at the pre-qualification stage). An alternative approach is to allow changes in the consortium only after the winning bid has been selected. However, in some countries, changes in bidding consortia are simply not allowed.

Obviously, no bidder should be allowed to participate in more than one consortium at the same time, as this could lead to leakages of information or collusion between consortia.

Procurement regulations may permit changes to the PPP contract after award, provided that they do not change the overall nature of the PPP contract or increase the price as a result of additional services required. This may be limited to no more than, say, 50% of the value of the original contract, because of unforeseen circumstances or where a new procurement would cause significant disruption in the provision of the service. There may also be an obligation to issue a public notice of such changes. Care needs to be taken that any changes would not have allowed other bidders to qualify or win if they had been included in the original procurement and that they do not change the risk/reward balance of the PPP contract in favour of the project company. The issue of PPP contract changes after contract signature is considered further in Chapter 16.

§10.7.3 Bonding

Bidders are sometimes required to provide bid bonds from their bankers, as security for their proceeding with the bid if it is successful. The bond is released when the PPP contract is signed, or when construction of the project begins. The amount of the bond may be quite significant in absolute terms (*e.g.* 1-2% of the project value). This helps to deal with the problem of 'deliverability'—*i.e.* presentation of an aggressive bid which cannot be financed, or where the bidders hope to improve their position once they are the preferred bidder. Bid bonds clearly add costs to the process so they should not be automatically required if other mechanisms exist to ensure deliverability, such as bids with finance already committed (*cf.* §22.2.8), due diligence on the financeability of bids (*cf.* §10.8.3) or the comfort that may be drawn from the commitment and costs incurred by bidders to go through the procurement process (*cf.* §20.4). For these reasons, the use of bid bonds varies across different PPP markets.

§10.7.4 Payment of Bid Costs

The corollary of bonding for bidders is an agreement by the contracting authority conducting the bid that if the process is cancelled at any stage, bidders should be compensated for a proportion (say a third) of the costs they have incurred, up to a defined limit. This limit could increase the further along the process the bid is cancelled. Losing bidders may even be given some compensation for their costs in any case, to encourage competition in a complex project, or to help cover the cost of securing financing commitments with their bids (*cf.* §10.8.3, §22.2.6). This approach was used effectively by Ireland to encourage bidders to return to its PPP programme after the 2008 financial crisis. More typically, contracting authorities retain discretion whether or not to reimburse bid costs. For example, they may choose, at their discretion, to reimburse bidding costs if a bid process is cancelled through no fault of the bidders and where the government wants to retain the good will of potential future bidders.

§10.7.5 Unsolicited Proposals

An issue which cuts across standard procurement procedures is that of unsolicited proposals (USPs) for PPP projects—*i.e.* a private-sector consortium proposes a PPP rather than responds to a public-sector request for bids. On the face of it, if private-sector innovation is a merit of PPPs (*cf.* §28.9.5), then such proposals could be a source of good ideas or help to identify bottlenecks or commercial opportunities not spotted by government.

However, USPs face a number of fundamental difficulties:

- A proposal is usually based on the interest of the proposer and not necessarily the needs or requirements of the contracting authority. It may also conflict with wider sector infrastructure plans, have little fit with broader strategic requirements for development of the sector and underestimate the risks for the contracting authority.
- There is an obvious issue as to how to ensure that the contracting authority is getting good VfM—some preference needs to be given to the original proposer to provide an incentive to put forward a USP but if too much preference is given there may be poor VfM; if there are no or limited competing bids, the pricing may easily become excessive.
- USPs are often poorly thought-through, in particular as to financing requirements, and hence tend to collapse later on in the procurement process.
- There may be a lack of transparency, causing the contract award to be challenged at a later stage (*e.g.* after a change of government).

Consequently, extreme caution is advised with USPs. In some countries, procurement regulations simply prohibit them. DFIs such as the World Bank (*cf.* §22.9.2) may also have difficulties in financing such projects if they believe that the procurement of the project does not comply with their own requirements, such as an effective competitive-bidding process.

Nevertheless, many countries do have procedures for USPs that aim to address the issues mentioned above. Some countries allow USPs to take place within a wider framework in which the contracting authority sets out its broad needs or project concepts. This helps to ensure that USPs respond to needs identified by government. USPs are then encouraged as a source of innovative approaches to meet these needs. Clearly the more structured the approach the more it will fall into line with standard PPP-procurement approaches that involve the contracting authority defining its outputs and leaving the private sector to come up with the best way to deliver them. Thus, some approaches to USP may get quite close to some of the procurement procedures mentioned above, such as competitive dialogue. Or to put it another way, some competitive-procurement approaches, such as those using dialogue, aim to achieve a similar objective of encouraging innovative solutions to be put forward but through a more structured competitive approach which avoids some of the other problems with USPs.

To address the VfM issue, USP procedures usually require a form of competition between the proposer of the USP and other providers. But in order to encourage proposals to be put forward, a limited advantage has to be given to the original proposer. This may involve some or a combination of:

- automatic pre-qualification in the bidding process;
- a scoring bonus when it comes to evaluating bids;
- a right to match the winning bidder (known as a 'Swiss Challenge'); and
- reimbursement of costs of the original proposer if its proposal is not chosen.

The proportion of bids that are consistently won by the original proposer varies between countries suggesting that some approaches involve more effective competition than others. One reason relates to the amount of time that other bidders are given to prepare their bids to compete with the original proposal—if this is too short then they are unlikely to provide a genuinely-competitive alternative.

Another way in which competition can be included in a USP is at the subcontractor level: the project developer is appointed on a USP basis, but the construction subcontractor, usually the largest cost component of the project, is appointed competitively. The benefits of this need to be passed through in the service fees (and it leaves the contracting authority with the risk that the construction subcontractor's bid may come in higher than expected, so affecting the affordability of the project).

It is also important that USPs do not disrupt the orderly development of a PPP programme and that the contracting authority does not get distracted by having to deal with so many different USPs that it cannot get on with its own investment priorities. The expected benefits of encouraging the private sector to develop the initial proposals may be diminished by the time and resources of the contracting authority needed to assess them. If used, USPs should therefore compliment rather than replace mainstream forms of public-investment procurement.

A contracting authority therefore needs to balance the potential benefits of innovation from USPs against the costs of a potentially-flawed project rationale, reduced competition, the direct costs, if any, of reimbursements to the original USP proponent and the marginal costs of assessing USPs and running the procurement. A contracting authority might also consider whether more attention should be focused on further developing its own internal capacity to identify the right public-infrastructure investment requirements and modes of delivery as discussed in Chapter 7 and in running a structured competitive-procurement process that allows for innovation, such as competitive dialogue, rather than rely on USPs.

§10.8 Due Diligence

The contracting authority needs to go through a 'due-diligence' process—*i.e.* a detailed review of the project contracts to ensure that they appear 'fit for purpose' and able to provide what is needed for the project to be successful. This should also confirm that their terms do not indirectly create onerous obligations for the contracting authority and are adequate—with respect to design (*cf.* §10.8.1), the subcontracts (*cf.* §10.8.2), financing documents (*cf.* §10.8.3), environmental regulations (*cf.* §12.2.4) and insurance arrangements (*cf.* Chapter 14)—prior to financial close (§10.8.4).

This process should ideally be completed at the bid-evaluation stage, but it may, at least partly, slip beyond that, *i.e.* after a preferred bidder has been appointed (*cf.* §10.6.8). A parallel process is carried out by the lenders (*cf.* §22.2.7), and by other parties such as subcontractors (*cf.* §12.5.1).

§10.8.1 Project Design

Design proposals submitted at the bid stage are typically conceptual in nature and are more often than not substantially modified during dialogue/negotiations. Even then detailed design is usually finalised after financial close. Design is thus a process where due diligence continues after financial close, as discussed in more detail in §19.3.2.

§10.8.2 Subcontracts

At the time of pre-qualification, the financial and technical capacity of the project company's main subcontractors—*e.g.* for construction, operation, maintenance or services—should have been approved by the contracting authority. These issues should therefore not need to be reopened unless there is a significant change since they were reviewed. However, during the due diligence of the bids, it is then necessary to review issues such as:

- the detailed costing and planning for the subcontracts, to ensure that they appear to be capable of delivering the requirements of the PPP contract;
- their detailed terms, to ensure that there is nothing in them obviously incompatible with the project company's own obligations under the PPP contract. For example, the levels of delay liquidated damages (*cf.* §12.4) in the subcontracts (and the bonding for this) should be adequate in relation to the project company's liabilities to the contracting authority for delay in completing the facility (*cf.* §15.4.1), and its debt-service and other costs that will still have to be paid during the period of delay; and
- the early termination provisions, to ensure that the contracting authority's potential liability in this situation is not excessive (*cf.* §17.6).

However, this does not imply that the contracting authority should 'sign off' on these subcontracts, and hence take the risk of any incompatibility between them and the PPP contract requirements (*cf.* §15.6.8).

§10.8.3 Financing

The purist view would be that the bidder is responsible for raising the debt for the project and therefore the contracting authority need not concern itself with the matter. In reality, the contracting authority will find it hard to keep the lenders at arm's length, as the latters' own due-diligence processes (*cf.* §22.2.7) may identify issues which the lenders wish to negotiate with the contracting authority directly. This is something best avoided (although this can be difficult), as it is likely to mean that bidders get 'two bites at the cherry', *i.e.* what they cannot win in their own negotiation with the contracting authority may be reopened and renegotiated by the lenders on their behalf. However, procurement rules have generally become less accommodating of such changes after the preferred bidder has been chosen (*cf.* §10.6.8). And in many cases the contracting authority may require the financing to be fully committed at the time of the bid with no further negotiation thereafter. (This requirement for fully-financed bids raises other issues that are discussed in §22.2.6.)

If finance is not committed, the financing plan should be reviewed during the bid evaluation by the contracting authority from its own due-diligence point of view. It is no use appointing a preferred bidder who does not have a realistic financing plan, and therefore the contracting authority needs to assess this plan in reasonable detail to ensure that it is both deliverable in the short term, and provides a stable long-term basis for the project company's operations.

The contracting authority also needs to understand the implications of the financing structure for the PPP contract as a whole, both as to the service-fee payment structure (*cf.* §15.3), and long-term flexibility and the cost of early termination of the PPP contract (*cf.* §17.2–§17.7), taking any financial hedging into account (*cf.* Chapter 24). Lenders' views on risk transfer (*cf.* §11.5) have to be taken into account. Attention needs to be paid to the lenders' security and reserve-account requirements (*cf.* §25.3) and whether the level of service fees bid is dependent on any assumed refinancings which may qualify from being exempt from gainsharing (*cf.* §26.2.7). It is clearly in the contracting authority's interests to make suggestions for any improvement to the financing plan during competitive dialogue (*cf.* §10.5), if this is possible, to be fed through as a reduction in the service fees; and if there is a funding competition (*cf.* §22.6), the contracting authority's involvement will be substantial.

Of course, this is why the contracting authority needs its own financial adviser (*cf.* §6.4.1).

§10.8.4 Financial Close

The formal legal requirements which have to be fulfilled to reach financial close usually consist of a very long list of documents, which if not managed effectively may seriously delay the start of construction. These are usually referred to as 'conditions precedent'. The preferred bidder needs the support of the contracting authority to manage this process. This includes gathering and checking off as much of the condition-precedent documentation as possible in advance of the signing of the PPP contracts and the financing documentation, to ensure the minimum delay before financial close. Checking off conditions precedent before signing the financing documentation also ensures that there are no unexpected surprises, *e.g.* from issues raised by lenders after the loan has been signed.

The financial-close conditions precedent is often circular in nature—*e.g.* the PPP contract does not become effective until the financing is available for drawing, and the financing does not become available for drawing until the PPP contract is effective—and so financial close is usually a simultaneous exercise in which all the parties to the PPP project structure are involved.

There may also be other forms of public-sector funding that are only available if the PPP is finalised. This may cause problems because the contracting authority is at risk of having to make up any shortfall if such funding is not forthcoming once it has committed itself under a PPP contract. Equally the bidders will not know if such funding is available until after financial close—if this was to be used to fund part of the capex, then the level of financing upon which they are bidding is unclear. An example of this problem was with EU funding of PPPs and was resolved by allowing for *conditional* approval of EU funding earlier on in the bid process, that then became available at financial close.

There may also be an interim 'commercial close' (also known as 'contractual close'), when the project contracts have been signed but are still subject to the completion of the financing or the satisfaction of other financial-close conditions, often so the politicians can say that the deal has been done. But this takes the pressure off the process and it is better to avoid this limbo stage if possible. If the PPP contract becomes effective before the lenders' terms are agreed, this may lead to forced renegotiation of the PPP contract terms. Bid bonds (*cf.* §10.7.3) may play a rôle here to ensure that financial close is reached by the sponsors within a specified period, as is the case, for example in India. Substantial delay may also cause bidders' costs to become unsustainable—*e.g.* the construction contract price may go up (*cf.* §12.3.3) or lead to the lenders no longer being able to offer the financing terms they may have committed to (*cf.* §22.2.8). This risks unravelling the whole procurement process. Of course, the cause for delay may be due to the contracting authority failing to meet its commitments in a timely way. This risk can be reduced by the contracting authority carefully assessing what remains to be done before declaring commercial close.

PART III

PPP RISK ANALYSIS AND ALLOCATION

Risk Analysis—Theory and Methodologies

§11.1 INTRODUCTION

Risk in a PPP relates to uncertain outcomes that have a direct effect either on the provision of the services (*e.g.* because the facility is not built on time), or the financial viability of the project (*e.g.* loss of revenue or increased costs). In either case the result is a loss or cost which has to be borne by someone, and one of the main elements of PPP structuring is to determine what the different risks are and who is best placed to bear them. Assessing the value of risks is also important for determining the VfM of the procurement option (*cf.* §8.3.2) and the affordability of the project (*cf.* §9.2).

This chapter therefore summarises the basic approaches to identifying project risks (§11.2), valuing them (§11.3) and allocating them to project parties (§11.4). Lenders are likely to be the most risk averse of the parties and therefore the lowest common denominator when it comes to structuring a project in a financially feasible way, so it is important to understand how they perceive risk (§11.5). The use of a risk register to track risks is also discussed, and an outline example of a typical risk register is provided (§11.6).

Chapters 12 and 13 then go through the typical key risks to be found in the construction and operation phases of PPP projects respectively and how these are allocated to, and managed by, the various parties involved in a PPP.

§11.2 IDENTIFYING RISKS

It is obviously important to identify all the relevant risks that are likely to be associated with the project before allocating them between the project parties. This is one of the most valuable disciplines of the PPP process. It helps to avoid the contracting authority under-estimating the true risks and costs of the project over its life. For the project's sponsors, understanding all the relevant risks is key to their decision whether or not to pursue the project. And for lenders, the project-finance approach to risk allocation means that attention has to be focused on detailed specific and identified risks, rather than relying on simple guarantees from the contracting authority or sponsors.

But what is risk? Risk is usually associated with the possibility of loss, *i.e.* a possible but nevertheless uncertain outcome. Risk, however, is not a one-way street: outcomes can also be better than expected, so risk is often referred to as an unpredictable *variation* in value (Irwin 2007). The overall value of a project is also the result of a large number of different particular risks (or risk factors) such as variations in construction costs, demand levels or operating costs. Some of these particular risks may be dependent on or correlated with other risks (*e.g.* construction costs may be linked to the risks of strikes or bad weather).

Risks can also be grouped according to their characteristics, which help in the allocation process later on: some risks are project-specific such as accidents or uncertain volumes of materials needed (often referred to as *non-systematic* risks). Other risks are based on wider economic factors such as interest rates or inflation or levels of demand (often referred to as *systematic* risks).

Establishing a complete picture as possible of all the possible risks and how they inter-relate is not easy. Nevertheless, various tools exist.

— Risk workshops

Contracting authorities often hold 'risk workshops' in the earlier phases of the project cycle such as during Phase 3 (Project Economic Assessment and Selection) (*cf.* §5.3.3) and/or during the PPP Procurement Review and Procurement Preparation phases (Phases 4 and 5) (*cf.* §5.3.4, §5.3.5). A workshop brings together information over the expected life of the project from different stakeholders and perspectives to help identify the different risk factors. External advisers (*cf.* §6.4) also bring their experience in identifying risks (as well as assisting in the management of risk workshops). A risk-breakdown structure can be used that identifies a hierarchy of potential sources of risks: lower levels in the hierarchy represent in increasing detail the sources of risks, often categorised over the different phases of the project. Or generic categories can be used to identify groups of risks such as PESTLE (political, economic, sociological, technological, legal/legislative and environmental)—this all helps the brainstorming in a risk workshop (although sometimes they are used *after* the workshop to check for any omissions).

— Risk lists

'Risk lists', often associated with VfM assessment (*cf.* §8.3.2) and other project-preparation guidelines, are available from different countries. These help to ensure that all the relevant risks have been identified. Multilateral organisations such as the Global Infrastructure Hub have also developed risk lists and suggested risk alloca- tion matrices for different PPP sectors (Global Infrastructure Hub 2016). Standardised PPP contracts (*cf.* §4.3.2) are another useful source for identifying risks and understanding how they can best be allocated.

As mentioned in the VfM context (*cf.* §8.6.1), experience with operational PPPs has shown that it is sometimes a third category of risks, the unknown risks, that unfortunately are the ones that will be most relevant in the future. Identifying individual risks and work- ing up from this to build a complete picture will obviously fail to include these. To help avoid this, those identifying risks also use a 'top-down' approach by looking qualitatively at the overall risk profile of the project and adding a contingency for unknown risks, pos- sibly based on past experience of overall outcomes.

§11.3 VALUING RISKS

The contracting authority has an interest in valuing risks in its VfM assessment of whether or not to retain or transfer a particular risk (*cf.* §8.6.1, §11.4). The basic question is whether the value of the risk it is transferring to the project company is justified by the price it expects to pay for doing so. Valuing risks is also relevant for assessing affordability where this requires estimating future costs and revenues.

Valuing risks is also important for sponsors so that they too have a realistic projection of the project's costs and revenues, and how certain these are. This enables them to esti- mate the risks they are taking on in relation to their expected returns.

Not all risks have to be valued: this depends on the purpose of the exercise. For exam- ple, when assessing the risk of the project-preparation process itself, the contracting authority does need to *value* those risks that are expected to take place *before* financial close. Instead it is more likely to identify the different possible outcomes—such as a long delay in preparing the project—and assign a low/medium/high likelihood to each of them.

Various approaches to valuing risks can be used.

— Deterministic approach

  This simpler approach involves multiplying the expected probability of a risk with its expected outcome value (this may be an adjusted average for a worst case, best case, most-likely value). The value for the different risk categories is added up and a certain percentage added to this for unknown risks. This can be repeated for a range of different underlying assumptions to build up a picture of the spread of the overall value of the project risk. This is referred to as the *deterministic* approach.

— Probabilistic approach

  A more sophisticated and complex (but not necessarily more reliable) approach, referred to as the *probabilistic* approach, uses distribution curves of different out- comes for particular risks. Agreed levels of required certainty (or 'risk averseness') are applied to these distribution curves to come up with a 'value at risk' figure for a particular risk (*i.e.* a percentage chance, say 95%, that the risk will not exceed a certain value). The 'risk value' is the difference between the most likely cost outcome and the cost outcome at the 95% probability level. Clearly this depends on the availability of data to establish probability distributions for each risk or category of risk. This is based on detailed analysis of data or techniques that take into account different risk relationships, such as Monte-Carlo simulation (named after the gambling habits of the uncle of one of the developers of this approach).

— Optimism bias

Optimism bias (*cf.* §8.3.3) is another approach used by contracting authorities to adjust costs for uncertainty using factors based on evidence of previous outcomes.

— Cost of insurance

The cost of insurance for certain risks is also a useful way to value risks if there is a reliable market available and it is clear that the contracting authority cannot manage or absorb the risk better than the market.

The above-mentioned approaches reflect the value of a risk by adjustment to the costs that are used in the financial models. Different risk categories can be valued in different ways. So, for example, in some countries, certain risks (such as economy-wide risk or systematic risks) are instead reflected by including a risk premium in the discount rate used to determine the PV of a particular variable (*cf.* §8.6.2). This is also the approach used when the private sector assesses returns (and risks) using tools such as WACC (*cf.* §20.3.1). It is important not to double-count the value of risks when combining these various approaches.

§11.4 RISK ALLOCATION

Risk allocation is at the heart of structuring a PPP project. Although the term 'risk-sharing' is often used in this context, PPPs do not generally involve risk-sharing in the sense of $x\%$ of the risk being taken by the contracting authority and $(100 - x\%)$ by the project company. If 'risk sharing' does take place, it usually involves fully transferring a risk to one side or the other for a defined band of outcomes such as traffic flows within a particular range (*cf.* §15.5.4) or a defined category of events such as a change in law (*cf.* §16.2.5).

When thinking about risk allocation, it is useful to bear in mind Figures 2.2 and 2.3 in Chapter 2. These figures show the key parties in a PPP arrangement, who each bear different risks, and the contractual relationships that distribute the risks between them. It is a sort of 'risk traffic diagram'.

Thus, there are only a limited number of ways in which any project risks can be allocated among these various parties:

- Risks can be retained by the contracting authority.
- Risks can be transferred to, and retained by the project company.

- Risks can be transferred to the project company, but then reallocated to third parties by:

    - passing them on a 'back-to-back' basis to subcontractors;
    - covering them by insurance (*cf.* Chapter 14); or
    - having them guaranteed by sponsors (*cf.* §23.7).

- In the case of concessions, risks can be transferred to users through the project company having a right to impose higher service fees.

The default position, which may be set out in the PPP contract, is that unless provided otherwise it is the project company's obligation to deliver the service as required, and bear or manage (by reallocation or otherwise) all risks accordingly. This is an important and fundamental distinction between PPPs and standard forms of contracting.

Risk transfer is important for the contracting authority, as it is at the heart of the VfM case for a PPP procurement (*cf.* §28.6). Setting aside balance-sheet issues (*cf.* §9.4), the main purpose of risk transfer from the public-sector point of view is to ensure that the project company and its investors are appropriately incentivised to provide the service which is the subject of the PPP contract. But it does not offer the best VfM for a contracting authority to try to transfer risks that are so difficult for the project company, its lenders or subcontractors to limit or control, that if they do take them on they must charge heavily for doing so.

The principle is that a particular risk should be transferred to the party best able to 'manage' it. But what does 'manage' actually mean? Some risks, such as the weather, cannot be controlled better by one party than the other. But they can be planned for better by a particular party to minimise their impact. Or there may be risks that cannot easily be controlled or planned for (such as civil unrest) but one party may be better able to manage or absorb the *consequences*. Thus, it is helpful to break this down further by considering which party is best able to:

- control or influence the *likelihood* of the risk occurring (*e.g.* choosing a particular building technique to reduce construction costs);
- control the *impact* of the risk on the project (*e.g.* planning certain construction activities to take place when the weather is expected to be better); and
- *absorb* the impact of the risk at the lowest cost (*e.g.* users may be best able to absorb user-charge increases within certain limits).

This implies that whoever assumes the risk must have the freedom to handle it as they think best. It also implies that the party *understands* the nature of the risk that is being allocated to it. It is therefore appropriate for the contracting authority to retain risks that relate to matters which the private sector cannot control cost-effectively (*i.e.* such a large risk premium would have to be built into the private-sector pricing that it is not VfM), or that the private sector cannot be given freedom to handle (perhaps because of the need to maintain the public service). If the contracting authority does retain risks, it should also benefit from any associated 'upside', *i.e.* where possible there should be symmetrical allocation of risks and benefits (*cf.* §15.5.2).

Of course, risk allocation in practice depends on those who *should* manage the risk actually doing so for the assumed cost. Good market sounding (*cf.* §10.4), a well-conducted procurement process (with relevant information provided to bidders), strong competition (*cf.* §8.8.3) and, perhaps most important of all, effective contract management (*cf.* Chapter 19) once the contract is in place, are all needed to ensure that this happens.

§11.5 HOW LENDERS PERCEIVE RISKS IN PPPS

A common mistake by the public-sector side in new PPP programmes is to push bidders to accept too much risk—in particular risks that have to be retained by the project company and cannot be reallocated elsewhere—with the result that when the lenders come into the picture the risk arrangements have to be renegotiated. As far as lenders are concerned, a risk that is transferred to and retained by the project company means that it effectively becomes the lenders' risk, because the project company has limited resources to bear any risks:

- It has a high level of debt, and limited reserves of cash or other resources.
- Most of its cash flow is needed to cover operating costs and debt service (*cf.* §25.2).
- Its investors generally have no obligation to make any further funds available beyond their initial equity investment (*cf.* §20.2.1).

As far as possible, therefore, the lenders wish the project company to be an 'empty box' (*cf.* §20.6.1), with all its risks reallocated elsewhere. The lenders' approach to risk in project finance is summed up by the maxim, 'A banker is a man who lends you an umbrella when it is not raining.' In other words, lenders are very reluctant to accept any but the most limited (and clearly-measurable) risks. This reflects the reality that the return the lenders get is not sufficient to absorb any substantial risk. A typical bank project-finance loan may earn a credit margin of 1-2% over cost of funds (*cf.* §23.4.1): a 1% margin means that if one in a hundred loans fails to repay, the bank could make a loss from its project-finance business. So even a 1/100th risk of failure is too great for a project-finance loan portfolio.

The lenders are not 'investors' in the project, although the sponsors or the contracting authority often like to use this expression in the heat of negotiation. If the lenders were investors they would get an equity rate of return, but they do not—typically in a successful project, the gross rate of return on the equity is at least twice that on the debt (*cf.* §20.3.3), which reflects the different risks taken by investors and lenders. Moreover, lenders have no 'upside'—*i.e.* the lenders' return is fixed, whereas the equity return can be improved by generating more value in the project (*e.g.* by more efficient operation, or financial restructuring—*cf.* Chapter 26). Turning this around the other way, lenders are able to offer project-finance loans with relatively-low credit margins because the risk is low.

Risk assessment by lenders is based as much on the financial impact that a particular risk may have on the project's viability as on the likelihood of it actually happening. So, a 'low possibility/high impact' risk will still be of concern to lenders. This means that the lenders assess risk by a series of 'worst-case' sensitivities (*cf.* §23.9.7), an analysis that is quite different from the weighting of risks which the contracting authority may undertake when considering VfM, as described above.

So the result is that since lenders are the most conservative party in a PPP, it is their view of risk that has to govern the approach that the contracting authority, investors and other parties take towards PPP project risks.

It is also important to note that any change in the project arrangements that may have an impact on the risk balance—*e.g.* alterations to the project contracts that change this balance—is always subject to lender control in some way (*cf.* §19.4.3). Similarly, any adverse change in performance under the PPP contract is likely to trigger lender controls over the project company's operations (*cf.* §25.3).

§11.6 THE RISK REGISTER

A standard project-management tool (irrespective of whether or not a project is procured as PPP) is a 'risk register' (or 'risk log') that identifies and keeps track of all the risks associated with the project, their expected impact and how they are expected to be managed. This is not an academic exercise—it is central to anticipating risks and ensuring that there is a plan for managing them. The risk register may first be established in Phase 3 (Project Economic Assessment and Selection) of the project cycle. Thereafter further information on risks is added to the register as the project is examined in increasing levels of detail and as more is learnt about the expected risks and their impact. The risk register continues to be used over the life of the project to help guide those responsible for managing risks, whether from the contracting authority's or the project company's perspective.

One of the important components of the risk register is information on the allocation of risks between the public and private sector as agreed in the PPP contract at financial close (or subsequently agreed following any amendment). This component of the risk register is often referred to as the 'risk matrix'. Thus, the risk matrix reflects how risks have been allocated, while the risk register is an over-arching dynamic management tool to help manage all the allocated risks.

Clearly once the PPP contract is signed, the allocation of those particular risks in the risk register cannot change unless the PPP contract is amended. But, depending on who is using the risk register, the risk register may also contain details of how risks are allocated *within* the public- or private-sector party. For example, those managing the project company need to track how the various risks for which the project company is ultimately responsible are allocated among its various subcontractors and how they will be managed (*cf.* §19.8.3).

There are also risks *outside* of the PPP contract that are relevant for the particular party using the risk register. For example, the contracting authority needs to manage a range of risks within the public sector such as:

- risks in managing the PPP-preparation process up to the point of financial close (*cf.* Chapters 7 and 10);
- risks arising from subsequent changes to the PPP contract terms (*cf.* §19.4.3);
- risks arising from its own internal-management arrangements such as a re-organisation of the contracting authority and its contract-management team (*cf.* §19.7); and
- risks arising from issues that are not immediately covered by the PPP contract but are related to the overall provision of the public service (such as stakeholder-management risks (*cf.* §6.5) or disaster recovery).

A risk register may therefore contain the following information (often in a spreadsheet form) for each risk:

- name, identification number and description of the risk;
- risk cause;
- project phase(s) of impact;
- likelihood of the risk (*e.g.* low, medium and high);
- the impact of the risk (*e.g.* low, medium and high);
- the party most affected;
- allocation of the risk and identification of the party responsible for managing it;
- risk value;
- outline of the commercial basis upon which the risk is handled in the PPP contract, where relevant; and
- outline of the risk-control measure (*e.g.* for the contracting authority if the risk register is written from its perspective).

The risk register can also be colour-coded to identify the risks that must be the most actively managed or monitored (such as high probability/high impact risks). This *prioritisation* of risks makes risk management more efficient.

Given the interrelationship between risks, a risk-relation map is another useful tool. This helps to visualise the relationship between a risk and what may contribute towards it (*e.g.* a cost overrun may be a result of, *inter alia*, poor design), which in turn may be a result of the risk of changes in the design team and conflicting design criteria (FHWA 2013). The risk-relation map also helps to categorise and list the risks in the risk register in a sensible order, say by phase and category, rather than having a random list of risks.

§11.6.1 Categories of Risks

Table 11.1 sets out a typical list of topics which may have to be considered when constructing a risk matrix; of course, there are always project-specific risks, and so this is only a general guide. As shown in Table 11.1, project risks can be divided into a few broad phases and categories.

Table 11.1 Key risks

Risk phase	Risk category	See	Nature of risk	See
General	Political		Political opposition to project	§4.4, §13.10
			Change in law	§16.2.5
	Economic	Chapter 24	Interest rates	§24.2
			Inflation	§24.3
			Foreign exchange	§24.4
Construction Phase	Project site	§12.2	Site acquisition	§12.2.1
			Ground condition	§12.2.2

(Continued)

Table 11.1 (Continued)

Risk phase	Risk category	See	Nature of risk	See
			Planning and permits	§12.2.3
			Environmental impact and risks	§12.2.4
			Archæology and fossils	§12.2.5
			Access, rights of way and easements	§12.2.6
			Connections to the site	§12.2.7
			Protesters	§12.2.8
			Disposal of surplus land	§12.2.9
	Construction	§12.3–§12.6	Construction subcontract	§12.3.1, §28.6.1
			Construction subcontractor	§12.3.2
			Price adjustments	§12.3.3
			Revenue during construction	§12.3.4, §15.5.3
			Delay by construction subcontractor	§12.3.5
			Performance	§12.3.6
			Construction subcontractor's risks	§12.5.1
			Contracting authority's risks	§12.5.2
			Design	§12.6
			Insurable risks	§14.3
Operation Phase	Operation	Chapter 13	Demand risk	§13.2, §28.6.2
			Network	§13.3
			Revenue payment	§13.4
			Availability and service	§13.5, §28.6.3
			Maintenance	§13.6, §28.6.4
			Other operating costs risks	§13.7, §28.6.4
			Interface risks	§13.9
	Termination	Chapter 17	Project-company default	§17.2, §28.6.5
			Termination by the contracting authority	§17.3
			Permanent *force majeure*	§17.4
			Hand back and residual value	§17.8

§11.6.2 Risk Mismatching

If risks are passed from the contracting authority to the project company, and then passed on again on a back-to-back basis to subcontractors, it is important to ensure that the definitions and consequences of these risks in the PPP contract and the relevant subcontract are the same. Examples of areas where risk mismatches may arise are:

- differences between the scope of the works under the construction subcontract and the requirements of the PPP contract, or the service required under an FM subcontract and those required under the PPP contract;
- a different definition of completion, or a mismatch between the level of delay LDs (*cf.* §12.4) under the PPP contract (*cf.* §15.4.1) and the construction subcontract (*cf.* §12.3.2);
- a different procedure for fixing the cost of a change in the project requested under the PPP contract by the contracting authority (*cf.* §16.2.1), and for fixing the cost of the same variation in the construction subcontract, so that the cost of the variation payable to the construction subcontractor may not be fully passed through the project company to the contracting authority;
- a similar issue arises with extra costs caused by a change in law (*cf.* §16.2.5); and
- different definitions of compensation or relief events (*cf.* §16.2, §16.4) between the construction subcontract and the PPP contract.

The need to ensure this matching may mean that subcontract negotiations effectively become multi-party, involving—directly or indirectly—the contracting authority (and sometimes also the lenders—*cf.* §10.8.3), the sponsors and the subcontractor.

§11.7 RISK INTERDEPENDENCIES

Another related issue arises where one PPP project depends on another. For example, a new concession road may rely on traffic generated by a new concession-based bridge, and *vice versa*. If the completion of the bridge concession cannot be guaranteed, the road concession will probably not be able to get financing; conversely if the completion of the road concession cannot be guaranteed, the bridge concession will probably not be able to get financing. The lenders to one project will have no interest in taking an extra risk on another project, with different investors and lenders, that they cannot properly assess or control. Financing the two projects as one may be a way out of this impasse, which may be one of the issues to consider when deciding on the project scope early on (*cf.* §5.3.2), but if they have been procured separately this will probably be impossible. In such cases the contracting authority may have to stand in the middle and guarantee each project's completion for the benefit of the other (which is obviously not ideal in risk-transfer terms). Similarly, where there is a coordinated country-wide programme for developing road concessions, this will probably be procured in stages, as otherwise it would be too big to be financed as a whole: a similar problem may then arise with each stage being dependent on the others being built as well.

§11.8 CONTRACTING AUTHORITY'S REQUIREMENTS

Finally, it is worth remarking that the contracting authority always retains the risk of having specified its requirements incorrectly, and so having to pay for a service which does not properly meet its needs. The requirements can be changed, but this is an expensive and relatively inflexible process (*cf.* §16.2.3).

12

Risk Allocation—Construction Phase

§12.1 INTRODUCTION

This chapter reviews the main risks over the construction phase of a PPP project and how they are generally allocated between the contracting authority, project company, sub-contractors and other parties to a PPP project. These risks are primarily considered from the lenders' point of view, since as explained in §11.5, they are usually the party with the lowest appetite for risk transfer from the contracting authority.

The construction phase is generally considered the riskiest stage of a PPP project (*cf.* §20.2.3). The primary categories of risk in this phase relate to the project site (§12.2) and construction (§12.3).

Most of the construction risks relate to the performance of the construction subcontractor: the project company is able to make substantial claims against the former should any of these risks crystallise, for which it also takes security (§12.4). And both the construction subcontractor and the contracting authority also need to consider what security they have, the former against non-payment by the project company, and the latter against failure to complete the facility (§12.5). The issue of design risk, a risk that overlaps the construction and operation phases, is also considered (§12.6).

Operation-phase risks are discussed in Chapter 13, and insurance, which plays an important rôle in mitigating risks both during construction and operation, is covered in Chapter 14.

Macroeconomic risks (relating to interest rates, inflation and foreign currency) are discussed in Chapter 24. Risks related to hand back of the facility at the end of the PPP contract are covered in §17.8.

§12.2 Project Site

A variety of risks related to the project site have to be allocated between the contracting authority, the project company and the construction subcontractor:

- site acquisition (§12.2.1);
- ground condition (§12.2.2);
- permits (for construction of the project) (§12.2.3);
- environmental permits and risks (§12.2.4);
- archæology and fossils (§12.2.5);
- rights of way (access to the site) and easements (right to use an adjacent site, *e.g.* for water discharge) (§12.2.6);
- connections to the site (§12.2.7);
- protesters (§12.2.8); and
- disposal of surplus land (§12.2.9).

Lenders aim to ensure that site risks should either be retained by the contracting authority, or passed on a back-to-back basis to the construction subcontractor, but should not be retained by the project company. If they are retained by the contracting authority, this implies that it will pay compensation to the project company should the risk materialise (*cf.* §16.2.4).

§12.2.1 Site Acquisition

The title to the project site (and hence anything built upon it) usually remains in the hands of the contracting authority (perhaps with a lease to the project company for the duration of the PPP contract),[1] and therefore generally cannot form part of the lenders' security (*cf.* §25.3). It is common for site acquisition to be the responsibility of the contracting authority (if the land is not already in public ownership), especially if this involves acquiring large areas of land in multiple ownership, for which a contracting authority's compulsory-purchase (eminent domain) powers may be needed; also, if there is any political controversy on the location of the facility, this is best dealt with by the contracting authority.

Moreover, if bidders have to estimate the cost of acquiring land (and a possible risk of not being able to acquire it), they will have to include a contingency in their bids which will probably not be good VfM for the contracting authority; also bidders' different site-acquisition costs could distort evaluation of the bids as a whole. At worst, if the acquisition costs are much higher than anticipated, the project company may not have sufficient financing to complete the project.

However, in cases where the facility does not have to be on a particular site, bidders may be allowed to propose various different solutions for its location, and to take responsibility for acquiring the site—in some cases allocating this task to the private sector may help to keep the costs (and timing) of site acquisition to reasonable levels.

---

[1] In countries where legal ownership of the facility is not connected to ownership of the land on which it is built, the PPP contract usually has a provision to ensure that the project company transfers its legal interest in the facility to the contracting authority.

If the contracting authority has to acquire the land specifically for the facility, the cost of doing so may reasonably be included as part of the project costs to be paid by the project company, but if the facility is to be built on a site already owned by the contracting authority, there is less of a case for any transfer payment being required from bidders if it is to revert to public-sector ownership at the end of the PPP contract (*cf.* §17.8).

Lenders will not normally lend until the project company has a clear right of access to the project site and any additional land needed during construction. This is most likely to be a problem in a linear project, *e.g.* where land has to be acquired for a road or a railway line, and acquisition is not completed at the time construction on one part of the project begins. Indeed, land expropriation can be a major cause of delay in transport projects, including PPPs, with consequent cost increases for the contracting authority.

If the contracting authority wants the project company to begin construction in advance of the former's acquisition of title to all the land, the PPP contract will have to indemnify the project company against the results of failure to acquire the balance of the land.

§12.2.2 Ground Condition

The risks that the geology of the site is not as expected is usally be passed from the contracting authority to the project company, and then to the construction subcontractor (*e.g.* the risk that unexpected extra piling may be required for foundations, or that past usage of the site, such as for underground mining, will cause construction problems). Site surveys may be carried out in advance of financial close to reduce this risk (if one party is willing to pay for them—one possibility is that the bidders collectively share the cost, another is that the contracting authority pays for them, but if possible avoids warranting their accuracy).

This can be a difficult area of risk transfer. A survey of the site can never provide 100% certainty that there is not a problem that has not been picked up by the survey. Similarly, a detailed knowledge of the history of the past usage of the site, while helpful, does not eliminate these risks. The problem is especially acute in:

- linear projects, *i.e.* projects not occupying one site, but being built over a long stretch of land where detailed site investigation may be impossible, such as a road;
- potentially-contaminated sites, *e.g.* previous use in manufacturing processes, or other activities that may result in an unclear level of contamination such as use by a petrol station (*cf.* §12.2.4); and
- 'brownfield' sites where there has been complex past use of the site, or where access for surveys may be difficult because there are old buildings sitting on the site (as compared to 'greenfield' sites where there have been no major structures on the site).

In such cases, there is a stronger case for the contracting authority to take responsibility for ground condition. It may therefore offer the contracting authority better VfM to take this risk on in such projects rather than pay (directly or *via* the service fees) for the project company including a large contingency in its costs that may never be required.

In cases where the contracting authority provides the site, to what extent should the contracting authority be held liable if information it has provided on ground condition proves to be incorrect and the project company suffers a loss as a result? This will probably be unavoidable in cases where the contracting authority is the only realistic source of information, and this cannot be independently verified by bidders at a reasonable cost and in a reasonable period of time.

From the lenders' point of view, a possible mitigation of such risks is that problems of this nature should often be apparent at an early stage of construction, when project costs may not yet have exceeded the amount of the equity investment; if so, they can drawstop (*cf.* §25.2.2) at that point, with their risk covered by the equity.

§12.2.3 Planning and Permits

Lenders also expect all necessary planning and construction permits to be obtained before they will advance funds. In fact, permitting is one of the commonest reasons for delays in reaching financial close on PPP projects (*cf.* §10.8.4). Procedures in this respect vary greatly from country to country. In some cases, the contracting authority obtains the key planning permits before the bids take place, which is the ideal procedure as it will probably speed up the whole progress of the project. However, this may not be a viable approach when each bidder is offering different solutions to the output specification.

Even if outline planning permits are obtained, detailed designs for the facility may require further permits. If the design work will not be complete until after financial close (*cf.* §10.8.1, §19.3.1), the risk of such detailed changes of design causing a construction-cost increase normally falls on the construction subcontractor as part of the overall responsibility for design.

§12.2.4 Environmental Impact and Related Risks

Most major projects require an environmental-impact assessment (EIA) as part of the permitting process. The EIA examines the environmental impact of the project in a variety of ways such as:

- the effect of construction and operation of the project on the surrounding natural environment (plant and animal habitats, landscape, *etc.*);
- the effect of construction on local communities, including noise, dust, other pollution and construction traffic;
- any emissions into the atmosphere caused by operation of the project;
- water supply and discharge;
- long-term effects of the project on local traffic, transport and utilities; and
- other long-term effects of the project on local communities or the natural environment.

As with planning and construction permits generally, lenders require any necessary environmental clearances to be obtained before they advance any financing.

An environmental audit of the project site may also be required; this examines the site for potential pollution or hazardous waste, taking account of its previous uses. If this is discovered, a programme for containing or removing it is required. The contracting authority may have to take responsibility for known problems, but unknown 'site-legacy' risk (*e.g.* on a brownfield site that has been used for industrial processes) may be taken on by the construction subcontractor as part of the responsibility for ground condition, discussed above.

If significant pollution or hazardous waste is known to be on the site, this is also likely to be a major issue with lenders, as they may end up with having liability for damage caused by pollution from a site over which they take security; in general, lenders feel vulnerable, as the parties with 'deep pockets', to the problem proving more difficult than expected or to long-term damage caused from site pollution. Insurance may be available to mitigate the risk (*cf.* §14.3.6).

§12.2.5 Archæology and Fossils

Discovery of important archæology or fossils on the project site may seriously delay construction or even require some revision of the construction plans. If the project is in a location where this is a high risk, the contracting authority normally undertakes site surveys (*e.g.* a geophysical survey and digging test trenches, or even a full-scale archæological dig) in advance of financial close. Thereafter, the project company may have to carry the risk of delay, at least to a certain level, which will thus be categorised as a relief event (*cf.* §16.4) both under the PPP contract and under the construction subcontract. If archæological remains are discovered, then another department of government usually has to be called in to deal with the issue—but it may be resource-constrained or have other priorities (although the PPP legislation may provide an extension of time for and/or compensation to the project company if there is a delay after a specified response time, as in Greece, for example).

§12.2.6 Access, Rights of Way and Easements

Site access is not normally a problem, except in cases where the facility is still being used during the construction phase. This is a particular issue with rail projects, for example, as the project company's subcontractors may only be able to get access for limited time windows during the night or at weekends. Construction risk in such cases becomes considerably greater because of the difficulty of managing this process.

The project company may also need to have rights of way (*e.g.* access to the site for construction or operation or to connect to utilities), or easements (*e.g.* a right to discharge water) from parties owning adjacent land, who may have no other connection with the project. Again, this is normally a risk which lenders will want to see dealt with before they advance any financing, and may be best dealt with by the contracting authority in advance of financial close.

Conversely, the contracting authority may wish to retain rights of way or access for other utilities or public services, which could include the right to enter the facility to undertake further works on these.

§12.2.7 Connections to the Site

The project may be dependent on the provision of connections to the site. For example, a water supply may have to be linked to the site, or a connecting road may be needed to enable traffic to use a toll road or bridge. The party providing the connection may also be dependent on others (*e.g.* for rights of way).

Furthermore, a party providing these connections that is not otherwise involved with the project may have no particular incentive to keep to the project timetable, and the damage to the project caused by late connection may be disproportionate to the cost of the connection. In such cases the project company can only assess the degree of risk by looking at the record of the third party in similar situations, and try to control the risk by close coordination with, and monitoring of, the third party. The construction subcontractor's relationship and experience with such third parties may also be relevant.

Similarly, projects such as construction of a road also need to arrange for diversion or relocation of utilities (*e.g.* a gas, water or sewage pipeline, or electricity supply, may need to be moved under the road). The utility concerned will probably have control of this procedure, and their cooperation is needed. In these cases, the risk that such events could delay progress may be passed to the construction subcontractor, as it is a relatively routine requirement in construction, although it may be treated as a relief event (*cf.* §16.4) thus exempting the project company from penalties for delay in completion, or compensating the project company for the costs of this delay such as loss of revenue.

If the connections are being provided by the contracting authority—a connecting road being a common case—then the contracting authority should clearly be responsible for the consequences of delay or failure to complete the connection, including loss of revenue that the project company suffers as a result. The issue becomes more complex where another public entity is providing the connection, since each may be unwilling to cover the other's delay or failure, and yet it is reasonable to expect the public sector as a whole to be responsible. If such risks are considered significant, they may affect the definition of the scope of the project (*cf.* §7.3.1).

§12.2.8 Protesters

As a sub-set of political risk (*cf.* §13.9), projects involving the construction of public infrastructure such as a road may be the subject of public protest that seriously affects the construction schedule. In general, the contracting authority should take some responsibility for delays of this kind. Ideally, it should be responsible for ensuring the provision of appropriate police protection for the construction subcontractor to carry out the work. Failing this, it should treat delays caused in this way as relief events (*cf.* §16.4).

§12.2.9 Disposal of Surplus Land

It is often the case that when a new facility is built, the site of an old facility is no longer needed by the contracting authority and can be sold to help fund the project (*cf.* §18.6). This reduces the level of the service fees, but raises the question who is to take the risks of the disposal (both as to timing and sale price), the contracting authority or the project company? Lenders are unwilling to take on this risk, so unless an advance sale can be organised, or one of the sponsors is willing to take the risk, the contracting authority will most likely have to do so.

Even if the old site is sold in advance, so there is no risk on the sale price, the completion of the sale may be dependent on construction progress on the new site, which enables the contracting authority to move out of the old site. Therefore, if there is a delay in construction, the advance sale may be lost because the old site is not available in time. The issue becomes more complex where a facility is being built in stages; this may involve a complex process of 'decanting', *i.e.* moving users from one old site to the new site (or maybe interim moves between old sites). This is a risk which the contracting authority may expect the project company to take on, and to pass to its construction subcontractor. However, this may cause difficulties with the latter, depending on the scale of the financial effect of failure to sell the land. The sponsors (*cf.* §20.2.1) may therefore have to consider giving support in this respect (*cf.* §22.8).

Wider risk-transfer issues also arise with the contracting authority using land sales to fund a capital grant (*cf.* §18.6).

§12.3 CONSTRUCTION

Construction risks[2] usually translate into an overrun in construction costs against the budget on which the financing structure has been based, or a delay in completion of the facility, which leads to loss of revenue for the project company. This may have various effects:

- There may be insufficient financing available to complete the project, thus forcing the sponsors to invest funds for which they have made no commitment to avoid a loss of their investment, or putting them at a severe disadvantage (and therefore liable to higher borrowing costs or other disadvantageous changes in loan terms) by having to ask the lenders to advance further financing or to agree to new financing arrangements.
- Even if additional financing is available, the project company's capex, and hence equity and/or debt costs, will increase, with no corresponding increase in revenue: therefore the investors' return will inevitably be reduced. In the worst case, this may lead to the investors abandoning the project because the increased costs destroy its viability.
- A delay in completion is likely to cause the project company to lose revenue (from either the contracting authority or users), with consequences similar to those discussed above.

---

[2] Also known as 'completion risks'.

'Hard' construction costs (*i.e.* payments to the construction subcontractor; other capex items are referred to as 'soft' costs) are invariably the most important item in the construction-phase budget, and may make up 80% or more of the total; the next-largest cost—interest during construction (IDC)—is largely an arithmetical product of drawing financing to meet the payment required by the construction subcontract, and other costs, such as the project company's own corporate costs, insurance and payments to advisers, are usually relatively small (*cf.* §23.9.2). It is therefore the risks related to the construction subcontract that require the closest review. These may be summarised as risks relating to:

- the construction subcontract itself (§12.3.1);
- the construction subcontractor (§12.3.2);
- price adjustments (§12.3.3);
- revenue during the construction phase (§12.3.4);
- delay in completion (§12.3.5); and
- failure to meet output specifications (§12.3.6).

A contingency reserve is often included in the project budget to further mitigate these risks (§12.3.7).

§12.3.1 Construction Subcontract

In the conventional design-bid-build public-sector procurement procedure for a major project, the contracting authority engages architects and consulting engineers to draw up the design, based on which bids for the construction are invited with detailed drawings, bill of quantities and so on; construction may be split into smaller works packages, and any specific equipment required is procured separately. Alternatively, a consulting engineer may be appointed as construction manager, with the responsibility for handling all aspects of the procurement of the project, against payment of a management fee, which may vary according to the final outcome of the construction costs. Neither of these approaches is usually acceptable to project-finance lenders:

- 'One-stop' or 'turnkey' responsibility for completing the project satisfactorily is necessary, since the project company must not be caught in the middle of disputes as to who is responsible for a failure to do part of the work correctly.
- A construction cost that is not fully fixed in advance is not acceptable because of the risk of a cost overrun for which there may not be sufficient financing, or that adds so much to the costs that the project cannot operate economically.
- A guaranteed completion date is also necessary, to match the requirements of the PPP contract for commencement of the service and to avoid loss of revenue.

In summary, therefore, a turnkey, fixed-price, date-certain construction subcontract is required. This should substantially eliminate the construction risk for the project company, and hence its lenders, of construction-cost overruns and delays, since this contract passes these risks to the construction subcontractor. This is clearly likely to be reflected in the construction subcontractor building more contingencies into the contract costings, and hence a higher contract price than in design-bid-build procurement (*cf.* §12.4.1).[3]

Two types of construction subcontract are seen in PPPs, depending on the nature of the project:

- Design and build (D&B), used for fixed infrastructure such as accommodation or roads; under this contract, the D&B construction contractor has responsibility for both the detailed design of the facility as well as its construction—this means that there is no room for later dispute whether any construction problems are caused by bad design.
- Engineering, procurement and construction (EPC),[4] used for process plant and equipment, again the turnkey nature of the contract is important in insuring 'one-stop' responsibility for it.

§12.3.2 Construction Subcontractor

Risk analysis of the construction subcontractor takes account of:

- the competence to undertake the work;
- the construction subcontractor's overall credit standing;
- conflicts of interest and
- the scale of the construction subcontractor's direct involvement in the works.

– Technical competence

The construction subcontractor's competence should be reviewed carefully by the contracting authority as part of the pre-qualification process (*cf.* §10.6.1), and should also be reviewed by the lenders' technical adviser (*cf.* §22.2.7). The construction subcontractor should be able to demonstrate experience to build the type of project required successfully—this would include providing references for similar projects already built, including, where appropriate, references for the technology being employed in the project. Similar references may be required for the construction subcontractor's own major subcontractors. The construction subcontract should provide the project company with a list of approved subcontractors, or the right to veto them (and it may give some rights of approval over the terms of these subcontracts, although subcontract prices are not usually revealed). If the construction subcontractor is working overseas, experience in the country of the project and good relationships with strong local subcontractors are also relevant. Finally, the expertise

---

[3] Under-pricing of the construction subcontract, by a construction company used to charging a very thin profit margin on the conventional design-bid-build approach and then making its real profit from contract claims and variations, may be a significant risk in markets where there has been a limited experience of the type of turnkey contract usually used for PPPs—the construction schedule may be seriously impacted, e.g. by the construction subcontractor raising as many disputes as possible, or at worst the construction contractor may become bankrupt.

[4] Also known as a design, procurement and construction or DPC contract.

of the construction subcontractor's key personnel who are actually working on the construction should be examined.

— Credit risk

Allocating project risk to the construction subcontractor is not worthwhile if the company concerned is not creditworthy. If the construction subcontractor's wider business gets into financial difficulties, the project is likely to suffer. The credit standing of the construction subcontractor therefore also needs to be reviewed as part of the pre-qualification to assess whether it could cause any risk to the project. In cases where the construction subcontractor is involved in PPP projects on a large scale, or as a major part of its business, the contracting authority and the lenders will need to consider whether it can adequately handle this work as a whole. This is especially the case if the construction subcontractor's involvement in the sector has grown rapidly.

The construction subcontract should also not be excessively large in relation to the construction subcontractor's other business. Otherwise there is a risk that if there are construction difficulties, the construction subcontractor may not be able to deal with these because of their financial effect on its business as a whole. The scale of the construction subcontract should therefore be compared with the construction subcontractor's annual turnover; if it is more than, say, 10% of this figure, the construction subcontract may be too big for the construction subcontractor to handle alone, and a joint-venture approach with a larger contractor may be preferable. If the construction subcontractor is part of a larger group of companies, guarantees of its obligations by its ultimate parent company may also be necessary to support the performance and credit risk.

Despite the turnkey nature of the construction subcontract, both the contracting authority's and the lenders' due diligence should include a review of the construction management and programme, covering issues such as the critical-path timing for each stage (including, *e.g.* allowances for bad weather during the winter), adequacy of the pricing for the works, *etc.*

— Conflicts of interest

A sponsor that is also the construction subcontractor has an obvious conflict of interest between this rôle and that of an investor in the project company (*cf.* §20.6.2). The risks of inappropriate contractual arrangements, or a less than rigorous supervision of the construction subcontract by the project company on an arm's length basis, are evident. These risks may be mitigated in several ways:

• Other sponsors not involved in the construction process may specify the work and negotiate the construction subcontract (assuming they have the relevant expertise or external advisers to do so).
• Supervision of the construction subcontract may be carried out by project-company personnel who are not connected with the construction subcontractor, with the assistance of an owner's engineer (*cf.* §20.7.3), or a checker (*cf.* §6.4.3).

- The construction subcontractor's directors on the project company's board should absent themselves from discussions on the construction subcontract, or at least be disbarred from voting on such matters.
- The lenders' technical adviser is likely to play a more prominent checking rôle.

But if the construction subcontractor is a major sponsor of the project, which is often the case with PPP projects (*cf.* §20.2.1), realistically, there is a limit to the extent that it can be isolated from the sponsor side of discussions on the construction subcontract.

− Limited involvement in the construction subcontract

A construction subcontractor often further subcontracts a significant part of the construction subcontract; for example, a main contractor whose primary business is that of equipment supply will normally subcontract the civil works, charging liquidated damages (LDs) and taking security from its subcontractors that parallel the terms of the main construction subcontract (*cf.* §12.4). This process, however, can be carried too far if the construction subcontractor is not a significant supplier of either equipment or works to the project but just providing an 'envelope' or 'wrap' for a contract largely carried out by its own subcontractors. This is especially to be avoided if the construction subcontractor has insufficient experienced in-house personnel to supervise the works and relies too much on its subcontractors.

In such a situation, the risk of poor overall control of the project may be reduced by requiring the construction subcontractor to work in joint venture with one or more companies that would otherwise have been its subcontractors.

§12.3.3 Price Adjustments

But a so-called fixed-price contract is never 100% fixed, and the risk of the construction subcontractor making claims for additional payments under various contract provisions has to be considered. These claims come under several categories:

− Changes in the project schedule

The start-up of the construction subcontract may be delayed, perhaps because of difficulties in raising the finance, other negotiation delays or satisfying all the lenders' conditions precedent (*cf.* §25.2.1). The construction subcontractor cannot be expected to keep the price fixed indefinitely, and therefore a cut-off date for the fixed price is normally set out in the sponsors' bid. The construction subcontractor may be willing to agree to a formula for adjusting the final fixed price against consumer-price inflation (CPI) (*cf.* §24.3.2) or another inflation index after the cut-off date; this may be manageable within the financing plan. If no formula is agreed, the lenders may be reluctant to continue with work on the financing, as one of the main cost elements is no longer fixed.

- Owner's risks

  Apart from making payments under the construction subcontract when these fall due, the project company (often called the 'owner' in this context) is responsible for 'owner's risks' such as:

  - making the project site available and ensuring access (*cf.* §12.2.1);
  - in some cases, ground conditions (*cf.* §12.2.2) or archæology and fossil finds (*cf.* §12.2.5);
  - obtaining outline planning permits (*cf.* §12.2.3);
  - again, in some cases, latent defects (see below); and
  - providing access to utilities needed for construction, such as electricity and water and ensuring that third-party contracts (*e.g.* an access road) are carried out as required (*cf.* §12.2.7).

  Some of these risks may be retained by the contracting authority (*cf.* §16.2.4), *i.e.* the construction subcontractor claims against the project company for consequential increases in costs, and the latter makes a matching claim against the contracting authority.

- Unforeseen events

  As between the project company and the construction subcontractor, the former normally takes the risk of changes in law affecting the construction-cost requirements (*e.g.* because of new public-health or safety requirements), which again may be covered off by the contracting authority (*cf.* §16.2.5). The arrangements between the contracting authority and the project company as to:

  - compensation events, including changes in specification by the contracting authority (*cf.* §16.2);
  - relief events, *i.e.* temporary *force majeure* (*cf.* §16.4)[5]—which should mainly be covered by insurance (*cf.* Chapter 14); and
  - permanent *force majeure* that causes construction to be abandoned (*cf.* §17.4).

  are therefore normally reflected on a back-to-back basis in the construction subcontract; hence, a compensation event under the PPP contract will be an owner's risk under the construction subcontract. This means that the contracting authority may find itself *de facto* negotiating these points with the construction subcontractor, either directly, or indirectly *via* the project company.

- Latent defects

  Particular problems arise on projects that do not involve construction on a 'greenfield' site (*i.e.* land that has not been used previously for any other purpose), but refurbishment, repair or maintenance of an existing ('brownfield') facility, in respect of latent defects (*i.e.* defects which no-one could reasonably have found and whose

---

[5] The French term *force majeure* is commonly used for unforeseeable circumstances that prevent someone from fulfilling a contract. Its literal translation is 'superior force'. The Latin term *vis major*, which has the same meaning, is also sometimes used.

effect does not appear until later). These may have the effect of making the reconstruction or maintenance of the facility more expensive than could reasonably have been anticipated. If the facility has been in the ownership of the contracting authority for many years, and it is difficult to investigate its condition, there is a strong case for the contracting authority to take some responsibility for latent defects—*e.g.* that they will be treated as compensation events above a certain limit, with the project company (and hence the construction subcontractor) taking on the first slice of the risk, with the contracting authority covering the risk thereafter.

§12.3.4 Revenue Risk during Construction

If interim revenues are receivable during the construction phase to fund part of the capex (*cf.* §15.4.2), the risk has to be assessed that such revenues will not be received as expected. Even a fairly small deviation from projections could leave the project company with an awkward hole in its financing plan, as Greece experienced with a number of its road concessions when road use fell during the economic crisis. Therefore, lenders will be concerned to ensure that projections of interim revenues during construction, if anything, are even more conservative than base-case projections of revenues during the operating phase (*cf.* §23.9.9), as at least in the latter case there is a cover ratio (*cf.* §23.3) to protect debt service, whereas 100% of the revenue during construction is needed to fund costs.

§12.3.5 Delay in Completion

A delay in completion of the project may have several consequences:

- Financing costs, in particular IDC (*cf.* §23.9.2), will be higher because the construction debt is outstanding for a longer period: this is, in effect, another form of construction-cost overrun.
- Revenues from operating the project will be deferred or lost.
- LDs (*cf.* §12.4.1) may be payable to the contracting authority (*cf.* §15.4.1).

The effect of delays is thus to increase costs and decrease revenues, and hence reduce investors' returns and the lenders' cover ratios (*cf.* §23.3). However, these consequences may be mitigated for the project company if they are the construction subcontractor's fault (*cf.* §12.4), or the ultimate responsibility of the contracting authority (*cf.* §12.3.3).

Project completion, which triggers the service availability date (*cf.* §5.3.7), is a concept that appears in the PPP contract (*cf.* §15.4.1), the construction subcontract (*cf.* §12.4) and the financing documentation (*cf.* §25.4). It is therefore important to ensure that the definitions of completion between all these different contracts fit together. If the project company is subject to penalties for late completion in the PPP contract, it will want the definition of service availability in the PPP contract to be as 'loose' as possible so completion can easily be achieved, but possibly impose an earlier completion date on the construction subcontractor.

Insofar as delay in completion results in loss of revenue or LD payments to the contracting authority (*cf.* §15.4.2), the project company and its lenders will want to ensure that this risk is minimised, and that if it materialises, the consequences are passed to the construction subcontractor.

The construction programme should contain adequate provision for such reasonably-foreseeable events such as bad weather during the winter, and hence the construction sub-contractor should not be excused for such delays. A delay in completion is often quite predictable if detailed programming for the project is in place, as it will become evident that critical-path items (*i.e.* aspects of the project that, if delayed, will delay the final completion) are falling behind schedule. The project company should supervise progress sufficiently closely to ensure that potential delays in the critical path are spotted, and then assist (or put pressure on) the construction subcontractor to catch up. The lenders' technical adviser also monitors this process.

As for cost increases (*cf.* §12.3.3), the financial effects of other causes of delays that are not the construction subcontractor's fault depends on whether they come into the category of compensation events (*cf.* §16.2), relief events (*cf.* §16.4), or are covered by insurance (*cf.* Chapter 14). Failing any of these, delay risks will be left wholly with the project company.

§12.3.6 Failure to Meet Output Specifications

This is an issue that primarily arises where process plant is involved, and is being constructed under an EPC contract (*e.g.* a waste-treatment facility), where equipment problems or inadequate technology may affect the ability of the project to perform as expected on completion. It is interesting to note that (to 2011) only 6 of the 700 or so PFI contracts in Britain had been terminated for project-company default (*cf.* §17.2, Bain 2011). These defaults related primarily to performance of some form of process plant, including a government laboratory, a medical-waste incinerator and two municipal-waste incinerators. Private-sector investors and lenders lost heavily in these cases, all of which involved excessive technology risks, *e.g.* because the technology was untried. From the public-sector point of view, this suggests that where there are high technology risks, or the technology is unproven, the VfM argument for risk transfer to the private sector through a PPP is a strong one (*cf.* §28.6). On the other hand, it could also be said that the contracting authorities concerned should not have chosen bidders that were using unproven technology, since the result was that the facility was not delivered as originally required, and public money was thus wasted on the procurement process.

Process-plant performance is measured by a (usually relatively limited) number of performance tests, which may measure both the ability to operate as specified, and meet emissions or other environmental requirements. As with completion generally, the contracting authority or an independent checker will be involved in this performance testing (*cf.* §6.4.3). If the performance tests are not passed (usually after several iterations to give the EPC contractor a chance to remedy the problem), performance LDs will become payable by the EPC contractor (*cf.* §12.4.1).

§12.3.7 Contingency Reserve

One protection against construction-cost overruns or a delay in completion is a contingency reserve. However well managed the budget, there is always a risk of unexpected events causing a cost overrun. Therefore, a contingency reserve covered by matching financing may be required by lenders (*cf.* §23.7). As a rough rule of thumb, a contingency of around 10% of the 'hard' construction cost, or 7-8% of total project costs is prudent. The contingency is also intended to cover the effects of delays in the completion of construction, where delay LDs are not payable by the construction subcontractor (see below). But contingency financing is not intended to cover macroeconomic risks such as interest-rate movements during the construction phase, which must be covered in other ways (*cf.* §24.2). During the operation phase, the lenders' requirement for reserve accounts (*cf.* §25.2.4) fulfils a similar function.

§12.4 CONSTRUCTION LIQUIDATED DAMAGES AND SECURITY

The construction subcontract will include LDs to provide the project company with compensation for the loss of revenue from a delay in completion or failure to reach the required performance level, where the latter is relevant (§12.4.1). If these LDs have been fully drawn on, termination of the construction subcontract may be necessary. This usually enables further claims to be made against the construction subcontractor (§12.4.2). These are substantial obligations for which the construction subcontractor usually has to provide the project company with security (§12.4.3).

§12.4.1 Liquidated Damages

– Delay LDs

If delay does occur and this is the construction subcontractor's fault (*i.e.* one of the justifications for delay discussed in §12.3.3 do not apply), the project company needs to be compensated for its losses that result from such a delay. This is covered by the LD provisions of the construction subcontract, based on agreed formulæ that both sides agree are sufficient to cover the project company's financial losses resulting from late completion of the project. If specific amounts are not agreed to in this way, there would be lengthy disputes about loss in each case: the uncertainty involved in this would not be acceptable to lenders, and the time spent in dispute could be financially disastrous for the project company. LDs are not intended as a penalty (indeed, many legal systems make a penalty payment of this type unenforceable), but a fair compensation for the loss suffered. Apart from the LD amounts, the project company cannot make claims against the construction subcontractor for loss of profits or extra costs, except on termination of the construction subcontract (see below). Delay LDs may be covered by insurance (*cf.* §14.3), where the cause of the delay is a *force majeure* event outside the construction subcontractor's control.

Delay LDs are calculated on a daily basis, at a rate that is a matter for negotiation, but should at the minimum be sufficient to cover the project company's interest costs and fixed overheads, plus any LDs payable to the contracting authority for late completion—*i.e.* the costs incurred as a result of the delay; ideally, they should be high enough to cover the total loss of revenue (less any variable overheads). The total sum payable as delay LDs is normally capped; depending on the project this cap may cover, say, a year to 18 months of delay in completion, some 15-20% of the construction subcontract value.

— Performance LDs

As mentioned above, these relate primarily to EPC contracts for a process plant such as a waste incinerator. They are calculated as sufficient to cover the NPV of the financial loss from poor performance for the life of the project. Performance LDs are normally used to reduce the debt so as to leave the lenders with the same cash-flow cover ratios as they would have had if the project had performed as expected (*cf.* §23.3), and any surplus is paid as a special distribution to investors to compensate them for their reduced equity return.

Obviously, the performance measurements of the project on completion are only a snapshot taken over a limited period of time, and there may still be further variations in performance as time goes on that will not produce further LDs. However, as it is difficult to separate the effect of how the project is operating from its original performance, LDs can really only be paid based on the performance on completion. Thus, there is also no opportunity, unless claims can be made under warranty (*cf.* §12.4.3), to go back to the EPC contractor several years after completion if performance gets worse.

LDs are likely to be higher than those in a construction contract that is not being project-financed. Obviously, the construction subcontractor takes the risk of providing high levels of LDs into account when proposing a construction schedule and pricing the contract, together with the higher risks inherent in being responsible for all its own subcontractors (to whom it may also pass on some of these risks—in which case its subcontractor will also charge for this extra risk). These additional factors mean that the price for a turnkey construction contract can be up to 20% higher than a design-bid-build approach with separate contractors,[6] a point which needs to be borne in mind when comparing a PPP with conventional public-sector procurement (*cf.* §8.5).

There is normally an overall cap for delay and performance LDs, typically around 25% of the contract value—again a figure higher than that usually found in non-project financed EPC contracts. But it is important to note, however, that LDs do not provide compensation for a complete inability by the EPC contractor to complete the contract: termination of the contract, discussed below, may provide further remedies in this case.

§12.4.2 Termination of the Construction Subcontract

Delay LDs should be sufficient to keep the project company financially whole for some time, and provide an incentive for the construction subcontractor to take any necessary

---

[6] It is also worth noting that design-bid-build contractors typically operate on a margin of 3-5%, which shows how much more risk they consider they are taking on with a turnkey contract. (However, much of their revenue on design-bid-build contracts tends to come from subsequent claims, *e.g.* that construction has cost more because of bad design.)

action to deal with prospective problems. But if the delay extends beyond a year or so, the delay LD cap will be reached, and this pressure then reduces considerably. Therefore, once the LD cap has been reached, the project company usually has the right to terminate the construction subcontract. The project company's loss in getting another contractor to finish the works then becomes the liability of the original construction subcontractor, although again the amount of this loss may be capped, *e.g.* at 100% of the original contract value.

§12.4.3 Security

The construction subcontractor normally provides the project company with specific security for its obligations as discussed above:

— Retainage

A percentage (usually around 5-10%) of each stage payment may be retained by the project company until satisfactory final completion of the project. This ensures that the construction subcontractor will deal expeditiously with snagging items at the end of the contract.

— Completion bond

The construction subcontractor is usually required to provide a bond (which may also be referred to as a 'construction bond' or 'performance bond') for 10-15% of contract value as security for general performance under the contract, including completion. This also provides further security to cover the obligation to pay LDs, insofar as any retention amount is not sufficient for this purpose.

— Advance-payment bond

If any payments have been made in advance of the work being done (for example, an initial deposit of say 10%, which is quite common), the construction subcontractor provides an advance-payment bond, under which the amounts concerned will be repaid *pro rata* if the contract is terminated before the work is complete.

— Maintenance bond

After completion of construction, the retention and completion bonds may be converted into a maintenance bond, covering the cost of remedying latent defects during the defects liability (construction warranty) period, which normally lasts for several years.

These obligations (if they are not covered by cash retainage) should be secured by bank letters of credit or insurance-company bonds that enable the project company to make an immediate drawing of cash rather than having to go through a dispute procedure or legal action before being paid anything. If this is not the case, the project company may face a cash crisis if the events being covered by the security arise and payment cannot be obtained immediately. Alternatively, the project company may accept a guarantee from the construction subcontractor's parent company if it is of sufficient financial substance (but of course this is not so easy to draw on immediately).

But the right to claim LDs, bonds and other security provided under the construction subcontract, even, when strengthened by bank bonding cannot substitute for the competence of the construction subcontractor. Even a termination payment that recovers all the money spent on the construction subcontract will not adequately compensate the project company for losses if the project is not built, since the construction subcontract price is only a part (though a large one) of the total capex. Similarly, the contracting authority wants to get the facility completed on time and to specification, and not to have to rely on the project company's claims against the construction subcontractor as a way of doing this.

It also has to be borne in mind that if something goes wrong with the construction subcontract, it may not be easy for the project company simply to terminate the contract and call on LDs. In this kind of situation, it is likely that the construction subcontractor will raise all kinds of counter-claims blaming the project company or the contracting authority for its problems. The result, as with termination of the PPP contract for default by the project company (*cf.* §17.2.9), is likely to be a negotiated settlement rather than a straightforward payment of a claim under the construction subcontract.

§12.5 RISKS FOR THE CONSTRUCTION SUBCONTRACTOR AND CONTRACTING AUTHORITY

There are also construction-phase risks that have to be reviewed from the points of the view of the construction subcontractor and the contracting authority.

§12.5.1 Construction Subcontractor: Payment Risk

A construction subcontractor could reasonably ask what security is offered that payments will be made by the project company? Lenders have first security over the project assets including bank accounts (*cf.* §25.3.1). Neither the sponsors nor the lenders normally provide the construction subcontractor with guarantees. (Of course, one of the sponsors may be the construction subcontractor—*cf.* §20.2.1.)

The construction subcontractor's key security is the existence of the financing arrangements, and the fact that it is seldom in the lenders' interests to cut off the financing for construction of the project. Therefore, the construction subcontractor does not normally begin work until financial close has been reached, and it is clear that financing has been made available by lenders on terms that should ensure that stage payments due under the construction subcontract can be made, and that the financing will not be withdrawn by the lenders on an arbitrary basis. The construction subcontractor may also review any contracting-authority funding arrangements (*cf.* Chapter 18).

The construction subcontractor should also ensure that the construction subcontract stage-payment schedule is linked as closely as possible to its own financial exposure to direct costs and payments to its own subcontractors and equipment suppliers. Thus, if the project company does collapse, the construction subcontractor's own losses can be limited.

§12.5.2 Contracting Authority: Completion Risk

Obviously, the contracting authority is concerned to see that the facility is completed on time and to specification, but how can it ensure this when it is not a party to the construction subcontract?

Although the contracting authority should not get involved in detailed negotiations with the construction subcontractor, it should ensure that the construction subcontract has appropriate levels of LDs, bonding and liability on termination, as these indirectly serve to protect the contracting authority's own interests (*cf.* §10.8.2). Similarly, although it (or its technical adviser) may have a right to supervise the construction process, this does not mean that it can interfere with it (*cf.* §19.3.1–§19.3.3).

The contracting authority could charge its own delay LDs (although this is really only appropriate if the delay causes it to incur additional costs), but in any case, it would not normally make any payments until the facility is complete, which is itself a substantial incentive for the project company to meet the schedule (*cf.* §15.4.3).

The contracting authority is not obliged to do anything to support a project company suffering construction-phase problems, but political pressures for the PPP not to be seen to be 'failing', or to ensure continuity of the public service, may put the contracting authority under pressure to provide some form of extra-contractual support or relief (*cf.* §28.6.5). So, although construction is primarily a private-sector risk, the contracting authority's due diligence before appointing a preferred bidder (*cf.* §10.8.2) should still take account of construction risks, and how they are mitigated.

§12.6 DESIGN

Design risk overlaps the construction and operating phases: on completion, the facility must be designed to meet the PPP contract's output specifications (*cf.* §12.4.1), but also during the early years of operations some flaw in design may emerge which, say, increases, heating or maintenance costs more than expected. The benefit of a 'whole-life' approach to design of the facility, and hence the issue of whether the project company should be responsible for design, is discussed elsewhere (*cf.* §19.3.1, §28.8): assuming that this is the case, a back-to-back responsibility for design is passed down by the project company to the construction subcontractor (*cf.* §19.3.2). This is then reflected in design warranties provided by the latter covering at least the first few years of operation, or in the terms of a hard FM contract. Thereafter, the benefits of whole-life design should emerge over time.

The construction subcontractor may also be required to take out professional-indemnity cover lasting some years, against liability for faults in the design of the facility.[7]

---

[7] However, it may not always be clear who is responsible for defects, since they may result from poor design or construction, subsequent poor maintenance by an FM/O&M subcontractor, or changes to the facility made by the contracting authority's staff without informing the relevant subcontractor. Again, integration of construction and operation is key here.

Risk Allocation—Operation Phase

§13.1 Introduction

Operation-phase risks may be summarised as:

- demand or usage (§13.2);
- network (§13.3);
- revenue payment (§13.4);
- availability and service quality (§13.5);
- maintenance costs (§13.6);
- other operating expenses (§13.7); and
- continuity of service (§13.8);

as well as the effects of 'unforeseeable' risks such as:

- changes in the project's specification by the contracting authority (*cf.* §16.2.3);
- changes in law, leading to a need for additional capex or opex (*cf.* §16.2.5); and
- *force majeure*—which may be covered by insurance (*cf.* Chapter 14), or lead to termination of the PPP contract (*cf.* §17.4).

There are also risks that can occur during construction and operation phases, but are more likely to arise in the operation phase given its relative length. These include interface risks (§13.9) and political risks (§13.10).

§13.2 Demand

Resources have to be committed up front to any kind of project in the expectation of a certain future level of demand or usage for the services that the project will deliver. So, any project, whether or not it is delivered as a PPP, involves a risk on the expected level of demand for the project's services.

In PPPs, this risk of future demand can either remain with the contracting authority, or part or all of it can be transferred to the project company. From a VfM perspective, the issue of deciding who best can manage the risk applies to the allocation of demand risk as with any other risk. In many cases the project company has relatively less ability to control this risk than the contracting authority, suggesting that allocating this risk to the project company may not be good VfM. But demand can also be affected by levels of service quality and the service fee (in the case of concessions) which may be more within the project company's control. Or looking at this the other way around, allocating demand risk to the project company can be an effective incentive to improve service quality and service fee levels for some types of projects (*e.g.* an airport where service levels may matter in competing for travellers).

The allocation of demand risk to the project company is also highly relevant to the willingness of investors and lenders to finance the project. This is perhaps the most significant risk that they need to consider. In general, private-sector investors are usually more willing to take demand risk on a facility:

- if it has an open-market use, *e.g.* an office building which is provided to the contracting authority under a PPP, but if the contracting authority chooses to leave the building it can be leased to a private-sector user; or
- if there is likely to be a consistent demand, *e.g.* for a road project with an existing record of traffic flows.

The private sector does not generally take demand risk where usage is dependent on the contracting authority's actions. For example, in the early development of PPPs in Britain, the idea of investors and lenders taking demand risk for PPP prisons was tested, but there was no appetite for this (quite apart from the perverse incentives that transferring this risk might create!).

Another factor that may influence the allocation of demand risk is its impact on how the project is likely to be classified for public-sector balance-sheet reasons (*cf.* §9.4). This may drive the contracting authority to transfer demand risk, which may be poor VfM and make the project difficult to finance. This illustrates that the contracting authority needs to consider and balance a range of competing issues (*e.g.* VfM, financial viability, service-quality incentives, balance-sheet treatment) when considering the level of demand risk to transfer.

It is sometimes assumed that if users are asked to pay for the service then demand risk is automatically transferred as a consequence. However, who pays for the project's services (*cf.* §9.2.3) can be a *separate* issue to who takes the demand or usage risk. In a concession (*i.e.* a PPP where the user pays for the service), demand risk may be taken either by the project company, or the contracting authority as in an LPVR concession (§15.5.2), or both depending on how the concession is structured. And even if the contracting authority is paying for the service, demand risk may still be transferred to the project company *via* a shadow-toll scheme (*cf.* §15.5.4) or retained by the contracting authority, as under an availability PPP (*cf.* §15.6).

PPP contracts with the project company taking demand risk generally relate to transport projects. As discussed above, finance can only be raised for such projects where there is a clearly-established demand for the service. For example, a project may consist of building a tolled bridge alongside an existing one to add capacity: the established traffic flows make projections of future toll revenues relatively easy. The risk assessment is more difficult if, for example, a toll road is to be built near to other roads with no toll. In these cases, however, if the current demand is clearly demonstrated by congestion on the roads, and the cost of tolls or fares is reasonable in relation to the cost of existing transport modes, investors and lenders are willing to consider taking the demand risk.

Demand projections for transport projects are based on modelling by the contracting authority, the project company's traffic consultants and the lenders' traffic advisers. Modelling of demand is based on traffic projections, which in a road project could take into account factors such as:

- overall population growth, distribution and movement;
- general and local economic activity;
- land use around the area of the project;
- travel at different times of the day or different seasons;
- distribution of travel (*i.e.* the split between local and long-distance travel);
- split between commercial and private traffic; and
- split between modes of travel such as bus, car or train.

These and other factors combine to produce a model of current traffic patterns, which it should be possible to validate by using it to project traffic growth from a date in the past up to the present and comparing the results with the actual growth figures. Future projections of traffic growth for project finance purposes are based on macroeconomic factors such as growth in the national and regional economy leading to growth in private and commercial vehicle ownership. These projections generally do not take into account extra traffic that may be created by the construction of the project itself.

Having said all this, traffic projections seem to be as much of an art as a science, and the record of failure in such projections is not encouraging. Perhaps around 10% of road concessions are financial failures, defining failure as a situation requiring financial support from either the investors and lenders, a renegotiation of the concession agreement, or a financial bail-out by the contracting authority. This is a much higher level of failure than found in other types of PPP, reasons for which include:

- the winning bidder taking too optimistic a view of traffic, often influenced by similar optimism from the contracting authority; this is known as the 'winner's curse';
- difficulty of valuing time saved, *i.e.* how much drivers are willing to pay to avoid spending more time on alternate but slower free routes;
- lower than expected usage by heavy-goods vehicles (HGVs), whose tolls usually constitute a major factor in total revenue projections as they are substantially higher than tolls for cars[1]; truck drivers typically take a much more conservative view on the value of time saved than car drivers (*cf.* §15.5);
- slower than expected ramp-up (*i.e.* initial growth in traffic);

---

[1] This is because damage to the road surface by HGVs is exponential, *i.e.* does not go up in proportion to the weight of the vehicle but at a much higher rate.

- unexpected public-sector investment in competing free roads, or failure to invest in anticipated connecting roads (*cf.* §13.3); and
- public opposition to tolls.

In addition to these obvious failures, projects may be undertaken primarily on the strength of revenue guarantees or other forms of financial support from the contracting authority rather than the inherent strength of the project, placing unexpected burdens on the contracting authority because investors' usage projections are not carried out rigorously (*cf.* Chapter 18).

In fact, road concessions tend to have either so little traffic risk (and a high risk of excess profits as a result) that there seems little value in transferring this risk to the private sector, or so much risk that it is better not to transfer it to the private sector because there is a high risk of the project collapsing and needing to be rescued (*cf.* §28.6.5). Similar problems exist with other types of transport concessions such as tram and light-rail projects, but can be made worse in such cases by competing modes of transport such as buses.

Transfer of demand risk to the project company can also occur in transport projects through the use of shadow tolls (*i.e.* where the contracting authority pays the project company on the basis of usage and not availability—*cf.* §15.5.4). As discussed in §15.5.3, demand-risk transfer in such cases is generally more limited than with real tolls under a concession, and the lenders' risk in particular is very firmly based on existing traffic-flow volumes and patterns. Shadow-toll structures have fallen out of favour partly because of this limited risk transfer and also because they may create uncertain payment liabilities for the contracting authority that turn out to be unaffordable.

In the case of availability PPPs, it is evident that demand risk is retained by the contracting authority. So, the contracting authority signs a long-term PPP contract to use the facility (or make the facility available to users), but may find that, some years later, it no longer fulfils its purpose—*e.g.* a school has become redundant because of local population changes and it would be better to move it elsewhere, or advances in technology have rendered a hospital unsuitable for up-to-date medical procedures. This is why determining the future levels of usage is such an important part of the early stages of the economic justification of a project, whether procured as a PPP or not (*cf.* §7.4.4). As discussed in §28.12, the usage risk for the contracting authority in such cases is much the same as if the facility had been constructed using public-sector procurement, where the same issues arise, but the PPP structure creates additional financial costs resulting from termination of the PPP contract, rather than just termination of the use of the facility (*cf.* §17.3).

§13.3 NETWORK

Any project involving demand risk also has to take into account the effect of public-sector policies on this demand. Policy changes that are local to a project are known as 'network' risks: these may result from construction of other roads that take traffic from a toll road, changes in local road layout, traffic management, or imposition or removal of tolls or other road-usage fees. It is typically difficult to define all network risks in advance, but insofar as they can be clearly defined, investors normally expect these risks to be borne by the contracting authority, *e.g.* through 'non-compete' provisions in toll-road concessions, under which the contracting authority undertakes not to build competing roads, or to compensate the project company for doing so (*cf.* §16.2.4, §28.9.1). However, if this is the case then the benefit of network changes that *improve* the project company's position (*e.g.* new connecting roads) should accrue to the contracting authority.

The risk of changes in general or national policies that affect the project (*e.g.* an increase in fuel taxes that reduces road-traffic volume in general) is generally left with the project company.

§13.4 REVENUE PAYMENT

Here the issue is not whether there will be sufficient demand to generate the projected revenues, as discussed above, but whether the project company can expect to be paid the revenues, *i.e.* the credit-risk aspect of these payments. In relation to concessions, this is a question of 'willingness to pay', discussed in §15.5.

For availability PPP projects, the credit issue is that of the contracting authority's ability to pay, especially where it is not a central-government entity (*cf.* §9.3.3). 'Sub-sovereign' contracting authorities, *e.g.* regional and local governments (municipalities), or state-owned entities such as utilities, may have limitations of legal capacity and credit-risk issues that do not apply to the central government:

- As to legal capacity, if a PPP intended to be off-balance sheet for such a contracting authority is later reclassified and placed on its balance sheet, its obligations may be outside its legal borrowing powers and hence the PPP contract could be unenforceable.
- The credit-risk question arises if the contracting authority is not a tax-raising body and relies on central or regional funding, or is otherwise restricted in its ability to raise tax revenues, or if it is, for example, a public-sector utility in poor financial condition.

Neither investors nor lenders are prepared to rely on a long-term stream of payments from a contracting authority if there is any doubt—however theoretical—about the contracting authority's legal or financial capacity to make these payments. This may mean making changes in national laws to give the necessary assurances.

In Brazil, for example, specific legislation exists to ensure that future appropriations for PPP payment obligations are to be treated in the same way as future debt-service payment obligations at central and state government levels. Brazil and a number of other countries have also established guarantee funds backed by identifiable and independently-managed state-owned assets that can be used to meet payments if the government fails to do so. The intention is to establish confidence so that, over time, such support is no longer needed. A public-sector fund in Korea fulfils a similar function.

Even if the availability of budgetary support is not a problem, the project company may still have concerns about payment *delays* by the contracting authority when undisputed payments are due. Contracting authorities are not always the fastest of payers even if they have the resources, due to slow payment-authorisation procedures. But a late payment of a service fee can have serious consequences for the financial viability of the project. The financing structure of the project company can include liquidity arrangements to cater for short-term payment problems (*cf.* §25.2.4) but these come at additional cost.

§13.5 AVAILABILITY AND SERVICE QUALITY

The consequences under the PPP contract of the facility not being available, or of poor quality of service, are set out in §15.6. The overall level of availability/performance risk, once a facility has been completed, is typically very low—*e.g.* none of the 800 or so British PFI projects have been terminated so far for unavailability or poor service.

§13.6 OPERATING EXPENSES—FM/O&M COSTS

The risks of opex being higher than projected have to be considered separately under the various categories of opex. The project company may only have a limited direct control over opex, if most of these expenses are covered by FM/O&M subcontracts. In these cases, the key to risk management is the matching of payments under these subcontracts to the service fees (The original construction subcontractor often provides the hard FM/routine maintenance for the facility).

FM/O&M costs can be split into several categories, although the dividing lines between them (and hence the scope of any subcontract) are not fixed.

In the case of a building, these categories may be:

— Soft FM

  This could include items such as cleaning, security and catering. If such services form part of the PPP contract, they are typically provided under a soft-FM subcontract, with the costs fixed and inflation-indexed to the extent that the PPP contract reflects this (*cf.* §23.9.3, §24.3): for example, inflation-indexation under the subcontract against a general CPI index rather than an industry-specific one,[2] if this is how inflation indexation under the PPP contract is calculated. But in general, soft-FM subcontractors are reluctant to take a very long-term risk on this basis, which means that a review of the projected pricing may be necessary through value testing (*cf.* §15.6.7); this raises the question of whether soft FM is a suitable component of a PPP contract (*cf.* §7.3.1, §15.6.7).

— Hard FM

  This is the routine maintenance for the building. It includes matters such as servicing and maintaining the heating, toilets and other utility systems, painting, replacing broken windows or light bulbs, *etc.*, maintaining paving, repairs to the roof, and so on, typically provided under a hard FM subcontract.

  In addition, the hard FM subcontract may cover 'lifecycle' costs. These costs relate to aspects of the facility that require renewal or replacement on a regular long-term cycle; for example, the heating boilers in a building may need to be replaced half-way through a PPP contract. Again, these costs may be included

---

[2] Typically, maintenance costs are affected by inflation of labour costs and any costs of specialised materials or equipment.

within the scope of the hard FM subcontract, but it is probably more common for this to be on a 'cost-plus' basis, *i.e.* leaving the real risk with the project company.

In the case of a road, maintenance requirements may consist of:

— Routine maintenance

   This covers such matters as repairing potholes or cracks, clearing any obstructions, cleaning drainage and signs, and maintaining grass verges, often *via* a maintenance subcontract.

— Major maintenance

   There is normally a cycle whereby the skimmed surface of the road is resealed say every five years, the road is resurfaced every 10–12 years and the underlying concrete layer strengthened or renewed every 18–20 years. The costs get greater for each of these procedures, and are difficult to estimate because they are so far ahead (and timing is very dependent on usage levels). The further ahead these costs are, the less likely it is that a maintenance subcontractor will take on their risk. Similarly, major maintenance is often a significant cost item for process plant (*e.g.* a waste incinerator may have to be shut down for major maintenance every five years or so).

Hard FM costs, maintenance and lifecycle/major maintenance costs are the main opex items where real risk transfer from the public to the private sector should take place. As discussed in §24.3, reallocating some of this risk to the contracting authority through value testing is not appropriate (unlike soft-FM costs). There are two aspects to this risk area: the effect on availability of the facility being out of service for maintenance and the costs of the maintenance.

A routine maintenance programme needs to be agreed in the PPP contract that gives a reasonable allowance for maintenance downtime against unavailability deductions or other penalties (*cf.* §15.6.1). It should also set out a basic schedule that ensures the minimum disruption—*e.g.* a school's heating system should be maintained, and its buildings repainted, during the school holidays. Unscheduled maintenance—*e.g.* because the heating system breaks down—is likely to lead to an unavailability deduction. Equally, issues can arise if the planned preventative maintenance (which is a risk the contracting authority has paid to transfer) cannot take place because it clashes with user requirements (*e.g.* lift maintenance in a busy hospital). This is particularly important when the facility is approaching scheduled major refurbishments (usually every five to ten years in the case of buildings).

Compliance with an agreed major-maintenance/lifecycle-renewal programme (*cf.* §23.9.3) may even be a requirement in the PPP contract,[3] so ensuring that the obligation to carry this out does not rely only on the payment deductions for unavailability or reduced quality of service. This is likely to be linked to the contracting authority having joint control of a reserve fund that is built up over time, so ensuring that the funds are not diverted for other purposes.

---

[3] The PPP contract may include a procedure to permit deferrals of maintenance in line with specified criteria (*e.g.* consistent with manufacturer's recommendations for a particular component), without reducing the project company's continuing performance obligations.

Performance failures may lead to penalties on the subcontractor, but such penalties are likely to be limited by reference to the overall level of profit that the subcontractor can earn. It is more difficult to pass on major maintenance/lifecycle risks to a subcontractor, since these are harder to predict.

If maintenance risk is not passed down to a subcontractor, it will remain significant for the project company, even if service fees in this respect are indexed against a construction-industry inflation index rather than a general (CPI) index (*cf.* §24.3.2). A maintenance reserve account helps to deal with predictable spikes in lifecycle costs or other major maintenance, but not a steady rise in other hard FM or routine maintenance costs (*cf.* §25.2.4).

Moreover, even if demand risk has been retained by the contracting authority, a high level of usage may result in higher maintenance requirements, and so in this sense the project company may be taking an element of usage risk too (*cf.* the similar case of utilities usage risk discussed below). In a concession, this higher usage cost would be matched by higher revenues. However, this is not the case with an availability PPP project where service fees are not based on usage, or are capped as with shadow tolls (*cf.* §15.5.4).

There may also come a point, in relation to any category of operating risk, whether passed down to a subcontractor or partially retained by the project company, that the cost of provision of the service has become so much higher than anticipated that the subcontractor's or project company's only commercially-sensible action is to default. This is then likely to leave the contracting authority with the choice of terminating the PPP contract or coming to some arrangement to take back some of this risk (*cf.* §28.6.5). This problem can become acute if the project company has taken over responsibility for a large and old building or network, rather than building something new: it is likely to be very difficult to assess the level of maintenance required, and thus passing this risk to the private sector may be unrealistic (*cf.* §12.3.3).

§13.7 OTHER OPERATING EXPENSES

Other categories of operating costs for the project company include:

– Utilities

Another opex item which may be included within the scope of the PPP contract, especially for accommodation projects, is utilities, *e.g.* for power and heating. There are two separate issues here:

- *The tariff risk: i.e.* the cost per unit, *e.g.* per kWh of electricity. This is a risk which is beyond the project company's control (unless it enters into a long-term purchase contract)—it may actually be more efficient for utilities to be purchased by the contracting authority if there are benefits from doing so as part of a bulk-purchase arrangement, and for the service fees to be adjusted for the actual tariff on this basis.
- *The demand (or volume) risk:* even if the project company is not taking the demand risk of the facility, as with maintenance (see above), the level of usage will affect utility costs. Furthermore, if the people working for the contracting authority go around leaving the heating on and the windows open, it is difficult to control this; on the other hand, a bidder should be incentivised to design a building

which is energy-efficient. There is a difficult balance here, although generally in projects where utility costs are a minor part of opex, this risk is left with the project company. Also, it may be possible for service fees to be adjusted after an initial 'bedding down' period to reflect the actual level of utilities usage, but this should not relieve the project company from responsibility for energy efficiency.

— Insurance premiums

This is another significant opex item that tends not to move in conjunction with CPI; as discussed in §14.10 this risk can also be shared with the contracting authority through adjustments to service fees, but once again the project company should still have some incentive to eliminate unnecessary insurance costs.

— Project company's direct costs

Unless the project company is running any significant part of its operations itself, instead of delegating to subcontractors, the project company's own direct operating costs are normally limited in nature and relatively easy to control. Lenders may impose rolling budgetary controls on these costs (*cf.* §25.2).

§13.8 Continuity of Service

From the contracting authority's point of view, the first priority for any PPP project must be the maintenance of the public service. There may be situations where the contracting authority needs emergency step-in rights to control the facility for service reasons, because of a health or safety risk, to carry out a legal duty (*e.g.* to provide the service), or for reasons of national security (*cf.* §17.6.1).

In any case, the contracting authority should have a general right of access to the facility and its financial and operating records, to monitor performance under the PPP contract (*cf.* Chapter 19).

§13.9 Interface Risks

One of the strong benefits of the PPP process is the potential to transfer interface risks to the private sector (*cf.* §28.9.3). These are the risks associated with the interaction between two parties, such as two subcontractors. Managing this risk means ensuring that the different parties that come together to deliver the facility and the service, work together smoothly. Interface risks exist both during the construction and operation phases, and so there will always be interfaces to manage (*e.g.* whether or not to include the clinical services in a hospital PPP, *i.e.* the interface between FM services and clinical services with the overall aim of delivering a health service to patients)—a point related to the unbundling discussion in §27.1. The issue goes right back to defining the scope of the project (*cf.* §7.3.1).

For the construction phase, these risks involve managing the interface between several construction or engineering companies undertaking different parts of the construction.

This requires strong project-management skills, and the private sector is usually a better source of these skills for complex construction and engineering projects than the contracting authority, hence the use of EPC contracts (*cf.* §12.3.1) to allocate the management of these risks to a single subcontractor.

During the operation phase, interface risks can arise when there are interfaces between the services provided by the project company and those that remain with the contracting authority but that are still required to provide the overall service for example, the contracting authority may retain responsibility for IT systems or security (because these are already being provided under existing different contractual arrangements) or soft-FM costs (*cf.* §15.6.7). However, excluding a significant proportion of services from the PPP contract starts to undermine the rationale for the use of a PPP (*cf.* §8.8.1) and increases the scope for interface risk for the contracting authority.

§13.10 POLITICAL RISKS

Just as developing a PPP programme requires political support (*cf.* §28.13), a PPP project that falls out of political favour is likely to face difficulties. From the project company's point of view, having a long-term PPP contract to which strong political opposition has developed puts it in a vulnerable position. Such opposition may be the result of a change in government, or in the form of a national campaign against PPP projects of this type, or local opposition to a particular project. This is why confirming the motivations to do a PPP (*cf.* §8.8.1) and managing stakeholders (*cf.* §6.5) is so important. A PPP contract also differs from normal commercial contracts because one party—the contracting authority—may be able to use its power to change the law, or take executive action, to the detriment of the project company.

So long as actions such as a change in law are taken in a non-discriminatory way, it can be argued that they are just the risk of doing business in a particular country and have to be accepted, although the contracting authority may have to compensate the project company for resulting costs or losses, especially where the change in law requires further capex (*cf.* §16.2.5).

But political pressure can take many subtle (and discriminatory) forms: for example, after a change in government the new government may claim that procurement procedures were not properly followed and use this as an excuse to cancel the PPP contract (which is why transparency in procurement is important).

It is also possible that, some years into the PPP contract, its terms are seen to be unduly onerous for the contracting authority. Sanctity of contracts is a pre-condition for long-term PPPs, but this does not prevent both sides recognising commercial realities—if contract is 'out of the market' or producing excessive profits for the project company and its investors, it may be better in such cases to find a compromise solution through a negotiated change or negotiated termination.

It should be noted that this book does not deal with 'cross-border' political risks, which may be more relevant in some jurisdictions. These risks include:

- foreign currency availability and transfer;
- war and civil disturbance;
- expropriation (*i.e.* a government take-over of the facility without compensation); and
- contract repudiation (by the authority).

Strictly speaking, these risks do not only relate to cross-border investors, but such problems are usually more likely to arise in a cross-border investment context.[4]

---

[4] *Cf.* Yescombe (2014), Chapters 11 and 16, for a detailed discussion on this topic and the use of political-risk insurance, as well as issues with the credit risk of a contracting authority in a developing country (*cf.* §13.4).

CHAPTER

14

The Rôle of Insurance

§14.1 INTRODUCTION

As discussed in §17.4, *force-majeure* risks that can be managed by insurance (*e.g.* natural disasters such as fire or flood) are generally left with the project company, and so it is up to the latter to arrange insurance cover for these risks. With some limited exceptions, all risks of physical damage (or economic loss arising from this) should be covered by insurance.

The insurances are usually arranged by the project company's brokers (§14.2) in two phases: first, the insurances covering the whole of the construction phase of the project (§14.3), taken out at financial close, and second, insurances when the project is in operation (§14.4), which are usually renewed annually. These insurances are all subject to deductibles (§14.5).

Both the lenders (§14.6) and the contracting authority (§14.7) have specific requirements on insurances to protect their interests, including how insurance proceeds are controlled (§14.8).

In some cases, however, it may not be VfM to require the project company to put in place commercial insurance, even if available (§14.9). The contracting authority may also give some protection against excessive increases in insurance premiums (§14.10), unavailability of particular insurance terms (§14.11) and the project becoming uninsurable (*cf.* §14.12).

§14.2 INSURANCE BROKERS AND ADVISERS

When bidding for a PPP project's development, the sponsors need to appoint an insurance broker with specific experience in insurance for project finance to advise on insurance requirements, and eventually place the insurance programme for the project company if the bid is successful (*cf.* §20.7). Brokers are often paid a percentage of the insurance premiums, but this is obviously not an incentive to keep premiums down, and it is preferable to negotiate a fixed fee for this work.

The project company's broker also plays an important rôle in communicating information about the project to the insurer, which is important in jurisdictions where insurance is an *uberrimæ fidei* ('of the utmost good faith') contract; in such cases, if any material information is not disclosed to the insurer, there is no obligation to pay under the policy (*cf.* comments on non-vitiation cover in §14.6). The broker must therefore work with the project company and the sponsors to ensure that this does not happen.

The contracting authority should not rely on project company's broker for insurance advice. This also applies to the lenders insurance adviser (*cf.* §22.2.7)—the lenders are primarily concerned about protecting their loan, for which insurance is a key part of their security, while the contracting authority is primarily concerned about protecting the public service. Therefore, the contracting authority needs its own insurance advisers to review and agree the insurance programme (*cf.* §6.4.4), which then becomes a requirement under the PPP contract. Having said this, however, the lenders' and the contracting authority's objectives have much in common.

§14.3 Construction-Phase Insurances

In construction contracts that are not being project-financed, it is common for the contractor to arrange the main insurances for the construction phase of the project and to include this as part of the contract price. This is logical, because under a standard construction contract the contractor is at risk of loss from insurable events; if part of the project is destroyed in a fire during construction, the contractor is required to replace it, whether it is insured or not. However, contractor-arranged insurance is not always suitable in PPP project finance for several reasons:

- As will be seen below, lenders require delay in start-up (DSU) insurance, which cannot easily be obtained by a construction subcontractor, who is not at risk of loss in this respect. If the project company takes out a separate insurance for this purpose, there is a risk that the two policies will not match properly.
- It is quite common in project finance to arrange insurance for the first year of operation as part of the package of construction-phase insurances, to ensure that there are no problems of transition between the two phases; again, this cannot be done in the name of the construction subcontractor.
- Lenders wish to exercise a close control on the terms of the insurance and on any claims, working through the project company rather than through the construction subcontractor.
- There are a number of specific lender requirements on insurance policies that may be difficult to accommodate if the policy is not in the project company's name (*cf.* §14.6).
- Lenders normally control application of the insurance proceeds (*cf.* §14.8).

Construction subcontractor-sourced insurance may appear cheaper, but this is usually because the coverage is less comprehensive than that required by lenders. However, the construction subcontractor will be a beneficiary of the project company's cover.

The main insurances required for the construction phase of a PPP project are discussed below.

§14.3.1 Contractor's All Risks

If the facility (or part of it) is damaged as a result of an insurable risk, contractor's all risks (CAR) insurance[1] ensures that financial resources are available to meet the project company's obligation under the PPP contract (and the construction contractor's obligation under its subcontract) to complete construction of the facility. It covers physical loss or damage to works, materials and equipment at the project site. The level of cover is normally on a replacement-cost basis. Insured events include most *force majeure* risks, such as acts of war, fire and natural disaster, as well as damage caused by defective design, material or workmanship.

The main exception for the requirement for replacement-cost coverage is if it is inconceivable that the whole construction site could be destroyed at once (*e.g.* a linear project such as a road or a long pipeline). In such cases, 'first loss' cover may be effected—a level of coverage sufficient to cover the largest possible individual loss which could occur.

§14.3.2 Delay in Start-Up (DSU)

This insurance[2] compensates the project company for loss of profit or additional costs (or at least the cost of the debt interest and fixed operating costs, plus any penalties payable for late completion of the project) resulting from a delay in start of operations of the project caused by a loss insured under the CAR policy. The DSU coverage pays an agreed amount per day of delay, for an agreed maximum period of time. The level of coverage should be sufficient to deal with the longest-possible delay caused by loss or damage to a crucial element of the project at the worst-possible time. It usually has to be issued by the same insurer as the CAR policy, because the losses on the two are linked—*e.g.* the insurer may agree to pay more to have the damage repaired faster (or, say, a spare part flown in instead of being sent by sea), to reduce the payment on the DSU policy.

DSU cover is expensive—roughly speaking it may double the cost of the construction-phase insurances, and may be the most difficult area to agree between the parties. Lenders will want a high level of cover, which the sponsors may resist on cost grounds.

Theoretically the contracting authority does not need to specify DSU as a required insurance under the PPP contract, since loss of revenue by the project company, as opposed to physical restoration of the facility, is of no direct relevance from its point of view. However, this loss of revenue may cause the project company to become insolvent and hence the project may collapse.

[1] Also known as 'builder's all risks', or 'construction and erection all risks' (CEAR) for an EPC contract.

[2] Also known as 'advance loss of profits' (ALOP).

§14.3.3 Marine All Risks/DSU

This insurance applies when a major component of the project, *e.g.* a power turbine, is being delivered by sea, providing similar cover to CAR/DSU for loss, damage or delay in transit.

§14.3.4 *Force Majeure*

The cover provided by *force-majeure* insurance[3] is to enable the project company to pay its debt-service obligations if the facility is completed late or abandoned following *force majeure* events that do not cause direct damage to the facility (which should be covered by DSU), such as:

- natural *force-majeure* events away from the project site, including damage in transit and at a supplier's premises (to the extent this is not covered under the DSU insurances);
- strikes, *etc.*, but not between the project company and its employees; and
- any other cause beyond the control of any project participants (*e.g.* damage affecting third-party connections), but not including a loss caused by financial default or insolvency.

Thus, *force-majeure* insurance may be used to cover any significant gaps in the DSU cover.

§14.3.5 Third-Party Liability

This insurance[4] is usually bundled up with CAR and covers all those involved in the project from third-party damage claims. As this insurance is relatively inexpensive, the levels of coverage required are usually high.

§14.3.6 Other Insurances

Insurance may also be available to cover the risk of finding hidden pollution or hazardous waste on the construction site (*cf.* §12.2.4). 'Efficacy' insurance, which covers the construction subcontractor's liability to pay LDs for poor performance on completion (*cf.* §12.4), may also be taken out.

The project company will also need to take out insurances required by law, such as employer liability and vehicle insurance (unless the O&M/FM subcontractor(s) do so).

§14.4 OPERATION-PHASE INSURANCES

The operation-phase insurance cover is similar in nature to that for the construction phase:

---

[3] N.B.: This is not directly-related to the definition of *force majeure* under the PPP contract (*cf.* §17.4).

[4] Also known as public liability.

§14.4.1 All Risks

This covers the project against physical damage. The level of coverage is normally the replacement cost of the facility (again unless a linear project is involved). This coverage may be split into 'property damage' (or 'material damage') insurance and 'machinery breakdown' (also known as 'boiler and machinery') insurance in the case of process plant.

§14.4.2 Business Interruption (BI)

This is the equivalent of DSU insurance for the operation phase (and therefore also has to be provided by the same insurer as for the all-risks cover). Again, the scale of coverage should be sufficient to cover losses (or at least debt interest, any penalties under the PPP contract, and fixed operating costs) during the maximum period of interruption that could be caused by having to replace a key physical element of the project. As with the DSU insurance, negotiations on the level of cover may be difficult and questions may arise as to how far the contracting authority should impose any requirements for, or accept any risk of failure to obtain, business-interruption (BI) insurance.

§14.4.3 Contingent BI

This insurance[5] is the equivalent of *force-majeure* insurance for the operation phase, and covers the project company against *force-majeure* events affecting a third-party's site that have a knock-on effect on the project company.

§14.4.4 Increased Cost of Working

If the result of an insurable event is not only a loss of revenue, but also that the project company has to incur increased costs to carry out the requirements of a PPP contract (*e.g.* in the waste sector—*cf.* §15.6.1), this category of insurance (usually an addition to the BI policy) covers such costs.

§14.4.5 Third-Party Liability

This is similar to the coverage during the construction phase. However, this risk may in certain cases be retained by the contracting authority where it offers better VfM to do so.

§14.5 DEDUCTIBLES

All these insurances are subject to deductibles (*i.e.* the loss to be borne by the project company before payments are made under the insurance cover). There is a simple trade-off—the higher the deductibles, the lower the cost of the insurance. The construction sub-contractor will try to make the CAR deductibles as low as possible, to limit its liability for

---

[5] Also known as BI supplier's extension.

such uninsured losses. The lenders will also try to keep all deductibles low to reduce their risk. The project company's investors may be more relaxed about higher deductibles. Insofar as lower deductibles increase the cost of the insurances, which feeds though to the level of service fees, the contracting authority has to strike a balance between increased cost and increased risk, and therefore straddles the positions of the project company and the lenders in this respect.

§14.6 LENDERS' REQUIREMENTS

As the insurance forms an important part of the lenders' security package, the levels of cover and detailed terms of the policies and the insurer's credit standing must be acceptable to them. There are also a number of specific requirements that lenders require to be included in insurance policies to ensure that they are properly protected (known as 'banker's clauses'):[6]

- Additional insured

  The lenders' agent bank or security trustee is named as an additional insured (or co-insured) party on the policies. As an additional insured party, the lenders are treated as if they were separately covered under the insurance policy, but have no obligations under the policy (*e.g.* to pay premiums). If this is not possible, the lenders' interests should be 'noted', on the insurance policy, preferably with a loss-payable clause, as below. Other parties with an interest in the project such as the construction subcontractor and the contracting authority are also named as additional insured.

- Severability

  The policies are stated to operate as providing separate insurances for each of the insured parties.

- Changes in and cancellation of the policy

  The insurer is required to give the lenders prior notice of any proposed cancellation of or material change proposed in the policies, and agrees that the policies cannot be amended without the lenders' consent. (The contracting authority may be given similar rights.)

- Non-payment of premiums

  The insurer agrees to give the lenders notice of any non-payment of a premium. As additional insured, the lenders have the option, but not the obligation, to pay premiums if these are not paid by the project company (and again these rights may apply to the contracting authority).

- Loss payee

  The lenders' agent bank or security trustee is named as sole loss payee on policies covering loss or damage (or sole loss payee for amounts above an agreed figure,

---

[6] Or 'bank interest clauses'.

with smaller amounts payable to the project company)—this is known as a 'loss-payable' clause. (However, payments for third-party liability are made direct to the affected party.) This may also give the lenders the right to take action directly against the insurer in some jurisdictions, but in any case, assignment of the insurance policies forms part of the lenders' security package.

— Waiver of subrogation

The insurer waives the right of subrogation against the lenders: in general insurance law, an insurer that makes payment under a policy claim may be entitled to any share in a later recovery that is made by the lenders; such a repayment to the insurer is not acceptable to the lenders until the debt is fully repaid.

— Non-vitiation

Lenders prefer to have a non-vitiation clause[7] included in the insurance policies which provides that even if another insured party does something to vitiate (i.e. invalidate) the insurances (e.g. failure to disclose material information), the lenders' coverage will not be affected. This can be a very difficult area to negotiate with the insurer, as it may add to their potential liability in a way that is not usual. In fact, in tighter insurance market conditions, it may not be possible to get the insurer to agree, and in such circumstances—if their insurance adviser advises there is no choice—lenders have to live without it.

It is sometimes possible to obtain separate coverage for this risk, and in some jurisdictions, it may be dealt with by naming the lenders as additional insured parties and including a 'severability' clause that gives lenders their own direct rights that cannot be affected by the actions of others.

§14.7 Contracting Authority's Requirements

The contracting authority also has a number of requirements for insurance policies, fairly similar to those of the lenders:

— Named insured

The contracting authority typically requires being one of the named insured under the insurance policies (with the exception of DSU/BI).

— Non-vitiation

As with the lenders the contracting authority requires this so that any claim it makes cannot be refused on the basis of the project company having failed to disclose or misrepresented any facts.

---

[7] Also known as a 'breach of provision' or 'breach of warranty' clause.

- Waiver of subrogation

  This is required to protect the contracting authority from being pursued for reimbursement by the insurer if a claim is raised by the project company under the insurances.

- Insured sum

  The contracting authority usually requires a minimum amount to be insured, *e.g.* to ensure that the full cost of reinstating the facility is covered.

- Payment of premiums

  The contracting authority should have the right to pay the insurance premiums if the project company does not do so (recovering the cost from service fees).

§14.8 CONTROL OF INSURANCE PROCEEDS

The lenders may wish to have the option of using the proceeds of an insurance claim for physical damage to repay their debt rather than restore the facility—the so-called 'head for the hills' option. This is unlikely to be realistic:

- Even a facility on one site is unlikely to be a total loss, and it is evident that will not be the case for a facility on several sites, or a linear project: in such cases, the insurance claim would normally not be enough to repay all the debt unless it came at a late stage in the project life.
- The insurer may require restoration of the facility as a condition for paying out under the claim.[8]
- The purpose of DSU/BI insurances is precisely to cover the situation where physical damage has occurred and the facility is being rebuilt, so it is perverse if lenders ask for DSU/BI cover but still want to walk away.
- The contracting authority also normally wants to ensure that insurance proceeds are applied to restoration of the facility, rather than used to reduce debt, so would include provision for this in the PPP contract.

Nonetheless, the lenders may be given this right if it can be shown that the facility would no longer be economically viable after the restoration works.[9] The meaning of economic viability (or 'economic reinstatement') may be a matter of much negotiation, but the most obvious test is one relating to the remaining LLCR (*cf.* §23.3.3). In any case the lenders generally supervise how the insurance proceeds are disbursed (*cf.* §25.2.4), although the contracting authority may also be involved in this process.

---

[8] Alternatively, the insurer may agree to 'cash out' the claim, *i.e.* a payment in cash but with no requirement to use this to repay the damage. The insurer's reason for agreeing to this would be that it would mean immediate stoppage of payments under the BI policy: but this is unlikely to be in the interests of the project company or the lenders (let alone the contracting authority).

[9] But this may have an impact on Eurostat balance-sheet treatment of the project (*cf.* §9.4.5).

In principle, any payment covering loss of revenue (*i.e.* claims on DSU or BI policies) is controlled by the lenders in the same way as they control the application of the general revenues of the project company. Thus, it is fed into the cash-flow cascade (*cf.* §25.2.3) and the contracting authority has no claim or control over such payments. However, the contracting authority may require that these proceeds are used to keep the facility operating (if this is possible) in priority to debt service, and that distributions should not be made to investors from these funds. It should also be noted that claims can only be made under these policies if the insurer is satisfied that efforts are actually being made to restart the business: the contracting authority's speed of response to plans for restoration of the facility is therefore important.

Third-party liability payments are usually paid directly to the claimant; the contracting authority may wish to control the litigation on any third-party liability claim if it could form a precedent for similar claims relating to public facilities which are not in the PPP—this will require negotiation with the insurer, who normally controls such litigation.

§14.9 CONTRACTING AUTHORITY-PROVIDED INSURANCE

In the overall context of transfer of risks to the private sector, the contracting authority should be very cautious about taking on the responsibility for insurance (for example, providing professional-indemnity cover against claims that relate to the project company's or its subcontractors' own negligence).

However, a contracting authority may not consider it necessary or feasible for some PPP projects to take out operating-phase insurances for physical damage through the project company (*e.g.* linear projects, projects where the facility is on a large scale or those where the assets are dispersed such as street lighting). Or the commercial market for insurance may be limited for a highly-specialised asset, so it is better VfM for the contracting authority to retain the risk of physical damage. Moreover, for a large centrally-procured programme of projects, it may be better VfM for the contracting authority to assume certain insurable risks in the operation phase, such as physical damage, and provide the project company with compensation for losses from this that would otherwise be insured.[10] But this is a difficult area: *e.g.*, the project company has little incentive to operate the project so as to limit claims for losses.

Another potential area of contracting authority cover relates to that for injury to third parties using the facility. This can be covered by insurance as discussed above, but this may not offer the best VfM. In the United States, for example, it is standard practice for the contracting authority to retain third-party liability for transport projects, rather than pass this to the project company.

§14.10 INSURANCE-PREMIUM COST RISK

The operation-phase insurances (other than perhaps the first year) cannot be arranged or their premiums fixed in advance. There was a big jump in insurance premiums after

---

[10] The project company should remain liable for a level of deductible losses, and pay for BI cover.

9/11, significantly affecting profitability of some older projects that had budgeted much lower costs. This phenomenon has not occurred again to date, but insurance premiums may still be one of the largest single cost risks left with the project company after other risks have been passed down to subcontractors. If bidders are only prepared to take the risk of large (above-inflation) increases in operation-phase insurance costs by building in large contingencies into their bids, it may be better VfM for this risk to be shared with the contracting authority. If so:

- Any such premium-cost risk-sharing should relate to movements in the market for comparable assets, *i.e.* should not be project-specific, and should exclude increases that are a result of a poor claims record by the project company.
- A band can be set for insurance-cost increases and decreases compared to the base case within which the project company bears the risks of increases or receives the benefits of reductions.[11] Thereafter these risks are transferred to the contracting authority through an adjustment to the service fee. However, a sliding scale whereby as the increases (or decreases) in insurance premiums become greater the contracting authority pays (or gets) a larger share is preferable as this incentivises the project company to continue controlling costs, *e.g.* by increasing deductibles.[12]
- These premium risk-sharing arrangements should only relate to insurances for physical damage, and possibly BI. Although the contracting authority does not benefit from the latter, it makes up a significant part of the total insurance premiums, and again a large contingency against BI premium-cost increases may not be good VfM for the contracting authority.

§14.11 Unavailability of Insurance Terms

In some cases, such as a large increase in deductibles, insurance may still be available but not on terms that fully comply with the requirements in the PPP contract (*e.g.* the maximum deductible required is lower than that available in the market). This can be dealt with by the PPP contract giving the project company a temporary exemption from the requirement but also leaving it with extra risk of loss.

§14.12 Uninsurability

It may no longer be possible to obtain one or more of the insurances that the contracting authority required, or the cost of such insurances may have become so high that it is no longer viable to pay the premiums. The issue will be peculiar to particular

---

[11] In such cases the contracting authority needs to ensure that bidders do not just increase the insurance premiums in the financial model by the amount of the banding, which effectively means that the contracting authority is paying 100% of premium increases within the banding that may never occur.

[12] Depending on the method of sharing costs, this may have an impact on Eurostat balance-sheet treatment (*cf.* §9.4.5).

sectors—*e.g.* prisons are one type of PPP where there have been temporary problems of this nature—or result from more general problems in the insurance market, *e.g.* unavailability of cover for terrorism.

In such cases the contracting authority may be prepared to indemnify the project company from carrying on without the required insurances, *i.e.* primarily those for physical damage and third-party liability (the lenders may press for BI cover as well, but the case for the contracting authority taking on these is not so strong as any benefit it receives is only indirect—the argument here is the same as for the risk of insurance-premium cost increases discussed above). If so, the project can continue on that basis, but if the contracting authority does not wish to do this, the PPP contract may be terminated for (permanent) *force majeure* (*cf.* §17.4). If the contracting authority does cover the uninsurable risks, there should be a deduction from the service fees equivalent to the saving in premiums (measured against the base case).

It is quite difficult to define uninsurability exactly—clearly if the insurance is not available at all then a risk is uninsurable, but, for example, does a large increase in deductibles result in the facility being uninsurable, or is this the unavailability of an insurance term as discussed above? Or at what point does an increase in premiums become so high that it is no longer viable to insure (especially if there are premium risk-sharing arrangements such as those described above)? The only real way to tell that a risk is uninsurable is if other parties operating similar facilities have ceased to insure.

Uninsurability provisions transfer the risk back to the contracting authority just at the time when—presumably—the insurance market thinks the risk is very high, and therefore the triggers for them need to be carefully limited.[13] And it is likely to be difficult in practice for the contracting authority to act as an insurer (which may even be outside its legal powers): *e.g.* investigating and qualifying claims.

---

[13] It is also important to ensure that uninsurability is related to genuine market reasons. Furthermore, if uninsurability is due to acts or omissions of the project company, under Eurostat rules this may result in the project being classified on the balance sheet of the contracting authority.

PART IV

THE PPP CONTRACT

CHAPTER

15

Service-Fee Payment Mechanism

§15.1 INTRODUCTION

This chapter sets out the basic structure of the service-fee payment mechanism for a PPP contract, *i.e.*:

- contracting for outputs (§15.2);
- service-fee payment structure (§15.3);
- start date for payments (§15.4);
- structuring service fees based on:
  - usage/demand (§15.5);
  - availability/service (§15.6) or
  - mixed usage and availability (§15.7); and
- dealing with third-party revenues (§15.8).

Chapter 16 deals with events that may give rise to a change in the PPP contract and Chapter 17 with termination provisions.

§15.2 CONTRACTING FOR OUTPUTS

As discussed in §7.2, a fundamental feature of PPPs is the concept of paying for defined outputs, such as the availability of road space to a defined standard: the PPP contract specifies the service required but not how to achieve it (which would be an input).

This leaves it to bidders to determine the best way to deliver the outputs, which is how scope for innovation is brought into the PPP-procurement process (*cf.* §28.9.5). Conventional public-sector contracting based on defining inputs makes it difficult to define quality (and procurement rules may prohibit reference to particular brands to help achieve this). On the other hand, as the project company is responsible for long-term performance outputs under a PPP contract, an incentive is created to ensure the quality of inputs to achieve these outputs.

Ideally, a contracting authority would like to pay for *outcomes* as that is what it is in the business of delivering for its citizens and the basis upon which it will be judged (*cf.* §19.9). However, outcomes, such as better educational attainment, are usually the result of combining several different activities or combinations of outputs, some of which may be impossible to contract the private sector to deliver (*cf.* §15.6.9).

Outputs, on the other hand, are easier to define and measure and can be bundled into packages that can be contracted to the private sector to deliver. However, contracting authorities are always seeking ways to contract for as close to outcomes as feasible and this is likely to be an area of continuing development. An example in the roads sector is the increasing use of active traffic-management systems ('smart lanes' or 'smart motorways') where the output that is paid for is reduced levels of congestion (measured through monitoring the speed of vehicles) as opposed to (or in addition to) lane availability.

A broad guiding rule to defining outputs is that they should be 'SMART', *i.e.* specific, measurable, achievable, relevant and time-bound.[1] In other words, they should be capable of being clearly set out a PPP contract and not paid for if they are not delivered. Table 15.1 gives some examples of SMART output specifications for a school PPP.

Table 15.1   Output specifications

	SMART	Not SMART
Specific	Build school to conform to Ministry of Education standards	Build school to good standards
Measurable	Ensure that all schools are structurally sound, with adequate ventilation, lighting and thermal comfort	Ensure that school is suitable for teaching
Achievable	Ensure that school can maintain internal temperature at $x°$ when outside temperature is between $y°$ and $z°$	Ensure that internal temperature is always maintained at $x°$
Realistic	Ensure that faults with heating system are rectified within 8 hours in school hours and 16 hours outside school hours	Ensure that faults with heating system are rectified within 2 hours
Timely	Maintain log of faults and report every month	Provide annual report on performance

Adapted from Attracting Investors to African Public Private Partnerships—A Project Preparation Guide (*World Bank, ICA, PPIAF, Washington DC, 2009*).

---

[1] The original term S.M.A.R.T. can be attributed to a paper by George T. Doran (Doran 1981) where the letters referred to specific, measurable, *assignable*, realistic and *time-related*, but common usage has led to a few changes over time.

§15.3 Service-Fee Payment Structure

A core aspect of any PPP contract is of course the basis on which the project company is entitled to receive service fees for providing the facility and associated services, and suffer penalties for failing to do so. Detailed formulæ for this are usually set out in a 'payment mechanism' schedule to the PPP contract.

The method of building up the service fee, and the levels of the payments, is discussed in §23.4. In summary, the revenue stream—whatever the type of PPP contract—must be sufficient to cover:

- operating and maintenance costs of the facility (opex);
- repayment of the project company's loans and interest (debt service); and
- equity returns to the project company's investors.

The latter two items are partly a function of the PPP contract tenor (§15.3.1) and payment profile (§15.3.2). Inflation must also be taken into account, as relevant, when structuring service-fee revenues and projecting costs (*cf.* §24.3).

§15.3.1 Contract Tenor

Arithmetically speaking, the longer a PPP contract lasts, the lower the level of service fees is. Thus, if the contracting authority wants to keep the service fees as low as possible, the PPP contract should be signed for as long a tenor as possible. For example, if a project costing $1,000 is financed at an overall return of 8% *p.a.* over 15 years, the annual annuity payments (*cf.* §23.2.2) to provide this return will be $117, but over 30 years the annuity payments will be $89. However, it should be borne in mind that the longer the tenor of the PPP contract, the longer the period of private-sector financing at a comparatively high cost, and therefore an annual 'saving' derived from lengthening the PPP contract period is somewhat of an illusion.

The natural limit for a PPP contract tenor is the life of the facility which is the object of the PPP contract, but a road, for example, really has no natural life, as it is continually being renewed with maintenance, and similarly a building such as a school has no obvious or predictable end to its life. So, the effective life of the facility is often of limited relevance. Conversely, if the facility has a very short life (*e.g.* because it is technology-related), a PPP is not likely to be appropriate anyway (*cf.* §28.12). Therefore, the main factors that need to be taken in to account in considering the appropriate tenor for a PPP contract are:

- *Affordability*: if the PPP contract tenor is too short, the service fees may be too high to be affordable either by end users in the case of a concession, or by the contracting authority in the case of an availability PPP;
- *Whole-life benefits*: also, if the PPP contract tenor is too short, the benefits from whole-life design and costing (*cf.* §28.8) will not be achieved (*i.e.* the tenor should cover at least the first major-maintenance/life-cycle renewal);
- *Lenders' tenor*: the length of the repayment tenor that lenders are willing to offer (*cf.* §23.2.1) may set a *maximum* length on the PPP contract tenor, since from the

contracting authority's point of view, it is not financially efficient to have a long 'tail' period after the debt is repaid (*cf.* §23.2.4);

- *The absolute financial benefit from extending the tenor*: *e.g.* in the example above, extending the tenor from 15 to 30 years cuts the annual payments from the public budget from $117 to $89, albeit increasing the total amount of the payments; if the tenor were increased to 35 years, the annual payment would be $85—*i.e.* the marginal benefit of each increase in the tenor, in terms of lower annual payments, gets smaller and smaller;
- *Long-term flexibility* (*cf.* §28.12): this is probably the most important limiting factor in setting the tenor—it makes little sense to make a small annual saving in payments while locking the contracting authority into a PPP contract that cannot be easily changed if its requirements or the technology used to deliver the service have changed substantially (and the chances of these requirements changing clearly increases over time);
- *The maintenance cycle for the facility*: *e.g.* does the contracting authority want to have the facility returned shortly after a major maintenance, or, say, half-way through the major-maintenance cycle (*cf.* §17.8)?

In the case of concessions, there may be a case for fixing the service fees and then letting bidders propose the tenor of the PPP contract as part of their bid (*cf.* §10.6.5, §15.5.2).

In some countries, the PPP regulations set a maximum contract period (such as 50 years) or require that the period should not be greater than that reasonably expected to repay the project company's debt and recoup the agreed equity return. In some cases, the service fee may be reduced once the debt financing is repaid, if the contract length is significantly longer than the maturity of the debt (but see below). This avoids excessive returns going to the equity investors (*cf.* §15.5.2).

§15.3.2 Payment Profile

The payment profile is also important. There is obviously a temptation for the contracting authority to 'back-end' the payment stream, so making the project cost less today and leaving someone else to worry about making higher payments in 20 years' time (*cf.* §9.2). Such behaviour pushes a PPP project towards being an expensive way of borrowing money. It also runs contrary to the principle that the payment should be related to the provision of the service, not 'sculpted' to the variation in costs or inputs (*cf.* §15.6.5). In principle, therefore, service fees should be level over the life of the contract.[2] The same public service is being provided by the project company over the life of the project, so the payments should be the same. This is a matter of 'inter-generational equity'—we should not expect our children to make disproportionate payments for benefits that we enjoy today. Conversely, investors usually prefer to 'front-end' the payments, to increase their equity

---

[2] In some instances, there may be a VfM argument for some limited variation to the payment profile, say for the periods when heavy maintenance is anticipated as this may help to reduce the level of cash tied up in reserve accounts (*cf.* §25.2.4), but the impact on risks to, and incentives for, major-maintenance/lifecycle renewals need to be taken into account.

IRR (*cf.* §3.4.3), which means that their long-term interest in project performance is reduced. A structure where service fees reduce sharply after the debt has been paid off may also be unsuitable for these reasons. This general level-payment principle is, however, subject to taking account of the effects of inflation (*cf.* §24.3.4).

§15.4 START DATE FOR PAYMENTS

Service-fee payments usually begin on the service availability date (§15.4.1), although there may also be revenue during construction in some circumstances (§15.4.2). Delay LDs may be payable to the contracting authority (§15.4.3).

§15.4.1 Service Availability Date

Formal acceptance of the facility by the contracting authority at the end of the construction phase triggers the service availability date. The conditions for acceptance are obviously very project-specific. At a minimum they include receipt of all necessary permits to operate the facility, and an inspection of the facility and confirmation that it appears to be able to deliver the services (*cf.* §12.3.5), for example by the appropriate safety-inspection authority. If equipment or engineering is involved, there will be acceptance trials to ensure that these function correctly.

As with design approval (*cf.* §10.8.1), acceptance does not imply that the contracting authority takes on responsibility for whether or not the facility can meet the service requirements under the PPP contract: it is merely the trigger for the service availability date. Acceptance is often certified independently by an independent checker (*cf.* §6.4.3), and the lenders' technical adviser (*cf.* §22.2.7) may also be involved. The level of scrutiny of construction completion by additional parties that is necessary for a PPP is sometimes surprising for a contracting authority used to traditional procurement approaches.

In some types of project, acceptance may be in stages—*e.g.* for a road, separate sections may be opened to traffic as they are completed, or a building project may also be completed in stages. Acceptance may also be on the basis that there are still minor rectifications to be completed which do not seriously affect the service delivery (*cf.* §12.3.5).

There may be a concept of 'practical completion'—*i.e.* the construction work has been substantially finished to the required specifications, and the facility is accepted for use by the contracting authority, but with small elements of the works such as landscaping (known as 'snagging' or the 'punch list') still outstanding. In this case, the project company commits to rectify these to the satisfaction of the checker within an agreed (short) period.

§15.4.2 Revenue During Construction

The contracting authority should not make payments for something that is not completed, and hence normally service-fee payments should not begin until the facility has met the required standard of completion, *i.e.* the service availability date. (In the case of a concession, clearly users will not pay until there is a service to pay for.)

However, if some form of interim service is being provided by the project company during the construction period—perhaps because construction is in phases—then an appropriate payment can reasonably be made for this.

Interim revenues can also be applied if the project company takes over an already-operating facility, typically a concession such as a road where tolls are already being paid, and uses these revenues as part-funding for further construction. Any such arrangement adds to the construction-phase risks for the project company (*cf.* §12.3.4), and raises similar VfM issues for the contracting authority to other types of public-sector funding (*cf.* §15.5.3).

In some cases, service-fee payments may be made to the project company for services provided during the construction phase that are separate from those for the facility being built (*e.g.* for maintenance of an existing asset that is included in the project scope). Where possible, these should be treated under a separate regime to that which applies to the facility that is being built so as not to affect the performance-based payment mechanism for the delivery of the facility and its associated services.

§15.4.3 Delay in Completion

The main incentive for the project company to ensure that the facility is completed on time is that service fees are not paid until it is complete. Late completion will eat into the operation phase, and thus reduce the return for investors (*cf.* §12.3.5). Assuming that the contracting authority would prefer to have the facility delivered late than not at all, there is no need for a 'hair-trigger' approach to termination for delay, and quite a lot of extra time can be allowed.

However, the contracting authority may itself suffer a loss resulting from late completion, because it has to make other arrangements for continued provision of the service. If such additional costs can be reasonably anticipated and quantified in advance, it is appropriate for there to be delay LDs under the PPP contract to cover them. As discussed in §12.4.1, delay LDs are not intended as a penalty, but a pre-agreed fair estimate of the losses the contracting authority will suffer from the delay; they may be secured by a bank bond (payment guarantee). The maximum amounts payable are normally capped—*i.e.* there cannot be unlimited delays.

Any delay LDs will probably be passed on by the project company to its construction subcontractor, who takes them into account in setting the construction price (*cf.* §12.4.1). Thus, delay LDs have a direct effect on the whole-life VfM of the PPP contract since this extra cost has to be covered by extra service fees. It may be worthwhile getting the bidders to bid for the PPP contract with and without delay LDs to assess the best VfM position.

There may come a point (sometimes referred to as the 'sunset date') where completion of the facility has been delayed so long that the contracting authority has the right to terminate the PPP contract (*cf.* §17.2). If the contracting authority is charging delay LDs, this backstop date would normally come when these LDs run out (or if they are not paid).

However, although most PPP contracts have a fixed tenor, *i.e.* the tenor is fixed from the date of financial close to a fixed final date (and hence if construction of the facility is delayed, the project company will lose revenue), the tenor may be based on a fixed operation period whereby it ends a defined number of years after the service availability date. In the latter case, the project company merely suffers a delay rather than an absolute reduction in service fees if the construction of the facility is delayed, removing a strong incentive for on-time delivery. This also has implications, *inter alia*, in cases of a compensation event for loss of revenue for the project company (*cf.* §16.2.1). Such a fixed operation period may make sense if significant life-cycle works are anticipated towards the end of the PPP contract.

§15.5 USAGE-BASED PAYMENTS

PPPs in the economic, as opposed to the social sector, often involve a usage-based payment mechanism, usually with the transfer of demand risk (*cf.* §13.2) to the project company, but not necessarily so.

For projects where demand or usage risk is transferred to the private sector, the usage-based payment mechanism can either involve payment by the user under a concession—in the road sector, these are often referred to as 'real' tolls—possibly with some public-sector financial or funding support (*cf.* Chapter 18), or payment by the contracting authority on behalf of the user—referred to as 'shadow' tolls (*cf.* §2.4.7, §15.5.4).

Alternatively, if the transfer of usage risk is not considered practical or does not provide VfM for the contracting authority but users are still expected to pay, the contracting authority can enter into an availability PPP where the project company simply collects tolls on its behalf,[3] or perhaps consider a concession with a variable length that is determined once the present value of toll revenue reaches an amount that is bid for (*cf.* §15.5.2).

Thus, the design of the particular usage-based payment mechanism is driven by two main issues: the appropriate allocation of demand or usage risk (*cf.* §13.2) and the approach taken as to who should pay for the service (*cf.* §9.2.3). In reality, the approach that is finally chosen is likely to reflect some sharing of demand risk and some sharing of payment for it between the contracting authority and the users.

In determining the best approach for a potential toll-road concession, for example, the following are the types of issues that need to be considered:

- With respect to transferring traffic risk:

  - traffic projections; as a rough rule of thumb, traffic lower than 10,000-20,000 vehicles per day (vpd) is likely to make it difficult to generate enough toll revenue to fund a stand-alone concession and therefore make it financially viable;
  - the level of tolls that could be generated on these assumptions;
  - if traffic levels are too low, whether the project would become viable with some level of funding support by the contracting authority (*cf.* §18.4);

---

[3] If the revenues collected are expected to contribute to 50% or more of the availability payment, then the project is considered on-balance sheet under Eurostat rules.

- the reliability of traffic projections and the costs or fM of asking the project company to take this risk (*cf.* §13.2).

- With respect to who pays any usage-based charges:
  - how charging drivers (tolling) fits within the overall national roads policy;
  - whether there is a free, albeit slower, alternative road—closure of free roads to force drivers onto the toll road is fairly certain to cause political problems;
  - whether there is a 'willingness to pay' on the part of drivers—*e.g.* there are usually strong objections if a road which has not previously been tolled is then made subject to tolls unless there are clear new benefits for drivers on that road; the tolls must take into account not only the financial requirements of the project, but also the 'reasonableness' of the toll level as perceived by drivers;
  - whether drivers not wishing to pay the toll would be diverted onto other less suitable roads, causing obstruction, or increasing local environmental problems (*e.g.* from additional noise and pollution through a town centre);
  - the behaviour of drivers of trucks and other heavy goods vehicles (HGVs), tolls from which are usually a major component of revenues as there is typically a substantial difference between tolls for cars and HGVs (*cf.* §13.2); HGVs are more likely to divert to free roads, so if HGV drivers decide to use alternative routes a toll road is unlikely to be viable (not to mention the significant additional road maintenance costs for the contracting authority caused by HGVs using the free road);
  - how easy is it to operate a toll system, whether e-tolling is viable and how well would this fit with connecting roads; (note that there are two ways of tolling a road—a 'closed' system measures where drivers get on and off the road, and charges are paid for distance, and an 'open' system where there is one fixed payment for using any part of the road); and
  - conversely, whether tolling the road would discourage local short-distance use of a road which is intended for long-distance traffic (the biggest problem with any new road which runs past a major conurbation).

If, having been through this exercise, it is clear that a real toll system is not a workable option (even with support from the contracting authority as discussed in Chapter 18), the contracting authority should consider availability-PPP or shadow-toll alternatives, as discussed further below. Similar principles can of course be applied to concessions in other sectors.

§15.5.1 Toll Levels

Again, looking at a toll-road concession, the level of tolls can be set in three possible ways:

- Bidders bid on the basis of fixed initial toll payments, which can then only be increased at, say, the rate of inflation during the concession period.
- Bidders are given freedom to set tolls throughout the concession term at whatever level the traffic will bear.

- The contracting authority sets the tolls, as part of a national road-tolling strategy (in which case the criteria for selecting the best bid will be another variable such as the lowest capital grant from the contracting authority (*cf.* §10.6.5; §18.6)).

The approach to this is therefore likely to be linked to the extent to which the contracting authority provides any funding or financial support for the concession.

§15.5.2 Limiting Revenues

The reverse issue, of whether there should be any limit on the revenues that can be earned under concession agreements by the project company, also needs to be considered by the contracting authority. There may come a point in concessions where the total usage level, and hence the service-fee income, is far above what either party to the PPP contract originally envisaged. It might be said that since the project company's investors have taken on the demand risk, they should be entitled to the rewards for doing so, and this may indeed be a fair point of view in a minority of circumstances where development of this demand is derived solely from the project company's efforts. But this is seldom entirely the case. If, for example, traffic on a concession road is well above the original forecasts, this is likely to be partly a product of other public-sector actions such as:

- the public sector having made it attractive to use the concession road by making other changes to the surrounding road network;
- public policy on issues such as fuel taxes, sales taxes on cars and road pricing elsewhere; and
- general economic growth, thanks to the government's economic policies.

Therefore, if the levels of traffic are so high that the marginal revenues (net of higher costs caused by greater usage) have become so great as to constitute a 'windfall' (*cf.* §26.1), it may be reasonable for both the public- and private-sector sides to share in this unexpected benefit. There is also an obvious case for this if the contracting authority has given any form of financial support as discussed in Chapter 18. It can be done in a number of ways:

- Capping revenues

  This approach and the issues that arise out of it are similar to the position where the contracting authority pays shadow tolls that include a cap on the revenues (*cf.* §15.5.4). The problem with a simple cap is that it may give the project company perverse incentives to limit traffic growth.

- Sharing surplus revenues

  This is the most straightforward approach, and especially appropriate where a minimum revenue guarantee has been given (*cf.* §18.4). Thus, under the Korean PPI Law, where such a guarantee has been given, when the revenue is 110-140% of base case projections, the surplus is divided between the project company and the contracting authority.

— Concession fee

Payment of a sliding-scale concession fee (*cf.* §10.6.5), based on the level of revenues, (*i.e.* in effect the contracting authority gets a share of excess revenues) is again a relatively-straightforward approach, and gives a greater incentive to maximise revenues than a simple revenue cap. However, this puts the contracting authority in the position of a *de facto* investor without the normal rights which an investor has to control the business.

Payment of a fixed concession fee, on the other hand, is open to similar objections as those against payment of an initial capital sum to the contracting authority (*cf.* §15.5.3): effectively, this can be an expensive way of raising revenue for the public sector as it means that the service fees have to be higher or the concession tenor has to be longer to fund these extra payments.

— Equity return cap

The project company's equity IRR can be capped at a certain level (higher than the base case), and surpluses paid over to the contracting authority. However, this is fraught with difficulties:

- It is difficult to create a 'leak-proof' system that prevents the surplus over the equity IRR cap being drained off through financial engineering, or manipulation of the subcontracts (especially if the project company's investors are also subcontractors).
- The IRR cap is unlikely to be reached until near the end of the PPP contract tenor anyway, as it is a cumulative calculation (*cf.* §3.4.3).
- Investors will be reluctant to make interim payments during the life of the concession, as demand may drop off later on, so reducing the overall project-life equity IRR below the cap. This means that any excess-IRR share may have to be set aside until the end of the concession, which is financially inefficient.

Alternatively, the concession may be terminated early if the equity IRR cap has been reached (*cf.* §10.6.5). This is a more straightforward approach, but may cause balance-sheet problems for the contracting authority, as this and any other cap on project-company returns would most likely lead to the project being on balance sheet under Eurostat accounting treatment (*cf.* §9.4.5) because the contracting authority in effect becomes an investor in the residual value of the concession. It is also again open to financial engineering or other manipulation.

However, it may be more appropriate to cap the overall rate of return, *i.e.* the project IRR, which looks at the financial return without splitting this between debt service and equity IRR (*cf.* §20.3.2). This at least avoids any distortion from artificial financial structuring as between debt and equity, and is the approach often used in regulation of privatised utilities.

— Least present value of revenues

LPVR is a more sophisticated alternative that offers particular merits in balancing risks and rewards from usage-based payments—the concession is awarded to the bidder that requires the lowest NPV of toll revenues (*cf.* §10.6.5). Once the bidder has received this NPV sum, the concession terminates. (The NPV calculation 'back-dates' the actual revenue flows to the date of signature of the concession.) Thus, the concession has no specific tenor, although there is usually a long-stop date by which it must finally terminate whatever the return. The benefits of this are:

- Traffic risk is largely retained by the contracting authority, which means that investors and lenders will concentrate on the ensuring the project is viable rather than just relying on public-sector support.
- It cuts the cost to the end user, as bidders should have a lower cost of capital (reflecting the lower risk) and do not have to build in large safety margins in their pricing.
- It reduces or eliminates the risk premium charged by the project company to bear demand risk which it cannot manage (*cf.* §13.2), so potentially improving VfM.
- It reduces the risk of the project company making politically-embarrassing, excessive returns.
- It gives the contracting authority greater flexibility; a fixed-tenor concession has to allow for compensation for some changes which affect traffic flows (*cf.* §16.2.4), but this may not be necessary in this case.
- It should ensure that the private sector eliminates political 'white elephants', *i.e.* projects that are promoted by the contracting authority for political reasons but are unlikely to recover their costs and be financially viable.
- It eliminates the 'winner's curse' (*cf.* §13.2).
- It simplifies calculation of compensation on optional termination by the contracting authority (*cf.* §17.3.2).
- It reduces the risk of renegotiations due to low traffic volume.
- It allows for a more flexible tolling policy.
- Because it is based on gross revenues not net return, it transfers construction- and operating-cost risks to the private sector, and also ensures that costs cannot be manipulated, unlike capping the equity IRR as discussed above.

However, there are some points that need to be borne in mind:

- The choice of the discount rate for the NPV calculation is obviously very important. In this case, the discount rate should relate to market-based project IRR (*cf.* §20.3.2) rather than using the PSDR (*cf.* §8.6.2), *i.e.* the rate will be relatively high. If this is not done, bidders have to build in an unnecessarily large safety margin: if revenues are generated more slowly than expected, this reduces their return on capital.
- This structure may provide fewer incentives to improve service and hence demand.[4]

---

[4] This depends on the sector and may be important where service levels are complex and difficult to regulate; Thus in some sectors, exposure to the risk of demand levels may be a more effective way of ensuring improved levels of service (*e.g.* an airport terminal with multiple service requirements rather than a road with fewer service requirements).

- • The lenders' estimate of demand and hence the concession length may make the tenor of the debt required difficult to finance in a particular market.
- • It may be classified as on balance sheet (again as in the case of Eurostat accounting treatment), because the contracting authority is taking too much 'risk/reward' on the project.

— Purchase option

If the contracting authority has an option to terminate the concession and then purchase the facility at a fixed price rather than a current valuation (*cf*. §17.3), this effectively caps the return that can be earned by the investors. However, this is more suitable for an availability-PPP project than a concession, where such a purchase option could leave the investors seriously at risk of not achieving their projected return if revenues are below projections.

§15.5.3 Initial Payment to the Contracting Authority

In a concession, the project facility may have been partly-built with public-sector funding, so that, for example, a section of a road may already be collecting tolls from users; this already-built road section may be included in the concession to make the project more viable by providing a stream of existing revenue while the new toll-road section is being built (*cf*. §12.3.4). The value of the toll revenues from the existing road section can obviously be taken into account by the project company (*cf*. §23.9.2), so reducing the tolls that have to be paid on the new road section, although such revenues during construction raise an additional risk issue (*cf*. §12.3.4).

However, this means that the general taxpayer has paid the cost of constructing the initial road section, and now there are no toll revenues to offset these past costs (and perhaps to service public-sector debt that was taken on to cover them). Therefore, the contracting authority may require bidders to include an initial lump-sum payment in their bids to cover this 'sunk cost'. The economic efficiency of this is open to question, as the end result is that the project company will have to take on more debt, at a higher cost than any public-sector debt that it is replacing, and feed this extra cost through its tolls. It can also lead to the size of the upfront payment dominating the choice of bidder at the expense of other requirements such as much-needed immediate new investment in the facility.

Payment for a franchise to operate an existing facility is similar in effect, but the motive is even more likely to be the benefit to the public budget despite any economic inefficiency. A toll road has a higher value for a contracting authority than it does for a private-sector purchaser investor if the contracting authority values the stream of revenues by discounting them at the PSDR, whereas the purchaser discounts at a higher cost of capital (which of course raises again the issue of whether the PSDR should be different to the private-sector cost of capital—*cf*. §8.6.2). On the other hand, if the proceeds of a franchise sale enable the contracting authority to pay off debt originally raised to pay for the facility, this may improve its credit rating and thus reduce its overall cost of borrowing. Alternatively, the contracting authority may use the proceeds to fund new infrastructure.[5]

---

[5] This is known in Australia as 'asset recycling'.

§15.5.4 Shadow Tolls

Shadow tolls are usage-based payments for transport PPPs that are paid by the contracting authority rather than users.[6] They are usually structured on a 'banded' basis, *e.g.*:

- *Band A*: a payment of $x per vpd or per vehicle-kilometre (vkm) for the first $(a \times 1,000)$ vpd/vkm;
- *Band B*: a payment of $y per vpd/vkm for the next $(b \times 1,000)$ vpd/vkm;
- *Band C*: a payment of $z per vpd/vkm for the next $(c \times 1,000)$ vpd/vkm; and
- *Band D*: all higher levels of vpd/vkm—no payment.

Band A represents a conservative view of the likely traffic levels: it will probably be the same or less than the banking case (*cf.* §23.9.9); total payments will be calculated to be sufficient to cover opex and debt service. Band B is the investors' base case, so total payments will thus be sufficient to provide the lenders' cover ratios (*cf.* §23.3) and the base case equity IRR (*cf.* §20.3.3, §23.9.9). Band C is an 'upside' case for the investors, which could say, take the equity IRR from 15% to 18%. Band D then ensures that the investors can earn no more than an 18% equity IRR whatever the level of traffic.

It is clearly reasonable to cap the revenues in this case, because the actual risk transfer to the private sector has itself been limited: Band A will be pitched at such a traffic level as to ensure that the lenders are taking little real traffic risk, and Band B is also likely to be at a sufficiently conservative level as to protect the investors as well. As a general principle, if usage risk transfer is not complete, there should always be a limit on revenues, as discussed above.

But since the risk transfer to the private sector is so limited, and the project company may have little real influence on traffic levels (*cf.* §13.2), there is clearly a question whether a shadow-toll system is appropriate. In fact, it was abandoned in Britain because it became clear that there was little risk transfer (and so the early shadow-toll projects had to be put back on the government balance sheet). If there is little real traffic-risk transfer, it is probably better to concentrate on payments for availability and service, where more risk and responsibility can be properly passed over to the project company, as discussed in §15.6.

§15.5.5 Penalties

The project company has an overall incentive to provide the services as required, since failure to do so will probably result in a reduction in revenue (although if revenues are guaranteed by the contracting authority, the incentive may not be as great—*cf.* §18.4). There is thus a natural regulator to this extent, but the monopoly nature of the services to be provided means that failure to reach agreed availability and service standards must also lead to some penalty payment by the project company in a similar way to deductions for unavailability or poor service quality in an availability PPP, also as discussed in §15.6.

---

[6] They are known in Portugal, which had previously been a large-scale user of this system, as SCUTs, short for *'Sem Combrança ao Utilizador'*—'without payment by the user'.

§15.6 Availability-Based Payments

Where service fees are to be paid on an availability basis, the process of establishing the base payment stream for the PPP contract is rather simpler than for usage-based service fees: it is a product of opex and financing costs, and the investors' required return (*cf.* §23.5), *i.e.* rather than the financing being structured to fit revenues, as in a concession, it is structured to fit costs. These base payments are then adjusted as set out below.

The essence of service-fee payments under an availability PPP is that they are only made when the facility is 'available' (which means capable of providing the service as required). This concept derives from availability charges for process plant, *e.g.* under PPAs (*cf.* §2.4.3), that are quite simple in nature. For a power station to be 'available', it has only to demonstrate its ability to start up, and produce a defined level of megawatts of power (while adhering to environmental requirements on emissions, *etc.*), subject to an allowance for downtime for routine and major maintenance. Similar fairly-limited requirements are all that are needed for other types of process plant.

But in the case of an availability PPP, the concept of availability is usually more complex than this. Availability is relatively easy to measure if a single-specific piece of equipment or service is being provided, but such cases form a small minority of availability PPPs. It is much more difficult to measure availability for a public-service building such as a prison, hospital or school, or a number of buildings such as accommodation units. Moreover, quality of service, which is not an issue with a process plant (since it either functions within specified limits or it does not) must also be taken into account.

Availability-PPP service-fee payment structures, therefore, normally have two main features:

- Payment deductions (abatements) are made—*i.e.* 'penalties'—are payable for any part of the facility which is *unavailable*, weighted according to the importance of the unavailable portion (§15.6.1).
- Service quality is monitored through *performance* indicators: failure to meet these also leads to payment deductions (§15.6.2).

Unavailability is crucial to the facility's operation, and therefore leads to immediate payment deductions; poor service quality does not prevent immediate use of the facility, but has an impact over time and hence more time may be given for rectification before payment deductions for poor performance are made.

However, it is highly unlikely that availability and performance deductions will ever substantially erode the service-fee stream to the extent of jeopardising debt service and indeed lenders are unlikely to finance a PPP contract where this is a likely scenario (*i.e.* deductions primarily affect investors not lenders). Once construction of a facility is complete, the chances of any prolonged period of unavailability are usually quite small.

It should be noted that this deduction régime is the contracting authority's only basis for claims against the project company (other than delay LDs—*cf.* §15.4.1); so, the contracting authority cannot make a separate claim for some other consequential loss because the services are not adequately provided. (This provision is known as an 'exclusive remedy' clause.) This may be a problem if the deductions are capped at a level that does not fully compensate for consequential losses (*cf.* §15.6.3).

§15.6.1 Unavailability

When dealing with a road project, it is easy to see that a particular stretch of the road is 'available' if it is open for traffic. But even in this simple case, a distinction has to be made between the reasons for unavailability, and hence the deduction to be made: unavailability due to unplanned maintenance (which is clearly the project company's fault) is different to unavailability due to heavy snow or a vehicle breakdown, and hence there should be a different level of deduction. Similarly, if the traffic has to slow down for some reason related to management of the road, this should also result in an unavailability deduction, but again on a different basis to the road not being available at all. And the time of day is also relevant: unavailability is obviously more of an issue during the rush hour than in the middle of the night.

These matters become more complex in an accommodation project. At what point is a building available or unavailable? Obviously, if the whole building has to be closed—perhaps because the heating system has stopped working—it is unavailable. But what if only part of the building has to be closed? Calculation of the *pro rata* share of this loss of availability is complex (and very project-specific)—and so to determine unavailability deductions in a building or similar facility, a detailed weighting scheme for each area or aspect of the facility has to be worked out in the PPP contract. For example, in a hospital the floor areas may be divided into three weighting categories:

- *Critical*: accident and emergency, operating theatres and patient services (wards, X-ray rooms, *etc.*);
- *Medium*: clinical support such as physiotherapy, pharmacy and waiting rooms and
- *Normal*: offices and training facilities.

Or each of the parts of a school may be divided into weighting factors such as:

- 1: storage rooms;
- 2: staff rooms;
- 4: standard classrooms;
- 6: specialised facilities, *e.g.* for laboratories, arts and drama, sports; and
- 10: assembly hall, kitchen, dining hall and IT system.

Thus, one classroom ('service area') is weighted as 4, whereas the kitchen is weighted as 10, so a classroom is said to be worth 4 'service units', while the kitchen is 10 service units. (Note that simple floor area is not used as a basis for weighting.) Multiplying the total of the individual areas by their respective service-unit weightings gives a total for the service units of the whole school. Suppose these come to 1,000—then if a classroom is out of action for a day, the unavailability deduction is the *pro rata* service fee for that day $\times 4 \div 1,000$.

In addition, the meaning of unavailability (which should be objective and clearly measurable) needs to be worked out with respect to each area, *e.g.* it may be decided that a school classroom will be unavailable if the heating is below a certain temperature (even if the pupils could theoretically wrap up warm and use the room). Thus, unavailability may include lack or inadequacy of:

- shelter from wind and rain;
- health and safety arrangements, or compliance with the law in other respects;

- heating, lighting, water or other utilities;
- key equipment, communications or IT infrastructure; and
- any other specific element required to keep the area in operation.

The PPP contract may also make provision for consequential unavailability so that even where a particular component itself meets the availability requirements, it is still deemed unavailable because another component to which it is linked is not deemed available (*e.g.* the hospital operating theatre is fully functional but the emergency back-up power source is not available).

There also has to be a reporting and recording system for determining when unavailability begins, and a remedy period before a payment deduction is made, which may be shorter for a critical area (perhaps less than an hour) than for a normal area (say, half a day), although performance points (see below) may still accrue during this period. However, if the matter is not remedied in this period, unavailability will be measured from the beginning of the problem. In some contracts, there may be an initial grace period at the start of the operational phase during which there is some relief from payment deductions, although the manner in which this applies varies either by the amount and/or scope of the relief. Or full deductions may be applied but they do not trigger early termination (*cf.* §17.2).

It is possible to turn this calculation the other way around—*i.e.* the project company is paid for the number of weighted service units available (which is the normal approach in a BOT contract for process plant), rather than having sums deducted from the PPP contracts for those service units that are unavailable. But this means that there cannot be a system of 'ratcheting' (or 'multiplying') unavailability deductions over 100%, often used to strengthen the incentive for the project company to perform, *i.e.* the payment for the service area may be $100, and so the deduction may be $100 for the first period of unavailability, but then it could increase to say $120, putting more pressure on the project company and its FM subcontract or (to whom these deductions would be passed) to remedy the problem.

There may be situations when a space or service is unavailable as defined in the PPP contract, but the contracting authority still wants to use it ('unavailable but used'). Obviously, if this use prevents the project company remedying the problem, there should not be a full payment deduction; this situation can be dealt with either by a lower rate of unavailability deduction or by accruing performance points instead.

Scheduled maintenance, which should be set out in the PPP contract, does not make the facility unavailable. The scheduling should of course fit the contracting authority's routine, *e.g.* a school should be maintained during the holidays or at weekends. However, unscheduled maintenance does make the space unavailable.

The proportionality of payment deductions may have an impact on the Eurostat balance-sheet treatment, which requires there to be genuine risk transfer to the project company. So, zero availability should mean zero payment over a meaningful period of time if the project is not otherwise to be classified as on the government balance sheet.

It should be noted, however, that in process-plant PPP projects such as municipal waste incinerators, payment is usually made based on the volume processed (*e.g.* a 'gate fee' per tonne of waste) on a 'deliver or pay' basis, *i.e.* if the contracting authority does not deliver a minimum volume of waste for processing it must still make a minimum payment similar to a capacity charge.[7] Even if a waste-processing facility is not available it usually still has to take the contracting authority's waste and make alternative arrangements for disposing of it, since the contracting authority may not be able to do so. (The extra cost involved would be covered by 'increased cost of working' insurance if the reason for unavailability is an insurable loss (*cf.* §14.4).)

§15.6.2 Service Quality

Quality of service is not a matter of great concern in a process-plant project: it is a fairly black-and-white issue whether a power plant works or not. If it works badly, it will not produce the level of power required, and so this failure will be caught under the capacity/availability payment provisions. Again, this question is more complex in an availability PPP, depending on the nature of the facility being provided. Broadly speaking, unavailability deductions relate to critical failures to provide what is intended under the PPP contract, while all other failures under the PPP contract relate to service quality. Also, availability measures should be objective, whereas some service measures may be subjective.

Service (which in this context includes routine maintenance) is often provided under an FM (or O&M) subcontract, and FM contractors are not prepared to suffer deductions or penalties that are out of scale with the (limited) fees that they charge for their work (*cf.* §15.6.7). Thus, any payment-deduction régime that penalises poor service quality generally is again likely to be limited, but at the same time there have to be sanctions for persistent poor service.

A typical approach to measurement of service quality is to create a matrix of 'key performance indicators' (KPIs) setting out the requirement for each service. For example, in a road project, performance may measure, *inter alia*, the quality of lighting, cleaning of the road surface, replacement of broken signage or more fundamental measures such as the speed of the traffic (an indication of how well traffic flow is being managed) and the number of accidents (an indication of how safely the road is being operated). Indeed, the latter cases may be dealt with under the availability heading, which illustrates the difficulty of drawing a precise borderline between availability and service quality.

KPIs may have to be very detailed—*e.g.* it may not be enough to say a room must be 'clean', the meaning of 'clean' may need to be defined too (and the definition will be different as between, say, a hospital ward and a school classroom)—and clearly FM subcontractors will interpret incomplete or ambiguous project-contract requirements to their advantage. The problem about this is that the more detailed the specification becomes, the more it becomes an input rather an output specification (*cf.* §15.2), and the more likely it is that some element of the specification will get lost in the detail.

Having established the KPIs, these are again weighted according to the importance of the service. Quality of service may be measured objectively, *e.g.* by speed of traffic, numbers of accidents or time of response to problems—one hour within which to remove a

---

[7] An alternative structure is for the contracting authority to agree that it will deliver all its household waste to the facility, meaning that the project company is left with the risk that the volume is less than projected. (However, this risk can be mitigated by taking in waste from other sources.)

broken-down vehicle once the project company is aware of it—or more subjectively, *e.g.* by inspection, or feedback from users of the service. Measurement of performance can be complex, and may depend to a considerable extent on records maintained by the project company if there is not to be a substantial extra monitoring cost for the contracting authority (*cf.* §19.4.1). Poor service often incurs 'performance points' based on the KPI weightings, rather than an immediate deduction from the service fee as for unavailability. There is often a 'ratcheting' mechanism whereby:

- More performance points may be imposed, *pro rata*, the longer the problem persists or the more frequently it occurs;
- Accumulation of a certain level of performance points within an agreed period eventually leads to a service-fee payment deduction; and
- If this accumulation passes a very high level such that there is a persistent failure of service, the PPP contract may be terminated (*cf.* §17.2).

The project company should not be penalised for unavailability and then incur performance points in relation to the same issue. The primary aim is to ensure availability and therefore these provisions take precedence.

One issue with this approach is the need to incentivise the project company to offer improvements in service, not just to operate to avoid payment deductions: the possibility of bonuses in some circumstances should therefore also be considered where better performance is self-funding in some way, or is sustainable within the contracting authority's budget. For example, in a road project an extra payment can be made for safety standards above the average for the contracting authority's whole road portfolio. Some account may also have to be taken of excess usage leading to higher maintenance costs (*cf.* §13.6). It is surprising however to find that, even for more straightforward projects such as roads, that there is still, after a number of years, a wide variety of approaches to developing KPIs across different contracting authorities. It is also quite common to find in less mature markets or in new sectors a tendency to have too many KPIs, which makes the management of the contract more complex than it needs to be, or may reduce focus on the performance criteria that really matter. In designing KPIs, it is useful to remember the adage 'measure less but measure well'.

§15.6.3 Calibration

'Calibration' refers to setting of unavailability or performance deductions that sufficiently incentivise the project company to perform and avoid the contracting authority paying proportionally more for the level of service. At the same time, calibration must avoid being excessively severe or unreasonably difficult for the project company to comply with. Developing the right level of unavailability or performance deductions is one of the more challenging aspects in preparing the PPP contract and it is not uncommon to find that the level of deductions is too small to drive performance. This is where experienced transaction advisers and those with contract-management experience can make a difference.

Examples of poor calibration include payment deductions that are too low to have any effect on performance (but *cf.* §15.6.7), setting caps to the level of deductions that are at a significantly lower level than the availability payment (so that the project company is always paid even if there is no availability), long lists of exclusions under which deductions will not be applied and deductions assessed relatively unfrequently (*e.g.* only annually) even though the service fee is paid monthly. Sometimes the deductions are only applied to a percentage of the availability fee in any month (*e.g.* 5% in the case of an accommodation PPP), to ensure some minimum level of cash flow for the project company (but often with any deductions that exceed the percentage carried forward to the following month).

There is also often a period (say the first six months) at the start of the operation phase when the full payment-deduction regime is not applied in order to allow the project company to reach its optimal performance. This may be the case where there are complex interfaces between the project and other activities that need time to settle down (but *cf.* §19.4.1).

Service-fee payments are typically invoiced monthly (or sometimes quarterly) by the project company—they may be invoiced at the end of the month with adjustments for any deductions in that month, or at the start of the month with adjustments for deductions from the previous month. (Alternatively, the contracting authority may make the deductions from the invoice.) Sometimes performance (as opposed to availability) deductions may be treated separately, say with the adjustment for any performance related deductions over the previous six months.

§15.6.4 Operational Gearing

Lenders may be concerned about the 'operational gearing' of an availability-PPP service mechanism, *i.e.* a project that is 'service heavy' (*cf.* §7.3.1). This looks at the ratio between the proportion of the service fees that is needed to repay debt and provide the equity return *versus* the proportion required to cover opex. Opex includes its own profit margin, and this profit margin also provides part of the lenders' cash-flow 'cushion' to ensure their debt service is paid (*i.e.* the cover ratios—*cf.* §23.3). But the operating margin is susceptible to deductions for unavailability or poor service, meaning that the lenders' cash-flow cover is more vulnerable if the proportion of service fees covering opex is especially high. In a typical availability PPP, the ratio between fixed costs (covering debt service and equity return) and variable costs (for opex) may be about 60:40 (*cf.* §24.3.5). So, if this ratio works out at say 50:50, lenders will be more concerned to ensure that unavailability or performance deductions from the service fees do not potentially eat up too much of their cash-flow cushion, *i.e.* they may want to reduce the maximum potential deductions, which may affect the overall calibration of such deductions. Similar concerns may be shared by financial investors (*i.e.* those not involved in the subcontracts).

§15.6.5 Unitary Nature of Payment

As mentioned in §2.4.7, the service fee comprises a single unitary charge or payment for a service. It is not a collection of payments for a bundle of different services or their different underlying costs (such as debt service). Equally, it cannot be split into different elements reflecting either availability and/or performance of the service. This would undermine the whole performance-payment mechanism as well as potentially destroy the performance incentives for one of the private-sector parties, *e.g.* the financiers if they are always entitled to their share of the service fee. After all one does not pay half the dry-cleaning bill (and pay that half to the cleaning company's lenders) if only half one's clothes are returned. Hence the word 'unitary'.

For a similar reason, it is generally not a good idea to vary (or sculpt) the unitary charge to changes in costs (*cf.* §15.3.2).

§15.6.6 Indexation of Service Fees

The service-fee mechanism also usually adjusts a proportion of the service fee for inflation. This issue is discussed in §24.3.

§15.6.7 Value Testing

As discussed in §13.6, two types of service may be included within the scope of a PPP contract for a building such as a school or hospital—hard FM, *i.e.* routine, major or life-cycle maintenance of buildings and equipment, and soft FM, *e.g.* cleaning, catering, security, *etc.* Hard FM is an inherent part of a PPP contract, since its whole basis is the provision of the facility in 'working order' throughout its tenor.

The provision of soft-FM services is less intrinsically embedded in a PPP contract. The arguments for including soft FM are:

- Bidders will take account of soft-FM requirements when bidding for and designing the facility (*cf.* §28.8).
- It removes the interface risk (*cf.* §13.9, §28.9.3)—*e.g.* the project company will not have the excuse that a failure of availability was actually caused by soft-FM providers not involved in the PPP contract.
- It gives the contracting authority a one-stop point of contact for all service issues on the facility.

Balanced against this:

- The level of payment deductions that can be made for poor service is limited, since the level of fees paid for soft services is such that the soft-FM subcontractor cannot realistically be expected to take on responsibility for disproportionate financial consequences for failure to perform (*cf.* §15.6.2).
- The soft-FM services are the point at which the facility interfaces with the users and general public: failure has a disproportionate effect on support for PPP projects in general.
- These services also tend to employ the most staff, and therefore raise the most difficult issues relating to transfers of staff from the public sector (*cf.* §28.13).
- The contracting authority's soft-service requirements may change substantially over the life of a PPP contract, and therefore a very long-term soft-FM subcontract is too rigid for this purpose.

- Soft-FM service providers are reluctant to sign very long-term subcontracts because of the difficulty of predicting their own costs.
- If there are provisions for value testing (see below), these really divorce the soft-FM subcontract from the rest of the PPP contract and further weaken the case for its inclusion.
- The contracting authority may already have its own internal- or external-contracted arrangements to provide soft services in its existing facilities, so a new arrangement for a single project may be inherently less efficient.

Exclusion of soft-FM services from the PPP contract does not mean that they cannot be provided by the private sector, as they can still be provided under an entirely separate contract on an outsourced basis (*cf.* §2.3-§2.5). If soft FM is not included, specifying service quality is likely to be less complex, since it will relate primarily to maintenance. So, where a relatively straightforward building project is involved, the case for including soft-FM services within the scope of a PPP contract needs to be carefully considered as the contracting authority may benefit from the greater flexibility of dealing separately with these services (especially if it already has arrangements in place for other similar facilities). But if the facility is complex, then there may be benefits in transferring the soft-FM interface risk to the private sector.

If soft-FM services are included, availability PPPs usually have provisions to rebase this element of the service fee periodically (usually every five years) by 'value testing'. This either involves obliging the project company to re-bid the services ('market testing'), which may lead to a change of the relevant subcontractor. Or to compare and re-align costs and performance with a sample of other current providers in the market ('benchmarking') but that would not lead to a change in subcontractor. These are usually service components whose delivery costs may improve with technology over time or where a large labour cost component means that it is expensive to get the project company to commit to such costs over the life of the PPP contract.

Market testing, as it involves the project company putting the services concerned out to tender, is generally more representative of cost changes than benchmarking, while benchmarking requires a mature market to provide comparable costs. However, it may not be practical to switch the specific service provider if the service component in question is intimately linked with the provision of other services. The two processes may also be combined, *e.g.* if the benchmarking process is inconclusive it can be followed by market testing.

Value testing does not necessarily lead to a reduction in the service fee and therefore cost savings for the contracting authority; it may lead to service-fee increases. Any adjustments to the service fee usually relate to the next value-testing period and may only apply if the prevailing rate is higher or lower than a specified band or threshold. Value testing can also be used as a process to price the cost of any contract changes required by the contracting authority (*cf.* §19.4.3).

§15.6.8 Dealing with Subcontractors

It is not the contracting authority's rôle to intervene with subcontractors, either to direct how they can improve the service, or to suggest their replacement: this is an inherent part of the project company's management rôle; the contracting authority has to rely on the PPP contract as a basis for enforcing its requirements (*cf.* §19.3.1).

The contracting authority generally does not have any control over changes to the terms of the subcontracts except where:

- they relate to provisions that have a direct effect on the contracting authority's own risks or liabilities (*cf.* §10.8.2); and
- they are linked to changes in the PPP contract itself (*cf.* §16.2.2).

The project company (or its lenders) may wish to deal with poor service by replacing the relevant FM subcontractor (although the number of times such a replacement is allowed should be limited). In such cases, it could be argued that there has to be a system for wiping out accumulated performance points, as otherwise the new subcontractor has no room for manœuvre before running into default. This may be dealt with by creating stricter triggers for termination in the FM subcontract than in the PPP contract. However, if a large number of performance points have accumulated, or there is a limited pool of prospective FM subcontractors, it may be necessary to reset the clock.

As the contracting authority would originally have approved the main subcontractors (*cf.* §10.8.2), it is reasonable for it to have a right of approving replacements, using similar criteria as to financial and technical capacity to those used at the time of the original procurement.

The contracting authority usually has the right to take over the subcontracts if it steps-in to take control of the facility or the PPP contract is terminated for default by the project company (*cf.* §17.6).

§15.6.9 Other Performance Measurements

It is possible to go beyond FM-based measures of performance in some circumstances, ideally measuring performance outcomes rather than outputs (*cf.* §15.2). For example, in a school project, the quality of the school buildings and the services provided should have some effect on the educational results which the school can achieve. Therefore, a payment deduction could be made if, say, measurable results (such as examination grades) do not improve by a certain percentage. However, it is evident that the project company only has a limited ability to influence such matters, and therefore deductions could only relate to a small proportion of the total payments receivable.

§15.7 MIXED USAGE AND AVAILABILITY PAYMENTS

Especially in transport projects, a mixed base of service fees is sometimes used:

- availability payments that are adequate to cover opex and debt service; and
- a demand-based service fee (or a toll), that is linked to usage, and provides the equity return.

As with any case where usage risk is not wholly transferred (*cf.* §15.5.2), there should be a cap on the demand-based payments under this structure. Other examples include projects where a particular demand-based service can be separated from the availability of the facility (*e.g.* in a school where demand-based payments in relation to school meals are made in addition to availability payments for the school facility).

§15.8 Third-Party and Secondary Revenues

Under some availability PPPs (*e.g.* accommodation projects), the project company may be allowed to earn additional revenues by making the facility available to third parties— *e.g.* a school hall may be hired out in the evenings for private functions.

Similarly, in a concession, the project company may be given the right to generate secondary revenues from the facility, for example the right to develop petrol stations, restaurants and lodging facilities on land adjacent to a concession road. (In such cases, investors may be reluctant to return such development to the contracting authority at the end of the concession, and hence will require a permanent—or much longer-term—right to exploit secondary developments.)

Third-party or secondary revenues may help to reduce the service fees, but normally lenders do not take such revenues into account in financial projections unless there is a high degree of certainty that they will occur. This means that the contracting authority may not in fact get the benefit of third-party revenues in the initial bid pricing. If third-party or secondary revenues are not taken into account in the bid pricing, these are often split between the contracting authority and the project company as and when they occur.

Third-party revenues are more significant in some sectors, *e.g.* waste-processing PPPs. Here there are several possible sources of third-party revenues, such as sale of electricity from a waste-to-energy incinerator, using excess plant capacity to process third-party waste, and sale of recycled materials (*e.g.* metals, paper, *etc.*). Some floor for such revenues, which can be used to reduce the service fees, may be guaranteed by the sponsors (*cf.* §22.8). These are built into the financial projections and hence taken into account by lenders. Also, if there is a free market, especially in the case of electricity, lenders may be prepared to assume a minimum sale price without a sponsor guarantee and again take this into account in their banking case (*cf.* §23.9.9).

16

Changes in Circumstances

§16.1 INTRODUCTION

This chapter deals with some of the key changes in circumstances after financial close which can affect the rights of either party to the PPP contract, namely:

- *Compensation events*, *i.e.* cases where there is a delay in completion, or increase in capex or opex for which the contracting authority has agreed to compensate the project company (§16.2)[1];
- *Excusing causes*, *i.e.* actions taken by the project company that affect its performance under the PPP contract but that do not result in any service-fee deductions by the contracting authority (§16.3); and
- *Relief events* (also known as 'temporary *force majeure*'), *i.e.* events outside the control of both the project company and the contracting authority resulting in a delay in completion of the facility, or failure to meet performance requirements after completion; in these cases, the contracting authority still has the right to make any payment deductions under the PPP contract (*cf.* §15.6.1, §15.6.2), but not to terminate it for default by the project company (§16.4).

Along with the service-fee mechanism (*cf.* Chapter 15), and the termination provisions of the PPP contract (*cf.* Chapter 17), the topics in this chapter are the key finance-related aspects of the PPP contract, *i.e.* the aspects to which lenders pay the most attention.

It should be noted that although in common-law countries, provisions covering changes and termination are set out in the PPP contract, in civil-law countries, many of them may

---

[1] The separate subject of payment of compensation by the contracting authority on early termination of the PPP contract is dealt with in Chapter 17.

be automatically implied by concession or PPP laws, or general public administrative law, and hence not set out in the PPP contract.

§16.2 COMPENSATION EVENTS

Compensation events, that cause a loss or cost to the project company, and give it the right to claim compensation from the contracting authority, usually fall into the following categories:

- change in PPP-contract specifications by the contracting authority ('contract changes');[2]
- failure by the contracting authority to carry out an action for which it is responsible, such as giving site access to the project company (*cf.* §12.2.6), which causes a loss to the project company;
- other specific risks that the contracting authority may assume on VfM grounds (*cf.* §11.4), again where these cause a loss to the project company;
- events not caused by the contracting authority's actions, but for which it takes on liability, such as unforeseeable site conditions, vandalism or protester action against the project (*cf.* §12.2); and
- change in law (§16.2.5).

In all of these cases, compensation-event provisions in the PPP contract may be mirrored in the relevant subcontract, or to turn it a round the other way, the project company may push for a particular item to be classified as a compensation event under the PPP contract because the relevant subcontractor insists on it being considered this way in the subcontract. As with other aspects of risk transfer, there is a price for anything, and the issue for the contracting authority is therefore whether it is better VfM to cover a particular risk as a compensation event, or get the risk transferred to and priced into the relevant subcontract (either as a relief event or with full risk transfer to the subcontractor) and thus fed through into the service fees (*cf.* §11.4).

§16.2.1 Economic Balance

The general principle in cases where the contracting authority is responsible for compensation events is that of 'economic balance'[3]—*i.e.* a level of compensation is required to put the project company, and thus its investors and lenders, in a position no better and no worse than it would otherwise have been had the compensation event not occurred.

If the compensation event only affects opex, the cost of this can be covered by a corresponding increase in the service fees. In concessions, the costs may sometimes be passed on to end users (so they pay for the consequence of the event and not the contracting

---

[2] Also known as 'contract variations'.

[3] Also known as 'economic and financial balance'.

authority); failing which, the contracting authority will have to pay them as they occur.[4] However, the change in opex may also imply some change in the risks involved in the project, which may be more difficult to quantify.

Where an increase in or additional capex is involved, the easiest and most economic approach is usually for the capex involved to be funded directly by the contracting authority, but of course there may not be a budget for this (and it can raise risk issues—*cf.* §18.6.1). If this is the case, the contracting authority may wish the project company to raise finance (which may be a mixture of new equity and debt), against compensation by way of an increase in the service fees. However, it is very difficult to impose a requirement to finance the capex on the project company: its own financial resources are limited to the existing capex requirements for the facility, and cannot be used for additional purposes. Existing lenders may agree to increase their loan, but they are also in a monopoly-supplier position, compounded by the fact that lenders cannot be forced to admit a new lender to share in their security (*cf.* §25.5).[5] It is unlikely to be economic to replace the whole of the original loan with an increased loan which both prepays the original loan and covers the new capex, so competitive bidding for financing the new capex is usually not realistic.

If the project company does finance the capex, the required increase in the service fees is normally calculated using the financial model such that the lenders' cover ratios (*cf.* §23.3) and the equity IRR (*cf.* §20.3.3) remain as in the original base case (*cf.* §23.9.9). However, there is an argument for the equity IRR reflecting the current rate of return on an investment of comparable risk: this may be more favourable to the contracting authority as the equity IRR for a mature project will be lower (*cf.* §20.3.3). There are also some problems in using the financial model for this calculation:

- The financial model was not originally designed for this purpose, and the parties may find it difficult to agree how it should be done (including both changes in assumptions and in the structure of the financial model); this cannot easily be provided for in advance in the PPP contract.
- Calculations must relate only to the cost increase: it is important to avoid being caught in the trap of calculating adjustments to the service fees based on the *total* cash flow, as opposed to the *marginal* change, as this would underwrite the lenders' risk and investors' return on the whole project.

A simpler approach for the contracting authority is to agree a supplementary service fee calculated to repay the financing for the marginal capex—*e.g.* on an annuity basis over the remaining tenor of the PPP contract—rather than trying to mix these with the overall financial model. However, care must be taken to check if this may change the balance-sheet treatment of the PPP project.

---

[4] If the project company has the right to increase user charges, this can be the means by which it is compensated and so the contracting authority is not responsible for the risk.

[5] The one exception to this, and an area in which, unusually, bonds may be more flexible than bank loans (*cf.* §22.5), is that 'variation bonds'—*i.e.* undrawn bonds which can be issued at a later date to pay for future capex, subject to certain conditions—can be included as part of an initial bond issue, albeit the pricing of these bonds will be affected by market conditions when they are issued.

Yet another alternative is for the PPP contract tenor to be extended (this can also apply where there is an increase in opex), which may be more 'painless' if it means that service fees do not need to be increased. This can seldom be provided for in advance, however, and would need to be specifically negotiated at the time as an alteration to the PPP contract.

A compensation event during the construction phase may not only involve additional capex, but also delay completion. Obviously, the project company should not be penalised for this (such as being required to pay LDs—*cf.* §15.4.1), and moreover compensation needs to be paid by the contracting authority for any loss of revenue.

How should delay that leads to a loss of revenue to the project company for the period of the delay be compensated? This depends on whether the PPP contract has an overall fixed tenor or a fixed tenor of operations (*cf.* §15.4.1). In the case of the former, the amount of compensation should be the service fee that would have been payable over the delay period less any opex costs the project company would not have had to pay. In the case of the latter, there is no revenue loss but the revenue shifts in time, and the project company should be compensated for costs or losses that arise as a result of this (*e.g.* additional finance costs or loss of equity returns).

In some countries, the concept of economic balance and hence the compensation-event mechanism is dealt with through the provisions of public (administrative) law. This is common, for example, in Latin-American countries. Public-law provisions are usually not very specific on how to restore economic balance and so it is left to the interpretation of the courts. In most cases, the courts have defined this quite narrowly (especially during the construction phase) and limited any award to the extent to which the project company's *financial* position is affected. This lack of clear definition makes it harder to develop a comprehensive risk register. It also means having to understand the provisions and application of local law, which can be an issue for non-domestic lenders, investors and contractors. As a result, over time, it has become increasingly common to define in the PPP contract itself the circumstances in which the project company can be compensated when a defined risk occurs and how the level of compensation is determined, *i.e.* the methodology to rebalance the PPP contract. While the project company cannot waive its rights of claim under public law, in practice the courts tend to follow the provisions of the PPP contract.

§16.2.2 Contract Changes

The contracting authority needs to have some flexibility to make changes in the specifications for the facility or the service to be provided under the PPP contract (*cf.* §19.4.3). It is evident that the project company should be properly compensated for such changes. Financing contract changes that involve capex is also an issue, since the project company will have little, if any reserve, for this purpose. Changes to the PPP contract also usually require the lenders' consent, as discussed further below.

Small changes in the detailed operation of the project that have limited effects on the service requirements of the PPP contract are the most common in occurrence, and should be easily dealt with—an annual and item-size limit can be agreed for such contract changes, and the contracting authority can just pay for the extra cost, be it capex or opex, as it occurs. The monopoly-supplier problem—*e.g.* the project company over-charging for, say, installing a new light fitment—may be overcome by agreeing general time and cost-plus rates at the time of the bid, for such cases. Thus, it should be not difficult for both sides to agree a quick and simple procedure for these minor contract changes. It is best to avoid such small contract changes requiring the consent of lenders, as this is a costly and time-consuming exercise, *e.g.* by delegation to approve changes below a certain value to the lenders' technical adviser or the agent bank (*cf.* §22.2.10).

Medium-size contract changes may be more difficult to pre-price, but it may still be possible to agree a framework of costs covering, for example, professional fees and an agreed profit margin.

Major contract changes, however, that require substantial additional capex or a significant change in the service provisions or opex, may raise risk issues, as well as issues on economic balance, and also procurement issues (discussed below). Taken together, these can have a serious effect on the long-term flexibility of PPP contracts (*cf.* §28.12).

As to risk, there must be some limitations on the scope of contract changes:

- The contract changes should not be so great as to alter the fundamental nature of the PPP contract. For example, a contract change that added over 50% to the construction cost would obviously be out of scale. Therefore, there has to be some overall limitation on contract changes if this not already limited by public-sector procurement regulations—*cf.* §16.2.3: 10% of the project value is a common limit in PPP contracts. Similarly, a facility cannot be halved in size, or a prison turned into a hospital.
- The changes cannot increase the risks undertaken by the project company under the PPP contract, *e.g.* by interfering with its ability to provide the services required, or by requiring them to be performed in such a way that operating permits may be invalidated.

It is possible that a contract change will save money rather than cost more. If so, this can be adjusted through the service fees, but the provisos above as to not changing the fundamental nature of the project, or its risks, apply here too. The savings in such cases may be retained by the contracting authority, or split with the project company, to encourage cooperation by the latter.

A 'change protocol' agreed as part of the PPP contract can set out ground rules for managing a change, such as minimum notice periods for a request for a contract change, the basis upon which a request for a contract change can be refused (*e.g.* if this could lead to a previously-granted consent being withdrawn) and how the contracting authority will fund or compensate for a contract change it requests. The PPP contract usually requires the project company to bear the cost of processing a contract change: the project company does not charge a separate fee for such processing as it is a routine part of the service (as opposed to the cost of the contract change itself), unless the contract change is particularly complex or the project company is required to assume additional risks (such as subcontractor insolvency risk—*cf.* §16.2.5).

A contract change may require re-calibration of the service fee (*cf.* §15.6.3). For this reason, it is better to group small-value changes together if at all possible for the purposes of updating the financial model (*cf.* §23.8). The PPP contract should allow the contracting authority to have access to agreed cost information and oblige the project company to keep full records of costs so that the former can understand the change in underlying costs involved in providing the service. If a service is transferred back to the contracting authority, the contracting authority also needs to assess any additional interface risks that it is taking on, the costs of which may outweigh the benefits of such a contract change in the first place. Those providing insurance for the project may also need to be notified.

The project company may also propose contract changes: this usually results in a saving in opex, with the benefit being split between the contracting authority and the project company. The contracting authority's share of any such contract change is normally reflected in a reduced service fee. The contracting authority usually has an absolute right to reject contract changes proposed by the project company.

§16.2.3 Contract Changes and the Lenders

It should be borne in mind that lenders usually have *de facto* control over major changes in the PPP contract. Even though there is usually nothing in the PPP contract that says this, the loan agreement will specify that no changes to the PPP contract (other than minor ones) can be agreed by the project company without the consent of the lenders (*cf.* §25.3.1).

Lenders start from the position that 'change means risk'; moreover, contract changes are unlikely to benefit them in any way, and in fact involve them in extra work getting the necessary credit approval. This means that lenders are unlikely even to consider changes without payment of a one-off fee (as well as coverage of their legal and technical advisers' costs), and even then, they do not want to keep receiving numerous requests for changes. If possible, changes should therefore be bundled together so the lenders can deal with all of them at once. Some lenders may simply not want to be bothered to process an approval for the changes, so if a majority vote is needed it may not be easy to get it. From the contracting authority's (and the lenders' agent's[6]) point of view, the best way of dealing with this is to have a 'you snooze you lose' clause in the loan agreement, meaning that if a change requires, say, 75% consent, this is 75% of the lenders actually voting, not 75% of all the lenders (*cf.* §25.5).

§16.2.4 Contract Changes and Procurement

If major capex is required as a result of a compensation event, this may raise procurement-law issues, and hence require competitive bidding. Even if this is not the case, procurement in such situations is a complex matter, as it is difficult to break away from the monopoly-supplier position of the project company and its subcontractors. The contracting authority can be given the right to benchmark costs by checking them in the market, if this is possible—but often comparable cost data cannot be obtained, and again there are discrepancies of information between the contracting authority and the project company, the latter being much better informed (*cf.* §28.9.9). Similarly, even if the

---

[6] *Cf.* §22.2.10.

contracting authority has the right to require the project company to procure through a competitive bidding procedure, this may not be very easy:

- If the project company's main contender for the work is one of its own shareholders, and an existing subcontractor, it will have inside knowledge, and an inherent advantage that will mean that other suppliers may be reluctant to bid.
- This reluctance on the part of other bidders will be enhanced if the existing subcontractor has a 'right to match' any bids received.
- It may not be possible for the work to be undertaken by a third party because this would invalidate the liabilities of the existing subcontractor, *e.g.* warranties under a construction subcontract (*cf.* §12.6).

EU procurement directives have provided some clarity on the right of contracting authorities to make changes without the need for re-bidding. For example, cumulative changes below 10% of the value of the contract are permitted. Equally changes that are necessary as a result of unforeseen circumstances are permitted, provided each change is no greater than 50% of the value of the original contract (and these must not change the overall nature of the contract). The same limit applies where additional works or services are required and a change of contractor would cause significant inconvenience or cost duplication for the authority. Similarly, changes as a result of restructuring or replacing the project company if it becomes insolvent are permitted. A contracting authority can also give itself more flexibility if potential changes are already identified in the initial procurement documents and provided for in a review clause in the contract that is 'clear, precise and unequivocal'. There must also be specified upper limits (value or duration) to the potential change.

§16.2.5 Contracting Authority's Risks

As has been seen, the contracting authority may be responsible under the PPP contract for certain aspects of the project risks during construction, especially related to the site (*cf.* §12.2). If such risks cause delay in completion or additional capex, the contracting authority must compensate for loss of revenue or extra costs. Such compensation should normally be paid direct by the contracting authority rather than by adjusting the service fees or expecting the project company to obtain extra financing (although if the project company is able and willing to finance the costs on the same basis as for a contract change, this is an alternative). Delay LDs (*cf.* §15.4.1) are obviously not payable by the project company in such circumstances. Similarly, the contracting authority may take on liabilities, *e.g.* to construct a connecting road, or a grid connection to a power station, and again if this is not done, the contracting authority has to compensate the project company for losses of revenue.

The contracting authority may also have continuing liabilities during the operating phase, for example relating to damage to the facility caused by its own staff, or persons for whom it is responsible, such as pupils at a school.

More complex changes in circumstances can affect some projects, especially where demand-risk transfer is involved—*e.g.* a decision to build a new road that affects an existing concession, where the project company would expect to be compensated for loss of revenue (*cf.* §13.3). But this loss may be difficult to isolate and measure with certainty. If the connection with the change in circumstance is less direct—*e.g.* an increase in fuel taxes reducing traffic in general—it becomes even more difficult to decide what compensation, if any, is reasonable. If it is agreed that such risks should be covered by the contracting authority, increases in tolls or an extension of the PPP contract tenor may be used to compensate the project company for loss, rather than direct compensation payments by the contracting authority, but this usually has to be negotiated on an *ad hoc* basis given the difficulty of providing for all eventualities in advance. This problem of providing for policy changes is another reason why transfer of demand risk to the private sector is often not appropriate (*cf.* §13.2).

§16.2.6 Change in Law

As a matter of basic public policy, a government generally cannot contractually fetter the right of its successors to change the law, and therefore provisions giving any protection of this kind are unlikely to be found in a PPP contract. However, a contracting authority can agree in the PPP contract that if the law is changed in a way that is detrimental to the project company or its investors, they will be compensated accordingly.

A change in law may be directly-related to the PPP project, *e.g.* by requiring a reduction in emissions from a waste incinerator, and hence additional capex, or a new safety requirement for the facility, which results in additional opex. Alternatively, the change in law may be of a more general nature, but still affect the project company, *e.g.* a change in corporate tax rates, or in requirements for pension provision for employees. The project company may have insufficient cash flow or financial resources available to it to accommodate any such changes in law (and even if it has, the extra costs reduce the equity IRR and lender's cash-flow cover).

One extreme viewpoint here is that as the contracting authority is part of the public sector that changes the law, the contracting authority should always compensate for the effect of such a change. The other extreme is that the project company is no different from any other company doing business in the country concerned, and should not be shielded from the business risks to which all other companies are subject; moreover, the particular contracting authority may have no influence at all over changes in the law. The typical PPP change in law risk transfer falls between these two extremes. At the more generous end for the project company, some PPP contracts provide for compensation for any changes in the law that were 'unforeseeable' by the private sector at the time of the bid (although the definition of what is and is not 'unforeseeable' varies). This may also apply to PPP contracts governed by public law. In other cases, the right to compensation is more restricted:

- Costs resulting from changes in law that are specific to PPP project companies or PPP-provided facilities (or indeed the particular project company or facility) should also be covered by the contracting authority, since these are in effect discriminatory against PPPs.
- Costs resulting from changes in law that are specific to the type of facility being provided in the PPP project can either be passed on to end users, in a concession, or are

covered by the authority in an availability PPP project: the argument for this is that if the facility were being provided in the public sector, the same costs would then apply.

- Other more general changes in law that affect opex, such as changes in tax rates, should be a project-company risk, the argument for this being that these are general costs of doing business, and all investors and lenders face these risks. Inflation indexation of the service fees (*cf.* §24.3) provides some protection against such cost increases; in the case of concessions, these extra costs may be passed on to the end users if this is commercially sustainable (and allowed under the concession agreement).
- General changes in law that require capex (for example new fire-safety regulations that apply to a wide range of buildings, not just those in the relevant PPP sector) are more difficult, since the project company does not have the resources to pay for any major costs of this type. Lenders may wish the project company to establish a change in law reserve (*cf.* §25.2.4) to build up funds to meet any such change or pay commitment fees to ensure additional financing is available: this is really not an effective use of cash flow or fees, given that the change may never occur, and if it does there is likely to be plenty of warning, which gives time to build up funds from regular cash flow. These costs will be reflected in the service fee. A contracting authority may find it better VfM to agree an overall cap on the effect of a change in law in such cases, above which the risk transfers back to the contracting authority. Alternatively, the contracting authority may agree to fund $x\%$ of the capex cost of such a change in law (perhaps on a sliding scale, where the first $x\%$ of cost is funded 100% by the project company, the next $y\%$ funded 75% and so on). This ensures that the project company has an incentive to fund this capex at the most economic cost. Apart from VfM, the policy argument for such risk sharing is again that, if the contracting authority were to operate the facility itself, it would face the same capex costs.

Change in law is usually a compensation event, but in some countries, it may be dealt with under the provisions of public law dealing with economic balance (*cf.* §16.2.1).

In some countries, PPP contracts include a wider concept of 'material adverse government action', which gives a greater scope for compensation claims where the power of the state has been used in a way that affects the project company. This is also referred to as 'political *force majeure*'.

§16.3 Excusing Causes

Unlike relief events, discussed below, an excusing cause is an event that does not give the contracting authority the right to make deductions under the PPP contract even though the project company is not performing. Such events are usually very limited—they could include, for example, the project company having to cease operations while it makes a contract change requested by the contracting authority, or as a result of a change in law.

§16.4 RELIEF EVENTS

Relief events are those that affect the project company's performance for a period of time, but which the parties agree are not directly controllable by the project company (hence the alternative term 'temporary *force majeure*').[7] These events may either be itemised in the PPP contract or be more broadly defined in case law. No service fees are payable if the service is not being provided, availability/performance deductions may be made,[8] and the project company must suffer any other increased costs or revenue losses (but these should generally be covered by insurance—*cf.* Chapter 14). However, the contracting authority cannot terminate the PPP contract for default by the project company (*cf.* §17.2)—*i.e.* the latter is given relief from termination. The project company obviously has to take reasonable steps to deal with the problem to benefit from of the relief-event provisions.

In summary, relief events give the project company 'time' (to sort the problem out), whereas compensation events give the project company 'time and money', but it should be noted that relief events do not normally give an extension of time for the PPP contract as a whole, *i.e.* its final termination date is not extended. The principle behind a relief event is recognition that while the event is outside the control of the project company, it is best placed to manage it and mitigate its effect.

Examples of relief events include:

- insurable events such as fire, explosion, accidental damages, *etc.*;
- civil disturbance;
- strikes applying to an industry as a whole (rather than specific to the project or any of the subcontractors);
- failure by third parties to carry out or facilitate works (*cf.* §12.3.3); and
- failure in utility supplies.

The effects of some types of event (*e.g.* archæological discoveries during construction) may be split between a relief event (*i.e.* no payment) for the first layer (or period) of loss and a compensation event thereafter. The compensation-event payment in these cases may, for example, be limited to a payment above a certain threshold, or that amount required to service the senior debt only, or a percentage of the revenue that the project company would otherwise have received less any insurance amounts received. Although it is not usual to allow any extension of the overall tenor of the PPP contract because of a relief event, in some cases this may offer better VfM than making the event concerned a compensation event.

The dividing line between compensation events and relief events is not a firm one, and will be affected by the extent to which subcontractors are willing to take on these risks. A compromise position may be reached, whereby the project company, and hence its

---

[7] Permanent *force majeure* is a event that makes it permanently (rather than temporarily) impossible to continue with the project and in this case either party usually has the right to terminate the PPP contract after a defined period during which the *force majeure* event has persisted (*cf.* §17.4).

[8] This is not always the case. For example, in the Netherlands, an adjusted payment is made to cover debt service during the period.

subcontractors, take on the first layer of the risk as a relief event up to a certain amount, with the balance being treated as a compensation event. Insurance may also play a part here.

How compensation and relief events are treated in the PPP contract clearly has an impact on the allocation of risk which in turn can affect the balance-sheet treatment of the project. For example, Eurostat guidance (*cf.* §9.4.5), which is based on risk/reward balance and can be taken as a guide as to what a 'reasonable' balance might look like, requires that the contracting authority's exposure to risks should be well defined and finite. So, risks such as changes in macro-economic conditions should not be allocated to the contracting authority. The events giving rise to a compensation or relief event should not have been reasonably foreseeable or estimable. Also, any compensation is strictly limited to the effects of the event in question and after any amounts recoverable under the required insurance.

CHAPTER 17

Termination

§17.1 Introduction

This chapter deals with early termination of the PPP contract under various scenarios:

- default by the project company (§17.2);
- early termination by the contracting authority, or default by the contracting authority, which is generally treated in the same way (§17.3);
- termination for *force majeure*—*i.e.* through no fault of either party, it is impossible to continue with the PPP contract (§17.4); and
- termination for corruption (§17.5).

The position of subcontractors on early termination (§17.6) and taxation of early-termination payments (§17.7) are also discussed.

This chapter also covers the possible options at the end of the PPP contract term, and associated hand-back requirements (§17.8).

§17.2 Early Termination: Default by the Project Company

It is unusual for the project company to be placed in default, and hence for the PPP contract to be terminated early. Even if the equity investment has effectively been lost, it is still usually in the lenders' interests for the situation to be sorted out by other means, *e.g.* additional finance to keep the project going (*cf.* §26.2.4), and if necessary exercise their 'step-in' rights (which delay the final termination) to deal with any problems rather than lose control of the situation through a default under the PPP contract (*cf.* §25.3.3). But of course, the contracting authority needs to have the default gun available to 'encourage' the lenders to take action.

Events of default (EoDs) by the project company that give the contracting authority the right to terminate the PPP contract should only be of so fundamental a nature that the facility is really no longer delivering the service required. A short-term unavailability or failure to perform to the required standard can generally be dealt with by penalties or deductions (*cf.* §15.6.1, §15.6.2) rather than a termination. Events that come under the 'fundamental' heading may include (in some cases with thresholds for materiality and defined remedy periods):

- failure to construct the project or reach the service availability date by the agreed backstop date (*cf.* §15.4.1);
- failure to continue construction for prolonged periods of time ('abandonment');
- a drawstop (*cf.* §25.2.2) by the lenders during construction: this is to ensure that the contracting authority has a relatively early seat at the table if the project's construction is going seriously wrong, but making this an EoD may face lender resistance if the lenders want the ability to sort out the problem by themselves;
- non-payment of LDs or penalties (*cf.* §15.5.5), or other fees such as a concession fee (*cf.* §15.5.2);
- unavailability deductions (*cf.* §15.6.1) reach more than a certain percentage of the service fees over a period of x months;
- accumulated performance points exceed a trigger level (*cf.* §15.6.2);
- other minor breaches (that do not incur performance points) keep occurring and the problems have not been rectified despite warning notices from the contracting authority—this is known as 'persistent breach' (and is typically very difficult to negotiate and enforce);
- insolvency/bankruptcy of the project company;
- a change of ownership without consent of the contracting authority (*cf.* §20.6.4); and
- breach of any other 'fundamental' provisions of the PPP contract, *e.g.* not taking out insurance (*cf.* §14.7), or a major failure to maintain the health and safety of the users of the facility.

Setting out clear and objective EoDs is important to avoid disputes and encourage investor and lender interest.

If—as is commonly the case—the contracting authority is the legal owner of the facility, and the project company only has contractual rights, the argument could be made that if the project company defaults and the PPP contract is terminated, then the project company and its creditors should get nothing. After all, the PPP contract is about providing a long-term service, and if the service is not provided, surely it is the contracting authority which should be compensated not the project company?

In the early British PFI road projects, payment of no 'termination sum', as such a payment on early termination is known,[1] was standard; this was based on the view, discussed above, that there would never be a default leading to termination and therefore setting a

---

[1] 'CompOnTerm' (= compensation on termination), is also used.

termination sum served no purpose. While there is logic in this, lenders are—not surprisingly—uneasy about this approach, and payment of a termination sum is more normal. Clearly a facility has been built, though perhaps not to the required standard, and it has a value. It would therefore be unreasonable for the contracting authority to have even a theoretical right to get a windfall gain by getting an asset for which it has paid nothing, although if the contracting authority chose not to take over the facility (cf. §17.8), there would be no reason for a termination-sum payment. (Similarly, in private-sector projects such as under a PPA, the power off-taker often only pays a termination sum if it opts to acquire the plant—and it is not obliged to do so.) This is not an aspect of the PPP contract that concerns investors too much, as the assumption can reasonably be made that if the project goes wrong to the extent of being placed in default, the value of the equity investment will have already been destroyed.

The contracting authority may also object to paying a termination sum for the simple reason that it will not have a budget for doing so. This problem can be alleviated by making the payment in instalments over the remaining life of the PPP contract (or removed altogether by the open-market sale alternative discussed later). Lenders should not object to payment by instalments, as rather than a high risk on the project company, they will then have a low risk on the contracting authority—indeed there is a case for interest on the deferred payments being at a lower credit margin than that being paid by the project company to reflect this reduction in risk.

There are several possible methods of calculating a project-company default termination sum:

- repayment of outstanding debt (§17.2.1);
- depreciated cost of assets (§17.2.2);
- estimated fair-market value (§17.2.3);
- adjusted base-case calculation (§17.2.4); or
- open-market sale through an auction of the PPP contract (§17.2.5)—here the contracting authority does not have to pay the termination sum: the buyer of the PPP contract will do so.

Any such payments (other than in an auction) may be liable to a cap and floor, i.e. an upper or lower limit (§17.2.6), and hybrids of some of the above can also be used (§17.2.7). Also, a different approach may be taken for default during the construction phase (§17.2.8).

As mentioned above, termination is primarily an issue for the lenders rather than the investors in the project company. There will inevitably have been a default in their loan as well as the PPP contract (cf. §25.4), the equity investment will probably have been lost anyway, and so the lenders are in charge doing their best to recover as much of their loan as possible (cf. §25.3). Realistically, payment of a termination sum is likely to be a matter for negotiation between the parties as the alternative is probably a prolonged legal dispute (§17.2.9).

In all cases but open-market sale, the value of any reserve accounts (cf. §25.2.4) or other security held by lenders (e.g. sponsor guarantees or undrawn equity) should usually be deducted from the payment. The contracting authority may also deduct its costs in dealing with the termination, including the cost of re-bidding to find a new service provider.

Other types of public-sector support, which may affect the amount received by the project company or its lenders on early termination, are discussed in Chapter 18.

§17.2.1 Repayment of Outstanding Debt

The early Turkish BOT model (*cf.* §2.4.4) guaranteed the debt after completion of construction, and thus paid the lenders in full on default termination, but paid nothing to the investors. This structure was also used in the first Greek PPPs, and had the advantage of making it easier to obtain debt, which might otherwise have been impossible at the time. But obviously the transfer of risk to the private sector is then capped at the amount of the equity (and such a structure may leave the project on the public-sector balance sheet). Moreover, it means that the lenders have little incentive to undertake due diligence, monitor the project closely or sort out any problems. It may also raise VfM issues if the link between the debt-based compensation amount and the value of the project is weak. In some cases, a proportion of the debt is repayable leaving the lenders with some 'skin in the game', *i.e.* loans still at risk to a limited extent.

This method of payment also raises a problem of who controls how much debt is outstanding:

- Should it be the amount of debt that was projected in the base case to be outstanding on the termination date?
- Or should it be the amount actually outstanding, which may include repayments deferred because of cash-flow difficulties, or extra amounts of debt added at the time of a refinancing (*cf.* §26.2.3), or because new money was needed to rescue the project company from financial difficulties (*i.e.* a rescue refinancing—*cf.* §26.2.4)?

The other issue here is breakage costs on any hedging, *e.g.* an interest-rate swap (*cf.* §24.2.3): if the intention is to keep the lenders whole, these have to be paid (though conversely if there is an breakage profit the contracting authority should benefit from this), but of course payment of any future swap credit premium should not be made as there is no reason to pay the swap provider for loss of future profits (*cf.* §24.2.6). Compensation is also required for outstanding or delayed interest costs, late payments and unpaid fees.

The issues on controlling debt outstandings and on breakage costs also reoccur in other termination scenarios, as discussed below, where the contracting authority specifically repays the debt. In such cases, the contracting authority should have a thorough understanding of the PPP's financing agreements before signing the PPP contract so that it is clear what it is committing to. It may also set a maximum debt percentage (*i.e.* leverage) used to finance the project (as is the case in Turkey).

§17.2.2 Depreciated Cost of Assets

This approach is used, for example, in the Spanish legislation relating to concessions and availability PPPs, which has a concept of '*Responsabilidad Patrimonial de la Administración*', under which the contracting authority must pay on project-company default termination for:

- the cost of land acquired by the project company;
- construction works, based on the base-case costs (*i.e.* excluding cost overruns); and
- operating equipment.

A deduction is made from this payment for the amount of any accounting depreciation (which should be roughly *pro rata* to the return on the project to date), and for 'damages' suffered by the contracting authority, which presumably includes the cost to bring the facility up to the standard required by the PPP contract. The PPP contract should also set out how any changes in accounting rules will be dealt with. There is uncertainty about how this is applied in practice, and there have been major court cases on this issue following the collapse of some of the road concessions in Spain after the 2008 financial crisis.

This approach ignores the cost of replacing the long-term service element and operating costs of the PPP contract. It deals only with capex, with no reduction in the value of the project because, *e.g.* operating or maintenance costs have proved to be higher than expected. But it reflects a view that PPPs are primarily about capex rather than long-term service provision, and also that since the project company will not be providing any long-term services it should not be paid for them (*cf.* §17.2.8).

§17.2.3 Estimated Fair-Market Value

A 'fair-market value' (FMV) calculation projects the future cash flow of the project company, taking account of its performance under the PPP contract to date (and hence likely revenue levels or payment deductions), and the further capex required to remedy any problem. This cash flow is discounted at a market rate for a project in this situation to produce the termination sum. (The discount rate would be relatively high to reflect the project's failure.) Obviously if the contracting authority is providing any support for the project's revenues (*cf.* §13.2), the value of this should be deducted in calculating the FMV.

While this provides a fair valuation in theory, in practice it may be difficult for the parties to agree on either the projections and rectification costs or the discount rate, and a third-party arbitrator will also find this complex. However, as default is so rare, it may be simplest just to keep to this approach.

§17.2.4 Adjusted Base-Case Calculation

Another approach for availability PPP projects is to calculate the FMV against an adjusted base case (*cf.* §23.9.9). This FMV is the PV of:

- future service fees, as in the base case, assuming no penalties or deductions; minus
- future capex and opex as in the base case; minus
- future additional costs (capex or opex) required to bring the facility or its operation up to the standard required by the PPP contract ('cost to remedy').

Note that:

- This is a pre-tax calculation (*cf.* §17.7).
- Nominal figures and a nominal discount rate should be used unless the service fees are fully indexed, in which case real figures and a real discount rate can be used (*cf.* §24.3.1).
- If nominal figures are used, an agreed basis is needed for projecting the rate of inflation: the lower the assumed rate of inflation the higher the NPV payment by the

contracting authority, because the fixed portion of the service fees, *e.g.* covering debt service, is discounted at a lower rate (*cf.* §24.3).

This method does not work well for a concession, because realistic rather than base-case revenue projections would be needed, as set out in §17.2.3.

A major problem with this structure is that the contracting authority does not actually know if the payment made to cover the cost to remedy will actually be sufficient, since this cost can only be an estimate and may be open to a lot of dispute (and hence decided by an arbitrator or a court) before the costs are actually incurred. It is preferable for part of the termination-sum payment to be held back in case the cost to remedy is greater than that projected.

Another difficult aspect of this method is the discount rate that should be used. If we assume that the project goes into default the day after completion, and requires no extra costs to be spent on it, then the base-case project IRR (*cf.* §20.3.2)—*i.e.* the IRR before taking the financing structure into account—is the correct rate, as the NPV amount will be exactly equal to the equity and debt which has been used to finance the project company, which is also the FMV of the project at that point. However, if the project IRR—a relatively high rate—is used to discount the third leg of the calculation, *i.e.* the cost to remedy, this is quite unfavourable for the contracting authority:

- Suppose the project IRR is 8%, and the additional costs are $1,000 in a year's time.
- The contracting authority would be paid $926 ($1,000 ÷ 1.08).
- The contracting authority's rate of return on this money is either:
  - the PSDR; or
  - the marginal cost to the contracting authority of obtaining funding, for which this cash can be used in substitution; or
  - the rate at which the contracting authority can place the funds on deposit in a bank.
- In any of these cases the rate of return may easily be below the project IRR (*e.g.* 3% instead of 8%), which means that in a year's time the contracting authority will have $926 × (say) 1.03 = $954, *i.e.* not enough money to pay the additional costs of $1,000.

There is thus an argument for using a different discount rate—the PSDR or one of the other alternatives set out above—for the future additional costs to remedy the project company's default, while retaining the project IRR as the discount rate for the base-case cash flows. This reflects the reality that a buyer of the project company in the open market would take into account the fact that the project had failed and required extra costs to remedy the position, and hence would apply a higher discount rate to the overall cash flows than that used for the original base case: applying a lower discount rate for the additional costs, combined with the base-case project IRR for the base-case costs, has the same net effect. The alternative approach is to decide what would be a reasonable discount rate at the time, and apply this to the whole cash flow, which actually comes to the same thing as the FMV calculation discussed in §17.2.3.

If the base-case project IRR is used as the discount rate, however, there is also an argument for adjusting it to reflect current-market interest rates, because these would be reflected in a new buyer's calculations. If interest rates have gone down this means that the contracting authority will pay more (because the discount rate will be lower), but on the other hand its cost of funding the termination sum will be lower, and *vice versa*. Similarly, changes in the underlying rate of inflation need to be taken into account. One formula for this adjustment, assuming a nominal discount rate is to be used, is:

$$\left(1 + \text{PIRR} + r^2 - r^1\right) \times (1 + i) - 1$$

where

PIRR = real project IRR,
r^1 = real government bond rate at financial close (for the average life of the debt (*cf.* §23.2.3)),
r^2 = real government bond rate at the time of default (for the remaining average life of the debt) and
i = projected rate of inflation at the time of default.

But the issue with this type of adjustment is that it assumes that the project IRR and government bond rates move in the same proportion, which is not the case, the former being affected also by the demand for and supply of PPP projects.

Overall, this system is likely to lead to a termination-sum payment over the true market value of the PPP contract, because a bidder in an auction (discussed below) would proba- bly use a higher discount rate to reflect the fact that the project has defaulted and therefore failed in some way and so is now high risk, as well as being conservative in estimating future costs to remedy the problem.

§17.2.5 Auction of the PPP Contract

The final alternative is not to terminate the PPP contract completely, but for the con- tracting authority to auction ('retender'), the project company's rights under the PPP con- tract in the open market on an 'as is' basis (*i.e.* bidders will have to spend extra costs on remedying problems, and/or take into account the fact that revenues are below the origi- nal base case, but no significant alterations are made to the PPP contract itself).[2] The con- tracting authority pays the amount bid, less its costs, to the project company. The PPP contract is then transferred to, or an identical PPP contract is signed with, the buyer. (The lenders can achieve a similar result through substitution under their direct agreement—*cf.* §25.3.3—which has the advantage of putting the procedure under their control rather than the contracting authority's.)

The benefits of this approach (which was first introduced with the British Treasury Task Force's standard PFI contract in 1999) are:

- It establishes the 'truc' FMV of the PPP contract.
- It avoids any windfalls from excess value (admittedly unlikely) being gained by the contracting authority, or (more likely) the contracting authority paying too much for the project.

---

[2] It may be appropriate to provide for some scope to make changes to the PPP contract if an aspect of it is not workable, but this is difficult as obviously neither the contracting authority nor the project company's investors will want to agree to changes to their detriment.

- It may offer better continuity of service than a complete termination in the ways described above.

When this method was first introduced in 1999, lenders could not be sure that there would be any investors willing to bid for the PPP contract. In the worst case, if nobody bid, the lenders would get nothing. Hence the inclusion of a 'liquid market' provision, that if there were less than *x* investors that would be likely to bid for the PPP contract,[3] the auction would be cancelled; the British standard PPP contract then allows the method set out in §17.2.4 to be used instead ('no retendering'). Lenders are very keen to claim that there is not a liquid market, precisely because the method set out in §17.2.4 is likely to lead to a higher termination sum. Some 20 years later, it is clear that there is a liquid market for most kinds of PPP projects (*cf.* §20.2), and it should no longer be necessary to 'prove' this before an auction takes place. Having said this, there have actually been no auctions of PPP contracts in Britain, as either the lenders have stepped in (*cf.* §25.3.3) or a settlement has been reached (*cf.* §17.2.9).

Retendering may not be so feasible in less-mature PPP markets with fewer market players. In such cases lenders may be unwilling to rely on a retendering outcome that is less predictable (and retendering itself may require skills, time and transaction costs that are unavailable to the contracting authority). On the other hand, if the view is taken that defaults are extremely unlikely, lenders can probably live with this approach.

§17.2.6 Caps and Floors

Some PPP contracts limit the termination-sum payment to a maximum payment cap or floor. For example, the payment could be the *lower* of the FMV and, say, 85% of the senior debt (*i.e.* the lenders never receive *more* than 85% of the debt outstanding) or the *higher* of FMV and 85% of the debt outstanding (*i.e.* lenders' never receive *less* than 85% of the debt outstanding).

§17.2.7 Hybrid Approaches

Finally yet another approach is a hybrid of those above: a combination of a partial debt guarantee, ensuring there will be an agreed minimum payment (*cf.* §18.9), but also allowing one of the other methods set out in §17.2.3-§17.2.5 to be used if this would produce a higher figure. Thus, in South Africa the standard form of PPP contract prescribes that lenders will be paid the greater of:

- the open-market value, as in §17.2.5;
- the adjusted base case, as in §17.2.4, if there is no open-market sale; or
- a fixed percentage of the debt, the requirement for which is to be set out in the original bid.

---

[3] There is a further rather strange proviso in the British standard contract that the price that is likely to be achieved through an auction should not be on the basis of 'a forced or liquidation sale'. Given that the whole point of the auction is that it is a forced sale (if not also a liquidation sale) this seems to negate the auction route!

§17.2.8 Default During the Construction Phase

All the above formulæ work for both the construction and operation phases. However, default during construction may be treated differently, on the grounds that this is the most serious type of failure by the project company, and there is no need to take theoretical future operating cash flow into account (*cf*. §17.2.2). If so, a standard approach is to pay a termination sum equal to the original base-case construction cost, less the NPV of costs to complete the facility to the required specifications. (In this case it is questionable whether 'soft' costs, such as interest during construction—*cf*. §12.3, §29.3.2—should be taken into account.)

§17.2.9 A Realistic View

Despite all the elaborate options set out above, in reality if the contracting authority wants to put the project company in default and terminate the PPP contract, the latter (or its lenders) is usually unlikely just to agree it is in default and hand the facility back. Prolonged legal disputes tend to occur, leaving the project in limbo for a considerable period of time. In the real world, the termination-sum payment is often likely to be a matter of negotiation between the parties, such a negotiated settlement usually being a far quicker and cleaner solution.

A negotiated solution should also make it easier to deal with the problem the contracting authority may face in taking the facility over after a project-company default (or even a voluntary termination, discussed later): the staff may be mainly employed by a sponsor rather than the project company (*cf*. §20.6.3), so how can the contracting authority step in and immediately run the facility? This may work for a relatively simple project such as a school, but not for more complex projects where the skills of the project company's staff are needed. Obviously if the staff came from the public sector originally (*cf*. §28.13), they can be reemployed (but otherwise an investor may quickly redeploy the experienced staff to another project). However, the parties can agree to a 'run-on' contract whereby the project company continues to run the project on a temporary basis as part of the negotiated settlement.

Another not unrelated issue is that a contracting authority may be reluctant to terminate a PPP contract for default because of 'reputation risk', *i.e.* it will be seen to have 'failed' as well as the project company, which may have political ramifications. This may handicap proper action on the contracting authority's part (*cf*. §9.3.4), but the contracting authority needs to consider the wider negative ramifications for the effectiveness of risk allocation across the whole PPP programme if it is seen as not prepared to follow through with enforcing its rights in the PPP contract.

§17.3 CONTRACTING-AUTHORITY DEFAULT OR OPTIONAL TERMINATION

Default by the contracting authority and authority voluntary termination (AVT)[4]—*i.e.* optional termination by the contracting authority—are usually treated in the same way as

---

[4] Also known as 'termination for convenience'.

far as the termination-sum payment is concerned, as otherwise if a default costs the contracting authority more, it would use AVT, and *vice versa*.

§17.3.1 Contracting-Authority Default

Default by a contracting authority is a rather unlikely event but, in most cases, gives the project company the right to terminate.[5] Action that could cause a default includes:

- non-payment of any sums due to the project company, after a reasonable grace period;
- expropriation of the facility or other assets of the project company;
- breach of obligations under the PPP contract (*cf.* §16.2.4) that make it impossible for the project company to complete or operate the facility—*i.e.* where treating this as a compensation event (*cf.* §16.2) is not sufficient (which it will be in most cases);
- the contracting authority transferring its rights under the PPP contract in violation of its provisions; and
- less common, though now an increasingly more frequent provision, a significant change in the legal status, powers or creditworthiness of the contracting authority.

In some countries, rather than the itemised list set out earlier, the definition of contracting authority EoDs may just be a broadly-defined material breach. But itemised lists can also add this item so the result is same. It is generally better to have a clear list: the contracting authority will prefer this to be limited to specific items while lenders will prefer a list including material breach. For availability PPPs, contracting-authority payment default is probably the most crucial issue; lenders may also push for EoDs that allow for early signals of future payment default.

§17.3.2 Authority Voluntary Termination

However, AVT is a more realistic possibility that has to be considered carefully in structuring a PPP contract. A contracting authority often cannot be certain that the PPP contract will serve its originally-designed purpose for its whole life (*cf.* §28.12), and there may come a point when such a fundamental change in the assumptions on which the contracting authority entered into the PPP contract has occurred, that the best thing to do for the public service is to terminate it. In some countries, however (such as France and Spain) the contracting authority may not have full freedom to terminate and AVT has to be qualified by a 'public interest' test (though usually quite broadly-defined in public law).

---

[5] In France and Portugal, the right of the project company to terminate on authority default is not recognised in the PPP contract. In France, the project company would have to take its case to an administrative court or, more likely, negotiate a way out. This is based on the administrative law principle of the contracting authority's obligation to ensure continuity of the public service which cannot be threatened by the private party (and so also allows for AVT). This approach, however, is widely accepted in France not least due to the strong underpinning of the contracting authority by the State in most cases (*cf.* §18.2).

§17.3.3 Compensation on Default or Optional Termination by the Authority

It is evident that the contracting authority must pay a fair termination sum to the project company in these circumstances, and should not make a windfall gain at the expense of the project company's investors, or deprive them of a reasonable return for taking the risks they have taken. The lenders, of course, would expect outstanding principal, accrued interest and any breakage costs (*cf.* §24.2.3) to be paid in full in this situation. Thus, there needs to be a reasonable formula to compensate both lenders and investors and also to meet any termination costs for subcontracts (*cf.* §17.6).

Simple reimbursement of the depreciated cost of the facility ('book value compensation'), used in some countries (*cf.* §17.2.2), may cover the lenders but is unlikely to provide fair compensation for investors. As it is independent of the financing, it can lead to an under- or over-payment of compensation and may be affected by changes in accounting rules.

A formula that values the project company as a whole should give fair compensation to both investors and lenders (and the lenders have first claim on this payment), but generally lenders prefer a separate formula to cover their debt outstandings. There are similar issues on defining these debt outstandings as discussed in §17.2.1—whether to cover additional borrowing above the base case, and whether the future credit premium or a make-whole payment should be paid as part of the breakage calculations. The case for making such 'extra' payments is clearly stronger in this situation, even though their cost may act as an impediment to the contracting authority's long-term flexibility.

The fairest formula for compensation to the investors is one that values the equity investment at the time of termination, and pays this as the termination sum, along with the debt repayment. Methods of calculating this equity valuation are:

- the NPV of the investors' future cash flows (based on a projection at the time of termination), discounted at the rate of return which could then be obtained by selling the investment in the secondary market (*cf.* §20.2.3)—'current market-value approach';
- to give greater certainty, a fixed formula can be used: the NPV of the originally-projected base-case cash flows from the date of termination, discounted at the base-case equity IRR, *i.e.* the originally-agreed equity return, but only for the period from the date of termination to the originally anticipated end of the PPP contract—'future-return approach'; and
- a variation on the last formula: payment of a sum that will bring the equity IRR up to the date of termination to the base-case level for the life of the PPP contract—*i.e.* an amount that, taking into account any amounts already paid to the investors, provides a return to the termination date at the rate that was agreed in the base case at financial close—'original-return approach'.

Using the assumptions and cash flow set out in Table 26.1, as an example, and assuming that there is an AVT at the end of year 5, just after the investors have received their cash-flow distribution for that year, Table 17.1 shows the results of using the different approaches set out earlier:

As can be seen, the current market-value approach, which is what a new investor would use when considering a secondary-market investment, produces a substantially

Table 17.1 AVT termination-sum calculations

	Payment
Current market-value approach, assuming a secondary-market yield of 8%	$289
Future-return approach	$217
Original-return approach	$241

higher termination-sum payment reflecting the lower secondary-market yield, and hence discount rate, that would be applied by a new investor to a project that is completed and operating successfully (cf. §20.2.3, §20.3.3, §26.3). The only reason that this might not be the case would be if the project was not operating well but the contracting authority does not have the grounds for a contractor-default termination (cf. §17.2).

From the project company's investors' point of view, the current market-value approach has the disadvantage of uncertainty since the appropriate discount rate would have to be determined based on the market at the time of termination, whereas the other approaches are based on pre-fixed calculation assumptions (and there may be a dispute about the cash-flow projections, especially for concessions), but this is far outweighed by its likely benefit.

Investors may nonetheless argue for a 'make-whole' approach whereby they are paid the higher of one of these two fixed formulæ and the then-current market value.

It should be noted that there is no reason to treat equity share capital and shareholder subordinated debt differently in these calculations, since the split between these is a matter of convenience for the investors and is of no relevance for the contracting authority (cf. §20.3.5).

Note that all cash flows and discount rates referred to should be calculated on a nominal, post-tax basis (cf. §24.3.1), and IRR calculations should take a consistent approach to investment in cash as compared to investors being on-risk (cf. §20.3.5).

Optional termination is an expensive exercise for the contracting authority, and is thus a serious impediment to long-term flexibility in a PPP contract (cf. §28.12). One way of giving more flexibility in this respect could be to ask bidders to offer fixed prices for a limited number of set termination dates, say one-third and two-thirds of the way through the PPP contract. Bid competition may ensure that these prices are lower than the 'fair value' amount. This also has the effect of capping investors' returns (cf. §15.5.2). However, bidders are unlikely to offer a much lower termination-sum payment than they would have received under the PPP contract on these dates anyway.

The termination sum is usually paid on a lump-sum basis but, in some countries, the debt portion can be paid in instalments at an agreed rate of interest (at least if AVT applies, but not in the case of a contracting-authority default).

Finally, the value of the facility has to be deducted from the termination sum if it is being retained by the project company (cf. §17.8).

§17.4 Early Termination: Force Majeure

As already discussed (*cf.* §16.4), a distinction has to be made between *force majeure* events which cause a *temporary* interruption in the provision of services under the PPP contract, which are dealt with as relief events, and those which are *permanent* and so make it impossible to continue with the project. Even a complete destruction of the project should generally be covered by insurance and treated as a relief event while the facility is being rebuilt (*cf.* §14.8).

There is a very limited range of events that cannot be covered by insurance, *e.g.* acts of war that destroy the project—events so unlikely in nature that there seems little point worrying about them (if they do happen, terminating the PPP contract will probably be the least of the investors' and lenders' worries). The simple view can therefore be taken that the essence of permanent *force majeure* in these cases is that each party has to suffer whatever loss it incurs.

§17.4.1 Unavailability of Insurance

However, it is also possible that the insurance cover for other temporary *force-majeure* risks that the parties had expected to be insured becomes unavailable. This is perhaps a more likely event to occur than the *force-majeure* risks that cannot be covered by insurance at all. If the contracting authority has an option to take on liability for this unavailable insurance (*cf.* §14.11), but chooses not to exercise it, the PPP contract will have to be terminated as the project company cannot carry on without insurance.

In such cases, if the contracting authority takes over the facility, it should reasonably expect to pay a termination sum of at least the outstanding debt and swap-breakage costs but no future profit margin in breakage costs (*cf.* §24.2.3). If the equity investment is to be covered by a termination-sum payment as well, investors cannot expect to be paid back more than their original investment, and perhaps only after deduction of distributions received to the termination date.

However, the argument for covering equity is not that strong, since as the *force majeure* is nobody's fault there should be some sharing of risk: an alternative to making no payment for equity is to pay the current market value of the facility (*i.e.* the physical facility not the PPP contract as for AVT) if this is higher than the level of debt outstanding.

If cover is provided by the contracting authority for loss of equity, it can logically be extended to the limited list of *force-majeure* events that cannot be covered by insurance in the first place.

§17.5 Early Termination: Corruption and Breach of Refinancing Provisions

Most countries have a provision for voiding public-sector contracts if corruption is involved. In some countries, this is treated in the same way as any other project company default. But it is arguably reasonable for the lenders to expect a termination sum payment equal to their debt outstanding, subject to the points already made on what debt outstanding means (*cf.* §17.2.1), on the basis that the lenders would not normally be involved in any corruption. However, the investors in the project company would lose their investment in these circumstances, since they are responsible for such actions.

In the case of a breach of refinancing provisions, *i.e.* the project company carrying out a refinancing without notifying the contracting authority and without paying the latter's share of the refinancing gain (*cf.* §26.2.7), it is common to treat this as a project-company default. But in some cases, the senior debt may be protected as with the treatment of corruption (although the logic of this is doubtful as the lenders would be involved in a refinancing).

§17.6 TERMINATION AND SUBCONTRACTORS

The subcontractors also suffer if an early termination takes place. Costs will be incurred in demobilising staff and equipment, and there will obviously be a loss of future profits. Whether they should receive any compensation from the contracting authority for this depends on the circumstances of termination.

In the case of AVT, it is reasonable for the contracting authority to pay both subcontractors' costs incurred as a result of the termination, and an element of foregone future profits. The PPP contract may state this in general terms, leaving the details to be set out in the subcontracts, but if so the contracting authority need to review the subcontracts as part of its due diligence before financial close (*cf.* §10.8.2), and obviously any future changes to these subcontracts that may affect the termination liability must be subject to the agreement of the contracting authority.

In the case of termination for default by the project company (where it is quite possible this default may have been caused by a subcontractor), there is no strong case for giving subcontractors any special protection. If the subcontractor is not involved in the default, it may be reasonable to protect their demobilisation costs if they are innocent parties, but obviously not their future profits.

This all assumes that the contracting authority actually wants to terminate all the subcontracts, which may not be the case, especially if a subcontractor is not involved in a default by the project company, or an AVT applies. The contracting authority should have direct agreements (*cf.* §25.3.3) with all major subcontractors that allow it to take over the relevant subcontract if it wishes to do so.

§17.6.1 Contracting Authority Step-In

Even if the project company is not in default, the contracting authority usually has the right to 'step-in' to the project, *i.e.* take it over on a temporary basis (*cf.* §13.8). If the project company cooperates with the contracting authority, the normal service fees should continue to be payable.

If the project company is in default, this probably implies that the contracting authority has to step in to rectify this default: in this case the contracting authority's costs should be deducted from service fees. However, this should not be used as a way of short-circuiting the normal termination provisions (*cf.* §17.2), *i.e.* the step-in is still only allowable in the specific circumstances mentioned in §13.8 and usually has to take second place to the lenders' security interests (*cf.* §25.3.3).

The contracting authority also needs to ensure that its step-in rights are reflected in the main subcontracts (as well as its rights to take over the subcontracts after termination as discussed earlier). The PPP contract usually specifies the notice periods required for contracting authority step-in, and limits the period of step-in and activities it can carry out to those reasonably required to address the problem.

§17.7 Tax Implications of a Termination-Sum Payment

Finally, the tax implications of any termination sum need to be considered. If the termination sum is taxable, the amount received by the investors and lenders may be insufficient to compensate them as intended (and at the same time the public sector will have made a termination-sum payment with one hand and taken some of it back in tax with the other hand). The termination sum therefore may need to be 'grossed up' (*i.e.* increased as necessary to produce the net amount required after tax). Obviously, this does not apply where the PPP contract is sold in the open market (*cf.* §17.2.5), or the termination-sum calculations are on a pre-tax basis (*cf.* §17.2.4).

In cases where part of the termination sum is specifically designated for debt repayment, it may be preferable for this payment to be made directly from the contracting authority to the lenders, instead of *via* the project company, even though the lenders have security over the cash as it flows through the project company, which may avoid raising unnecessary tax issues.

§17.8 Final Maturity, Residual-Value Risk and Hand Back

PPP contracts can take a variety of legal forms (*cf.* §2.4, §2.5), which may or may not give legal ownership (or other legal title) of the facility to the project company during the tenor of the PPP contract. Legal ownership is a matter of policy for the contracting authority and is otherwise of little importance during the tenor of the PPP contract: it is the PPP contract itself that creates value for investors and security for lenders, not the physical asset (*cf.* §21.3, §25.3). However, it obviously becomes important at the end of the PPP contract, and residual ownership of the facility may also affect balance-sheet treatment (*cf.* §9.4).

Most PPP projects assume that there will be no residual value at the end of the PPP contract, or that the facility's specialised use makes it inappropriate for it to be transferred away from the public sector. Thus, the facility simply reverts to the contracting authority's control (assuming it is already under its ownership), or the ownership is transferred for no payment or a nominal sum. In cases where the facility site has, or may have, a residual value because it has an alternative private-sector use, such as housing or office accommodation, the choice is between:

- giving the contracting authority an option to take over the facility at nil cost as above, in which case bidders will obviously not take any residual value into account in their pricing;
- leaving the facility in the hands of the project company: this implies that the original bid will have attributed some residual value to the facility (or the land on which it is built), and reduced the service fees accordingly;
- obliging the contracting authority to acquire the facility for a pre-agreed fixed sum, that has to be proposed at the time of the original bid;
- giving the contracting authority an option to acquire the facility for a pre-agreed fixed sum; and
- giving the contracting authority an obligation or an option to acquire the facility for the then-current market value, perhaps with a cap on the price.

If the contracting authority is obliged to acquire the facility for a fixed sum, bidders can take this into account and thus offer lower service fees, but less so if the contracting authority only has an *option* to purchase at the end of the contract, as the project company is then left with the 'downside' risk on the residual value. If the final payment depends on market value (whether through purchase by the contracting authority or sale into the open market), this obviously becomes more speculative. As this is so far into the future bidders may attribute little current value to it, and hence it will have little effect on the service fees. Obviously, the contracting authority should not effectively pay for the full cost of the facility through the service fees and yet leave the residual value with the project company. Other than a market-value purchase, any of these options may raise balance-sheet issues for the contracting authority (*cf.* §9.4) as this may be construed as guaranteeing a payment to the project company irrespective of performance and thus transferring risk back to the contracting authority.

Apart from taking over the facility at final maturity of the PPP contract, the contracting authority may have:

- an option to renew the PPP contract instead of taking over the facility (on a pricing basis which reflects the fact that its capital cost has been paid off)—this encourages the project company to keep the facility in good condition in case the renewal option is exercised; and
- an option to put a new PPP contract out for a competitive bid (in which the existing project company may participate) as a franchise (*cf.* §2.4.2); the winner of the bid will take over the facility from the project company at no cost. (Of course this option does not necessarily have to be written into the PPP contract as the contracting authority can make this decision when the time comes.)

§17.8.1 Hand Back

If the facility is to be transferred to the contracting authority at the end of the PPP contract, there is an obvious temptation for the project company to neglect maintenance during the final years of operation. By the time of the hand back, the project company may have paid over all its remaining cash to its shareholders, and ceased to have enough financial substance to pay compensation for poor maintenance. The contracting authority can ensure that the maintenance is actually carried out by:

- a requirement to achieve maintenance standards before the end of the PPP contract, so that if this is not done, payment deductions can be made (in this case the technical specifications in the PPP contract defining the acceptable return condition of the facility are crucial);
- alternatively, a requirement that for the last few years of the PPP contract part of the service fees should be paid into a maintenance reserve (*cf.* §25.2.4) under the control of both the project company and the contracting authority, to cover the cost of any maintenance to meet the required standard; this fund is used for maintenance as needed, and any final surplus (once all specified maintenance has been carried out) is returned to the project company;
- requiring an independent assessment of the condition of the facility and estimated remedial costs, say two to five years before contract expiry, and setting aside funds for the required works out of service fees in the same way as above; and
- a requirement to provide security—a sponsor guarantee or bank bonding—to ensure that the final maintenance obligations are carried out.

Provisions are also needed for the transfer of building plans, operating information, manuals, and so on, as relevant.

There is a mirror issue to the above in cases where the facility is not transferred to the contracting authority at the end of the PPP contract. If there has been new capex for which the contracting authority is responsible (because it results from a compensation event—*cf.* §16.2), and so pays for it either through a lump-sum payment or increased service fees, and the facility's assets including those on which this expenditure has been made have a useful life after the end of the PPP contract, the payments by the contracting authority should take this into account. Thus if, 10 years before the end of the PPP contract, capex of $100 is incurred, after which the economic life of the facility is 20 years, the contracting authority's payments should be reduced in proportion: so, if payment is to be made through the service fees, the cost should be amortised over 20 years instead of 10, with the contracting authority only being responsible for payments covering the first 10 years.

Public-Sector Support for PPP Contracts

§18.1 INTRODUCTION

There are a variety of ways in which the public sector can provide support to PPP contracts, if this can be justified on VfM grounds (*cf.* Chapter 8), is affordable (*cf.* §9.2, §9.3) and does not create public-sector balance-sheet problems (*cf.* §9.4). The aims of this support may include:

- reducing the cost of the project to make it affordable;
- reducing the risk transfer to make the project financeable; or
- providing finance where there is a financing gap (*i.e.* the available private-sector finance is insufficient or only available on unsuitable terms).

In the case of availability PPPs, the project company's revenue is of course derived from the contracting authority, itself a direct form of support which means—assuming there are no credit-risk issues with the contracting authority (*cf.* §13.4)—that the project company is not taking the demand risk (but *cf.* §13.7).[1] Partial debt assumption can be used to extend this support further (§18.2).

---

[1] Of course, under shadow-toll schemes (*cf.* §15.5.4), the project company does take (some) demand risk, even if the source of payment is the contracting authority.

Public-Private Partnerships for Infrastructure
DOI: https://doi.org/10.1016/B978-0-08-100766-2.00018-8

As to concessions, if the projected demand and service fees produce insufficient cash flow to make the project financially viable, public-sector support can be justified by the wider externalities produced by the concession (*cf.* §7.4.1), although it could also be argued that the very fact that these externalities cannot be priced into a service fee paid by the user suggests that these should be used with caution. Support for concessions can take a variety of different forms:

- revenue subsidies (§18.3);
- revenue guarantees (§18.4); or
- flexible concession tenor (§18.5).

Other types of public-sector support that may be used for both availability PPPs and concessions include:

- capital grants (§18.6);
- part-construction of the project (§18.7);
- debt financing (§18.8)—also *cf.* §22.9 for public-sector loans or guarantees on a more commercial basis;
- *pro-rata* debt guarantee (§18.9);
- debt underpinning (§18.10);
- credit guarantee finance (§18.11); and
- equity investment (§18.12).

Whatever the type of support provided, there may be public-sector balance-sheet implications (§18.13).

§18.2 Partial Debt Assumption

In French availability PPPs, the administrative law concept of *cession de créance* ('loan transfer') can be applied to an availability PPP, under which, on satisfactory completion of the facility, the project company's right to a part of the service fee, capped at up to 80% of its financing element, is transferred to the lenders such that the lenders are paid this part of the service fee irrespective of project performance. This effectively turns a part of the debt into public-sector borrowing, *i.e.* debt assumption by the public sector. (If deductions exceed the remaining service fees, they remain a claim against the project company.) Similar provisions can be found in Germany with the forfeiting model ('*Forfaitierungsmodell*').

This reflects the reality that even the poorest performance post-completion by the project company is unlikely to result in the service fees being reduced below the level where debt service is jeopardised (*cf.* §15.6.4). Thus, it makes sense to guarantee what is without significant risk, and to benefit from the lower cost of financing that this attracts (although this may be offset by a higher cost of finance on the debt that has not been assumed). The effect is similar to a minimum revenue guarantee under a concession (*cf.* §18.4), and to debt underpinning (*cf.* §18.10).

§18.3 REVENUE SUBSIDIES

A fixed subsidy towards operating costs can be provided if it is necessary to reduce service fees to make a concession viable (*cf.* §10.6.5, §13.2). Clearly this is a fairly crude approach, which makes it possible for the project company to earn windfalls from unexpected usage growth. A preferable method of subsidy is therefore payments on a sliding scale, reducing as usage increases.

§18.4 MINIMUM REVENUE GUARANTEE

If the issue is not one of reducing the service fees, but uncertainty of whether there may be enough revenue in a concession (even though the base case gives a reasonable expectation that enough revenue can be generated), then a minimum revenue guarantee (as it is known in the case of a toll-road concession)[2] may be provided by the authority, *i.e.* the break-even level of vehicles/tolls that covers opex and debt service is agreed, and insofar as the actual level of toll revenues is below this, the contracting authority pays the amount required to reach the guarantee level. If the toll revenues are over the guarantee level, the benefit of this is usually split on a sliding-scale basis between the project company and the contracting authority. The contracting authority's support can be limited to a 'ramp-up' guarantee, whereby minimum usage levels during the first few years of operation are guaranteed. The assumption here is that all parties expect the projected usage levels to be reached, and the only doubt is how long it will take to achieve these levels.

In all such cases, the proportion of support needs to be carefully considered: it is obviously unreasonable for the contracting authority to guarantee 100% of the base-case revenues or passenger usage, as this not only negates any real risk transfer but also removes the incentive on the part of the project company to maintain or improve service quality (and to increase the numbers of passengers, if that is a policy objective). Therefore a minimum revenue guarantee should either be for a fixed percentage of projected revenues (*e.g.* 70% as under the Chilean 1991 concession law), or a sliding scale of support, as previously applied in Korea which takes the ramp-up point discussed above into account: thus 80% of the projected usage may be guaranteed for the first five years, 70% for the next five years, 60% for the next five years and nothing thereafter, the practical effect being to provide cover for opex and some but not all of the debt service, leaving equity fully at risk.

However, there is a fairly sorry history in various countries, *e.g.* Mexico in the early 1990s (Ruster, 1997) and subsequently in Korea (Noumba Um, 2005), of concessions being undertaken on the strength of revenue guarantees rather than a proper evaluation of the usage risks, with consequent heavy costs falling on the contracting authority as the guarantees are called in.[3]

---

[2] The same principle applies to other usage guarantees, *e.g.* for passengers, where the term 'fare-box guarantee' is commonly used.

[3] Korea subsequently abolished its minimum revenue guarantee scheme in 2009. A new risk-sharing scheme provides a revenue subsidy up to a 'risk-sharing revenue' level (based on the revenue that produces a project IRR equal to the government bond yield). If subsequent revenue is greater, any previously paid subsidy is repaid.

If support is provided for revenues rather than capex (*cf.* §18.6), this means that the project company has to raise more private-sector financing, with a consequent effect on the service fees.

§18.5 CONCESSION EXTENSION

Rather than providing direct financial support, the contracting authority may agree that if usage falls below a mutually-agreed level, the concession tenor can be extended *pro rata*: the additional revenue at the tail-end may thus help to make up any deficit. This has a similar effect to bids on the basis of an equity IRR cap, or lowest NPV of revenues (*cf.* §10.6.5).

§18.6 CAPITAL GRANT

A capital grant[4] is a (non-repayable) funding contribution from the contracting authority towards capex (for an availability PPP or a concession) to reduce the construction cost of the project and hence the service fees. By lowering the amount of finance needed this may also make the project more financially viable, especially if there are concerns about the level or terms of long-term finance available in the market. Another reason may be to improve VfM by reducing the amount of relatively more-expensive private finance required. Finally, it may be a condition for government to make a capital grant as a condition to receiving grants from elsewhere (*e.g.* EU structural funds—see below—require a national contribution to be made as well).

An example of a capital-grant scheme is the use of 'viability gap funding' (VGF) in India (and other countries). Here the contracting authority's funding contribution is established though a competitive process. For road concessions, as the level of user fee per kilometre is already set by policy, bids are assessed on the minimum level of funding from the contracting authority required by bidders to make the project financially viable for the private sector, but with a maximum grant of 20% of capex (*cf.* §10.6.5). The affordability assessment for the contracting authority therefore focuses on the expected VGF in the relevant project, within the overall budget of the VGF programme.

Grants from the various EU 'Structural and Investment Funds' for eligible projects are an example of capital grants at a supranational level.

In addition to direct funding from the contracting authority, the capital grant may be derived from the proceeds of sale of surplus land as a result of building the new facility (*cf.* §12.2.9).

Capital grants raise risk-transfer issues, namely the appropriate level of capital grant (§18.6.1), its timing (§18.6.2) and ensuring that long-term risk transfer is not eroded (§18.6.3).

---

[4] Also known as a 'capital contribution'.

§18.6.1 Level of Capital Grant

The level of capital grant is usually between 20% and 50% of capex, but no higher due to concerns about the impact on incentives for the project company to perform, and overall risk transfer. Clearly the higher the grant the lower the overall risk transfer to the project company.

§18.6.2 Timing of Capital Grant

As to timing, it is obviously inappropriate for the public-sector money to go in first and thus bear the whole initial construction risk on the project—so it should go in at least after the equity finance has been paid in and the debt fully drawn. Indeed, the ideal position is that the project company should fund construction fully, and then only if completion takes place should any public-sector funding be injected. Otherwise the contracting authority is effectively taking back some of the construction-phase risk (*cf.* §12.3). The project company should be able to arrange interim financing that would be repaid from the public-sector contribution after completion.

However, capital grants are nonetheless often made during the construction period, albeit conditional upon defined milestones being achieved during the construction of the facility. An alternative approach is to require the investors in the project company to guarantee repayment of any such capital grant if construction is not completed (or to provide bank guarantees for this).

§18.6.3 Long-Term Risk Transfer

If a capital grant is part of the overall project-financing structure, some care has to be taken to ensure that if there is an early termination of the PPP contract, the contracting authority does not end up paying twice, once through the capital grant and once through payment of a termination sum (*cf.* §17.2-§17.5). If the termination sum is based partly on discounting future service-fee payments, the capital grant will be taken into account because these payments will have already been reduced to take account of it. However, in other cases there may be a need to take direct account of the capital grant in the termination-sum calculation.

§18.7 PART-CONSTRUCTION OF THE PROJECT

As one alternative to a capital grant, the contracting authority may itself construct part of the project. For example, this has been used in rail PPPs—the contracting authority constructs the track and the project company provides the rails, signalling, *etc.*, and perhaps also the trains and rolling stock. This is quite risky from the contracting authority's point of view: it is likely that there will be interface problems, *i.e.* the contracting authority and the project company both blaming the other for construction problems—and any delay by the contracting authority in completing its construction to schedule will delay the PPP project's completion and hence probably result in LD payments (*cf.* §12.2.7).

§18.8 DEBT FINANCING

A contracting authority, the government (or a government agency), may itself act as a lender to the project company. This may be done for two reasons:

— Bridging a financing gap

A public-sector loan may be provided due to a lack of liquidity in the debt-financing markets that causes a gap in the project company's financing. (A number of countries did this in different ways after the 2008 financial crisis.) If so, it is usually on the same terms as any other senior lender. Such loans are often covered by separate documentation, *i.e.* not included in the PPP contract itself (as, *e.g.*, a capital grant would be). This provides flexibility for the contracting authority (or other public-sector lender) to sell the loan at a future date.

— Lower cost or longer tenor of finance

In this case, the aim of using public-sector debt is to narrow the financing-cost gap between public-sector procurement and PPPs, perhaps to make the PPP project financially viable. But it does not eliminate this gap, firstly because it only reduces the cost of debt and an equity return is still required, and secondly because any retention of risk in the private sector still has a cost (*cf.* §28.4).

If public-sector debt is provided on concessional terms to reduce the overall cost or lengthen the overall tenor of the available financing, it is usually treated as mezzanine debt, *i.e.* subordinated to the other (senior) lenders (*cf.* §22.7, §25.5.4).[5] Therefore interest payments and principal repayments may be postponed until net cash flow after the senior lenders' debt service has reached a certain level, or surplus cash flow may be divided between payments on the public-sector financing and distributions to investors (*cf.* §25.2.3, §25.2.5). This form of contribution as mezzanine debt can be more attractive than a capital grant insofar as it can leverage in an increased level of senior debt and reduce the overall cost of financing for the project.

However, it should be borne in mind that a loan is a greater risk for a contracting authority than a capital grant. This is because the effect of a capital grant is to reduce the service fees: should the project company default on the PPP contract, and the contracting authority's termination-sum payment is based on future service-fee revenues (*cf.* §17.2), these revenues have been reduced because of the capital grant, and so the contracting authority effectively recovers the balance of its capital grant, while the lenders probably will not recover all of their loan. (And if a contracting authority provides a mezzanine loan its situation is even worse.)

Public-sector debt or guarantees on a more commercial basis, often in parallel with private-sector debt, are discussed in §22.9, along with debt from multilateral sources.

---

[5] This type of lending is also known as a 'financial instrument' or even 'a repayable grant'.

§18.9 PRO-RATA DEBT GUARANTEE

If the contracting authority and the investors consider that the project is viable, but there are concerns about the availability of long-term debt, another cost-effective way of providing support to enable the project to proceed is for the contracting authority to guarantee some of the debt. This should also reduce its overall cost.

The contracting authority can specify that the guaranteed and unguaranteed debt must be 'stapled', *i.e.* must be held *pro rata* and cannot be split and sold off separately, to ensure that lenders have an incentive to protect both tranches of debt (although it is probably impossible to prevent one of the tranches being *de facto* sold off through a sub-participation or derivative contract).

The guarantee is usually supplemented by an indemnity agreement between the contracting authority and the project company such that in the event of a payment being made to the lenders, the project company agrees to indemnify the contracting authority (although it probably will not have the funds to do so).

§18.10 DEBT UNDERPINNING

Another form of partial debt guarantee (also referred to as 'underpinned financing') is based on the assumption that it is highly unlikely that the default termination sum payable to lenders after a facility has been completed would ever be less than, say, 75% of their debt outstanding. Therefore, once the facility has been completed and has operated for an initial period, the contracting authority guarantees 75% of the debt, but unlike the *pari-passu* type of guarantee discussed above, the first loss (up to 25% of the debt) is borne by the lenders. This is obviously similar in effect to partial debt assumption (*cf.* §18.2).

The contracting authority may seek to argue that its guarantee liability should not be on the public-sector balance sheet because there is no realistic chance of the guarantee being called upon (*cf.* §9.3.4), as the open-market value of the project will always be more than 75% of the debt.

§18.11 CREDIT GUARANTEE FINANCE

Under this structure, the government or a government agency lends to the project company, on similar terms as to repayment profile, cover ratios, security, *etc.*, as private-sector lenders, but at a lower cost because the loan is at or near to the cost of government bonds. The debt is guaranteed by private-sector commercial banks or has an insurance-company 'wrap' (*cf.* §22.4.4). Thus, risk remains with the private-sector lenders as in a standard PPP, but financing is provided by the public sector. Some pilot projects using this scheme were undertaken by the British Treasury, who gave it the name 'credit guarantee finance'.

The lower cost of finance is of course reflected in lower service fees, but the absolute benefit will be limited. Commercial banks will charge the same guarantee fee as the credit margin that they would have charged had they lent directly, and the insurance-company guarantors will also charge the same guarantee fee as they would have charged for a bond issue. The benefits are therefore limited to the relatively-small difference between the base cost of funds for the public sector and that for the lenders. However, there is also a political benefit as it takes the sting out of the argument that public-sector funding is 'cheaper' (*cf.* §28.4).

Moreover, a bank or insurance-company guarantee does not mean that risk has been entirely eliminated for the public-sector lender: there is still a risk on the guarantor (as was shown in the case of the monoline insurers (*cf.* §22.4.4)). If the public sector is too restrictive on which private-sector banks or insurance companies qualify as acceptable guarantors, this can easily turn a few institutions into monopoly suppliers, with obvious cost results (and also result in an excessive buildup in exposure to these institutions). Conversely, an over-liberal approach could result in guarantees of limited or diminishing value from poor credits. Moreover, the guarantee has to last for 25-30 years, which could easily mean that an institution which appeared acceptable at financial close ceases to be so some years in the future. In fact, it is bad practice to rely only on a guarantee, without any review or monitoring of the underlying credit of the project company. There is a parallel here with the practice of rating agencies when rating PPP bond issues which are wrapped by a monoline insurer: the agencies look at both the credit of the monoline insurer and the credit of the underlying project.

The public-sector lender therefore has to put systems in place to:

- monitor and review policy on exposure to guarantors;
- review financing and other documentation to ensure that it follows required principles;
- manage loan disbursements and administration;
- deal with changes in the project that have an effect on financing (*cf.* §16.2.2);
- monitor and control the credit standing of its guarantors; and
- be prepared, in the worst case, take direct control of the underlying loan because the guarantor is no longer acceptable, and is unable to provide alternative security, such as cash collateralisation, or find a new guarantor to take its place.

A government department is not well equipped to manage such issues, and the better approach for public-sector financing, discussed in §22.9, is to use public-sector or multilateral development-banking institutions that have developed the necessary specialised expertise to evaluate and take on project risks.

Credit guarantee finance is also biased against commercial-bank finance:

- Syndication of guarantees will require the approval of the public-sector lender (since the effect is to change its guarantor), which reduces the attraction of the structure for banks compared with a direct loan (*cf.* §22.2.9).
- Banks lose their swap profits (*cf.* §24.2.8), and so may have to increase credit pricing to compensate for this.
- Insurers may charge less for their guarantees than the credit margins required by banks (*cf.* §22.4.4), which means that if banks are to be brought in as guarantors, projects have to be 'ring-fenced' for them to make it worthwhile for them to bid for the business.

Therefore, it is not surprising that the credit guarantee finance structure has had little impact in the PPP financing market.

§18.12 EQUITY INVESTMENT

The contracting authority may choose to invest in the project company. This is not usually done as a way of providing public-sector financial support to a project, but rather for transparency reasons, or to capture part of the equity return for the public sector. See §27.4 for further discussion on this.

§18.13 BALANCE-SHEET IMPLICATIONS

In considering the level of public-sector support to provide by any of the means set out above, the contracting authority may also need to consider any impact on the overall public-sector balance-sheet treatment of the PPP project. For example, under Eurostat rules (*cf.* §9.4.5) public-sector support of 50% or more of the value of the capex leads to the PPP project being recorded on the government balance sheet.[6]

There may also be other restrictions on the level of government support. Within the EU, for example, such support is only allowed if it does not constitute 'state aid', effectively using public resources to support one economic operator to compete unfairly with another. To help determine that state aid is not being provided, procurement should be conducted in a transparent and non-discriminatory manner, and the contracting authority should act as if it were a 'market-economy investor', *i.e.* operating like any other rational investor would do under normal market economy conditions and not providing advantages to a particular economic operator. If the subsidy is found to constitute state aid, it must be refunded, and the enforceability of any government guarantees may be affected.

---

[6] Rather strangely, capex in this context is considered by Eurostat to consist only of capital expenditure incurred for the construction of the asset, *i.e.* the 'hard' construction costs (*cf.* §23.9.2).

Public-Sector Contract Management

§19.1 Introduction

The contracting authority needs to ensure adequate contract management throughout the whole life of a PPP contract, not just up to financial close. Poor understanding of what this involves and inadequate preparation and capacity to do this properly may undo all the hard work that has gone into getting the project to this phase of the project cycle. One of the main challenges is a change in mindset for the contracting authority from delivering services itself (which may be described as the 'public-works approach') to overseeing their delivery by a third party.

Apart from ensuring that the project company delivers the service contracted for, the contracting authority needs to:

- manage those risks for which it is responsible (*cf.* Chapter 12);
- monitor the project company's performance (*cf.* §13.9);
- deal with changes that occur over the life of the PPP contract (*cf.* Chapter 16); and
- manage relationships, not only with the project company (and possibly its investors and lenders) but also with other stakeholders (*cf.* §6.5).

Contract management should be viewed as a continuous and active process with both parties seeking to improve the service and the way it is delivered. A cooperative relationship (not a one-sided one which uses 'partnership' as a façade for commercial gain), with both parties seeking to achieve agreed common goals, is the best way to ensure long-term success for a PPP.

Contract management therefore involves particular practices and behaviours that may at first be unfamiliar to the contracting authority (§19.2). There are specific activities

261

required during the construction phase (§19.3) and the operation phase (§19.4). If disputes to do arise between the parties, the PPP contract usually includes a process to resolve these while seeking to preserve a constructive relationship (§19.6).

Contract-management resourcing requirements are often under-estimated by the contracting authority (§19.7). However, various tools are available to help the contracting authority with these complex tasks (§19.8).

The contracting authority is ultimately responsible for the provision of the public service and can expect to be subjected to external reviews, not only to demonstrate that the PPP arrangement itself is delivering VfM, but also to ensure that the originally-identified objectives are being addressed (§19.9). Transparency as between the project company and the contracting authority, and as far as possible in providing information to the general public, is important to maintain support for PPP projects (§19.10). The interests of staff transferred from the public authority to the project company also have to be appropriately protected (§19.11).

§19.2 PRACTICES AND BEHAVIOURS

In the run-up to or shortly after financial close, the contracting authority's contract-management team takes over management of the PPP project. It is important to have the maximum-possible continuity with the project-management team who have been managing the PPP project up to this point (*cf.* §6.2.2). If contract managers are not actually part of the project-management team, they should still be involved in the detailed final stages of negotiating the PPP contract. As part of the handover process, the project-management team should draw up a contract manual (*cf.* §19.8.1).

A positive and business-like relationship between the contracting authority and the project company is crucial. Ideally, the relationship should work as a partnership with both parties acting as a single team continually seeking performance and efficiency improvements. In reality, it is often at best a more traditional client-contractor relationship. Although the contracting authority's contract-management team can expect to have weekly or even day day-to-day contact with the project company (especially for an availability PPP where the contracting authority itself is the user of the services provided), the two parties will also have contact points at different levels of seniority in their respective organisations. This is important in case an issue needs to be escalated to a higher authority or the relationship between opposite managers breaks down.

There should also be regularly-scheduled formal meetings between the two parties' managers, and less frequent but scheduled meetings at the higher levels of seniority. It is good practice for both parties to take formal minutes of meetings and record decisions to avoid misunderstandings later on. The two parties should also be aware of the approval procedures of the other party. A third useful form of contact is for the project company to hold forums from time to time for the contracting authority and key subcontractors to share issues and build a common sense of purpose.

Apart from acting as a team and having regular communication, other signs of an effective relationship between the contracting authority and project company are:

- mutual understanding of the PPP contract's terms, of the services required and of the respective business objectives of the other party;
- confidence in the other party's ability to meet its responsibilities;
- supportive and fast responsiveness; and
- good consultation on staff changes so that staff turnover on the part of either party does not affect the relationship.

Contract management imposes new and different pressures on the contracting authority. A good example of this is in decision-making, linking into the responsiveness point above—there may be obligations under the PPP contract for the contracting authority to respond to information or proposals from the project company within agreed time frames and so the contracting authority's decision-making processes may need to adjust for these. This may require direction from the contracting authority's senior management at first until these new priorities are understood and new behaviours have been embedded. There may also be a perception that reporting more information is better reporting. But if the contracting authority does not know what to do with such information or act upon it, it is an unnecessary cost.

§19.3 CONSTRUCTION PHASE

§19.3.1 Subcontractors

It is difficult for a contracting authority used to procuring its own requirements to step back and allow the project company to do so on its behalf. However, an essential element of a PPP is that the project company is fully responsible for its subcontractors, which means that the contracting authority generally cannot interfere in this relationship. Therefore, communications with subcontractors should generally be *via* the project company.

The contracting authority's rights to approve changes in the subcontract terms or in the subcontractors are limited (*cf.* §15.6.8). Again, some comfort can be taken from the lenders' much wider controls over changes such as as part of their security package (*cf.* §25.3.1), their interests in this respect being virtually identical with the contracting authority's.

§19.3.2 Project Design

Detailed design (and engineering, where relevant) of the facility after financial close is normally the responsibility of the project company (*cf.* §10.8.1). Although the basic design is set out in the PPP contract (perhaps based on an outline design from the authority), much of the detailed design work may not be undertaken until after financial close. The PPP contract just specifies the outputs required (*cf.* §15.2), and it is the project company that must take the risk that the detailed design will not fulfil these requirements (*cf.* §12.6, §28.9.5).

This does not mean that the contracting authority pays no attention to the project company's design development (or, more commonly, design development by the construction subcontractor): it is not in the contracting authority's interests for the project company to develop a design that fails to provide the service required under the PPP contract. It is therefore quite normal for the contracting authority to have a right to review and comment on detailed designs, but this would not usually involve the contracting authority in approving or 'signing off' the designs, either in stages or as a whole, as it would mean the risk of responsibility for a design error being transferred back to the contracting authority. The review process may be taken a stage further, giving the contracting authority the right to raise objections to the design if it considers it not to be in accordance with the PPP contract specification: if the parties cannot agree at this stage, the dispute-resolution procedure (DRP) (*cf.* §19.6) needs to be used.

The contracting authority should also be given flexibility to require small design changes that do not significantly affect costs or the ability to provide the service.

§19.3.3 Construction Supervision

The position on construction supervision is much the same as on design: while the contracting authority should not 'approve' any aspect of the construction stages, it should have a right to check what is being done, and point out any aspects which seem to be deviating from the PPP contract requirements. It should also be careful not to 'over-monitor' the project and treat it like a public-works project. Again, this could result in taking risks back from the project company—*i.e.* if something later goes wrong, the project company must not be able to claim that this was caused by the contracting authority requiring it to construct the project in a particular way. At the same time, the contract-management team should not over-rely on the work of the independent checker (and, indirectly, the lenders' technical adviser). They should take a close interest in these reviews and assure themselves that the checker has done its work properly.

§19.3.4 Position of the Lenders

Lenders need to continue to monitor and control the activities of the project company to ensure that the basis on which they originally assessed the project's risks is not undermined. This may also leave the equity investors with much less independent management of the project than would be the case with a corporate financing. (The controls imposed by lenders and the rôle of the lenders' technical adviser are discussed in Chapter 25.)

Once the financing is signed up, the contracting authority has no formal or regular relationship with the lenders. (The direct agreement—*cf.* §25.3.3—is a document which only comes into action in a crisis.) Nonetheless, the lenders share many of the same aims: it is in their interests for the project company to meet the requirements of the PPP contract in full. Aligning the lenders' aims with that of the contracting authority to ensure good performance is one of the key risk-allocation enforcement mechanisms of the PPP arrangement.

§19.3.5 Revenue during Construction

Some projects, especially involving refurbishment of an existing facility, or an extension to it, may involve the project company taking over an existing facility and providing services from it immediately after financial close, while construction of the new facility proceeds. In such cases, the operation-phase régime discussed in §19.4 will also apply with respect to these services.

§19.3.6 Preparing for the Operation Phase

Prior to moving on to the operation phase, performance monitoring and the payment mechanism (*cf.* Chapter 15) should be tested in trial runs to ensure that they work and that both parties know what to expect. Joint training of the contracting authority contract-management team and the project company's team may take place. To the extent possible, users of the facility should also be told what level of service to expect and what to do if there is a fault in the service. The risk register (*cf.* §11.6), as well as communications and stakeholder-management plans are also updated (*cf.* §6.5). In some countries, the transition to the operation phase is a point for a gateway review (*cf.* §5.4).

§19.4 OPERATION PHASE

§19.4.1 Monitoring the Service

The rôle of the contract-management team once the project company is delivering the service is to monitor the service provision and maintenance of the facility to ensure that the agreed standards are being met. For concessions, the contracting authority also ensures that the agreed user charges, and any changes to them, are in line with the terms of the PPP contract (*cf.* §15.5). This is similar in some respects to the activities of a regulator of a privatised public utility (*cf.* §27.6) but in this case regulation is achieved through the terms of the PPP contract—often referred to as 'regulation by contract' (although in some countries a regulator may play such an oversight rôle in a concession). In the case of availability PPPs, where the contracting authority is itself paying for the service, it administers the regular payment of the service fees and ensures that the appropriate contractual penalties and deductions are made (*cf.* §15.6).

There may be some reluctance to insist on a strict interpretation of the PPP contract penalties or deductions during the start-up of operations (say the first 6-12 months), but enforcement of the PPP contract's terms is probably the best way to ensure that the project company quickly does whatever is needed to sort out initial problems (but *cf.* §15.6.3). Sticking to the terms of the PPP contract from an early stage has also been shown to lead to a better long-term working relationship between the contracting authority and the project company, not least because it is clear and consistent what each party's rights and obligations should be.

In availability PPPs, especially if the contracting authority is not the direct user of the facility, there is usually a 'help desk' arrangement, *i.e.* a single point where the users of the facility (for example teachers or hospital staff) can report faults and other service issues that need to be addressed by the project company. (This may be staffed by, for example, a facility manager from the project company who is permanently on-site at the facility or cluster of facilities, or at least readily accessible at all times of operation.) The service fault and speed with which it is rectified in line with the agreed response times will be recorded. This is an important feature of the performance requirements in the PPP contract payment mechanism (*cf.* §15.6.2). Frequent deductions are a sign that there may be more systemic problems with the project company, the contracting authority, the relationship between the two or the PPP contract itself.

Most of the performance information required to calculate payment deductions will actually be generated by the project company (sometimes referred to as 'self-reporting'), with the contracting authority retaining the right to verify this whenever it wishes. The PPP contract therefore needs to specify the reporting obligations of the project company on technical, financial and legal issues. The structure of reporting and the level of detail, format and deadlines should be clear and reasonable, and of course the contracting authority will have audit rights.

Some reporting may be real-time and some monthly, quarterly or annual (*e.g.* annual financial statements). Much of this is done using IT tools such as Computer Assisted Production Management Systems (CAPMS). It is important that these are adapted to and reflect the specific requirements of the project, especially where the investors in the project company may have a number of PPP projects (*cf.* §20.6.3)—there have been instances where systems used for previous projects have not been adequately adapted for the project in question. In some cases, the contracting authority may have a system it wants the project company to use. The detail of these arrangements should be set out clearly in the PPP contract, including allowing the contracting authority to access the project company's record-keeping and management tools.

Periodic user-satisfaction surveys, say annually, may be required in the PPP contract. This helps to measure the more subjective elements of the quality of service, although this also means that, due to their subjective nature, they may not lead to significant deductions in the service fee. Nevertheless, apart from a useful monitoring tool, surveys can act as an incentive to improve service delivery and push the project company to put in place a remediation plan or carry out a performance audit at its own expense. Users surveyed may also include wider stakeholders such as school pupils' parents. The contract-management team should also consider regular meetings with user-group representative bodies, especially where user-satisfaction surveys may be more difficult to arrange (for example for a transport facility).

Another cost component that usually needs to be monitored and reviewed periodically is the project company's insurances to check that the required cover is being maintained.

Given the tendency for the costs of insurance to vary significantly over the life of the PPP contract, there may be mechanisms in the PPP contract to share the risk (or benefit) of changes in costs (*cf.* §14.10).

§19.4.2 Value Testing

An activity that is likely to take place periodically during the operation phase, especially for availability PPPs, is value testing of certain components of the soft-FM service (*cf.* §15.6.7). The required timing and scope will be established in the PPP contract and it is the project company's responsibility to carry out the process. Nevertheless, the contracting authority has a close oversight involvement in the process. It should expect to sit down with the project company 9-12 months in advance of the process to discuss how the process will be conducted, especially in the case of market testing. This may also involve adjustments to the service that is being market tested to suit the updated requirements of the authority.

§19.4.3 Managing Contract Changes

Change is almost inevitable over the life of a PPP contract. Experience has shown that there may be literally thousands of contract changes (*cf.* §16.2.2), albeit many of them being minor, over the life of a large PPP contract. In fact the term 'contract change' is rather a misnomer, as most such changes are allowed for *within* the terms of the contract as opposed to being changes *to* the contract. The degree of flexibility to respond to changes first needs to be considered during the consideration and preparation of the PPP contract. The need to manage contract changes can be reduced in the first place by excluding elements of the service from the PPP arrangement that are most likely to change (such as soft-FM services—*cf.* §15.6.7), shortening the PPP contract tenor (so the likelihood of a change of requirements over time is lower—*cf.* §15.3.1) or using financial structures with lower levels of debt (so changes are less likely to affect the financing structure). Most PPP contracts allow for the ultimate change, which is for the contracting authority to terminate the PPP contract (*cf.* §17.3.2). But such flexibility almost always comes at a cost, so there is a point at which the PPP route is no longer VfM if significant contract changes are anticipated (*cf.* §8.8, §28.12).

While standard PPP contract terms have improved over time to accommodate contract changes, particularly those required by the contracting authority, managing these is still one of the most challenging aspects of PPP contract management. This can be a result of a failure to appreciate that managing PPP contracts is an *active* business for the contracting authority, which is still ultimately responsible for ensuring that the public service is delivered and remains VfM.

For contract changes that require significant additional cost, or revision of the PPP contract terms, development of a business case and its review and approval should be used to ensure VfM (*cf.* §5.4). Competitive tendering for the service component involved should be used where possible. Changes to the subcontracts generally require the lenders' consent (*cf.* §16.2.3, §25.4).

§19.4.4 Savings

While good contract management is about getting the service one is paying for, not necessarily cost reduction, the contracting authority's contract-management team should keep an eye out for potential cost savings and efficiencies. Sometimes, this may simply be a case of securing savings that are due to the contracting authority but may have been overlooked, such as a share in third-party income (*cf.* §15.8) or a rebate on insurance costs (*cf.* §14.10)—hence, the value of a contract-management manual (*cf.* §19.8.1). In other cases, there may be changes in the operating environment or service requirement that create an opportunity to make savings. Finally, the contracting authority may be under pressure to find savings because of increasing budgetary pressures. The contract-change mechanism is used to manage and process such savings (*cf.* §16.2.3).

However, savings are unlikely to be found in construction costs, as these are sunk costs. Equally seeking savings from changes to the core maintenance and life-cycle costs may significantly disturb the risk allocation and VfM of the PPP contract—effectively seeking short-term savings at the expense of higher long-term costs, which is exactly the sort of behaviour the PPP approach is seeking to address.

This leaves potentially four main sources for savings:

- getting more services for the same price, such as improving asset use (*e.g.* increased occupancy of an office accommodation PPP or generating third-party income from facilities at weekends of a PPP school) or extending coverage of the service (*e.g.* extending the existing service to other users);
- paying less for the same level of service through value testing (*cf.* §15.6.7), insurance costs savings (*cf.* §14.10) or refinancing (*cf.* §26.2);
- reducing the required scope or performance levels of the service and paying less for it (*e.g.* reducing the frequency of window cleaning, cutting the grass on road verges less often, reducing fault-repair response times, especially if this brings the project into line with practices elsewhere); and
- taking the provision of a soft-FM service out of the PPP contract to be provided, if possible, more cheaply elsewhere (*cf.* §15.6.7).

But reducing the scope or performance levels of the services is, however, unlikely to be VfM—the value of any reduction negotiated in the service fee is often more than the reduction in cost to the contracting authority.

For larger central government-funded PPP programmes, contracting authorities may need to be encouraged to pursue savings by allowing them to keep any savings achieved (rather than having to hand them back to, say, the Ministry of Finance).

Of course, there is also scope for savings outside the PPP contract such as ensuring user practices lead to more efficient energy use (*cf.* §13.7) but this should not reduce incentives for the project company to design and operate the facility efficiently. Thus, contract management is part of a wider activity of using the facility efficiently and effectively.

§19.5 HAND BACK

Issues which arise towards the end of the PPP contract's life are discussed in §17.8. Well in advance of the hand back, the contract-management team needs to ensure that the project company keeps to its obligations to maintain the facility (and there may be additional mechanisms in the PPP contract to ensure this) while also arranging for the procurement of a follow-on service contract from a new private-sector operator after hand back.

At hand back itself, the project company needs to ensure that the asset register (*cf.* §23.9.2) is up to date and provide a list of all assets transferred to the authority, together with all project records and documents. It may also be necessary to arrange for the transfer of employees to the contracting authority (*cf.* §28.13).

§19.6 DISPUTES

Disputes can arise due to changes in the environment or issues arising in the project that are unclear or not provided for in the PPP contract (*e.g.* what is the definition of 'clean'?). The first defence is a good PPP contract, which is why thorough contract preparation and a procurement process that ensures as far as possible all issues are mutually understood and agreed is so important. The dispute-resolution procedures (DRP) in the PPP contract should encourage issues first to be resolved at the day-to-day management level, and then if necessary through consultation between senior management at the contracting authority and the project company within a specified period of time. Only if an issue cannot be resolved through consultation, would it then go to an expert or a board appointed from a panel of experts whose members have been jointly agreed by the two parties. Arbitration and ultimately court proceedings should be used as a last resort. Multiple contact points between the contracting authority and the project company can also help prevent problems turning into conflicts. One of the objectives is to avoid the resolution of the dispute itself irreparably damaging the relationship between the two parties wherever possible.

The contracting authority's key weapon if a dispute arises is that it can withhold disputed amounts from the service-fee payments (in the case of availability PPPs), which obviously puts financial pressure on the project company. However, should the DRP find in the project company's favour, the contracting authority would have to pay interest on the disputed amounts withheld. On the other hand, the contracting authority may not want to pursue disputes where these involve relatively small amounts of money and the project company is stubborn about settlement, since the legal costs of any dispute, especially one that moves from arbitration to a court, are likely to be significant. So, unless the contracting authority is prepared to pursue DRP, withholding part of the service fee may not achieve very much: as soon as the project company gives notice that it intends to pursue DRP, the contracting authority may have to give in and pay the withheld amount.

§19.7 Contract-Management Resourcing

As can be seen, contract management is a not a passive undertaking for the contracting authority and requires dedicated resources and funding. The level of resourcing the contract-management team needs is often under-estimated by the contracting authority.[1] This may be understandable if the contracting authority has little experience of what is involved. However, these costs should be anticipated in PPP Phase 4 (Procurement Review) and form part of the decision to procure the project as a PPP.

Contract management requires the 'soft skills' of relationship and stakeholder management, negotiation and management of change, together with more specialist skills in financial and technical areas. Furthermore, contract management involves periods of routine and continuous activities combined with periods of high intensity such as at the start of the construction phase, at handover from construction to operation, at points during the operation phase when a contract change needs to be managed or the project gets into difficulty and, finally, around hand back. PPP units (*cf.* §4.7) can support contract-management teams at critical points: for example, during a refinancing (*cf.* §26.2) or when a project gets into difficulty. For smaller national programmes or for sector programmes, such a unit may play a more active and regular rôle under a suitable support arrangement with the contracting authority.

A large hospital PPP could typically have the equivalent of four full-time people overseeing the project company's performance in hard and soft FM (*cf.* §13.6) and other services, as well as the administration of payments and financial reporting.[2] The minimum requirement to manage a PPP contract for a contracting authority should be at least one full-time person equivalent.

Creating a central team that oversees several PPP projects in a programme may bring benefits in terms of economies of scale and depth of expertise, as well as collecting central data on performance and costs and disseminating good practice (but this requires that individual projects share such information with the central team). This is one reason why programme approaches (*cf.* §4.6) can be attractive. For example, the French prisons programme involves over 50 prisons using various contractual structures, including PPPs. A central unit of eight people provides technical support to regional and facility-based contract managers at each prison with reporting mechanisms up and down the line. This ensures that performance information is shared and that the day-to-day contract-management teams are well supported for more complex, non-routine issues. In some cases, a central unit may provide professional mediation services to the contracting authority contract-management team to resolve disputes (*e.g.* Britain's Department of Health's Private Finance Unit provides this and other central contract-management support services to individual hospital PPPs).

---

[1] Although it can occasionally be over-estimated, with the contracting authority treating the project as a traditional public-works project and interfering too heavily in the day-to-day management and operations.

[2] In some cases, even more: the larger hospital PPPs in Britain have teams of up to 13 people managing the PPP contract (National Audit Office 2010).

Most availability PPPs involve provision of the 'accommodation' by the project company while the main services are provided by the public sector—*e.g.* schools or hospitals where the teachers and clinicians, respectively, are 'users' of the facility as part of the public sector. This 'triangle' of contracting authority, users and project company needs to be recognised in such projects in setting up the contract-management arrangements. These users are the 'front line' in observing and reporting on the availability and quality of the facility. Contract management should therefore ensure that they understand the extent and limits of the project company's responsibilities and know how to report service issues. This may even involve educating users in how to use the facility (*e.g.* not opening windows in a climate-controlled environment, or putting up shelves themselves, *etc.*, which they may have been used to doing before). Attention should also be paid to ensuring that there is effective integration between the users' activities and those of the project company (such as allowing for user and maintenance schedules to be coordinated) and that there is a constructive partnership approach to resolving issues.

§19.8 CONTRACT-MANAGEMENT TOOLS

§19.8.1 Contract Manual

While the PPP contract should always be the ultimate point of reference, this is a large and complex document, not well designed for practical operational-management issues. A contract manual is a useful tool to set out in everyday language what the contract-management team is expected to do. The manual should be developed by the project-management team before financial close, ideally in collaboration with the contract-management team. It should cover matters such as:

- governance arrangements (contracting authority's hierarchy, decision-making processes, delegated powers, management of communication and stakeholders, including the users);
- organisation and composition of the contracting authority's contract-management team, as discussed above;
- organisation and composition of the project company's team (*cf.* §20.6.3);
- the purpose and frequency of meetings between the contracting authority and the project company;
- the service-specification requirements and service-fee adjustment mechanisms (*cf.* Chapter 15);
- requirements for reporting and collection of data;
- an explanation of the payment mechanism;
- risk-management arrangements, including updating the risk register (*cf.* §11.6);
- how contract changes are managed (*cf.* §19.4.3); and
- the dispute resolution process (*cf.* §19.6).

The contract manual needs to be updated to take account of any changes internal to the PPP contract or as a result of developments in the external environment (such as the way the contracting authority is organised).

The project company should be asked to provide feedback on relevant parts of the manual. Guidance in other areas such as protocols on communication, service continuity and disaster recovery should also be provided. It is also helpful if the contract-management team has access to the records that reflect the activities and decisions over the prior phases of the project.

In countries with highly-standardised PPP contracts for certain sectors, the contract manual for the relevant sector may be also be standardised and readily available. This is the case in India, for example.

§19.8.2 Financial Model

The financial model is another critical management tool (*cf.* §23.8). A base case of the financial model has to be agreed at financial close for the purposes of agreeing how the effect of changes will be calculated (*cf.* §23.9.9), such as contract changes, calculating refinancing gains (*cf.* §26.2.6), monitoring of user-charge adjustments and revenue or profit-sharing/capping mechanisms.

§19.8.3 Managing Project Risks

One of the most important activities in contract management is the management of risk (*cf.* Chapters 11-13). The risk register (*cf.* §11.6) is used to enable the contract-management team to oversee how the risks of the project are being managed, who is responsible for managing each risk and to support the management of those risks that it has retained. The risk register, which should have been developed in the earlier phases, therefore needs to be continually updated and reviewed by the contract-management team.

§19.9 Reviews and Ex-Post Evaluation

During the construction and operation phases, the contracting authority may carry out periodic reviews of the overall performance of the PPP contract (apart from any contractually-envisaged value-testing reviews—*cf.* §15.6.7), or reviews may be carried out by an independent public body such as a national audit office.

Such reviews may focus on the performance of the PPP contract or the performance of the contracting authority's contract-management team. They may also focus on plans for future improvements in VfM, innovation and on how well or otherwise the performance of the PPP contract has adapted to any changes in circumstances. Reviews also aim to identify any lessons learnt that can be used to assist the development of future PPP policy. Typically, a review may take place 18 months into the operation phase and every five years thereafter but may also be driven by specific events such as a major change or if there are concerns about the project. However, such periodic reviews should not be considered a substitute for active day-to-day contract management.

In other cases, however, the reviews carried out by an oversight body are at a strategic level. These may cover a programme of projects or review the performance of the project overall, *i.e.* not just the PPP element. In this case, such reviews usually assess the *outcomes* of the project in relation to the originally identified *needs* and *objectives* (*cf. §7.2*). This is usually done by an *ex-post* assessment of VfM looking at the '3 Es' of 'economy' (reducing the cost of the way things are currently done), 'efficiency' (doing more for less) and 'effectiveness' (improving the quality of a service that addresses the needs and objectives) (*cf. §8.2*). If the needs and objectives for the project have not been clearly defined *ex-ante*, then such reviews are difficult to carry out and the risk for the contracting authority is that they are then judged on the basis of whatever the reviewing body decides at the time should be the measure of success.

Frameworks for how assessments are carried out have been developed in various parts of the world such as the 'programme logic model' used by the European Court of Auditors, the 'investment logic map' of Victoria State's Department of Treasury and Finance (Victoria State Department of Treasury and Finance, 2017) and the US Department of Transport Federal Highway Administration's 'performance-based approach to planning and programming' (FHWA, 2013). It is therefore important for the contracting authority to be aware of how, and on what basis, the project is likely to be assessed before the public audit body comes knocking on the door.

§19.10 Transparency and Disclosure

Contracting authorities are under increasing pressure from within government and wider stakeholders to make information publicly available on matters such as:

- the level of PPP activity;
- the PPP contract terms entered into;
- the status, progress, condition and performance of PPP projects; and
- the documents that underpin public-sector decisions to procure PPPs.

PPPs often operate in an environment where there is suspicion of the motivations for PPP projects and of their true performance and rationale for them. The long-term nature of PPP contracts, the potential commercial benefits that accrue to the private partner for the provision of a public service and the levels of public money involved all require proper accountability. There may also be concerns that the contracting authority does not properly understand the true level of returns of the private partner.

However, a balance has to be struck between the levels of disclosure, the legitimate commercial interests of the public and private sectors and the cost of providing information. Other restrictions, such as disclosure of personal data, also need to be taken into account. At the same time, there may be public-disclosure laws (such as freedom of information legislation) that require disclosure under certain conditions. Or there may be disclosure requirements if the project company or its owners are listed on a stock exchange or finance is raised through the capital markets.

For the public sector, disclosure may include regular publication of the status of preparation of projects, of the long-term payment and other commitments under the PPP contract (not least for sound fiscal reporting—*cf. §9.4*), publication of the PPP contract or its principal terms. It may even include publication of the documents, such as business cases (*cf. §5.4*), that justified the investment and the decision to procure the project as a PPP.

With regard to disclosure of information by the private sector, the PPP contract may require the project company to disclose to the contracting authority costs such as life-cycle costs (and provision for them), costs of changes (*cf.* §19.4.3) on an open-book basis, the accrued and forecast investment returns for the project company's shareholders, details of beneficial ownership of the project company and the terms of the principal finance agreements. To help ensure access to information, there may be provision for the contracting authority to participate as a shareholder (*cf.* §27.4) or at least have an observer on the board of the project company, or to have the right to see all correspondence with the lenders (who usually get detailed management information from the project company).

There is generally an acceptance that a limited amount of the information is commercially sensitive and not for disclosure, but determining what this should be and for how long it should remain confidential, is tricky. This varies between sectors but normally includes any information that is proprietary to a sponsor and that if disclosed would enable a competitor to obtain a commercial advantage over the sponsor. Nevertheless, national audit bodies are likely to have over-riding rights to information (whether or not confidential) and to be able to report to parliament. Furthermore, as mentioned above, whatever is agreed to be treated as confidential should not conflict with legal requirements to disclose information. The PPP contract should clearly list what information is to be treated as confidential, making a distinction between information that the project company will not disclose to the contracting authority on the grounds of commercial confidentiality, and information that the contracting authority will not disclose on the same grounds should it receive a freedom of information request; the extent of this list can be one of the livelier issues discussed during the bidding phase.

§19.11 STAFF TRANSFERS

The employment conditions of staff that are transferred to a new employer under the PPP arrangement may be protected by law. An example is TUPE (Transfer of Undertakings Protection of Employment) Regulations 2006 in Britain, which applies to organisations of all sizes and is designed to protect employees' rights when the organisation or service they work for transfers to a new employer (British Department for Business Innovation and Skills 2014).

In the context of a PPP, this means that staff transferred from the contracting authority to the project company or subcontractors carry with them their continuous service from their public-sector employer and should continue to enjoy the same terms and conditions of employment with the incoming employer (staff may also retain access to their public-service pension scheme—British Treasury 2013).

Following a transfer, employers often find they have employees with different terms and conditions working alongside each other and wish to change/harmonise terms and conditions. However, TUPE protects against change/harmonisation for an indefinite period if the sole or principal reason for the change is the transfer.

Another approach used to protect the terms and conditions of soft-FM staff (such a cleaning staff) is for the public-sector employer to second such staff to the PPP for the duration of the PPP contract.

PART V

THE PRIVATE-SECTOR PERSPECTIVE

Sponsors and Other Investors

§20.1 INTRODUCTION

Having considered in the previous chapters how the contracting authority goes through the process of developing and signing up to a PPP contract, this chapter considers the parallel process on the part of private-sector investors, *i.e.*:

- sources of investment for PPP projects (§20.2);
- the financial basis for the investment decision (§20.3);
- bidding and project development (§20.4);
- joint-venture issues (§20.5);
- formation and management of the project company (§20.6); and
- the use of external advisers (§20.7).

§20.2 SOURCES OF INVESTMENT FOR PPP PROJECTS

A clear distinction has to be made between the two main sources of private-sector finance for PPPs—investors and lenders. In order to obtain debt financing for the project company, its investors (*i.e.* the parties that own the project company's shares) have to offer priority payment to the lenders out of the project company's cash flow, thus accepting that they will only receive any return on their investment after the lenders have been satisfied (*cf.* §2.4, §25.2.3). Therefore, investors assume the highest financial risk, but at the same time they receive the highest return from the project company's (*pro rata* to the money they have at risk) if all goes according to plan.

The rôle of investors is discussed in this chapter. The following chapters cover the use of project-finance techniques by lenders, the ways in which debt is raised for PPP projects and the integration of debt and equity in the overall financial structure.

§20.2.1 Sponsors

Investors in project companies are usually very limited in number: no more than two or three is quite common, as this makes the complex arrangements for developing and controlling a PPP project easier to coordinate. The key investors are those responsible for bidding for, developing and managing the project, known as the sponsors (*cf.* §2.3).

Even though the project company's debt will probably be 'non-recourse', *i.e.* have no guarantees from the sponsors (*cf.* §21.3) or very limited guarantees (*cf.* §22.8), their involvement is important. Both the contracting authority and the lenders have to consider whether the sponsors of the project are appropriate parties, taking into account factors such as:

- Do the sponsors have experience in the sector concerned and, hence, the ability to provide any technical support required by the project? (This experience may be divided between several sponsors with different backgrounds.)
- Have the sponsors worked together successfully before?
- Do the sponsors have a reasonable amount of equity invested in the project company, which gives them an incentive to provide support to protect their investment if it gets into difficulty (even though they have no legal requirement to provide such support, but it may make commercial sense for them to do so if they can)? If so, do they have the financial resources to provide such support?
- Do the sponsors have arm's-length contractual arrangements with the project company (where they act as subcontractors, *e.g.* for construction of the facility)?
- Is there a reasonable return on the sponsors' investment? (If the return is low—*e.g.* because there is a high construction subcontract price—there may be little incentive for the sponsors to continue their involvement with the project company once construction is complete.)
- Do any of the sponsors have a clear interest in the long-term success of the project, or is their interest limited to the construction phase only?

Typical sponsors for PPP projects can be divided into two main categories:

- 'operational' investors—*i.e.* companies for whom investment is part of a strategy for securing other business as subcontractors to the project company, although some of these have also become significant long-term investors in PPPs; and
- 'financial' investors—*i.e.* entities only interested in the investment and not in ancillary business as subcontractors; these may be banks, life-insurance companies, pension funds or infrastructure-investment companies or funds.

To look at these in more detail:

— Subcontractors

PPPs offer a way of expanding business (or compensating for loss of other public-sector business that may now be procured as a PPP) for both construction and service or maintenance contractors, who will sign subcontracts with the project company. The return on their investment in the project company thus becomes part of their overall return along with the profit on the subcontracting work they undertake.

Support from potential subcontractors is essential for the development of a PPP programme, and there are some countries (*e.g.* Spain) where most PPP investment is undertaken only by subcontractors (or closely-associated lending institutions) some of which are substantial global businesses. But in many markets, local contractors team up with international contractors as well as with financial investors who can bring PPP structuring expertise to the table.

— Banks

It is a natural step for banks to move from acting as lenders (for which see Chapter 22) to investors in PPP projects. An equity investment may be a relatively small addition to the financing they have already committed to the project, and while the risks are higher they are similar in nature to the risks which are also assessed before providing the debt financing (*cf.* §11.5).

— Institutional investors

Life-insurance companies and pension funds (known collectively as 'institutional investors') are natural investors in PPPs, as the long-term PPP investment cash flows match their long-term liabilities. However, there are some obstacles to this source of investment:

- Institutional investors tend not to be well equipped to evaluate and monitor PPP investments (since they form a small part of their total portfolios, it is not worth their while to recruit the staff for this).
- Many institutional investors only really want to invest in deals that are prepared and 'ready to go'. But the PPP market is generally based on developing a project through a risky procurement phase that takes a lot of work and high-risk capital.
- Finally such investors tend to avoid construction risk (*cf.* §12.3), preferring to come into projects as 'secondary' investors (*cf.* §20.2.3), when the facility has been constructed and is operating successfully, or to invest indirectly at that stage in specialist infrastructure funds as discussed below. However, a number of such institutional investors (for example in Canada and the Netherlands) have increasingly developed in-house capability to participate as sponsors and take early-stage project risks, partly to reduce the fees they would otherwise be paying to the managers of separate infrastructure funds.

In some countries, there has been political pressure for public-sector pension funds to invest in PPPs, especially where the investment pool is too small for a major PPP programme (*e.g.* Nigeria), or where the private sector is perceived to be making 'windfall' profits (*cf.* §26.3) at the public-sector or taxpayers' expense (*e.g.* Britain).

From pensioners' point of view, this is a rather dangerous approach if the result is that investments are made on a political rather than a sound financial basis.

— Infrastructure investment funds

Infrastructure investment funds—investing both in privatised infrastructure such as airports and utilities and privately-developed and -owned infrastructure such as mobile-phone networks, but also in PPPs—have become a world-wide phenomenon. Such funds are managed by investment banks, fund managers specialising in infrastructure investment (which may themselves invest in infrastructure as well as manage infrastructure funds) and major insurance companies (as part of their over-all fund-management business). Again, institutional investors are typically the largest investors in infrastructure funds, but in this case smaller entities can invest as they rely on the fund manager to carry out evaluation and monitoring of projects. In some cases, infrastructure funds are quoted on stock exchanges, which widens the market further to individual investors, as well as making it easier for institutional investors to value and trade in such PPP investments.

Infrastructure funds have become probably the most important source of equity for PPP projects (as well as for privatised/private-sector infrastructure projects). The largest fund managers in this sector are to be found in Australia, Canada and the United States. Macquarie Group, of Australia, is by far the largest infrastructure-fund manager, with $96 billion of funds under management in mid-2017, $69 billion of which was from pension funds; other smaller categories of investors in its funds include insurance companies, sovereign-wealth funds, wealth-management companies and banks (Willis Towers Watson 2017).

Such funds are sometimes criticised for their high management fees or for taking an investment approach that is too short term (*i.e.* they seek to realise their returns by selling their investments within a relatively short period) in relation to the long-term nature of infrastructure investment (*cf.* §20.3.3).

Although some investors only get involved with PPPs and other infrastructure in their own country, there is also a large international pool of such investors. A contracting authority has to bear in mind that while its particular project may be the only one in the country, it may have to compete for investment with other similar PPP projects going on elsewhere in the world.

The contracting authority or another public-sector entity may also invest in the project company (*cf.* §18.11, §27.4).

§20.2.2 Conflicts of Interest

It has to be borne in mind that each of these categories of sponsor may have conflicts of interest:

— Subcontractors

There are inherent conflicts of interest in subcontractors acting as investors in the project company, when it comes to dealing with issues arising on the subcontracts, although it could also be argued that equity investment means that a subcontractor is more committed to the success of a project. Subcontractors with a substantial equity involvement usually keep this investment separate from the contractual relationship with the project company to ensure that their own decisions are made in a balanced way.

There is also a more fundamental conflict arising from the fact that each subcontractor may only be interested in a limited phase or aspect of the PPP contract; in particular, the construction subcontractor may have little long-term interest in the project after it is built, and will often prefer to dispose of the investment in the project company at that time. But another reason for selling at that time is for the subcontractor to recycle the proceeds into bidding for new projects, which is of course beneficial to PPP programmes as it increases market liquidity and competition.

But some construction contractors—e.g. from France and Spain—have transformed themselves into long-term investors in infrastructure projects, treating construction and investment as separate albeit linked businesses. If a construction contractor can be re-rated by the stock market as an infrastructure investor, this is likely to add considerable value to its shares, as its revenues will then be considered by the market to be long term in nature, instead of continually vulnerable to the short-term fluctuations of the construction industry. In some cases, however, this has led contractors to bid too aggressively for projects to transform themselves into infrastructure businesses and ultimately face difficulties.

Companies with long-term maintenance or other operating subcontracts, on the other hand, usually maintain their investment while they have this contractual relationship with the project company.

— Financial investors (*i.e.* banks, institutional investors and infrastructure investment funds)

If a sponsor, such as a bank, is both an investor and a lender, there are potential conflicts of interest between these rôles (although some banks only act as lenders or investors, not both, depending on the overall business model).

If a bid is put together by a financial investor, with major subcontractors in a secondary rôle, this may raise questions about the whole-life integration of the design and construction, and so weaken one of the arguments in favour of PPPs (*cf.* §28.8). On the other hand, financial investors perform an independent due-diligence rôle and have an incentive to get the best possible terms out of subcontractors, whereas sponsor subcontractors obviously have a conflict of interest in this respect, however well controlled, as discussed above. This independence may also be beneficial if a project gets into difficulty and a 'blame game' develops between the subcontractors: the financial investor will try to ensure the issue is resolved quickly for the benefit of the project.

If the sponsors of the project are primarily infrastructure fund managers, whose interest is in placing the investment in managed funds, a significant part of their return may come from arrangement or advisory fees that are paid out of the initial financing (known as development fees—*cf.* §23.9.2), rather than out of the long-term operating cash flow of the project. This may encourage a riskier approach to structuring the financing, as well as increasing its development costs.

— Contracting authority

Here the conflict of interest is self-evident (*cf.* §27.4).

§20.2.3 Secondary Investors

Some sponsors' business models depend on selling off their investment shortly after the project has been completed and has demonstrated that it is producing net revenues as expected. Even where the investment is long term in intention, investors that have built up a portfolio of PPP investments may also choose to sell off parts of their portfolio from time to time, as a way of establishing its overall value, or to raise funds for new projects.

Once a PPP programme is established therefore, there is likely to be a reasonably active 'secondary market', into which other new investors may enter, *e.g.* a 'secondary' infrastructure investment fund. Primary funds invest in the project from the beginning, as discussed above, and therefore usually form part of the bidding consortium. They aim at a higher target return because of the higher risk inherent in the bidding and construction phases of a project. Secondary funds usually purchase their investments from primary investors (both financial investors and subcontractors) once the project is complete, and risks have reduced, offering a correspondingly lower return (*cf.* §26.3).[1]

§20.3 THE INVESTMENT DECISION

§20.3.1 Cost of Capital and Its Relationship to PPP Investments

In deciding whether to invest in a new project, an investor has to consider whether the investment provides an adequate return. The baseline against which this is measured is normally the investor's own cost of capital. For a company, the 'weighted average cost of capital' (WACC) is used, *i.e.* the weighted average of the costs of its own equity and debt funding. A simplified WACC calculation would be:

$$\text{WACC} = \left(\frac{E}{E+D} \times \text{Re} \right) + \left(\frac{D}{E+D} \times \text{Rd} \times (1 - T\%) \right)$$

where

E = market value of company's equity;
D = company's outstanding debt;
Re = return on equity, expressed as a rate of return;
Rd = return on debt, *i.e.* the cost of borrowing expressed as a rate of interest; and

---

[1] However primary investors may face the problem that while it is not difficult to sell out to a secondary investor, replacing a profitable primary investment with a new one that is equally profitable is becoming more difficult given increasing competition for such investments.

T% = effective tax rate (as debt is tax-deductible)—a more sophisticated calculation might distinguish between initial tax benefits on investment, and later tax charges on net income.

While 'Rd' (the cost of debt) is quite easy to measure, 'Re' (the cost of equity) is more complex. This measurement has to take into account both the general risk premium applied to any company compared to a risk-free investment in government debt, and the particular risk premium which the stock market attributes to the company's own business. The calculation (known as the 'capital asset pricing model' (CAPM)) is thus:

$$Re = Rf + \beta(Rm - Rf)$$

where

Rf = the risk-free rate, *i.e.* the cost of government debt;
Rm = the market-risk premium, *i.e.* the average rate of return which investors expect from investing in the equity market; and
β (beta) = the risk premium for the particular company's business compared to the market as a whole; if the company is considered to have the same risk as the market as a whole, $\beta = 1$.

Thus, if a company is financed 50% by equity whose cost (Re) has been calculated as 15% *p.a.* using the CAPM, and 50% by debt costing 6% (Rd), with a tax rate of 30%, the calculation would be:

$$WACC = \left(\frac{50}{100} \times 15\%\right) + \left(\frac{50}{100} \times 6\% \times (1 - 30\%)\right) = 9.6\%$$

The WACC, used as a discount rate to discount future pre-financing cash flows expected from the company's business, will produce a NPV calculation of the current value of the company (*cf.* §26.3). Since the WACC is thus the overall required return on the company's business, pre-financing cash flows from new investments must at least match this rate of return to preserve the company's value.

In corporate-finance theory, changes in a company's leverage (*i.e.* the ratio between equity and debt, also known as 'gearing') do not change its WACC (if the risk inherent in the business has not changed); so, if the leverage increases (*e.g.* debt goes above 50% in the example above), the relative costs of Re (*i.e.* the CAPM calculation) and Rd will adjust such that WACC remains at 9.6% (but *cf.* §21.5.1).

The above might suggest that the WACC in a separate project company should equal the investor's own WACC, but this is not the case: the project company's own cost of capital has to be taken into account. This may differ from that of its investors because of:

- the different risk profile of the project company and its investors' other businesses; only businesses with the same overall risk should have the same WACC;
- different investors in the project company having different WACCs;
- substantial changes in leverage over the project's life (high to begin with and low at the end), so there is no consistent weighting of equity and debt, unlike the assumption in the WACC model (these changes in leverage reflect the fact that a

project company's debt has to be repaid by the end of PPP contract; normally non-PPP companies do not pay off all their debt); and

- the tax position of the project company is likely to be quite different from that of its investors, and also to change substantially over time (*cf.* §23.6.1).

§20.3.2 Project IRR

WACC is thus not really an appropriate measure for a project company. The usual measure of the cost of capital for PPP projects is the project IRR. This is calculated as the IRR on the original investment, derived from the projected net operating cash flow (before financing costs) over the project. The project IRR for a PPP project company is not the same as its WACC, because WACC is a snapshot at the beginning of the project (which assumes it continues indefinitely in the same constant state), whereas project IRR is based on a projection over the project life (and hence allows for changing leverage and the finite nature of the project). Project IRR thus gives a more accurate view of the expected cost of capital over the life of a typical PPP project.

§20.3.3 Equity IRR

However, as far as a bidder for a PPP project is concerned, the standard approach for pricing the bid is to determine the leverage and cost of debt, and then to apply the required equity IRR to the balance of the financing (*cf.* §23.4). Thus, the bidder does not start with a required project IRR (although experienced bidders will know roughly what this should be), but the eventual project IRR is a result of this calculation.

The equity return in PPP projects is calculated using the equity IRR. This is the IRR of the cash flow derived from:

- the initial investment in the project company;
- the projected cash flow from this investment over the life of the project (after debt service and all operating costs, including hard FM); and
- any residual value, if the project company retains the facility (*cf.* §5.3.9, §17.8, §19.5).

It should be noted that the equity IRR includes any margin charged by the project company on its operating costs, *i.e.* the profits on the continuing services or the return on continuing risks, such as maintenance. This cannot be compared with a 'pure' return on the capex. Also, it does not take into account profit margins earned by subcontractors and then charged on to the project company; so, from the contracting authority's point of view, the equity IRR does not represent the overall return that the private sector as a whole is getting for providing the facility *and* associated services.[2]

---

[2] And the profits earned by lenders should also be taken into account in this respect.

§20.3.4 Factors Affecting the Equity IRR

The investor's own WACC often provides the base for the equity IRR pricing, to which is added an allowance for the additional risk that applies throughout the project life, given the nature of the project: thus, a road concession with high traffic risk would be at the top end of the scale, and an availability-PPP project with no usage risk at the low end.

Very roughly speaking, investors looking at a project at its earliest phase (*i.e.* as bidders) might target a nominal equity IRR (*i.e.* without deducting the effect of inflation—see §24.3.1) of 10-14% in markets open to general international competition. Investors also commonly require a maximum payback period (*cf.* §3.4.3) of, say, seven years.

Equity IRRs tend to decline as a PPP programme develops, the project risks are better understood by investors, and the investment pool becomes deeper. Ensuring real competition in the procurement process is obviously a key factor here.

Once the facility has been completed and is operating normally, secondary investors will accept a lower equity IRR, and hence the value of the project goes up, creating a profit for the sponsors or other primary investors (*cf.* §20.2.1, §26.3).

There has been concern that PPP primary equity IRRs seem to be higher than is really reflected in a project's risks (National Audit Office 2012). The problem here is partly political: perceived excessive rates of return on equity investment for a low risk can undermine the PPP programme (*cf.* §26.1, §28.13). The reasons for this discrepancy may include:

- The need to take account of the costs of losing bids—if a bidder wins one deal in four this one deal must pay for the bid costs on the other three.
- Similarly, once a bidder has won a bid and reached financial close, the value of the equity immediately increases (*cf.* §26.4), which may suggest that the bidder is not paying full value for the investment, or that it is overpriced from the contracting authority's point of view—but part of the reason for such a rise is that the bidding/development risk has been removed from the project, so any investor coming in at this point will accept a lower return reflecting this lower risk, and hence pay more for the equity.
- The use of standard hurdle rates for investments that do not take account of the lower long-term risk of a PPP investment, with a secure income stream, compared to investors' other business where there is greater uncertainty—so it is not necessarily correct to assume that the corporate WACC is a base to which a project-specific return should be added, as the corporate WACC already has an allowance for risk.
- Competition from other high-yield investments in the private-equity field, especially relevant where a significant part of the equity investment comes from financial investors or fund managers—although it is certainly questionable whether it is appropriate to measure the relatively low risk of equity investment in a PPP against the high risk of a private-equity fund.
- The effect of combining high leverage and the lenders' loan-cover requirements, which has a direct effect on the equity IRR (*cf.* §23.3, §23.5).

It should also be noted that the standard equity IRR calculation usually does not take into account any development fees, *i.e.* profits earned by the sponsors on their development costs (*cf.* §20.4).

§20.3.5 Shareholder Equity and Subordinated Debt

Instead of investing only in the share capital of the project company, investors often provide subordinated debt (*i.e.* debt that is only paid when third-party 'senior' lenders such as banks have been paid what they are due), typically at an interest rate roughly equal to the equity IRR. Such shareholders' subordinated debt is used instead of share capital (at least to some extent) for several reasons:

- It is more tax-efficient if subordinated-debt interest payments by the project company are tax-deductible (provided 'thin capitalisation' or other tax provisions do not treat shareholder-provided subordinated loans as equity for tax purposes rather than as debt).
- It eliminates the 'dividend trap' problem (*cf.* §23.6.4).
- It is easier to return funds to investors by prepaying a shareholder subordinated loan rather than repaying equity shares if a refinancing takes place and the senior debt is increased (*cf.* §26.2), or in the later years of the project when the investors may wish to have their equity investment gradually paid back.
- Returning funds in this way may also have a tax advantage, if repayment of subordinated debt is not taxable, whereas a dividend payment on the equity is.

From the point of view of the contracting authority or the lenders, it makes little difference how the 'equity' is made up, *i.e.* the split between share capital and subordinated debt: it is only necessary to ensure that:

- The investors' funding, in whatever form, is fully committed to the project (and thus cannot be withdrawn or cancelled half-way through the construction phase if it has not already been spent by then—*cf.* §25.3.2).
- Investors have a long-term commitment to the project derived from earning their return—whether by dividends or subordinated-debt service—over the full life of the PPP contract (and, *e.g.* not skewed towards the early years of the PPP contract).
- Investors do not get any extra rights at the lenders' expense as a result of financing through subordinated debt instead of share capital (*cf.* §25.5.5).

A contracting authority may feel that it should specify that bidders should invest at least $x\%$ as share capital (and not subordinated debt) in the project company—a common provision in rules on foreign investment in developing countries. But the result may be to force bidders to use a less efficient shareholding structure, and hence offer a less attractive pricing for the PPP contract (although on the other hand this may produce a higher tax revenue for the country concerned).

When calculating their return, investors that also provide subordinated debt normally amalgamate the two, *i.e.* the cash flow from both types of investment is added together and a 'blended equity IRR' calculated on this basis ('equity IRR' hereafter is intended to mean the total equity-return calculation, *i.e.* the blended equity IRR where this is relevant).

Blended equity IRR calculations are normally done using the project company's cash flows as paid out to the investors. (The combination of dividend payments on shares and debt service on shareholder subordinated debt is known as 'distributions'.) The calculations will thus take account of any tax payable by the project company; a separate calculation may take account of tax payable by investors on the receipts from the project company, but this is normally internal in nature, as each investor's tax position is likely to be different.

The equity IRR may also be used to recalculate the service fees at financial close (*cf.* §24.2.13) or after changes in the PPP contract (*cf.* §16.2.1), and to calculate the termination sum, should the contracting authority choose to terminate the PPP contract early (*cf.* §17.3.3). This is why an agreed financial model (*cf.* §23.8) is important as it sets out an agreed way in which such a calculation should take place.

§20.3.6 Equity Commitment *versus* Investment Returns

The use of equity IRR calculations as the main measure for investors' returns leads to some strange distortions of behaviour. Lenders would clearly prefer investors to invest their money into the project first (rather than, say, *pro rata*, with the debt). The earlier the investment is paid in—given that the rest of the cash flow from the project does not change—the lower the investor's equity IRR (*cf.* §3.4.3). This therefore leads investors to find ways of making a commitment to invest in a way that satisfies lenders, but that does not require their IRR calculation to run from day one of the project, *e.g.*:

- committing to pay in the equity in cash towards the end of the construction period (when the debt has been fully used), and if necessary providing an on-demand bank guarantee for this payment; or
- arranging an 'equity-bridge' loan: this is a loan, usually provided by the lenders to the project company and guaranteed by the sponsors *pro rata* to their shareholding, which is drawn in lieu of the equity; it is repaid by a committed equity subscription at the end of the construction period, meaning that the equity is paid in later than the above structure; the cost of the loan is relatively low as it represents a corporate risk on the sponsors rather than a risk on the project company, thanks to the equity commitment.

Neither of these two structures makes the slightest difference to the sponsors' actual risk: whether they invest the equity on day one, or commit to do so in future, the risk is exactly the same. Should there be a loan default during the construction phase, the equity must be paid in immediately. A proper assessment on the part of investors would take account of the commitment rather than the cash investment, *e.g.* by notionally charging the project the investor's cost of funds less a redeposit rate during the period when the investment is undrawn (*cf.* §3.4.6), but this is not usually done.

However, there are categories of investor that do not usually use such structures—*e.g.* an infrastructure investment fund, as the fund would have collected cash investments and would not want to have the cash lying idle during the construction period: this would reduce the fund's IRR even more than subscribing the cash up-front, because this IRR is based on when the cash is subscribed into the fund, not when it is used to make an investment.

So long as a simple IRR approach is taken by investors, whatever the timing of their investment, the contracting authority should of course try to encourage the use of an equity guarantee or bridge, because this reduces the cost of capital during the construction period, and hence the eventual service fees.

§20.4 BIDDING AND PROJECT DEVELOPMENT

Successful PPP project management requires a systematic and well-organised approach to carrying out a complex series of interrelated tasks, in a similar way to the contracting authority (*cf*. Chapters 6 and 19). The sponsors' bidding and project-development team needs a mixture of disciplines, depending on the nature of the project:

- design and construction;
- service delivery/operation;
- legal, covering site acquisition, planning, project and loan documentation;
- accounting and tax;
- financial modelling; and
- financial structuring.

As the bidding and development process (to financial close) on all projects runs into months, and on some projects into years, sponsors should not underestimate the scale of costs involved. High costs are unavoidable—the sponsor's own development staff will have to work for long periods of time on one project, and the costs of external advisers (*cf*. §20.7) have to be added to this. There are also limited economies of scale—large projects also tend to be more complex in structure, so the bidding and project-development costs also grow in proportion, but it is probably true to say that if a project is small, the bid costs will not reduce proportionally and so can become out of proportion with the size of the project.

Bid costs alone can reach a significant proportion (5-10%) of the project cost, and clearly if there are three shortlisted bidders each may have a 66% chance of losing these costs. Regular participants in bidding for PPP contracts, therefore, have to judge carefully which projects they want to bid for, and ensure that they have adequate cost-control systems. A project manager should thus expect to face a high level of scrutiny when making the case to the investor's board to bid for a project given the high level of costs and risks involved.

§20.5 JOINT-VENTURE ISSUES

As has been seen, the investment in the project company is often split between several sponsors. Developing a project through a joint venture adds a further layer of complexity to the process: one partner may have a good understanding of PPPs and related financing issues while the other does not; corporate cultural differences become more acute under the heat of third-party negotiations (*e.g.* with the contracting authority or the lenders), or negotiations may be undertaken before all intra-partnership issues have been clearly resolved. Indeed, it is not unknown for the development of a PPP project to be held up, not because the contracting authority or the lenders raise problems, but because the sponsors have not agreed on key issues among themselves. If a bid is to be credible in front of a contracting authority, the bidders must speak with one voice, and resolve any differences behind the scenes.

Sponsors bidding for and developing a PPP project together therefore usually sign a project-development agreement, which covers matters such as:

- the scope and structure of the project;
- exclusivity and confidentiality commitments;
- equity allocation;
- project-management rôles and responsibilities;
- an agreed programme for feasibility studies, appointment of advisers, negotiations with subcontractors and other potential parties to the project contracts, and approaches to other prospective investors and lenders;
- rules for decision-making;
- arrangements for funding of bidding and project-development costs, or the crediting of these costs against each sponsor's allocation of equity (taking account of both the amount of the costs and the timing of when they were incurred);
- provisions for 'reserved rôles' (if any)—*e.g.* if one of the sponsors is to be appointed as a subcontractor without being subject to third-party competition; and
- arrangements for withdrawal, or transfer, of a sponsor's interest.

Major decisions on the project have to be taken unanimously, because if the project develops in a direction not acceptable to one partner, that partner will not wish to keep financing it. Lesser issues—such as appointment of an adviser—may be taken on a majority-vote basis. If a sponsor wishes to withdraw, the other sponsors usually have a right to purchase its share. The development agreement is usually superseded by a share-holder agreement when the project company has been set up and takes over responsibility for the project (*cf.* §20.6.2).

There are particular issues where the contracting authority itself is a joint-venture investor (*cf.* §18.12).

Sponsors developing a project may bring in another investor to commit the balance of the equity (or to purchase some of the original sponsors' investment) at financial close (*i.e.* the end of the bid phase). In this case, they expect to be compensated for having assumed the highest risk, which can be achieved by:

- requiring the new investor to pay a premium for its shares (a higher price per share than that paid by the original sponsor); or
- crediting the original sponsor with a notional high rate of interest on cash already spent on the project, and including this when allocating shares based on the amount invested; or
- allowing the original sponsor to charge the project company a development fee, which is usually payable at financial close: obviously, any such fee has to be partly financed by the lenders as part of the project company's costs, and therefore cannot be at a level which upsets the project company's long-term financial viability, or leaves the original sponsor with little incentive to support the project thereafter.[3]

---

[3] A development fee may be charged to the project company anyway, as a way for the sponsors to take out an initial profit on their development costs (*cf.* §23.9.2).

All of these methods increase the original investor's equity IRR at the expense of the new investors, but the first method can offer the contracting authority a way of alleviating the problem of high initial equity IRRs, as discussed below.

§20.6 THE PROJECT COMPANY

§20.6.1 Structure

The project company lies at the centre of all the contractual and financial relationships in a PPP project. Where project finance (*cf.* Chapter 21) is being used, these relationships have to be contained inside a separate 'box', known as a special-purpose vehicle (SPV),[4] *i.e.* the project company as an SPV cannot carry out any other business that is not part of the project. The reasons for using an SPV include:

- ensuring that there is no recourse to the sponsors, by isolating the project in a separate legal entity; and
- ensuring that the business of the project company is not affected by problems with any unrelated businesses.

Since the project company should have no assets or liabilities except those directly related to the project, a new company should be formed specifically to carry out the PPP project rather than reusing an existing one that may have accrued liabilities. The corporate form of borrower (*i.e.* a project company) is generally preferred by lenders for security and control reasons (*cf.* §25.3.2).

The project company may not always be directly owned by the sponsors; the sponsors may use a holding company for this purpose, *e.g.* because:

- lenders require this for security reasons (*cf.* §25.3.2); or
- there is some tax benefit from doing so—for example the holding company may be incorporated in a favourable jurisdiction, *e.g.* to ensure that withholding tax is not deducted from distributions before they flow on to the investors; however, PPP laws or government policy often specifically require that the SPV is registered in the same country as the contracting authority.[5]

In some PPP projects, a form other than that of a limited company is used. This is usually a partnership, with the sponsors as limited partners, so their liability remains limited in the same way as if they were shareholders in a limited company. Reasons for this include:

- 'tax transparency', *i.e.* enabling the income of the project to be taxed directly at the level of the sponsors, or tax depreciation on its capex (*cf.* §23.6) to be deducted

---

[4] The term special-purpose entity (SPE) is also used.

[5] A contracting authority should be aware of the politically-sensitive issue that arises if the project is owned through an offshore structure, as this does not sit easily with the involvement of public money and public services in PPPs.

directly against sponsors' other income, rather than in the project company, which may be more tax-efficient;

- different tax positions of the sponsors: an obvious example being a PPP in which the contracting authority is also a shareholder in the project company (*cf.* §27.4), where the contracting authority, as an investor, is not subject to tax—it may be considered preferable for tax not to be 'lost' at the project company level, *i.e.* for the contracting authority's share of the income, which would otherwise be tax-free, to be taxed; similarly, a PPP fund may be taxed differently to a corporate investor; and
- if lenders' cover ratios (*cf.* §23.3) are based on post-tax cash flow, eliminating tax from the project company's cash flow increases the cash flow that the lenders take into account in their cover-ratio calculations, and hence increases the amount that can be borrowed against this cash flow (*cf.* §23.3.6).

§20.6.2 Shareholder Agreement

If there is more than one sponsor/investor, at or before financial close, once the project company has been set up and is responsible for managing the implementation of the PPP project, the project-development agreement previously signed by the sponsors (*cf.* §10.6.1, §20.5) is normally superseded by a shareholder agreement (although it is possible to have one agreement for both phases of the project). The shareholder agreement covers issues such as:

- subscriptions to equity and shareholder subordinated debt;
- board representation;
- governance issues such as conflicts of interest (*e.g.* if a subcontractor is a sponsor, participation in voting on issues relating to the relevant subcontract is not allowed, although the subcontractor's director may be allowed to participate in board discussion on the subject);
- appointment and authority of management;
- budgeting;
- policy on distributions (*cf.* §20.3.5);
- voting of shares at company meetings; and
- sale of shares by sponsors, usually with a first refusal (pre-emption) right being given to the other sponsors, or there may be 'tag along' rights (*i.e.* should one of the sponsors transfer its shareholding to a third party the other sponsors have a right to receive an offer from that third party on the same terms).

Some provisions may require unanimous consent of the shareholders and/or be included in the project company's corporate articles rather than a separate shareholder agreement. The sponsors may also have a separate agreement with the project company to pay in their agreed levels of equity or subordinated debt (if this is not paid in at financial close); if so, this agreement is assigned to the lenders as part of their security (*cf.* §20.3.6).

50:50 joint ventures are not uncommon in the PPP field, and they give rise to obvious problems in decision-making. In cases with more sponsors, it may still not be possible to get a consensus where a minority partner can block a vote on major issues. Arbitration or other legal procedures are seldom a way forward in this context. Clearly, if there is a deadlock, one partner will have to buy out the other, for which a suitable process has to be established—typically whichever partner offers the highest price can buy out the other.

§20.6.3 Management and Operations

The project company is often formed at a late stage in the project-development process, because it normally has no function to perform until the project contracts and financing are in place. Sponsors may even sign some of the project contracts to begin with (*e.g.* for construction) and transfer them in due course to the project company. However, even if the project company comes into formal existence late in the development process, as mentioned previously (*cf.* §20.2.1) arm's-length arrangements need to be in place from an early stage for negotiating any subcontracts which it is going to sign with its sponsors.

Similarly, the project company may not have a formal organisation and management structure until a late stage, as the sponsors' staff will be doing the project-development work. There is, however, only a limited overlap between the skills needed at this development stage and those needed once the project company is set up and the project itself is under way, and arrangements must be made to ensure that there is a smooth transition between the two phases of the project, as in the similar case of the contracting authority (*cf.* Chapter 19).

Project management after financial close may be undertaken by a combination of the project company's own staff and subcontractors. There are various models for this: at one extreme, the project company may have no permanent staff at all: all its key functions—*i.e.* construction, operation and maintenance—are subcontracted out. Supervision of these subcontracts, as well as corporate functions such as accounting, is carried out by one or more sponsors. The only 'permanent presence' that the project company has in this model is the board of directors. This is not an untypical structure for a low-risk accommodation project, and if a sponsor has a large portfolio of PPP projects, there are clearly economies of scale in this approach.[6]

At the other extreme, the project company may only contract out the construction of the facility and retain all other aspects of the project in-house. This approach is often used in concessions.

While there is obviously merit—both financial and operational—in subcontracting project functions to experienced organisations, it is generally preferable for the project company to have a minimum level of staff, which probably consists of a general manager (reporting to the board) and one or two assistants. This gives a clear point of contact for the contracting authority, and a 'public face' for the project company—*e.g.* it may be required to meet with user groups such as the parents' association in a school project.

---

[6] This structure may cause a problem for the contracting authority if it terminates the PPP contract (*cf.* §17.2.9).

Furthermore, it is preferable to have a person dedicated to supervising subcontractors regularly, rather than having to juggle this with other work.

The contracting authority should consider during bid evaluation whether the plans for long-term management of the project company will be adequate for providing the quality of service required—*e.g.* whether there will be a single point of contact with responsibility for the total relationship under the PPP contract.

§20.6.4 Changes in Ownership

The sponsors are often required by either the contracting authority or the lenders (or both) to retain their investment at least until construction of the project is complete (a 'lock-up period'), since they are both relying heavily on the ability of the sponsors to manage the completion of what is usually the riskiest phase of a project. Where particular technical skills are required for long-term operation, relevant subcontractor sponsors may be required to maintain their shareholdings for longer periods.

In some cases, the contracting authority may be more relaxed about shareholders that are not involved in construction or service delivery selling their shares but there may also be concerns about the reputational impact of a new shareholder or its origin, especially in the case of highly-sensitive projects (*e.g.* defence). In this case, objective criteria need to be set out to define the basis upon which approval for a new shareholder would be required.

Subject to these controls, a secondary market in PPP investments, as described above, creates liquidity in the primary market that is valuable to a continuing PPP programme because it enables primary investors to recycle their capital back into new projects. Also, from the public-sector point of view, although there is some security in a committed long-term ownership of the project, liquidity in primary investments will tend to increase their value, and thus make the cost of investment lower in future. Conversely, if excessive restrictions on investment transfers are put in place, this will reduce the value of these investments in the secondary market, and thus tend to push up the primary-market pricing, which feeds through to higher service fees in future bids. It also makes the PPP sector less attractive to investors, and so may reduce bid competition. Moreover, in practice, it is very difficult to restrain transfers of the benefits of ownership, even if legal title to shares is retained by the original sponsors (*cf.* §26.3).

The contracting authority should therefore only exercise any control over transfers of ownership:

- during the construction phase, to ensure that the original sponsors are not just bidding to take a quick profit turn, but have a real financial commitment to get the PPP up and running; typically, this may mean a restriction on transfers for a year or so from completion of construction;
- where this could reasonably have an effect on the long-term service provision: this is a difficult area—even if a subcontractor sells its shareholding in the project company, it will still have to carry out the contractual obligations, but may have less financial incentive to do so without capital at risk (*cf.* §28.9.7); similarly, the argument for whole-life costing and maintenance-risk transfer (*cf.* §28.8) may be weakened if the project is put together by a financial investor intending to sell out early;

- where there are issues of national security, *e.g.* in a PPP for defence equipment; and
- in the case of a limited number of 'reputation' objections—*e.g.* it may be reasonable to bar companies in the tobacco or pornography business from being shareholders in a school PPP, however remote their ability to have any influence on the school through the PPP.

It should also be noted that similar 'commitment' issues arise with debt refinancing, since this usually has the effect of reducing the investor's capital at risk in the project (*cf.* §26.2.3).

It is also important for contracting authorities to recognise the importance of the corporate skill and experience needed to put together a bid for a PPP project and subsequently ensure the contracting and investing activities work well together. This capacity to 'glue' the various components of a PPP project together can be one of the main market capacity constraints, especially in a new market, where contractors are more used to bidding for traditionally-procured projects that do not require this. This is another reason why allowing contractors who develop this capacity to recycle their capital and bid for new projects is relevant.

§20.6.5 Changes to the Project Company

While the special-purpose nature of the project company limits its activities to the project and this is closely controlled by the lenders, the contracting authority is also usually concerned to control any changes to the permitted activities of the project company outside of the project (so that it does not risk becoming insolvent for reasons not connected with the project).

The contracting authority's consent may also be required to other changes such as the project company's tax domicile (which can be a particularly sensitive issue) or constitutional documents.

In some cases, consent may also be required for changes in the leverage (*cf.* §21.3; §26.2) of the project company above a certain limit, or the replacement of key personnel.

§20.7 External Advisers

Various external advisers are used by the sponsors during the bidding and project-development processes. They can play a valuable rôle since they will probably have had greater experience in a variety of projects than the sponsors' in-house staff; if a sponsor is not developing a continuous pipeline of projects, employing people with the necessary expertise just to work on one project may be difficult. Using advisers with a good record of working in successful projects also gives the project credibility with lenders. In addition to these sponsors' advisers, the contracting authority has its own advisers (*cf.* §6.4) and lenders use a parallel set of advisers as part of their due-diligence process (*cf.* §22.2.7), but the largest part of the advisory work is likely to be done by the sponsors' advisers.

Advisers may be prepared to work on a 'contingency' basis during the bidding stage, on the understanding that they will be engaged (at an enhanced rate) if the bid is successful. Thereafter, the options for fee-payment structures are similar to those available to the contracting authority (*cf.* §6.4.6).

§20.7.1 Financial Adviser

Unless the sponsors are experienced in PPP project development, problems are highly likely to be caused by negotiation (or even signature) of PPP-contract or subcontract arrangements that are later found to be unacceptable to the project-finance debt market. Therefore, bidders for or developers of PPP projects—even those with in-house project-finance expertise—usually make use of external financial advice to make sure that they are on the right track as they bid on and develop the project. The financial adviser obviously needs to have a good record of achieving successful financing on similar PPP projects. Bidders also need to ensure that the individual actually doing the work has this experience, rather than just relying on the general reputation and record of the financial adviser.

The financial adviser for a PPP project has a wider ranging rôle than would be the case for a corporate loan (where the work would be centred around financial structuring). One of the most common errors during project development is for the sponsors to agree on a project contract that is commercially sound, but not acceptable from a project-finance point of view—for example, the PPP contract may leave too much risk with the project company instead of passing risks down to the subcontractors, perhaps because the contracting authority has tried to pass too much risk to the private-sector side of the table (*cf.* §11.4)—and so the financial adviser must anticipate all the issues that could arise during the lenders' due-diligence process (*cf.* §22.2.7), ensuring they are addressed in the project contracts or elsewhere.

The terms of the financial adviser's engagement are set out in an advisory agreement, usually signed with the sponsors. (The sponsors may transfer the advisory agreement to the project company in the latter stages of the project-development process.) The financial adviser's scope of work under an advisory agreement may include:

- assisting in preparing a financial model for the project (*cf.* §23.8);
- advising on sources of debt and likely financing terms (*cf.* §23.2-§23.4);
- advising on the optimum financial structure for the project (*cf.* §23.4);
- advising on accounting and tax issues (*cf.* §23.6);
- advising on the financing implications of project contracts;
- assisting in bid preparation (*cf.* §20.4);
- assisting in negotiations with the contracting authority (*cf.* §10.6.3);
- preparing an information memorandum to present the project to the financial markets (§22.2.9);
- advising on selection of commercial-bank or other lenders, or placement of bonds (§22.4.2); and
- assisting in negotiation of financing documentation (*cf.* §22.2.8).

As has been seen (*cf.* §6.4.1), the public sector relies mainly on large accounting firms for financial advice on PPP projects. Major international banks (or domestic banks in particular markets) do provide advisory services to bidders for PPP projects, though usually in conjunction with lending, as discussed in §22.2.5. Financial advice is also provided to bidders by investment banks (*i.e.* banks that arrange finance but that do not normally lend money themselves), specialist project-finance advisory 'boutiques' or individual advisers. Table 20.1 sets out the leading advisers to bidders for projects in general (not just PPP projects, although these probably constitute a large part of the total). As can be seen, there are two firms of accountants in the list, but in general bidders make greater use of banks as advisers (in many cases because they are expected to provide the debt required in due course).

Table 20.1   Project-finance debt advisory mandates from bidders, 2016

Firm	Category	Advisory mandates
EY	Accountants	31
Synergy Consulting	Project-finance advisers	28
Green Giraffe	Project-finance advisers	23
Crédit Agricole	Bank	14
Bank of Tokyo-Mitsubishi	Bank	13
Société Générale	Bank	12
Sumitomo Mitsui	Bank	12
BNP Paribas	Bank	11
PwC	Accountants	10
Portland Advisers	Project-finance advisers	10

Source: *Project Finance International* (Issue 593, 25 January 2017).

Financial advisers are usually paid by a combination of fixed or time-based retainer fees, and a success fee on conclusion of the financing. Major out-of-pocket costs, such as travel, are also paid by the sponsors. These costs, and those of the other advisers discussed below, are charged on to the project company in due course as part of the development costs (*cf.* §23.9.2). However, as is the case with other advisers, they often work for the sponsors during the bid phase on a contingency basis, *i.e.* they only start to earn substantial fees when their client has been appointed as preferred bidder, or perhaps not until financial close.

These financial-advisory services may be essential to the successful development of the project, but they are necessarily expensive (costing around 1% of the capex on an average-sized project). Costs may be reduced by using smaller advisory boutiques or individual consultants, but less experienced sponsors may feel uneasy about not using a 'big name' adviser. There is also always some risk that the financial adviser—however well qualified—thinks a project is financeable but the lending market does not agree.

§20.7.2 Legal Adviser

Legal advisers have to deal not only with the project contracts, but also with how these interact with project-finance requirements, as well as being familiar with project-finance documentation. This work tends to be concentrated in a small pool of major law firms who have built up the necessary mixture of expertise.

§20.7.3 Owner's Engineer

The project company may not need a third-party technical adviser (known as the owner's engineer, *vis-à-vis* the construction subcontractor) if this function can be carried out by one of its shareholders. However, if one major shareholder is the construction subcontractor, other shareholders may wish to ensure that their work is checked and supervised on behalf of shareholders as a whole, although of course there is also checking by the contracting authority (*cf.* §6.4.3) and the lenders (*cf.* §22.2.7).

§20.7.4 Planning and Environmental Consultant

If the contracting authority has not already obtained planning permission for the project, the sponsor may have to take on advisers to deal with this process (*cf.* §12.2.3), albeit with support from the contracting authority. Separate advice may be required on environmental issues (*cf.* §12.2.4).

§20.7.5 Market Consultant

Market-risk advisers are required for a concession, or availability-PPP project involving usage risk, *e.g.* traffic consultants (*cf.* §13.2). The expertise of these advisers, and the degree of their involvement in the project, may be significant factors in obtaining initial lender support for a bid even though the lenders will have their own advisers in due course.

§20.7.6 Accountants

Accountants are often retained to advise on the accounting and tax aspects of the project (*cf.* §23.6), both for the project company itself and for the sponsors.

§20.7.7 Insurance Adviser

For the rôle of the insurance broker, *cf.* §14.2.

Project Finance and PPPs

§21.1 INTRODUCTION

PPPs are closely linked to the financing technique known as 'project finance': the vast majority of PPP projects are financed in this way. An understanding of project-finance techniques and their application in PPPs is therefore necessary when considering policy-related financing issues in PPPs.

Project finance is a method of raising long-term debt financing for major projects. It is a form of 'financial engineering', based on lending against the cash flow generated by the project itself, and depends on a detailed evaluation of a project's construction, operating and revenue risks, and their allocation between investors, lenders and other parties through contractual and other arrangements. As such, it is well suited to financing PPP projects. 'Project finance' is not the same thing as 'financing projects', because projects may be financed in many different ways; alternative approaches to financing public-infra-structure projects are discussed in Chapter 27.

This chapter therefore provides a general background on project finance:

- its development (§21.2);
- key features (§21.3);
- comparison between project finance and other types of structured finance (§21.4); and
- why project finance is used for PPPs (§21.5).

Chapter 22 looks in more detail at sources of project finance, and Chapters 23-25 cover financial and legal structuring.

The main other method of financing PPPs is corporate finance, in which there is a single sponsor who provides all the finance for the project rather than raising external project-finance debt (§21.6).

§21.2 DEVELOPMENT OF PROJECT FINANCE

The development of project finance is linked to some of the same factors which led to the growth in PPPs. Some successive waves of development in project-financing techniques and coverage can be identified:

- Finance for natural resource projects (mining, oil and gas), from which modern project-finance techniques are derived, developed first in the Texas oil fields in the 1930s; this approach was first used in Europe for development of North Sea oil fields in the 1970s.
- Finance for independent power projects in the electricity sector (primarily for power generation) using BOO/BOT structures developed in the 1980s as discussed in §2.4.3. Linked to this was the growth in the use of gas for power generation, which also led to project financing of gas pipelines and liquefied natural gas receiving terminals (*i.e.* gas delivery as opposed to gas production).
- Finance for public infrastructure (*i.e.* PPPs) was revived with the Channel Tunnel project in the 1980s and thereafter with the creation of the British PFI programme from the early 1990s (*cf.* §2.4.7).
- Similarly, various countries such as Australia and Chile revived the use of private finance for concessions around the same period.
- Finance for mobile-telephone networks was also a large part of the market from the mid-1990s until the build-out of most of these networks was complete in the early 2000s, but finance for telecommunications-satellite systems remains a significant sector.

Accordingly, the three main legs on which project finance stands today are the natural resources, energy and infrastructure sectors.

Other changes in financing techniques, developed from the early 1970s, which helped the evolution of project finance included:

- long-term commercial bank lending to corporate customers—previously commercial banks only lent on a short-term basis, to match their deposits (*cf.* §24.2);
- the use of export credits for financing major projects, albeit the risk in such cases is substantially borne by public-sector export-credit agencies (*cf.* §22.9.4);
- shipping finance, where banks make loans to pay for construction of large vessels, on the security of long-term charters—*i.e.* construction lending against a contractual cash flow, with the borrower being a separate special-purpose company owning the ship, in a way very similar to later project-finance structures;
- property (real-estate) finance, again involving loans for construction secured against long-term cash-flow (rental) projections; and

- tax-based financial leasing, which accustomed banks to complex cash-flows (*cf.* §21.4).

The final vital element in the development of project finance was the creation (in the mid-1980s) of user-friendly spreadsheet software, without which project financing would be practically impossible.

§21.3 FEATURES OF PROJECT FINANCE

Project-finance structures differ between various industry sectors and from deal to deal: there is no such thing as 'standard' project finance, since each deal has its own unique characteristics. But there are common principles underlying the project-finance approach. Some typical characteristics of project finance are the following:

- It is provided for a 'ring-fenced' project (*i.e.* one which is legally and economically self-contained), carried out through a project company (*cf.* §20.6).
- It is usually raised for a new project rather than an established business (except for sales of franchises—*cf.* §2.4.2; also, project-finance loans may be refinanced).
- There is a high ratio of debt to equity ('leverage')—roughly speaking, project-finance debt may fund 70-95% of a project's capex.
- There are no guarantees from the investors in the project company (*i.e.* it is non-recourse' finance—*cf.* §20.2.1), or only limited guarantees (*i.e.* limited-recourse financing—*cf.* §22.8), for the project-finance debt.
- Lenders rely on the future cash flow of the project for payment of their debt service, rather than the value of its assets or analysis of historical financial results.
- Therefore, the project contracts are the main security for lenders; the project company's physical assets are likely to be worth much less than the debt if they are sold off after a default on the financing.
- Lenders exercise a close control over the activities of the project company to ensure the value of these project contracts is not jeopardised, *e.g.* by performance failures.
- The project has a finite life, based on such factors as the length of the contracts or licences, or the reserves of natural resources, so the project-finance debt must be fully repaid by the end of this life.

Hence project finance differs from a corporate loan,[1] which:

- is primarily lent against asset values in a company's balance sheet, and projections extrapolating from its past cash flow and profit record;
- assumes that the company will remain in business for an indefinite period and so can keep renewing ('rolling over') its loans;
- has access to the whole cash flow from the spread of the borrower's business as security, instead of the limited cash flow from a specific project—thus even if an individual project fails, corporate lenders can still reasonably expect to be repaid;
- can use buildings and equipment as security; and

---

[1] To be distinguished from corporate finance for projects, discussed in §21.6.

- generally, leaves the management of the company to run the business as they see fit, so long as this does not have significant adverse financial consequences, *i.e.* the lenders do not have the same level of control over the borrower's cash flow as they do in project finance.

Project finance is made up of a number of 'building blocks'. One set of blocks relates to the financing for the project company, which has two elements:

- equity, provided by investors in the project company (*cf.* Chapter 20); and
- project finance-based debt, provided by one or more groups of lenders to the project company.

The project-finance debt has first call on the project company's net operating cash flow—it is thus 'senior' to other claims (hence the term 'senior debt'), especially those of the investors (equity shareholders), including their subordinated debt (*cf.* §20.3.5), or third-party mezzanine debt (*cf.* §22.7). The investors' return is therefore at a higher risk because it is more dependent on the success of the project—hence investors' returns are higher than lenders'.

The other major building blocks relate to the project contracts entered into by the project company—namely the PPP contract, and subcontracts for construction, operation and maintenance of the facility. These are the means by which risks are transferred from the project company to other parties (*cf.* Chapters 11-13), and form the most important part of the lenders' security package. Of course, none of these structures or contractual relationships are unique to project finance. However, the relative importance of these matters, and the way in which they are linked together, is a key factor in a project-financed PPP.

The close resemblance between the use of project finance for a power-generation project, as described in §2.4.3, and its subsequent development in different types of PPP, can be seen from the structural diagrams in Chapter 2 for a PPA (Figure 2.1), a concession (Figure 2.2) and an availability PPP (Figure 2.3).

§21.4 PROJECT FINANCE AND STRUCTURED FINANCE

The broad term 'structured finance' covers any kind of finance where an SPV has to be created to raise the financing, with its debt structured to fit the cash flow. This should be distinguished from corporate financing in which loans are made to a borrower already in business, as discussed above. Various types of structured finance overlap with project finance to a certain extent, and also compete with it for resources within the financial institution concerned (*cf.* §22.2).

§21.4.1 Asset Finance

This is based on lending against the value of assets easily saleable in the open market, *e.g.* aircraft or real-estate (property) financing, whereas project-finance lending is against the cash flow produced by the asset, which may have little open-market value other than through its linkage with the PPP contract.

§21.4.2 Receivables Financing

This is based on lending against the established cash flow of a business and involves transferring a cash-flow stream to an SPV similar to a project company (but normally off the balance sheet of the true beneficiary of the cash flow). This cash flow may be derived from the general business (*e.g.* a hotel chain) or specific contracts which give rise to this cash flow (*e.g.* consumer loans, sales contracts, *etc.*). The SPV then borrows against this cash flow, without any significant recourse or guarantee to the owners of the original business, who are thus able to raise financing off the balance sheet of the original business, as well as reduce their own business risks.

The key difference from project finance is that receivables financing is based on an established cash flow, whereas project finance is based on a projection of cash flow from a project yet to be established. However, the sale of a franchise for an already-constructed road is a form of receivables finance, even though it may be classified by the parties concerned as project financing.

§21.4.3 Securitisation

If receivables financing is procured by raising funds in the bond market (*cf.* §22.4), it is known as securitisation of receivables. There have also been securitisations of receivables due from banks' project-finance loan books, but so far this has not been a significant feature in the market. Such securitisations can take two forms—a transfer of the loans from the bank to an SPV, to provide a pool of security for bondholders ('real' securitisation), or a 'synthetic' securitisation, where the risk is transferred but the loans remain on the bank's balance sheet (albeit with a low or nil capital requirement for the bank, because of the risk transfer), financed by a bond issue.

§21.4.4 Leveraged Buyout (LBO) or Management Buyout (MBO) Financing

This highly-leveraged financing provides for the acquisition of an existing business by portfolio investors (LBO) or its own management (MBO). It is usually based on a mixture of the cash flow of the business and the value of its assets. It does not normally involve finance for construction of a new project, nor does this type of financing use contracts as security, as does project finance. The term 'private equity' is also used where the acquisition is made by an investment fund.

§21.4.5 Acquisition Finance

Probably the largest sector in structured finance, acquisition finance, enables company A to acquire company B using highly-leveraged debt. In that sense, it is similar to LBO and MBO financing, but based on the combined business of the two companies. The risks and returns on these sectors are higher than those for PPPs, but as the financing sources overlap, they have tended to drag up pricing for PPP projects (*cf.* §20.3.3).

§21.4.6 Leasing

Leasing is a form of asset finance in which ownership of the asset financed remains with the lessor (*i.e.* lender), with the lessee (*i.e.* borrower) paying for the right to use it. A major motive for leasing in the past was that it enabled tax benefits from large capital investments to be transferred to the lessor, and fed back to the lessee *via* lower lease payments than would have been made under an equivalent loan (*cf.* §21.2). These tax benefits have been substantially eroded in most countries, and leasing finance is now seldom used in the PPP field, especially as many PPPs involve substantial investment in buildings or civil works (such as for a road), that generally does not receive as favourable tax treatment as investing in equipment.

§21.5 WHY USE PROJECT FINANCE FOR PPPS?

Like PPPs, project finance is complex, slow and has a high upfront cost. Adding the two together obviously makes these problems worse. It also severely restricts the ability of the owners of a project to manage it freely. Nonetheless, there are good reasons why project finance is commonly used for PPP projects, since it has benefits both for the private-sector investors in such projects, and for the contracting authority.

§21.5.1 Benefits for Investors

There are a number of reasons why investors use project financing for PPP projects.

– High leverage

As has been seen, investors in PPPs typically require a hurdle-rate equity IRR which—despite corporate-finance theory—looks more at the risk of the project than its financing structure (*cf.* §20.3.3). It follows arithmetically from this that the higher the leverage, the easier it is to earn a higher level of equity IRR, taking advantage of debt being cheaper than equity. This also reflects the fact that in a project-finance transaction, higher leverage does not necessarily imply proportionately higher risk for lenders (*cf.* §23.5). Hence, although the cost of debt goes up, this is not in proportion to the increase in leverage.

Table 21.1 sets out a (very simplified) example of the benefit of leverage on an investor's return. Both the low-leverage and high-leverage columns relate to the same investment of $1,000 which produces revenue of $75 *p.a.* If it is financed with 50% debt, as in the low-leverage column (a typical level of debt for a good corporate credit), the return on equity is 10%. On the other hand, if it is financed with 90% (project-finance-style) leverage, the return on (the reduced level of) equity is 21%, despite an increase in the cost of the debt (reflecting the higher risk for lenders).

Table 21.1 Benefit of leverage on investors' returns

		Low leverage	High leverage
Project cost		$1,000	$1,000
(a) Debt		$500	$900
(b) Equity		$500	$100
(c) Revenue from project (p.a.)		$75	$75
(d) Interest rate on debt (p.a.)		5%	6%
(e) Interest payable	[(a) × (d)]	$25	$54
(f) Profit	[(c) − (e)]	$50	$21
Return on equity	[(f) ÷ (b)]	10%	21%

But it must be emphasised that this example is highly simplified,[2] and as will be seen below, leverage is dictated largely by the lenders' requirements for a cash-flow cushion, which in turn may actually dictate the equity IRR on the project, and even its overall financial structure (cf. §23.4).

Another important factor encouraging a high level of debt in project companies is that it may be more difficult to raise equity than to raise debt. The need to raise more equity can make the project more complex to manage (especially during the bidding and development phases) if this means that more investors have to be brought in. Moreover, if more investors have to be brought in, this means that the original sponsors may lose control of the project.

− Risk spreading and limitation

Project finance involves a structure under which groups of investors can easily work together, thus easily enabling the risk of the investment to be divided up.

Moreover, an investor in a project raising funds through project finance does not normally guarantee the repayment of the debt—the risk is therefore limited to the amount of the equity investment only, and the investor's business as a whole is not usually at risk from failure of the specific project, i.e. there is limited 'risk contamination' between the project and the rest of the investor's business. In effect, in return for a relatively small fee (its equity share), a sponsor has established an 'option price' at which it may retain the investment if successful or walk away if its failure could otherwise have a high impact on its other business.

It is also worth noting that one of the highest areas of risk for a PPP project is the expenditure on bidding, and so forming a partnership at the bidding stage obviously reduces this risk too.

---

[2] For example, the debt has to be repaid, as does the equity investment.

- Unequal partnerships/combining skills

  Thanks to high leverage, the relatively small amount of equity required for a major PPP project where project finance is used enables parties with different financial strengths to work together. It would be quite normal for example, for the investors in an availability PPP school project to consist of a financial investor (say an infrastructure fund), a construction company, and an FM company, whose balance-sheet strengths would probably be very different, but with each bringing particular skills to this partnership. This aspect of a project-finance structure also makes it easy for the contracting authority to be brought in as a shareholder if this is considered appropriate (*cf.* §27.4).

- Long-term finance

  Project-finance loans typically have a longer tenor than corporate loans. Long-term financing is necessary if the assets financed have a high capital cost, which cannot be recovered over a short tenor without pushing up the project's service fees. So, loans for PPP projects may run for 20-30 years, compared to a normal corporate loan of perhaps 5-7 years.

  Paradoxically, a longer-term loan may reduce the risk of financial default during a PPP project's early years of operation, when the cash flow may be most uncertain, by reducing the level of cash flow required for annual debt-service payments.

- Borrowing capacity

  The non-recourse nature of project finance raised by a project company means that such finance is not normally counted against the sponsors' corporate credit lines. It may thus increase an investor's overall borrowing capacity, and hence the ability to undertake several major projects simultaneously. Similarly, a sponsor's credit rating is less likely to be downgraded if its risks on project investments are limited through a project-finance structure, again enabling it to invest in more projects.

- Off-balance sheet

  If the investor has to raise the debt and then inject it into the project, this will clearly appear on the investor's balance sheet. A project-finance structure may allow the investor to keep the debt off the consolidated balance sheet, but usually only if the investor is a minority shareholder in the project—which may be achieved if the project is owned with other partners.

  Keeping debt off the balance sheet is sometimes seen as beneficial to a company's position in the financial markets. However, a company's shareholders and lenders should normally take account of risks involved in any off-balance-sheet activities. These are generally revealed in notes to the published accounts even if they are not included in the balance sheet figures. So, project finance is not usually undertaken purely to keep debt off the investors' balance sheets.

  However, there is another related benefit, which is that investment in a project through an unconsolidated affiliated company is useful during the construction phase of a project. The high capital investment that is not producing revenue during this period would otherwise be on the sponsor's balance sheet and a 'dead weight' on the rest of a company's business for this period.

Also, a project-finance structure enables subcontractors to make a clearer separation between their contracting and investment activities (*cf*. §20.2.1).

§21.5.2 Benefits for the Contracting Authority

Equally, encouraging investors to use project finance for PPP projects may bring benefits to the contracting authority, and to the overall PPP programme in the country concerned.

— Lower cost

The higher leverage inherent in a project-finance structure helps to ensure the lowest cost to the contracting authority. This can be illustrated by doing the calculation in Table 21.1 in reverse: suppose the investor in the project requires a return of at least 15%, then, as Table 21.2 shows, to produce this return, revenue of $100 *p.a.* is required using low-leverage finance, but only $69 using high-leverage finance, and hence the service fees reduce accordingly. (But as with Table 21.1, it must be emphasised that this example is highly simplified.)

Thus, if the contracting authority wishes to achieve the lowest long-term cost for the project, and if it is able to influence how it is financed, this suggests that the use of project finance should be encouraged, *e.g.* by agreeing to sign a PPP contract that fits project-finance requirements as to risk transfer between public and private sectors. Nevertheless, this does not suggest that a contracting authority should require that bidders should be restricted only to using project finance (*cf*. §21.6)—a competitive process should leave it to bidders to identify the most cost-competitive financing structure.

— Increased competition

For the reasons set out above, project finance enables investors to undertake more projects by increasing their financial capacity, the effect of which should be to create a more competitive market for projects, to the benefit of the contracting authority.

Table 21.2 Effect of leverage on the service fees

		Low leverage	High leverage
Project cost		$1,000	$1,000
(a) Debt		$500	$900
(b) Equity		$500	$100
(c) Return on equity required	[(b) × 15%]	$75	$15
(d) Interest rate on debt (*p.a.*)		5%	6%
(e) Interest payable	[(a) × (d)]	$25	$54
Service fee required	[(c) + (e)]	$100	$69

— Increased market participation

Project finance brings together a wide range of investors, some of whom may not have the balance sheet on their own to support a project, which encourages more entrants into the market and therefore more competition. Also, if PPP opportunities are limited to a handful of large players, then there will be suspicions of collusion and the risk of reduced political support for the PPP programme.

— Rôle of lenders

The contracting authority may benefit from the independent due diligence and control of the project exercised by the lenders (*cf.* §22.2.7), who will want to ensure that the project is viable, and that all obligations to the contracting authority can be safely fulfilled. Project-finance techniques are based on risk allocation, and so this due diligence fits well with the overall philosophy of risk transfer which is one of the arguments for PPPs (*cf.* §28.6). The involvement of third parties, especially lenders and their advisers, in a PPP structure should therefore mean that a rigorous review of the risk transfer is carried out, and any weaknesses exposed, before the contracting authority has made a commitment to go ahead. However, it must be borne in mind that lenders will always want to ensure that project risks are taken primarily by subcontractors or the contracting authority rather than the project company (*cf.* §11.5), and so their objectives are not the same as those of the contracting authority. Moreover, lenders can be used as proxies by sponsors to re-open PPP contract negotiations (*cf.* §10.8.3)—*i.e.* if they are on anybody's side, it is the sponsors rather than the contracting authority.

In addition, once a PPP contract has been signed, project-finance lenders exercise continuing controls on the activities of the project company (*cf.* Chapter 25), thus helping to ensure that the requirements of the PPP contract are fulfilled.

— Transparency

As a project financing is self-contained (*i.e.* it deals only with the assets and liabilities, costs and revenues of the particular project), the true costs of the service can more easily be measured and monitored. This fits well with the need for transparency in a PPP (*cf.* §28.10.1).

§21.6 CORPORATE FINANCE

While project finance provides the commonest method of financing PPPs, there are many cases where a corporate-finance approach—in which the funding for the project is provided from the investor's own financial resources rather than external project-finance debt—is a suitable alternative.

Since project financing is a specialised form of finance, in some markets corporate finance, which is a more mainstream form of bank lending, may indeed be the only form of financing available. In this case, the investor's available cash and credit lines are used to pay for the project, or if necessary new credit lines or even new equity capital are raised to finance the project's cost. Provided it can be supported by the investor's balance sheet and earnings record, a corporate-finance loan to finance a project is normally fairly simple, quick and cheap to arrange. In a corporate-finance structure for PPPs, the project company is usually a wholly-owned subsidiary of the investor, or the investor may enter directly into a project agreement with the contracting authority.

Clearly, both the cost of finance and ancillary costs are lower in this case than in a project-financed transaction. This may translate into a lower cost for the contracting authority, depending on the overall level of the investor's cost of capital. But this approach is obviously dependent on the investor having the necessary balance-sheet and financial capacity, and is therefore typically used for smaller PPPs for which the considerable transaction costs of a full-scale PPP with external debt would be disproportionate to the level of financing (*cf.* §7.5.1), or those in which the level of capital investment, as opposed to long-term service provision, is lower. But as the financial capacity of the investor itself is used up, so the capacity of such sponsors for new projects is likely to be an increasing constraint on further projects.

Project-Finance Debt—Sources and Procedures

§22.1 INTRODUCTION

This chapter reviews the main sources of private-sector debt for PPP projects (assuming finance on a project-finance rather than corporate-finance basis—*cf.* §21.6).

Private-sector project-finance debt is provided from two main sources—loans and bonds. Commercial banks provide long-term loans to project companies (§22.2). Non-bank lenders are also becoming more active in some markets (§22.3). Bond holders—typically long-term investors such as insurance companies and pension funds—purchase long-term bonds (tradable debt instruments) issued by project companies (§22.4). ('Lender' is used in this book to mean any of a bank lender, a non-bank lender or a bond investor.) Although the legal structures, procedures and markets are different, the criteria under which debt is raised in the private-sector loan and bond markets are much the same, but they each have advantages and disadvantages (§22.5).

The contracting authority may wish to ensure that the project company has the most competitive debt terms by requiring competitive tenders for the debt towards the end of the procurement process (§22.6).

Mezzanine debt (third-party subordinated debt) can also play a limited rôle in financing PPP projects (§22.7). Similarly, limited recourse to the sponsors may be used to support any risks that are unacceptable to lenders, or to reduce the cost of external debt (§22.8).

Loans or guarantees may also be provided by public-sector or multilateral development or infrastructure banks, usually on a similar basis to commercial banks, often in markets where the latter may not be active (§22.9). Other types of public-sector funding or financing for PPPs are discussed in Chapter 18.

311

§22.2 Commercial Banks

Commercial banks are the most important source for project finance for PPPs: in 2016, they provided $231 billion of project-finance debt, although it should be noted that some of this was not new money, but refinancing old loans on better terms (*cf.* Chapter 26).

§22.2.1 Scale of the Market

Table 22.1 sets out the overall scale of the world project-finance market (for both bank loans and bond issues—*cf.* §22.4), from which the division into the three legs of energy, natural resources and infrastructure are evident:

- Power-generation projects remain the bedrock of the project-finance industry, including an increasingly large proportion of renewable-energy projects in sectors such as wind and solar power. (Some power-generation projects may also be classified as PPPs, where the power off-taker under the PPA is a public-sector owned electricity company.)
- The recent commodity-price boom and its subsequent decline are reflected in the figures for the natural-resources sector (which includes oil and gas and petrochemicals as well as mining).
- Infrastructure, which includes private-sector and privatised infrastructure as well as PPPs, had shown continued and steady growth in business volume, but this fell back in 2016, partly because the 2015 figures reflect a $12 bn railway refinancing in Taiwan.

Table 22.2 provides the same data by location. The largest activity in the Americas market relates to the United States, the increases in 2014-2015 reflecting the boom in shale gas, which led to major projects for LNG export terminals as well as gas-fired power stations. The reductions in the Asia-Pacific market after 2012 relate to drops in major natural-resources projects, especially in Australia. Volumes in Europe and the former Soviet Union still remain below those of 2008.

Overall, the commercial-bank project-finance market has struggled to expand since the financial crisis of 2008, before which the total market volume was some $250 billion. Apart from reductions in investment since that time, another key factor has been balance-sheet pressure from regulatory controls, discussed in §22.2.4.

Table 22.1 Commercial-bank project-finance loans by sector, 2010-2016

($ millions)	2010	2011	2012	2013	2014	2015	2016
Power	73,300	80,499	66,308	69,380	83,534	106,338	111,097
Natural resources	46,115	54,272	69,223	55,936	96,075	78,247	62,855
Infrastructure	55,160	45,329	54,853	57,611	62,165	79,468	48,525
Other	33,599	33,387	8,362	21,100	17,951	13,162	8,679
Total	**208,174**	**213,487**	**198,746**	**204,027**	**259,725**	**277,215**	**231,156**

Source: *Project Finance International,* Annual project-finance league tables (data summarised).

Table 22.2   Commercial-bank project-finance loans by location, 2010-2016

($ millions)	2010	2011	2012	2013	2014	2015	2016
Americas	25,535	38,383	39,321	51,420	92,884	93,277	55,902
Asia-Pacific	98,708	91,764	91,523	63,646	72,226	76,263	51,942
Europe/FSU	63,480	63,725	45,847	52,395	64,780	69,095	86,936
Middle East/N. Africa	16,774	13,829	13,142	25,534	22,063	28,713	30,957
Sub-Saharan Africa	3,678	5,786	8,913	11,032	8,244	10,382	5,419
Total	**208,174**	**213,487**	**198,746**	**204,027**	**259,725**	**277,730**	**231,157**

Source: *Project Finance International,* Annual project-finance league tables (data summarised).

Unfortunately, there are no good statistics that clearly distinguish project-financed PPPs from other categories of infrastructure finance: as can be seen the *Project Finance International* figures for infrastructure in general are lower than the PPP estimates in Figures 2.4 and 2.5, but the figures for the bond market in Table 22.4 need to be added to those for Table 22.1. Also, neither of these tables includes equity investments, whereas Figures 2.4 and 2.5 do. Other issues also affect these published statistics:

- Financial institutions draw the boundaries between project finance and other types of lending based on convenience rather than theory, taking into account that skills used by loan officers in project finance may also be used in similar types of financing. Many deals have project finance as part of their structured-finance operations (§21.4). As a result, project-finance market statistics may be affected by inclusion or exclusion of large deals on the borderline between project finance and other types of structured finance.
- The figures do not distinguish between loans to new projects and to projects that have become established and are then refinanced (*cf.* §26.2).
- The statistics are based on lending by private-sector financial institutions, and hence do not include projects financed by development finance institutions, export-credit agencies or other public-sector sources of finance (*cf.* §22.9), other than for any private-sector component of this financing.
- Clearly, the financial institutions that supply their figures have an interest in making the market, and their own involvement, look as large as possible.
- The figures from different financial databases differ quite widely, again because of issues of reporting and classification.
- Specifically, in relation to PPPs, lender figures relate to the amount of debt raised, whereas figures produced by the public sector (reflected in Ministry of Finance or PPP unit reports of project activity) relate to the 'cost' of the project, which may mean either the capex or the NPV of the service fees, which will clearly be significantly more than the capex.

Nonetheless, the year-to-year figures give a fair picture of overall trends in the project-finance market, which can be compared to the attempt in Figures 2.4 and 2.5 to extract PPP projects from the wider project-finance market.

§22.2.2 Major Lenders

Within the international project-finance market, there is a fluctuating 'inner circle' of perhaps 20-30 international banks, predominantly Japanese and European, that play a key rôle in putting together major transactions wherever these are located. However, if a country has a strong PPP programme, local banks not otherwise extensively involved in project finance also typically play leading rôles in PPP project financing. Table 22.3, which sets

Table 22.3   Major project-finance banks, 2016

		Total underwriting ($ millions)	No. projects	Average underwriting ($ millions)
Bank of Tokyo-Mitsubishi UFJ	Japan	14,216	150	95
China Development Bank	China	13,203	3	4,401
Sumitomo Mitsui Banking Corp.	Japan	11,079	110	101
Mizuho Financial	Japan	7,752	64	121
Crédit Agricole	France	7,390	79	94
Société Générale	France	5,967	67	89
BNP Paribas	France	5,808	63	92
ING	Netherlands	5,591	65	86
State Bank of India	India	5,278	12	440
Natixis	France	4,389	58	76
Santander	Spain	4,120	62	66
Commonwealth Bank of Australia	Australia	3,805	35	109
HSBC	Britain	3,745	31	121
Norddeutsche Landesbank	Germany	3,359	66	51
Sberbank	Russia	2,998	3	999
National Australia Bank	Australia	2,814	28	101
Intesa SanPaolo	Italy	2,751	23	120
Gazprombank	Russia	2,412	5	482
UniCredit	Italy	2,355	30	78
Citigroup	United States	2,354	19	124
Others (225)		119,770		
	Total	**231,156**		

Source: *As for Table 20.1.*

out the 'top 20' project-finance commercial banks in 2016, illustrates this mix.[1] It is also conspicuous that apart from Citibank, there are no US or Canadian banks on the list: in fact, bank finance to PPPs in the United States and Canada is provided mainly by the same Japanese and European banks, as US and Canadian banks have a limited interest in long-term project-finance lending (*cf.* §22.4.3).

In total, major lenders in the project-finance market underwrote 766 projects in 2016.[2]

§22.2.3 Organisation

Most international commercial banks have specialist departments that work on putting project finance deals together. There are three main approaches to organising such departments:

- Project-finance department

  The longest-standing approach is to have a department purely specialising in project-finance transactions. Larger departments are divided into industry teams, covering the main project-finance sectors such as energy, infrastructure (including PPPs) and natural resources. Concentrating all the project-finance expertise in one department ensures an efficient use of resources and good cross-fertilisation, using experience of project finance for different industries; however, it may not offer clients the best range of services. But probably only a minority of banks now maintain this structure.

- Structured-finance department

  As mentioned in §21.4, the divisions between project finance and other types of structured finance are quite blurred, and therefore nowadays project finance often forms part of a larger structured-finance department. This approach may offer a more sophisticated range of products, but there is some danger that project finance may not fit easily into the operation since other structured-finance business is based on a much shorter time horizon.

- Industry-based departments

  Another approach is to combine all financing for a particular industry sector (*e.g.* electricity, oil and gas/mining, or construction/infrastructure/PPPs) in one department; if this industry makes regular use of project finance, project-finance experts

---

[1] It will also be seen that several of the 'commercial banks' on the list are actually owned or controlled by the state, namely China Development Bank, State Bank of India, Sberbank and Gazprombank. These banks typically finance only a few large projects, and underwrite much larger amounts of debt than the private-sector commercial banks.

[2] This is less than the total number of projects for the 20 project-finance banks in Table 22.3 because where more than one bank is lead arranger for a loan (*cf.* §22.2.5), *Project Finance International* credits each bank with the project, while splitting the underwritten amount between them *pro rata*.

form part of the team. This provides one-stop services to the bank's clients in that particular industry, but obviously may diminish cross-fertilisation between project-finance experience in different industries.

It has to be said that banks do not always pursue consistent policies towards project-finance business. Some major banks such as Bank of America, Deutsche Bank and UBS, that formerly were very successful in project finance, closed these activities down. The problem with project finance from the perspective of such banks is that the process is much slower and more people-intensive than other structured-finance activities, and the revenues are also unpredictable (in the sense that one large project will push up fee income in one quarter, but the income cannot be sustained in the next quarter). Having said this, the *Project Finance International* statistics show that over 200 banks are active in the project-finance market, indicating that the disappearance of some of the traditional market leaders has been counterbalanced by new entrants.

So long as a country's PPP programme offers a steady and reliable stream of business, this should ensure that commercial banks are prepared to make the staffing and balance-sheet commitments that are needed to ensure that there is enough market competition for this programme to get financing on the best terms available. But this is not necessarily the case in smaller newer markets where domestic banks may hitherto have had little experience of project finance. These banks may find it difficult to justify the establishment of such capacity for just a few projects (and international banks may also be less interested in such markets).

§22.2.4 Regulation

It is also important to understand the way bank regulators oversee the project-finance activities of banks: this is another limiting factor in bank project-finance lending, especially since 2008. The Basel Committee on Banking Supervision, consisting of the representatives of central banks or other banking supervisory bodies from major financial centres, develops common approaches on requirements for bank capitalisation. This is to ensure banking stability and that banks compete internationally on the same basis. In 1988 the Committee introduced capital-adequacy rules for banks (known as the Basel Capital Accord), which were based, *inter alia*, on the simple measure that banks should hold capital equal to 8% of their commercial loans (including project finance). Subsequent accords—Basel II (2004) and Basel III (2011)—are sophisticated revisions of the 1988 Accord, which stipulate the quantity and quality of capital that banks must allow to underpin their lending. Basel III, in the wake of the 2008 financial crisis, considerably tightened up the Basel II requirements for capital required to underpin banks' trading activities and lending and also introduced tougher requirements (and hence higher costs) in relation to how banks finance less liquid assets (such as long-term project-finance loans). Basel IV, for which proposals were released for initial discussion in 2016, aims at greater standardisation of how banks calculate credit risks and regulatory capital, the effect which has been that, especially in Europe, banks have become less willing to provide the long maturities required for project-finance loans (*cf.* §23.2.7).

Therefore, a bank's appetite and costing for risk, and provision of long-term lending, is not wholly within its control but is subject to how changing regulations affect its project-finance business.

§22.2.5 Lead Arrangers and Financial Advisers

The normal approach to arranging a project-finance loan is to appoint one or more banks as 'lead arranger(s)',[3] who will ultimately underwrite (*i.e.* guarantee the availability of) the debt and place it in the market (but retaining a significant share of the debt on their own books). As with a financial adviser, experience of lending to similar PPP projects is a key factor in selecting a lead arranger; a wider banking relationship with one or more of the sponsors is often another element in the decision. Lead arrangers' fees are predominately based on a successful conclusion of the financing, although there may be a small retainer, and other out-of-pocket costs, such as travel, are usually covered by the sponsors.

One of the first questions sponsors have to consider on the financing side is when the lead arrangers should be brought into the transaction. Ideally, to ensure the maximum competition between banks on the financing terms, the whole of the project package should be finalised (including all the project contracts) and a number of banks then invited to bid in a competition to underwrite and provide the loan—which may actually be required by the contracting authority (*cf.* §22.6). This implies either that the sponsors make use of a financial adviser to put this package together (*cf.* §20.7.1), or do it themselves if they have the experience.

An alternative approach is to agree with a bank at an early stage of the project development process that it will act both as financial adviser and lead arranger. This should reduce the cost of the combined financial advisory and banking underwriting fees. It also ensures that the advice given is based on what the bank is itself willing to do and therefore that the project should be financeable. Moreover, many of the major banks in the market are not interested in 'pure' financial advisory work (*cf.* §20.7.1), which is also even more unpredictable in income. Such banks are therefore usually only interested in doing advisory work if it is combined with being the lead arranger.

If this approach is used, a mandate letter is normally signed between the sponsors and the lead arranger, which provides for services similar to those of the financial adviser set out above, but also expresses the bank's intention—subject to due diligence, credit clearance and agreement on detailed terms—to underwrite the debt required; some indication of pricing and other debt terms may also be given, although this may be difficult at an early stage of the transaction. This mandate letter does not impose a legal obligation on the bank to underwrite or lend money for the project—it is merely a statement of intent, albeit a serious one (since if the deal is not signed the bank will have done a lot of work for little, if any, fee).

---

[3] Other terms are used for this rôle, such as lead manager.

The obvious problem with this approach is that the bank is not in a competitive position (even if there may have originally been some kind of bidding process for the mandate), and therefore the sponsors will probably not get the most aggressive final terms for the financing. However, this may be a reasonable price to pay for the saving on advisory fees, greater efficiency of the process and greater certainty of obtaining finance that this method affords. Clearly the general relationship between the sponsors and the bank(s) concerned may also affect this decision. Some competition can also be retained by appointing at least two banks as joint lead arrangers, with each committed to underwrite all of the financing if necessary. If one bank steps too far out of line, it can be dropped and the other will take up the slack. However, this cannot be done for small projects.

In major projects, however, both a financial adviser and lead arranger(s) are often appointed separately at an early stage to provide more balanced advice, although obviously this adds to bid costs.

§22.2.6 Commitment Letters and Letters of Intent

If a contracting authority wants a fully-committed bid, on which there will be no further negotiation, it may require the financing to be committed at the time of the bid (*cf.* §10.8.3). This means that banks have to complete their due-diligence process (*cf.* §22.2.7), put together a detailed financing package (*cf.* Chapter 23), obtain internal credit approvals, perhaps even have agreed loan documentation with the bidders, and set out their commitment in a formal letter, for the bidders to demonstrate that the financing can be provided and thus the project can begin without delay. The disadvantage of this approach is that a full underwriting commitment by banks will involve fees (*cf.* §23.4.3) and substantial legal and other advisory costs. Bidders may be unwilling to pay for all this with no certainty that they will win the bid, in which case it is not uncommon for losing bidders' costs to be covered up to an agreed level by the contracting authority (*cf.* §10.7.4). There may also be market limitations—committed finance for three bids means committed finance worth three times the requirement of the project, for which there may not be market capacity. But there is often no strong reason for the contracting authority to require full commitments with each bid, unless there is something novel about the structure or risk of the PPP, and hence some doubt about the terms on which it may be financeable.

Therefore, an alternative approach is for banks to provide letters of intent (or letters of interest) to sponsors to support their bids for a PPP project. These are usually short—perhaps two pages long—and

- confirm the bank's basic interest in getting involved in the project, based on a review of the draft project contracts (on which they may have taken legal advice);
- set out outline terms and commitment levels for their share of the financing;
- confirm that the bank sees no reason not to be able to achieve financial close on the schedule required by the contracting authority, but
- state that the letter is not a legal commitment on the bank's part, and is subject, *inter alia*, to full due diligence and final credit approval.

If the letter requires the sponsors to deal exclusively with the bank concerned, this may become a lead arranger's mandate letter as described above. Alternatively, the sponsors may collect a number of such letters from different banks. Letters of this nature provide initial reassurance to the sponsors that their planned bid is reasonably realistic, and to the contracting authority that the required finance can be delivered. Although banks treat such 'support letters' seriously, they should not be regarded as a real commitment on their part. Many banks issue these letters without going through any internal credit-approval procedure. They are often used to ensure that they keep their foot in the door of the project, and therefore should not be interpreted too strongly.

In new or smaller markets, the contracting authority may need to take a view on whether even such letters of support may preclude other (smaller) bidders from bidding. This can happen if the support of a bank is tied exclusively to a bidder, which may lead to a more restricted number of bidders (due to the number of banks available). Apart from reducing competition, this can create a perception of collusion and a sense that only a small privileged number of contractors have access to the PPP market. The rôle of DFIs (cf. §22.9.2), which cannot usually be tied to one bidder but can indicate conditional support and terms for the project's financing requirements, helps counter this problem. This also reduces the financing that has to be raised by bidders from the commercial-banking market.

If a separate financial adviser is used, the adviser normally also provides a support letter for the bid, confirming that in its view the project can be successfully financed.

§22.2.7 Lenders' Due Diligence

A project company, unlike a corporate borrower, has no business record to serve as the basis for a lending decision. Therefore, lenders have to be confident that they will be repaid, especially taking account of the additional risk from the high level of debt inherent in a project-finance transaction. This means that they need to have a high degree of confidence that:

* The project can be completed on time and on budget.
* Major subcontractors have the experience and financial capacity to support their obligations, especially during construction (cf. §10.8.2, §12.3.2).
* Revenues and opex can be predicted with reasonable certainty.
* There will be enough net cash flow from the project's operation to cover their debt service adequately; project economics also need to be robust enough to cover any temporary problems that may arise.

So, the lenders need to evaluate the terms of the project contracts insofar as these provide a basis for the latter's construction costs and operating cash flow, and quantify the risks inherent in the project, with particular care. As the project company has a limited ability to absorb risk (because of its high leverage), lenders need to ensure that project risks are allocated to other appropriate parties, or, where this is not possible, mitigated in other ways (cf. §11.5). This due-diligence process may cause slow and frustrating progress for a PPP project, especially if it leads lenders to get involved—directly or indirectly—in the negotiation of the project contracts (cf. §10.8.3), but it is an unavoidable aspect of raising project-finance debt.

To help with this due diligence, the lead arrangers—like the contracting authority (*cf.* §6.4) and the sponsors (*cf.* §20.7)—employ external advisers (at the sponsors' or project company's expense):

— Legal adviser

Lawyers will be required both to prepare loan and security documentation and to review the project contracts. Their own and the lenders' legal costs are one of the main categories of bidding and development costs for the sponsors. These ultimately feed through to the service fees as they become part of the total capex (*cf.* §23.9.2), although it is generally the sponsors who are at risk if these costs exceed the levels assumed in their bid. It is preferable for legal work to be done on a fixed-fee basis (*cf.* §6.4.6), but if this is not possible costs need to be carefully controlled. If their lawyers are working on time-based fees, the lenders—who normally receive fixed fees—have every incentive to try to shift due-diligence work onto them to get a better return on the time of their staff involved in the project. Typical examples of this are the use of lawyers to act as secretaries of meetings that are primarily discussing commercial or financial (rather than legal) issues, or to draw up the term sheet (*cf.* §22.2.8). The sponsors must therefore agree to the lenders' legal advisers' scope of work and carefully supervise the time spent.

— Technical adviser

A consultant (a surveying or engineering company) will be needed to advise the lenders on:

• the cost and feasibility of the construction;
• FM costs and the maintenance cycle;
• other operating costs (where relevant);
• the technical aspects of the project contracts;
• progress of the construction as a condition to loan disbursements (*cf.* §25.2); and
• completion of the construction (*cf.* §15.4.1).

— Market-risk adviser

In the case of a concession, or an availability PPP project that transfers usage risk, an adviser will be required to review this risk, *e.g.* by modelling or reviewing models for traffic flows and tolls (*cf.* §13.2).

— Insurance adviser

The major international insurance brokers all have departments which specialise in advising lenders to major projects, insurance being an important part of the lenders' security (*cf.* §14.6).

— Financial-model auditor

The rôle played by the financial model, and the model auditor, in project development and due diligence is discussed in §23.9.8.

Throughout the due-diligence process, the financial advisers or lead arrangers are likely to play an active rôle in any further negotiation (or renegotiation) of the project contracts, to ensure that financing implications of these contracts are taken into account. Any changes in the project contracts that are good for the sponsors are generally good for lenders too, and so the banks may be used by sponsors to improve their commercial position in any negotiations with the contracting authority (*cf.* §10.8.3).

So long as it is not used to re-open negotiations (*cf.* §10.8.3), this whole due-diligence and control process can be of value to the contracting authority, despite the extra work and cost it may create, as it helps to 'validate' the project and ensure its long-term viability (*cf.* §28.9.8). However, the contracting authority must also conduct its own due diligence on the financing structure and terms (*cf.* §10.8, §21.5.2).

§22.2.8 Term Sheet, Underwriting and Documentation

As the financing structure develops, a term sheet is drawn up, setting out in summary form the basis on which the finance will be provided (as discussed in detail in Chapter 23). This can develop into quite an elaborate document, especially if the bank lawyers are involved in drawing it up, which can add substantially to the sponsors' legal costs. It is preferable for term-sheet discussions to concentrate on commercial rather than legal issues, although the dividing line may be difficult to draw.

A term sheet may be drafted by the sponsors' financial adviser as a basis for requesting financing bids from prospective lead arrangers, or at a later stage by the lead arrangers to crystallise their commitment to the financing.

The final term sheet provides the basis for the lead arrangers to complete their internal credit proposals and obtain the necessary approvals to go ahead with the loan. The work of a bank's project-finance team, and the consequent proposal for a loan, is normally reviewed by a separate credit department, and it may be presented to a formal credit committee for approval. Banks must have a well-organised interface between the credit team and the project-finance team, especially where a bank is acting as a lead arranger: it may take a long time to develop a PPP project, and if the loan is turned down at the end of that process on credit grounds, this obviously has serious consequences for both the sponsors and the contracting authority (and does not help the bank's project-finance business very much). On the other hand, the bank cannot obtain full credit approval at the beginning of the development process, because the structure of the transaction will probably not be sufficiently finalised. The sponsors and the contracting authority therefore need to have confidence that a lead arranger has the experience and credibility to manage this internal-review process.

After obtaining the credit approval, lead arranger(s) may 'underwrite' the debt, usually by signing the agreed term sheet. The term sheet provides for a final date by which documentation should be signed, as banks usually have to reapply for internal credit approval if their loan is not signed within a reasonable period. This signature of a term sheet is still normally no more than a moral obligation, as the commitment by the banks is usually subject to further detailed due diligence on the project contracts and agreement on financing and security documentation. Bank technical or other advisers may also still have due-diligence work to do. Nonetheless, the term sheet is treated seriously, and banks normally only withdraw from an underwriting if there is a major change of circumstances, either in relation to the project itself, the country in which it is situated, or the market in general.

The next phase in the financing is the negotiation of financing documentation, typical terms for which are discussed in the following chapters; when this is signed, the sponsors have finally obtained committed financing for the project company. But even at this stage, the banks may not actually provide the financing, as there are numerous conditions precedent that have to be fulfilled before the project reaches financial close and a drawing can be made (*cf.* §25.2.1).

It is evident from this description that arranging project finance is not a quick process. If the project is presented to potential lead arrangers as a completed package, with all the project contracts in place, it is likely to take a minimum of three months before signature of the loan documentation by the lead arrangers. But there is clearly a lengthy process to go through before such a package can be completed, and issues may well arise during banks' due diligence that further slow down the matter. Finance is therefore usually an important critical-path item, and it is not uncommon for banks to work for a year or more on the financing side of a major PPP project.

§22.2.9 Syndication

For larger loans, the lead arrangers may wish to reduce their loan exposure by placing part of the financing with other banks in the market, while retaining arranging and underwriting fees. There are many banks participating in the project-finance market at the next level down as sub-underwriters or participants in syndicated loans. Some of these participate in domestic lending in their own countries, others in syndications of a wider range of loans around the world originally arranged and underwritten by the larger players in the market.

The lead arrangers prepare an information package to facilitate this loan-sale process (which is known as 'syndication'), at the heart of which is an information memorandum. This may be based on a preliminary information memorandum (PIM) originally prepared by the sponsors or their financial adviser to present the project to prospective lead arrangers. The information memorandum probably also imports a lot of information from the bid documents prepared by the contracting authority (*cf.* §10.6.2)—this information on the project provided by the contracting authority is sometimes confusingly referred to the '*project* information memorandum'. The information memorandum prepared by the lead arranger provides a detailed summary of the transaction, including:

- a summary overview of the project, its general background and *raison d'être*;
- the project company, its ownership, organisation and management (*cf.* §20.6);
- financial and other information on sponsors, including their experience in similar projects and the nature of their involvement in, and support for, the current project (*cf.* §10.6.1, §20.2.1, §23.7);
- similar information on the parties to the project contracts;
- technical description of the construction and O&M of the project;

- where relevant, information relevant to usage of the facility, *e.g.* historic and projected traffic flows;
- summary of the PPP contract and other project contracts;
- project costs and financing plan (*cf.* Chapter 23);
- risk analysis (*cf.* Chapters 11-13);
- financial analysis, including the base-case financial model (*cf.* §23.9.9) and sensitivity analyses (*cf.* §23.9.7); and
- a detailed term sheet for the financing (*cf.* §22.2.8).

In other words, the information memorandum provides a synopsis of the structure of the project and the whole due-diligence process, which speeds up the credit analysis by prospective participant banks. (If well-organised and written, it also provides the project company and the contracting authority with a useful long-term reference manual on the project and its financing.) The information memorandum is accompanied by supplementary reports and information:

- a copy of the financial model, with the model auditor's report (*cf.* §23.9.8);
- the technical adviser's report (*cf.* §22.2.7), summarising their due-diligence review;
- if relevant, the relevant adviser's report on usage-risk aspects of the project and its revenue projections;
- the legal advisers may provide a summary of legal aspects of the project, including the main project contracts;
- a report on insurances from the insurance adviser (*cf.* §20.7.7); and
- annual financial statements or other information on the various parties to the project.

The sponsors are actively involved in the production of the information memorandum, which is normally subject to their approval and confirmation of its accuracy; the contracting authority may also review the draft.

A formal presentation is often made to prospective participant banks by lead arrangers, the sponsors and other relevant project parties, which may include the contracting authority, sometimes through a 'road show' in different financial centres for major projects. Prospective participant banks are usually given 3-4 weeks to absorb this information and come to a decision whether to participate in the financing. They are generally given the documentation to review after they have taken this decision in principle to participate, and may sign up for the financing 2-3 weeks after receiving this.

The project company does not usually take any direct risk on whether the syndication is successful or not; by then the loan should have been signed and thus underwritten by the lead arrangers. The contracting authority and sponsors should resist delay tactics by lead arrangers who try to avoid signing the financing documentation until after they have syndicated the loan and thus eliminated their underwriting risk. Similarly, syndication should not be of concern to the contracting authority. (In some cases, 'market-flex' provisions give bank underwriters some flexibility to increase their loan pricing, for a large loan before syndication, to reflect changes in the loan markets, but this is not common in the PPP project-finance market.)

Participant banks may also transfer part or all of their loans to other banks at any time during the life of the loan. This is important as part of their portfolio management—commercial banks are not naturally lenders for the 20 years or more of financing required for a PPP project, since their deposits are mainly short-term in nature (*cf.* §24.2), and portfolio liquidity is therefore important.

The contracting authority should not control either the syndication process or subsequent transfers by banks to other lenders, since a change in lenders should have no effect on the services provided under the PPP contract. Any such restrictions will reduce the liquidity of the bank loan, which has an associated cost. (The project company may be more restrictive if the result would be that it has to pay additional withholding tax—*cf.* §23.4.2.) Of course, new lenders must assume any obligations to the project company such as advancing the undrawn balance of the loan, or those that exist in favour of the contracting authority under the direct agreement (*cf.* §25.3.3), *e.g.* as to confidentiality.

§22.2.10 Agency Operation

Once the financing documentation has been signed, one of the lead arrangers acts as agent for the bank syndicate as a whole: this agent bank acts as a channel between the project company (and the contracting authority if necessary) and the lenders. Without this arrangement, the project company could find that it is spending an excessive amount of time communicating with individual banks. The agent bank:

- collects the funds from the syndicate when drawings are made and passes these on to the project company;
- holds the project security on behalf of the lenders (this function may be carried out by a separate security trustee, acting on the instructions of the agent bank);
- calculates loan interest payments and principal repayments;
- receives payments from the project company and passes these on to the individual syndicate banks;
- gathers information about the progress of the project, in liaison with the lenders' advisers, and distributes this to the syndicate at regular intervals;
- monitors the project company's compliance with the requirements of the financing documentation and provides information on this to the syndicate banks;
- arranges meetings and site visits as necessary for the project company and the sponsors to make more formal presentations to the syndicate banks on the project's progress;
- organises discussions with and voting by the syndicate if the project company needs to obtain an amendment or waiver of some term of the financing, or a change in the subcontracts (*cf.* §19.4.3); and
- takes enforcement action against the project company or the security after a default.

The agent bank seldom has any discretion to make decisions about the loan (for example, as to placing the project company in default), but acts as directed by a defined majority of the banks. Requiring collective voting by the banks in this way ensures that one rogue bank cannot hold the rest of the syndicate (and the project company) to ransom.

§22.3 NON-BANK LENDERS

Non-bank lenders, in particular life-insurance companies, have been playing an increasing part in providing project-finance debt for infrastructure in lieu of or alongside commercial banks, particularly in Europe and North America. To a certain extent, they have filled the gap in long loan maturities from which some banks have retreated (*cf.* §22.2.4, §23.2.7). Moreover, this type of lending is usually at a fixed rate, similar to bonds (see below), which is advantageous. However, the overall scale of this activity remains small by comparison with commercial banks.

Similar solvency regulations for insurance companies to the Basel regulations discussed in §22.2.4 (such as the 2009 Solvency II directive of the EU) also aim to regulate how much capital these institutions must hold when they invest in assets such as long-term project-finance loans. So far this seems to have had little effect on the appetite of insurance companies interested in providing project-finance debt.

The majority of institutional interest in project-finance debt is still to be found in the bond market, as discussed below. One advantage for a non-bank lender of making a direct loan instead of buying a bond is that a lender has more direct controls over any decisions that have to be taken about the loan, should any issues arise that need such decisions (*cf.* §22.2.10, Table 22.6).

§22.4 BOND ISSUES

A bond issued by a project company is similar to a loan from the project company's point of view. As the borrower—known as the 'issuer' in this context—the project company agrees to repay to the bond holder the amount of the bond plus interest on fixed future instalment dates. (A 'bond' in this context has nothing to do with 'bonding' or 'bonds' issued as security, *e.g.* when making a bid (*cf.* §10.7.3), or to support a subcontractor's liabilities (*cf.* §12.4.3).) Bonds may also be referred to as 'securities', 'notes' or 'debentures'.

Buyers of project-finance bonds are usually institutional investors that require a secure long-term return on their investment without taking equity risks, in particular insurance companies and pension funds. Although these parties also invest in equity (*cf.* §20.2.1), this is a more recent phenomenon. Bonds are often held by bond-investment funds, with a similar client base to infrastructure-equity funds.

The key difference between loans and bonds is that bonds are tradable instruments (*i.e.* they can be bought and sold in financial markets or stock exchanges) and therefore have at least a theoretical liquidity, which loans do not. This difference is not as great as it at first appears, because many PPP bonds are sold on a private-placement basis (§22.4.2) to investors who do not intend to trade them in the market, and loans are in fact traded on an *ad hoc* basis between banks and with non-bank lenders. However, the project company and the contracting authority will have less knowledge of, and potential contact with, bond holders than with bank lenders.

§22.4.1 Due Diligence

Investors in bonds generally do not get directly involved in the due-diligence process to the extent that banks do, and rely more on the project's investment bank and a rating agency to carry out this work. An investment bank (*i.e.* a bank that arranges and underwrites financing but does not normally provide the financing itself, except on a temporary basis) is appointed as lead arranger for the bond issue, and assists in structuring the project in a similar way to a financial adviser on a bank loan (*cf.* §22.2.5).

The investment bank then makes a presentation on the project to a credit-rating agency (the leaders in the field as far as project-finance bonds are concerned are Standard & Poor's and Moody's Investors Services). The rating agency assigns the bond a credit rating based on its independent review of the risks of the project, including legal documentation and independent advisers' reports (using external advisers in a similar way to banks—*cf.* §22.2.7). This review considers the same risk issues as a commercial bank would do. As project-finance bonds usually form a very small part of a bond investor's portfolio, it is more cost-effective to rely on the rating as the main basis for the credit decision, rather than have to employ staff to undertake the kind of detailed due diligence undertaken by banks.

Credit ratings by Standard & Poor's and Moody's are graded from the prime credit level of AAA/Aaa respectively down to the minimum 'investment grade' rating of BBB-/Baa3 (below which many bond investors will not—and in some cases legally cannot—purchase a bond issue).[4] Most PPP-project ratings are at the lower end of this range, *i.e.* just within the investment grade. Some bank loans are also rated by the rating agencies, to assist in a wider syndication, and because some institutional investors participate in (or lend in parallel to) bank syndicated loans. However, this is not a widespread practice in the project-finance market.

From the borrower's point of view, the disadvantage of dealing with credit through a rating agency, as compared to negotiating with a bank lender, is that the former is not under the same competitive pressure to do the deal. This can mean that the bond has to be issued on less aggressive terms than might be the case if banks were competing for the business, or sponsors may be forced to provide extra security or other credit support (*cf.* §23.7).

Having obtained the rating, the investment bank prepares a preliminary bond prospectus that covers similar ground to an information memorandum for a bank syndication (*cf.* §22.2.9), although in less detail. The work done by the investment bank and the rating agency reduces the need for due diligence by bond investors—provided the bond rating fits the bond investor's maximum risk profile, such investors can just decide to buy it without substantial due diligence.

§22.4.2 Bond Placement

After any necessary preliminary testing of the market (which may include a road show of presentations to investors), the investment bank issues the final bond prospectus

---

[4] Below the investment-grade level, the ratings continue from BB+/Ba1, *etc.*

and underwrites the bond issue through a subscription agreement. The coupon (interest rate) and other key conditions of the bond are fixed based on the market at the time of underwriting (*cf.* §23.4.6), and the bond proceeds are paid over to the project company a few days later. The investment bank places (or resells) the bonds with investors, and may also maintain a liquid market by trading in the bond. As can be seen, the timing of this process means that the underwriting does not take place until the underwriter already knows that there are buyers for the bonds, and the price at which they can be sold: thus, unlike a bank underwriter (§22.2.5), the bond underwriter takes little if any market risk.

Bonds may either be public issues (*i.e.* quoted on a stock exchange and—at least theoretically—quite widely traded), or private placements, that are not quoted and are sold to a limited number of large investors who typically hold them throughout their life. It is possible for a private placement to take place without the intervention of an investment bank (*i.e.* the sponsors can deal directly with investors, as they can deal direct with banks, without the use of a financial adviser), although this seldom occurs.

Paying agents (also known as fiscal agents) and trustees are appointed for the bond issue, with similar rôles to that of an agent bank for a loan (*cf.* §22.2.10). The paying agent pays over the proceeds of the bond to the borrower and collects payments due to the bond investors. The bond trustee holds the security on behalf of the investors, and calls meetings of bond holders to vote on waivers or amendments of the bond terms.

§22.4.3 The Project-Finance Bond Market

As Table 22.4 illustrates, the market for project-finance bonds is far smaller in scale than that for bank loans (*cf.* Table 22.1), and has shown little growth in recent years.

Table 22.4   Project-finance bond market by sectors, 2010-2016

($ millions)	2010	2011	2012	2013	2014	2015	2016	No.*
Infrastructure	9,839	11,348	10,757	21,527	19,564	16,772	15,184	48
Power	4,877	5,448	7,108	9,099	10,950	15,054	10,543	3
Natural resources	4,474	5,483	6,262	18,515	19,593	3,185	12,489	15
Telecommunications	0	0	0	114	225	274	1,271	1
Other	600	0	0	0	0	0	3,410	51
Total	**19,790**	**22,279**	**24,127**	**49,255**	**50,332**	**35,285**	**42,896**	**118**

*Number of projects, 2016.
Source: *Project Finance International,* Annual project-finance league tables (data summarised).

Table 22.5   Project-finance bonds by country, 2016

($ millions)	2010	2011	2012	2013	2014	2015	2016
Americas	9,822	13,220	17,059	26,563	24,807	19,253	22,402
Of which: United States	4,905	4,264	7,111	13,506	12,306	10,880	13,653
Canada	4,521	4,131	2,076	2,064	3,315	4,913	3,679
Asia-Pacific	6,432	2,628	2,952	2,986	4,951	5,284	3,645
Of which: Australia	4,550	935	0	1,944	3,148	1,149	1,511
Europe/FSU	3,536	5,432	2,642	16,323	18,276	10,748	16,544
Of which: Britain	3,276	4,732	2,538	4,214	4,862	3,209	4,010
Middle East/N. Africa	0	999	1,300	3,272	1,998	0	306
Sub-Saharan Africa	0	0	174	111	300	0	0
Total	**19,790**	**22,279**	**24,127**	**49,255**	**50,332**	**35,285**	**42,896**

Source: *Project Finance International,* Annual project-finance league tables (data summarised).

The market is also heavily concentrated in certain countries, as illustrated by Table 22.5. The US market for project-finance bond issues is by far the largest. This reflects the combination of reluctance by American banks to lend for long tenors (*cf.* §22.2.2), and the high demand for bonds from institutional investors, especially pension funds. There are two separate project-finance bond markets in the United States:

- Municipal bonds

  The United States has a large municipal-bond ('muni') market: this market provides debt to local governments, including for specific projects where repayment relies on the cash flow of a particular project, *i.e.* on a project-finance basis. Such projects may be owned by the municipality, a public trust (*cf.* §27.5.3) or, under some circumstances (where services are being provided to or on behalf of an authority), a private-sector project company.[5] The structuring of project-finance bonds is derived from this market. (Table 22.5 does not include munis on a project-finance basis.) Coupon (interest) payments on munis are tax-free: this means that institutional investors—which generally do not pay tax—do not invest in this market because munis' interest rates are comparatively low, reflecting their tax-free status.

- Rule 144a

  The institutional project-finance bond market in the United States is based on Rule 144a, adopted by the Securities and Exchange Commission (SEC) in 1990. A private

---

[5] These are known as 'private-activity bonds (PABs)'. They are estimated to make up 25-35% of the total muni market.

placement of a bond issue does not have to go through the SEC's lengthy full registration procedure, but cannot be sold on to another party for two years. This lack of liquidity is generally not acceptable to US bond investors. However, Rule 144a allows secondary trading (*i.e.* reselling) of private placements of debt securities, provided sales are to 'qualified institutional buyers' (QIBs) with a portfolio of at least $100 million in securities. Rule 144a bonds are therefore sold by the project company to an investment bank, which then resells them to QIBs. Thus, Rule 144a provides an efficient and effective way of raising project finance in the world's largest bond market. This is the main basis on which project-finance bonds are issued in that market, whether they are limited private placements or more widely-traded issues, although they have to be relatively large in size—at least $100-200 million. Rule 144a US $-denominated project-finance bonds are the only important source of cross-border (international) project-finance bond financing, primarily for projects in the Americas.

The non-$ bond market is concentrated in a few locations. This partly reflects the fact that European and Asian banks are more aggressive lenders to the project-finance market, and tend to have closer relationships with major project sponsors, and partly that the bond markets are also much smaller. In Europe, the British (£ sterling) market is the most important for project-finance bonds. The minimum size for public placements is around £100 million; smaller amounts can be raised through private placements. Bonds are typically used for large projects (£300 million and above), where there may be more limited bank liquidity, and also for refinancing (*cf.* §26.2). There are similar markets in other European countries, Australia and Canada for infrastructure-related bonds.

Inflation-indexed bonds, where interest and principal repayments are linked to inflation, are discussed in §24.3.6.

§22.4.4 Debt Insurance

Until the 2008 financial crisis, a key element of both the general project-finance bond market and the US muni market was that a large proportion of the bonds, in the infrastructure field in particular, were 'wrapped', or guaranteed by 'monoline' insurance companies (so called because they specialise in bond insurance, *i.e.* they have only one line of business). Most of the PFI bonds issued in Britain, for example, had monoline cover. This meant that bond holders were not taking any project risk. However, as it turned out, they were taking more risk on the monolines than they thought. Most of them became effectively insolvent during the financial crisis, not because of their insurance of project-finance bonds, but because they also insured sub-prime mortgage bonds. Since that time only one monoline assurer, Assured Guaranty, has written new business.

Another insurance market has been developing in more recent years to provide 'non-payment insurance' for bank loans. As the name implies, it was originally intended to cover non-payment by a buyer of goods of some kind, but it has been extended to non-payment under bank loans, including project-finance loans. Typically, and unlike monoline cover, this type of insurance covers only 35-50% of the loan. Maximum capacity for a single loan is around $500 million. Claims can only be made as and when a loan instalment is not paid, *i.e.* if loan repayments are accelerated on a default (*cf.* §25.4), the insurance company still only pays out as and when the original loan repayments were due.

§22.5 Bank Loans versus Bonds

The key factors that are likely to affect a project company's decision whether to use commercial-bank or bond financing (in a market where bond financing is available) are:

- *Size*: Bonds can only be used for larger projects, as investors want the bond issue to be sufficiently large for the issue to have market liquidity. For very large (say more than $250 million) projects, there may be more limited bank liquidity and so bonds may be more suitable.
- *Cost*: Bonds have tended to have a lower cost than equivalent bank loans, partly because there is a wider investor base.
- *Tenor*: Bonds have always been used to provide very long-term finance, whereas until the mid-1990s it was unusual for a bank project-finance loans (or any other loans) to be for longer than 20 years. Tenor has also become an issue in some banking markets in more recent times (*cf.* §22.2.4, §23.2.7). It remains the case that for very long-term loans (say 30 years or more) bonds are usually more competitive.

There are a number of other more detailed or technical pros and cons between loans and bonds, summarised in Table 22.6.

Because of some of the uncertainties about the final availability or terms of bond financing, sponsors may arrange a bank loan as an 'insurance policy' in case the bond issue falls through, or put together a bank loan with the intention of refinancing it rapidly with a bond. Obviously, this involves extra costs.

In general, bonds are suitable for 'standard' projects. They are also especially suitable if a project is being refinanced after it has been built and has operated successfully for a period. Conversely, the greater flexibility of bank loans tends to make them more suitable for the construction and early operation phases of a project, projects where there are likely to be changes in the contracting authority's requirements, more complex projects, or projects in more difficult markets. However, the distinction between the two is becoming blurred, as investment funds and some other categories of non-bank lenders may buy into both bank loans and bonds.

From the contracting authority's view, enabling projects to have access to both bank and bond financing can help to create competition in the market from these two different sources of long-term finance and lead to lower financing costs. In more mature markets, governments have used strategies to encourage both markets to develop, particularly bond markets, especially when there is concern about the capacity of banks to provide project financing in relation to the needs. DFIs have also played a market-development rôle in this respect.[6]

---

[6] The European Investment Bank's (EIB's) 'Project Bond Initiative' was one such example in which the EIB provided forms of credit support for projects to encourage bond institutional investors to finance projects, especially in the aftermath of the credit crisis (*cf.* §22.9.3).

Table 22.6 Bank loans *versus* bonds

Bank loans	Bonds
Banks can be involved in and effectively (though not legally) committed to the project from an early stage	Bond investors only come in at a very late stage, and may be more affected by short-term market sentiment
Although banks do not formally commit to loan terms (including credit margin) in advance, they are more likely to stand by the terms they offer at an early stage (unless market-flex provisions apply)	The terms for the bond and the market appetite for it are only finally known at a late stage in the process, when the underwriting takes place
The sponsors' corporate-banking lines may be used up in project-finance loans (but *cf.* §21.5.1)	Bonds bring a different investor base, thus avoiding the need to tie up bank credit lines.
Project-financing contracts kept confidential, in a loan syndicated to a restricted number of banks	The terms of the bond financing, including information on the project, may have to be published in a public rating report (*cf.* §22.4.1) or bond prospectus: this may not be acceptable to the sponsors for reasons of commercial confidentiality
Generally, only offer fixed rates of interest through hedging arrangements (*cf.* §24.2.2)	Fixed rates of interest
Interest-rate pricing is based on open-market quotations (but *cf.* §24.2.8)	Interest-rate pricing is a 'black box' (*cf.* §22.4.2), although the likely outcome can be monitored by watching the prices of comparable bonds already issued
Inflation-indexed loans generally not available or only available through hedging arrangements (*cf.* §24.3.9)	In some markets bonds can be issued on an inflation-indexed basis (*cf.* §24.3.6)
Funds from the loan drawn only when needed	Funds from the bond may have to be drawn all at once, and then redeposited until required to pay for capex—there is likely to be a loss of interest (known as 'negative arbitrage') caused by the redeposit rate being lower than the coupon on the bond (*cf.* §24.2.11)
Banks can offer flexible loan repayment schedules (*cf.* §23.2.5), and short-term working capital loans	Bond loan repayment schedules are inflexible and cannot offer short-term funding

(Continued)

Table 22.6 (Continued)

Bank loans	Bonds
Banks exercise control over all changes to project contracts, and impose tight controls on the project company	Bond investors only control matters that significantly affect their cash flow cover or security, and Events of Default leading to accelerated repayment of the financing are more limited in bond issues
Decisions on waivers and amendments to loan terms are taken on a case-by-case basis by banks; this is more flexible, especially during the construction phase	Bond investors cannot easily take complex decisions (because of the widespread and number of investors), and so rely mainly on mechanical tests such as cover ratios (*cf.* §23.3); this may be less flexible if amendments to these ratios are required (although bond holders may allow any parallel bank lenders to take decisions on their behalves)
Banks tightly control the addition of any new debt, and are unlikely to agree the basis for this in advance	It is may be easier to add new debt (*e.g.* for a project expansion) to bond financing as bond investors will agree the terms for this in advance through 'variation bonds' (*cf.* §16.2.1—footnote)
Low penalties for prepayment (*e.g.* because the debt can be refinanced on more favourable terms)	High penalties for prepayment (*cf.* §24.2.12)
It is easier to negotiate with banks if the project gets into difficulty	If the project gets into serious trouble, it can be difficult to have a direct dialogue with bond holders, who are more passive in nature than a bank syndicate; banks are often wary of lending in partnership with bond holders for this reason
If a project gets into difficulty, negotiations with banks should remain private	Negotiations with bond holders may be publicised

§22.6 Funding Competitions

Competitive bids by prospective lender syndicates may be required by the contracting authority after the appointment of the preferred bidder. (Of course, the project company may decide to hold its own funding competition at this point—if so, this will be a matter entirely under its control, without any contracting authority involvement.)

§22.6.1 Purpose of a Funding Competition

Although a bidder has every incentive to secure the best terms from lenders at the time of submitting the bid, there may nonetheless be a case for the contracting authority to require a competitive procurement for the financing (known as a 'funding competition'[7]), if the terms offered for the financing in the bid are felt to be uncompetitive, thus resulting in higher than necessary service fees. The competition takes place after the appointment of the preferred bidder. This is because:

- lenders are likely to offer more competitive terms to a preferred bidder; and
- lenders are less likely to raise issues on the PPP contract (or other project contracts) if faced with competition from other lenders, which cuts down the risk of deal creep (*cf.* §10.6.8).

A funding competition is not all negative from the lenders' point of view, as it means that they know by then that the PPP project should go ahead with the particular preferred bidder and they are therefore bidding on a 'real deal'.

It could be argued that a funding competition introduces a kind of separability (*cf.* §2.4.7), and that it is inappropriate to pick on just one of the factors which affects the bidder's pricing and open this up to competition after the bid has been submitted. But there is a substantial difference between the rôle lenders play in a PPP bid and that played by other subcontractors.

Having said this, however, it is unlikely that a funding competition will add much value to a 'standard' deal, where there is good competition from bidders, and financial structures and terms are already well-established. It is also an additional stage in, and adds to the costs of the procurement process. This means that it should only be considered in cases where:

- A country is at the early stage of developing a PPP programme, so that market terms are not yet well-established (but this also assumes a certain level of sophistication on the part of the contracting authority to manage the process which may not be available early on).
- The project involves a new type of PPP, so there may be a considerable variation of views amongst lenders on its financing terms.
- There has been a long period after the appointment of the preferred bidder, and hence the lenders' terms are no longer in line with the market.
- The preferred bidder's existing lenders have been raising new issues on the PPP contract that are not in conformity with the original bid. (Of course, a funding competition would only be used here if the contracting authority considered that the existing lenders' views would not be shared by others.)

However, a funding competition, if initiated by a contracting authority, can also create a number of risks such as:

- Less interest in bidding for PPP projects where finance is not part of the original package because prospective bidders may be uncomfortable with having to deal with lenders with whom they have no existing relationship.

---

[7] Although it would be more correct to call it a financing competition—*cf.* §9.2.1.

- Bids turn out to be more expensive than expected.
- Extra costs for the contracting authority, *e.g.* from its financial advisers having to undertake more work (and reimbursement of extra costs for the bidder, unless these have been built into the bid), which need to be justified by improved terms achieved in the funding competition.
- Bidders may employ separate financial advisers rather than just lead arrangers (*cf.* §22.2.5), so adding to bid costs and hence the cost of the project.
- Lenders will be less willing to spend time on due diligence at the time of the bid, with the risk that the resulting project contracts may prove not to be 'bankable' (*cf.* §10.8.3, §28.9.8).

Accordingly, funding competitions for projects much below $100 million are rare, not least because of the additional complexity, transaction costs and delay involved.

In the end, the threat of a funding competition—so long as it is credible—may be enough to keep the bidders' original lenders competitive, and therefore at a minimum the contracting authority can make it a condition in the bid documents (*cf.* §10.6.2) that it reserves the right to require one.

§22.6.2 How a Funding Competition Works

The first point to make here is that even if the contracting authority is the driver for holding a funding competition, it is the preferred bidder that must be responsible for negotiations with lenders. But it is necessary for there to be an agreement between the project company and the preferred bidder as to procedure, evaluation and costs.

- Procedure

    The preferred bidder negotiates the PPP contract with the contracting authority (to the extent that is allowed under the relevant procurement procedure), as well as the other project contracts. Once they are at a relatively final stage, these project contracts are reviewed by 'shadow' legal, technical and other advisers appointed on behalf of the prospective lenders by the preferred bidder: these advisers will prepare due-diligence reports which form part of an information memorandum package (*cf.* §22.2.9) to be sent to prospective lead arrangers. (The shadow advisers become direct advisers to the lead arrangers in the normal way (*cf.* §22.2.7) once these lead arrangers have been mandated.) The information package is then sent out to an agreed list of financial institutions.

- Evaluation

    'Non-conforming' bids—*i.e.* bids that require changes to the project contracts, or to the financing term sheet included in the information memorandum—are excluded from the process (unless the changes are acceptable to both the preferred bidder and the contracting authority and allowable under the relevant procurement procedure). Evaluation is thus primarily on financing terms and structure: however, even some of these terms can be more or less fixed in advance, especially the repayment structure (*cf.* §23.2) and hedging arrangements (*e.g.* interest-rate swaps—*cf.* §24.2.2). This leaves the bidding to cover:

* lending margins and fees (*cf.* §23.4);
* cover ratios and leverage (*cf.* §23.3, §23.5); and
* reserve-account requirements (*cf.* §25.2.4);

in the case of a bank loan, and in the case of a bond issue:

* margin over government bond rates, underwriting and other fees (*cf.* §23.4.6);
* cover ratios and leverage (*cf.* §23.3);
* reserve-account requirements (*cf.* §25.2.4);
* the GIC rate (*cf.* §24.2.11—this may be bid separately); and
* prepayment penalties (*cf.* §24.2.12).

The lenders will have to take the preferred bidder's equity IRR requirement (*cf.* §20.3.3) into account, and so structure their loan proposals in the most cost-effective and financially efficient way to ensure that this equity IRR is preserved (*cf.* §23.5).

The contracting authority may join meetings with the financiers, and is generally kept informed on progress. The choice of the winning bid is made by the preferred bidder (who may wish to take its existing banking relationships into account), but subject to ratification by the contracting authority. The service fees are then adjusted to take account of these final financing terms.

If the preferred bidder has been using a lead arranger as a financial adviser (*cf.* §22.2.5), the latter may be given a 'right to match', *i.e.* if the original lead arranger does not win the funding competition but if it offers the same terms as the winner, it will be allocated 50% of the financing.

— Costs

A definition of the marginal costs of the funding competition (on top of the preferred bidder's other bids costs) should be agreed between the contracting authority and the preferred bidder in advance. These marginal costs (*e.g.* additional work by advisers) will have to be funded by the bidders, but offset against the benefit of the funding competition when calculating the final service fees, unless they were allowed for in the original bid.

At the end of this process, the result of the funding competition is fed into the financial structure for the project, and hence the final service fees. There is no reason why the contracting authority should not get 100% of the benefit of the funding competition. But perhaps as an incentive to creativity for the bidder, if the service fees can be reduced by more than an agreed level, part of this extra benefit can be left for the project company (in the form of a reduction in service fees of less than 100% of the benefit).

§22.6.3 Refinancing

A funding competition should also generally be used to ensure that the best possible terms are obtained from a refinancing (*cf.* §26.2).

§22.7 MEZZANINE DEBT

Mezzanine debt is subordinated debt provided by third parties rather than the investors in the project company (*cf.* §20.3.5).[8] These may include non-bank investors, such as insurance companies or specialised funds. Such debt may also be provided by the contracting authority, or another public-sector institution (*cf.* §18.8).

Mezzanine debt may be used in cases where either there is a gap between the amount that senior lenders (*i.e.* the lenders with the highest priority in security and repayment) are willing to provide and the total debt requirements of the project, or in lieu of part of the equity to produce a more competitive bid. This is because the pricing of mezzanine debt lies between that for senior debt and that for equity. Mezzanine debt may also be provided by institutional investors as part of a debt package including bond financing, or by the contracting authority (*cf.* §18.8).

Bringing third-party debt into the financing package obviously creates greater issues of repayment priority and control over the project between the different levels of lenders than when subordinated debt is provided by shareholders (*cf.* §25.5.4).

Although mezzanine debt is common in other forms of structured finance, it has not been widely used in project finance, probably because the relatively high levels of leverage leave little space for it: it is thus more common in concessions where leverage is typically lower.

§22.8 RECOURSE TO THE SPONSORS

The only financial obligation that sponsors have in all PPP project financings is to subscribe their equity share in the project company, *i.e.* the lenders provide a loan to the project company with no guarantee of repayment from the sponsors—thus the loan is 'non-recourse' to the sponsors (*cf.* §21.3).

The contracting authority may feel uneasy about contracting with a project company which has no track record and no significant assets beyond the PPP contract itself, and so may want to request some form of completion guarantee or performance bonding from either the sponsors or the subcontractors (*cf.* §12.4, §12.5). This is usually impossible for the project company to provide, especially as the lenders will want first claim on any security of this type. The contracting authority has to rely primarily on:

- the fact that it does not make any payments until the service is provided (*cf.* §15.4);
- its own due diligence on the sponsors, and the quality and financial strength of the subcontractors (*cf.* §10.8); and
- the considerable financial incentives under the PPP contract (and its financial penalties for failure—*cf.* §15.5.5, §15.6.1).

---

[8] Both shareholder subordinated debt and third-party mezzanine debt are often referred to as 'junior debt', to contrast with the 'senior' debt provided by lenders (*cf.* §22.1). Given its ambiguity, the term junior debt is not used in this book.

However, while in principle sponsors do not provide loan guarantees to the project company's lenders either, limited guarantees may sometimes be provided to lenders to cover a risk that proves to be unacceptable. Examples of such 'limited-recourse' guarantees are:

- *land sale proceeds guarantee*: underwriting disposal of surplus land (*cf.* §12.2.9);
- *contingent equity commitment*: the sponsors agree to inject a specific additional amount as equity into the project company to meet specified cash-flow requirements;
- *cost-overrun guarantee*: the sponsors agree to inject additional equity up to a certain limit to cover any cost overruns during construction (or operating cost overruns);
- *completion guarantee*: the sponsors undertake to inject extra financing if necessary to ensure that construction of the project is completed by a certain date, thus taking on the risk that more financing for construction or initial debt service may be required; this can also be cast in the vaguer form of taking responsibility for completion, thus leaving lenders to prove what loss they have suffered if completion is late;
- *financial completion guarantee*: the sponsors provide a guarantee not only that the project will be physically completed, but also that it will achieve a minimum level of operating revenues or cash flow, and so make up any debt shortfall caused by a cash-flow deficit;
- *buy-down commitment*: the sponsors guarantee that minimum cover ratios will be achieved on completion; if this is not the case, the sponsors pay down the loan until the required cover ratios are met;
- *performance guarantee*: the sponsors agree to provide additional equity financing for debt service if the cash flow is reduced by the project not operating to a minimum performance standard;
- *claw-back guarantee*: the sponsors agree to make up any deficiency in the project company's cash flow for debt service, to the extent they have received distributions;
- *interest guarantee*: the sponsors agree to pay the interest on the loan if the project company cannot do so—in practical terms this is very close to a full guarantee of the loan; if it is not paid back, the sponsors will have to keep paying interest indefinitely;
- *cash-deficiency guarantee*: the sponsors agree to make up any debt service that cannot be paid because of a lack of cash in the project company—this is, of course, virtually a full financial guarantee;
- *shortfall guarantee*: a guarantee to pay any sums remaining due to lenders after termination of the PPP contract and realisation of other security; and
- *third-party revenue guarantee*: guarantee of a minimum level of third-party revenue (*cf.* §15.8).

But it should be emphasised that sponsor support in any of these ways is the exception rather than the rule.

§22.9 PUBLIC-SECTOR DEBT FINANCE

Another approach is to leave the PPP structure, risk transfer and private-sector equity in place, but to source the debt financing from the public sector. As discussed in §18.8, this may be done either to reduce the cost of debt, or to fill a debt-financing gap.

Such public-sector debt can be provided in a number of ways:

- direct public-sector lending with private-sector bank or insurance-company guarantees (*cf.* §18.11);
- loans from national DFIs or infrastructure banks (§22.9.1);
- loans from multilateral DFIs (§22.9.2), an important example of this being the European Investment Bank (§22.9.3); and
- other sources of cross-border debt (§22.9.4).

Some DFIs also invest in equity, but otherwise in all the above cases, equity is raised from private-sector investors in the usual way (*cf.* §20.2.1).

§22.9.1 National DFI or Infrastructure-Bank Finance

Making a 25-year loan to a PPP project company has very limited appeal to a commercial bank in many countries, if banks prefer to concentrate on much shorter-term consumer or commercial lending at rates which may be equal to or better than those for a long-term PPP loan. This is especially the case in developing or newly-industrialised countries, but is also true in the United States (*cf.* §22.4.3, §23.2.6). Therefore, unless financing can be raised from the bond market, or a multilateral or cross-border source as discussed below, the government will be forced to use public-sector debt financing if a PPP programme is to be developed. This may sound paradoxical if the main purpose of a PPP programme is avoid using the public budget to fund infrastructure. However, although a public-sector development or infrastructure bank will require some capital investment by the public sector, it should be able to raise most of the funding required for loans to PPPs and similar projects from the private sector on a stand-alone basis, *i.e.* outside the public-sector budget.

A typical example of using an established public-sector development bank for PPPs is the rôle of the state-owned Korea Development Bank (KDB) in the growth of the Korean PPI programme. Similarly, the National Economic and Social Development Bank (BNDES) of Brazil has played a significant rôle in financing Brazil's PPP programme.

Public-sector banks specifically aimed at financing infrastructure are a newer development. They are much talked about, and have been set up in some countries, but have not made a significant impact on infrastructure finance to date.

The inherent problem with public-sector financing of this type is that due diligence may be at less than arm's-length. Sometimes, the assumption is made that the contracting authority will ensure that the lender does not suffer a loss if things go wrong. Even worse, the lender may be forced to lend because of political pressure. This means that there is a risk of badly-structured projects being put together, and any cost-saving in financing (and the wider benefits from the PPP) may therefore be wiped out by the effects of poor due diligence.

§22.9.2 Multilateral DFIs

These are institutions set up by international treaties to provide development finance. Some of those active in the PPP context are:

- International Finance Corporation, part of the World Bank Group;
- Inter-American Development Bank;

- Asian Development Bank;
- African Development Bank
- European Bank for Reconstruction and Development; and
- European Investment Bank (EIB)—the EIB is different in nature and of particular importance for PPPs, and is therefore discussed separately below.

As these multilateral DFIs are independent of an individual country's budget, and are accustomed to financing public-sector infrastructure, it is a natural step for them to deal with PPPs. However, for many of them their business is largely confined to developing countries, and has to be 'additional' to lending by commercial banks and other private-sector sources, *i.e.* if financing is available on reasonable terms from the latter, the DFI must step out of the picture.[9] DFIs are generally required to lend on arm's-length commercial terms to the private sector and to avoid 'crowding out' commercial sources of finance if they are available. Indeed their measures of success usually include the mobilisation of commercial lending as a result of their activities.

DFIs have become steadily more active in the project-finance field, and in PPPs as a sub-set of this. In Africa, for example, very few PPPs are financed without DFI or other cross-border debt (other than in South Africa where there is a fully-developed financial sector).[10]

§22.9.3 European Investment Bank

The EIB is the world's largest multilateral borrower and lender and the most important public-sector institution lending in the PPP field. Unlike the other multilateral DFIs discussed above, its lending is predominantly to developed countries.

The EIB supports both public and private-sector entities. Most of its financing activities are through lending but it also provides guarantees, microfinance and equity.

Infrastructure is one of the EIB's core areas for financing support (alongside small business, environment/climate and innovation financing) and PPPs are a significant part of this (the EIB also supports infrastructure through public sector loans or loans to private sector corporates such as regulated utilities). EIB's cumulative lending to PPPs from 1990 to 2016 was some €50 billion (for 227 projects) making it a larger lender to PPPs than any individual private-sector bank. About 30% of these loans to PPPs have been in Britain; other countries in which EIB has a large PPP portfolio include France, the Netherlands, Portugal and Spain, with the remainder of the portfolio quite diversified. It is therefore worth considering EIB's activities in more detail, as these provide an interesting model for multilateral financing.

- Structure

    Under the 1958 Treaty of Rome, which established what is now the European Union (EU), EIB was created as an autonomous body within the EU as the long-term lending institution of the EU. Under its Statute, the mission of the Bank is to contribute towards the integration, balanced development and economic and social cohesion

---

[9] Note that this is nothing to do with 'additionality' of PPPs (*cf.* §28.3,§28.4).

[10] For a much fuller discussion on this topic, *cf.* (Yescombe 2014, Chapter 16), and (Yescombe 2017) for the position in sub-Saharan Africa.

of the EU Member States. To achieve this, the EIB raises substantial volumes of funds on the capital markets and lends these funds on favourable terms to projects furthering EU policy objectives.

The EIB operates on a non-profit-making basis. As such, the Bank does not have a specific target for return on equity, but rather aims at generating an income that shall enable it to meet its obligations, to cover its expenses and risks and to build up a reserve fund.

EIB's shareholders comprise all EU Member States which have subscribed €243 billion capital of which €22 billion was paid up as of the end of 2016.

The EIB raises its funding on the capital markets (i.e. primarily through public and private placements of bond issues). Apart from governments, EIB is probably the largest bond issuer in the European markets.

- Cost of finance

Finance can be provided both in Euros and other major currencies, on a fixed or floating-rate interest basis (cf. §24.2). EIB's public-sector ownership and high credit rating enables the Bank to raise its own funding on terms at least as good as many European governments. These, combined with the fact that it only has to cover its costs rather than lend on commercial terms or make a return on its capital, mean that it is able to lend to projects at a cost that is highly competitive with commercial-banking and bond markets. This advantage has meant that EIB's lending has expanded substantially: in 2016, the Bank signed up €76 billion in new loans of which €68 billion was to borrowers with projects in the EU. Cumulative outstanding loans disbursed amount to €455 billion.

Although lower cost and long tenor are major reasons for the use of EIB financing in projects, where there are problems of capacity in the private-sector financing markets, either because of the size of the project or because the local financing market is not adequately developed, the EIB can offer additionality of financing, as well as act as a catalyst for other financing. This was the case in the 2008 financial crisis when EIB was able to play a counter-cyclical rôle as commercial sources of long-term lending dried up. Depending on credit risk profile and linked to the economic life of the project (assets), tenors are typically up to 15 years or longer (even up to 30 years) on a case-by-case basis. Its loans can be senior, subordinated, secured or unsecured, also decided on a case-by-case basis. Pricing is determined on the internally assessed credit risk profile of the borrower and not by market demand considerations.

- Eligible projects and co-lending with commercial banks

The EIB does not usually lend to projects where the total investment in less than €25 million and in many cases the projects it supports are much larger. Projects must be financially, technically and environmentally sound and meet minimum economic return criteria. This requirement for economic viability is another feature that at times distinguishes the EIB from commercial lenders. Its loans can cover up to 50% of the total project costs although on average this is around one third.

Commercial-bank lenders lending in parallel may finance about the same amount in total to a PPP project as the EIB, but in much smaller individual shares if they syndicate the loan (*cf.* §22.2.9). As there have to be inter-creditor arrangements (*cf.* §25.5), this generally means that EIB has the largest vote, and usually a veto over most actions by the lenders as a whole.

The EIB treats potential borrowers for eligible PPP projects at the bidding stage on an equal basis, although its terms of finance may differ based on the individual proposals of the bidders. It usually confirms the eligibility of a project for potential EIB support prior to the bidding process but commitment of finance and final terms are subject to due diligence on the winning bidder. EIB's potential support adds credibility to the project (as commercial lenders take comfort from EIB's due diligence) and this may help to attract commercial long-term lenders. In turn this increases competitive interest in the project, enhancing VfM for the public sector.

– Blending

Over the years, the EIB has developed various instruments to provide support for projects with a higher risk profile than it would normally accept. Such instruments are often provided in collaboration with the European Commission and involve helping to leverage the EU's significant multi-annual programme of funding initiatives, an exercise often referred to as 'blending'. The most recent example of this is part of the Investment Plan for Europe (the 'Junker Plan'). One 'pillar' of this is the European Fund for Strategic Investments ('EFSI') which effectively uses an EU Commission and EIB funded endowment to underpin a proportion of EIB finance for riskier investments. The idea is that, on a portfolio basis, for every €1 of endowment support, EIB can lend €3 to projects on a basis that attracts a further 5 times of privately sourced financing, creating a 15 times multiplier of the original endowment. At the time of writing, the original target of €315 bn is on track to be met over three years and a further enlargement of the plan is underway.[11]

– Advising

The EIB has obviously developed a lot of in-house expertise on PPPs, and apart from bankers also has a large department of engineers and economists involved in this sector. So its third and growing area of activity is advising. For example, in 2008 EIB set up the European PPP Expertise Centre (EPEC). This is in effect a regional club of PPP units hosted, funded and supported by EIB, providing policy advice and market information to its 41-member PPP units as well as a platform to share good practice on PPP issues between members. EPEC also provides upstream project support to contracting authorities as well as assisting EU Commission bodies in developing appropriate PPP-related policies.

---

[11] Other examples of blending public funds and private finance include the $600 m Emerging Africa Infrastructure Fund of the Private Infrastructure Development Group, which has helped mobilise cumulative investment commitments of $16 bn since its establishment in 2001 on the back of $388 m of funding from its public-sector funders (four government aid agencies) and a further $210 m of private/DFI financing in the Fund.

Other areas of advisory technical support related to PPPs (though not exclusively) involve assessing the case for, and supporting the establishment of, funds that can provide equity, loans and guarantees ('financial instruments') in targeted areas (such as urban development) as part of the deployment of EU Commission structural funds (*i.e.* effectively helping the blending activity). The EIB also administers the European Investment Advisory Hub, a second 'pillar' of the Investment Plan for Europe that offers a single access point to the EIB's and participating national development bank sources of advisory and technical assistance services as well funding for such assistance.

§22.9.4 Other Sources of Cross-Border Finance

The other main categories of cross-border project finance, *i.e.* loans to projects in other countries, mainly in developing countries for PPPs are:

- National DFIs

  National DFIs such as Japan Bank for International Cooperation, Korea Development Bank and KfW (Germany) provide cross-border finance. These are often, but not always, linked to investment in the project from the country concerned.

- Export-credit agencies (ECAs)

  As their name implies, ECAs provide finance (or debt guarantees) linked to exports from the country concerned (either by direct lending or by providing guarantees to commercial lenders). A PPP project with significant investment in equipment, such as a waste incinerator, may be eligible for this type of finance. Examples of major ECAs include the export-import banks of the United States, Japan and Korea, as well as COFACE (France), Hermes (Germany) and SACE (Italy).

23

Financial Structuring

§23.1 INTRODUCTION

This chapter deals with the process by which bidders and their lenders structure the financing for a PPP project. The service fees (*cf.* Chapter 15) are the final output of this process, since these have to cover the project company's financing and operating costs, and provide a return on the bidders' equity investment. A similar process is usually followed by the contracting authority and its advisers during the preparation stages of the project to assess VfM (*cf.* §8.4) and affordability (*cf.* §9.2) of the project as a PPP.

Financial structure of the project finance has to work within various constraints:

- the contracting authority's requirements for the PPP contract tenor and service-fee profile (*cf.* §15.3.1, §15.3.2);
- investors' equity IRR requirements (*cf.* §20.3.3);
- lenders' requirements for the tenor and payment profile of their debt (§23.2);
- lenders' requirements for a 'cushion' of cash flow, known as a cover ratio, in excess of debt service (§23.3);
- the cost of debt finance (§23.4);
- the complex interplay between all of these (§23.5);
- accounting and taxation requirements (§23.6); and
- any requirement for contingent or standby funding (§23.7).

The financial model (§23.8), which is used in a variety of different ways by the different parties—contracting authority, sponsors and lenders—at different stages of the project, plays a central rôle in financial structuring. The key inputs to a model, and the outputs it produces, are discussed in §23.9. The financial model also has to take account of any financial hedging against macroeconomic risks, mainly interest rates and inflation (*cf.* Chapter 24), as well as the controls lenders exercise over the cash flow of the project company (*cf.* §25.2).

Another important tool for the project company and contracting authority is the asset register, which is used to keep track of the project assets for maintenance and accounting purposes over the life of the project (§23.10).

§23.2 DEBT PROFILE

§23.2.1 Debt Tenor

While project-finance loans in general (*e.g.* to the power or natural resources sectors) have long repayment tenors—say 15-18 years—PPP project cash flows may require debt service (*i.e.* the payment of interest and scheduled loan repayments) to be spread out over 20 years or more. This may better match the natural life of PPP projects and also debt service is smaller for each year the longer the tenor of the loan, so the service fees can be lower, producing a more affordable cost for the contracting authority or users (*cf.* §15.3.1). PPP projects offer a high level of certainty of long-term cash flow, and therefore provide a good basis for such long-term project-finance-based loans. Typically, when a new PPP market opens up, loan tenors are initially shorter and lengthen as lenders become used to the risks involved.

Another factor that determines the length of a loan is the lenders' cover-ratio requirements (*cf.* §23.3)—the shorter the loan the higher the debt-service payments, and so the worse the cover ratios become; so, from this point of view, paradoxically, the longer a loan the safer it appears.

But the 'long-term' nature of a loan to a PPP project may be misleading. Most commercial banks' deposits are short-term in nature, so lending long term leaves them with a mismatch—despite this they are prepared to make long-term loans for PPP projects because a large proportion of PPP loans are refinanced after the end of the construction period (*cf.* §26.2).

In developing countries, there may be no private-sector lenders willing to provide long-term loans, partly because banks can earn a high return from short-term lending, so there would no good reason for them to divert funds to long-term loans, whether for PPP projects or anything else. In such cases, other sources of long-term finance have to be found (*cf.* §22.9).

§23.2.2 Repayment Profile

Loan repayments usually begin around six months after the construction of the facility is complete, and are usually made at six-monthly intervals. (In the case of a project with demand risk, an initial ramp-up period may be allowed for, with lower debt service while the usage is building up.)

The standard bond-market practice is for a bond to be repaid in one amount on its final maturity date. Thus, a sinking fund could be built up to repay the whole amount of the bond on its final maturity but this obviously adds to the financing cost, especially over a long period of time. Project-finance bonds are therefore generally amortised (repaid) in a similar way to loans.

If the service fees are to be kept level, as discussed in §15.3.2, the debt service has to be level as well. But if a loan of $1,000 is paid back over 10 years in equal annual instalments of $100, and at an interest rate of say 5%, the debt-service payments will not be level. At the end of year 1 there will be a payment of $150, being $100 of principal and $50 of interest on the $1,000 loan outstanding over the first year, while at the end of year 10 there will be a payment of $105, with an interest payment of $5 on the final loan balance of $100. This is not a viable approach.

Therefore, debt service has to be based on an 'annuity' schedule, in a similar way to a home-mortgage annuity payment. In the case of the $1,000 loan above, the annual debt-service payment required to pay the loan off and cover interest over its 10-year period is $129.5, *i.e.* in between the debt service of $150 in year 1 and $105 in year 10 produced by the 'straight-line' repayment schedule above. An annuity cash flow is set out in Table 23.2.

Having said this, it is unlikely that a precise annuity-repayment schedule will work for the project company, given the contracting authority's requirement that the service fees resulting from this should also be level. This is because there will most probably be other fluctuations in the cash flow, and the loan payment schedule will need to be 'sculpted' to smooth these out (a complex modelling process) and so maintain the service fees level. These include:

- the maintenance schedule, if this is cyclical in nature;
- taxation payments: a typical project company does not pay tax in its early years of operation because of a high level of write-off of project costs against its tax liability; there is then a sudden drop in cash flow when tax payments begin; and
- the effect of inflation, which can be very significant (*cf.* §24.3.4).

Predictable temporary cash-flow swings such as major maintenance or a large tax payment can be smoothed out by the establishment of reserve accounts (*i.e.* accumulating cash in advance from the cash flow—*cf.* §25.2.4) to maintain constant cover ratios but it is not efficient from the investors' point of view to have cash tied up in the project company unnecessarily, and, as far as possible, debt sculpting is a preferable way of dealing with this.

But the project company cannot expect *carte blanche* to make repayments whenever it chooses within the overall debt tenor. Lenders want to see investors having a long-term incentive to manage the business well, and will not be comfortable with debt repayments being pushed towards the back end of the project cash flow if this means that the investors are getting higher than appropriate payments at the front end.

§23.2.3 Average Life

Apart from the overall tenor of the loan, lenders also look at the repayment schedule to assess how rapidly their risk reduces over the tenor. There is obviously a considerable difference in risk between a loan of $1,000 repaid in 100 instalments over 10 years, and a loan of $1,000 repaid in one instalment at the end of 10 years. This is measured by looking at the loan's average life, which is used by lenders as a check to ensure that the repayment schedule is not over-extended, in a similar way to the payback-period calculation by investors (*cf.* §3.4.3). The average life of a loan is the average number of years that the principal is outstanding.

§23.2.4 The Cash-Flow 'Tail'

Another factor which determines the length of the debt financing is the requirement that lenders have for a cash-flow 'tail'. This is the period between the scheduled final repayment of the debt and the end of the PPP contract, during which the service fees continue. This builds in a safety margin, so that if the project gets into temporary difficulties, or cash flow is a bit below expectation, there may still be enough cash flow left to ensure that the debt is paid off, albeit later than expected (*cf.* §23.3.4).

The greater the inherent revenue risk in the project, the longer the tail period that will be required. So, for an accommodation project in an established market, where the lenders' risk is relatively small, it may be possible to negotiate a tail period as short as a year. On the other hand, a road concession project with a high level of traffic risk may require a tail of some years. The longer the tail period:

- the higher the service fees will have to be (because the debt is being repaid over a shorter period within the overall 'envelope' of the PPP contract tenor); and
- the more the receipt of distributions will be pushed to the back of the cash flow, making them less valuable in equity IRR terms (*cf.* §3.4.3, §3.4.4).

Therefore, bidders usually aim to keep the tail period as short as possible. A contracting authority should also not enter into PPP contracts that are going to require long tail periods (*cf.* §15.3.1), as this is financially inefficient (and liable to lead to later windfall gains on refinancing the debt if the market becomes more favourable—*cf.* §26.2.9).

§23.2.5 Flexible Repayment

Projects where there is demand risk may often face an initial problem in meeting the required usage levels because the ramp-up is slower than anticipated. To provide the project company with some room to manœuvre in this respect, lenders may agree to build some flexibility into the repayment structure.

One way of doing this is to build two repayment schedules into the loan structure: one is the level that the lenders actually wish to achieve if the project operates as expected ('target' repayments), and one is the minimum level of repayment required to avoid a default by the project company under the loan. If the project company has cash flow available, it must make a repayment sufficient to bring the loan outstanding down to the target schedule, but if not, it must at least achieve the minimum schedule. The difference between the two decreases as time goes on, so that in any case the loan is fully repaid by the originally-scheduled date.

§23.2.6 Balloon Repayment

It is possible for a 25-year PPP contract to be financed with 15-year debt, which is refinanced after 15 years over the remaining tenor of the PPP contract. This ensures that the debt-service payments will not be too high in relation to the level of service fees that the contracting authority is trying to achieve (*cf.* §23.2.1). However, it also means that a large element (but not all) of the debt has to be left as a 'balloon'—*i.e.* repayable at the end of the 15 years, on the assumption that it will be refinanced at that point. For example, a balloon-repayment structure may involve debt-service payments profiled for 14 years at the same level as for a 25-year loan, with the balance of the loan outstanding repayable at the end of the 15-year period. So, using the repayment schedule set out in Table 23.2, a seven-year $1,000 loan would have annual debt-service payments of $73, and a balloon principal repayment at the end of seven years of $766.

The risks in a balloon-repayment structure are:

* The project company may not be able to obtain replacement financing—the risk of this is usually quite limited: either, by the time the financing is needed, the project company's business will be well established and able to service the replacement debt, in which case it should not be difficult to find a lender, or things are going badly, in which case a longer-maturity loan would be in difficulty, if not default, by then anyway. However, if the project-finance debt market as a whole freezes up, as happened in the 2008 financial crisis, then there is a serious problem: this was what happened in Spain, where the banks were generally making seven-year loans to toll-road concessions but found they could not get out of the loan at the end of seven years.
* It leaves the project company exposed to interest-rate risk (*cf.* §24.2.7) after the initial loan tenor—this is the main objection to a balloon structure, which explains why it is not widely used.

§23.2.7 Mini-Perms

However, in markets where lenders are reluctant to lend for the total tenor required to make the project viable, a balloon-repayment structure is the only way of bridging this financing gap.

In the US real-estate market, banks provide three- to five-year construction loans, which are refinanced by long-term 'permanent' mortgage loans from institutional lenders on completion and when the building has been let to tenants, so producing a stable cash flow. This initial short-term loan is known as a 'mini-perm' (*i.e.* it is not a long-term permanent loan). Similarly, in the PPP case, the initial loan may be arranged to mature two to three years after completion of construction, to allow flexibility of timing for the refinancing. In a mini-perm repayment structure, any Principal repayments after completion of construction are based on a long-term debt-service schedule, but cut off after three to five years, so giving rise to a balloon repayment of the balance of the loan.

In fact, from the point of view of long-term flexibility of PPP contracts, there is some logic in a greater use of mini-perms, reflecting the reality that loans are often refinanced anyway (*cf.* §26.2), although this is only viable where lenders are happy that there is no significant refinancing risk and the project can accommodate the risk of higher market interest rates at the time of the refinancing. This is easier if the initial leverage (*cf.* §23.3) is in the 70-80% range rather than 90%, and also if there is a significant tail (*cf.* §23.2.4) at the end of the PPP contract, giving extra room for manœuvre—which implies that a mini-perm is easier for a concession where these conditions are more likely to apply.

This type of mini-perm is known as a 'hard' mini-perm, meaning that the loan has to be repaid on the due date. 'Soft' mini-perms are a related approach that has been used quite widely, especially in Europe, since the 2008 financial crisis as a way of giving lenders some assurance that their loan will be prepaid by a refinancing, but not throwing the project company over the cliff of a firm balloon-payment date. This is linked to the fact that commercial banks, especially in Europe, may be reluctant to lend for more than seven years or so, partly because of the Basel IV regulations (*cf.* §22.2.4).

In the case of a soft mini-perm, the lenders agree a repayment profile as discussed in §23.2.2, but after, say, seven years, the credit margin is increased sharply, and a cash sweep, discussed below, is applied. This is highly disadvantageous to the equity investors, who will probably also be blocked from receiving distributions from the project company (assuming there is any free cash flow left), and is an obvious incentive to refinance the loan if this is possible.

In either case, soft or hard, the base-case financial model agreed with the contracting authority, which is the basis on which the service fees are calculated (*cf.* §23.8), has to be structured on the assumption that a refinancing will take place, as otherwise the investors have no incentive to refinance at all in the soft mini-perm case, or no incentive to get the best terms in the hard mini-perm case. In other words, the refinancing risk must not be assumed by the contracting authority.

§23.2.8 Cash Sweep

If a mini-perm structure (soft or hard) is used, this may be linked with a 'cash sweep' in say years 3-5 after completion, which requires some or all of the cash flow that would otherwise have been equity distributed to investors (*cf.* §25.2.3) to be used for debt prepayment instead (or placed in a reserve account to secure the debt). This effectively forces the investors in the project company to refinance the debt as soon as possible.

A cash sweep may also be useful for debt structuring in other circumstances:

- If there is uncertainty about the growth of future revenues, which could apply in a concession, or an availability PPP project with demand risk transferred to the project company (*i.e.* a shadow-toll project (*cf.* §15.5.4)). In such projects, after an agreed level of distributions to the investors, the balance of the cash flow is used to prepay the debt or split between prepayment and a further distribution to the investors. Thus, if the project performs according to the agreed base case (*cf.* §23.9.9), the investors will receive the base-case equity IRR, but cash flow from the project above this level is split between investors and debt repayment. In this way, surplus cash generated in good times is used to reduce debt and so provide a buffer against a downturn.
- If costs have to be incurred a long time in future, and are too substantial to be covered by setting aside spare cash in a reserve account (*cf.* §25.2.4). For example, an

additional traffic lane may have to be built for a road concession once traffic has reached a certain level after, say, 15 years, and the cost of this is to be covered by tolls over the following 15 years. The initial loan may run for 20-25 years (*i.e.* past the date when additional financing may be needed). It is likely to be very difficult to fix the costs of the major works 15 years in advance (or even to know whether it will be, say, 15 or 17 years until the extra lane is required), and raising debt that would not be used for 15 years is virtually impossible (and uneconomic). The solution may be a cash-sweep arrangement beginning several years before the date for the new works, linked to traffic growth, to build up cash for the new works. This would also encourage the investors to refinance the loan and raise the additional debt required when it becomes feasible nearer that time.

• If lenders are concerned about the tail risk (*cf.* §23.2.4). In such cases, several years before the tail begins, some or all of the cash flow after debt service is not distributed to the investors, but is used for debt prepayment, or placed in a reserve account.

§23.2.9 Debt Accretion

In the case of very long (50 year-plus) concessions, where bond rather than bank financing would be used (*cf.* §22.5), 'capital accretion bonds' may be issued. Under this structure, drawdown of debt can continue, and hence the loan amount increase, *after* completion of construction, rather than the lenders requiring repayments to begin from that point. Subject to the performance of the project, this is done by capitalising part of the interest on the bond and adding this to the principal amount, such that the peak loan balance occurs after 15-20 years, and the bond is then repaid thereafter. This reflects the slow but steady long-term growth in traffic or other usage which might be expected in such a project. In effect debt accretion is an advance commitment by the lenders to keep increasing the loan if the project meets expectations (*cf.* §26.2). The same result can be produced through an accretion swap (*cf.* §24.2.10). However, experience—again after the 2008 financial crisis—has shown that it cannot be assumed that traffic will keep increasing indefinitely: traffic growth is quite closely linked to GDP growth, so if there is an economic recession, traffic may reduce instead of increase.

§23.3 DEBT-COVER RATIOS

Financial ratios are a basis for corporate lending (*cf.* §21.3)—typical measures are:

• Liquidity ratio (also known as the 'current ratio'), *i.e.* short-term assets (primarily cash and debtors) divided by short-term liabilities (*e.g.* trade creditors and debt due within one year); lenders may require a liquidity ratio of, say, $1.5\times$.

• Interest cover, *i.e.* earnings before interest, depreciation and amortisation (EBITDA— a simple proxy for the company's cash flow), divided by the interest payable during the relevant period; lenders aim to ensure that at all times they have an interest-cover ratio of, say, $2\times$.

- Leverage, *i.e.* the ratio of debt to equity; lenders may require that the borrower's debt is not more than, say, 50% of its equity; this can also be expressed as a 'loan-to-value' ratio, *i.e.* the ratio of the loan to the value of the company's assets in general, or the particular assets given to the lender as security.

These measures are not appropriate for a PPP project financing, because:

- The short-term liquidity of a project company is assured by the creation of reserve accounts (*cf.* §25.2.4).
- A corporate borrower always has some outstanding debt, which is refinanced again and again, but a project company has a finite life, during which all its debt must be repaid as discussed above (*cf.* §21.3) and therefore an interest-cover ratio—which only looks at the ability to pay interest, but does not assess the ability to repay debt—is inadequate.
- A leverage ratio is based on the assumption that the assets of the borrowing company will be worth a proportion at least of their book value if the company is wound-up, and hence the leverage ratio is an indication of the safety margin for lenders, as it is the excess of liabilities, excluding equity, over assets; however, as discussed above, such a residual value cannot be assumed for a project company's physical assets, as its value is based primarily on its project contracts (in particular the PPP contract). Having said this, however,
  - As discussed in §23.3.3, the loan-life cover ratio is in fact a form of loan-to-value ratio in a project-finance context.
  - The lenders to a project company expect the sponsors to have a 'reasonable' amount of equity at risk: 100% debt financing, even if theoretically possible using the cover-ratio approach set out below, would not normally be acceptable (but *cf.* §27.5.1).
  - A leverage ratio is often used in the construction phase to keep the sponsors' and lenders' exposures in parallel, *e.g.* where sponsor equity is being paid in *pro rata* with debt drawings, or to 'true up' the leverage ratio at the end of the construction phase, if an equity bridge (*cf.* §20.3.6) is used.

Thus, the amount of debt which can be raised by a project company (and hence the split in financing between debt and equity, *i.e.* the leverage) is primarily determined by its projected ability to pay its debt service, with a comfortable margin of safety; this margin is of course the same as the distributions to investors. To assess this safety margin, lenders calculate 'cover ratios', which measure cash flow against debt service (§23.3.1), assessed both on a period-to-period basis, and over the life of the project, namely:

- annual debt-service cover ratio (ADSCR) (§23.3.2),
- loan-life cover ratio (LLCR) (§23.3.3); and
- project-life cover ratio (PLCR) (§23.3.4).

Taken together, these determine the maximum loan amount (§23.3.5), although it should be noted that there are various issues arising on precisely how the calculations are done (§23.3.6).

§23.3.1 Cash Flow Available for Debt Service

The basis for all these ratio calculations is the cash flow available for debt service (CADS), *i.e.* revenues less opex—taking account of any transfers to or from the maintenance reserve account or similar reserve accounts covering anything other than debt service (*cf.* §25.2.3), and ignoring any non-cash items such as depreciation. This may look similar to the EBITDA measure above, but should be based strictly on cash flow rather than accounting results. Thus, income or expenditures accrued but not actually paid during the period being measured should be excluded, as should, *e.g.*, tax accruals where the tax is not actually payable until a later period.

§23.3.2 Annual Debt-Service Cover Ratio

The ADSCR assesses the project company's ability to service its debt from its annual cash flow, and is calculated as CADS divided by debt service. Thus, if CADS for the year is $120, interest payments are $55, and loan repayments are $45, the ADSCR would be $1.20 \times (120 \div (55 + 45))$. The debt-service figures are adjusted to take account of any financial hedging (*cf.* Chapter 24).

The ADSCR is usually calculated semi-annually, on a rolling annual basis. The ratio can obviously only be calculated when the project has been in operation for a year, although because it may affect the ability to pay distributions to investors (*cf.* §25.2.5), it may be calculated for the previous six months only for the first period after the project begins operation.

The ADSCR is the primary determinant of the maximum loan which can be raised against the project, as illustrated by Table 23.1. The assumptions are that there is $1,000 *p.a.* of cash flow after opex, with a 25-year debt tenor. Assuming the lenders' interest rate is 6%, and they have an ADSCR requirement of $1.50 \times$, the maximum annual debt service allowable is $667 ($1,000 \div 1.50$), which means that the maximum amount of debt that can be raised is $8,522—*i.e.* an annual payment of $667 is required to pay interest at 6% and repay a loan of $8,522 on an annuity basis over 25 years. However, if the cover ratio is reduced to $1.25 \times$, the amount of debt which can be raised goes up to $10,227.

In their base-case projections, the lenders structure both the amount and the repayment schedule of their loan such that projected ADSCR for each period throughout the tenor of

Table 23.1   Effect of ADSCR on loan amount

		25 years	25 years
	Debt tenor	25 years	25 years
	Interest rate	6%	6%
[a]	Project cash flow (pre-debt service) *p.a.*	$1,000	$1,000
[b]	**Required ADSCR**	1.50	1.25
	Maximum annual debt service ([a]÷[b])	$667	$800
	Amount of debt that can be raised (annuity repayment)	**$8,522**	**$10,227**

the loan does not fall below their required minimum at any time. The minimum ADSCR requirement, which thus effectively determines the maximum loan, is a function of the risk inherent in the project from the lender's point of view—the greater the uncertainty of the cash flow, the higher the risk, and hence the higher the cover-ratio requirement. In the PPP sector, the highest-risk category of projects is usually that involving demand risk, on which a minimum ADSCR in the range 1.5-2.0× may be required, depending on the perceived level of risk (or certainty of the cash flows). The lowest-risk category is that of accommodation projects, where the minimum ADSCR may be in the range 1.25-1.5×.

The actual ADSCRs are reviewed (and projections may be recalculated) once the project is in operation (*cf.* §25.2.5).

§23.3.3 Loan-Life Cover Ratio

The LLCR is based on a similar calculation, but taken over the whole tenor of the loan, *i.e.*

- projected CADS for the life of the loan, discounted to its NPV at the same interest rate as that assumed for the debt (again taking account of any financial hedging); *divided by*
- debt outstanding on the calculation date.

LLCR is a useful measure for the initial assessment of a project company's ability to service its debt over its whole tenor, but clearly it is not so useful if there are likely to be significant cash-flow fluctuations from year to year. ADSCR is thus a more significant measure of a project company's ability to service its debt as it falls due.

The minimum initial LLCR requirement in lenders' base-case projections for 'standard' projects is typically around 10% higher than the figures shown above for minimum ADSCR.

Apart from the initial LLCR on project completion, the LLCR may be recalculated throughout the project life, comparing the projected operating cash flow for the remainder of the loan tenor with the remaining loan outstanding on the calculation date, as part of the lenders' continuing controls, in a similar way to the continuing use of the ADSCR, although this is of dubious value for a PPP (*cf.* §25.2.5).

§23.3.4 Project-Life Cover Ratio

Another point that lenders check is whether the project company has capacity to make repayments after the original final maturity of the debt, but within the tail period of the PPP contract (*cf.* §23.2.4). This is in case there have been difficulties in repaying all of the debt in time.

The value to lenders of the tail can be calculated using the PLCR; here projected CADS for the whole life of the project (not just the tenor of the debt as for the LLCR) is discounted to its NPV, and this figure is divided by the debt outstanding. Obviously the PLCR will be higher than the LLCR; lenders may wish to see it around 15-20% higher than the minimum ADSCR.

Since the 'value' of a project company is effectively the NPV of its future revenues (*cf.* §26.3), it could be said that the PLCR is a kind of loan-to-value ratio.

§23.3.5 Cover-Ratio Calculations

Table 23.2 sets out cover-ratio calculations for a typical project, based on an annuity-repayment loan. Thanks to this loan structure, the contracting authority's service fees are also kept level (*cf.* §15.3.2): bidders always use an annuity-payment structure for the debt

Table 23.2   Cover-ratio calculations—annuity loan

Assumptions

- Project cost $1,000
- Debt/equity ratio   90:10
- PPP contract tenor   25 years
- Loan tenor: 23 years, repaid on an annuity basis
- Interest rate   6% p.a.
- Required equity IRR   15%

($)	Year:	0	1	2	3	20	21	22	23	24	25	Total
(a) CADS			88	88	88	88	88	88	88	88	88	2,200
Lenders' viewpoint:												
(b) Loan repayments			19	20	22	58	61	65	69			900
(c) Interest payments			54	53	52	15	12	8	4			782
(d) Total debt service [(b) + (c)]			73	73	73	73	73	73	73	73		1,682
(e) *Year-end loan outstanding*		*900*	*881*	*861*	*839*	*196*	*134*	*69*	*0*			
ADSCR	[(a)÷(d)]		*1.20*	*1.20*	*1.20*	*1.20*	*1.20*	*1.20*	*1.20*			
LLCR	[(NPV* (a)† ÷(e)]	*1.20*	*1.20*	*1.20*	*1.20*	*1.20*	*1.20*	*1.20*				
PLCR	[(NPV (a)÷(e)]	*1.25*										
Average life of loan		*14.5*	Years									
Investors' viewpoint:												
Equity investment:		−100										
Distributions	[(a) − (d)]		15	15	15	15	15	15	15	88	88	518
Equity IRR	15%											
Payback period	c. 7 years											

*at 6% discount rate.
†to year 23.

rather than level principal repayments, because the latter 'front loads' the debt service, as discussed in §23.2.2, and hence results in a higher NPC for the contracting authority.

§23.3.6 Other Issues with Cover-Ratio Calculations

There are some issues which may arise on the mechanics of cover-ratio calculations:

— Other calculations

Lenders often use other cover-ratio calculations, in particular the loan-life average ADSCR and average LLCR in incremental 6-monthly calculations. It is difficult to see what extra benefit is derived from these.

— Treatment of cash balances

The project company may have cash balances in reserve accounts (*cf.* §25.2.4): since both the ADSCR and the LLCR measure the ability to repay debt, and cash balances can also be used for this purpose, should these be taken into the calculation? In respect of the ADSCR, the answer is that they should not—this ratio measures the ability to pay debt on a year-to-year basis, and if the cash balance is used to improve the ratio in year 1, it is then no longer available in year 2. In the case of the LLCR, it is reasonable to take into account cash in a reserve account intended to cover debt service, as it is part of the total picture of resources available for debt service over the project life. The project company may argue that balances on other reserve accounts such as for maintenance should also be deducted in the LLCR calculation for the same reason; lenders may, however, point out that this cash is not intended for debt reduction.

There are two ways of bringing these balances into the LLCR calculations—add them to the CADS NPV or deduct them from the debt balance. The latter produces a higher cover ratio, but the former is probably the commoner project-finance market practice.

— Payments to and from reserve accounts

In calculating the ADSCR and LLCR, payments to reserve accounts other than for debt service are treated as a deduction from the operating cash flow in the period concerned, and drawings from such accounts (*e.g.* to pay maintenance costs) are added back to the cash flow (and hence offset the actual expenditure). Payments to and from any reserve account for debt service are ignored in the ADSCR calculation (which is intended to show the project company's ability to service its debt on a regular basis without using reserves).

Interest earned on reserve accounts is normally added to the operating income when calculating cover ratios, unless the balance of the reserve account concerned is below the minimum required (which would mean that the interest earned cannot be taken out of the reserve account).

— Taxation

Strictly speaking, CADS does not include taxation payable by the project company, because tax is calculated *after* interest payments. Nonetheless, it is a fairly common practice to deduct projected tax payments (when paid in cash) from cash flow to arrive at CADS (even though interest payments, that are offset against tax, are not included in the CADS). Thus, using a limited-partnership structure for the project company (*cf.* §20.6.1), where there is no tax in the financial model, can be advantageous for investors if lenders do not increase their cover-ratio requirements to compensate for this.

§23.4 DEBT-FINANCING COSTS

Apart from the lenders' advisers' fees (*cf.* §22.2.7), the main financing costs payable by the project company for commercial-bank loans are:

- the lenders' own cost of funds in the wholesale money market, most probably on a 'floating-rate' basis, and costs relating to financial hedging, if any (*cf.* §24.2);
- the lenders' credit margin (§23.4.1);
- a cost-of-capital charge, and other additional costs (§23.4.2);
- advisory, arranging and underwriting fees (§23.4.3);
- commitment fees (§23.4.4); and
- agency and security trustee fees (§23.4.5).

The pricing for bonds is similar to this (§23.4.6).

§23.4.1 Credit Margin

Project-finance loans for PPP projects typically have credit margins in the range of 0.75-2.5% over the lenders' cost of funds. The top end of this range would relate to high-risk projects such as concession roads, whereas the bottom end would relate to low-risk projects such as availability-PPP accommodation projects. Pricing is also affected by the location of the project, with those in high-risk countries obviously paying more than those in low-risk countries. Pricing is usually higher until completion of construction, reflecting the higher risk of this stage of the project, then drops down, and then may gradually climb back again over time. Thus, an accommodation project with a loan covering a two-year construction and 25-year operation period could have a credit margin of 1.25% for years 1-2, 1% for years 3-5 and 1.25% thereafter. The increase in the margin is partly intended to encourage refinancing (*cf.* §26.2).

§23.4.2 Additional Costs

Bank lenders are also exposed to additional funding costs, which would erode their credit margin, arising from:

- Liquidity and capital costs

  Banks may face a requirement from their central bank for liquidity reserves against long-term lending, or for increased capital to support such lending; these are known as 'minimum liquidity requirements' (MLRs), or 'minimum liquid asset' requirements

(MLAs). If these costs are of any significance (usually the effect is minimal), they are borne by the borrower.

Banks may also be required to raise the ratio of capital which they have to hold against different classes of asset (as a protection for their depositors) or for longer-term loans. The cost of such loans may then have to be increased to preserve their return on capital.

— Taxes

In cases where loans are made from outside the project company's country, lenders may not be able to offset withholding taxes on interest payments from the project company against their other tax liabilities.

If withholding taxes do apply, the project company usually has to 'gross up' its interest payments (*i.e.* increase them by an amount sufficient to produce the amount of net interest payment to the lenders after deduction of tax). A lender may agree that if it can offset this amount of tax against its other tax liabilities in due course, the withholding will be refunded to the borrower. However, lenders are not prepared to get into debates about how they manage their tax affairs, and therefore any refund relies entirely on a lender's good faith.

Apart from withholding taxes, lenders should not be able to charge any of their tax liabilities to the project company.

— Market disruption

The project company also takes the risk, where the bank financing is on a short-term floating-rate basis (*cf.* §24.2), that the banks may not be able to roll over their financing due to disruption in the market—this could mean changing the market-interest pricing basis, or if the banks cannot extend the finance at all, prepaying the loan. If one or two banks get into trouble because of their own, rather than general market problems, these provisions do not apply.

Where appropriate, these costs are charged in addition to the credit margin and are not peculiar to the project-finance market. But they should only be used to cover the banks actually affected, not the whole syndicate of lenders.

§23.4.3 Fees

Arranging and underwriting fees charged by lead arrangers are derived from several factors:

- the size and complexity of the financing;
- the time and work involved in structuring the financing;
- the risk that a success-based fee may not be earned because the project does not go ahead;

- the bank's overall return targets for work of this kind (bearing competitive pressure in mind), taking into account both the fees earned and the return on the loan balance that it keeps on its own books;
- the length of time the underwriting bank has to carry the syndication risk (where the loan is being syndicated)—for a variety of reasons there can often be a considerable time lag between the signing of loan documentation and hence underwriting, and syndication to other participating banks in the project-finance market; and
- the proportion of the fee that has to be reallowed to sub-underwriting or participating banks to induce them to join the syndication (which is itself a function of the time the participating bank has to spend on reviewing it, the overall return the market requires for the risk, taking credit margin and fees together into account, and perhaps competition from other transactions in the market at the same time).

As a rough rule of thumb, the arranging and underwriting fees are usually about the same as the credit margin, *i.e.* 1-2.5%. If the arranging bank is also acting as financial adviser, this may increase the fees by around 0.5%, although this does not always apply.

§23.4.4 Commitment Fees

Commitment fees are paid on the available but undrawn portion of the debt during the construction period, *i.e.* so long as drawings may be made on the loan. As most project-finance loans are drawn down very slowly (during, say, a two- to three-year construction period), banks need the commitment fee to give them a reasonable rate of return on their risk during the construction of the project when they are not earning the full loan margin. Commitment fees are usually around half of the credit margin in project-finance loans.

§23.4.5 Agency Fees

Finally, there are the agency fees payable to the agent bank or security trustee (*cf.* §22.2.10). The time that a bank has to spend on agency work can be quite considerable, and it is in the project company's interests to ensure that a reasonable annual agency fee covers this work adequately, but this should be based on a fair assessment of costs, not a major source of extra profit for the agent.

§23.4.6 Bonds and Other Fixed-Rate Finance

The pricing for bonds, *i.e.* their interest-rate coupon (*cf.* §22.4.2), is based on that for government bonds of a similar maturity. However, most bonds have bullet repayments, *i.e.* the principal is repaid in *one* amount on the final maturity date. Project-finance bonds, however, have to be repaid over the whole life of the financing tenor, and hence the pricing for such bonds is based on the market price for a series of bonds each maturing on the dates when a repayment is made. The same pricing principles apply where non-bank lenders are providing fixed-rate loans.

The pricing premium over the government-bond rate—known as the 'issue spread'—is based on a combination of the bond's credit rating, and the general supply and demand in the market. Thus, when placing a new bond, it should be possible to see what a reasonable pricing for it should be, by comparing it with the pricing of other bonds with a similar credit rating and average life/maturity already being traded in the market. The issue spread is often fixed only at the time of placing the bond, although it may be possible to negotiate a cap in advance.[1] Overall pricing in most bond markets is, however, likely to end up being broadly similar to that in the banking markets.

Fees for bonds are a combination of a financial-advisory fee and an underwriting fee. Financial-advisory fees are comparable to those for bank loans—indeed at the beginning of the financial-advisory process, it may not be clear whether a bank or bond financing offers the best option, so the financial adviser may have to consider both as part of the advisory work. Bond-underwriting fees tend to vary between domestic bond markets, and are affected by the degree of competition for underwriting mandates. In some markets, there are effectively fee cartels which tends to keep fees relatively high, and to charge the same percentage fee however large the bond issue, but in general competition breaks down this approach. Given the very limited level of risk in a bond underwriting—as has been seen (*cf.* §22.4.2), bonds are not underwritten until the underwriter is already confident they can be sold, as the sale takes place very shortly after the underwriting—there is no reason for fees over 0.5% of the amount of the bond. Commitment fees do not apply to bonds, as they are drawn immediately, and trustee fees are similar to bank agency fees. As with bank loans, other due-diligence costs, including the costs of the rating agency (*cf.* §22.4.1), are payable by the project company.

§23.5 RELATIONSHIP BETWEEN COVER RATIO, LEVERAGE AND EQUITY IRR

There is a complex interplay between leverage (the debt/equity ratio), cover-ratio requirements, the cost of the debt and the investors' required return—a bidder needs to balance all these factors to offer the most competitive level of service fees. This is illustrated by Table 23.3.

There are four scenarios in this table:

- Case 1 has a project cost of $1,000, with the lenders being willing to fund 90% of this cost so long as they have an ADSCR of 1.5×. Debt is provided over 25 years, on an annuity-repayment basis, at a rate of 6% *p.a.* This produces an annual debt-service payment of $70. Investors require an equity IRR of 15% (also on an annuity basis), which produces an annual distribution of $15. Thus, the total service fees required to cover both debt service and equity IRR (ignoring the further payments to cover opex) amount to $86 ($70 + $15)[2]. But these payments are insufficient to provide the lenders

---

[1] Bond private placements and other fixed-rate finance from non-bank lenders may be priced at a margin over the interest-rate swap rate (*cf.* §24.2.2), so also fixing the project-specific credit margin in advance in the same way as a bank loan.

[2] Figures are rounded.

Table 23.3   Relationship between leverage, cover ratio, debt interest rate and equity IRR

Assumptions	Case 1: Maximum debt	Case 2: Lower leverage	Case 3: Lower cover ratio	Case 4: Lower interest rate
Project cost ($)	1,000	1,000	1,000	1,000
Leverage	90%	80%	89%	81%
Debt interest rate	6.0%	6.0%	6.0%	5.5%
Debt tenor (years)	25	25	25	25
(a) Lenders' required ADSCR	1.50×	1.50×	1.25×	1.50
Investors' required equity IRR	15.0%	15.0%	15.0%	15.0%
Annual payments ($)*				
(b) Debt service (annuity)	70.4	62.4	69.4	60.1
(c) Distributions (annuity)	15.5	31.2	17.4	30.0
Annual service fees ($)*				
- to cover debt service + equity IRR [(b) + (c)]	85.9	**93.7**	**86.8**	**90.1**
- to satisfy ADSCR [(b) × (a)]	**105.6**	**93.7**	**86.8**	**90.1**

*Figures are rounded.

with a 1.5× ADSCR, for which $106 ($70 × 1.5) is required. This would obviously be an unattractive structure for a bidder for a PPP project, who would not want to bid $106 when this produces a higher service fee than actually needed to cover the debt service and equity IRR.

- Case 2 gets the figures back into equilibrium, paradoxically (cf. §21.5.1) by reducing the leverage to 80%. The annual debt service is thus reduced to $62, although the distribution to provide the equity IRR goes up to $31. These changes increase the required service fees to $94 ($62 + $31) but this is sufficient to give the lenders a cover ratio of 1.5× ($62 × 1.5). The result is that the bidder can reduce the annual service fee from $106 in Case 1 to $94 in Case 2.
- Case 3 supposes that the lenders are willing to reduce the cover ratio from 1.5× to 1.25×. This means that leverage can be increased to 89%, and service fees are reduced to $87. This illustrates the importance of the cover ratios in structuring the finance.
- Case 4, instead of reducing the cover ratio, reduces the cost of the debt from 6 to 5.5%. As can be seen this results in an annual service-fee requirement of $90, compared to the $87 achieved by reducing the cover ratio. Thus, a reduction in the cover ratio may be more valuable for a bidder (and perhaps less painful for a lender) than reducing the cost of the debt.

Of course, these calculations are highly simplified, to illustrate the principles involved, and they do not take account of:

- the LLCR requirement (*cf.* §23.3.3);
- tax (see below);
- inflation (*cf.* §24.3); and
- the effect of any tail on the equity IRR (*cf.* §23.2.4).

§23.6 ACCOUNTING AND TAXATION ISSUES

Although a financial model (*cf.* §23.8) for a PPP project financing is concerned with cash flows rather than accounting results, it is usually necessary to add accounting calculations—*i.e.* profit and loss accounts (income statements) and balance sheets for each calculation period—to the model, because:

- The accounting results are important to the sponsors, as they will not wish to report an accounting loss from investment in a project company affiliate.
- Tax payments are based on accounting results rather than cash flow (§23.6.1, §23.6.2).
- Value-added tax (VAT) may distort the cash flow, especially during the construction phase (§23.6.3).
- The accounting results affect the project company's ability to pay dividends, and could affect its ability to keep trading (*cf.* §23.6.4).
- Adding a balance sheet is a good way of checking for errors in the financial model: if the balance sheet does not balance, there is a mistake somewhere.

§23.6.1 Tax Calculations

The main differences between cash flow and accounting results in a financial model for a PPP project company relate to the calculation and payment of corporate taxes on the project company's income.

A PPP project involves the project company a high initial capex. If the project company had to charge off the costs of the project as they were incurred, the result would be an enormous loss in the construction phase of the project, followed by enormous profits in the operating phase. This obviously does not represent the real situation of the project. In most countries, the project's capex is capitalised (*i.e.* added to the asset side of the balance sheet). As discussed in §23.9.2, capex includes not only the construction (or 'hard') cost, but also the 'soft' costs incurred until the project is in operation (*i.e.* bidding, development and financing costs, payments to advisers, *etc.*). The total of these costs is then written off (depreciated) over the life of the asset, and it is these write-off amounts which are charged against tax.[3] The write-off may be increased in the early years of the project by an acceleration of the tax-depreciation allowances. In some countries (*e.g.* Britain and the United States), depreciation may be dealt with in different ways for accounting and tax purposes: for *accounting*

---

[3] *Cf.* §18.13 for the Eurostat treatment of capex (for statistical rather than accounting purposes), which is more restrictive.

purposes, the project asset is depreciated over its useful life, thus spreading the cost of the asset against the earnings it generates and increasing the reported profits in the early years of the project, whereas for *tax* purposes accelerated depreciation is used. The difference between the two is taken directly to (or later deducted from) a tax reserve on the liability side of the balance sheet. In other countries (*e.g.* France and Germany), the accounting and tax depreciation must be the same.

Alternatively, the project company's investment in the project may be treated as a financial claim under the PPP contract, and depreciated so as to produce a level income over the life of the PPP contract (a system known as 'contract debtor' accounting in Britain).

§23.6.2 Tax Payments

Any of these methods of calculating tax is likely to produce tax payments that are not in proportion to CADS for the relevant period. A common pattern is that the project company pays little corporate tax in its early years, because of a high level of write-off of its investment against tax, but makes higher tax payments in the later years of the project. Since the rest of the opex is likely to remain reasonably constant (subject to inflation), this makes the process of producing level service fees (*cf.* §15.3.2) that much more complex. Moreover, a sudden 'blip' in the cash flow can be caused by the project company having to start making tax payments once it has written off its initial tax losses; if tax is included in CADS for the purpose of lenders' cover-ratio calculations (*cf.* §23.3.6), this is likely to be the point at which the ADSCR is lowest, and hence may determine how much debt can be raised (*cf.* §23.3.2). (This problem can be reduced by setting up a tax reserve account— *cf.* §25.2.4—to accumulate the tax payment in advance)

The timing of tax payments also has to be taken into account in the financial modelling. Again, systems vary from country to country—in some cases corporate taxes are paid in the year following the relevant tax year, while in others payments are made on account during the year, and adjusted thereafter based on the final taxable income for that year.

§23.6.3 Value-Added Tax

Some forms of taxation may require the government to put in place specific measures of support for contracting authorities. Value-added tax (VAT) is one such example. VAT is a tax that arises during the supply chain in the production of a good or service. Through a system of charging and recovery, it does not fall on the individual producers along the supply chain but on the ultimate consumer, the last entity in the chain, who cannot recover the tax. One problem arises when the 'consumer' is a public entity, such as the contracting authority in an availability PPP. The contracting authority is not able to levy or recover VAT, due to its classification as a non-taxable entity and the nature of the public service it is buying and providing to citizens. The contracting authority therefore finds itself paying the full amount of VAT (as part of the service fee), which is an additional cost that it may not easily afford. Taking government as a whole this is not an issue (government is simply paying itself the tax), but for a particular contracting authority this additional cost comes out of its own budget. Because the PPP contract involves paying for all the inputs for the service being provided, unlike traditional procurement, where some of the inputs may be sourced from within the authority, the PPP represents a more expensive option for the contracting authority simply because more external inputs are involved that give rise to the VAT element.

To alleviate this problem, some governments have established mechanisms for PPPs that allow the contracting authority to claim for direct reimbursement of the VAT costs from central government.

A further VAT issue relates to the project company itself during the construction phase of a PPP project. VAT will be payable by the project company on the construction subcontractor's and other bills, but since the project company is not trading, in some countries it cannot recover the VAT until it starts billing the contracting authority (or charging users in the case of a concession). This means that it needs a separate short-term VAT financing loan until it can recover the VAT paid. Obviously, this is an unnecessary complication in the financing structure, and adds a cost that will ultimately be passed on to the contracting authority or users. However, there may be little choice in the matter if that is how the country's VAT system works.

§23.6.4 The Dividend Trap

Another reason that accounting projections are required in a financial model is to ensure that the project company is legally able to pay dividends on its shares when the model shows that there is sufficient cash flow to do so. The project company may make accounting losses in its early years because of a higher level of depreciation of its assets (while the revenues remain constant over the whole tenor of the PPP contract, other than inflation indexation—*cf.* §24.3), but still be generating a positive cash flow after debt-service payments. A company generally cannot pay a dividend to its shareholders if there is a negative balance on its profit and loss account, *i.e.* if accumulated accounting losses (plus past dividends) are greater than accumulated accounting profits. This is a function of the difference between tax depreciation and debt principal repayment; if the former is much greater than the latter, a negative profit balance develops, which disappears as the situation is reversed. (It is clearly less of an issue in countries where the accounting depreciation does not have to mirror the tax depreciation.) The structure of the investment in the project company therefore has to be adjusted to take account of this 'dividend trap', which can be done by

- making part of this investment in subordinated debt rather than equity share capital (*cf.* §20.3.5); the financial model is used to check that this structure should work properly by reviewing the accounting results over the life of the project;
- making temporary loans to its own shareholders of surplus cash flow which cannot otherwise be distributed, to be repaid from later dividends; this is likely to have complex tax implications, and would therefore only be used if a subordinated-loan structure did not work for some reason.

On the other hand, if the project company has a relatively small proportion of equity, with a large proportion of the equity investment financed with shareholder-provided subordinated debt, there is a danger that accumulated accounting losses in the early years of operation may be greater than the book amount of the equity. If a company has a 'negative equity', it may have to go through a court-approved capital restructuring, or cease trading. Again, therefore, the financial model is used to ensure that the mix of funding provided by the investors should not create this problem.

§23.7 CONTINGENT FUNDING

Although the likelihood of capex cost overruns should be limited (*cf.* §12.3.2), a prudent lender would generally require the project company to have some contingent financing in hand to meet unexpected events. The simplest way of doing this is to add a contingency to the capex budget (*cf.* §12.3.7)—if it is not needed, the undrawn financing for this can be cancelled. More formally, additional 'standby' equity and debt can be provided separately. In this case the contingency financing, if required, is drawn after the base-case equity and debt is fully drawn.

§23.8 THE FINANCIAL MODEL

A financial model is used in different ways during the bidding and development phase of a PPP project:

- by the contracting authority as part of assessing and preparing the PPP option during the Procurement Review and Procurement Preparation phases (Phases 4 and 5); subsequently in the procurement phase (Phase 6), it may be used to provide a template for bidders or to calibrate the preferred bidder's model and test the affordability of bids; a 'shadow' financial model is produced by the contracting authority's financial adviser, that attempts to predict the bidders' costs, financing structure and other assumptions (in Australia this is called the 'private financing predictor' (PFP)), and hence whether the outcome in terms of service fees is likely to be affordable from the public-sector point of view (*cf.* §9.2.2);
- by bidders (or project developers) to structure their financing, review the benefits of different financial terms and arrangements and calculate of the service fees required to cover capex, opex, debt service and the investors' return as a basis for the bid;
- by lenders as part of their due-diligence process (*cf.* §22.2.7); and
- to fix the service fees where these depend on interest rates at financial close (*cf.* §24.2.13):

After financial close, the model continues to be used:

- as a basis for lenders to review the changing long-term prospects for the project and thus their continuing risk exposure (*cf.* §25.2.5);
- to price contract changes (*cf.* §16.2.1, §19.8.2);
- to calculate termination-sum payments (*cf.* Chapter 17);
- to calculate any refinancing gain to be shared between the contracting authority and the project company (*cf.* §26.2.6); and
- as a budgeting tool for the project company.

However, given that the original objective of the model changes after financial close, it will require some adaptation to undertake these tasks, if not a complete re-build.

As there are three parties involved—the contracting authority, the sponsors and the lenders—there could theoretically be three parallel financial models, but this is seldom the case. The more usual course is for the contracting authority's financial adviser and the lenders to review the model prepared by the preferred bidder (or the latter's financial adviser), calibrate it against the contracting authority's shadow financial model to ensure that the results are the same (given the same assumptions), and then use the bidder's model thereafter, in the ways listed above. Alternatively, there is some merit in the contracting authority providing a template financial model to be used, with suitable adaptation, by all bidders, to make comparison of bids easier.

It may be asked why the contracting authority should have access in this way to the bidders' financial models—isn't the data in these models commercially confidential? But this is unlikely to be the case because:

- The contracting authority needs to be able to check whether the bid is financially viable, and can thus deliver the initial investment in the PPP project and its long-term service requirements (*cf.* §10.6.7).
- If the financial model is used to calculate the service fees at financial close (*cf.* §24.2.13), it obviously has to be agreed by both parties.
- There has to be an agreed base case (*cf.* §23.9.9), because should compensation be required later (*cf.* §16.2.1, §17.3), it has to be measured against the outcome in the PPP contract which both parties originally agreed was reasonable.

Therefore, transparency between the parties on model assumptions and calculations is the better practice.

§23.9 MODEL INPUTS AND OUTPUTS

It is not the intention to discuss modelling techniques in any depth in this book. But it is necessary to have a basic understanding of what goes into and comes out of a financial model for a PPP, and how this output is used.

The model's initial purpose is to calculate the service fees, based on various 'building blocks' of inputs. The basis for the inputs must be clearly documented; the standard way of doing this is for an 'assumptions book' to be compiled. This takes each line of the financial model and sets out the source for the input (or the calculation based on these inputs) in that line, with copies of the documentation to back this up.

§23.9.1 Macroeconomic Assumptions

Background assumptions are needed for interest rates and inflation (*cf.* Chapter 24). The contracting authority should ensure, at the bidding stage, that the same assumptions are used by all bidders if changes in these would affect the service fees (*cf.* §24.2.13).

§23.9.2 Capital Expenditure

The capex budget for the project takes into account costs incurred during the bidding, development and construction phases of the project, *i.e.* both 'hard' construction costs and the 'soft' costs for financing, advisory fees and administration.

As discussed in §12.3, the construction subcontract, which obviously forms the largest part of the capex, should normally be on a fixed-price turnkey basis, with payments made *pro rata* to the progress of construction. Taxes such as VAT on this price (and any other costs) also need to be taken into account if they cannot be recovered before the end of the construction period (*cf.* §23.6.3).

The main soft costs are likely to include:

— Bidding and development costs

These are the main pre-financial close costs, *i.e.* the sponsors' own staff costs and those of external advisers (*cf.* §20.7), including lenders' advisers (*cf.* §22.2.7). There is often a time gap between when the total capex budget is agreed with the lenders, and financial close, and during that time there is a risk that legal and similar costs which are not fixed may mount up more than budgeted. If they are not treated as part of the initial equity investment, such development costs are normally reimbursed to the sponsors at financial close. If such costs are above budget by that time, lenders may require reimbursement of the excess to be deferred until the end of the construction period, at which time reimbursement may be allowed if sufficient undrawn funds are then available.

— Development fees

Project economics may allow one or more sponsors to take out an initial fee from the project company for developing the project, and thus make a profit on the development costs (*cf.* §20.2.1, §20.5). This figure may fluctuate (or be eliminated entirely) as the financial evaluation of the project develops, or like the over-budget costs referred to above, may be deferred until the end of the construction period and then paid if enough undrawn finance is available to do so.

— Project company costs

These include costs after financial close such as:

- staff and administration; some administration costs such as accounting may be subcontracted (cf. §20.6.3);
- office and equipment;
- continuing external advisory costs, e.g. for construction supervision; and
- construction-phase insurance (*cf.* §14.3).

Apart from insurance premiums, the amounts should be relatively small in the context of the overall capex budget if most of the project company's activities have been contracted out to O&M or FM subcontractors.

— Working capital

The working capital is the amount of money required to cover the time difference between payment of the project company's opex and receipt of revenues in cash. In effect, it is the short-term (usually 30-60 day) cash-flow cycle of the project, which cannot be calculated directly in a financial model that runs for six-monthly periods during the operating phase of the project. It is thus the initial costs that the project company has to incur until it receives its first revenues. These costs are unlikely to be substantial for the project company as long as its subcontractors are paid on a cycle that matches its revenue cycle. The most significant initial cost may be payment of the first operating-phase insurance premium (as these premiums are normally paid annually in advance).

— Reserve accounts

Reserve accounts (*cf.* §25.2.4) are normally funded as part of the capex rather than from operating cash flow, as this improves the investors' equity IRR. (If they are funded as part of the capex this means that most of the funding will come from the lenders, whereas if they are funded out of cash flow this effectively means that all of the funding is provided by the investors, who have to give up distributions to do this, hence reducing their equity IRR.)

— Interest during construction (IDC) and finance drawdown

Project costs as set out above then give rise to a requirement for the total financing (in debt and equity) required for the project. However, there is a circularity about this calculation (*i.e.* the answer changes the inputs), because:

* IDC, which is funded by further drawings on the financing sources (*cf.* §24.2), itself needs to be included in the total financing requirement and
* the financing split between debt and equity is determined by the ability of the operating cash flows to support that debt.

This means that various iterations of the calculations are required to get the right balance of debt and equity.

— Contingency

Finally, an overall contingency may be added to the project cost to allow for unexpected events (*cf.* §12.3.7, §23.7).

§23.9.3 FM/O&M Costs

The next block of modelling deals with the operation phase. Opex, which is typically smaller than the debt service for a PPP project with a heavy initial investment in infrastructure and a consequent high level of debt (say, a 40:60 ratio), would include:

* the project company's own direct costs (*cf.* §20.6.3);
* subcontract payments;
* operating-phase insurance (*cf.* §14.4); and
* taxation (*cf.* §23.6.2).

FM/O&M costs are likely to form the largest part of the operating costs, whether incurred *via* subcontractors or by the project company, and can be difficult to predict if this cost risk has not been subcontracted (*cf.* §13.6).

A cost model is often used to establish the relevant input costs that need to be built up from a range of underlying data available. This should not be confused with the financial model itself.

§23.9.4 Debt Service

Cf. §23.2–§23.4.

§23.9.5 Revenues

Although the financial model is initially used to calculate the service fees, there are natural caps on the level of these that can be fed into the financial structure at the time of bidding:

- In the case of a concession, projected demand and 'willingness to pay' will determine the levels of usage and the rates to be charged for tolls, *etc.* (*cf.* §15.5).
- In the case of an availability PPP project, the contracting authority's VfM (*cf.* Chapter 8) and affordability (*cf.* §9.2) requirements have to be taken into account.

Subject to these overall constraints, there is again some circularity about calculating the minimum required service fees as these have to be sufficient to pay debt service and provide the investors' return, *i.e.* there is a requirement for a certain level of CADS. There is thus a logical sequence in arriving at the level of service fees to bid—these need to be sufficient to:

- cover opex
- fit within the 'envelope' of the contracting authority's requirements
- meet lender debt-service and other requirements; *and*
- give the investors their required rate of return.

Having established the first of these requirements as above, the interplay between the latter three requirements is quite complex, as discussed in §23.5.

§23.9.6 Model Outputs

The model outputs[4] are a series of calculations:

- capex;
- drawdown of equity;
- drawdown of debt;
- service fees;
- other operating revenues (*cf.* §15.8);

---

[4] Just to be clear, these outputs have nothing to do with outputs under a PPP contract (*cf.* §15.2).

- opex;
- interest calculations;
- tax;
- debt repayments;
- profit and loss account (income statement);
- balance sheet;
- cash flow (source and use of funds);
- lenders' cover ratios (*cf.* §23.3);
- investors' returns;
- the NPV of these payments, to enable the contracting authority to compare bids (*cf.* §10.6.5);
- project IRR (*cf.* §20.3.2); and
- equity IRR (*cf.* §20.3.3).

A summary sheet in the financial model usually sets out the key results on one page.

§23.9.7 Sensitivities

The financial model also needs to be sufficiently flexible to allow both investors and lenders to calculate a series of 'sensitivities' (also known as 'cases') showing the effects of variations in the key input assumptions. Such sensitivities may include calculating the effect on lenders' cover ratios and the equity IRR of:

- construction-cost overrun;
- delay in completion (say for six months);
- deductions or penalties for failure to meet availability or service requirements (*cf.* §15.6);
- reduced usage of the project (where the project company assumes demand risk);
- higher opex;
- higher interest rates (where these are not fixed—*cf.* §24.2); and
- changes in inflation (*cf.* §24.3.3).

In summary, the sensitivities look at the financial effect of the commercial- and financial-risk aspects of the project not working out as originally expected. Lenders also usually run a 'combined downside case' to check the effects of several adverse things happening at once (*e.g.* three months' delay in completion, a 10% drop in usage (if relevant) and 10% increase in opex). This calculation of several different adverse events happening at once is also called 'scenario analysis', and the aim is to see if, despite these combined problems, the debt can still be repaid, albeit probably not as scheduled.

As can be seen, the approach to assessing risk by the private sector is somewhat different to the approach used by the contracting authority (*cf.* §11.3) and reflects the fact that the sponsors and lenders tend to focus on the consequences of usage or cost levels for the financial viability of the project within the parameters of acceptable cover ratios and equity returns.

§23.9.8 Model Audit

The lenders usually require the model to be audited by a model auditor, a service provided by specialist departments within major firms of accountants, or by specialised financial-modelling companies. The functions of the model auditor are to confirm that:

- the model properly reflects the project contracts and other stated assumptions (*e.g.* as to the rate of inflation);
- accounting and taxation calculations are correct; and
- the model has the ability to calculate a reasonable range of sensitivities, as discussed above.

The contracting authority should also be a beneficiary of this audit if its own financial advisers do not audit and certify the model (which it is preferable they should do, because of the various ways in which it may be used—*cf.* §23.8).

If another entity, such as a PPP unit is responsible for reviewing the preparation status of the project and the results of the contracting authority's financial model to test for affordability (*cf.* §9.2), rather than getting lost in the minutiae of the financial model, a useful approach is to use a simplified generic financial model to check if the result using broad revenue, costs and financing assumptions is similar to the service-fee projections of the more detailed model that the contracting authority is using.

§23.9.9 The Base Case

Once the contracting authority, sponsors and lenders agree that the financial model's structure and calculation formulæ reflect the project and the project contracts correctly, the basic input assumptions are settled, and the financial structure and terms discussed below are agreed to and also incorporated in the model, the final run of the model—which is known as the 'base case'[5]—usually takes place at or just before financial close:

- to enable the lenders to check that, using fully up-to-date assumptions, and the final versions of the project contracts, the project still provides them with adequate coverage for their loan;
- in some cases, to fix the level of the service fees to reflect interest rates at financial close (*cf.* §24.2.13).

§23.10 ASSET REGISTER

In addition to the financial model, the project company usually establishes a register of each of its assets in an 'asset register'. This is normal business practice for both private- and public-sector entities and is important for managing the maintenance of the

---

[5] The assumptions of the financial model agreed between the project company and the contracting authority may differ from that agreed between the project company and the lenders (the latter being typically more conservative). The model agreed with the lenders is known as the 'banking case'.

assets, scheduling asset replacement, for accounting purposes including the calculation of depreciation and for insurance coverage and claims. It also particularly relevant if the project involves refurbishment of assets as the nature and condition of the assets taken on by the project company is an important consideration for all parties concerned—if so, this would need to be completed as part of the Phase 5: Procurement Preparation (*cf.* §5.3.5).

Macroeconomic Risks and Hedging

§24.1 INTRODUCTION

This chapter covers the main macroeconomic issues likely to arise in the financial structuring of a PPP project, namely dealing with risks relating to interest rates (§24.2), inflation (§24.3) and exposure to foreign-exchange risks (§24.4). All of these require some kind of 'hedging' to eliminate these risks as far as the project company is concerned, either in the PPP contract itself (as is typically the case with inflation), or through financial hedging (as is typically the case with interest-rate and foreign-exchange risks).

Such hedging may have a direct or indirect effect on the contracting authority, by affecting either the original service fees (*cf.* §24.2.13), or the amounts the contracting authority has to pay on termination of the PPP contract in some circumstances (*cf.* §17.2.1). It is also a key element in the overall viability of a bid for a project (*cf.* §10.6.7). Review and approval of financial-hedging strategies is therefore an important part of the contracting authority's due-diligence process (*cf.* §10.8).

§24.2 INTEREST-RATE RISK

A project company may need a loan for 20-30 years to finance its PPP project. Although project-finance bonds for PPP projects always carry a fixed-rate coupon (except inflation-indexed bonds—*cf.* §24.3.6), commercial banks do not generally lend for such a long tenor at a fixed rate, because they cannot fund the loan with matching deposits. Therefore, most long-term bank loans have a 'floating' interest rate, whereby the interest rate on the loan is adjusted, usually every 6 months, to current-market rates for their short-term deposits. The credit margin (*cf.* §23.4.1) is then charged on top of this. Examples of such floating rates are LIBOR (the London inter-bank offered rate), in which floating rates are quoted both in domestic £ sterling and a variety of international currencies such as the US$, or its cousin Euribor (the € inter-bank offered rate).[1]

Fluctuating interest rates can obviously have a significant effect on the long-term financial viability of a PPP project. This is an inevitable consequence of the high leverage and tight debt-service cover inherent in project finance—small changes in interest rates make a big difference to the net cash flow.

So, a floating interest rate on a project company's debt is not viable for investors (since higher interest costs could destroy their equity IRR), or lenders (since higher interest costs will erode their cover ratios), nor is it in the interests of the contracting authority for the project company to be financially vulnerable to changes in interest rates, which could threaten delivery of the service under the PPP contract. Financial hedging is therefore required to eliminate this risk.

There is a similar issue with respect to IDC. During the construction period, the interest is not paid in cash, but capitalised (*i.e.* added to the loan amount), or paid by making a new drawing on the loan. Thus, IDC becomes part of the project's capex budget (*cf.* §23.9.2), and so there is a risk that if the interest rate for the IDC is not fixed, and is eventually higher than originally projected, there will be a construction-cost overrun (*cf.* §12.3). Lenders do not normally allow any general construction-cost contingency to be used to cover this risk, as this is primarily intended to cover overruns in the 'hard' costs (mainly the construction contract), or the effect of a delay causing higher total interest costs.

§24.2.1 Hedging by the Contracting Authority

The simplest (and cheapest) way of hedging the risk would be for the service fees to be adjusted for movements in the floating-rate interest on the project company's debt (*cf.* §24.2.13). This is not unknown in other sectors of the project-finance market, but is seldom seen with PPPs, because it is likely to give the contracting authority a balance-sheet problem with availability PPP projects. There is also the more fundamental problem that it may not be easy for contracting authorities to access additional funds to pay for interest costs higher than expected, at least in a timely way (*cf.* §9.3), and if the project collapses the contracting authority may suffer a loss if it has hedged its own interest-rate risk (*cf.* §24.2.3). This approach is also impossible with concessions, as users would not accept constant changes in user fees to match changes in interest rates. This therefore means that the project company is likely to have to undertake the hedging instead (but *cf.* §24.2.14).

§24.2.2 Interest-Rate Swaps

The most common form of financial hedging used to cover floating interest-rate risk—indeed almost universal in a project-finance context—is the interest-rate swap. Under an interest-rate swap agreement,[2] one party exchanges an obligation to pay interest on a

[1] After the decline of the inter-bank lending markets following the 2008 financial crisis, and some scandals around fixing LIBOR rates, LIBOR will be phased out by the end of 2021, with a range of replacement reference rates under discussion at the time of writing.

[2] Also known as a 'coupon swap'.

floating-rate basis for an obligation to pay interest on a fixed-rate basis, and the other party does the opposite. Interest-rate swaps are a long-established form of financial derivative (dating back to the late 1970s),[3] and banks in the derivatives markets run large swap books. The market for swaps is far deeper than for other interest-rate derivatives, especially for the long maturities which are characteristic of PPP projects and hence pricing is usually more competitive—but *cf.* §24.2.8 for issues on competition.

Under an interest-rate swap, a project company with an obligation to pay interest at a floating rate under its loan agrees to pay its counterpart (a bank or banks—the 'swap provider'), the difference between the floating rate and the agreed-upon fixed rate if the floating rate is below this fixed rate, or will be paid by the swap provider if the floating rate is above the fixed rate. These payments take place when the floating interest rate is adjusted, say every six months, the dates for payment being known as 'settlement dates'.

For the swap provider, arranging a matching swap in the market is far easier than raising long-term fixed-rate financing and on-lending this to the project company, since its own financial-market counterparts take a much lower credit risk in providing a swap than making a long-term loan. The swap provider can thus make use of its access to short-term floating-rate financing, on the assumption that this will always be renewed, and then swap this to a fixed rate. Although the swap provider does not have to be the lender, this is usually the case (*cf.* §24.2.8).

The calculation of the net payment amount between the project company and the swap provider is based on the 'notional principal amount' for each period (*i.e.* the amount of the loan on which the interest is being calculated), although in a swap agreement neither side lends the other any money, but simply pays over the difference between the two interest rates. Table 24.1 shows how an interest-rate swap works in practice, assuming that:

- the project company borrows $1,000 (*i.e.* this is the notional principal amount), and repays the loan in one instalment at the end of 5 years;
- this loan is at a floating interest rate, re-fixed annually;
- the project company swaps its floating interest-rate payment obligation against a fixed rate of 5%; and
- the floating-rate interest actually increases from 4% in year 1 to 8% in year 5.

As can be seen, the project company has turned its floating-rate interest payments into the equivalent of a fixed rate of 5%, and the swap provider has done the reverse. Had the project company not entered into the swap, it would have been $50 worse off.

Of course, this can work the other way around: if floating interest rates go down against the fixed swap rate, the project company will 'lose' money—but this is not a real loss, just being wise after the event. For the project company not to fix its interest rate would be a gamble that would not be acceptable to the lenders, and ought not to be acceptable to its investors; moreover, the contracting authority should also be concerned about the long-term financial stability of the project company.

---

[3] A derivative contract is a financial contract that derives its value from the performance of another financial entity such as an asset (for example, a quoted stock), index (for example, an inflation index) or interest rate (for example, LIBOR).

Table 24.1   Interest-rate swap

($)		Year:	1	2	3	4	5	
(a) Notional principal amount			1,000	1,000	1,000	1,000	1,000	
(b) Floating rate (*p.a.*)			4%	5%	6%	7%	8%	
(c) Swap fixed rate			5%	5%	5%	5%	5%	
(d) Floating-rate interest	[(a) × (b)]		40	50	60	70	80	
(e) Fixed-rate interest	[(a) × (c)]		50	50	50	50	50	
(f) Difference	[(d) − (e)]		−10	0	10	20	30	
Project-company position								
(g) Interest on loan	[= (d)]		40	50	60	70	80	
(h) Swap payment/(receipt)	[= −(f)]		10	0	−10	−20	−30	**Total**
Net interest cost	[(g) + (h), = (e)]		**50**	**50**	**50**	**50**	**50**	**250**
Swap provider position								
(i) Interest on notional principal	[= (e)]		50	50	50	50	50	
(j) Swap payment/(receipt)	[= (f)]		−10	0	10	20	30	**Total**
Net interest cost	[(i) + (j), = (d)]		**40**	**50**	**60**	**70**	**80**	**300**

§24.2.3 Interest-Rate Swap Breakage

Although neither side of the swap arrangement is lending the other any money, each side is taking a credit risk on the transaction if the swap arrangement has to be cancelled, *e.g.* because the project company defaults on its debt. In this situation, the swap provider has to terminate the original swap and enter into another swap for the balance of the tenor (*i.e.* another party effectively takes over the obligations of the project company). But if long-term fixed interest rates have gone down since the swap was originally signed, the new counterpart will not be willing to pay the same high rate of fixed interest as the project company. The NPV of the difference between the original fixed-rate payment and the new fixed-rate payment (discounted at the new fixed rate) represents a loss to the original swap provider. This is known as the 'breakage' (or 'unwind') cost. Of course, if, when the default takes place, the long-term fixed rate for the remainder of the swap tenor is higher than the original rate, there is no breakage cost to the swap provider; on the contrary, there is a breakage gain which is due to the project company.

For example, as shown in Table 24.2, an interest-rate swap with a notional principal of $1,000 is provided for 15 years, at a fixed rate of 6%. If after 3 years the project company defaults and the swap is terminated, and the swap provider is only able to redeploy the swap at 3%, the swap provider's loss on termination amounts to $30 *p.a.* for the remaining 12 years. The breakage cost is the NPV of these amounts, discounted at 3% (the new swap

Table 24.2   Calculation of swap-breakage cost

Assumptions:
- Notional principal amount $1,000
- Tenor of loan and swap   15 years
- Original swap fixed rate   6%
- Swap rate on termination   3%

($) Year:	3	4	5	6	7	8	9	10	11	12	13	14	15
Fixed-rate payment													
- original amount		60	60	60	60	60	60	60	60	60	60	60	60
- revised amount		30	30	30	30	30	30	30	30	30	30	30	30
Swap provider's annual loss:		30	30	30	30	30	30	30	30	30	30	30	30
NPV of loss		299	278	256	234	211	187	163	137	112	85	57	29

rate), which can be calculated as $299. This is therefore what would be owed by the project company on termination of the swap (*cf.* §25.5.1). If the default occurs at the end of year 4, the payment goes down to $278, at the end of year 5 to $256, and so on—other things being equal, the later in the loan tenor that the swap is terminated the lower the swap-breakage cost, because the swap provider's future losses reduce over time. (On the other hand, if the swap rate on termination at the end of year 3 goes up to 8%, there is a break-age profit of $226, which would be due to the project company.)

Table 24.2 assumes that the $1,000 loan is repaid in one amount at the end of 15 years, but of course this would not be the case in a project-finance loan. This means that, again other things being equal, the swap-breakage cost declines more rapidly over time because the notional principal amount is going down instead of staying the same.

The process of valuing a swap against current-market rates is known as 'marking to market'; a swap that shows a profit on being unwound is said to be 'in the money', and one which shows a loss is 'out of the money'. The breakage-cost risk is therefore not a fixed figure, but depends on:

- the remaining profile of the notional principal amount(s);
- the remaining tenor of the swap(s);
- the way market rates have changed, when the default takes place; and
- whether the original swap was at a historically high or low rate (if at a low rate, the likelihood of a breakage cost is less because long-term rates are less likely to go even lower).

The risk of there being a breakage cost is relevant to:

- the swap provider, for whom the breakage cost is the amount it has at risk if the project company defaults;
- other lenders, as the swap provider will have a claim *pari-passu* with their loan if the project company defaults (*cf.* §25.5.1);

- the project company, if the original loan is refinanced (*cf.* §26.2); and
- the contracting authority, in cases where the contracting authority pays off the loan, *e.g.* when exercising an option to terminate the PPP contract (*cf.* §17.3)—which also means paying associated breakage costs.

It should be noted that a floating-rate lender also may have a small breakage cost if the project company defaults between the two interest-rate fixing dates.

§24.2.4 How Interest-Rate Swap Rates Are Determined

The fixed rate quoted by the swap provider is based on three elements:

— Government bond rates

These provide the 'base rate' for the swap; for example, a swap, in $ for 7 years, would be based on the current yield of a US Treasury bond for the same period.

— The swap-market premium[4]

This reflects supply and demand in the swap market and also in the fixed-rate corporate-bond market (*cf.* §22.4), since corporate-bond issuers and other market participants can arbitrage between the fixed-rate market and the floating-rate market with a swap. Swap-market rates are quoted in the financial press and on dealing screens.

— The credit premium

This is the charge for taking the particular credit risk of the project company. If the swap provider assumes that the maximum likely level of breakage risk is, say, 10% of the initial notional principal amount, and the credit margin on the loan to the project company is, say, 2%, then the credit premium added to the swap rate should be 10% of 2%, *i.e.* 0.20% *p.a.* Note that this is a separate figure from the credit margin charged in the underlying loan (*cf.* §23.4.1).

The swap market works on the basis of bullet repayments of notional principal—*i.e.* the type of loan repayment schedule shown in Table 24.1, that assumes none of the notional principal of $1,000 is repaid until the end of the five-year schedule. However, a project-finance cash flow is of course based on repayment in annuity instalments over a period of time (as shown in Table 23.2). The way the swap provider deals with this is to quote a weighted average rate for a series of swaps covering each repayment date, with the notional principal being the amount repayable on that date (known as an 'amortising swap').

The swap quotation also has to take into account that the notional principal may not be drawn all at once; most projects have a drawing period of 2-3 years or so during construction, so swap rates are quoted in advance for an increasing notional principal amount during the construction/drawing period (this is known as an 'accreting swap').

---

[4] In fact, due to the distortions of the government bond and inter-bank markets since the 2008 financial crisis, swap rates have sometimes been at a discount rather than a premium against the equivalent government bond.

§24.2.5 ISDA Documentation

Interest-rate swaps are documented in a standard form produced by the International Swap and Derivatives Association (ISDA), and on which there is limited room for negotiation. This is necessary because swap dealers want to be able to trade their entire swap book on the basis of standard terms. The specific terms of the swap (nominal amounts, rates, payment dates) are attached as a schedule to the ISDA documentation.

There are currently two standard forms of ISDA documentation being used in the market, those of 1992 and 2002. The most important difference between them in this context relates to the calculation of breakage costs on termination. The 1992 documentation allows the parties to choose between the 'Market Quotation' method (where the breakage is priced in the market) and the 'Loss' method, where it is priced by the swap provider. The latter should be chosen by the project company. The 2002 documentation only has one method ('Close-Out Amount'), which uses market quotations except where these are not available.

§24.2.6 The Credit Premium and Breakage Costs

As mentioned above, the pricing of a swap includes a credit premium, which in effect equates to the credit margin on a loan. However, when the swap rate is fixed and documented, this credit premium is usually just added to the total rate, not dealt with separately. The effect of this is that if the swap is terminated early, the swap provider will get the NPV of all the future credit premiums, which is really the same thing as a lender getting all the future credit margin if a loan is terminated early (which does not usually happen).

If the swap credit premium is dealt with in this way, it creates a *de facto* termination fee on the swap. Roughly speaking, assuming a 0.10% swap credit premium, this will be of about 1% of the loan outstanding in the early years of the project, declining over time.

This has various implications for both the project company and, potentially, the contracting authority:

- It eats into the benefit of a refinancing (*cf.* §26.2), unless the original swap provider also provides the refinancing.
- It inhibits optional termination of the PPP contract by the contracting authority, and hence long-term flexibility (*cf.* §17.3).
- In cases where the contracting authority repays debt, including breakage costs, on a 'no fault' termination (*cf.* §17.4), it is clearly inappropriate for this payment to include the lenders' future profits.

There is no good reason for lenders to make a windfall profit on early termination of a swap, when they do not do so on early termination of the loan to which this swap is linked. The credit premium can be separated from the swap, and hence dealt with differently on early termination, in one of two ways:

- It can be documented separately in the ISDA schedule, with a provision that it should not be taken into account in the breakage calculation.
- It can be paid under a separate swap-premium agreement, which terminates without any penalty payment if the swap is terminated.

If the loan is refinanced by a different lender, the original swap provider may offer to 'roll over' (*i.e.* transfer) its swap from the project company to the new swap provider instead of terminating it.[5] This is helpful insofar as termination of the swap incurs a cost, not taken into account above, reflecting the market bid-offer spread. However, it also means that the original swap provider continues to receive the original credit premium (even though the risk is now the new lender, not the project company), while a further credit premium will be charged by the new swap provider.

§24.2.7 Scale and Timing of Interest-Rate Hedging

In a highly-leveraged financial structure, as has already been seen above, there is little scope for a project company to absorb fluctuations in interest rates. However, even in this case there is still a need for some flexibility in the interest-rate hedging programme:

- Some flexibility needs to be left for the drawdown timing, which will depend on the progress of construction (*cf.* §25.2.1).
- It may be possible to delay the swap transaction until shortly after financial close, if market rates are felt to be unfavourable.
- If there is a flexible repayment schedule (*cf.* §23.2.5), hedging must allow for this.
- The interest-rate risk on contingent financing (*cf.* §23.7), which may never be drawn at all, need not be hedged at the beginning of the construction period.
- If, say, the loan is for 20 years, the project company could choose to hedge for 15 years if the fixed rate is relatively low and the risk for the last 5 years is also small. Interest-rate risk obviously diminishes over the life of the project as the loan is repaid and the interest payments reduce as a proportion of the total debt service.
- Alternatively, the hedging may run for only five years, because the project company intends to refinance the debt then, even though this creates a greater interest-rate risk at that time (*cf.* §23.2.7), and hence is unattractive to the original lenders.

If the project company's leverage is lower—*e.g.* the typical 70-80% found in a concession project—the need for hedging may also be lower, as the project company may be more able to absorb changes in interest rates without unduly undermining the lenders' cash-flow cover. It may therefore be easier in such cases for the investors in the project company to decide—taking a view on where they think interest rates will be over the project life—to hedge less than the full amount of the debt, or to hedge for less than the full tenor of the debt.

§24.2.8 Competition in Swap Pricing

The simplest way for the project company to cover its interest-rate risk through a swap is to have its syndicate of banks providing the floating-rate loan also provide the swap *pro rata* to their share of the loan; however, the problems with this are:

---

[5] This has been less the case since the 2008 financial crisis, and the subsequent decline in scale of the inter-bank dealing markets.

- The final syndication of the loan may not be completed until after financial close (*cf.* §22.2.9), and swap arrangements have to be concluded at or shortly after financial close. (In which case, the swap would have to be provided by the lead arranger(s).)
- Some of the syndicate banks may be less competitive than others in their swap pricing, and the project company may end up having to pay the swap rate of the most expensive bank.
- It leaves the syndicate banks (or the lead arranger(s)) with no competition, and therefore the project company may not get the best rates for the swap.[6]

Although interest-rate swap rates are quoted and can be checked on trading screens, this is not the case for an interest-rate swap on a project-specific debt-service schedule, for which a 'blended' rate has to be produced, reflecting the drawdown and repayment schedule over the life of the project (*cf.* §24.2.4). While it would not be fair to say that the pricing of such a blended swap, which is done under time pressure at financial close, is a complete 'black box', it is difficult for the project company to check that the most competitive price has been obtained from its lender. Indeed, it is notorious that excess profits on interest-rate swaps have formed a significant part of project-finance banks' revenues in some PPP sectors.

If there are several banks in the lending syndicate, it may be possible to get them to bid against each other for the whole of the swap business, which is probably the simplest way of achieving a competitive bidding situation, but of course this will not work if syndication has not taken place and there is only one lead arranger.

It is not normally possible for the project company to go directly to other banks in the market and ask them to quote for the swap, firstly because a bank not already involved in lending is unlikely to want to spend the time bringing in its project-finance department to analyse the risk involved, and secondly because if a swap is provided by a bank which is not also a lender to the project company this causes inter-creditor problems (*cf.* §25.5.1).

A structure that gives the project-company access to the best market rates is for one or more of the banks in the lending syndicate to act as a 'fronting bank'. The project company goes into the swap market for quotations, based on the swap provider entering into a swap with the fronting bank; the project company then enters into an identical 'back-to-back' swap with the fronting bank. (The fronting bank itself can still quote in competition for the market swap.) The fronting bank charges the credit premium discussed above (or is counter-guaranteed by the syndicate banks and charges a smaller premium reflecting this). This structure also has the advantage of documenting the swap credit premium separately, making it easier to provide for the premium not to be payable on early termination (*cf.* §24.2.6). However, if the swap provider charges a significant credit premium for taking the risk of the fronting bank,[7] this structure will not be viable.

---

[6] In fact collusion between the banks' dealing rooms is likely. One way to lessen the chance of this is to get individual swap quotations at different times during the rate-fixing day.

[7] Again something that is more liable to happen with the reduction in scale of the inter-bank dealing markets since 2008.

§24.2.9 Roll-Over Risk

The notional principal schedule used as a basis for the swap is based on estimates of when drawings on the loan will be made during construction, and when loan repayments will be made (beginning when the project is completed). These estimates may prove incorrect—*e.g.* a delay in the construction programme affects the timing of drawings, or the final completion of the project is delayed, which may also delay the repayment schedule, if this is calculated from the completion date.

If the shift in timing is a relatively short period of a month or so, this does not matter, and the swap can be left to run on the original schedule (assuming that the project company will have funds available to make any net payment that is due) since any extra loss in a one-month period is likely to be compensated by a profit in another. If a significant shift in the schedule takes place—say six months—because of a delay in completion of the project, it is preferable to 'roll over' the swap (*i.e.* terminate the original swap and enter into a new one on the new schedule). Any breakage cost on termination would be largely matched by the benefit of a lower long-term fixed rate, and any profit would compensate for a higher fixed rate.

However, the project company may face some difficulty with the swap provider:

- The swap provider may no longer wish to provide the swap and try to use the roll-over request as a way of getting out of it.
- If there is no competition on the rate for the roll-over, the project company could pay too much for it.

If the fronting-bank structure described above has been used, roll-over of the swap should be less of an issue; in other cases, it may be possible to agree to a competitive approach in advance. If not, the project company (and its lenders) may just have to take this risk as one of the inevitable adverse consequences of a delay in completion. A similar issue arises if the loan amount is increased (*e.g.* by drawing on contingent financing because of a delay in completion), and the swap needs to be increased correspondingly. The risk may also flow on to the contracting authority if the delay is its fault (*cf.* §16.2).

§24.2.10 Other Types of Interest-Rate Hedging

The interest-rate swap market is the largest and most liquid of the derivatives markets in interest rates. This liquidity is especially evident at the longer maturities required for project-finance cash flows, which is the reason that interest-rate swaps are generally the instrument of choice for this purpose. However, there are some other derivative structures which can be used in a project-finance context.

   — Interest-rate cap

      Under an interest-rate cap, the cap provider agrees to pay the project company if floating interest rates go above a certain level (known as the 'strike rate' or 'cap rate'). For example, the current floating rate may be 5%, and the cap rate set at 7%. So long as the floating rate remains below 7%, the project company just pays the floating rate. If the floating rate goes above 7%, the cap provider pays the project company the difference between the two in the same way as in an interest-rate swap. For budget purposes, the project company can thus assume an interest cost of 7% fixed, and insofar as the floating rate cost comes out below this level, this is a bonus.

Caps are a form of option, and their pricing is based on complex formulae which base the pricing on forward interest rates (*i.e.* market quotations for interest on deposits to be placed in future). Payment for the cap is usually made by way of an up-front premium (unlike an interest-rate swap, where, as seen above, payment if any is made throughout the life of the swap). The amount of the premium will depend on how far the cap is out of the money—*e.g.* if the forward rate is 5% on average, a cap at 6% will cost more than a cap at 7%.

Interest-rate caps may provide a short-term solution to interest-rate hedging, for example, if a floating-rate loan during the construction period is to be refinanced by a fixed-rate loan on completion of the project. They have the advantage that the provider does not take a credit risk on the project company, because (after payment of the initial premium) payments only ever flow from the provider to the project company, and so can be obtained from any provider in the market. However, the disadvantage is that the up-front premium adds to the project's development costs. They are therefore seldom used for long-term hedging.

— Interest-rate collar

An interest-rate 'collar' combines an interest-rate cap with its reverse, an interest-rate floor (*i.e.* a maximum rate of say 6% is fixed with a cap as above, while if the floating rate goes below a floor rate of say 4% the project company pays the difference to the provider). Interest-rate collars may be obtained at no cost (*i.e.* without an up-front premium) because the cap and the floor have the same cost, and one is being bought and the other sold by the project company. However, the taker of the floor rate has a credit risk on the project company, albeit usually a lower level of risk than that for an interest-rate swap provider. But although a collar offers flexibility, the relative illiquidity of the market at longer maturities makes it difficult to use for long-term hedging of a PPP project.

— Swaption

A swaption (or 'contingent swap') is the right (or option) to enter into a swap at a future date, which may give some flexibility if the timing of drawings and repayments by the project company is not completely fixed. Swaptions are seen in a PPP context primarily in the situation where construction of part of the project is to go ahead while construction of the rest (and hence the need for financing) is not yet certain, *e.g.* because this latter part is dependent on planning approvals.

— Accretion swap

This type of swap[8] achieves the same result as debt accretion (*cf.* §23.2.9); instead of the fixed payments by the project company under an interest-rate swap merely hedging its floating interest payments, a part of these payments is shifted to later dates.

---

[8] Also known as a 'step-up swap'.

§24.2.11 Bond Proceeds Redeposit (GIC)

Although long-term interest-rate hedging is not an issue with a fixed-rate bond, the nature of bond issues does introduce an indirect short-term interest-rate risk which has to be hedged. A bank loan can be drawn by the project company as and when needed for the costs of the PPP project during the construction period. A bond issue, on the other hand, usually has to be drawn in one amount at financial close—bond investors will not usually commit to buy bonds in the future, least of all at a rate fixed today. (Although some bond markets are becoming more flexible in this respect.) The result is that the project company has to pay interest on the whole of its borrowing from financial close, rather than paying interest only on the money as it is drawn. On the other hand, the proceeds of the bond issue can be kept on deposit by the project company until they are needed, and the interest on this deposit used to offset the extra interest cost on the bond. But under normal market conditions—when short-term rates are lower than long-term rates—there will be a net loss on this offset (*i.e.* the interest on the deposit will be less than the equivalent interest payable on the bond), known as 'negative arbitrage', which has to be taken into account when considering the overall cost of the bond financing.

The redeposit of the bond proceeds also creates an interest-rate risk. The bank taking the deposit will normally only pay interest on a floating-rate basis, and so if interest rates go down the offset against the bond interest costs will be less than expected, which could result in a deficit in the project company's construction budget. It is therefore necessary for the project company to obtain a fixed rate on the re-deposit, which is provided by a bank swapping the floating-rate interest on the deposit for a fixed rate. This is known as a 'guaranteed investment contract' (GIC).[9] As the GIC provider takes no risk on the project company, a GIC can be procured from the market on a competitive basis.

§24.2.12 Breakage Costs on Bonds or Fixed-Rate Loans

A bond investor, or any lender providing a fixed-rate loan, also has a breakage cost if a bond is prepaid early, *e.g.* if the project company defaults, for exactly the same reason as the swap provider: if the rate at which the fixed-rate funds can be re-lent has gone down when the project company defaults, the bond investor makes a loss. However, the breakage cost on prepayment of a bond issue can be significantly higher than the breakage cost for an interest-rate swap, which magnifies the implications for both the project company and the contracting authority discussed above, because:

- The breakage cost is calculated as the NPV of all of the future bond debt service typically discounted at or near the equivalent government bond rate—a relatively low rate considering that the bondholder should be able to buy an equivalent bond with a higher yield, which of course would significantly reduce the breakage cost.

---

[9] Note that this term is also used with wider meanings in the United States, *e.g.* long-term deposits by pension funds with insurance companies.

Table 24.3   Bond breakage costs

Assumptions:
- Bond amount $1,000
- Repayment   20 years, annual annuity payments
- Interest rate (coupon)   6%

($) Year:	0	1	2	3	4	5	16	17	18	19	20
Interest payment at 6%		60	58	57	55	53	22	18	14	10	5
Principal repayment		27	29	31	32	34	65	69	73	78	82
Total debt services		87	87	87	87	87	87	87	87	87	87
Outstanding amount	**1,000**	**973**	**944**	**913**	**881**	**847**	**302**	**233**	**160**	**82**	**0**
Termination payments											
Lower rate (4%)	1,185	1,145	1,104	1,061	1,016	969	316	242	164	84	
Higher rate (8%)											
- without par floor	856	837	817	795	772	746	289	225	155	81	
- with par floor	1,000	973	944	913	881	847	302	233	160	82	

- The breakage calculation for a bond may be in one direction—*i.e.* if interest rates have gone down, the bondholder is compensated by the borrower, but if they have gone up, the bondholder does not pay over this profit to the project company. This is known as a 'par floor'.

The combination of these two requirements is known as a 'make-whole' clause.[10] Table 24.3 illustrates how it can work, based on the assumption of a $1,000 bond issue, at a coupon of 6%, with two examples of prepayment on early termination: one with an increase and the other with a decrease in interest rates at the time of termination. So, in year 5, when the outstanding amount is $847, if the termination discount rate has gone down to 4%, a breakage payment of $969 will be due, the extra amount being required to cover the loss on redeploying the funds from 6% to 4%. On the other hand, if the termination discount rate is 8%, a profit is made on redeploying the funds at this higher rate, and taking this into account the breakage payment should be $746, but if a par floor operates, the payment will be the outstanding principal amount of $847 instead.

The par floor may seem unfair, but it should be borne in mind that the alternative is a capital loss by the bondholder, which may obviously be unattractive because of its effect on accounting results (unless the bondholder marks the value of its bonds to market anyway), and cause tax problems (because the bondholder may not be able to offset the

[10] Or a 'Spens' clause in the British bond market, named after the investment banker who imported it into this market.

capital loss against tax). It may be possible, in some bond markets, to avoid a make-whole payment by paying a higher coupon for the debt.

If the government-bond rate is taken as the termination discount rate, this means that the NPV of the whole of the difference between government bond rates and the rate charged to the project company—*i.e.* not just the market premium, but the credit margin as well (*cf.* §22.4.2), has to be paid. This is unreasonable, since the bond investor can easily go out and invest in another corporate-bond issue of a similar rating. The discount rate should therefore be somewhere between the government bond rate and the coupon on the project company's bond: this is typically a matter of *ad hoc* negotiation. The issue here is similar to that already discussed, of paying the NPV of future credit premiums on a swap breakage (*cf.* §24.2.6) but the potential costs involved are much greater, because the difference between the discount rate and the coupon rate is greater than a typical swap premium.

§24.2.13 Bid to Financial Close

So far, this discussion of interest-rate risks and hedging has dealt with the situation at financial close, and how interest-rate risk is hedged thereafter. But the bidder for a PPP project has an inherent interest-rate risk from the day of the bid. In order to offer a fixed price for the service fees, a cost of debt, including the underlying interest rate, must be assumed. If, by the time financial close is reached—perhaps a year or more after the bid— interest rates have gone up, the bidder's return will diminish, and in the worst case the project may become unfinanceable. The greater the leverage, and the longer the period between bid and financial close, the more serious the problem becomes. The sponsors can theoretically deal with this problem in two ways:

- include a safety margin for interest-rate movements in the bid—but of course this may make the bid uncompetitive; or
- hedge the interest rate in advance of financial close (perhaps through a swaption—*cf.* §24.2.10), and then transfer the hedge to the project company at financial close—but if the sponsors do not win the bid, or the project does not reach financial close, the cost of this hedging would not be recovered if it has gone out of the money; therefore, this is a course of action which a bidder would only take very near to financial close.

The first alternative is the general course of action in projects with lower leverage (70-80%), especially concessions, and indeed is the normal procedure in other sectors of the project-finance market besides PPPs. But in cases with high leverage, *e.g.* availability PPP accommodation projects, it may not offer the contracting authority the best VfM (unless all parties can be confident that the period from bid to financial close will be limited). This is because it implies paying for what may amount to an expensive option to cover the risk of interest-rate movements from the bid to financial close—*i.e.* this is part of the process of deciding which particular risks of a PPP contract it is cost-effective to transfer to the private sector, and which it makes sense for the public sector to retain (*cf.* §11.4). Moreover, if the public sector as a whole is undertaking a programme of PPPs, it is reasonable to suppose that losses from interest-rate movements on one project will be offset by gains on another as time goes on.

If the contracting authority is thus prepared to take the risk of interest-rate movements up to financial close, the bid documents (*cf.* §10.6.2) should specify standard market interest rates (*e.g.* swap rates) to be used by bidders to enable bids to be compared on a like-to-like basis (*cf.* §23.9.1). To give the contracting authority some assurance that it will not be faced with a project which becomes too expensive (unaffordable), these assumed rates should build in a reasonable safety margin over the current market.

The project company remains formally responsible for the interest-rate fixing at financial close: the rate produced is then used to calculate the final actual level of service fees, while maintaining the lenders' cover ratios and the investors' equity IRR at the same levels as those originally bid. However, it is self-evident that the project company has little interest in getting the best possible rates in this situation. The process therefore has to be supervised by the contracting authority (with its financial advisers), and the contracting authority has to agree to the final terms for the swap. If this procedure is used, the argument for competitive bids for the swap, either by syndicate banks bidding against each other or through the fronting-bank structure (*cf.* §24.2.8), becomes even stronger.

A further complication is introduced if the project company does not hedge its debt for the full tenor of the loan because the lenders and investors are willing to absorb some level of interest-rate risk based on their view of the financial market (*cf.* §24.2.7). If the contracting authority is adjusting the service fees to reflect the rate-fixing at financial close, should this be based on the actual rate paid for the shorter swap, or the notional rate that would be charged for the longer swap? In principle, it should be the latter, especially if it is a lower rate, but of course this raises difficult questions on how competitive pricing can be achieved.

As far as bond issues are concerned, pricing is more of a 'black box', and introducing competition is difficult (other than for underwriting fees and other ancillary matters such as the GIC rate). The bond underwriter is normally paid a fixed fee, irrespective of the final pricing of the bond, and therefore has a clear incentive to be less than aggressive on the pricing to ensure that the bonds are not left on its hands. It is possible to have a more competitive approach for a private placement, but whether the pricing for a publicly-quoted bond is competitive cannot really only be judged by comparing it with other similar quoted bonds already in the market; as the market for project-finance bonds, and their liquidity, is limited, this may be difficult to do.

In general, it is not prudent for a contracting authority to give any advance protection for interest rates before financial close, any more than any other part of the PPP contract arrangements should be activated before everything is signed and effective. However, there is one aspect of interest-rate fixing where this may be necessary. If a very large bond issue is to be placed in the market, the effect may be to push up market rates and so also the service fees. The investment bank placing the bond issue may therefore undertake a 'market stabilisation' exercise in advance of the bond issue—in effect hedging against a future rise in rates by selling government bonds forward. If rates for the bond issue do go up, the profit on the forward sale of the government bonds will offset this. A similar exercise can be carried out if a large interest-rate swap is to be placed in the market. In such cases the contracting authority has to underwrite any loss which arises from this exercise, *i.e.* if rates go down, but this stabilisation will still have effectively fixed the price of the bond in advance of its issue.

§24.2.14 Should the Project Company Have to Hedge Interest Rates?

The interest-rate hedging by the project company discussed in this chapter is highly ineffi-cient from the public-sector point of view. It ignores the fact that individual PPP projects are normally part of a larger programme, and hedging them one-by-one is far more expensive than dealing with them on a pool basis. Moreover, the hedging of a PPP programme has to be put in the context of the government's economic policy, which determines the very inter-est rates which may require hedging—in other words the government is hedging itself.

The only reason interest rates cannot be hedged through adjusting the service fees (and then hedged on a pooled basis for all PPP projects by the contracting authority or central government) is that, as discussed in §24.2.1, it is likely to raise balance-sheet issues for the public-sector budget. If this is not the case, it makes most sense to adjust the service fees for floating-rate interest movements and hedge these on a pooled basis.

Possibly the contracting authority could enter into separate interest-rate swap agreements with project companies. The difficulty with this is that the contracting authority then assumes the breakage risk on the project company, but will not be allowed by the lenders to have a *pari-passu* claim with them on the project company's assets, or to exercise any serious controls on the project company to limit the breakage risk (*cf.* §25.5.1). Hence there is a credit risk (which could be covered by the lending banks guaranteeing the swaps).

It might also be possible for the contracting authority to enter into a swap or other hedging instrument in advance of financial close, to fix its own costs, and then transfer this at financial close to the project company. However, this is quite complex from a legal point of view, and just as pre-fixing interest rates has dangers for the investors, it obvi-ously also involves extra risk for the contracting authority, and may put pressure on the contracting authority to rush the financial close.

Another approach to interest-rate hedging is for fixed-rate financing to be provided by the public sector, but with the credit risk taken by banks (*cf.* §18.11).

§24.3 INFLATION ISSUES

Unfortunately, issues relating to the effect of inflation on PPP contracts can be far more complex than those relating to interest-rate risk. Because of the cumulative effect of infla-tion, relatively small annual changes have a substantial effect over the 20-30-year tenor of a PPP contract. The contracting authority will also inevitably be far more involved in these issues because service fees are usually at least partially indexed against inflation, for which there are several reasons:

- Payments under FM subcontracts are always inflation-indexed.
- Bidders are likely to charge heavily for project-company exposure to the risk of infla-tion on their opex ('variable costs'), which is unlikely to be good VfM from the con-tracting authority's point of view.
- The contracting authority's own resources, *e.g.* from tax revenues, may themselves be linked to inflation, and therefore it is logical to index accommodation-PPP service fees to match this. The same can apply to user fees for concessions.

- Value testing may deal with soft-FM costs, but inflation of the hard-FM costs cannot be dealt with in this way (*cf.* §15.6.7).
- If the facility had been procured by the public sector, these variable costs would have been subject to price inflation anyway; it is therefore logical to index part of the service fees against inflation, insofar as these payments relate to similar project-company costs.

§24.3.1 Nominal and Real

By way of introduction, the rather confusing terminology of inflation needs to be explained. A 'nominal' cash flow is one that *includes* the effect, if any, of inflation, and a 'real' cash flow is one that *excludes* the effect of inflation. Thus, a real payment is one in 'money of today' even if at a future date, whereas a nominal payment is the amount actually paid (or expected to be paid) in 'money of the future'. Furthermore, a payment in a PPP cash flow may be described as 'fixed', *i.e.* a nominal payment unaffected by inflation, or 'variable', *i.e.* a real payment subject to inflation.[11]

To give some examples of real and nominal figures in the context of the cash flow for a PPP project:

- Service fees are priced on a real basis, but partly or wholly subject to inflation indexation. So, for example, a real payment of $100 *p.a.*, 50% indexed against inflation, assuming inflation of 4% *p.a.* [50 + (50 × 104%)], will produce a nominal payment of $102 after one year.
- Debt service is normally a fixed series of payments, which are thus on a nominal basis (except for inflation-indexed financing, for which see below). Therefore, a debt-service payment of $100 in a year's time, where inflation is 4%, is $96.15 in real terms (*i.e.* $96.15 × 104% = 100), and $100 in nominal terms. (This reduction of a future fixed nominal amount to a real amount is called a deflation calculation.)
- Similarly, bidders usually assess their equity IRR on a nominal basis.
- Construction subcontract costs are normally fixed, and hence these costs are nominal payments like debt service, as are most of the other elements of the capex (there may be small exceptions such as the project company's staff costs during the construction phase, which will be variable).
- The project company's opex is usually projected on a real basis, and then increased for the expected rate of inflation. (Operating subcontract payments may be payable on a variable basis, *i.e.* indexed for inflation.)

If a DCF calculation is required (*e.g.* for a bid comparison—*cf.* §10.6.5—or to calculate a termination sum—*cf.* §17.2.3), both the cash flow to be discounted and the discount rate itself must be on the same basis, *i.e.* either nominal or real. Therefore if, the discount rate,

---

[11] A 'nominal' interest rate is sometimes referred to, but, to avoid confusion, not in this book. This expression is used where interest is payable less than annually; the nominal rate is the stated annual rate. Thus, if the nominal rate is 5%, and payment is made, and thus interest is compounded, semi-annually, the actual rate of interest—known as the effective annual rate—is 5.06%, because the amount of interest received at the end of one year includes a half-year's interest compounded at 2.5%. Other terms used include 'constant' for real figures and 'current' for nominal.

such as the PSDR, is a real rate, and it is to be used to discount nominal cash flows, then the discount rate has to be converted into a nominal rate, using the 'Fisher formula':

$$n = (1 + r) \times (1 + i) - 1$$

where: n = nominal discount rate, r = real discount rate and i = rate of inflation.

Thus, if the PSDR is 3.5% real and inflation is projected at 2.5%, the nominal discount rate is

$$n = (1 + 3.5\%) \times (1 + 2.5\%) - 1 = 6.0875\%$$

and not, as might be thought, 6% (3.5% + 2.5%). So, if we have $1,060,875 in a year's time, and want to discount this at a rate of 3.5% real plus 2.5% inflation, the discount calculation (*cf.* §3.2) is:

$$\frac{1,060,875}{(1 + 6.0875\%)} = \$1,000,000$$

Alternatively, the cash flow can be converted into real figures, and then discounted at the real rate. So, to use the same example, $1,060,875 nominal after one year, with inflation of 2.5%, equates to $1,035,000 real ($1,060,875 ÷ 1.025), which when discounted at 3.5% is $1,000,000 today.

It might be thought that if the service fees are fully indexed against inflation, it is unnecessary to take account of inflation in the cash-flow projections, but this is not likely to be the case, as illustrated by Table 24.4, which shows the effect of mixing nominal and real figures in the calculation. This table shows two identical cash flows. (A) ignores the effect of inflation, and produces a level annual cash flow, but this is not correct because the debt-service figures are not affected by inflation and therefore have to be deflated to produce a real cash flow. (A) thus mixes up nominal and real cash flows, and the correct nominal and real figures are those in (B).

To avoid confusion between real and nominal figures, it is thus generally best to prepare financial models with the cash flows calculated on a nominal basis, *i.e.* taking account of projected inflation. Another reason for preparing cash-flow figures on a nominal rather a real basis is that tax calculations are based on nominal cash flows. In the example in Table 24.4, if the nominal cash flow in (B) were taxed at 50%, tax actually payable in year 3 would be $81, or $74 in real terms, and it would be wrong to prepare a real cash flow as in (A), which would show tax payable as $63. Moreover, tax depreciation (*cf.* §23.6.1) is based on the original nominal cost of the project, and no allowance is normally made for inflation over the years during which this depreciation allowance is offset against tax.

§24.3.2 Inflation Indices and Projections

In a PPP project's cash flow, 'inflation' can be on more than one basis:

- If service fees are adjusted for inflation, this adjustment will be linked to a specific inflation index (*e.g.* consumer price inflation—CPI).

Table 24.4 Effect of inflation on project cash flow

Assumptions:
- Revenues $1,000 p.a., indexed for inflation
- Opex $400 p.a., also subject to inflation
- Debt $2,000
- Repayment   5 years, annuity basis
- Interest rate   6%

($) Year:	1	2	3	4	5	Total
(A)—0% inflation						
Debt outstanding	2,000	1,645	1,269	870	448	
Revenues	1,000	1,000	1,000	1,000	1,000	5,000
Opex	− 400	− 400	− 400	− 400	− 400	− 2,000
Debt interest	120	− 99	− 76	− 52	− 27	− 374
Debt repayment	− 355	− 376	− 399	− 423	− 448	− 2,000
Net cash flow	**125**	**125**	**125**	**125**	**125**	**626**
ADSCR	1.26	1.26	1.26	1.26	1.26	
(B)—3% inflation						
Inflation index	1.03	1.06	1.09	1.13	1.16	
Revenues	1,000	1,030	1,061	1,093	1,126	5,309
Opex	− 400	− 412	− 424	− 437	− 450	− 2,124
Debt interest	− 120	− 99	− 76	− 52	− 27	− 374
Debt repayment	− 355	− 376	− 399	− 423	− 448	− 2,000
Net cash flow (nominal)	**125**	**143**	**162**	**181**	**201**	**812**
Net cash flow (real)	**122**	**135**	**148**	**161**	**173**	**738**
ADSCR	1.26	1.30	1.34	1.38	1.42	

- The project company's payments under, say, an O&M subcontract are usually adjusted against the same inflation index (cf. §24.3.12).
- Other opex for the project company, e.g. insurance costs or staff costs, while variable, and hence affected by inflation, will not be linked to any specific inflation index. In fact, changes in costs such as insurance may vary dramatically from general inflation (cf. §24.3.12).

The contracting authority has to consider the most appropriate inflation index to use for indexing the PPP payments (this should not be left to bidders as it could make comparing different bids difficult); there are two schools of thought on this:

- The index should relate to the business sector in which the project company is operating, *e.g.* a construction- or building maintenance-specific index.
- A general consumer-price index such as CPI should be used, on the grounds that the subcontractors providing the relevant services over the life of the PPP contract can themselves influence a specific index.

The choice between the two relates to the nature of the costs being indexed: if they constitute a long-term and large-scale element of the overall service fees, there will be more pressure for an industry-specific index. The other factor is whether subcontractors are willing to accept a contract with a non-specific index, as it is generally imprudent for the project company to agree with the contracting authority to receive payments indexed on one basis, and then also to agree to make payments to subcontractors indexed on a different basis (*cf.* §24.3.12). A minor divergence between the two indices can have a very major effect on the cash flow over a period of time, and hence subcontractors may be reluctant to sign very long-term contracts. A compromise between the two choices, to reduce this risk, is to index at CPI plus $x\%$.

However, there is an argument for only allowing indexation at 'inflation minus $x\%$', on the grounds that this encourages long-term efficiency savings by the project company. Otherwise the PPP contract 'freezes' the efficiency requirements on day one and prevents the contracting authority from making such savings it the way it could were it operating the facility itself (*cf.* §28.9.4). Arguably as FM or O&M costs generally inflate faster than CPI, using CPI alone as the inflation index for the PPP contract achieves this result.

§24.3.3 Inflation Forecasts

Whether variable costs are specifically indexed against inflation in the PPP contract or not, an assumption has to be made in the financial model on the projected rate or rates of inflation to be applied against each element of variable costs. The public sector as a whole should have a common approach to inflation assumptions to be used by bidders and in bid evaluation (including the PSC if there is one), but there tends not be an obvious source for such assumptions. Government or central bank inflation projections (as well as those produced by independent sources such as the Organisation for Economic Co-operation and Development (OECD)) may run for no more than five years, whereas a PPP may need assumptions for 20-30 years. If the central bank has an inflation target, this can be used for projections, but of course this is a target rather than reality. A long-term inflation rate based on market views can be derived from government inflation-indexed bonds, but for the reasons discussed in §24.3.8 this will be somewhat artificial. In the end, the choice of an inflation assumption may be no more than a rough guess, but in making this choice various questions arise, *e.g.*:

- Should this assumption be the same for all the elements of revenues and costs mentioned above?
- Is the prudent assumption a high rate of inflation or a low rate?

Sensitivities should be run on the financial model to show the effect of different approaches on these questions. Bidders and lenders also have to consider these issues, and for the purposes of their own evaluation may take a different view of inflation than that used by the contracting authority.

§24.3.4 Effect of Indexed Service Fees on Financing Structure

As discussed in §15.3.2, service fees should be level throughout the life of the PPP contract. However, it is generally accepted that the arguments against a 'back-ended' payment profile do not apply insofar as this is caused by indexing the payments for inflation—*i.e.* inflation-indexed service fees are kept level from year to year in real rather than nominal terms.

In concessions, service fees are usually fully indexed against inflation; in availability PPPs, as discussed below, payments may also be wholly indexed, or only partially indexed. Concentrating for now on the case where service fees are fully indexed, this has a significant potential effect on both the financing structure and the service fees, as illustrated by Table 24.5. As this table shows, the annual debt service over 25 years for a loan amount of $1,000 at an interest rate of 6%, on an annuity repayment basis, is $78. If the lenders require a minimum ADSCR of 1.20×, this means that the annual service fees (ignoring the further amounts needed to cover opex, and assuming the cover ratio also covers the equity IRR—*cf.* §23.5) have to be $94 ($78 × 1.2).

But if the service fees are indexed against inflation, which is assumed in the calculations to be projected at 2.5% *p.a.*, the year 1 service fee can be reduced from 94 to 74, if the loan repayments can be 'back-ended' to take advantage of the indexed revenues increasing over time. As can be seen a steady 1.20× cover ratio is maintained (although this does increase the average life of the loan). However, in total the service fees are greater, reflecting the fact that the loan is being repaid more slowly, and more interest is thus paid, as can be seen in the totals of the relevant columns. Similarly, the indexed service fees are greater in real terms.

§24.3.5 Should Service Fees be Fully Indexed?

Table 24.5 and (B) in Table 24.4 may suggest that the contracting authority, the project company and its lenders should all be quite happy with a fully-indexed stream of service fees. However, the issues here are quite complex, and the different parties may have different views on the matter.

As Table 24.5 shows, the result of 100% indexation is that in real terms the PPP contract becomes more expensive because the debt is repaid more slowly, and thus harder to justify on VfM grounds. Nonetheless, there is obviously a political temptation to get a PPP facility built at a cost which may be affordable in year 1 and leave someone else to worry about affordability in later years.

But other problems arise from such 'over-indexation' of service fees (*i.e.* the indexed proportion being greater than the proportion that the project company's costs affected by inflation—mainly opex—bear to the total costs). In a typical accommodation PPP, for

Table 24.5   Effect of inflation-indexed service fees

Assumptions:

Loan amount ($)	1,000
Tenor	25 years
Interest rate	6.0%
Inflation	2.5%
Required ADSCR	1.20×

($)	Year: 0	1	2	3	4	10	11	12	24	25	Total
Fixed service fees											
Service fees (nominal)	94	94	94	94	94	94	94	94	94	94	**2,347**
Loan outstanding		1,000	982	962	942	791	760	727	143	74	
Interest		60	59	58	57	47	46	44	9	4	**956**
Loan repayment		18	19	20	22	31	33	35	70	74	**1,000**
Total debt service		78	78	78	78	78	78	78	78	78	**1,956**
ADSCR (×)		*1.2*	*1.2*	*1.2*	*1.2*	*1.2*	*1.2*	*1.2*	*1.2*	*1.2*	
Average life of loan	*15 years*										
Service fees (real)		92	89	87	85	73	72	70	52	51	**1,730**
Inflation-indexed service fees											
Service fees (nominal)	72	74	76	78	80	92	95	97	130	134	**2,526**
Loan outstanding		1,000	998	995	990	914	892	866	202	105	
Interest		60	60	60	59	55	54	52	12	6	**1,105**
Loan repayment		2	3	5	7	22	25	29	97	105	**1,000**
Total debt service		62	63	65	66	77	79	81	109	111	**2,105**
ADSCR (×)		*1.2*	*1.2*	*1.2*	*1.2*	*1.2*	*1.2*	*1.2*	*1.2*	*1.2*	
Average life of loan	*17 years*										
Service fees (real)		72	72	72	72	72	72	72	72	72	**1,803**

example, only about 40% of its costs relate to opex and so are subject to inflation, with the fixed-cost balance relating to debt service and distributions to investors.

On the one hand, the contracting authority is taking a substantial risk on inflation not being higher than the projected rate, which may or may not be an issue depending on whether the contracting authority's own resources move in step with its liabilities under the PPP contract, *i.e.* whether it can be confident that these resources will also increase in line with inflation. This is obviously a matter of central government policy. In Britain, for example, where central government funding is often used to fund local governments' PPP service fees, such funding comprises a fixed stream of payments intended to cover some or all of the capex inherent in the service fees. However, the remaining funding needed—largely to cover opex—has to be paid from the local government's other sources of revenue (which are likely to vary with inflation).

The result may be that, say, 60% of a local government's resources for the PPP project are fixed and 40% are variable. Clearly lower initial service fees can be produced by making them 100% variable against inflation instead of 40%. But this means that the local-government contracting authority is taking the risk of a long-term mismatch in its resources for paying the service fees—its own resources to be used for the 40% of variable service fees have to increase by $2^1/_2$ times the rate of inflation—which is difficult to justify on policy grounds. This is of course part of the wider issue for the contracting authority and the central government, of ensuring that the overall public-sector budget will support a PPP programme in the long-term (*cf.* §9.3, §28.3).

On the other hand, in the case of a concession, as already mentioned, 100% indexation of service fees is not uncommon. (To be precise, the project company may have the right to index service fees up to a cap equal to 100% of inflation, but may choose not to do so.) Assuming the initial service fees are acceptable (*cf.* §9.2.3), users would not normally object to them being increased each year by the rate of inflation.

Even if the contracting authority can initially satisfy itself that 100% indexation of the service fees is appropriate, this may still raise issues for the project company's lenders and investors. The danger of over-indexation is that a large part of the project company's cash flow is required for debt service, which is fixed—if the outturn (actual) inflation is *lower* than the projections on which the financing structure was based, and hence revenues are lower than projected, there will be problems with this debt service.

This is illustrated by Table 24.6, which assumes that the debt-service schedule in Table 24.5 has been adopted, with inflation projected at 2.5%, but in fact outturn inflation is 1%.

As can be seen, the result is bad from the lenders' point of view, with debt-service coverage disappearing and eventually there would be insufficient cash flow to repay the debt, as well as for the investors since they would lose money from year 13 onwards.

This risk of over-indexation and low inflation is most acute where the leverage is relatively high, and projected inflation is also relatively high. (The latter is always a temptation for a project company with service fees inflation-indexed 100%, as it makes the operating cash flow higher, and hence more debt can be raised.) So as mentioned previously 100% inflation indexation for concessions, where the leverage is typically lower, is less of an issue.

Table 24.6   Effect of lower outturn inflation on an over-indexed service fee

($) Year:	1	2	3	4	10	11	12	24	25	Total
Service fees (nominal)	73	73	74	75	79	80	81	91	92	2,058
Total debt service	62	63	65	66	77	79	81	109	111	
ADSCR	*1.18*	*1.16*	*1.14*	*1.13*	*1.03*	*1.02*	*1.00*	*0.84*	*0.83*	

§24.3.6 Inflation-Indexed Loans

Just as interest-rate risk can be eliminated by fixed-rate financing or an interest-rate swap, the lenders' and investors' low-inflation risk discussed above can also be eliminated by an inflation-indexed loan (which may be a bond or a loan, the latter usually by a non-banking institution such as an insurance company or pension fund), or an inflation swap (for which *cf.* §24.3.9). As will be seen, this type of financing may bring other benefits for both the project company and the contracting authority, but it also carries hidden risks.

The pricing and structure of inflation-indexed bonds is based on that for inflation-indexed government bonds[12] in the same way as the pricing for fixed-rate loans is linked to that of fixed-rate government bonds (*cf.* §22.4.2). Such bonds are issued with a real interest-rate coupon, and interest and principal payments under the bond are then indexed against the agreed inflation index. For example, if an inflation-indexed loan of $1,000 is made at a real interest rate of 2%, and inflation for the first year is 2.5%, the amount owing at the end of the first year is:

- principal: $1,000 \times (1 + 2.5\%) = $1,025.00
- interest: $20 \times (1 + 2.5\%) \quad = $20.50
- total: $\qquad\qquad\qquad\qquad = $1,045.50.

This result can be checked using the Fisher formula:

$$n = (1 + 2.0\%) \times (1 + 2.5\%) - 1 = 4.55\%$$

The NPV of $1,045.5 discounted at 4.55% for one year is $1,000.

This demonstrates that the lender has received a real return of 2%.

In year 2, the calculation (assuming the same rate of inflation) is:

- principal: $1,025 \times (1 + 2.5\%) = $1,050.63
- interest: $20 \times (1 + 2.5\%)^2 \quad = $21.01
- total: $\qquad\qquad\qquad\qquad = $1,071.64.

Note that the interest is still calculated on the real amount of the loan ($1,000) not the nominal amount ($1,025), but then adjusted for two years' cumulative inflation. The total cash flow is now $20.5 in year 1 and $1,071.64 in year 2 (assuming the loan is repaid at that point). Using the same discount rate of 4.55% to discount this cash flow gives an NPV of $1,000—again confirming that the real return is 2%. It can also be seen from these calculations that the principal amount outstanding under an inflation-indexed loan initially increases over time (assuming there are no principal repayments), unlike a fixed-rate loan, where the amount outstanding never increases.

The calculations are more complex for a project-finance cash flow, since unlike government bonds, an indexed bond for a project financing is repaid in instalments. A typical calculation for an inflation-indexed bond, repaid on an annuity basis, is set out in Table 24.7. This can be used to hedge inflation-indexed service fees which would

---

[12] These have a variety of names such as 'treasury inflation-protected securities' or TIPS (the United States), 'commonwealth treasury indexed bonds' (Australia), 'indexed gilts' (Britain) and 'real return bonds' (Canada).

Table 24.7   Inflation-indexed bond

Assumptions:
- Loan amount *($)*   1,000
- Loan tenor   20 years
- Inflation-indexed loan:
  - Annuity repayment (in real terms)
  - Real interest rate   2%
  - Projected inflation   2.5%

($) Year:	0	1	2	3	4	5	16	17	18	19	20	Total
Real payments												
Interest		20	19	18	17	17	6	5	4	2	1	
Principal repayment		41	42	43	44	45	55	56	58	59	60	
Total debt service		61	61	61	61	61	61	61	61	61	61	1,223
Loan balance	1,000	959	917	874	830	786	233	176	119	60	0	
Nominal payments (=real payments × inflation index)												
Inflation index	1.000	1.025	1.051	1.077	1.104	1.131	1.485	1.522	1.560	1.599	1.639	
Interest		21	20	20	19	19	9	7	6	4	2	250
Principal repayment		42	44	46	48	50	82	86	90	94	98	1,288
Total debt service		63	64	66	68	69	91	93	95	98	100	1,539
Loan balance	1,000	983	963	941	917	889	346	268	185	96	0	

otherwise be financed with a 'back-ended' fixed-rate loan similar to that in Table 24.5. If inflation goes down, reducing the service fees, the debt service for the inflation-indexed bond will go down *pro rata*, so maintaining the lenders' cover ratios. This avoids the problem set out in Table 24.6. If inflation goes up both the service fees and the debt service go up. The real equity IRR is also maintained at a constant figure thanks to this inflation hedging.

§24.3.7 Breakage Costs

As with bonds or fixed-rate loans (*cf.* §24.2.12), the potential breakage cost on an inflation-indexed bond has to be borne in mind. The breakage cost of an inflation-indexed loan is calculated by:

- taking the stream of future real payments;
- inflating these by the implied inflation rate (for the remaining tenor of the loan) at the time of the breakage; and
- discounting them at the current-market fixed rate (for the remaining tenor of the loan) at the time of the breakage.

Table 24.8   Inflation-indexed bond—breakage costs

($)	Year:	0	1	2	3	4	5	16	17	18	19	20
2.5% inflation		1,000	983	963	941	917	889	346	268	185	96	0
3.5% inflation		1,000	992	982	969	953	933	404	317	221	115	0
Increased breakage cost		0	10	19	28	36	44	58	48	35	19	0

On the basis of the repayment schedule set out in Table 24.7, the amount that has to be repaid if the inflation-indexed loan is terminated early with no change in any of the assumptions is the balance shown as the nominal loan balance, *e.g.* $889 in year 5, identical to that for the fixed-rate loan.

But if the inflation outturn is above the projected 2.5%, the result can be serious, as illustrated in Table 24.8. This takes the same real debt-service payments as set out in Table 24.7, but increases the outturn inflation from 2.5% to 3.5% from year 1; the discount rate for the breakage calculation is assumed to derive from the unchanged 2% real interest rate and a 3.5% projected inflation rate, *i.e.* 5.57%. The resulting increases in breakage costs are shown. Note that the effect of any make-whole clause (*cf.* §24.2.12) is ignored in these breakage calculations.

The 2.5% inflation figures produce a similar pattern of breakage costs as a fixed-rate bond (*cf.* Table 24.3). But as can be seen the increased outturn inflation means that breakage of the indexed bond initially becomes relatively more and more expensive over time. (In the example in Table 24.8 the peak breakage cost is $74 in years 11-12, after which it declines.) This is because past history is of no relevance for an interest-rate swap breakage calculation, which is only affected by market rates for the remainder of the loan tenor at the time of the breakage. However, on an inflation-indexed loan, a higher rate of inflation builds up the nominal principal balance, and the breakage calculation in this case reflects this. A relatively small cumulative annual excess over the projected rate of inflation therefore has a relatively large effect on the breakage costs for an inflation-indexed loan. So, although an inflation-indexed loan may bring benefits, it does involve significant extra contingent risks.

§24.3.8 Inflation Arbitrage

Inflation-indexed loans have another pricing advantage—under normal financial market conditions— as they can produce a lower debt-service cost than equivalent fixed-rate loans. This is because the underlying government inflation-indexed bonds tend to have a lower real yield than equivalent fixed-rate bonds. This is the result of:

- governments issuing limited quantities of indexed bonds, even though there is usually a high demand from institutions such as pension funds; and
- indexed bonds effectively offering 'insurance' against high rates of inflation (which lead to high interest rates, which in their turn erode the value of fixed-rate bonds); this has an inherent value which is also reflected in the lower real yield for indexed bonds.

For example, a fixed-rate government bond may have a nominal yield of 4.5%, whereas an equivalent inflation-indexed bond may have a real yield of 1.5%. The implicit rate of inflation in the inflation-indexed bond is 2.96%—*i.e.* this is the 'break-even' inflation rate which would result in the indexed bond's nominal outturn cost being the same as that for the equivalent fixed-rate bond. (Again, using the Fisher formula this is calculated as [(1 + 1.5%) × (1 + 2.96%) − 1 = 4.5%].) Typically, break-even inflation is higher than the real market expectation for inflation, because the yield of the inflation-indexed bonds has been pushed down for the reasons discussed above.

Suppose the project company is happy with an inflation projection of 2.5% compared to the implicit rate of 2.96% above: if it raises debt on an inflation-indexed basis, the nominal cost (ignoring the market and credit premiums—*cf.* §22.4.1) will be projected as 4.04% [(1 + 1.5%) × (1 + 2.5%) − 1], compared to 4.5% for fixed-rate debt, thus saving 0.46% *p.a.* In effect, the project company can arbitrage between the rate of inflation implicit in inflation-indexed bond yields, and its own expectation of inflation. This is another strong motivation, apart from hedging variable service fees, for using inflation-indexed debt as this benefit may of course be fed through to the contracting authority by way of lower service fees in the original bid.

A bidder can easily mix together the over-indexation and inflation arbitrage points by saying to a contracting authority, 'if you will index *x*% of the service fees I can take out an inflation-indexed loan and offer you a $*y* reduction in the initial payment.' In such cases the contracting authority has to distinguish between the risks of a higher level of indexation and whether an indexed financing offers a lower real cost than fixed-rate financing, and consider the benefits and drawbacks of each.

§24.3.9 Inflation Swaps

As with fixed-rate finance, inflation-indexed loans are primarily provided by the bond market, but the banking market produces the same 'synthetic' result through inflation swaps.[13] The inflation-swap rate (the 'strike price') is based on the implicit rate of inflation on an inflation-indexed government bond (*e.g.* 2.96% in the example in §24.3.8), to which is also added a market spread and a credit premium as for an interest-rate swap (*cf.* §24.2.4).

An inflation swap can work in two ways, both of which have the same final effect:

- As with an inflation-indexed loan, the project company can swap a stream of fixed payments equal to the debt service for equivalent variable payments. The project company is then receiving a variable income from the service fees, and paying a variable debt-service stream under the swap, so the two hedge each other.
- Alternatively, the project company can swap a stream of variable receipts equal to the service fees (or the portion of these which is to be hedged), for a stream of fixed receipts, thus hedging the fixed debt service.

---

[13] Known as 'RPI swaps' in Britain. RPI = Retail Price Index, the particular inflation index used for index-linked government bonds in Britain.

The net result of either in cash-flow terms is identical to an inflation-indexed loan, just as the net result of a fixed-rate loan, and a floating-rate loan with an interest-rate swap, are also identical, assuming of course that the market and credit premiums are the same in each case.

§24.3.10 LPI Swap

It should also be mentioned that, just as a collar is an alternative to an interest-rate swap (*cf.* §24.2.10), it is also possible to enter into a 'limited price inflation' (LPI) swap, whereby there is a floor and a ceiling on inflation increases and decreases. However, if the floor is made so high as to eliminate all downward movements in inflation, the pricing will be little different from a simple swap.

§24.3.11 Position of the Contracting Authority

From the point of view of the contracting authority, inflation hedging, whether by an inflation-indexed loan or an inflation swap, does not in any way hedge its own service-fee payments (in the availability PPP). In this respect, it is quite different from an interest-rate swap, which can fix service fees for the contracting authority as well as the project company and its lenders. In fact, the greater the level of inflation indexation on the service fees, the greater the risk on inflation which the contracting authority is taking, whether this is hedged by the project company or not. In principle, therefore, only if the contracting authority is confident that its resources will in fact rise in line with inflation over the whole life of the PPP contract (of which it is difficult to be certain), should over-indexation of the service fees be considered. Unfortunately, the affordability benefit of over-indexation may overwhelm objective consideration of its long-term risks.

If the service fees are over-indexed, inflation hedging may offer a saving in the debt-service costs which can feed through to the service fees (*cf.* §24.3.8). Even if such a saving is not offered, if the lenders are unhappy about the inflation risk, hedging may be an alternative to the lenders requiring a higher cover ratio for inflation-indexed service fees, with consequent effects on the level of these. Obviously, it is important to ensure that this issue is dealt with when the bidders and their lenders are still competing (or in a funding competition—*cf.* §22.6).

If the contracting authority is taking the risk of interest rates at financial close (*cf.* §24.2.13), a combined interest-rate and inflation swap very difficult to monitor, and therefore any cost benefit may be eroded at this stage. Inflation hedging may also significantly increase termination payments (*cf.* §24.3.9), where the contracting authority is liable for breakage costs (*cf.* §17.3-§17.5). On balance, therefore inflation hedging is quite difficult to justify from the contracting authority's point of view, especially in availability PPPs.

So, if service fees are over-indexed, can the contracting authority discourage inflation hedging by offering something in lieu? One possibility is to offer take back some of the inflation risk, if this offers better VfM than inflation hedging. This is done by indexing the service fees by a fixed amount for inflation—say 2.5% *p.a.*—which means that if inflation goes over 2.5% the contracting authority gains but if it goes below 2.5% it loses. Alternatively, the contracting authority can offer the equivalent of an LPI swap (*cf.* §24.3.10), *i.e.* a floor and ceiling on inflation adjustments in the service fees. (A one-way bet—*i.e.* only putting a floor on service fees—is obviously undesirable.) These structures avoid the problem of termination payments.

But clearly the simplest and most risk-free way of dealing with inflation is to balance the service fees between fixed and variable proportions which broadly match the project company's fixed and variable costs. This also reflects the structure of what the contracting authority's own costs would have been had it procured and operated the facility itself.

§24.3.12 Inflation-Index Mismatch Risk

It has already been mentioned (*cf.* §24.3.2) that it is not advisable for the project company to enter into subcontracts where the payments are indexed for inflation using a different index to that used for service fees. However, the project company may find it difficult to find subcontractors, especially for soft FM services (cleaning, catering, security, *etc.*), that are prepared to sign long-term contracts with the pricing only indexed against general rather than industry-specific inflation.

If soft-FM costs included within the scope of the PPP contract are a significant part of the variable opex against which the service fees are inflation-indexed, and the project company cannot get a subcontract with the costs indexed against the same inflation index as the service fees, there will be concern about a discrepancy between inflation of revenues and costs in this respect. Alternatively, the soft-FM subcontractor may agree to this matching of indexation on a short-term basis (say for 5 years) but not for the life of the PPP contract. Lenders may also have concerns about the long-term viability of the FM subcontract if its commercial basis is eroded through inflation.

Bidders can deal with this risk by adding a large contingency into the initial soft FM costs, but this is not necessarily the best VfM solution for the contracting authority. An alternative is therefore to use value testing (*cf.* §15.6.7). Care obviously has to be taken that this does not cause a problem for the contracting authority's balance-sheet treatment, and if the soft FM services are effectively split out in this way, this raises the question of whether they should be included in the scope of the PPP contract at all, as discussed in §15.6.7. Moreover, there is a problem of information asymmetry between public and private sector as to the bench-marks used in value testing, given the lack of publicly-available data on the pricing of such services, and value testing can encourage short-term under-pricing in bids.

Value testing as a method of hedging inflation mismatches can also be used for insurance costs (*cf.* §14.8), but it is less suitable for maintenance costs because these are partly a function of the original design and therefore something which should be taken into account in the bid (*cf.* §28.8). Value testing the cost of maintenance work destroys this link—if this risk is not left with the project company, there will be no incentive to control maintenance requirements through the original design of the facility.

§24.4 FOREIGN-EXCHANGE RISKS

Another possible macroeconomic risk is that of foreign-currency exchange-rate movements.[14] This can occur if the financing, service fees, capex or opex are in different currencies such as:

- concessions where users pay in foreign currencies, *e.g.* port or airport projects;
- in cases where there is a high component of imported capital equipment in the project, which is not so common in the infrastructure field (other than the power sector or in developing markets); or
- in countries where the long-term debt is raised in a foreign currency because it cannot be provided by the domestic banking market.

In most markets where there is access to deep domestic financing resources (or resources in the national currency), foreign-exchange risk is not a significant issue and if it does arise, the contracting authority would expect the project company to put in place its own hedging arrangements to mitigate any risk.

The issue can be more serious for where levels of financing in the national currency are less readily available particularly due to mismatches between the currency of debt-service obligations and the service fees, because the availability of hedging arrangements may be more limited. In this case the contracting authority may need to retain some of the risk of devaluation of the local currency if this is necessary for the economic viability of the project. This could include a subsidy arrangement for the contracting authority to meet the cost impact of the devaluation beyond a certain level (and a reduction of the service fee if the currency moves in the other direction) or a threshold could be established to trigger termination for *force majeure* with an agreed basis for a termination-sum payment (*cf.* §17.4).

In some sectors, parts of the service fee may be adjusted for variations in the exchange rate. For example, in the power sector, it is not uncommon to see the contracting authority assuming currency risk within the availability-charge payment mechanism (*cf.* §2.4.3). However, in other sectors, such as transport, where the levels of service fee can significantly affect levels of demand, passing the currency risk on to users through higher local currency charges may simply swap a currency risk problem for a demand risk problem (and probably also cause political problems).

DFIs have developed some hedging tools to help mitigate exchange risk; one approach, apart from lending in local currencies, is to provide guarantees to local banks or bond markets. However, this depends on the availability of long-term domestic sources of finance, which either may not be available or available at unattractively high rates of interest.

---

[14] This topic is covered in more detail in (Yescombe 2014, Chapter 10).

Apart from risks associated with the level of the exchange rate, there may also be risks with regard to currency convertibility or restrictions on repatriation of funds. These are political risks that have to be assessed by foreign investors and lenders. Again, DFIs, other multilateral bodies or the commercial insurance market can provide forms of insurance to mitigate this risk.

If the contracting authority (or relevant national public-sector body) is assuming foreign-exchange risk, it needs to take account of the contingent liability that is being assumed to ensure that it will be affordable if it occurs (*cf. §9.3.4*).

Lenders' Cash-Flow Controls, Security and Enforcement

§25.1 Introduction

This chapter looks at how the financial structuring and hedging issues discussed in the last two chapters feed through to the lenders' documentation, and in particular:

- how the lenders control the project company's cash flow (§25.2);
- the nature of the lenders' legal security (§25.3);
- loan default procedures (§25.4); and
- relationships between different classes of lenders (§25.5).

These are largely issues between the lenders and the project company (and its investors), but the contracting authority needs to review the lenders' documentation to ensure that there are no provisions which weaken or unduly inhibit the project company's ability to carry out its responsibilities under the PPP contract.

§25.2 Control of Cash Flow

The project company's cash flow is closely controlled by the lenders, both during the construction phase of the project, to ensure that the funds are being spent as planned, and during the operating phase, to ensure cash flow is applied according to the agreed priorities.

During the construction phase, a construction-cost budget (*cf.* §23.9.2) is agreed with the lenders, and any actual or projected excesses over the amounts set out in the major cost categories normally need to be approved by them as they occur or are projected, even if there is still enough overall financing available to complete the project. However, lenders should be discouraged from trying to set up too detailed a 'line-item' control of the budget; most of the construction-cost budget is contractually fixed, or represents financing costs, and some flexibility needs to be given to the project company to manage remaining minor variations in cost categories, especially if the overall project cost is not significantly affected. Similarly, during the operating phase, the lenders also exercise some control over the budget for costs under the project company's direct control (*i.e.* excluding those costs under subcontracts).

Apart from these budgetary controls, during the construction phase, the lenders control expenditure *via* the disbursement account (§25.2.1), and have the ability to stop disbursing funds if something goes wrong (§25.2.2).

During the operation phase, lenders set out priorities for application of cash flow (§25.2.3), require funds to be kept in reserve accounts to provide an additional cushion (§25.2.4) and also control distributions to investors (§25.2.5).

§25.2.1 Disbursement Account

The procedure for drawing on the loan to finance construction usually involves the project company presenting a formal drawing request several days in advance of the date on which funds are required (there is usually only one drawing a month). This drawing request:

- attaches a payment request from the construction subcontractor, certified by the lenders' technical adviser (*cf.* §22.2.7);
- summarises the purpose for which other disbursements are required (*e.g.* for project-company costs or debt interest);
- sets out how these costs are to be funded (*i.e.* by equity or debt, and if there are several loans, which one is to be drawn);
- compares the monthly and cumulative project costs with the construction budget;
- demonstrates that enough funds remain available to complete the project; and
- demonstrates compliance with any other conditions precedent to disbursements.

Both equity investment and loan disbursements are paid into a disbursement account[1] in the project company's name, one of a number of project accounts[2] or they are paid directly to the beneficiaries, *e.g.* the construction subcontractor. Although this and other bank accounts are in the project company's name, withdrawal of funds may require the consent of the agent bank or security trustee, and the account balances form part of the lenders' security. (Note that this procedure relates to bank loans—bond proceeds are drawn from the GIC account (*cf.* §24.2.11) as and when required, but the result in terms of budgetary control is similar.)

---

[1] Also known as the 'proceeds account'.

[2] Also known as 'control accounts' or 'escrow accounts'.

Lenders may control all payments from the disbursement account or allow the project company to make the payments for the purposes set out in its disbursement requests, only taking control of payments if there is a default. The latter is a more practical procedure—if a disbursement-request procedure as set out above is being used, there is no need for lenders to do anything other than monitor payments out of the account.

§25.2.2 Drawstops

If there is an event of default under the loan documentation (*cf.* §25.4), the lenders may refuse to advance further funds for construction of the project until this default is remedied to their satisfaction. This is known as a 'drawstop', and can be used, for example, to force the project company's investors put in more equity to fill any financing gap that has appeared, *e.g.* due to a cost overrun.

§25.2.3 The Cash-Flow 'Cascade'

Once the project company has started operating and earning revenues under the PPP contract, the lenders control its cash flow through the operation of a cash-flow cascade (or 'waterfall'), setting out their required order of priorities for the use of this cash. A typical order of priorities is:

1: Payment of opex, including the subcontractors and taxes, *i.e.* all the costs that the project company needs to pay to continue operating the project.
2: Fees and expenses due to the agent bank and security trustee, if any.
3: Interest on the debt and any swap or other hedging payments.*
4: Debt repayments (to the 'minimum' schedule if there is one—*cf.* §23.2.5—if so, remaining payments to the 'target' schedule come at 6).*
5: Payments to reserve accounts (*cf.* §25.2.4).
6: Cash sweep, if any (*cf.* §23.2.8).
7: Distributions to investors (*cf.* §25.2.5).
(* These may be accumulated on a month-by-month basis in a debt-payment reserve account—see below.)

Once all the funds required for the first category have been paid, remaining cash available is moved down to the second, and so on (like water flowing down a series of pools—hence the names for this system of cash-flow allocation). It follows that if there is insufficient cash to pay the first five items, no cash is distributed to the investors. Items 6 and 7 are usually only paid half-yearly, during a limited time window after calculations of the project company's results and hence the lenders' cover ratios for the previous six months (*cf.* §25.2.5).

Revenues can flow into the cascade in two ways:

- Lenders may require the project company to segregate funds for the first category of costs in a separate operating account under the project company's day-to-day control, leaving the other funds in a revenue account under the joint control of the agent bank or security trustee and the project company until the other cascade payments need to be made.
- Alternatively, all revenues may flow into one account, from which the cascade payments are made by the project company when required.

The latter is obviously preferable for the project company and generally more practical for day-to-day operations.

§25.2.4 Reserve Accounts

Cash is paid out of the cascade, as necessary, into various reserve accounts, which are under lenders' control like the other project accounts. These serve to protect the project company's liquidity should there be a temporary shortage of revenues or increase in opex, build up funds for particular purposes such as maintenance, or segregate special funds such as insurance proceeds. Although the contracting authority does not usually have any direct security or control over these accounts (except perhaps for maintenance, for which see below), as they are for the benefit of the lenders, there is an indirect benefit to the authority. This is because such accounts give some assurance of continuity of service while any cash-flow problems are being dealt with. On the other hand, it is in the interest of neither the contracting authority nor the investors in the project company for cash to be tied up unnecessarily in reserve accounts, since this delays distributions, so reducing the equity IRR, and may thus be reflected in higher service fees in the original bid than would otherwise have been necessary.

Reserve accounts may include:

— Debt-service reserve account (DSRA)

This account contains sufficient funds to pay the next debt-service (principal and interest) instalment, usually six months' worth of debt service. If the project company cannot pay some or all of the debt service from its normal cash flow (or a debt-payment reserve account, if any—see below), funds are taken out of this account to do so. The DSRA has to be established at the beginning of the operating phase. There are two ways of doing this:

  • including the DSRA as part of the construction-cost budget for the project, and filling it up at the end of the construction phase; and
  • funding the DSRA from operating cash flow under the cascade (which means that it is filled up as cash flow comes in from initial operations, and thus until it is filled up no distributions can be made to the investors).

The first approach is preferable from the investors' point of view, because most of the funds required for the DSRA are funded by the lenders (i.e. pro rata to the debt portion of the debt/equity ratio) rather than out of the equity cash flow. It also has the benefit from the lenders' point of view that they know that the DSRA is funded as soon as the project begins operation. As a halfway house between these two alternative approaches, the project company may be allowed to draw funds for the DSRA at the end of the construction phase from any unused or contingency funding not required for any other purpose.

To improve their equity IRR, the sponsors may provide the lenders with a bank letter of credit (L/C) or, if acceptable, corporate guarantees, in lieu of a DSRA, which avoids this cash being trapped in the project company (but in such cases, they cannot have a claim against the project company for any drawings on the L/C, as this creates inter-creditor problems—*cf.* §25.5). And another variant on this theme is for the lenders themselves to provide a standby debt-service loan in lieu of the DSRA: this can be drawn, and must be paid back, in the same way as drawings on a DSRA.

Some lenders may accept the provision of an interest reserve account only (*i.e.* with a balance equal to the next interest payment due), perhaps coupled with the establishment of a debt-payment reserve account, as follows.

— Debt-payment reserve account

This account may be used (in addition to a DSRA) to accumulate funds on a month-by-month basis to pay the next instalment of principal and interest, instead of leaving the funds in the project company's operating account (usually if the project company's revenues flow into one account, instead of being split into operating and revenue accounts as described above). If so, the account is emptied at the end of each payment period to pay the interest and principal instalment then due.

— Maintenance-reserve account (MRA)

The original purpose of an MRA in project-finance structures was to deal with projects that have a major-maintenance cycle (*e.g.* a power plant that has to be maintained every five years, with most of the maintenance costs thus being incurred every five years rather than annually); in such cases, the MRA smooths out this maintenance 'spike', and ensures that the funds are there when they are needed, by placing one-fifth of the estimated maintenance costs in the MRA every year, and then emptying the account to pay for the maintenance in year five. This is obviously relevant to PPP projects involving process plant with this kind of maintenance cycle, such as a waste incinerator. It is also relevant to fixed infrastructure projects such as roads, which may have to fund major maintenance such as a resurfacing, say, after 15 years (although in such cases, the build-up of the MRA may not be continuous, but begin, say, 5 years before the maintenance work is required), and other projects where lifecycle costs are significant. However, the effect is to add another cost to PPPs compared to public-sector procurement, because in the latter case, there would not be a need to accumulate maintenance reserves (and hence pay extra financing costs as a result) years in advance.

There is also a danger that if the project company defaults, it is the lenders who have security over and so will take the cash in the MRA, if necessary, to repay part of their loan, so the contracting authority will end up paying twice for the same maintenance; this suggests that the contracting authority should have a prior claim on the MRA in case of default by the project company, or its balance should be offset against any termination sum (*cf.* §17.2).

While the interests of the contracting authority and lenders are usually aligned in ensuring that there is adequate funding available for major maintenance/lifecycle costs, in some cases the contracting authority may also require that an MRA is a condition of the PPP contract, especially if corporate finance is being used (*cf.* §21.6) or the debt is of a maturity well short of the tenor of the PPP contract. The contracting authority may even have some rights over how and when cash from the MRA is used.

An MRA is less relevant to accommodation and other projects where hard FM may fluctuate somewhat from year to year, but not dramatically (other than perhaps some lifecycle costs such as replacement of a heating boiler). Some lenders require a 'rolling' MRA in such cases—e.g. the MRA should be funded with enough cash to cover the next two or three years' maintenance (or say 100% of what is required next year, 50% of the following year and 25% of the following year), the amounts required being agreed by the lenders' technical adviser. This does not remove the long-term risk of such costs being higher than expected (cf. §13.6) and there is really no reason for cash to be trapped in the project company to this extent. The creation of such unnecessary reserve accounts reduces the investors' equity IRR, and so will probably push up the level of the service fees.

On the other hand, at the time of a refinancing (cf. §26.2), there may be a temptation for the project company to persuade new lenders to reduce the balance of the MRA. If the contracting authority has to consent to the refinancing, this is an aspect which should be considered carefully as it may not be in the long-term interests of the project and continuity of service.

— Tax reserve account

If the project company is projected to incur a significant tax liability in one year, but does not have to pay the tax until a later year (§23.6.2), a tax reserve account is normally established to set aside the cash for this purpose. Other 'smoothing' reserve accounts of this nature may be established to cover deferred liabilities or irregular costs if they would have a significant effect on the lenders' ADSCR.

— Change in law reserve account

The project company may have to take the risk of having to fund the cost of certain changes in law (e.g. capex to meet new fire-safety requirements); the rôle of a reserve account in this situation is discussed in §16.2.5. Again, it is preferable not to trap cash in the project company for nothing, in the same way as establishing an MRA when there is no spike in maintenance costs.

— Insurance proceeds account

A separate reserve account may be established into which the proceeds of insurance claims are paid, and from which amounts are paid under the lenders' control for restoration of the project or reduction of the debt (cf. §14.8). Similar accounts may be used for other types of compensation received by the project company, such as liquidated damages from the construction contractor (cf. §12.4). In these accounts, where money has been received for a specific purpose, the cash does not flow through the cascade, but directly into the account, to be applied on a specifically-agreed basis.

§25.2.5 Controls on Distributions to Investors

The investors come at the bottom of the cash-flow cascade. Once opex, tax, fees, debt-service and reserve-account requirements have been met, in principle distributions to investors can be made. If the project company cannot immediately pay distributions over to the investors (*e.g.* because there may be a delay before the annual general meeting can be held and a dividend declared), they are paid into a shareholder distribution account in the name of the project company. The lenders may wish to take security over the distribution account, along with the other reserve accounts, but as the cash in this account is supposed to be out of their control, the case for doing so is not strong. However, this would only make a difference if the project company went into default under the loan, at which time the lenders would be able to block payments from the account (*cf.* §25.3.1).

But it is not quite as simple as seeing if there is any cash left at the bottom of the cascade and just paying it to the investors: there are other hurdles to be jumped. The project company obviously has to demonstrate that sufficient cash will remain or be generated in the future to repay debt after the distributions have been made. This is dealt with by establishing a 'distribution-block' ratio.[3] For example, if the base-case average ADSCR was 1.25×, distributions cannot be made if the previous year's actual ADSCR is lower than, say, 1.10×. The calculation of whether there is sufficient cash to make distributions is usually carried out on a rolling annual basis once every six months (and hence distributions can only be made once in every six months). If cash flow cannot be distributed, because distribution-block ratio requirements are not met, any cash available may be used to reduce the debt or held in a special reserve account, until the cover-ratio calculations again fall on the right side of the line after allowing for the debt reduction or funds held in the special reserve account.

If the base-case cover ratios are low (*e.g.* an ADSCR of 1.15×), and hence close to the distribution-block ratio (*e.g.* an ADSCR of 1.10×), this is quite a dangerous situation for investors. A small drop in cash flow will result in their cash flow being blocked. So, while low cover ratios are advantageous in winning a bid (*cf.* §23.5), they may not be so advantageous later on.

An issue in calculating the distribution-block ratio is whether 'forward-looking' ratios (*i.e.* the projected ADSCR for the next year, or the LLCR or average ADSCR as projected for the rest of the loan) should be also used for this purpose. Once the project is operating, the best way of projecting how it will operate in the future is to look at how it has actually operated in the past, so it is the actual ADSCRs achieved that should mainly concern lenders. Especially in a project with a regular assured cash flow under a PPP contract, it is difficult to conceive why the projections of cash flow for the next year should be much lower than those for the last year (predictable fluctuations, *e.g.* maintenance, should be dealt with using reserve accounts). This approach is more relevant to mining or other natural resource projects. Therefore, although beloved by lenders, forward-looking ratios are largely a waste of time in this situation, and doing away with them also eliminates the problem of deciding what assumptions should be used in the financial projections for this purpose. However, if a project company is taking demand risk on a concession, there is more of a case for forward-looking ratios, as future changes in usage may be projected.

The project company will have to fulfil yet further requirements before making distributions, in particular no event of default should have occurred under the PPP contract (*cf.* §25.4) or the financing documentation.

---

[3] Also known as a 'dividend stop' or 'lock-up' ratio.

§25.3 Lenders' Security

Lenders to a project company cannot expect to take security over the facility which is the object of the PPP contract. Maintenance of the public service has to take priority over any claims by the lenders in this respect—clearly, the idea of lenders foreclosing on a public-sector school and selling it would be unacceptable, and selling off a road or a bridge is impossible. Even if they could theoretically be sold, the specialised nature of most PPP assets means that they have little open-market value. And if the contracting authority originally provided an asset to the PPP contract with a wider market use, such as commercially-zoned land or an office building, this should not form part of the lenders' security unless this can be done without disturbing the contracting authority's own continuing rights.

Therefore, lenders in a PPP project-financing can only rely on the cash flow of a successful continuing project company for their repayment. However, it remains important for the lenders to hold security to ensure that:

- the lenders are involved at an early stage if the project begins to go wrong;
- the lenders can take over and run the project if necessary;
- third parties (such as unsecured creditors) do not gain any prior or *pari-passu* rights over the project assets;
- project assets are not disposed of without the lenders' agreement; and
- lenders can 'encourage' co-operation by the project company if it gets into trouble.

The lenders' security normally has four layers:

- control of cash flow, as discussed above;
- security over the project company's contracts and financial assets (§25.3.1);
- security over the project company's shares (§25.3.2); and
- the ability to step in to the project under direct agreements (§25.3.3).

§25.3.1 Security over Project Contracts and Financial Assets

In the absence of security over physical assets, lenders expect a comprehensive package which assigns to them the project company's rights over all its major contracts, *e.g.*:

- the PPP contract;
- subcontracts, and any bonds or guarantees for these contracts (*cf.* §12.4.3);
- insurances (*cf.* Chapter 14); and
- any continuing advisory contracts (*cf.* §20.7).

Changes to project contracts cannot be made without the lenders' consent (*cf.* §16.2.3). In addition, security is taken over financial assets, *e.g.*:

- pledges over the project company's bank accounts, including reserve accounts, with dual signatures from the project company and the agent bank or security trustee required where lender approval is needed to transfer funds from an account;

- assignment of the project company's right to receive payments of equity (including share-holder subordinated debt) from the sponsors;
- assignment of the project company's right to receive any payment due to it if the financial hedging is broken (*cf.* §24.2.3); and
- assignment of insurance policies (*cf.* §14.6).

Consent to pledges or assignments by the other parties to the relevant agreements will also be necessary, preferably accompanied by direct agreements as discussed below.

Depending on the particular legal jurisdiction, there may be problems with security where there are preferential creditors (*e.g.* tax claims with priority over a secured creditor), or high levels of stamp duty or other fees to register security.

§25.3.2 Security over the Project Company's Shares

Lenders normally take security over the investors' shares in the project company. This is done:

- in cases where the equity is not fully paid-in at the beginning of the construction phase, to ensure that it can be called on if there is a default during this phase (*cf.* §20.3.5); and
- to enable the lenders to take over management of the project company after a default more quickly than may be achieved by taking action under contract assignments.

There may be some difficulties with this in some legal jurisdictions where the procedures for enforcing security may be too cumbersome for lenders who want to be able to take over control of the project quickly, especially if lenders are required to sell the assets in a public auction or after a court action rather than take over their control and operation immediately through an administrator or receiver. On the other hand, this may be the only way in which the lenders can take over management of the project company in some countries, as local bankruptcy laws (such as 'Chapter 11' in the United States) may prevent them from doing so *via* their security over the project company's assets.

An investor's corporate lenders may have imposed 'negative pledge' provisions, under which the investor is not to give security over its assets to any third party, which would prevent a pledge being given over their holding of project company's shares. It is preferable for the investor to negotiate a waiver of this provision in the case of its project company shares.

It is fairly common for the project company to be owned by an intermediary holding company (*cf.* §20.6.1), whose shares are owned by the investors and then pledged to the lenders. Reasons for this include:

- Lenders want to ensure that the project company is not affected by one of its investors getting into financial difficulties (*i.e.* it is 'bankruptcy remote'). For example, if an investor is made insolvent, this should not result in its project company subsidiary or affiliate being made insolvent as well, or remove the benefit of a pledge of the project company's shares. An intermediary holding company between the investors and the project company may reduce this risk.

- The holding-company security may also give the lenders greater control in the case of insolvency of the project company itself.
- There may be tax advantages to the structure.
- If the lenders are also investors in the project company, they may not wish to own it as a direct subsidiary or affiliate in case there is adverse publicity if something goes wrong with the project.

§25.3.3 Direct Agreements

The contracting authority and other key project-contract counterparties are all normally required to sign direct agreements[4] with the lenders (to which the project company may also be a party).[5] These are also known as 'acknowledgments and consents', since they acknowledge the position of the lenders, and consent to them taking an assignment of the contracts as security. This may not be strictly necessary in legal systems that allow a contract to have a *stipulatio altri* (provisions for the benefit of a third party), but in view of their complexity, it is still probably easier to use a separate agreement.

The PPP contract direct agreement is normally the only legal link between the contracting authority and the lenders, and is therefore probably the most important of these documents. Under the direct agreement, the contracting authority:

- acknowledges the lenders' security interest in the PPP contract;
- agrees to make payments to a specific project account or as notified by the lenders;
- agrees that amendments will not be made to the PPP contract without the lenders' consent;
- gives the lenders various rights to intervene if the project company is in default, as discussed below; and
- may agree that if the lenders enforce their security, the PPP contract will automatically be terminated, thus ensuring the termination sum is paid (*cf.* §17.2). (In return, the contracting authority may also want the right to terminate the project agreement immediately if the lenders cease to make funds available for construction of the project.)

The contracting authority may be reluctant to sign such a direct agreement, on the grounds that the lenders should not have any extra rights that are not in the PPP contract. It could be also argued that the practical value to the lenders of many of the provisions of such a direct agreement is questionable. In practice, if a project is going wrong, all parties have to sit around the table and try to find a solution, whether there is a direct agreement or not. However, from the lenders' point of view, the PPP contract is the most important part of their security, and a direct agreement may help them to step rapidly into the picture after a project company default to preserve the position, and find another party to take over responsibility for the project contracting authority.

---

[4] Also known as 'tripartite deeds'.

[5] As noted in §17.6, the contracting authority also has direct agreements with major subcontractors, in case it has to take over the project from the project company.

Similar direct agreements are signed with, for example, the construction subcontractor, that will ensure that if the project company gets into trouble during the construction phase, the lenders can take over and complete the project on the basis of the original construction subcontract.

The lenders may also obtain collateral warranties with respect to construction or operation of the project, *e.g.* from the construction subcontractor, under which direct liability is accepted (to the extent agreed in the relevant contract with the project company) *vis-à-vis* the lenders.

If the project company gets into difficulties, it is in the contracting authority's interests to get these problems sorted out by the lenders rather than terminating the PPP contract, while also ensuring that the risk allocation and service provision are not disturbed in the process. Although the lenders' general security over the project company should give them the ability to intervene, *e.g.* by replacement of subcontractors, their direct agreement with the contracting authority provides them with time and a framework to deal with the most serious problems without being frustrated by the contracting authority itself taking premature action. Various stages and options for lender action can be set out in the direct agreement:

– Notification

   The contracting authority agrees to notify the lenders if it is considering terminating the PPP contract because of a default by the project company, or if the project company has accumulated penalties, payment deductions or performance points (*cf.* §15.6.2) beyond a trigger level, and gives the lenders the right to join in any discussions with the contracting authority at that time.

– Cure periods

   If the project company is in default under the PPP contract (and assuming this default can be remedied, or 'cured'), the direct agreement gives the lenders 'cure periods' (*i.e.* extra time to take action to remedy the project company's default, in addition to that already given to the project company) before the PPP contract is terminated. These cure periods are limited in length—perhaps only a week or two—where the project company has failed to pay money when due, but substantially longer for non-financial default (*e.g.* failure to operate the project to the required minimum availability or service level)—usually around six months if the lenders are taking active steps to find a solution to the problem (*i.e.* they have stepped in or exercised their right of substitution as discussed in the following).

– Step-in

   The direct agreement should give the lenders the right to step in to the PPP contract, which means that they can appoint a nominee to undertake the project company's obligations in parallel with the project company; the nominee is effectively in charge of the project, but the project company remains the contracting authority's formal counter-party under the PPP contract. Step-in is supposed to be a *temporary* remedy to allow time to find a longer term solution to the project company's problems, and so the length of time allowed for this may be limited, say to six months (linked to the cure periods discussed above).

Normal unavailability and other deductions from service fees, and accrual of performance points (*cf.* §15.5.5, §15.6.2) should continue during a step-in period but should not give rise to a right to terminate the PPP contract so long as the lenders are taking active steps to remedy the problems.

Lenders will resist any requirement to guarantee the project company's obligations in return for allowing them to step in, as this leaves the contracting authority in a better position than if the project company had not got into trouble at all: the contracting authority, on the other hand, may argue that the lenders should accept this as they are delaying its ability to take control of the situation by terminating the PPP contract.[6] Even if lenders accept some responsibility for liabilities which cannot be offset against service fees, they will not accept long-term liabilities, *e.g.* to bring the maintenance of the facility to a specified condition before returning it to the contracting authority (*cf.* §17.8), which is reasonable if the step-in is only for a limited period.

The contracting authority also has step-in rights (*cf.* §13.8).

— Substitution

The lenders normally also have the right to 'substitution', in other words, appointment of a new obligor in the place of the project company. The contracting authority should have some control over the choice of new obligor. An absolute veto is unlikely to be acceptable to the lenders, although they may settle for the use of applying pre-agreed selection criteria. (Lenders will prefer specific qualification criteria rather than some basis of 'reasonable opinion' on the contracting authority's part.) Once the new obligor is appointed, the 'old' project company then ceases to have any further involvement with the project, other than a possible re-transfer of the project agreement after the lenders have been repaid (as the project company retains the right to any surplus cash-flow from the project after the repayment). In such cases, the new obligor must take on any accrued liabilities, but the accrual of any performance points needs to start from zero or it will be difficult for the lenders to find anyone to take over. This is meant to cover sale of the project to a long-term buyer, and is in effect a lender-controlled version of the market sale discussed in §17.2.5. (As such, it may raise concerns that an arm's length public-procurement procedure is not being followed.)

The technical and financial capacity of the lenders' step-in nominee or substitute obligor will have to be acceptable to the contracting authority.

The contracting authority may also allow the lenders to exercise their step-in and substitution rights when an event of default under the financing documentation has occurred, even if the PPP contract is not in default.

---

[6] In Hungary, for example, those stepping in are jointly and severally liable for the project company's liabilities, including those arising before step-in.

In reality, as discussed in §25.3, the main purpose of these powers is for the lenders to ensure that they are kept fully in the picture if things start going wrong, and that they can force the project company to take any remedial action. The existence on paper of step-in and substitution rights means that they seldom have to be used.

Not all countries use the direct agreement approach to step-in. In some countries, such as Poland and Spain, a similar result is achieved through the lenders taking security over the shares in the project company (*cf.* §25.3.2). Similarly, in countries where step-in is used, it does not necessarily involve a direct agreement. Thus, in France, Germany and Italy, for example, lender step-in rights are granted under provisions of the PPP contract or by law. There are also variations in the liabilities that lenders may have to take on and in some countries (such as France and Germany), the contracting authority has to consent in all cases to lender step-in. Contracting authorities should therefore be careful to ensure what their legal framework allows for in the case of lender step-in provisions.

§25.4 EVENTS OF DEFAULT

Project-finance lenders do not want to have to wait to take action until the project company has run out of funds to service the debt; they therefore create a defined set of triggers which give them the right to take earlier action against the project company. These are 'events of default' (EoDs). Once an EoD has occurred, the project company is no longer able to manage the project without lender involvement. It should be noted that these events do not of themselves put the project company in default under the loan (*i.e.* bring the financing to an end and allow the lenders to enforce their security): a positive decision to take this next stage of action has to be made by the lenders after the EoD has occurred. The threat of moving to this next stage gives the lenders a lever to ensure that they can sit at the table with the project company, subcontractors and the contracting authority to find a way out of a problem that either exists already, or is indicated by the trigger events to be on the horizon.

Some of these EoDs (such as failure to pay, insolvency, *etc.*) would apply to any corporate financing, but others are peculiar to project finance, *e.g.*

- a projected construction-cost overrun;
- failure to complete the project, *i.e.* achieve the service availability date (*cf.* §15.4.1) by an agreed backstop date;
- any default under the PPP contract;
- changes made to the project documents or the facility without lenders' consent (*cf.* §16.2.3);
- ADSCR falls below a certain level; thus, the initial base-case average ADSCR could be 1.25×, the distribution-block level (*cf.* §25.2.5) 1.10× and this 'default ratio' level 1.05×; as with distribution blocks, there is the issue of whether forward-looking ratios should be used in this context; or
- a similar drop in LLCR, which means that the project company's ability to pay the debt off over its remaining life is seriously jeopardised.

Various courses of action are open to the lenders after an EoD, partly depending on what stage the project has reached:

- to waive (*i.e.* ignore) the EoD;
- if the project is still under construction, to impose a drawstop (*cf.* §25.2.2);
- if the project is in the operating phase, to require that all net cash flow be applied to reduction of debt or held in a separate reserve or escrow account under the lenders' control, rather than distributed to investors; or
- to enforce the lenders' security.

Once the EoD has occurred, it is entirely within the lenders' discretion which of these actions they choose to take. The project company may also ask the lenders to waive or amend a particular term of the financing documentation, so it does not fall into default in the first place.

If there is a syndicate of banks or a group of bond holders providing the loan, there has to be a decision-making process, or one rogue lender could pull the house down by taking individual action against the project company while the rest are trying to find a solution. (Indeed, it is not unknown for a small lender to blackmail the larger ones by threatening to do this, so that the larger lenders will buy out the smaller lender's loan.) The agent bank or security trustee also needs to have clear instructions from the lenders as a whole on what action is to be taken on their behalf. Voting mechanisms therefore have to be agreed to in advance between lenders; the project company also has an interest in these arrangements, to try to ensure that one or two 'hostile' lenders cannot dictate the action taken, against the wishes of the majority. So minor decisions may require only say 75% of the lenders to be in favour, whereas a vote to declare a default would require a smaller percentage.

§25.5 Inter-Creditor Issues

If there is only one lender, or group of lenders in a syndicate, the situation is quite straightforward—these lenders hold their security and claims on the project company through their agent bank (or trustee), take decisions collectively as discussed above, and the project company also deals with them as necessary through their agent or trustee. Between themselves, the lenders have a vote on decisions proportionate to their loan amount (*cf.* §16.2.3). However, it may not be quite as simple as this, and if there are different groups of lenders, or senior lenders and mezzanine lenders, or other parties with financial claims such as swap providers, some complex negotiations may result. Although the project company may not be a direct party to these inter-creditor arrangements, it has a strong interest in ensuring that they are practical and workable, and should therefore be aware of such issues when considering the basic financial viability of a bid.

Each of the lending groups will have its own loan or other financing documentation with the project company, but they also need to establish machinery for working together, or the project company will soon find itself like a bone between two dogs, with the project in pieces after being pulled in different directions. This is usually done through a 'common terms agreement', under which, apart from sharing security, the parties agree on a common approach, *e.g.* to the cash-flow cascade (*cf.* §25.2.3), and to voting on amendments and waivers to the loan documentation or on agreeing changes to the project contracts.

As discussed below, particular classes of financial claim can raise various issues.

§25.5.1 Interest-Rate Swap Providers

If an interest-rate swap is provided *pro rata* by all the banks in a lending syndicate, there is obviously no need for any special inter-creditor arrangements to take account of this, but if—as is commonly the case—the swap is being provided just by one or two banks (either for their own account or acting as a fronting bank as discussed in §24.2.8), their voting rights and share in security *vis-à-vis* the rest of the syndicate need to be considered. Because their breakage costs at any one time cannot be predicted (and may be zero if rates move the right way), the extent of their risk—if any—on a default by the project company cannot be fixed in advance. Theoretically, the swap provider would wish to have a vote in the syndicate equal to whatever proportion the breakage cost at the time of the vote bears to the rest of the debt: this uncertainty is usually not acceptable to the other lenders. The end result is often that:

- the swap provider does not take part in voting on waivers and amendments (the swap provider is usually also a lender and thus still has a voice that can be heard in this way);
- the swap provider may only terminate the swap independently if the project company is in default under a limited number of categories (such as non-payment and insolvency); and
- once the claim has been crystallized by termination of the swap, the swap provider's vote on enforcement is also fixed *pro rata* to this.

This explains why swap quotations direct from the market are not usually feasible—a swap provider who is not also a lender to the project company cannot easily be fitted into the control and security structure—hence another way has to be found to introduce competition for swap pricing (*cf.* §24.2.8).

However, the voting rights are structured, the swap provider shares *pro rata* in any enforcement proceeds based on the crystallized breakage cost.

Similar principles apply to a lender providing a fixed-rate or inflation-linked loan when there are other lenders.

§25.5.2 Fixed-Rate Lenders

Fixed-rate lenders are in a similar position to interest-swap providers when a default takes place: they may also have a breakage cost. This does not normally give them any extra voting rights, but is taken into account in determining their *pro rata* share of any enforcement proceeds.

A problem may arise, however, if the fixed-rate lender has a make-whole clause (*cf.* §24.2.12), and other floating rate lenders do not. This may lead to a large discrepancy in the relative size of the claim that the different groups of lenders have on a default in relation to their actual loan outstanding.

§25.5.3 Inflation-Indexed Loans or Swaps

The problem becomes more acute if one group of lenders has an indexed-linked loan or inflation swap, and the other does not. The discrepancy between relative loan outstandings and actual claims can become much greater in such cases (*cf.* §24.3.7, §24.3.9), and so it is quite difficult to structure a financing with both inflation-indexed and fixed-rate finance from different groups of lenders.

§25.5.4 Mezzanine Lenders

Mezzanine debt may be provided by third parties unconnected with the sponsors or other investors (*cf.* §22.6), usually secured by a second mortgage or junior position on the senior lenders' security. This raises a number of difficult inter-creditor issues:

— Drawing priority

Senior lenders prefer mezzanine loans to be drawn first by the project company, in a similar way to equity financing. If financing is being drawn on a *pro rata* basis, senior lenders will want there to be only very limited conditions precedent to drawing the mezzanine lenders' financing (*cf.* §25.2.1), to ensure they cannot exercise an independent drawstop (*cf.* §25.2.2).

— Cash-flow cascade

In principle, mezzanine lenders are placed in the cash-flow cascade above distributions to investors, and so are repaid if sufficient cash flow is available after senior debt-service payments have been made. The senior lenders will probably require their DSRA, MRA or other reserve accounts to be filled up before mezzanine lenders can be paid, and to be able to block payments to mezzanine lenders in a similar way to distributions to investors (*cf.* §25.2.5)?

— Default and enforcement

Mezzanine lenders accept that if the financing package as a whole is in default, and enforcement action is taken, they will only be repaid if the senior lenders are fully repaid. But senior lenders will be concerned about 'Samson in the temple' behaviour by mezzanine lenders—if the project goes wrong and there is only enough money to repay the senior lenders, the mezzanine lenders have nothing to lose so they can threaten to pull the whole project to pieces unless the senior lenders share some of the value that their loans still have. Therefore, senior lenders restrict the rights of mezzanine lenders in a number of ways to try to avoid this happening:

• Senior lenders want freedom to make amendments to their loan terms, including the repayment schedule and interest rate, and the ability to increase the amount of senior debt if the project gets into trouble. Obviously, this may make the mezzanine lenders' position worse: a compromise may be to limit the amount of extra debt or other costs that can be added on to the senior debt at various points in the project life.
• Any amendments to the project contracts require senior lenders' consent; they normally require freedom to allow such amendments without interference by mezzanine lenders, unless the result is to increase the senior debt amount, as discussed above.

- Mezzanine lenders want to have the right to take enforcement action if they are not paid when due. It is difficult for senior lenders to exclude the mezzanine lenders completely from taking action; a common compromise is to require the mezzanine lenders to wait, say, six months after a payment default before they can take action (and of course such action will trigger action by the senior lenders, so ensuring that any enforcement proceeds still accrue to them first).

If mezzanine debt is provided by the contracting authority or another public-sector party (*cf.* §18.8, §22.9), the provider is likely to have fewer rights than an independent third-party mezzanine debt lender.

§25.5.5 Subordinated Lenders

The position of subordinated lenders, *i.e.* loans provided by investors as an alternative way of investing their equity into the project company (*cf.* §20.3.5) is quite different from that of mezzanine lenders. The investors cannot expect to get any rights which they would not otherwise have had, just because of the form in which they make their investment.

The senior lenders (and any mezzanine lenders) will therefore require them to agree that they have no security rights and cannot take any independent enforcement action to recover their debt, or otherwise obstruct the senior lenders, until all the senior lenders' debt has been fully repaid.

Debt Refinancing and Equity Sale

§26.1 INTRODUCTION

Having looked in Chapter 23 at the initial financial structuring for a project company, it is worth considering what can happen to this financial structure if the project proceeds as expected, *i.e.* construction is completed on time and on budget, and the project company begins to generate revenues as originally projected. Once the project has entered into this new phase, its risks have significantly decreased (*cf.* Chapters 11-13), which opens up new possibilities for its investors—a refinancing of the debt on better terms (§26.2), or a profitable sale of their equity investment (§26.3).

Refinancing the debt or selling equity at an early stage in the project life may have an adverse effect on the public perception of PPPs, hence potentially reducing political support for a PPP programme: the debt and equity were supposed to be long-term commitments, and yet somehow the investors in the project have made large 'gains' two to three years into the PPP contract? The private-sector market has long since recognised this political danger, so in many countries part of the 'refinancing gain' is paid to the contracting authority.

In relation to equity, the most straightforward approach is for the contracting authority to become a shareholder in the project company, so sharing in equity gains, although this raises issues including conflict of interest (*cf.* §27.4). It may also be possible to arrange an auction to sell part of the equity just before financial close, with part of the benefit of this accruing to the contracting authority (§26.4).

§26.2 DEBT REFINANCING

It may seem strange to talk about refinancing the project company's debt (which might have a tenor of, say, 20 years), perhaps only two to three years after financial close. But construction and start-up of operations are generally considered to be the high-risk phases of a PPP project. Thereafter the project company usually has a steady and reasonably predictable cash flow (more so in the case of availability PPPs, less so in the case of concessions). As a result, lenders are likely to be more comfortable with the project company's prospects and so offer improved terms for financing the project compared to the debt terms at financial close, even though that was not long ago.

Debt refinancing can result in various different benefits:

- reducing the interest cost;
- increasing minimum cover ratios (*cf.* §23.3);
- increasing the debt amount;
- extending the debt-repayment tenor, *i.e.* reducing the tail (*cf.* §23.2.4); and
- otherwise improving loan terms, *e.g.* by reducing reserve-account requirements, especially the MRA (*cf.* §25.2.4).

Apart from these financial benefits, a refinancing may give the project company greater flexibility because some of the more restrictive controls on its operations imposed by the original lenders may be negotiated away. It may also offer the investors an opportunity to structure the financing for their PPP business as a whole more efficiently, by combining the financing for several completed and operating projects, as well as providing additional capital for investment in new projects.

§26.2.1 Benefit of a Refinancing to Investors

Determining the financial benefit of a refinancing (known as a 'refinancing gain') to the project company's investors is a more complex process than might be supposed at first sight, as can be seen by considering each of the above elements of a refinancing:

— Reduced interest costs

It might be thought that if market interest rates have gone down, refinancing the original debt at a lower rate will be a profitable exercise, but this is generally not the case. Although there will be a benefit from the lower cost of the new debt, at the same time there will be a balancing breakage cost from prepaying the fixed-rate finance or interest-rate swap on the original debt (*cf.* §24.2). Therefore, only a reduction in the credit margin (*cf.* §23.4.1), not the underlying interest rate, is beneficial.

— Increasing the debt amount (*e.g.* by reducing the required cover ratios, reducing the tail or because the cash flow has turned out better than the original banking case)

If a PPP project requires $1,000 of funding, which has been provided as to $900 by debt and $100 by equity, and on a refinancing the debt is increased to $950, it might be thought that the increase of $50 represents the refinancing gain. But we do not make ourselves richer by borrowing more money, and in fact the debt-service payments will increase over the remaining tenor of the debt (as there is more interest to pay on a higher level of debt, and more debt to repay), so reducing distributions to the project company's investors.

– Extended debt-repayment tenor

Similarly, extending the debt-repayment schedule by a year or so at the end of the project, reducing the cash-flow tail, does not create an obvious benefit. Debt-service payments do reduce year by year (assuming the amount of the debt is not increased), but over the life of the project interest payments will increase, and hence the investors' distributions after the refinancing will decrease over the remaining life of the PPP contract.

– Reductions in reserve accounts

Reductions in reserve accounts only accelerate a process that happens over the life of the project anyway—by the end of the loan tenor the reserve accounts are usually reduced to zero. So again, the refinancing gain is not the amount of the free cash released by the refinancing.

It is evident therefore that the benefit of undertaking a refinancing of a project company's debt is more complex than at first appears.

§26.2.2 Refinancing Calculation

To understand the real benefit which investors receive from a refinancing, it is necessary to look at a typical cash flow by way of a worked example set out in Table 26.1. As shown:

• The annual pre-refinancing cash flow, after the construction period, consists of $95 of CADS, less $70 of debt service, leaving $25 of surplus cash flow to be paid out as distributions to the investors in the project company. Before the refinancing, the projected base-case equity IRR was 11.5%.
• The refinancing, which takes place at the end of year 4, i.e. 2 years from completion of construction, reduces the lenders' initial 1.35 × ADSCR to 1.25 ×, extends the debt tenor by two years (i.e. leaving a one-year tail instead of three years as previously), and reduces the debt interest rate from 6% to 5.5% assuming no change in the underlying interest rate, so the loan margin is reduced by 0.5%.
• The refinancing raises $150 of additional debt, which is paid out straight to the investors, e.g. by way of prepayment of their subordinated debt (cf. §20.3.5).
• The investors' original investment was $193; they received $25 in years 2 and 3 (the first two years of operation), and $150 from the refinancing; thereafter, the investors' annual cash flow diminishes from $25 to $19 (with a greater reduction in the tail years), so that the total equity cash flow over the project life goes down from $585 to $482.
• However, the effect of the refinancing is to increase the equity IRR (over the project life) from 11.5% to 17.2%.

So, the benefit of the refinancing for the investors is based on an improvement to the equity IRR, not an increase in their revenue over the remaining project life; which actually decreases. The IRR improves because the refinancing has brought the equity cash-flow distributions forward, and the IRR calculation gives a much greater weight to this early cash (cf. §3.4.3). Of course, the result is also a sharp improvement in the investors' reported

Table 26.1 Effect of refinancing

Assumptions:

At financial close

- Tenor of PPP contract — 25 years
- Project cost — $1,000, split over a two-year construction period
- CADS — 95, after operating costs, but before debt-service costs
- Initial debt:equity ratio — 81%:19%
- Debt interest rate — 6.0% p.a.
- Debt tenor — 22 years (20 years from completion of project)
- ADSCR — 1.35×

Refinancing

- Timing — End of year 4 (two years from completion)
- Additional debt — $125, two years after completion of project
- Debt interest rate — 5.75%
- Debt tenor — 22 years from completion, *i.e.* 20 years from refinancing
- ADSCR — 1.25×

($)	Year: 0	1	2	3	4	5	6	22	23	24	25	Total
Pre-refinancing												
Project cost	−333	−333	−333									1,000
CADS				95	95	95	95	95	95	95	95	2,185
Interest payments				−48	−47	−46	−44	−4				−600
Principal repayments				−22	−23	−25	−26	−66				−807
Total debt service	269	269	269	−70	−70	−70	−70	−70				2600
Equity cash flow	**−64**	**−64**	**−64**	**25**	**25**	**25**	**25**	**25**	**95**	**95**	**95**	**585**
Year-end debt	269	538	807	785	762	737	711	0				
Post-refinancing												
Project cost	−333	−333	−333									−1,000
CADS				95	95	95	95	95	95	95	95	2,185
Additional debt					**150**							
Interest payments				−48	−43	−50	−48	−11	−8	−4		−703
Principal repayments				−22	−27	−26	−27	−65	−68	−72		−957
Total debt service	269	269	269	−70	−70	−76	−76	−76	−76	−76		
Equity cash flow	**−64**	**−64**	**−64**	**25**	**174**	**19**	**19**	**19**	**19**	**19**	**95**	**482**
Year-end debt	269	538	807	785	908	882	854	140	72	0		

profits for year 3. This example also illustrates that refinancing in the project-finance context is not just about reducing the interest cost, but also often increasing the debt amount through lowering cover ratios and (where possible) lengthening its tenor.

§26.2.3 Should Refinancings be Subject to the Contracting Authority's Consent?

Debt refinancing may be of concern to the contracting authority because:

- It may have an effect on the project company's ability to continue delivering the services under the PPP contract (*e.g.* if its financial position is destabilised by taking on too much new debt, or if lenders less familiar with the requirements of a PPP are introduced or if it introduces less flexibility in the PPP structure).
- It may increase the contracting authority's termination-sum liabilities in some scenarios (*cf.* §17.2.1, §17.3).
- If the original sponsors have been able to accelerate the return on their investment, they may only have a much-reduced long-term financial interest in the success of the project company (*cf.* §20.2.1).
- It may create large 'windfall gains' which suggest that the original PPP contract was not good VfM for the public sector; this may create political problems which reduce general public support for a PPP programme (*cf.* §28.13).
- It may alter the balance-sheet treatment of the project (*cf.* §9.4.5).

A debt refinancing may well require some form of cooperation from the contracting authority, even though it is not a party to any loan documentation. This is because the contracting authority may have a general right to approve any increases to the debt amount, or the PPP contract may cap the contracting authority's termination-sum liability to pay off the debt in some scenarios based on the original debt schedule, which effectively give it a similar approval right (*cf.* §17.2.1, §17.3-§17.5). Furthermore, the new lenders will probably want the contracting authority to sign a new direct agreement (*cf.* §25.3.3), and again the contracting authority does not have to do this.

In 2002, the British Treasury introduced into its standard form of PFI contract (*cf.* §2.4.7, §4.3.2) an unrestricted right for the contracting authority to give its consent to (and hence control) a refinancing so long as this gave rise to a refinancing gain (*cf.* §26.2.6). This enables the contracting authority to take account of the concerns about a refinancing discussed above, but a requirement for its consent also helps to ensure that the contracting authority gets its share of a refinancing gain (*cf.* §26.2.7). Countries such as Ireland and Portugal also require approval from a public body.

§26.2.4 Rescue Refinancings

A requirement for the contracting authority's consent to a refinancing is made more complex by having to deal with 'rescue refinancings', where the project company has got into financial difficulty and needs to raise more financing for this reason, *i.e.* a 'bad' refinancing rather than a 'good' refinancing. Lenders may claim that if they are willing to take on the risk of injecting more financing than they originally committed to save the project, the contracting authority should not interfere with the process. But the contracting authority's response may well be that if it is to be in any way responsible on termination for more debt than was originally scheduled to be outstanding (*cf.* §17.2.1), it must always have the right to agree to this additional debt. Even if the contracting authority is willing to accommodate a rescue refinancing, the problem remains of distinguishing this from a 'good' refinancing. There are several possible answers to this:

- The British approach of 2002 mentioned above, namely that consent for refinancing is only needed if it produces a refinancing gain (discussed below); a rescue refinancing should not do so and so would not require consent.
- A specific cap of, say, 10% extra on the debt outstandings, which in principle is only available for rescue refinancings, but without trying to define this too closely (if there is no general cap as suggested above). In fact, this is what now applies in Britain, the 2002 solution having proved unacceptable to the lending market.
- To define the circumstances in which additional debt for a rescue refinancing will be covered—for example the LLCR for the project has dropped below a default level (*cf.* §25.4). The contracting authority may be concerned that any such scenario could be manipulated by the project company and the lenders, but it is difficult to see how this could be done in reality.

§26.2.5 Should the Contracting Authority Share in the Refinancing Gain?

If the contracting authority can control increases in debt through having to agree any potential increase in termination liabilities, it is clearly in a good position to negotiate a share of any benefit that the investors receive in return for doing so. In 2002 the British Treasury introduced into its standard form of PFI contract a specific requirement for the contracting authority to share 50% of the benefit of a refinancing.[1] The arguments put forward for sharing in the refinancing gain—to which the main concern was that the right of consent discussed above should not be used as a lever to increase the contracting authority's share over 50%—were:

- The 'value' in the project company which provides a basis for the refinancing is the revenues which the public sector provides (in an availability PPP), or facilitates (in a concession).
- The fact that better terms are available is partly the consequence of the public sector having continued to develop its PPP programme since the original PPP contract was signed, creating greater interest in loans to this sector.

---

[1] This was subsequently increased to a sharing of 60% in favour of the contracting authority of gains between £1 and £3 million and 70% above £3 million. Eurostat has since issued specific provisions on the balance-sheet treatment of refinancings (Eurostat 2016), under which a sharing by the contracting authority of more than *one third* of the gains leads to the PPP being on the government balance sheet based in the principle that sharing of rewards as well as risks has an impact on the balance-sheet treatment.

- Public support for the PPP programme will be reduced if investors are seen to be making 'windfall' profits only a short time after making what is supposed to be a long-term investment in a project company. (This was the primary motive for introducing the concept into the British PFI market of sharing 50% of refinancing gains, as there had been adverse publicity about such large gains from projects signed early in the PFI programme.)

The Treasury accepted that private-sector investors in a project company were entitled to keep the benefits of a refinancing that arose because the risk of the project had reduced (because construction was complete and it was operating profitably), or because the cash flow had increased above initial projections because of efficiency gains on the part of the management of the project company. But as it is very difficult to isolate the effects of these factors from the others set out above, a 50:50 sharing mechanism was initially introduced as an approximate basis which took these factors into account. There was little objection by the investment market—investors understood the political importance of the issue.

This approach has been widely adopted in other PPP programmes involving project finance. Countries that have adopted the British standard form of PFI contract (*e.g.* South Africa) took over its refinancing provisions at the time. Others have negotiated for a share of refinancing benefits on an *ad hoc* basis (*e.g.* Portugal). PPP legislation may also cover this issue—Korea's 2005 amendment of its PPI Act included a provision for 50:50 sharing of refinancing gains.

In view of the potential gains for the contracting authority (especially if there is a view that current terms, such as lending margins, are likely to improve in time), the PPP contract may also give the right to the contracting authority to request the project company to instigate a refinancing, although it may be difficult to implement such a clause (for example the project company cannot be forced to take on more senior debt, which is likely to be a key element of a beneficial refinancing as discussed above).

The arguments for sharing in refinancing gains are not so strong where concessions are concerned, although similar provisions are to be found in some concession agreements, typically copied from the British standardised PFI contract even though it is not meant for concessions. In an availability PPP, project revenues are largely fixed, and the scope for increasing cash flow through operating efficiencies is also likely to be limited. However, in a concession, there is much greater risk on revenues, and lenders will inevitably be more conservative until these are established (*cf.* §23.3.2), at which point a potentially large refinancing can take place. A refinancing gain is therefore much more the product of project-specific factors in a concession than in an availability PPP project. Probably the better approach on concessions is for the contracting authority to take a share of windfall revenues (*cf.* §15.5.2).

§26.2.6 Calculating the Refinancing Gain

But even if the principle of sharing the refinancing gain, say, 50:50 between the contracting authority and the project company's investors is agreed, a method has to be found to do this. There is no refinancing gain—*i.e.* just one amount of money—which can be split 50:50. So how can it be calculated?

- The reduction in credit margin?—But even if there is such a reduction, as Table 26.1 illustrates, the total interest payments increase not decrease (as the debt has increased).
- The increased loan amount (*i.e.* the extra amount the shareholders take out at the time of the refinancing)?—But this does not take account of the later reductions in return to investors.
- The difference between the pre- and post-refinancing cash flows?—But if this is a negative number, as it is from year 5 in Table 26.1, it cannot be a gain?
- The increase in (short-term) reported profits?—May be a motive for the refinancing, but will be again be offset by later decreases.

As can be seen, this is a complex question. The answer devised in Britain was that the refinancing gain is the NPV of the change in the investors' cash flow (*i.e.* distributions), pre- and post-refinancing. Note that the pre-refinancing cash flow is adjusted from the base case to reflect the current performance of the project, so that insofar as the project is performing above base case, the investors get the benefit of this rather than the contracting authority (albeit if there is a higher CADS than in the base case, this also increases the project company's borrowing capacity, which is another reason for the rough 50:50 split).[2]

Three methods for a refinancing-gain calculation are set out in Table 26.2, which uses the results from Table 26.1. Methods 1 and 2 involve discounting the difference between the pre- and post-refinancing cash flows and paying 50% of the NPV to the contracting authority (assuming that it is getting a 50% share of the refinancing gain). This therefore takes account of both the positive cash flow in the year of the refinancing, and the reductions in the equity distributions thereafter (which are caused by the increase in the loan amount).

An immediately obvious question is, what is the discount rate to be used for the NPV calculation, since it is clear that this will have a major impact on the answer, and hence the size of any share of the refinancing gain to be paid out to the contracting authority? As Table 26.2 shows, the higher the discount rate the higher the NPV, and hence the higher the refinancing gain on which the contracting authority's 50% share is calculated. This is counter-intuitive, as a higher discount rate normally creates a lower NPV, but in this case the changes in the cash flow after the refinancing has taken place are negative, and so a higher discount rate reduces this negative effect.[3]

---

[2] Provision was, however, made to ensure that if the project had been operating poorly at some stage before the refinancing, such that the original investors were no longer projected to achieve their required equity IRR over the life of the project, any sharing of refinancing gain with the contracting authority would only take place after allowing for the projected equity IRR to increase back to the base-case level. So this is rather a one-way arrangement: if the project does well, the investors keep all the benefit of the excess over the base case, but if it does badly, the contracting authority lets the investors get the base case return. But in reality if the project does badly, a refinancing is less likely.

[3] But this is not the case if the only refinancing change is a reduction in loan margin, as in that case all the future pre- and post-refinancing cash-flow differences are positive not negative.

Table 26.2 Different methods of calculating a refinancing gain

($)	Year:	4	5	6	22	23	24	25	Total
Method 1									
• Post-refinancing cash flow		174	19	19	19	19	19	95	482
• Pre-refinancing cash flow		25	25	25	25	95	95	95	585
• Difference		150	−6	−6	−6	−76	−76	0	−103
• Discounted at base-case equity IRR (11.5%)	81								
• **Contracting authority 50% share**	40								
Method 2									
• As for Method 1 but discounted at current market equity IRR (8%)	59								
• **Contracting authority 50% share**	30								
Method 3									
Pre-refinancing equity IRR	11.5%								
Post-refinancing equity IRR	17.2%								
∴ Adjusted equity IRR	14.3%								
∴ **Contracting authority 50% share**	41								

So, what is the correct discount rate to use? One argument might be that it should be the PSDR (*cf.* §8.6.2), but this is a 'risk-free' rate which is not appropriate in this context. An equity risk-related discount seems to be more appropriate, and in fact in the British case the rate chosen for this purpose is the base-case (post-tax) equity IRR, a relatively high rate. It could be argued that a more appropriate rate would be not the primary equity IRR, but the (lower) secondary equity IRR, *i.e.* the rate of return a new investor would expect when coming into the project at the time of the refinancing—with its lower risk profile (*cf.* §20.3.3). The difficulty about this is that the original equity IRR is clear from the base-case financial model, in which it is calculated, whereas determining what the market would consider a fair secondary equity IRR is more difficult.

Method 1 in Table 26.2, therefore, uses the base-case equity IRR as the discount rate, resulting in a payment to the contracting authority, assuming it gets 50% of the refinancing gain, of $40. Method 2 uses an assumed secondary-market equity IRR of 8%, resulting in a payment of $30.

Method 3 does the calculation in a different way: the contracting authority's share of the refinancing gain is the sum of money today which equates to half of the increase in the base-case equity IRR as a result of the refinancing. So, in the case set out in Table 26.1, where the equity IRR has increased from 11.5% to 17.2%, after payment of the contracting authority's share of the refinancing gain, the projected equity IRR should increase by half of the difference between 1.15% and 17.2%, *i.e.* to 14.3%. A payment of $41 achieves this result. This is virtually the same as the payment under Method 1, which suggests that Method 3 is more straightforward, in the sense that there need be no dispute about a discount rate.

§26.2.7 Sharing the Refinancing Gain

But calculating the refinancing gain to fix the amount to be shared between the contracting authority and the investors in the project company is still not the end of this rather tortuous story. In the example in Table 26.2 (with a 11.5% discount rate), the refinancing gain is $81; if this were to be split 50:50, this implies a payment of $40 to each party. In this case there is $150 of extra cash available from the refinancing, so it is not difficult for the contracting authority to be paid its share, and for all the rest of the surplus cash ($110) to be paid to the investors in the project company—the extra amount compared to that paid to the contracting authority thus compensating them for the reductions in distributions which occur afterwards.

There may, however, be cases where the contracting authority's share of the gain needs to be paid over the remaining life of the PPP contract, rather than in an initial lump sum as described above:

- The public-budgeting system may mean that such lump-sum receipts are taken off the contracting authority's other budget allocations, so giving the contracting authority no incentive to agree to a refinancing unless another way can be found of paying its share of the refinancing gain.
- There may not be a lump sum of money immediately available, from which the contracting authority's share of the refinancing gain can be paid, *e.g.* because there has only been an interest-rate reduction or a rescheduling of debt-service payments over a longer period, rather than an immediate increase in the debt amount.

In such cases an alternative method is needed for spreading the payment of the contracting authority's share of the refinancing gain over time. There are two possible approaches here:

- Assuming that the cash-flow changes after the refinancing are all positive (as they would be with an interest-rate reduction or debt rescheduling), the contracting authority and the project company's investors can just 'split the difference', *i.e.* get half of the reduced cost each. But this means having one system in one case and one in other types of refinancing, which is not ideal.
- The second approach is to calculate the refinancing gain on an NPV basis as above, agree an interest rate to be credited on its deferred payment and spread the payments out evenly over remaining PPP contract. The interest rate which should be charged should take account of the risk involved in the deferral from the contracting authority's point of view.

This latter risk is a function of where the deferred payment comes in the cash-flow cascade (*cf. §25.2.3*). If the payments to the contracting authority are made *pari-passu* with payments to the investors in the project company, *i.e.* from surplus cash flow after opex and debt service, this leaves the contracting authority in the *de facto* position of being an equity investor, but without the control over the project company's business which its other investors have. A more suitable approach, therefore, is to make these payments by way of reductions in the service fees. If this approach is adopted, the risk of non-receipt is limited, and it would be appropriate to use a lower interest rate on the deferred payments than that used for the original discount rate when calculating the refinancing gain—*e.g.* instead of, say, a 11.5% rate it should be something closer to the PSDR (risk-free rate).

However, deferred payments should not be the preferred route for a contracting authority if the lump-sum option is available, as this in effect means that the contracting authority lends the money that it would otherwise take as the lump sum to the project company, and will be paid back from increased PPP payments. This is both economically inefficient, and allows the project company's investors to take this extra amount out of the project company at the time of the refinancing, which reduces their financial incentive to ensure that the project company meets the requirements of the PPP contract in future.

§26.2.8 Refinancing and Authority Voluntary Termination

Another issue that has to be considered when looking at refinancing provisions of a PPP contract is the possible interaction between these provisions and the AVT termination-sum payment, in cases where compensation for the debt and equity is calculated separately (*cf. §17.3.3*). The effect of a refinancing having increased the debt on the three approaches to the AVT termination sum set out in Table 17.1 is as follows:

- *Current market-value approach*: The payment for the debt increases because the debt has increased. However, the payment for equity decreases since the lower future distributions after a refinancing reduce the current value of the equity.
- *Future return approach*: Using the financial-close base case (*cf. §23.9.9*) to calculate the NPV of the future equity distributions in clearly incorrect, as these go down after the refinancing. This is dealt with by a provision in the PPP contract that the financial-close base case has to be revised to reflect a refinancing.
- *Original return approach*: Since the equity IRR to the date of the refinancing will include the effect of the refinancing, the termination-sum payment will reduce accordingly.

§26.2.9 Refinancing and Contract Extensions

Yet another refinement of the debate on refinancing arises if the project company offers the contracting authority a 'package deal' of an extension to the PPP contract tenor, and a reduction in annual service fees, along with a payment for refinancing gain-sharing similar to what would have been paid normally.

This may seem like a 'win-win' for the contracting authority, but of course the lower annual payments are achieved by lengthening the debt tenor. Effectively the contracting authority is borrowing money (the refinancing-gain payment and the annual reductions in service fees), and paying it back from the additional annual payments made during the extension period. This extra borrowing is at the project company's relatively high borrowing rate, not the lower rate at which the contracting authority could borrow in its own name. So, the justification for a contracting authority agreeing to an extension in the PPP contract tenor in these cases is not any saving in cost (because this is illusory), but that this is a way to use a PPP to raise additional funds for the contracting authority outside the public budget. (This situation is thus similar in nature to selling off a franchise to the private sector—*cf.* §2.4.2.)

§26.2.10 Should Refinancing Gain-Sharing Apply in All Cases?

The whole issue of sharing refinancing gains between the public and private sectors is thus very complex, and the question must be asked whether the issue is sufficiently important to deserve attention. It has received a great deal of attention in Britain, but this was because the early PFI projects were financed on much less attractive terms than the later generations of such projects, especially as to the tenor of the debt, where tail periods of five years were not unusual. This left a lot of scope for subsequent refinancing gains. The pace of refinancings subsequently slowed down substantially, because:

- Later projects were financed on more competitive terms, so reducing the room for any refinancing gains.
- Having to pay away half of the refinancing gain to the contracting authority obviously reduces the incentive to refinance, especially since sale of the equity shareholding provides an alternative way of making an early gain (*cf.* §26.3).
- Also, some refinancings were done 'behind the curtain' to avoid paying out any refinancing gain, *e.g.* by refinancing though a holding company (*cf.* §20.6.1), leaving the original lenders of record notionally in place, rather than an individual refinancing through the project company.
- Some refinancings ran into tax problems as to the treatment of the refinancing-gain payment received by the investors (the issue being whether it is treated for tax as income, where there would be tax due, or a capital repayment, where tax would not be due).
- Refinancings involve a lot of management time on the part of investors which could be more profitably spent on bidding for new PPP projects; this is especially the case for smaller projects, where the relative costs (legal and financial) of a refinancing are high in relation to the likely level of benefits.

'Excess' or 'windfall' refinancing gains are therefore really only likely to be an issue:

- When a PPP programme is in an early stage of development, and there is likely to be a rapid improvement in financing terms offered by the market.
- For a 'non-standard' project, where financial market perception of its risks may change substantially.

- When there has been 'deal creep' on a project (*cf.* §10.6.8), and no funding competition (*cf.* §22.6), so that the debt-financing terms are out of line with the general market.
- Where a project has been initially financed on adverse financial terms, as happened after the 2008 financial crisis (*cf.* §23.2.7).

It is also difficult for a contracting authority to define a refinancing in a PPP contract in such a way as to catch all possible ways of investors restructuring the debt, directly or indirectly, so as to accelerate withdrawal of equity cash flow out of the project company. Apart from the project company simply borrowing more money, drafting has to cover matters such as:

- refinancings that were already taken into account in the bid, and hence the base case service fees: if bidders take the risk of refinancing in this way they should not be expected to share the benefit;
- refinancings that do not involve lending new money, such as:
  - lengthening the repayment schedule such as in a mini-perm (*cf.* §23.2.7);
  - reducing the loan margin and
  - reducing requirements for reserve accounts (*cf.* §25.2.4);
- the fact that refinancing gains are calculated based on changes in distributions to investors, not just dividends (*cf.* §20.3.5); however, there may be other movements of cash which are not obviously distributions, but which should still be caught, *e.g.* extra payments under the subcontracts where subcontractors are linked to the investors in the project company as this may be an alternative way of getting money out of the project company without sharing any refinancing gain;
- refinancings through holding companies, as discussed above;
- syndication of the loan (*cf.* §22.2.9) or placement of bonds (*cf.* §22.4.1) which should be excluded from the definition of refinancing;
- raising new debt to finance PPP contract variations (*cf.* §16.2.1);
- rescue refinancings (*cf.* §26.2.4); and
- sale of equity (§26.3).

There must also come a point where any refinancing gain is so *de minimis* that the original policy reasons for paying a share to the contracting authority, or for the contracting authority having any control over the matter, have really disappeared. Normal day-to-day waivers and amendments of loan documentation should not be caught in the definition of a refinancing (even if they produce a notional refinancing gain); investors and lenders will not wish refinancing provisions in a PPP contract to be used by the contracting authority to control the normal business activities of the project company.

In a fully competitive market, the benefits that can be achieved by a refinancing should be factored into the initial bids for a PPP project, and therefore if a sharing of refinancing gains is imposed, it may well result in bidders increasing the service fees they would otherwise have proposed, which leaves the contracting authority in a worse position, as lower service fees at financial close are clearly better than the hope of offsetting higher service fees by a future uncertain prospect of a share in any refinancing gain.

If windfall gains of whatever nature (*i.e.* on debt, or on equity as considered below) are considered likely, the simplest way for a contracting authority to share in these may be to take a substantial minority shareholding in the project company, rather than try to catch these through provisions in the PPP contract. This may also give the contracting authority greater access to information on the project company's activities to help reduce the risk of 'hiding' refinancing gain that should otherwise be shared. But as mentioned in §27.4, this may raise conflict of interest and balance-sheet issues.

§26.3 Equity Sale

While refinancing may involve the investors in the project company in complex negotiations with the contracting authority, and result in a significant share of its benefit being paid away to the contracting authority in return for permission to go ahead, sale of the equity shareholding (along with any shareholder-provided subordinated debt) is usually subject to less control by the contracting authority. There may be an initial period during which the original sponsors cannot sell their shares, but thereafter the contracting authority's right to object to equity disposals is likely to be limited (*cf.* §20.6.4).

Sale of equity thus is a highly-likely scenario, as it is based on the substantial difference between the equity IRR required by an original bidder for a PPP project, and that required by a secondary purchaser who comes in after the initial construction risks of the project have passed (*cf.* §20.2.3, §20.3.3). Table 26.3 illustrates the benefit of this from the point of

Table 26.3   Equity sale

($)	Year: 0	1	2	3	4	5	6	22	23	24	25	Total
Buyer												
Total cash flow					− 291	25	25	25	95	95	95	585
Equity IRR = 8%												
Seller												
Project cash flow	−64	−64	−64	25	25							−144
Sale					291							291
Total cash flow	−64	−64	−64	25	315							147
Equity IRR = 36%												
Original investment	193											
Profit on investment	147											

view of both the original investors, and the new buyer, using the same assumptions as Table 26.1 for this purpose.

In this example, the buyer of the equity is a secondary investor willing to accept an equity IRR of 8% on a 'mature' investment, such as a completed and operating PPP, whereas the original investor won the bid on the basis of a 11.5% return. Therefore, using the same cash flow as in Table 26.1, such an investor would pay $291 at the end of year 4, in return for the project company's cash flow from year 5 onwards. The seller of the equity is the original primary investor, who finances the original investment and receives the cash flow until the end of year 4, and then the lump-sum payment of $291 from the buyer. In absolute terms, the original investor has made a profit over a four-year period of $147 on an original investment of $193, or an equity IRR of 36%.

As can easily be seen by comparing these results with Table 26.1, in terms of immediate gain, the sale of equity may be more attractive than a refinancing from the original investor's point of view. This is especially the case if this gain does not have to be shared with the contracting authority (although the remaining revenue from the project company over the life of the project is then lost). It should be noted that a refinancing reduces the future cash flow of the project, and thus its value to another equity purchaser, so it may not be beneficial for the original investor to refinance the debt if the intention is to sell the equity.

It is also apparent from these figures that the political embarrassment for a PPP programme of such equity-sale profits is potentially just as great, if not greater, than from refinancing gains. This therefore raises the question whether the contracting authority should seek to share in such profits as well as refinancing gains. It is possible to construct a 'super profit' formula, whereby all cash flow received by investors, whether by way of refinancing or equity sale, is measured, and if the resulting IRR exceeds a threshold level (obviously higher than the base-case equity IRR), part of this excess is shared with the contracting authority. But problems of definition and legal drafting, already complex enough with refinancing gain-sharing, become far worse with a structure of this type. Moreover, it could again be argued that a profit on the sale of the equity is taxable, so the public sector will benefit in this way instead.

The simpler approach, where equity windfalls are likely to be an issue, is again for the contracting authority to take a minority shareholding in the project company, and thus benefit to that extent by the primary/secondary equity IRR difference through selling this shareholding when the facility is operating (cf. §27.4). Alternatively, as discussed below, another method of sharing in equity gains may be through an equity competition just before financial close.

If there is an especially high level of equity-sale profits, the most important reason for this is likely to be a discrepancy between primary- and secondary-market equity yields, discussed above (cf. §20.3.3): the figures used, of 15% and 8%, are not out of line with those seen in some mature PPP markets such as Britain and Australia. It is evident that if the gap between primary and secondary yields were lower, profits on equity sales would reduce. But as has been seen (cf. §23.5), if the leverage is high, it is the lenders' cover ratio which really determines the equity IRR. So, the issue of equity-sale profits is linked to wider issues of financial structuring for PPPs.

§26.4 EQUITY COMPETITIONS

A competition for part of the equity may help to address the issue of excessive primary equity IRRs (*cf.* §26.3). For example, the original bidders may underwrite half of the equity required for the project, and sell the other half at financial close to the best bidder. (Competition for all of the equity could be considered, but this would make it unlikely that any investor would bid in the first place.) Bidders at financial close should offer a reduction in the equity IRR required by the original bidders (because the high-risk bidding and development phase is over), which can be achieved by paying a premium price (*i.e.* above par value) for the project company's shares.[4] This premium can be split between the contracting authority and the original bidders (as a requirement for the original bidders to underwrite and then sell the equity in this way is not necessarily attractive to them).

However, although there may be some financial benefit from this process, it is also important not to lose sight of the fact that equity investors are more than just sources of finance for projects: they may also bring valuable experience to the project company. Thus, the forced introduction of new shareholders, perhaps without experience in the relevant PPP sector, may not be in the contracting authority's interest.

Equity competition was introduced in the British government's PFI programme (renamed 'PF2'[5]) in 2012 (British Treasury 2012), along with an option for a public-sector 10% shareholding in the project company (*cf.* §27.4). However, it has only been used once so far at the time of writing. There is little enthusiasm on the part of financial sponsors (i.e. institutional investors and infrastructure fund managers—*cf.* §20.2.1) to take the considerable development risks and then have their equity watered down at the last minute in this way. The position of potential subcontractors may be more flexible in this respect if their main driver is the subcontracting work rather than the equity investment.

---

[4] The bidder would pay for the equity based on an NPV valuation between the primary and secondary markets, reflecting the fact that it has taken less risk than the sponsors, but there is still more risk than applies in the secondary market because construction risk still applies.

[5] This is not an abbreviation but the actual name for the programme.

ALTERNATIVE MODELS—SUMMING UP

CHAPTER

27

Alternative Models

§27.1 INTRODUCTION

This chapter looks at some alternatives to the PPP model discussed in the rest of this book. To examine such alternatives, it is useful first to recall some of the key building blocks of the PPP model. These include:

- a PPP contract integrating finance, construction and operation of the facility;
- carried out by a project company with most of the project risks transferred to subcontractors;
- with debt financing from private-sector commercial banks, non-bank lenders or the bond market; and
- equity investment by private-sector sponsors and other investors.

The alternative routes all involve 'unbundling'—*i.e.* the contracting authority procuring one or more of the PPP building blocks separately instead of as one bundle within the PPP contract. (This is of course in conflict with the basic PPP concept of non-separability—*cf.* §2.4.7). Unbundling has already been discussed in relation to:

- *Project scope* (*cf.* §7.3.1)—insofar as any aspect of the project is outside the scope of the PPP contract, this is a form of unbundling. Soft-FM services are an example of this— as previously discussed, there is a case for excluding these services from the PPP contract (*cf.* §15.6.7).
- *Equity competition*—as discussed in §26.4, this allows part of the equity to be procured separately with the aim of reducing the project's cost and hence the service fees.

Public-Private Partnerships for Infrastructure
DOI: https://doi.org/10.1016/B978-0-08-100766-2.00027-9

- *Funding competition*—similarly this allows the debt to be procured separately instead of in an integrated bid (*cf.* §22.6).
- *Public-sector debt finance* (*cf.* §22.9)—which may be agreed separately between the contracting authority and the public-sector lender, meaning that bidders may not have to include private-sector finance in their proposals. Such financing may replace private-sector lenders, or be lent in parallel with them.

However, more radical approaches to unbundling, including removal of some elements of the standard PPP package, can be considered:

— Public-sector procurement (§27.2)

Conventional public-sector procurement may be adapted to achieve the main benefits of a PPP structure, without some of the drawbacks of the higher cost of private finance and the inflexibility of a long-term PPP contract. However, this will probably involve funding wholly provided by (or at the risk of) the public sector, with the budgetary implications that this entails as well as less effective 'whole-life' risk allocation and facility maintenance.

— Post-construction take-out (§27.3)

As the highest-risk phase for a PPP is usually during construction, a post-construction take-out (or assumption of risk) by the contracting authority cuts out the 'higher' cost of private-sector financing thereafter in return for taking operation-phase risks. This also at least allows the facility to be kept off the public-sector balance sheet during the construction phase, if this is important but, again, has implications for 'whole-life' risk allocation and facility maintenance.

— Public-sector equity investment (§27.4)

The contracting authority (or another public-sector entity) becomes one of the project company's equity investors, the idea of this being to ensure that the public sector shares in equity returns and any other 'windfalls' (*cf.* §26.1). However, this is liable to lead to a conflict of interest which may not be in the contracting authority's best interests.

— Not-for-profit structures (§27.5)

Another approach to reducing the cost of capital for PPP projects is to eliminate the equity return which goes to the private sector, or retain it for the benefit of the public sector. Paradoxically, however, this may result in higher initial service fees.

— 'Regulated asset base' (RAB) structure (§27.6)

This introduces a regulatory system similar to that used in some countries for privatised utilities.

§27.2 PUBLIC-SECTOR PROCUREMENT

Ignoring the question of whether public-sector funding is really 'cheaper' (*cf.* §28.5), it is possible to adapt conventional public-sector procurement so that it takes advantages of some of the benefits inherent in a 'fully-fledged' PPP structure, while still using public funding.

§27.2.1 Design-Build-Operate

A turnkey construction contract can eliminate the construction risk without the need for the full panoply of a PPP structure. A Design-Build-Operate (DBO) Contract is an extension of the D&B structure that tries to alleviate this problem. It takes the 'F' out of DBFO, and just requires an integrated bid for construction of the facility, together with provision of long-term FM services.[1]

Under a DBO Contract, the contracting authority pays for both construction and FM/O&M contract costs as they are incurred, in the same way as a project company pays for these in the standard PPP structure. If felt necessary, a private-sector project-management company can supervise and manage these contracts on behalf of the contracting authority, in a similar way to a PPP project company. There is also greater long-term flexibility to make changes in the DBO contract because it is not bundled up with 'external' financing, *i.e.* there are no financing stakeholders and associated contractual obligations that have to be dealt with. Consequently, the DBO structure is less complex (fewer parties are involved) and so should be quicker to complete and inherently reduce costs.

However, there must be some question whether the same long-term risk transfer can be achieved as in the conventional PPP structure, especially as to maintenance risk (*cf.* §13.6) and the benefit of the 'whole-life' approach to this (*cf.* §28.6.1, §28.8). What happens if the DBO contractor fails to maintain the facility? Clearly there will be penalties, but these can never be as significant as the potential loss of capital (equity and debt) that arises when a PPP contract is terminated for failure to perform (*cf.* §28.9.7). Thus, any apparent transfer of risk in this structure may be illusory, because it may be cheaper for the DBO contractor to walk away than to deal with a long-term problem with maintenance costs.

In any case a DBO contract requires public-sector funding, which may not fit with an objective for a PPP programme (*cf.* §28.3).

§27.2.2 'Public-Public Partnerships'

Another approach makes use of the organisational benefits of a project company to manage the construction and operation of the facility, still using (generally private sector) subcontractors for most, if not all construction and operating services in the same way as a PPP, but with all the financing being either provided or guaranteed by the contracting authority. This is a fairly common structure and it is often found in the water sector where a separate but publicly-owned entity works under 'corporate' disciplines (an example being the partnership between the Stockholm public water utility and a number of public utilities in the Baltic States). This approach was also used in financing construction of the

---

[1] An alternative term is 'design, construct and maintain' (DCM).

first motorways in France: the main motive for this at the time was that the financing was outside the state budget, but this would be more difficult to achieve now.

The 2012 Olympics and the Crossrail projects in London are other examples of public-public partnerships. These were both very large projects that were able to support sophisticated project governance and contractual arrangements to manage a vast range of subcontractors effectively.

Nonetheless, a publicly-run project company may be less effective than a private-sector project company's sponsors in negotiating with subcontractors, especially if these sponsors are not themselves subcontractors, and hence have no conflict about squeezing subcontract costs (*cf.* §20.2.2); and because the debt financing is public-sector provided or guaranteed, lender discipline over the process is lost. Thus, a public-public partnership's lower financing costs may be offset by higher subcontract costs. And again, there is no risk capital in this structure. Furthermore if the objective is to introduce private-sector financing that is outside the public-sector budget this structure will not achieve this (unless the contracting authority itself is not classified as a public entity for public debt purposes).

§27.3 Post-Construction Take-Out

The idea here is to leave the construction risk with the private sector, but for the contracting authority to take over responsibility either for the project as a whole, or for its debt at least, thereafter. This reflects the fact that even if a facility is on the public-sector balance sheet, this need not apply when it is still under construction, when construction and initial financing risks remain with the private sector. As the construction period may last several years, this both keeps the high-risk construction phase with the private sector, as well as postponing any budgetary problem.

— Design-build-guarantee-operate (DBGO)

This is a development of the DBO approach discussed above: the key extension is that commercial banks or other private-sector financial institutions guarantee construction financing provided by the contracting authority, the guarantee being released on completion of the facility. DBGO has the advantages of using lower-cost public-sector finance while bringing lender discipline back into the picture during the highest period of risk.

— Construction finance with a take-out

A further development of the DBGO model is to require an SPV to raise private-sector financing for construction of the facility, which will be repaid by the contracting authority when it is completed. 'Equity' may be provided by the construction contractor, but in effect this is nothing more than a deferral of its profit on the construction and is also paid off on completion.

This structure has been used in Italy, for example, under the 2001 *Legge Obiettivo* ('Target Law'), intended to finance major infrastructure projects. The law provides for DBFO structures, but alternatively for financing by the construction contractor during the construction period, with a take-out by the public sector on completion. (*Cf.* the French and German systems described in §18.2, of which the latter still leaves some operation-phase risk with the lenders.)

However, structures like these described above may be difficult to negotiate with lenders. The problem is that if there is a default on the construction contract, or a lengthy completion delay going beyond the agreed backstop completion date, the lenders may be in a poor security position. In many standard PPP contracts, the termination-sum payment in these circumstances would include an amount relating to the NPV of the long-term PPP contract cash flow (*cf.* §17.2.3-§17.2.7), but no such amount would be payable under this structure. Of course, it could be said that the NPV of future cash flow should not be taken into account if the facility has not even been constructed (*cf.* §17.2.8). Also, in the conventional PPP approach, the lenders can hope that even if there are cost overruns, or delays and loss of revenue, which have forced an increase in the debt or additional rolled-up interest (which also causes an increase in the debt), the future revenues may be used to pay off this excess, at the expense of the equity investors. The result may be that in the absence of this future cash flow the lenders require a 'sunset date' by which their debt has to be repaid by the contracting authority even if the facility has not reached completion. If so, this radically changes the risk transfer and would probably not represent VfM for the contracting authority.

A variation on this theme is a PPP-contract tenor between a post-construction take out and the full tenor of a standard PPP contract, which ends after the first major-maintenance/life-cycle renewal in order to help ensure there are reasonable incentives for good design and high quality construction (*cf.* §15.3.1). This limits the need for private financing over tenors that may not be available in some markets (especially in developing countries) and may help provide greater flexibility for the contracting authority in the medium-term. However, the higher service fees required to amortise the capital expenditure over this shorter tenor may raise affordability issues.

§27.4 PUBLIC-SECTOR EQUITY INVESTMENT

The contracting authority (or another public-sector entity) may require the sponsors to allow it to invest in the project company's equity.[2] The motivations for this approach vary:

— Concessions

 Here the reason may just be in order to share in the profits of the project company (but there may be balance-sheet classification issues depending on the level and type of control—*cf.* §9.4.2).

---

[2] The term 'institutional PPP' is often used to describe structures with public-sector equity, but these are generally joint-venture arrangements between the public and private sectors for the purpose of exploiting or commercialising a public-sector asset or jointly managing an activity (*cf.* §4.6) rather than providing a service under a PPP contractual arrangement. In many cases, the asset (such as land or intellectual property) may be contributed to the venture by the public sector, with cash and management skills coming from the private-sector partner.

— Availability PPPs

In this case the motivation is usually driven by policy considerations about transparency, *i.e.* the problems arising from the project company having better access to information (*cf.* §19.10), and also sharing in 'windfall' equity gains (*cf.* §26.3). In these cases, the equity share is typically around 10-30% with a right to appoint a member of the board of the project company. The terms of the shareholding, set out in the shareholder agreement (*cf.* §20.6.2), are similar to those that a commercial minority shareholder would expect (*e.g.* right to veto changing the project company's constitutional documents, changes in dividend policy or levels of indebtedness and allowing for the flexibility to sell the shareholding). However, there need to be certain provisions to address obvious conflicts of interest when it comes to issues such a dispute under the PPP contract with the contracting authority.[3] Again though, the level of equity and the rights attached may have an impact on balance-sheet classification.

There are some significant questions that arise relating to the choice of the private-sector partner, and maintenance of an arm's-length relationship between the contracting authority and the project company. These issues occur at various stages:

- Procurement:
  - Should there be a two-stage procedure, first for choosing a partner and then for the PPP contract itself?
  - What procedure is appropriate if the contracting authority first sets up a public-public partnership (*cf.* §27.2.2) and then sells a shareholding in the project company to private-sector investors?
- PPP contract negotiations—how can the contracting authority be on both sides of the table?
- Long-term management of the PPP contract—the same question arises;
- Will the contracting authority-appointed director have the time and capacity to do this extra job? (The nature and level of workload can be greater than expected);
- What happens if the project gets into difficulty—will the contracting authority be forced to rescue it to protect its own shareholding, because it is concerned about 'reputation risk', *i.e.* if the project fails and the contracting authority is a shareholder it will be seen to have failed as well (*cf.* §9.3.4, §17.2.9)?
- Is the contracting authority prepared for a potential loss?

So, while a PPP with public-sector equity has obvious political attraction, this is a structure that the contracting authority has to handle with considerable care to ensure that the wrong decisions are not taken because of its dual role.

---

[3] A public-sector shareholding of up to 10%, combined with an equity competition, are two key additions in the PF2 changes to the British PFI model for availability PPPs (*cf.* §2.3). This shareholding is effectively managed by the British Treasury on behalf of the contracting authority, so helping to deal with potential conflicts of interest. But the use of this structure is quite recent and has been fairly limited to date (*cf.* §26.4).

§27.5 NOT-FOR-PROFIT STRUCTURES

Even if some form of public-sector debt financing is provided as discussed above, the marginal difference compared to private-sector loans is relatively limited. The highest return is of course made by the equity investors in the project company, and it is this equity return which can be a key factor in making PPPs politically unacceptable. 'Not-for-profit' structures are a way of dealing with this issue. Such structures should also ensure that insofar as there are unexpected financial windfalls from a project, these will accrue to the public sector. Three not-for-profit models are discussed below:

- 'pinpoint equity' or 'debt-only' structures (§27.5.1);
- the Scottish 'Non-Profit-Distributing' (NPD) structure (§27.5.2) and
- public trusts (§27.5.3).

§27.5.1 'Pinpoint Equity' Structures

As it is the relatively-high equity return that is most vulnerable to any political opposition (*cf.* §28.13), a 'debt-only' structure has an obvious attraction. In a typical debt-only structure, the project company's shares continue to be owned by private-sector investors, but the actual share capital is negligible in size (hence the term 'pinpoint equity'[4]), and no distributions are made.[5] Such structures can be used where there is a very secure cash flow, *e.g.* a road concession which expands the capacity of an existing road bridge by building another in parallel (and hence the traffic and toll-revenue flows are already well established), which was the case in the early British projects for the Dartford and Severn bridges, and the Portuguese second Tagus bridge.

The immediate objection to such structures is that they are inevitably more expensive in service-fee terms. This is because the debt must still have a cover ratio; the result can be seen in Table 27.1, which compares a standard PPP financing with 90% debt with one financed with 100% debt:

- The figures at (A) set out the 'standard' structure: calculating in a similar way to Table 23.3, the service fees required to cover the debt service provide the lenders' required 1.2× ADSCR, and a 15% equity IRR, amount to $84 *p.a.* (N.B. This calculation ignores the further service fees required to cover opex.)
- (B) then assumes that the project is financed with 100% debt, on the same terms. The debt service is $77 *p.a.*, which means that with an ADSCR of 1.2× the service fees have to go up to $92. Therefore, (B) is immediately more expensive for the contracting authority—however, (B) is also producing a surplus of $15 *p.a.* which cannot be used to provide an equity return but has to go somewhere.

[4] This would also be the case where most of the equity investment is in the form of shareholder subordinated debt (*cf.* §20.3.5), but the difference in the pinpoint equity structure is that dividends are not paid on the equity shares.

[5] Other corporate forms can be used for this purpose, such as the English 'company limited by guarantee', instead of by shares.

Table 27.1 100% debt financing

Assumptions:
- Project cost   1,000
- Debt interest rate   6%
- Required ADSCR   1.20 ×
- Debt tenor   26 years
- Required equity IRR   15%

PPP contract tenor   28 years

($)	Year: 1	2	3	18	19	20	26	27	28	Total
(A) *Standard structure*										
Debt/equity ratio 85:15										
Annuity debt service	65	65	65	65	65	65	65			
15% equity IRR	15	15	15	15	15	15	15	80	80	
Total service fees	**80**	**80**	**80**	**80**	**80**	**80**	**80**	**80**	**80**	**2,246**
ADSCR	1.2 ×	1.2 ×	1.2 ×	1.2 ×	1.2 ×	1.2 ×	1.2 ×			
(B) *100% Debt*										
Opening loan balance	1,000	983	965	523	478	429	73			
Interest payments	60	59	58	31	29	26	4			
Principal repayments	17	18	19	46	48	51	73			
Total debt service [a]	77	77	77	77	77	77	77			2,000
Closing loan balance	983	965	946	478	429	378	0			
Total service fees ([a] × 1.2) **[b]**	**92**	**92**	**92**	**92**	**92**	**92**	**92**	**92**	**92**	**2,584**
Surplus ([b] − [a])	15	15	15	15	15	15	15	92	92	**584**
(C) *Surplus used for debt service*										
Opening loan balance	1,000	968	933	89	2					
Service fees (=[b])	**92**	**92**	**92**	**92**	**2**					**1,663**
Interest payments [c]	60	58	56	5	0					
Principal repayments ([b] − [c])	32	34	36	87	2					
Closing loan balance	968	933	897	2	0					

- (C) therefore assumes that all surplus cash flow after debt interest payments is devoted to principal prepayments, and the PPP contract is terminated when the debt has been paid off; as can be seen, this occurs in year 19, instead of year 28 in the standard structure. (The result is similar to the LPVR model—*cf.* §15.5.2.) This structure has the further advantage that if subsidies have to be paid to make it viable, and too much is handed over in subsidies, these do not benefit equity investors. It can also be combined with a minimum revenue guarantee by the contracting authority (*cf.* §18.4).

  However, although the cost is much lower over the life of the project, the higher initial service fees (which remain at $92 to provide the required ADSCR) may raise an affordability problem. Nonetheless this structure—*i.e.* once the debt is paid off the facility is toll-free—has commonly been used in public-public partnerships, and was also used in the road bridge PPPs in Britain and Portugal mentioned above.[6]

But if structure (C) is used, someone has got to own and run the project company. There is a danger that the construction subcontractor may be the only person who has an interest in doing this, but there is an obvious conflict of interest here during the construction phase and little or no involvement during the operation phase. The lenders, on the other hand, have an incentive to ensure that the facility is built on time and to budget, and operated as required, to ensure that their debt is repaid, so the project company can be owned by them (assuming this does not cause them any balance-sheet or other regulatory problems).

In fact, a more likely structure is for there to be two layers of debt—senior and mezzanine (*cf.* §22.6)—with the mezzanine lenders, who may include the subcontractors, controlling the project company. This may have the effect of lowering the initial service fees, because the mezzanine debt, although more expensive than the senior debt, should require lower cover ratios.

Care still needs to be taken, however, with the governance of the project company: the lenders have no incentive for their loan to be paid off quickly, and could be tempted to use the cash-flow surplus for other purposes (*e.g.* to pay themselves a higher credit margin), and if the construction subcontractor is a mezzanine lender, the conflict of interest remains. Therefore, such governance controls need to be imposed *via* the PPP contract. This position is likely to be less than ideal (and also occurs in the NPD model, discussed below), which is why a public-trust route may be preferable. Indeed, the incentive issue is wider than this, since although the lenders have loan capital at risk, the greater risk/return incentive from the equity finance being at risk has been lost.

Moreover, the contracting authority's evaluation of structures (B) and (C) requires some care. If the evaluation is based on the NPV of the service fees (*cf.* §10.6.5), a distinction has to be made between the gross service fees, which can be discounted at the PSDR (*cf.* §8.6.2) and the surplus cash flows. The risk on the latter is quite different, and akin to the risk on an equity investment, meaning that an equity IRR rate should be used as the discount rate for the surpluses.

---

[6] However, under Eurostat rules (*cf.* §9.4.5), this structure would put the project on-balance sheet for the public sector because the contracting authority is effectively an equity shareholder (*i.e.* it receives all the profits of the project after the debt is paid off). It is also difficult to use this structure for availability PPP projects as the real level of risk transfer to the private sector becomes very limited.

§27.5.2 Non-Profit-Distributing Model

The NPD model was developed in Britain by the Scottish regional government as there were political objections to the equity profits generated by standard availability PPPs. At the same time projects needed to be off-balance sheet for the public sector. The key points of comparison with the standard PPP structure were:

- The financing was split between senior and subordinated debt in the same way as a standard project financing, and with the pinpoint equity majority owned by the subordinated lenders, as in a standard PPP structure.
- The contracting authority did not own any of the shares.
- No dividends were to be paid on the equity—surpluses after debt service were to be donated to a charity (*e.g.* in the case of a hospital project the surpluses could be paid to a charity associated with the hospital).
- The charity could nominate an independent director (to a board where a majority of the directors were appointed by the subordinated lenders).
- An independent director was appointed by another public-sector body unrelated to the contracting authority. This director had various blocking and other rights to ensure that any conflicts of interest were dealt with appropriately and also had the power to direct the charity on how any surpluses were to be applied.
- The PPP contract could be terminated before its final maturity if all the debt were to be paid off (*i.e.* there would actually be no surplus payable to the charity).

This was initially a structure suitable for keeping such projects off-balance sheet, and this remained the case when the structure was refined further, including elimination of the charity and having the 'independent' director appointed by the contracting authority. However, it subsequently failed the Eurostat balance-sheet tests.

§27.5.3 Public Trusts

The concept of a not-for-profit PPP owned by its lenders, although shown to be possibly viable by the projects already mentioned, is still inherently a bit strange. The alternative is for the project company to be, or to be owned by, a public trust. The term 'trust' as used here is not a legal term of art, but means an entity which is:

- independent of the contracting authority;
- not owned or controlled by private-sector investors; and
- not-for-profit.

We have come around in a large circle to get to this point, because an 18th-century school or hospital owned by a charity, or a turnpike road operated by a turnpike trust (*cf.* §2.4.1), both fit into this definition.[7] And interestingly enough the first specific project

---

[7] 'Is there anything whereof it may be said See this is new? it hath been already of old time, which was before us.'—*Ecclesiastes* I, 10.

which the authors have found officially described (by President Eisenhower) as a 'public-private partnership' (in *Time* magazine, 14 November 1955) was the construction, with part-funding from the federal government of the Priest Rapids and Wanapum Dams on the Columbia River, Washington State, by the Grant County Public Utility District, a public trust providing electricity. (However, this was not a PPP as defined in this book, as the federal funding was just a construction subsidy with no long-term contractual relationship.)

Since a public trust is another debt-only model, it faces the cover-ratio problem discussed above. In this case, a cover ratio can be created in one of two ways:

- by providing an existing cash flow to the trust as a 'starter'; using the example in Table 27.1, if the trust has a surplus cash flow of $15 *p.a.*, it will be able to raise financing for the new investment; this works well if the trust is formed to, say, upgrade an existing toll road; and
- by higher service fees, as shown in Table 27.1.

In either case, the trust will of course have a running cash-flow surplus: this can be used to retire debt early as in the pinpoint equity structure, subsidise service fees, or spend on other related public services. A 'snowball' effect can develop—as new infrastructure produces increasing cash flows, the surpluses from these can be used to back new borrowing and further investment. Public trusts are quite common in the United States, and were used for some of the first modern toll roads, the Pocahontas Freeway in Virginia and the Southern Connector in South Carolina. Similarly, public trusts (housing associations) are now the main providers of social housing in Britain: these may begin their activities with transfers of social housing from the public sector, and are then able to raise financing for further investment based on this existing rental cash flow, with all their surplus cash flow being ploughed back into further investment. The public-trust approach thus works well for concessions.

It is also easier to use a public-trust than a pinpoint-equity approach for financing social infrastructure using availability PPPs, because again something has to be done with the surplus. As said above, the surplus cannot just be used for debt reduction (or paid back to the contracting authority) as this would most probably put the project on the public-sector budget. But a project company owned by a public trust can develop, say, a school PPP project, with the public trust devoting the surplus cash flow that arises from the lenders' cover ratios to building another school. From the contracting authority's point of view, this may offer good VfM compared to the standard PPP structure if this application of the surplus by the public trust can be used within the contracting authority's own VfM calculations: *e.g.* if the surplus is applied by the public trust within the geographical area for which the contracting authority is responsible. (There may be further tax benefits from the public trust being a charity, or the project company making tax-deductible donations of its cash-flow surplus to a similar charity.)

However, the contracting authority may still struggle to demonstrate that this structure provides VfM compared to the standard PPP structure. The easiest way to compare the two is to take the NPV of the service fees under the standard structure, and compare this with the NPV of the service fees under the public-trust *minus* the NPV of the running surplus. Taking the examples in Table 27.1, assuming a PSDR of 6% and a discount rate for the surplus of 15% (the same as the private-sector equity IRR for the reasons mentioned above (*cf.* §27.5.1), the results are as follows:

- Case (A): Standard PPP structure:
- Case (B): Debt-only structure:

NPV of service fees	=	$1,075
NPV of service fees	=	$1,237
Minus: NPV of surplus cash flow =		$104
Net NPV cost	=	$1,133

So, using these assumptions, Case (A) actually offers better VfM for the contracting authority. The results are highly-sensitive to the discount rates used, especially for the cash-flow surplus; a lower discount rate for the latter will turn the result around: *e.g.* 12% produces an NPV cost of $1,108, so making Case (B) apparently the better choice. Similar issues arise in the pinpoint-equity structure.

There are also governance problems involved in using a public-trust structure: lenders may be concerned that the lack of a commercial imperative means that the project company will not be managed effectively, *i.e.* the benefit of private-sector project management and other skills (*cf.* §28.9) will be lost.

In summary, therefore, although the real financial benefit of eliminating private-sector equity from PPPs may be more limited than might at first be thought, this may be balanced by not-for-profit structures being more politically acceptable, and avoiding the transfer of later financial windfalls to the private sector. However it is difficult to keep such structures off-balance sheet for the public sector, especially in the case of availability PPPs.

§27.6 REGULATED ASSET BASE STRUCTURE

It could also be argued that PPP contractual structures—however adapted—are too rigid for dealing with long-term public-infrastructure requirements, and so if such infrastructure is to be financed by the private sector, this may be better done though a regulatory régime. Under the RAB structure, the project company's long-term service standards and investment returns are controlled by independent regulators rather than set out in PPP contracts, in a similar way to privatised utilities (*cf.* §2.5). The investment-return calculation is based not on what the facility actually cost but what the regulator decides is a reasonable cost (and allowing for depreciation). This is different to the PPP approach in which the capex, investment return and service costs are in effect fixed in advance (provided the project performs as expected) for a long period of time.

This approach has not been widely adopted,[8] but could have a rôle to play in concessions, and possibly availability PPP projects. It may have the advantage of eliminating windfalls by capping total investment returns, however derived, while allowing for changes in capex, opex and capital structure over time. It would probably also make it easier for the contracting authority to introduce changes into the scope and nature of the service being provided. However, this approach relies on a credible and effective regulatory system and can be open to criticism as to what level of costs and equity return are deemed 'acceptable'.

---

[8] It was used in the early 2000s in Britain for availability PPPs that were to upgrade the infrastructure in the London Underground system, but these collapsed mainly because of the difficulty of the regulator and the sponsors (all construction companies) agreeing the costs of these improvements at the regulator's first review date. The structure was also used in 2015 for the Thames Tideway Tunnel, a major sewage project in London.

PPPs—For and Against

§28.1 Introduction

Why has there been such a worldwide growth in interest in PPPs? The public-sector reform movement that began in the 1980s, known as 'New Public Management' (NPM), provides the theoretical background for PPPs (§28.2). In reality, however, one of the main drivers for growth in many, but not all, countries is that PPPs avoid limitations on public-sector budgets (§28.3).

The debate on the additional merits and demerits of PPPs is a highly-complex one. A variety of arguments are used by governments for promoting PPP projects, but many of these are of a somewhat *ex-post* nature, *i.e.* they are used to justify a decision that has already been taken for budgetary reasons. These arguments have appeared throughout this book, but it is probably worth summarising the issues. The main elements of the debate revolve around:

- the benefits of accelerated delivery of investment in public infrastructure (*cf.* §28.4);
- the higher financing costs implicit in PPPs (§28.5);
- whether risk transfer (such as construction completion) and VfM from PPPs can be offset against higher financing costs (§28.6);
- economies of scale (§28.7);
- the benefits of whole-life costing and maintenance (§28.8);
- the value added through the use of private-sector skills and allowing the public sector to focus on its core activities (§28.9);
- PPPs as a catalyst for public-sector reform and the concept of contestability (§28.10);
- complexity (§28.11); and
- the effect of PPPs on public-sector flexibility (§28.12).

Finally, the political context of this debate has to be borne in mind (§28.13).

§28.2 New Public Management, Privatisation and PPPs

PPPs must be seen within the overall context of the public-sector reform movement known as New Public Management (NPM), which encourages:

- decentralisation of government;
- separating responsibility for the purchase of public services from that of their provision;
- output or performance-based measurements for public services;
- contracting-out public services to the private sector; and
- privatisation of public services.

All of these increasingly blur the boundary between the public and private sectors. So, while the BOT contract and its variants provided the *technical* basis in the 1990s for a new generation of PPPs (*cf.* §2.4.4), the *theoretical* or *political* basis was provided by NPM.

The privatisation of public services, championed by the Thatcher government in Britain and other countries in the 1980s, was driven by NPM-based beliefs that there should be a 'roll-back of the state' with the private sector providing services where this is more efficient. This was especially prevalent in the utilities sector, underpinned by the belief that the introduction of competition leads to a better service and lower cost for the citizen (or customer), as well as less waste of economic resources (especially if services are supplied free or below cost by the state). The NPM trend reversed the 20th-century trend for public services to be provided by the state (whereas before that charities or private-sector capital usually took the initiative (*cf.* §2.2)). The subsequent (post-Thatcher) British PFI programme (*cf.* §2.4.7) was aimed at extending the benefits of its privatisation experience to core public services that could not be privatised. VfM and other arguments (discussed in Chapter 8 and below in §28.6) derive from this NPM way of thinking. However, there are important differences between privatisation and PPPs, some of which make it difficult for a PPP to achieve the same results as a privatisation:

- The contracting authority remains directly politically accountable for a PPP-provided service, but not for a privatised service.
- The citizen is usually not especially conscious that a PPP-based service is being provided by a private-sector company rather than the public sector, whereas this is obvious for privatised services.
- In a PPP, ownership of physical assets normally remains with (or reverts to) the public sector, whereas in a privatisation they become permanently private sector-owned.
- A PPP usually involves the provision of a monopoly service, whereas a privatisation usually means the introduction of competition to provide the service (or in its absence, regulation with a view to working towards competition).
- In a PPP, the scope and cost of services is fixed by a specific contract between the private and public sectors, whereas in a privatisation they are controlled, if at all, by some form of licensing or regulation which allows for regular cost changes, or are simply left to the forces of market competition.

In addition to the efficiency strand of thinking in the NPM, there is also an equity (in the sense of fairness) strand. Proponents of PPPs may claim that PPP can better match the delivery of a service to when it has to be paid for. This is fairer to society over time as today's taxpayers do not have to pay for most of the costs of a facility that will mainly be enjoyed by future taxpayers. This argument, however, is weakened if today's investment is financed by borrowings, the repayment burden of which will fall on future taxpayers. But it can also be argued that a PPP, especially a concession, helps to ensure that the costs of a project fall more directly on those who will use it when they use it—thus a toll road is directly paid for by drivers. This cannot be taken too far as it soon starts to raise issues of which forms of public infrastructure this could apply to and how to account for the benefit of having a service readily *available* to citizens even if they decide not to use it.

§28.3 BUDGETARY BENEFIT

While NPM has provided a theoretical basis for PPPs, a major attraction for govern ments is that PPPs do not require public-sector funding today. In many cases, PPPs may allow the capital cost of a public-sector facility to be spread out over its life, rather than requiring it to be charged immediately against the public budget (*cf.* §9.3). This cost is then either (for concessions) paid for by users instead of paying taxes, or (for availability PPPs) charged to the public-sector budget over the life of the PPP contract, in either case through the payment of service fees. A PPP programme may thus enable the public sector to break free of short-term constraints on investment in public infrastructure imposed by insuffi- cient tax revenues and limits on public-sector borrowing. In economic terms, PPPs there- fore allow the benefits of a project to be delivered sooner than might otherwise be possible, although the benefit of this is not often measured (*cf.* §28.4).[1]

Some of the names given to PPP programmes, such as Britain's former 'Private *Finance* Initiative' or the terms 'innovative finance' or 'alternative financing and procurement', reveal the view that PPPs are at least then partly about private-sector *finance* for public- sector investment.

This is fine so long as using PPPs as a finance tool does not create the affordability illu- sion (*cf.* §9.2.1), *i.e.* encourages projects today that turn out not to be affordable in the long term. This may eventually worsen the original constraints that led to the adoption of the PPP route in the first place, which is a particular danger where an availability PPP pro- gramme is large in relation to the budget for the overall sector: the problem was evident in Portugal (Abrantes de Sousa, 2011), for example, where payments for a major and rapidly-developed PPP road programme had a significant effect on the public budget and led to a subsequent restructuring of these road PPPs (and ironically also reclassifying them as 'on-balance sheet' projects in the process).

---

[1] It is arguable from a macroeconomic point of view that if public investment increases, private investment decreases, and so the net result is the same whether investment is public or private, but there seems to be little evidence that PPPs 'crowd out' private-sector investment elsewhere (although they may affect the construction industry, as discussed later on). Similarly, it is generally clear that PPPs are indeed undertaken in addition to other forms of public-sector investment, not in substitution for it.

While the financing element may be a way temporarily to ignore the fact that the project eventually has to be paid for, it may also enable the original capital cost not to show up as expenditure in the public budget or to be classified as public-sector borrowing at all, *i.e.* to be off the government's balance sheet (*cf.* §9.4). Escaping the normal public-sector budgeting processes may lead to projects that in other respects represent poor VfM, to inappropriate project prioritisation and potentially unsustainable future obligations.

Putting aside the issue that a PPP project, just like any other infrastructure investment, eventually has to be paid for and whether such future costs are justified, it can on the other hand be claimed that a PPP improves budget *certainty* by giving visibility to, and fixing today, the long-term costs of construction and operation. This enables easier and more transparent long-term budget planning. Of course, this depends on the long-term payment obligations of the PPP being recorded and monitored in some form.

The budgetary benefit and its potential downside are therefore not necessarily a 'for or against' argument for PPPs. PPPs are merely a tool: they can be useful if used for the right purpose or in the right way, but destructive if used for the wrong purpose or in the wrong way, *i.e.* it is the motives and responsibility of the user of the PPP tool, not the tool itself, that is the issue.

While PPPs can shift *when* services are paid for, they can also shift the burden as to *who* pays. Concessions are attractive to governments as a means of taking the payment burden off the public sector as users, not government, pay for the service (§9.2.3). This is perhaps the main attraction of this form of PPP. Furthermore, it may be argued that concessions are also more efficient as payments from the user pass directly to the provider avoiding the inefficiencies and administrative costs of passing through government. This benefit, however, has to be considered in light of other factors, such as the VfM of transferring demand risk (§13.2). Moreover, there may still be payment obligations for government, even if contingent, that need to be considered (*cf.* §9.3.4).

§28.4 Benefit of Accelerated Delivery

As mentioned above (*cf.* §8.8.2, §28.3), by enabling resources to be made available sooner, a PPP enables the benefits of the project to be delivered earlier than might otherwise be the case. In countries that face severe current resource constraints, but are expected to grow in the future, the benefit of receiving services today rather than much later on can be considerable. However, the benefit of earlier service delivery is often not specifically recognised or measured (as compared to the benefits of risk transfer, which are exhaustively assessed in the various quantitative approaches to VfM assessment (*cf.* §8.3). If a benefit-cost analysis of the project is carried out (*cf.* §3.4.2), these benefits of earlier delivery can be estimated. In France, for example, this can be done by applying the PSDR and assuming that a project's benefits are least equal to its costs (otherwise the project would not go ahead anyway on a benefit-cost basis). Say a conventionally procured project costs $100 in NPC terms but will be operational in 5 years and the project procured as PPP costs $105 but will be operational in 3 years. The question then is whether the value of the earlier delivery of the PPP is worth the additional $5. If we assume that PV of the benefits of the project are at least $100, then the additional value of bringing this benefit of $100 forward by 2 years is the difference between this benefit of $100 *compounded* by two years at the PSDR under the PPP and the later benefit of $100 under the conventional procurement: assuming a PSDR of 4% this is therefore $100 \times (1.04)^2 - \$100 = \$8.16$. $8.16 is greater than the additional cost of the PPP ($5), so the PPP is better VfM in this instance (EPEC 2011).

§28.5 FINANCING COST AND RISK TRANSFER

Private-sector finance for a PPP clearly costs more than if the project were procured in the public sector and financed with public-sector borrowing: the cost of capital for a PPP is typically around 2-5% *p.a.* higher than that of public-sector funding, even for an availability PPP where the payment stream is still derived from the public sector.

Public-sector borrowing is cheaper because lenders to the government are not taking any significant risk with their money, whereas lenders to a PPP are obviously taking a greater risk. But a project's risks do not disappear just because the public sector is funding it—these risks are retained by the public sector when it funds a project and constitute a concealed cost of the project, which should be added to the lower cost of public-sector financing to make this comparable with a PPP's financing costs.

There is an alternative view that the public sector is better able to spread out risks than the private sector—hence there is a real difference between public- and private-sector risk assumption, and so the real cost of public-sector funding of a project, even taking account of risk, is actually lower than financing and managing the project by the private sector. But if this view were carried to the extreme, it would mean that the government should finance everything. And it can equally be said that companies in the private sector are owned by many individual shareholders (directly or *via* investment or pension funds) who diversify their risks by owning a wide range of shares. There is therefore not a strong case for suggesting that there are fundamental differences in the abilities of the public and private sectors to absorb risk.

But quantifying the risk transfer to a PPP (or the corresponding risk that would be retained in a public-sector procurement) is difficult, as already discussed (*cf.* §8.6.1), as is quantifying the case for other possible benefits from a PPP, discussed below. The realistic approach is that debate about comparative financing costs assumes that there is a free choice between public-sector funding and a PPP, whereas most of the time, given public-budget constraints, no such choice exists and the choice is actually between a PPP and no project at all. The issue then becomes whether the facility is being procured cost-effectively as a PPP, irrespective of what might theoretically have been the outcome with public-sector procurement. This could be based on evidence from previous similar PPP projects, on the benefits of the PPP delivered service compared with having no service at all or a combination of these.

§28.6 RISK TRANSFER AND VALUE FOR MONEY

Despite this difficulty of quantification, risk transfer remains a key element of the VfM argument in favour of PPPs (*cf.* §8.3)—namely, that certain risks that are transferred can be better managed by the private sector, and thus the cost of doing this will be lower than if such risks are retained by the public sector. Hence the transfer of certain risks improves VfM. In this context, VfM is not based on just what is initially cheapest, but takes account of the combination of risk transfer, whole-life cost (§28.8) and service provided by the facility, as a basis for deciding what offers the best value. VfM arguments are of considerable political importance in gathering support for a PPP programme. The risk-transfer element of VfM is also inextricably linked with the fact that projects cannot generally be taken out of the public-sector balance sheet unless sufficient risk transfer to the private sector can be demonstrated (*cf.* §9.4).

There is no doubt that PPPs encourage the public sector to identify whole-of-life project risks and think about risk transfer in a way that has not been usual in conventional public-sector procurement. The way in which risk transfer works in PPP contracts is a complex process as discussed in detail in Chapters 11-13, but in summary a PPP transfers the risks of construction and either the market/usage risk or the availability/service delivery risk to the private sector. The arguments for or against PPP for each of these main risk categories are discussed briefly below.

§28.6.1 Construction Risk

Procurement of major projects by the public sector can result in large construction-cost overruns (*cf.* §8.3.3), whereas a contracting authority's payments for a PPP are fixed by contract. Therefore such overruns should not (and generally do not) occur. Thus, it is clear that construction risks are transferred to the private sector in a PPP.

But the reason for this is not so much the PPP structure itself, as the fact that construction costs are fixed under a turnkey (or 'design-build') contract (*cf.* §12.3.1), in which the project company (through the construction subcontractor) also takes design risk, *i.e.* the risk of any errors or omissions in the design, or other unforeseen work. Turnkey contracts do not completely eliminate the risk of cost overruns or failure to complete the facility (*cf.* §12.3.3). Nevertheless, they do avoid the problem, endemic in public-sector design-bid-build procurement, of initial low bids from contractors being inflated by change orders as the contracting authority develops and changes the design. However, a turnkey contract's initial cost is inherently higher than a design-bid-build approach (*cf.* §12.3.5), which leaves room for cost overruns in the latter. Also, there can be large increases in PPP-project costs (which may be hidden by a reduction in the scope of the project) between the time that bids are received and the final signing of the PPP contract (*cf.* §10.6.8)—*i.e.* cost overruns do occur, but at a different stage in the process. Procurement rules have tightened in some regions and countries to reduce this type of behaviour (*cf.* §10.5).

In any case, turnkey construction contracts can also be used in public-sector procurement substantially to eliminate cost overruns, provided the contracting authority can specify, negotiate and supervise these contracts effectively (*cf.* §27.2). Similarly, the combination of design and build inherent in a PPP contract should ensure faster completion of construction, as these activities can be partly carried out in parallel instead of in sequence. Again, this benefit could be secured by the contracting authority entering into a design-build contract instead of using design-bid-build.

However, it should be borne in mind that in a PPP it is not only the construction subcontractor who is at risk, but also the private-sector equity and debt. If something goes seriously wrong with the construction subcontract, such as the subcontractor itself getting into financial difficulty, further losses can be imposed on the investors and lenders, which is not the case in a public procurement of a turnkey contract.

§28.6.2 Demand Risk

In concessions, demand risk is usually transferred to the project company (but it may be underpinned by the contracting authority—*cf.* §18.4), and to some extent also in availability PPPs. However, this may not always be cost-effective if the private sector has to charge heavily for taking on demand risk. For this, as well as for reasons of financeability, in Europe and the United States, PPPs have moved away from using concessions in favour of availability PPPs. And for some time now the general trend in PPP projects where the contracting authority pays, has been for demand risk to be retained by the contracting authority, rather than using shadow tolls (*cf.* §15.5.4). On the other hand, some of the main arguments in favour of transferring demand risk usually centre around the avoidance of white-elephant projects (*cf.* §28.9.1) and the impact it may have on driving service performance in a competitive market, particularly in the transport sector (poor service leads to lower demand and therefore lower revenues for the project company).

§28.6.3 Availability and Performance Risks

Although these risks may be transferred to the project company, the real level of such risks, once the facility has been built, appears to be quite low (*cf.* §15.6). However, as many projects have yet to reach the end of their contract lives, time will tell if this is the case and evidence in some markets is starting to suggest that some performance (and long-term maintenance and lifecycle risks, discussed below) may have been under-estimated by bidders.

§28.6.4 Operation and Maintenance Costs

The risks of operating-cost overruns are generally transferred to the project company (*cf.* §13.6); as discussed in §28.8, this 'whole-life' approach to building and maintaining the facility, which is fundamental to the PPP process, so that the contractor has to live with the consequences of its quality of design and construction, is one of the strongest VfM arguments for PPPs. Again, however, these risks are not always transferred in full (*cf.* §14.10, §16.2.4).

§28.6.5 Reality of Risk Transfer

But how real is any risk transfer? A PPP, by definition, provides an essential public service. If the private-sector investors in the PPP get it wrong they may lose their investment (*cf.* §28.9.7), but they have no obligation to put further money in to rescue the project (*cf.* §21.5.1). If the PPP fails, it is quite likely that the contracting authority will incur extra costs to maintain the public service, so risk transfer will fail to this extent anyway.

Moreover, as the contracting authority's main concern is to ensure that the PPP continues to provide the contracted service, the easiest way of achieving this may be to provide extra support for the project rather than terminate the PPP contract and then try to sort out new arrangements. Such a support process may mean that the contracting authority takes back responsibility for risks that had been transferred to the private-sector investors (*e.g.* traffic flow), thus negating the intended risk-transfer benefit of the PPP. This process has been characterised as 'privatising profits while socialising losses'.

However, it would not be correct to suggest that this is what always happens if PPP projects get into trouble, so long as there are good financial incentives for the private-sector side of the table to sort the matter out (*cf.* §28.9.7). In particular, the lenders, as opposed to investors, may play an important rôle: the contractual design of the PPP usually seeks to encourage the lenders to sort out the problem first before government has to, on the simple premise that they will not get their money back unless they do so. This is why allowing lenders to step into the shoes of the project company is so integral to the financing structure of a PPP (*cf.* §25.3.3), and, conversely, why fully guaranteeing the lenders that they will get their money back (*cf.* §17.2.1), destroys this incentive.

Another key factor is the availability of other private-sector investors and operators prepared to take over a troubled project (for a price that reflects its current status) instead of the contracting authority being required to do so. Again, the contractual structures of a PPP often set out the specific mechanisms to enable this (*cf.* §17.2.5). So, in this case risk transfer depends on there continuing to be a healthy supply of contractors and operators who are available and willing to replace those who fail to deliver on a PPP contract. And even mature programmes may find that the supply of contractors is limited if there has been a process of consolidation in the industry.

But, most fundamentally, the reality of risk transfer may come down to political will. While it is a truism that risk transfer is limited if there is no mechanism in the PPP contract for making deductions for poor performance, there is no point in this mechanism if the contracting authority is unwilling to exercise its rights in this respect. The politically-expedient but expensive option may be for the contracting authority to sort out the problem rather than sticking to the terms of the PPP contract, when the more politically-challenging option would be to risk letting the project company fail, using the PPP contract mechanisms correctly (*cf.* §9.3.4, §17.2.9, §17.6.1). If the contracting authority takes the latter route it can demonstrate that it is serious about risk transfer. This further reinforces the incentive for the private party to bear risks in future projects in accordance with the PPP contract's terms. This was a positive lesson learnt in the early days of the British PFI schools programme when contracting authorities stuck to the contractual provisions. Despite dire forecasts of the PPP school projects concerned opening late and the potential for political embarrassment, the project companies were told that they had no choice but to sort out the failing projects. In the end most of the schools opened with minimal delays and without additional costs falling on the public sector.

A more common problem with risk transfer is that the contracting authority may simply not be aware of all its contractual rights and so fail to exercise them due to poor day-to-day contract management (*cf.* Chapter 19). Risk transfer is therefore not only about what the PPP contract should or should not say, but about how well the contract is actively managed over the long-term (*cf.* Chapter 19) and how tools, such as a risk register, are used (*cf.* §11.6).

§28.7 ECONOMIES OF SCALE

Because a PPP allows investment in public infrastructure to be accelerated, in some cases a project which might otherwise have been procured by the public sector in smaller parts (*e.g.* a road divided into sections) can be procured as a whole. The economies of scale in construction (*e.g.* because construction contractors do not need to mobilise for operations for each section separately, or because this enables the use of specialised heavy equipment) should result in a saving in capital costs; also in some cases speeding up construction can avoid construction-cost inflation.

On the other hand, a large increase in demand for construction works on PPPs can cause problems of capacity in the local construction industry, and so lead to an increase in prices, offsetting other benefits that might be derived from the PPP route. Significant increases in construction costs have thus been seen for British schools and hospitals, and Portuguese roads, all sectors where there have been large PPP programmes. Similarly, the size and complexity of PPP projects often discourages smaller contractors from bidding, so reducing competition, which may also affect the final cost. To some extent these issues can be addressed if the public sector better recognises the limitations of the market and the impact that its own demand has on the market. Taking a more strategic approach to developing market capacity, sometimes referred to as 'market shaping' involves tools such as market sounding (*cf.* §10.4), programme approaches (*cf.* §4.6) and managing an orderly flow, or 'pipeline', of projects to market (*cf.* §4.2).

One practical advantage of the PPP arrangement is that separate public-sector procurement processes are no longer required for the individual components of each project or over the life of the project (*e.g.* when a component needs replacing). The private party is free to procure the relevant inputs as and how it sees fit. The VfM for the contracting authority has already been established at the level of one single procurement of the overall project outputs.

§28.8 WHOLE-LIFE COSTING AND MAINTENANCE

Whole-life costing is perhaps the most important element of the VfM case for PPPs. Because the investors are responsible both for the construction of the facility and for its operation and service delivery, they are incentivised to design it to produce the best 'whole-life' cost—*e.g.* private-sector investors may be prepared to spend more on the initial capex if this will result in a greater saving in hard-FM or even soft-FM costs over the life of the PPP contract, whereas a typical public-sector procurement approach is to go for the lowest initial capital cost. However, in cases where investment in PPP contracts is finance-driven rather than contractor-driven, integration of the whole-life design approach may also become weaker (*cf.* §20.2). And the case for 'bundling' construction and long-term services together is also weaker in relation to soft-FM services (*cf.* §7.3.1, §15.6.7).

But it is the risk-transfer argument which is more significant here. A PPP transfers the maintenance-cost risk—probably the most difficult to predict (*cf.* §13.6). Having capital at risk ensures that the investors in, and lenders to, the project company cannot easily walk away from this risk (*cf.* §28.9.7).

It can also be said that the long-term contractual nature of a PPP forces the public sector to provide for maintenance (through the service fees) of its assets, without regard to short-term budget constraints. This prevents the omission of routine maintenance, which is typically what happens when public-sector budgets are squeezed, which leads to higher costs in the longer term. At the same time, the performance-based nature of payment provides the incentive for the private sector to carry out the maintenance, if service fees are not paid (or deductions are made) when maintenance standards are not met. A PPP contract thus should ensure that the facility is maintained to pre-determined standards throughout its life (*cf.* §17.8).

Of course, the benefits of 'tying the hands' of the authority to ensure that it does not omit routine maintenance, also means that when budgets are tight, a contracting authority may have to accept denying, say, a clinical service because its budget is already committed to the hospital's building-maintenance costs or not repainting a school wall quite so often to maintain the standard in the contract which may no longer be considered affordable.

§28.9 PRIVATE-SECTOR SKILLS

It is also argued that the involvement of the private sector in PPPs brings particular benefits that are not available to public-sector procured projects.

§28.9.1 Project Selection

Where service fees are dependent on demand, and assuming these are not underwritten by the contracting authority in any way (*cf.* §18.4), the private sector has an incentive only to back good projects, and avoid 'white elephants'.

However, there is a danger that the ability to transfer some types of risks and not others may distort the decision on how to proceed with a project. For example, a road which can be funded through tolling may be preferred to an untolled alternative which produces greater economic, environmental or other benefits: *e.g.* 'non-compete' provisions in toll-road concessions may inhibit the development of other public-sector roads (*cf.* §13.3).

§28.9.2 Project Management

It is claimed that the private sector has greater expertise in managing complex projects, and hence delivering them on time and on budget, as well as maintaining services thereafter. This may well be the case, given that public-sector management of major projects has a fairly poor record, but projects can be managed by the private sector without private-sector finance as well (*cf.* §27.2.1).

§28.9.3 Single-Point Responsibility

A PPP contract provides the contracting authority with a single point of responsibility for the construction and operation of the facility, thus eliminating 'interface' problems, where each contractor blames the other for problems. Again, it may be possible to produce a structure that could achieve this result without using private-sector financing (*cf.* §27.2.1).

§28.9.4 Efficiency

The proposition here is that the private sector is fundamentally more efficient than the public sector, because the profit motive is the main incentive for efficiency. But there is a problem with this in the PPP context where the private sector is not really paid for being efficient, but for performing what is required under the PPP contract. By 'fixing' the required level of efficiency through the performance regime of a PPP contract (*cf.* §15.6), the contracting authority loses the opportunity to make future efficiency savings of its own over the tenor of the PPP contract, unless the operating-cost element of the service fees is indexed at a rate below that of FM/O&M inflation (*cf.* §24.3.2), or unless such savings can be achieved through contract changes (*cf.* §16.2.2), improving asset use (*cf.* §19.4.4) or value testing (*cf.* §19.4.2).

This argument is much stronger when it is used in relation to privatisation of services in a competitive market, rather than in a PPP context where there may be no competition, especially in the case of an availability PPP once the PPP contract has been signed. However, it does at least illustrate the importance of competition when awarding PPP contracts (*cf.* §10.2).

And although there may well be scope for improvement on how a contracting authority operates, unless careful quality controls are in place, private-sector 'efficiency' may actually consist of no more than employing fewer staff at lower salaries (*cf.* §19.11), or other action that lowers the quality of the public service being delivered.

However, this argument is not without merit: it is evident that the combination of the PPP contract deductions and penalties for failure to perform, and controls by investors and lenders over the project company, should ensure that management inefficiency and other remediable performance failures are detected and dealt with swiftly, compared to public-sector procurement where such failures are more easily buried.

§28.9.5 Innovation

It is also argued that PPPs give private-sector bidders the opportunity to come up with a variety of different solutions, and so give the public sector the benefit of innovatory approaches, whether in design of the facility or the method of delivering the service. This is linked to a key feature of PPPs, namely that the contracting authority usually specifies outputs rather than inputs when calling for private-sector bids. Service fees are then only made if output specifications are met (*cf.* §15.2, §15.6.1, §15.6.2). It is the greater flexibility of how to meet output specifications that gives bidders the opportunity to come up with innovatory solutions.

Having said this, many private-sector bidders for PPPs rely heavily on staff who originally worked in the public sector: it is difficult to believe that such staff suddenly become innovative just because they have changed jobs. So, if they cannot be innovative in the public sector, there is something wrong with the system rather than the people. It can indeed be argued that public-sector officials are not incentivised to innovate if this means taking more risks, but on the other hand it can also be questioned how much room for innovation there really is in many PPPs. A contracting authority that already operates similar facilities is likely to have the best detailed knowledge of what can (and cannot) be done to make them better. This is an argument for the design of 'standard' PPP projects (such as a school building) to be specified by the contracting authority rather than using output specifications which require individual bidders for the projects to spend time and money drawing up their own designs. However, some care is needed here; if the contracting authority specifies inputs, this may jeopardise the risk transfer—*e.g.* if the contracting authority gets the design wrong, it may have to be responsible for this. (A way of getting around this problem is for the contracting authority to require bidders to accept the design risk anyway.)

Moreover, lenders to PPP projects generally discourage innovation if this creates additional or unknown risks from their point of view, particularly with regard to technical innovation, where untried and untested technologies are usually not bankable. Innovation can therefore mean different things and PPPs can be inappropriate for some forms of innovation.

§28.9.6 Third-Party Revenues

In some types of PPP, the project company may be able to generate additional revenues when the facility is not fully utilised as public-sector infrastructure (*cf.* §15.8). Although the same thing could be done by a contracting authority as owner of the facility, private-sector management skills may be more effective in this respect. Any such additional revenue may help to reduce the service fees and hence improve VfM for the contracting authority. It is tempting though for contracting authorities to over-estimate the level of third-party revenues when making the case for the affordability of a project.

§28.9.7 Capital at Risk

Where public services are outsourced (*cf.* §2.3), if private-sector companies do not perform well, they will lose the profit from this work, but (generally speaking) that is all. In a PPP, the private-sector investors and lenders have capital at risk, and therefore a greater financial incentive to ensure that the service is provided as required. This is the key risk-allocation driver in the PPP structure, since it underpins the transfer of long-term maintenance risk discussed in §28.8.

§28.9.8 Third-Party Due Diligence

The lenders' involvement in PPPs means that a third party will check the project's viability (*cf.* §22.2.7), which can be beneficial to the contracting authority (*cf.* §21.5.2). This discipline is likely to be stronger for concession projects where lenders may be exposed to demand risk. Users will only use the project if it makes sense for them, so lenders have a strong incentive to assess the expected demand for the service.

§28.9.9 Principal-Agent Problem

In economic theory, there is a principal-agent problem if the agent who controls a business has access to more information than the principal who owns it, and this asymmetry of information can be used to give the agent an unreasonably large share of the benefits of a business. Asymmetry of information may arise in any kind of public-sector procurement, so giving rise to potential excess profits for a private-sector supplier. The long-term relationship inherent in a PPP may give more time for this asymmetry to develop. For example, the contracting authority may find it difficult to determine if the project company's proposed costs for making changes to the specifications of the facility are reasonable (*cf.* §16.2.3, §19.4.3). This may point to a strategy of using a mix of procurement approaches and not relying on a single one. Furthermore, each of these approaches can drive improvements in the others as discussed further below.

§28.10 PUBLIC-SECTOR REFORM

A PPP programme can serve as a catalyst for wider public-sector reform in a number of different ways:

§28.10.1 Transparency and Accountability

A PPP makes the real long-term cost of the facility clear—it cannot be cut into pieces and buried in the depths of public-sector accounting. In particular it shows the whole-life cost of the facility, including operation and maintenance, in a transparent way, and forces the public sector to make choices about how services are to be delivered and paid for. Public-sector accounting does not deal with the cost of public infrastructure in this integrated way. The result of transparency is accountability: as public-sector officials cannot hide the cost of choices, they must justify them, however uncomfortable this is.

In this connection, when comparing the costs of a PPP and public-sector procurement, it is important to ensure that like is being compared with like. Operation and maintenance costs, even in a relatively simple accommodation PPP contract such as a school, may amount to 30% of the annual service fees, and up to 50% for a more complex building such as a hospital. These costs are all bundled together as part of the total cost of the PPP contract, and it is clearly inappropriate to compare them only with the funding of the initial capital cost for a public-sector procured facility.

However, although the costs may thus be transparent to the contracting authority, this does not necessarily mean that they are similarly transparent to the general public. Commercial confidentiality tends to be the main reason for this (*cf.* §19.10). But if information is not made publicly-available, over-simplified 'apples and oranges' comparisons between PPPs and public-sector procurement are inevitable (*cf.* §28.13), as are wider criticisms of lack of public accountability.

In the same way that costs are made clear, PPPs also sharpen the assessment of risks in delivering a project (*cf.* Chapters 11-13). Clearly identifying what these risks are, how they are managed or mitigated and who should best manage them is central to any decision on public investment, PPP or otherwise. However, the nature of risks is they do not have an immediate cash implication (unless there is insurance against them). It is therefore easy for a contracting authority to ignore or bury their impact. Because PPPs involve having to define and allocate these risks over the long-term to various parties, a PPP can force the contracting authority to acknowledge the true costs of risks. This is an important benefit of quantitative VfM assessment (*cf.* §8.7), despite its shortcomings. Following on from this, it is sometimes claimed that PPPs can be looked at as a form of insurance policy: the additional costs in finance and preparation of a PPP are in effect an insurance premium, *i.e.* a defined and certain cost paid by the public sector to insulate it from potentially greater and uncertain costs materialising in the future. Assessing VfM is then about answering the question whether or not this 'insurance premium' is justified in relation to the likelihood and cost impact of the risks covered.

§28.10.2 Procurement Skills

The PPP process, if properly handled, develops better procurement skills in the public sector. This is because public-sector requirements have to be analysed and clearly set out in advance, and once decided cannot easily be changed (at least without a cost which cannot be buried elsewhere). A major factor behind public-sector construction-cost overruns is that the contracting authority does not specify what it wants in sufficient detail, or keeps changing its mind about what it wants during the construction phase of the project. While cost overruns are not impossible with a PPP (because the contracting authority will probably retain some construction-related risks—*cf.* §16.2.4), they are certainly less likely.

Furthermore, the contracting authority has to consider the long-term service delivery, operation and maintenance of the facility as part of the overall cost when negotiating a PPP contract, instead of looking only at its initial capital cost. Lessons in 'joined-up thinking' learned from PPP procurements can be applied by the public sector in a much wider context. Ideally the transparency of PPP procurement would also spill over to public-sector procurement. In some more mature PPP markets, it can be argued that this has been happening, with the PPP approach to the project assessment, assurance and approval process being incorporated into wider public-sector processes.

On the other hand, new procurement skills that are developed may subsequently be lost because a particular contracting authority may only undertake one or two PPP projects. Thus, once a deal is done, the project team is disbanded (*cf.* §6.2.2). Furthermore, public-sector officials with good PPP experience tend to move to often better-paid jobs in the private sector, so PPP expertise is also lost in this way. On the other hand, private-sector companies are obviously able to move their teams from project to project, allowing them to accumulate experience, so creating a greater discrepancy between the public and private sectors in this respect.

§28.10.3 Management

A PPP allows the contracting authority to act as a contract manager and not as a service provider, and thus concentrate on service planning and performance monitoring instead getting tied up in the day-to-day delivery of the services. However, the loss of day-to-day management control of public facilities raises its own issues since the ultimate responsibility for these services still lies with the contracting authority. The flexibility issues discussed below may also affect the contracting authority's ability to manage the delivery of services.

§28.10.4 'Contestability'

If a small number of PPPs are undertaken in a particular sector (*e.g.* education), these can serve as a benchmark against which costs and service delivery in respect of the large majority of facilities still under public-sector control can be compared rather like holding up a mirror to the public sector. This may lead to improvements in public-sector procurement and service delivery as well. In some cases, such contestability can help make the case for change so obvious that it can help to force improvements to less efficient engrained practices. This was one of the benefits of the Britain's prisons PPP programme, in which custodial services were transferred to the private sector as part of the package. This forced the contractors to think carefully about long-term operating costs, which in turn drove changes to prison design. Less than 10% of Britain's prisons are PPPs, but the effect has spilled over to prison design in general.

§28.11 COMPLEXITY

It has probably become evident to the reader that a PPP adds a substantial layer of extra complexity to the already complex task of procuring a project. This complexity translates itself into a longer procurement period, which means that part of the accelerated delivery advantage discussed in §28.4 may be eroded, and into higher procurement costs, including the costs of specialised legal and financial advisers who would not be required for a public-sector procured project. PPP procurement costs can reach 5-10% of the 'hard' capital cost for a reasonably large project, and these costs do not reduce *pro rata* for smaller projects (*cf.* §20.4). It follows from this that PPPs are not cost-effective for very small projects, unless these can be 'packaged' together (*cf.* §7.5.1) or delivered as part of a highly standardised programme (*cf.* §4.6). Equally, it is questionable whether PPPs are suitable for very large projects where the addition of extra complexity to the structure may make the project collapse under the weight of its own complications (not to mention the risk of reduced market capacity and therefore competition).

The size and complexity of PPPs therefore limits competition from private-sector bidders, since smaller construction contractors, in particular, do not have the necessary financial resources to sustain the risks of a PPP contract (*cf.* §12.3.2), at least in the eyes of lenders. This is another factor that tends to increase construction costs where there is a large PPP programme.

On the other hand, some of the perceived additional 'complexity' may simply reflect the activities that should be carried out when undertaking any form of public-sector investment activity, such as thorough risk analysis or estimations of long-term costs. The PPP process, involving more parties from outside the public sector and greater transparency (*cf.* §28.10.1), is less forgiving about taking shortcuts in these respects. So, the genuinely additional complexities of a PPP are likely to stem more from the contractual structuring issues: it is the cost of these that have to be set against the benefits of having private sector capital at risk and a payments process that depends on long-term performance. At the same time, a PPP removes a different set of complexities associated with the management of the design and construction of the facility from the public sector. The balance of increased complexity is not as obviously against PPPs as might first appear.

More recently, it has become apparent that the long-term project management of PPP contracts by contracting authorities introduces its own set of complexities, in addition to those involved in preparing and procuring the PPP (*cf.* Chapter 19). This can be particularly the case when it comes to monitoring and checking performance, and dealing with disputes that arise from this, or managing contract changes (*cf.* §16.2.2, §19.4.3). Similarly, the refinancing of a project (*cf.* §26.2), which would simply not be an issue for a public-sector project, may require highly specialist financial skills, not least to ensure that the originally-designed allocation of risks is not disturbed. In one sense, a PPP has just transferred the shorter-term complexities of managing a construction contract to a set of longer-term complexities in managing a long-term services contract. Yet the prevailing attitude among many contracting authorities is that a PPP will virtually run itself once the PPP contract is signed—nothing could be further from the truth.

§28.12 FLEXIBILITY

Lack of flexibility during the relatively short-term construction phase of a project has considerable merit, if, as discussed above, it ensures that the contracting authority cannot keep changing its mind about what it wants and the costs that go with this. But there are longer-term issues resulting from a contracting authority entering into a commitment which may extend for 20-30 years' of operation. A PPP contract is of a type known in legal theory as an 'incomplete contract'—*i.e.* the contract cannot provide for all possible eventualities in the future. The longer and more complex the contract the more this is the case, and therefore the more it is impossible for the contracting authority to abdicate or transfer responsibility for dealing with unforeseeable circumstances.

For example, it is very difficult for the public sector to predict the usage requirement for some types of facility over a long period of time—*e.g.* population changes may make a school or hospital redundant, or alternatively require it to be expanded. Similarly, there may be a change in technology which requires a significant part of the facility to be replaced or make it no longer needed. PPP contracts do not accommodate such events easily, and major amendment to, or cancellation of, a PPP contract part-way through its life is inevitably expensive. There is a direct relationship between flexibility and VfM, albeit one that is difficult to quantify financially. This needs to be taken into account in considering the whole-life costing of the facility and, ultimately if the choice of a PPP route is appropriate.

It follows from this that projects with a stable long-term planning horizon, such as roads or other transport facilities, fit well with the PPP approach (*cf.* §15.3.1), although even here there can be problems—*e.g.* non-compete provisions preventing the contracting authority from undertaking other road improvements (*cf.* §13.3, §16.2.4). Conversely, those projects where the contracting authority cannot clearly specify and stick to its long-term requirements, or where technology is changing rapidly, are not suitable for PPPs. It is mainly for the latter reason that PPPs are less commonly used for IT projects. (Other reasons can be problems in achieving enough risk transfer to the private sector, a different cost structure—low initial costs and high continuing costs—which can make financing difficult, and the high failure rates for such projects.) Social infrastructure projects fall somewhere between the transport and IT positions.

However, it must be remembered that if the public sector builds a facility, this too represents a long-term commitment, albeit buried in government accounting. If such a facility becomes a 'stranded asset' (*i.e.* no longer viable for the purpose for which it was originally designed), it still cannot be knocked down or moved without considerable loss. It could therefore be argued that all a PPP does is make this issue transparent—but there are issues of flexibility that are peculiar to a PPP, in particular the cost of making major changes to the facility when there is effectively a monopoly supplier in place (*cf.* §16.2.3), and the extra financial costs of terminating the PPP contract if the facility is no longer required (*cf.* §17.3). For this reason more varied approaches to PPP contract tenors may develop, even if this may require greater/earlier levels of funding from the contracting authority.

§28.13 PPPs AND POLITICS

Given the public-service nature of PPPs, it is inevitable that they are subject to heavy political debate. Unless there is a strong political will on the public-sector side of the table, and the ability to communicate the case for pursuing PPPs clearly and fairly (*cf.* §4.4), political winds can easily blow the process off course and a PPP programme will struggle for success.

One aspect of this debate is that despite being clearly different (*cf.* §28.2), PPPs may still be regarded as a form of privatisation, which gives rise to various reasons for political opposition:

— 'Private profit at the public's expense'

It may be claimed that PPPs give private-sector investors the opportunity to make profits by providing services that could be provided by the public sector more cost-effectively. But many of the individual elements of a PPP structure, such as construction of the facility, would have been provided by the private sector anyway. The marginal extra profit that the private sector makes from investing in a PPP project, as compared to the profits on direct public-sector procurement, is probably not great enough to sustain this argument. In any case if the public sector does not have the budget capacity to undertake the project, this argument is based, like that of comparing costs of public- and private-sector procurement, on the false premise that there is a choice between public-sector procurement and a PPP.

It should also be borne in mind that the private sector makes losses as well as profits on PPP projects, especially during the construction phase. There are many cases of construction subcontractors underestimating costs for fixed-price turnkey contracts or suffering LD payments if the facility is completed late, in the worst case leading to bankruptcy (*cf.* §12.3). Similarly, equity investors' returns may be squeezed down by long-term operating and maintenance costs being higher than projected (*cf.* §13.6).

However, if private-sector investors are perceived to be making 'windfall' profits, for example through high initial rates of return on investment (*cf.* §20.3.3), debt refinancing (*cf.* §26.2) or sale of their equity shareholdings (*cf.* §26.3), this certainly does weaken a PPP programme from the political point of view.

- Poor operating standards

  It may be argued that a facility operated by a private company will 'sacrifice safety for profit'. But a PPP is under close supervision by the contracting authority, and safety standards should be clearly laid down in the PPP contract: in this respect, a contracting authority probably has more ability to control and supervise safety than could be applied to a privatised company. In any case, the private company is subject to numerous wider health and safety regulations whether it is operating under a PPP or more conventional arrangements. The highly-specified and fixed nature of operating standards required of a PPP structure also drives greater *consistency* in the quality of service (irrespective of whether the standards themselves may be better or worse than public-sector delivery).

- Erosion of working conditions

  It may also be claimed that a PPP erodes the working conditions of public-sector workers in cases where this work—*e.g.* in cleaning and catering—is taken over as part of the PPP. This is the one aspect of a PPP where the position is the same as that of a privatisation—in both cases public-sector workers may be taken over by a private company, and it is up to the contracting authority to ensure that private-sector investors in a PPP are not encouraged to treat the workforce unfairly, *e.g.* by concentrating on 'efficiency gains' that are only obtained by cutting the pay and numbers of staff. In some cases, staff working conditions may be protected by law or through secondment arrangements (*cf.* §19.11) to prevent this happening.

Political opposition to PPPs is often quite misconceived. For example, specifications (*e.g.* the number of beds in a hospital) are a matter for the contracting authority to decide when procuring the PPP contract, but those opposed to PPPs may claim that private investors have made such decisions. PPPs may also be disadvantaged by their greater transparency with regard to overall costs, (*cf.* §28.10.1), so the costs of a PPP, including long-term operation, may be wrongly compared to the initial capex for public-sector procurement only. Similarly, the greater transparency required of PPPs with regard to reporting performance levels as part of the service fee payment mechanism (*cf.* Chapter 15), means that mistakes are more obvious.

On the other hand, the case made by a contracting authority for a PPP can be equally one-sided, *e.g.* with claims of large cost savings compared to public-sector procurement that cannot be proved objectively (*cf.* §8.6, §19.9), or that do not compare like with like, and PPPs may be promoted for short-term political advantage.

It does not help that the range and often quality of *ex-post* assessments of projects delivered both as PPPs and through more traditional means is not as extensive as it ought to be even after several decades of PPP activity. However, the challenges of carrying out such assessments—such as the availability of long-term operating cost and service-level data for traditionally procured and operated facilities—and making comparisons of like-for-like service levels should not be under-estimated.

It can thus be difficult to maintain a balanced debate on the pros and cons of a PPP programme, especially, as this chapter has made clear, because the arguments for and against PPPs are by no means black and white.

References and Further Reading

The references cited in the text, as well as other useful publications on PPPs, are set out below. Most of these are available for free Internet download.

The following websites gather together a large amount of information on PPPs that can be used to supplement this list:

PPP Knowledge Lab, launched in 2015 by Asian Development Bank, European Bank for Reconstruction and Development, Inter-American Development Bank, Islamic Development Bank and the World Bank Group, with support from the PPP Infrastructure Advisory Facility (PPIAF). Other multilateral bodies, such as EIB/EPEC, ESCAP, GPOBA, OECD and UNECE also contribute materials.

Public-Private-Partnership in Infrastructure Resource Center (PPIRC), maintained by the World Bank; this includes a database of PPP agreements and related documents, as well as the *Private Participation in Infrastructure (PPI) Project Database*, covering PPPs and other private-sector investments in infrastructure projects in developing countries.

European PPP Expertise Centre (EPEC), part of the European Investment Bank, publishes guidance materials on PPPs and maintains a database of PPP projects in a European context.

Global Infrastructure Hub (GIH), established by the G20, provides guidance and data on infrastructure policy and project development globally.

Abrantes de Sousa, Mariana, *Managing PPPs for Budget Sustainability* (Henley-in-Arden: Association for European Transport and Contributors, 2011)

Allen & Overy, *Contractual Terms in PPP Projects* (London 2016)

Auditor General of Ontario, *Infrastructure Ontario—Alternative Financing and Procurement*, 2014 Annual Report of the Office of the Auditor General of Ontario (Toronto 2015), Chapter 3 Section 3.05

Australian Department of Infrastructure and Regional Development,
— *National Public Private Partnership Guidelines, Volume 1: Procurement Options Analysis* (Canberra 2008)
— *National Public Private Partnership Guidelines, Volume 4: Public Sector Comparator Guidance* (Canberra 2008)
— *National Public Private Partnership Guidelines, Volume 5: Discount Rate Methodology Guidance* (Canberra 2013)

Bain, Robert, 'Construction Risk—What Risk?', *Project Finance International* (London: Thomson Reuters, 2010)
— 'Is it time to revisit PPP ratings?' *Infrastructure Investor* (February 2011)

Blanc-Brudé, Frederic & Dejan Makovšek, *Construction Risk in Infrastructure Project Finance* (Lille: EDHEC Business School, 2013)

Boardman, Anthony & Mark Hellowell, *Comparison and Analysis of Specialist PPP Units' Methodologies for Conducting Value for Money Analysis* (Vancouver, BC/Edinburgh: University of British Columbia/University of Edinburgh, 2015)

British Department for Business Innovation & Skills, *Employment Rights on the Transfer of an Undertaking: A Guide to TUPE Regulations* (London 2014)

British Infrastructure and Projects Authority, *OGC Gateway Process Reviews 0-5* (London 2016)

British National Audit Office,
— *Private Finance Projects* (2009)
— *Performance of PFI Construction* (2009)
— *Lessons From PFI and Other Projects* (2011)
— *Equity Investment in Privately Financed Projects* (2012)
— *Review of the VFM Assessment Process for PFI* (2013)
— *Savings From Operational PFI Contracts* (2013)
— *PFI and PF2* (2018)

NAO has produced over 40 published reports on individual PFI projects or more general aspects of PFI; most of these have been the subject of hearings by the House of Commons Public Accounts Committee, which then also publishes reports on these topics.

British Treasury,
— *Value for Money Assessment Guidance* (London: HM Stationary Office, 2nd edition 2006)
— Office of Government Commerce, *Competitive Dialogue in 2008: OGC/HMT Joint Guidance on Using the Procedure* (2008)
— *Green Book Supplementary Guidance: PFI* (2013)
— *Green Book Supplementary Guidance: Optimism Bias* (2013)
— *Fair Deal for Staff Pensions: Staff Transfer From Central Government* (2013)
— *Public Sector Business Cases: Using the Five Case Model, Green Book Supplementary Guidance on Delivering Public Value From Spending Proposals* (2013)
— *Standardisation of PF2 Contracts, Draft* (2017)
— *The Green Book: Appraisal and Evaluation in Central Government* (3rd edition 2003)

Bull, Matt, Anita Mauchan & Lauren Wilson, *Toll-Road PPPs: Identifying, Mitigating and Managing Traffic Risk* (Washington DC: PPIAF, 2017)

Burger, Philippe & Ian Hawkesworth, 'How to Attain Value for Money: Comparing PPP and Traditional Infrastructure Public Procurement', *Organisation for Economic Co-operation and Development Journal on Budgeting* Volume 2011/1 (2011)

Buso, Marco, Frédéric Marty & Tran Phuong Tra, *Public-Private Partnerships From Budget Constraints: Looking for Debt Hiding* EPPP DP No. 2016-1 (Paris: Chaire Economie des Partenariats Public-Privé, Institut d'Administration des Enterprises, 2016)

Chen, Can & John R. Bartle, *Infrastructure Financing: A Guide for Local Government Managers* (Omaha, NE: University of Nebraska at Omaha, 2017)

Deloitte Touche Tohmatsu Limited, *IFRIC 12 Service Concession Arrangements—A Pocket Practical Guide* (New York: Deloitte IFRS Global Office, 2011)

Dewulf, Geert, Anneloes Blanken & Mirjam Bult-Spiering, *Strategic Issues in Public-Private Partnerships* (London: Wiley-Blackwell, 2nd edition 2012)

Doran, George, 'There's a S.M.A.R.T. Way to Write Management's Goals and Objectives', *Management Review AMA Forum*, 1981

Engel, Eduardo, Ronald D. Fischer & Alexander Galetovic, *The Economics of Public-Private Partnerships—a Basic Guide* (New York: Cambridge University Press, 2014)

European Commission/IMF/OECD/UN/World Bank, *System of National Accounts 2008* (New York 2009)

European Commission, *Guide to Cost-Benefit Analysis of Investment Projects Economic-Appraisal Tool for Cohesion Policy 2014-2020* (Brussels 2014)

European Parliament and Council,
— *Directive 2014/24/EU of the of 26 February 2014 on Public Procurement and Repealing Directive 2004/18/EC* (Brussels 2014)
— *Directive 2014/23/EU of the of 26 February 2014 on the Award of Concession Contracts* (Brussels 2014)

European PPP Expertise Centre (EPEC),
— *State Guarantees in PPPs: A Guide to Better Evaluation, Design, Implementation and Management* (Luxembourg 2011)
— *The Non-Financial Benefits of PPPs—Review of Concepts and Methodologies* (Luxembourg 2011)
— *Procurement in PPP and the Use of Competitive Dialogue—A Review of Public Sector Practices Across the EU* (Luxembourg 2011)
— *Termination and Force Majeure Provisions in PPP Contracts—Review of Current European Practice and Guidance* (Luxembourg 2013)
— *VAT and PPP Contracts—Review of Key Issues Arising in the European Context* (Luxemburg, 2013)
— *Establishing and Reforming PPP Units—Analysis of EPEC Member PPP Units and Lessons Learnt* (Luxembourg 2014)
— *Programme Approaches to PPPs* (Luxembourg 2015)
— *Value for Money Assessment—Review of Approaches and Key Concepts* (Luxembourg 2015)
— *A Guide to the Statistical Treatment of PPPs* (Luxembourg 2016) jointly published with Eurostat
— Further guidance materials and market data are available on the EPEC website (www.eib.org/epec) including the *EPEC PPP Project Preparation Status Tool*

Eurostat,
— *European System of Accounts: ESA 2010* (Luxembourg 2013)
— *Manual on Government Deficit and Debt* (Luxembourg 2016)
— *A Guide to the Statistical Treatment of PPPs* (Luxembourg 2016) (jointly published with EPEC)
Farquharson, Edward, Clemencia Torres de Mästle & E.R. Yescombe, with Javier Encinas, *How to Engage With the Private Sector in Public-Private Partnerships in Emerging Markets* (Washington, DC: PPIAF/World Bank 2011)
Federal Highway Administration U.S. Department of Transportation; FHA provides a comprehensive collection of guidance documents on the economic appraisal of projects and on PPPs in the US highways sector (www. FHWA.dot.gov). These include
— *P3 Toolkit* (2012)
— *Guidebook for Value for Money Assessment* (2013)
— *Performance-Based Planning and Programming Guidebook* (2013)
— *Public-Private Partnership Oversight: How FHWA Reviews P3s* (2015)
— *Availability Payment Concessions Public-Private Partnerships Model Contract Guide—Draft* (2015)
— *Benefit-Cost Analysis for Public-Private Partnership Project Delivery: A Framework* (2016)
Flyvbjerg, Bent (with COWI A/S), *Procedures for Dealing With Optimism Bias in Transport Planning* (Report for Department of Transport) (London 2004)
France Ministère de L'Economie et des Finances,
— *Les contrats de partenariat : Guide Methodologique* (Paris 2011)
— *Guide d'utilisation du Modèle Financier d'Evaluation Préalable* (Paris 2014)
— *Plan type du rapport d'évaluation préalable du mode de réalisation* (Paris 2016)
Funke, Katja, Timothy Irwin & Isabel Rial, 'Budgeting and Reporting for Public-Private Partnerships', *OECD International Transport Forum Discussion Papers Series, no 7* (Paris: Organisation for International Co-Operation and Development, 2013)
Global Infrastructure Hub, *Allocating Risks in Public-Private Partnership Contracts* (Sydney 2016)
Gómez-Lobo, Andres & Sergio Hinojosa, *Broad Roads in a Thin Country: Infrastructure Concessions in Chile* (Policy Research Working Paper 22790) (Washington, DC: World Bank, 2000)
Grout, Paul A. 'Value-for-money measurement in public-private partnerships', *EIB Papers*, Vol. 10, No. 2 (Luxemburg: European Investment Bank 2005), p. 32
IFRS Interpretations Committee, IFRIC 12 (London 2006)
Indian Ministry of Finance, *PPP Toolkit for Improving PPP Decision-Making Processes*—this is an online toolkit with a comprehensive collection of guidance materials with a focus on the highways, ports, solid waste management, urban transport and water and sanitation sectors
Infrastructure Ontario, *Assessing Value for Money—An Updated Guide to Infrastructure Ontario's Methodology* (Toronto 2015)
International Monetary Fund, *Government Finance Statistics Manual* (Washington, DC 2014), Appendix 4, paragraphs 4.58—65
International Monetary Fund, World Bank Group, *PPP Fiscal Risk Assessment Model (P-FRAM)* (Washington, DC 2016)
International Organisation of Supreme Audit Institutions, *Guidelines on Best Practice for the Audit of Risk in Public/ Private Partnership (PPP)* (Vienna 2004)
International Public Sector Accounting Standards Board (IPSASB), *IPSAS 19—Provisions, Contingent Liabilities and Contingent Assets* (New York 2002)
— *IPSAS 32—Service Concession Arrangements: Grantor* (New York 2011)
Ireland Department of Finance,
— *Framework for Public-Private Partnerships* (Dublin 2001)
— *Guidelines for the Provision of Infrastructure and Capital Investments Through Public Private Partnerships: Procedures for the Assessment, Approval, Audit and Procurement of Projects* (Dublin 2006)
— *Discount Rate Principles for Public Private Partnership Capital Investment Projects, Central Guidance Note No. 7* (Dublin 2006)
— *Assessment of Projects for Procurement as Public Private Partnership, Central Guidance Note No. 6* (Technical) (Dublin 2006)
— *Technical Note on the compilation of a Public Sector Benchmark for a Public Private Partnership Project* (Dublin 2007)
Irwin, Timothy & Tanya Mokdad, *Managing Contingent Liabilities in Public-Private Partnerships— Practice in Australia, Chile, and South Africa* (Washington, DC: World Bank Institute/Public-Private Infrastructure Advisory Facility, 2010)

Irwin, Timothy, *Government Guarantees: Allocating and Valuing Risk in Privately Financed Infrastructure Projects* (Washington, DC: World Bank, 2007)

Kim, Jay-Hyung, Jungwook Kim, Sung Hwan Shin & Seung-yeon Lee, *Public—Private Partnership Infrastructure Projects: Case Studies From the Republic of Korea* (Manila: Asian Development Bank & Korean Development Institute, 2011)

Leighland, James, 'Is the Public Sector Comparator Right for Developing Countries?', *Gridlines Note No. 4* (Washington, DC: Public-Private Infrastructure Advisory Facility, 2006)

Lorenzen, Carlos Cruz & María Elena Barrientos with Suman Babbar, *Toll Road Concessions: The Chilean Experience* (Private Finance Group Discussion Paper 124, Washington, DC: World Bank n.d.)

Makovšek, Dejan & Marian Moszoro, 'Private Sector Participation in Infrastructure: Can the Price of Risk Transfer be Efficient?', *Organisation for Economic Co-operation and Development International Transport Forum Discussion Paper 2016.08* (Paris: International Transport Forum, 2016)

Monteiro, Rui Sousa, 'Public-Private Partnerships: Some Lessons From Portugal', *EIB Papers*, Vol. 10, No. 2 (Luxemburg: European Investment Bank 2005), p. 72

Mott Macdonald, *Review of Large Public Procurement in the UK* (Report for British Treasury) (London: HM Treasury, 2002)

Netherlands Ministry of Finance,
— *Public Sector Comparator* (The Hague 2002)
— *Public Private Comparator* (The Hague 2002)

"Norwegian Road Projects Are Now Profitable—The Government Reduces the Discount Rate", *Nordic Road and Transport Research*, No. 2/3 (Stockholm: VTI 2005)

Organisation for Economic Co-operation and Development, 'Public Governance and Territorial Development Directorate Public Governance Committee', *Towards a Framework for the Governance of Public Infrastructure* (Paris: OECD Report to G20 Finance Ministers and Central Bank Governors, 2015)

Partnerships British Columbia, *Methodology for Quantitative Procurement Options Analysis, Discussion Draft* (Vancouver 2009)

Ruster, Jeff, 'A Retrospective on the Mexican Toll Road Program (1989—94)', *Public Policy for the Private Sector* No. 125 (Washington, DC: World Bank, 1997)

Sherwood, Monika, 'Medium-Term Budgetary Frameworks in the EU Member States', *Discussion Papers 21 European Commission Directorate-General for Economic and Financial Affairs* (Brussels: European Commission Directorate-General for Economic and Financial Affairs, 2015)

South African National Treasury,
— *Standardised PPP Provisions* (Pretoria 2004)
— *National Treasury PPP Manual* (Pretoria 2004)
— *Capital Planning Guidelines 2017 MTEF* (Pretoria 2017) Victoria State Government, Department of Treasury and Finance, *Investment Management Standard 2017, A guide for Victorian departments and agencies* (Melbourne 2017)

World Bank Group, *Guidance on PPP Contractual Provisions* (Washington, DC 2017)

World Bank Institute/Public-Private Infrastructure Advisory Facility, *Value for Money Analysis-Practices and Challenges* (Washington, DC 2013)

World Trade Organisation, *Revised Agreement on Government Procurement* (Geneva 2014)

Yescombe, E.R., *Principles of Project Finance* (San Diego, CA: Academic Press, 2nd edition 2014)

Yescombe, E.R., *Public-Private Partnerships in Sub-Saharan Africa: Case Studies for Policymakers* (Dar-es-Salaam: Uongozi Institute, 2017)

Glossary and Abbreviations

Term	Definition	Refer to:
Abandonment	Failure by the project company to construct or operate the facility for a prolonged period of time	§17.2
Acceptance	Confirmation by the contracting authority or the independent checker that conditions for the service availability date have been met	§15.4.1
Accommodation projects	PPP projects involving the provision of buildings such as schools, hospitals, government accommodation or prisons	§2.4.7
Accreting swap	An interest-rate swap drawn in instalments to match drawing of the notional principal amount	§24.2.4
Accretion swap	An interest-rate swap that allows part of the fixed-rate interest payment to be deferred to a later date; *cf.* debt accretion	§24.2.10
Acts of God	*See force majeure*	
Additionality	The question whether PPPs result in additional or faster investment in public infrastructure than relying only on public-sector procurement	§28.3, §28.4
Additionality	The requirement for DFIs only to lend if financing cannot be provided by the private-sector markets	§22.9.2
ADSCR	Annual debt-service cover ratio, the ratio between CADS and debt service over any one year of the project	§23.3.2
Advance-payment bond	Security provided by the construction subcontractor for amounts paid in advance under the construction subcontract by the project company	§12.4.3
Affermage	*See* Franchise	§2.4.2, §2.5

(Continued)

(Continued)

Term	Definition	Refer to:
Affordability	The ability of the contracting authority to pay the service fees from its budgetary resources over the life of an availability PPP contract; *cf.* 'willingness to pay' in relation to a concession	§9.2
Agent bank	The bank liaising between the project company and its lenders	§22.2.10, §23.4.5, §25.4
All-risks insurance	Insurance against physical damage to the facility during operation	§14.4
ALOP insurance	Advance loss of profits insurance; *see* DSU insurance	§14.3.2
Amortising swap	An interest-rate swap reduced in instalments to match reductions in the notional principal amount	§24.2.4
Annuity repayment	A debt repayment schedule that produces level debt-service payments	§15.3.1, §23.2.2
Asset register	A register in which all the fixed assets of the project company are recorded for asset management, accounting and insurance purposes	§23.9.2
Assumptions book	The source data for the financial model	§23.9
Authority	*See* contracting authority	
Availability	The period when the facility (or the relevant part thereof) is able to provide the service as required under the PPP contract	§15.6
Availability charge	The fixed-charge element of a PPA or other process-plant tariff, payable whether or not the product or service is required, intended to cover debt service and equity return; *cf.* gate fee; usage charge, unitary charge	§2.4.3
Availability PPP	A PPP in which the service fees are paid by the contracting authority when the facility is available for use; *cf.* concession, shadow tolls	§2.4.7, §15.6
Average life	The average period that the loan principal is outstanding	§23.2.3
AVT	Authority voluntary termination, or termination of the PPP contract at the option of the contracting authority	§17.3

(Continued)

(Continued)

Term	Definition	Refer to:
Backstop date	*See* sunset date	
BAFO	Best and final offer, a final-stage bid in a public procurement	§10.5
Balloon repayment	A large final principal repayment of a loan (after a series of smaller payments); *cf.* bullet repayment, mini-perm	§23.2.6
Banker's clauses	Additional lender requirements on insurances	§14.6
Banking case	The projected cash-flow assumptions on which the lenders' loan is predicated; *cf.* base case	§23.9.9
Base case	The projections of project cash flow for the purposes of the PPP contract at or shortly before financial close	§23.9.9
Basel process	The procedure for agreeing capital requirements for international banks under the ægis of the Bank for International Settlements, Basel	§11.5, §22.2.3, §23.4.2
BCR	Benefit to cost ratio; the ratio of the PV of the benefits of a project to the PV of its costs (from the public-sector point of view)	§3.4.1, §7.4.2
Benchmarking	Adjustment to the service fees based on comparable market costs for soft FM services; *see* value testing; *cf.* market testing	§15.6.7, §19.4.2
BI insurance	Business-interruption insurance, *i.e.* insurance against the loss of revenue after physical damage to the project during the operation phase; *cf.* contingent BI insurance	§14.4
BI supplier's extension	*See* contingent BI insurance	
Bid documents	The package of documents that is provided to bidders as part of the PPP procurement process	§10.6.2
Blended-equity IRR	The investors' IRR based on the combined return on equity and shareholder subordinated debt; *cf.* distributions, equity IRR	§20.3.5
BLOT	Build-lease-operate-transfer	§2.5
BLT	Build-lease-transfer	§2.5

(Continued)

(Continued)

Term	Definition	Refer to:
Bond	A tradeable debt instrument	§22.4, §23.4.6
Bonding	Security provided by bidders, subcontractors or the project company	§10.7.3, §12.4.3, §17.8.1
BOO	Build-own-operate	§2.4.4, §2.5
BOOT	Build-own-operate-transfer	§2.5
BOT	Build-operate-transfer	§2.4.4, §2.5
Breach of provision clause	*See* non-vitiation clause	
Breach of warranty clause	*See* non-vitiation *See* non-vitiation clause	
Breakage cost	The cost of early termination of a swap, bond or other fixed-rate or inflation-indexed loan	§24.2.3, §24.2.6, §24.2.12, §24.3.7, §25.5.1, §25.5.3
Brownfield project	Project involving refurbishment of an existing facility, or building on a site where there have previously been major structures; *cf.* greenfield project	§12.2.2, §12.2.4, §12.3.3
BTL	Build-transfer-lease; in Korea refers to availability PPP projects	§2.4.7, §2.5
BTO	Build-transfer-operate	§2.4.4, §2.5
Builder's all-risks insurance	*See* CAR insurance	
Bullet repayment	Repayment of a loan in one final instalment rather than a series of principal repayments; *cf.* balloon repayment	§23.4.6, §24.2.4
Business case	The document that sets out the evolving status of the project at various points in the project cycle; often used for the purposes of assurance and formal presentation for approval within the contracting authority and to other branches of government	§5.4, §5.5, §19.4.3, §28.10.1
CADS	Cash flow available for debt service, *i.e.* revenues less opex	§23.3.1, §23.9.3

(*Continued*)

(Continued)

Term	Definition	Refer to:
Capacity charge	*See* availability charge	
Capex	Capital expenditure; the initial costs of constructing the facility or any investment required thereafter; *cf.* opex	§2.4.6; §23.9.2
Capital accretion bonds	*See* debt accretion	
Capital contribution	*See* capital grant	
Capital grant	A payment made by the contracting authority towards a PPP project's capex, in return for a reduction of the service fees	§18.6
CAPM	Capital asset pricing model, a method of measuring the cost of equity	§20.3.1
CAR insurance	Contractor's all-risks insurance against physical damage during construction	§14.3.1
Cascade	The order of priorities under the financing documentation for the application of the project company's cash flow	§14.8, §25.2.3, §25.5.4, §26.2.7
Cash sweep	Dedication of surplus cash flow to debt prepayment, often part of a soft mini-perm structure; *cf.* soft mini-perm	§23.2.8
CEAR insurance	Construction and erection all-risks insurance; *see* CAR insurance	
Certifier	*See* checker	
Cession de créance	Concept in French administrative law that enables the contracting authority to take over direct responsibility for part of the project company's debt after completion of construction; *cf.* debt underpinning	§18.2
Change in law	A change in the law affecting the project company or the project, resulting in additional capex or opex	§13.9, §16.2.6, §25.2.4
Checker	An engineering firm not linked to any party to the project contracts, that confirms that project construction has been carried out as required by the PPP contract and construction subcontract (also known as the certifier, contract administrator, independent engineer, *maître d'œuvre* or verifier)	§6.4.3, §12.3.2, §12.3.6, §15.4.1, §19.3.3

(Continued)

Term	Definition	Refer to:
Claw-back	Requirement for sponsors to repay distributions if the project company is later short of cash *cf.* distributions	§22.8
Collateral warranties	Agreements under which subcontractors accept liability to the lenders for the performance of their subcontracts	§25.3.3
Commercial banks	Private-sector banks, the main suppliers of debt to PPP projects	§22.2
Commercial close	Signature of project contracts subject to completion of the financing	§10.8.4
Commitment fee	Percentage fee charged on the available but undrawn portion of a bank loan	§23.4.4
Common terms agreement	Common lending conditions agreed between different groups of lenders	§25.5
Compensation event	Event for which the contracting authority is required to compensate the project company for its increased costs or loss of revenue; *cf.* excusing cause, *force majeure*, relief event	§16.2
Completion	*See* service availability date	§5.3.7
Completion bond	Security provided by the construction subcontractor for performance under and completion of the construction subcontract	§12.4.3
Completion risks	*See* construction risks	
CompOnTerm	*See* termination sum	
Concession	A PPP in which users pay service fees in the form of tolls, fares or other charges for using the facility; *cf.* availability PPP	§2.4.1
Concession agreement	A PPP contract relating to a concession	§15.5
Concessionaire	The private-sector party to a concession agreement; *see* project company	
Conditions precedent	Conditions to be fulfilled by the project company before drawing on the debt, or before project contracts become effective	§10.8.4, §25.2.1

(*Continued*)

(Continued)

Term	Definition	Refer to:
Consortium	A group of contractors and investors that have agreed to come together for the purposes of putting forward a bid	§10.6.1, §10.7.2
Construction bond	*See* completion bond	
Construction phase	Phase 7: The period from financial close to the service availability date	§5.3.7
Construction risks	Risks relating to the construction of the facility; *cf.* site risks	§12.3
Construction subcontract	A D&B or EPC contract entered into by the project company for the construction of the facility	§2.4.3, §2.4.6, §2.4.7, §12.3.1
Construction subcontractor	The subcontractor responsible for the construction subcontract	§12.3.2
Contingency	Unallocated reserve in the capex budget, covered by contingent or standby financing	§12.3.7, §23.7, §23.9.2
Contingent BI insurance	Insurance cover for a loss of revenue caused by physical damage away from the project site; *cf.* BI insurance	§14.4
Contract administrator	*See* checker	
Contract changes	Change in PPP-contract specifications by the contracting authority or the project company	§16.2.2, §16.2.3, §16.2.4, §19.8.2
Contract debtor	A system of taxation and accounting in Britain under which the NPV of the capex portion of the service fees is shown as a financial claim in the project company's accounts, rather than showing the facility as a fixed asset	§23.6.1
Contracting authority	The public-sector entity party to a PPP contract	§2.3
Contractual close	*See* commercial close	
Control accounts	*See* project accounts	
Corporate finance	Finance for a PPP project provided from an investor's own resources rather than using project finance	§21.6

(Continued)

Term	Definition	Refer to:
Corporate loan	A loan against a company's balance sheet and existing business	§21.3
Cost-benefit ratio	*See* BCR	
Cost-effectiveness analysis	A comparison of the costs of different project options, where benefits are not easily calculable or are not expected to vary between options; *see* BCR	§7.4.2
Coupon	The interest rate payable on a bond	§22.4.2
Coupon swap	*See* interest-rate swap	
Cover ratio(s)	Ratio(s) of the cash flows from the project against debt service, *i.e.* ADSCR, LLCR or PLCR	§23.3, §23.5
CPI	Consumer price index, a measure of inflation	§24.3.2
Credit guarantee finance	The British Treasury's scheme for public-sector financing of PPP project companies, with private-sector debt guarantees	§18.11
Credit margin	The margin over cost of funds charged by a lender to cover its credit risk and provide a return on capital	§23.4.1
Credit premium	The margin over the market swap rate charged by a swap provider to cover its credit risk and provide a return on capital	§24.2.4, §24.2.6
Cross-border risks	Risks that arise when a loan or investment is made from one country to a project in another	§13.9
Cure period	A period of time allowed for lenders to remedy a default under a project contract	§25.3.3
D&B Contract	Design and build contract, a fixed-price, date-certain, turnkey contract for design and construction of infrastructure such as roads or buildings; *see* construction subcontract	Figure 2.2, 2.3
DBFM	Design-build-finance-maintain; *see* DBFO	
DBFO	Design-build-finance-operate, a type of PPP contract	§2.4, §2.5
DBGO	Design-build-guarantee-operate, a contract similar to a DBO contract, but in which the construction funding provided by the contracting authority for the facility is guaranteed by commercial banks or other private-sector financial institutions	§27.3

(Continued)

(Continued)

Term	Definition	Refer to:
DBO	Design-build-operate, a form of long-term contract for construction and operation of a facility, in which funding is provided by the contracting authority	§27.2.1
DCF	Discounted cash flow, a calculation of the value today (NPV) of a future cash flow	Chapter 3
DCM	Design construct and maintain; *see* DBO	
DCMF	Design-construct-manage-finance; *see* DBFO	
Deal creep	Gradual deterioration in the terms of the PPP contract compared to the original bid during subsequent negotiations, usually caused by the project requirements not being initially specified in enough detail by the contracting authority, or by changes in requirements	§10.6.8, §22.6.1, §26.2.10
Debt	Finance provided by the senior lenders; *cf.* junior debt, mezzanine debt, senior debt	Chapter 22
Debt accretion	Increasing the debt amount during the operation phase of a very long-term concession; *cf.* accretion swap	§23.2.9
Debt/equity ratio	Ratio of debt to equity	§23.3.5, §23.5
Debt service	Payment of interest and debt-principal instalments	§2.4.3, Chapter 23
Debt underpinning	Guaranteed repayment by the contracting authority of a minimum proportion of the project company's debt	§18.10
Decanting	Moving the facility (or parts of it) from an old site to a new site during the process of construction	§12.2.9
Deductible	Initial loss amount that is not covered by an insurance company	§14.5-§14.11
Deductions	Sums deducted from service-fee payments for failure to meet availability or service requirements of an availability PPP contract; *cf.* penalties	§15.6
Default ratio	Minimum cover ratio(s) below which an EoD occurs under the loan documentation	§25.4

(Continued)

Term	Definition	Refer to:
Deflation calculation	Reduction of a future nominal sum to a real sum	§24.3.1
Delay LDs	LDs payable by the project company to the contracting authority for failure to complete the facility by the agreed date; or LDs payable by the construction subcontractor to the project company for late completion of the facility causing a loss of revenue or payment of delay LDs to the contracting authority	§12.4.1, §15.4.3
Depreciation	Writing-down the capex incurred on the facility for tax or accounting purposes	§23.3, §23.6, §23.10
Derivative	A contract for payments and receipts over a period of time, at prices 'derived' from an underlying financial-market movement, *e.g.* an interest-rate swap	§24.2.10
Derogations	The process of approving changes to a standardised PPP contract	§4.3.2
Design-bid-build	A standard method of public-sector procurement whereby the contracting authority designs the facility and then calls for bids to construct it	§2.4.7, §2.5, §12.3.1, §12.4.1, §28.6.1
Development costs	Costs incurred by the sponsors before financial close	§20.2.1, §20.5, §22.2.7, §23.9.2
DFI	Development-finance institution, a national or multilateral entity that may provide financing to (or debt guarantees for) a project company	§22.9
Direct agreement (s)	Agreement(s) between the lenders and the contracting authority or subcontractors, protecting the lenders' interests under project contracts, or similarly between the contracting authority and subcontractors	§17.6, §25.3.3
Disbursement account	The project company's bank account into which equity subscriptions and debt drawdowns are paid, and from which payments are made for the facility's construction costs and other capex	§25.2.1

(Continued)

(Continued)

Term	Definition	Refer to:
Discount rate	The percentage rate used to reduce a future cash flow to a current value, and so calculate its PV	§3.2.1
Distribution block	Cover ratio(s) below which the lenders prevent payment of distributions	§25.2.5, §25.4
Distributions	The project company's net cash flow paid to investors as dividends, subordinated-debt interest or principal repayment, or repayment of equity; *cf.* equity IRR	§2.4.3, §20.3.5, §25.2.5
Dividend stop	*See* distribution block	
Dividend trap	Inability of the project company to pay dividends, despite having cash available to do so, because of accounting losses	§23.6.4
DPC Contract	Design, procurement and construction contract; *see* EPC contract	
Drawing request	The formal procedure for drawings on the debt by the project company	§25.2.1
Drawstop	Suspension of loan advances by the lenders after an EoD	§25.2.2, §25.4
DRP	The dispute resolution procedure under the PPP contract (and subcontracts)	§19.6
DSRA	Debt-service reserve account, a reserve account with a cash balance sufficient to cover the next scheduled debt-service payment	§25.2.4
DSU insurance	Delay in start-up insurance, insurance against the loss of revenue or extra costs caused by a delay in completion after damage to the project	§14.3
Due diligence	Review and evaluation of project contracts, financial projections and their related risks, carried out by both the contracting authority and the lenders	§10.8, §12.3.2, §12.5.2, §21.5.2, §22.2.7, §22.4.1, §28.9.8
Easement	A right to use adjacent land, *e.g.* for discharge of water	§12.2.6
Economic infrastructure	Public infrastructure required for day-to-day economic activity, such as transport and utilities; *cf.* social infrastructure	§2.2

(Continued)

Term	Definition	Refer to:
Effective date	*See* financial close	
Efficacy insurance	Insurance that covers the construction subcontractor's liability to pay LDs for delay or poor performance	§14.3
EIA	Environmental-impact assessment, a study of the effect of the construction and operation of the facility on the natural and human environment	§12.2.4
EIB	European Investment Bank, the long-term financing institution of the European Union	§22.9.3
Emergency step-in	The right of the contracting authority to take over operation of the facility to maintain the service, or for reasons of safety, public security, *etc.*	§13.8
Environmental risks	Risk relating to the environmental effect of the construction or operation of the facility	§12.2.4
EoDs	Events of default, that give parties to project contracts the right to terminate them after due notice, or the lenders the right to drawstop or terminate the financing	§17.2, §17.3, §25.4
EoI	Expressions of interest (call for); *see* PQQ	§10.6.1
EPC contract	Engineering, procurement and construction contract, a fixed-price, date-certain, turnkey contract for design and engineering, equipment procurement or manufacture, and construction and erection of process or other plant; *see* construction subcontract, D&B contract	§2.4.5, §12.3.1
EPEC	European PPP Expertise Centre, part of the EIB and an initiative that also involves the European Commission, EU member states, candidate and certain other states, providing PPP policy and project advisory support to the public sector in these countries	§9.3.5, §10.3, §22.9.3
Equity	The portion of the project's capex contributed by the investors to the project company, either as share capital or subordinated debt	§5.3.7, Chapter 20
Equity competition	Auction of part of the project company's equity shortly before financial close, as a way of reducing project costs; *cf.* funding competition	§26.4

(Continued)

Term	Definition	Refer to:
Equity IRR	The IRR on the equity paid in by the investors, derived from dividends; this term is also commonly used for the blended-equity IRR (*q.v.*)	§15.5.2, §20.3.3, §20.3.6, §23.5, §26.2.2, §26.3
Equity-bridge loan	Finance provided by lenders during the construction period for the amount of the equity investment	§20.3.6, §23.3
ERR	Economic rate of return, a method for the public sector to measure the net benefits of a project; *cf.* FIRR	§7.4.4
Escrow account	A bank account under the joint control of two parties; *see* project accounts	
EU	European Union	
Eurostat	The Statistical Office of the EU, which has published detailed rules for the statistical treatment of PPPs	§9.4.5, §14.10, §14.8, §15.5.2, §15.6.1, §15.8, §18.4, §18.13, §26.2.5
Ex-ante	prior to, before; *cf. ex-post*	
Exchange-rate risks	Macroeconomic risks resulting from changes in currency exchange rates	§24.4
Exclusive remedy clause	Provision in a PPP contract that the deductions or penalties in that contract are a contracting authority's only basis for a claim against the project company	§15.6
Excusing cause	Non-performance by the project company, for which it is not penalised; *cf.* compensation event, *force majeure*, relief event	§16.3
Ex-post	retrospective; *cf. ex-ante*	
External economies/ diseconomies	*See* externalities	
Externalities	Economic, social, environmental or other effects of a project, the benefit or cost of which cannot be charged to users of the facility	§2.2, §7.4.1, §18.1

(Continued)

(Continued)

Term	Definition	Refer to:
Facility	The public infrastructure provided under the PPP contract	§2.3
Fare-box guarantee	*See* minimum revenue guarantee	§18.4
Financial adviser	The contracting authority's adviser on financial aspects of preparing, procuring (and managing) a PPP, or the sponsors' (separate) adviser on arranging finance for the project company	§6.4.1, §9.2.2, §10.8.3, §20.7.1, §22.2.5, §23.4.3, §23.8
Financial balance	A mechanism to put the project company, and its investors and lenders, in a position no worse than they would otherwise have been had a compensation event not occurred	§16.2.1
Financial close	The date at which all project contracts and financing documentation have been signed, and their conditions precedent have been fulfilled	§5.3.6, §10.8.4
Financial model	The financial model(s) used by the contracting authority, investors and lenders to review and monitor the PPP project	§3.5, §9.2.2, §10.6.2, §16.2.1, §19.8.2, §23.8, §23.9
FIRR	Financial (internal) rate of return, the direct cash-flow return of a project from the point of view of the public-sector (as opposed to its economic benefit—*cf.* ERR)	§7.4.4
Fiscal agent	*See* paying agent	
Fisher formula	A formula for adjusting cash flows for inflation	§24.3.1, §24.3.6, §24.3.8
Five-case model	A framework for analysing a business case	§5.5
Fixed costs	The project company's costs not subject to inflation (primarily debt service and distributions); *cf.* variable costs	§24.3
Floating interest rate	An interest rate revised at regular intervals to the current market rate; *cf.* LIBOR	§24.2
FM	Facilities management (for a building); *see* hard FM, soft FM; *cf.* O&M	§2.4.7, §13.6, §23.9.3

(*Continued*)

(Continued)

Term	Definition	Refer to:
FM subcontracts	Subcontracts with the project company for the provision of hard FM or soft FM services	§2.4.7, §13.6
FMV	Fair market value, a method of calculating the termination sum	§17.2.3, §17.2.6
Force majeure	A event that is not the fault of either party to the PPP contract, that makes it temporarily or permanently impossible to continue with the PPP contract; *see* permanent *force majeure*, relief event	
Force-majeure insurance	Insurance against third-party *force-majeure* events affecting the construction subcontractor that cause the facility to be completed late or abandoned	§14.3
Franchise	The right to operate existing public infrastructure and receive user fees; differs from a concession because no substantial new investment is required by the private sector	§2.4.2, §2.5, §15.5.3
Franchisee	The private-sector party to a franchise	§2.4.2
Fronting bank	A bank acting as a channel for competitive interest-rate swap quotations	§24.2.8
Funding competition	A competitive bidding procedure to provide the debt financing that takes place after the appointment of a preferred bidder; *cf.* equity competition	§22.6
Gate fee	Payment method used in process-plant projects such as waste incinerators, in lieu of service fees	§15.6.1
Gateway	A review point during the project cycle	§4.5, §5.4, §19.3.6
Gearing	*See* leverage	
GIC	Guaranteed investment contract, a fixed rate of interest paid by a depository bank on the proceeds of a bond issue until these are required to pay construction costs	§24.2.11
Government procuring entity	*See* contracting authority	
GPA	Agreement on Government Procurement, the framework for public procurement under the WTO	§10.5

(*Continued*)

(Continued)

Term	Definition	Refer to:
Green-field project	Project involving constructing a completely new facility, or building on a site where there have previously been no major structures; *cf.* brownfield project	
Hand-back	The reversion of the facility to the contracting authority's control at the end of the PPP contract	§5.3.9, §17.8.1, §19.5
Hard FM	Routine maintenance of the facility; *cf.* FM, lifecycle costs, soft FM	§2.4.7, §13.6, §23.9.3
Hard mini-perm	A mini-perm that has to be repaid on a balloon-repayment date; *cf.* mini-perm, soft mini-perm	§23.2.7
Hedging	A financial-market contract to protect the project company's capex, revenues or costs against adverse movements in interest rates, inflation or currency movements	Chapter 24
Help desk	A single location where the users of the facility (for example teachers or hospital staff) can report faults and other service issues that need to be addressed by the project company	§19.4.1
HGV	heavy goods vehicle, *i.e.* truck	§13.2, §15.5
Hurdle rate	The discount rate or minimum IRR used to determine if an investment produces the minimum required return	§3.2.3, §3.3, §3.5.2, §7.4.4, §20.3.4
IASB	International Accounting Standards Board, the body that sets international financial accounting standards	§9.4.1
ICD	Invitation to competitive dialogue, an invitation to bid in a public procurement using the competitive dialogue procedure	§10.6.2
IDC	Interest during construction, which is capitalised and forms part of the capex budget	§23.9.2, §24.2
IFRS	International Financial Reporting Standards, issued by IASB	§9.4.1
IMF	International Monetary Fund	§9.4, §9.5

(Continued)

(Continued)

Term	Definition	Refer to:
Independent engineer	*See* checker	
Inflation-indexed loan	A loan whose debt service is indexed against inflation	§24.3.6
Inflation risks	Risks to the project company's capex, revenues or opex resulting from changes in the rate of price inflation	§24.3.4
Inflation swap	A hedging contract to convert a cash-flow subject to inflation adjustment to a fixed cash flow (or *vice versa*)	§24.3.9
Innovative finance	A term used in the United States for alternative methods of funding public infrastructure	§28.3
Institution	*See* contracting authority	
Institutional investors	Mainly life-insurance companies and pension funds	§20.2.1
Institutional PPP	An agreement between public-sector and private-sector partners to partner in a venture to develop an asset, *e.g.* land or intellectual property, owned by the former with both parties usually sharing in the risks of the venture (not a PPP as defined in this book)	§27.4
Insurance	Cover against the effects of temporary *force majeure* on construction or operation of the facility	Chapter 14
Inter-creditor	Relationship between different groups of lenders	§25.5
Interest-rate cap	A hedging contract that sets a maximum interest rate	§24.2.10
Interest-rate collar	A hedging contract that sets a floor (minimum) and ceiling (maximum) interest rate	§24.2.10
Interest-rate risks	Risks to the project company's capex or opex resulting from changes in interest rates	§24.2
Interest-rate swap	A hedging contract to convert a floating interest rate into a fixed-rate (or *vice versa*)	§24.2.2

(Continued)

(Continued)

Term	Definition	Refer to:
Interface risk	The risk that arises as a consequence of the interaction between two parties such as between two subcontractors	§7.3.1, §13.9, §15.6.7
Investment bank	A bank that acts as a financial adviser, places bonds and manages PPP investment funds but does not usually provide debt	§20.2.1, §20.7.1, §22.4
Investment-grade rating	A credit rating of BBB-/Baa3 or above	§22.4.1
Investors	Sponsors and other parties investing equity into the project company; the owners of the project company	§20.2
IPSAS	International Public Sector Accounting Standards, financial accounting standards for the public sector similar to the private-sector IFRS	§9.4
IRR	Internal rate of return, the rate of return on an investment calculated from its future cash flows	§3.3
ISDA	International Swap and Derivatives Association, the body that produces standard-form documentation for hedging contracts	§24.2.5
IT	Information technology	
ITB	Invitation to bid; *see* RfP	
ITT	Invitation to Tender; *see* RfP	
Junior debt	*See* mezzanine debt, subordinated debt	
km	Kilometre	
KPIs	Key performance indicators, measuring service standards under the PPP contract; failure to attain these leads to payment deductions and/or performance points	§15.6.2, §15.6.3
Latent defects	Defects in the facility that no-one could reasonably have found and whose effect does not appear until a later date	§12.3.3, §12.4.3
L/C	Letter of credit, a form of on-demand guarantee issued by a bank	§25.2.4

(Continued)

(Continued)

Term	Definition	Refer to:
LDs	Liquidated damages, the agreed level of loss when a party does not perform under a contract; *see* delay LDs, performance LDs; *cf.* penalties	§12.4
Lead arranger(s)	Bank(s) arranging and underwriting the project company's debt	§22.2.5
Lead manager	*See* lead arranger	
Lead transaction adviser	One of the contracting authority's advisers, that subcontracts and manages the other advisers	§6.4.5
Lease	A form of debt in which the asset being financed is owned by the lessor (a finance lease); or the right to use a facility or other property for a specified period of time; *see* franchise	§2.4.1, §2.5, §12.2.1, §21.4.6
Lenders	Banks, non-banks or bond investors, *i.e.* the senior lenders to the project company; *see* senior lenders	§10.8.3, §11.5, Chapter 22
Lenders' advisers	External advisors employed by the lenders	§22.2.7
Lessee	The obligor under a finance lease (equivalent to a borrower)	§21.4.6
Lessor	The provider of finance under a finance lease (equivalent to a lender)	§21.4.6
Leverage	*See* debt/equity ratio	
LIBOR	London inter-bank offered rate, a floating interest rate	§24.2
Lifecycle costs	The costs of major renewals of equipment over the tenor of the PPP contract	§13.6, §15.3.2, §25.2.4
Limited-recourse	Project-finance debt with limited guarantees from the sponsors; *cf.* non-recourse	§21.3, §22.8
Linear project	A project involving construction of a facility over a long stretch of land, *e.g.* a road	§12.2.1, §12.2.2, §14.3, §14.4, §14.8
LLCR	Loan-life cover ratio, the ratio of the NPV of CADS during the remaining tenor of the debt to the debt-principal amount	§23.3.3-§23.3.6, §25.2.5, §25.4
Lock-up	*See* distribution block	

(Continued)

(Continued)

Term	Definition	Refer to:
Lock-up period	The period during which the sponsors cannot sell their shares in the project company, usually at least during the construction phase	§20.6.4
Logic model	A tool used by a national performance-audit body to assess the *ex-post* performance of a public intervention including its delivery as a PPP *cf.* need, objectives, outputs, outcomes	§7.2, §19.9
LPI swap	Limited price-inflation swap, whereby there is a floor and a ceiling on inflation increases and decreases	§24.3.10
LPVR	Least present value of revenue; an LPVR concession is one without a fixed tenor that terminates when the NPV of a set revenue level has been achieved	§9.2.3, §10.6.5, §15.5.2
Macroeconomic risks	Risks to the project company's capex, revenues or opex related to inflation, interest rates, or currency exchange rates	Chapter 24
MAGA	Material adverse government action; *see* political *force majeure*	
Maintenance bond	Security for the construction subcontractor's obligations during the warranty period	§12.4.3
Maître d'œuvre	*See* checker	
Make-whole clause	A provision in a bond financing, whereby on prepayment of the bond the amount payable is the NPV of the future debt service, but must not be less than the par value of the bond	§24.2.12
Market flex	A pricing arrangement that gives banks the right to change pricing before syndication of a large loan to reflect market-pricing changes	§22.2.9
Market sounding	The process of consulting with the market prior to formal procurement to determine market interest, expected costs and the acceptability or feasibility of the proposed features or terms of the PPP project	§7.3.1, §9.2.2, §10.4, §11.4
Market stabilisation	A hedging exercise in advance of placement of a large bond or swap, to ensure that the placement itself does not move market rates	§24.2.13

(Continued)

(Continued)

Term	Definition	Refer to:
Market testing	Obliging the project company to re-bid soft-FM services to allow the contracting authority to test the cost of the services in the market—*see* value testing; *cf.* benchmarking	§15.6.7, §19.4.2
Merit goods	Infrastructure and services that the public sector needs to provide to ensure availability for all, *e.g.* schools	§2.2
Mezzanine debt	Subordinated debt provided by third parties other than the investors; *cf.* subordinated debt	§18.8, §22.7, §25.5.4, §27.5.1
Minimum revenue guarantee	A guarantee from the contracting authority to the project company that revenues from a concession will not be less than a set amount; *cf.* fare-box guarantee	§9.3.4, §15.5.2, §18.4, §27.5.1
Mini-perm	A loan for the construction period and first few years of operation of a project, to be refinanced in due course by longer-term debt; *cf.* balloon repayment, bullet repayment, soft mini-perm, hard mini-perm	§23.2.7-§23.2.8
MIRR	Modified IRR, an IRR calculation with a reduced reinvestment rate for cash flow taken out of the project	§3.4.3
MLAs	Minimum liquid asset requirements; *see* MLR	
MLRs	The cost of banks' minimum liquidity-ratio requirements, if any	§23.4.2
Model auditor	An independent firm of accountants or financial-modelling company that reviews and certifies the financial model	§23.9.8
Monoline insurance	Insurance of an individual financial risk (rather than general casualty insurance)	§18.11, §22.4.4
MRA	Maintenance reserve account, a reserve account used to set aside cash for the maintenance of the facility	§13.6, §17.8.1, §25.2.4
NDFA	National Development Finance Agency, the 'trading' name for the National Treasury Management Agency of the Government of Ireland and the statutory financial adviser to State	§6.3, §8.9.3

(Continued)

(Continued)

Term	Definition	Refer to:
	authorities in respect of all public investment projects with a capital value over €20 million including responsibility for the procurement and delivery of PPP projects in certain sectors.	
Need	The gap between objectives and existing arrangements, which a public intervention (*q.v.*) aims to solve or overcome *cf.* objectives, outputs, outcomes	§7.2
Negative arbitrage	The loss of interest caused by having to draw the whole of a bond financing at financial close and then redeposit the funds until required; *cf.* GIC	§22.5, §24.2.11
Negative equity	A cumulative accounting loss exceeding the amount of project company's share capital	§23.6.4
Negative pledge	An agreement by a borrower with its lender not to give security over its assets to any third party	§25.3.2
Network risk	The risks for the project resulting from connections outside the project	§13.3, §15.5.2
Nominal cash flow/return	The cash flow or return on an investment including inflation, if any—*i.e.* 'money of the future'; *cf.* real cash flow/return	§24.3.1
Non-conforming bid	A bid that offers an alternative solution for the project to that in the contracting authority's bid requirements	§10.7.1
Non-payment insurance	Insurance partially covering the risk of non-payment by the project company of a bank loan	§22.4.4
Non-recourse	Finance with no guarantee from the sponsors; *cf.* limited-recourse	§20.2.1, §21.3, §21.5.1, §22.8
Non-vitiation clause	Provision in an insurance policy that the rights of lenders or the contracting authority will not be affected by action by the project company that invalidates the insurance	§14.6, §14.7
Not-for-profit	A form of ownership that eliminates private-sector distributions from a PPP project; *cf.* NPD, pinpoint equity	§27.5
Notional principal amount	The amount of debt that is the subject of an interest-rate or inflation swap	§24.2.2, §24.3.9

(*Continued*)

(Continued)

Term	Definition	Refer to:
NPC	Net present cost; the NPV of the cost of a PPP to the contracting authority net of any revenues	§3.2.2
NPD	Non-profit-distributing model, a form of PFI-based PPP used in Scotland; *cf.* not-for-profit	§27.5.2
NPM	New Public Management, one of the theoretical bases for PPPs	§28.2
NPV	Net present value, the discounted present value of a stream of future cash flows, offsetting benefits against costs	§3.2
O&M subcontract	Operation and maintenance subcontract, *e.g.* for a process-plant PPP; *cf.* FM	
	(also referred to as the Intermediate Business Case)	
Objectives	The initially intended outcomes to be achieved by the public intervention (*q.v.*); *cf.* need, outcomes, outputs	§7.2
OECD	Organisation for Economic Co-operation and Development	
Operation phase	Phase 8 of the project cycle: the period between the service acceptance date and the end of the PPP contract	§5.3.8, §19.4
Operation-phase risks	Risks relating to the operation phase that may affect the project company's revenues or opex, or require further capex	Chapter 13
Operational gearing	In a PPP project context, the ratio between the portion of the service fees covering operating costs and that covering financing costs	§15.6.4
Opex	Operating costs, including maintenance but excluding financing costs; *cf.* capex	§2.4.6, §23.9.3
Optimism bias	The tendency for the public sector to underestimate project costs or delivery times, which need to be taken into account in considering project risks	§8.3.3, §11.3
Outcomes	The changes that arise from the implementation of a public intervention related to the objectives of the intervention (they may be expected or unexpected, positive or negative) *cf.* need, objectives, outputs	§7.2, §8.3.3, §15.2, §19.9

(Continued)

(Continued)

Term	Definition	Refer to:
Outputs	Service requirements under a PPP, defined on the basis of the contracting authority's requirements rather than how these requirements are to be delivered. Outputs are directly measurable and either singly or collectively deliver an objective/outcome *cf.* need, objectives, outcomes	§2.4.7, §7.2, §7.3.1, §15.2, §28.2
Outsourcing	Provision of soft FM or other services by the private sector under contract to a contracting authority; not considered a PPP as it does not involve substantial provision of fixed assets	§2.3, §2.5, §15.6.7, §28.9.7
Over-indexation	Inflation indexation of the service fees by a proportion greater than the project company's variable costs	§24.3.5, §24.3.8, §24.3.12
Owner's engineer	The adviser supervising the construction subcontract on behalf of the project company	§12.3.2, §20.7.3
Owner's risks	The responsibilities of the project company under the construction subcontract	§12.3.3; §12.3.5
p.a.	*per annum*, yearly	
P3	A term used in North America for PPPs	§2.3
PABs	Private-activity bonds: tax-exempt bonds in the US municipal bond market that may be used to finance PPPs	§22.4.3
Par floor	*See* make-whole clause	§24.2.12
Pari-passu	Equal and *pro rata*; relates to security shared by different lenders, or payments to other claimants	
Payback period	The period of time in which distributions to investors equal their original investment in the project company	§3.4.3, §20.3.3
Paying agent	A company distributing debt-service payments from the project company to bond investors	§22.4.2
Payment mechanism	The provisions in the PPP contract that are used to calculate service-fee payments or charge deductions or penalties	§15.3, §15.6.5, §19.4.1
Penalties	Payments by the project company for failure to meet service requirements under a concession; *cf.* deductions	§15.5.5

(Continued)

Term	Definition	Refer to:
Performance bond	*See* completion bond	
Performance LDs	LDs payable by an EPC contractor if the facility is unable to meet the output specifications on completion (usually relates to process plant); *cf.* delay LDs	§12.3.6, §12.4.1
Performance points	Penalties for failure to meet KPIs, accumulation of which results in deductions from the service fees and may eventually lead to termination of the PPP contract	§15.6.2, §15.6.8, §17.2, §25.3.3
Permanent *force majeure*	An uninsured event that makes it impossible to continue with the project	§12.3.3, §17.4
Permits	Planning, environmental or other permissions required to construct and operate the facility	§12.2.3, §12.2.4, §12.3.3, §15.4.1
Persistent breach	Consistent failure by the project company to observe any provisions of the PPP contract that are not covered by penalties or deductions, or otherwise an EoD	§17.2
PF2	Revisions to PFI that included options for equity competitions and public-sector equity investment in the project company	§2.3, §26.4, §27.4
PFI	Private Finance Initiative, the United Kingdom's PPP programme, prior to PF2	§2.4.7, §12.3.6, §13.5, §17.2, §21.2, §26.2.3, §28.2, §28.6.3
PFP	Private financing predictor, a term used in Australia for the 'shadow' financial model prepared for the contracting authority to assess the initial financial feasibility of a PPP	§23.8
PIM	Preliminary information memorandum, prepared by the project company as a basis for obtaining financing bids from prospective lead managers	§22.2.9
Pinpoint equity	A not-for-profit structure that can be used for a PPP; *cf.* NPD	§27.5.1

(Continued)

(Continued)

Term	Definition	Refer to:
PLCR	Project life cover ratio, the ratio of the NPV of CADS during the remaining life of the PPP contract and the outstanding debt amount	§23.3.4
Political risks	Risks related to government action affecting the project company or its operations	§12.2.8, §13.9
Positive PPP test	A test that requires a PPP option to be considered when assessing the procurement options for a project	§4.4.1
P-P Partnership	*See* PPP	
PPA	Power purchase agreement, a contract under which an electricity distributor agrees to purchase electricity from a project company	§2.4.3
PPI	Private Participation in Infrastructure; used in Korea to refer to concessions; *see* PPP	
PPP	Public-private partnership, a long-term contractual arrangement under which a private-sector party invests in a facility to provide a public service to or on behalf of the public sector involving a sharing of risks between the public- and private-sector parties, where payment is based on outputs rather than project inputs, taking account of the whole life cycle implications for the project. Payment for services is either by users or the contracting authority; *cf.* availability PPP, concession, shadow toll	§2.3
PPP contract	The contract between the contracting authority and the project company for design, construction, finance and operation of the facility; *see* concession agreement, project agreement	§2.3, Chapters 15-17
PPP unit	A specialised centre of PPP expertise in the public sector	§4.7, §5.4, §6.3, §8.9.2, §8.9.3
PQQ	Pre-qualification questionnaire, used in the first stage of a public-procurement process that involves pre-qualifying potential bidders for their suitability to bid	§10.6.1

(Continued)

(Continued)

Term	Definition	Refer to:
Preferred bidder	A bidder with whom the contracting authority intends to sign the PPP contract subject to various final conditions being met	§10.5, §10.6.6, §10.6.8, §10.7.3, §22.6
Prepayment	Early repayment of a loan or bond	§22.5, §23.2.8, §24.2.3, §24.2.12
Pre-qualification	The first stage of a public-procurement process that involves pre-qualifying potential bidders for their suitability to bid; *cf.* PQQ	§6.4, §10.6.1, §10.6.5, §12.3.2
Primary investors	The original investors in the project company, including the sponsors; *cf.* secondary investors	§20.2, §20.3
Principal-agent problem	In the context of a PPP, asymmetry of information between the contracting authority and the project company	§28.9.9
Private party	*See* project company	
Prior information notice	Or PIN: notice issued by a contracting authority to the market of a forthcoming procurement	§10.6.1
Private placement	Bonds not quoted on a stock exchange	§22.4.2
Privatisation	Transfer of ownership of public infrastructure to the private sector, as compared to PPPs where ownership remains in the public sector	§2.5, §28.2
Proceeds account	*See* disbursement account	
Project	A series of works, activities or services intended to accomplish an indivisible task of a precise economic and technical nature that has clearly identified goals or objectives	§7.3.1
Project agreement	A PPP contract relating to an availability PPP project	
Project board	The *ad hoc* board (or steering committee) established by the contracting authority to oversee and take decisions with respect to the preparation and implementation of a PPP project and provide support to the project team	§5.4, §6.2
Project company	The private-sector SPV that is the contracting authority's counterparty under the PPP contract	§2.3, §20.6

(Continued)

(Continued)

Term	Definition	Refer to:
Project company costs	Costs of running the project company itself, excluding subcontract costs	§23.9.2, §23.9.3
Project contracts	The PPP contract and the subcontracts	§2.3
Project cycle	The sequence of phases in the life of a project from initial needs assessment to, in the case of a PPP project, the hand-back of the facility to the contracting authority	§5.2
Project director (or manager)	The individual in the contracting authority responsible for managing the project team and reporting to the project board	§6.2.2
Project finance	A method of raising long-term debt financing for major projects through 'financial engineering', based on lending against the cash flow generated by the project alone; it depends on a detailed evaluation of a project's construction, operating and revenue risks, and their allocation between investors, lenders and other parties through contractual and other arrangements	§2.4.5, chapters 21–25
Project IRR	The IRR of CADS against the original capex	§3.5, §20.3.2
Project team	The *ad hoc* team established by the contracting authority to manage the preparation and procurement of the PPP project usually until financial close (in some cases the same team continues to be responsible for management of the subsequent PPP contract)	§6.2.2
Project-development agreement	An agreement between sponsors relating to bidding for and development of the project; *cf.* shareholder agreement	§10.6.1, §20.5
Promoter	*See* contracting authority	
PSB	Public-sector benchmark; *see* PSC	
PSC	Public-sector comparator, a theoretical measurement of the cost of public-sector procurement of a facility, that is compared against the cost of the PPP	§8.3-§8.7, §8.9.1, §10.6.6

(Continued)

(Continued)

Term	Definition	Refer to:
PSDR	Public-sector discount rate, the discount rate used by contracting authorities when evaluating spending on public infrastructure	§7.4.3, §8.6.2, §15.5.3, §24.3.1, §27.5.3
Public authority	*See* contracting authority	
Public entity	*See* contracting authority	
Public goods	Public infrastructure that has to be freely available for all, and for which it is difficult to charge users, *e.g.* street lighting	§2.2
Public infrastructure	*See* economic infrastructure, social infrastructure	§2.2
Public intervention	A set of financial, organisational and human resources mobilised to achieve, in a given period of time, an objective or set of objectives, with the aim of solving or overcoming a problem	§7.2
Public party	*See* contracting authority	
Public procurement	The process of competitive bidding for a PPP contract with a contracting authority; *cf.* public-sector procurement	§2.4.7, Chapter 10
Public trust	A not-for-profit structure that can be used for a structure similar to that of a PPP	§27.5.3
Public-liability insurance	*See* third-party liability insurance	
Public-public partnership	A structure substantially similar to a PPP, but with the project company owned and funded by the public sector	§2.5, §27.2.2
Public-sector procurement	Conventional procurement of public infrastructure by the contracting authority instead of through a PPP contract	§2.4.7
PV	Present value; the result of a DCF calculation; *cf.* NPC, NPV	§3.2
QIB	Qualified institutional buyer, an institutional investor to whom Rule 144a bonds can be sold	§22.4.3
RAB	Regulated asset base, by which a regulator sets the level of tariffs charged by utilities based on assumptions about their costs and levels of investment return	§27.6

(Continued)

(Continued)

Term	Definition	Refer to:
Ramp-up	The early years after completion of a project, when usage is still building up (*e.g.* for a concession road)	§13.2, §18.4, §20.3.3, §23.2.2, §23.2.5
Rating agency	A company providing an independent view on the creditworthiness of the project company	§22.4.1
Raw PSC	The first stage in development of the PSC prior to adjustment for the cost of risks *cf.* PSC	§8.3.1
Real cash flow/ return	The cash flow or return on an investment excluding inflation, if any—*i.e.* in 'money of today'; *cf.* nominal cash flow/return	§24.3.1
Real tolls	Tolls paid directly by the users of the facility; *cf.* shadow tolls	§15.5
Refinancing	Prepayment of the debt and substitution of new debt on more attractive terms; *cf.* rescue refinancing	§17.5, §26.2
Refinancing gain	The benefit of a refinancing of a project company's debt	§26.2.5, §26.2.6
Relief event	Temporary *force majeure* preventing the completion or continuous operation of the facility, for which the project company is not penalised but receives no compensation from the authority; *cf.* compensation events	§11.6.2, §12.2.5, §12.2.7, §12.3.3, §12.3.5, §16.4, §17.4
Reputation risk	Concern by the contracting authority that if the PPP project fails, it will be seen (especially politically) to have failed as well, sometimes leading to it not enforcing its legal right under the PPP contract. Or a similar concern that a new shareholder in the project company may be unsuitable	§9.3.4, §17.2.9, §17.6.1, §28.6.5§20.6.4
Rescue refinancing	A restructuring of project company's debt made necessary by the project being in financial difficulty	§17.2.1, §17.3.3, §26.2.4
Reserve accounts	Accounts controlled by the lenders (or their trustee or escrow agent) in which part of a project company's cash flow is set aside to provide security for the debt or to cover future costs; *cf.* DSRA, MRA	§13.6, §17.2, §23.2.8, §23.3.6, §23.9.2, §25.2.3, §25.2.5, §25.3.1, §25.5.4, §25.2.4

(Continued)

(Continued)

Term	Definition	Refer to:
Restricted procedure	A public-procurement procedure whereby suppliers are pre-qualified to submit bids and no negotiation takes places after bids have been made	§10.5, §10.6.1, §10.6.2
Retainage	The proportion of each payment under the construction subcontract retained by the project company as security until the service availability date	§12.4.3
RfP	Request for proposals; an invitation for bids in a public procurement	§10.6.2
RfQ	Request for qualifications; *see* PQQ	
Right of way	A right of access to the facility through adjacent land	§12.2.6
Risk matrix	A matrix that reflects how risks are agreed to be allocated and that also forms a part of the risk register	§11.6
Risk register (or risk log)	A risk management tool that involves the use of regularly updated information on risks including their identification, allocation, management and mitigation measures	§11.6, §19.8.3
Roll-over risk	The risk that an interest-rate swap contract may not be amended on acceptable terms if the amount of debt or the repayment schedule changes	§24.2.9
RPI swap	*See* inflation swap	
Rule 144a	SEC provisions that allow trading in bond private placements with QIBs	§22.4.3
SCUT	*Sem Combrança ao Utilizador* ('without payment by the user'), the former Portuguese system of shadow tolls	§15.5.4, §28.3
SEC	Securities and Exchange Commission (of the United States), which regulates the investment markets	§22.4.3
Secondary investors	Investors that invest in the project company after financial close (usually in the early years of the operation phase), purchasing their shares from the primary investors	§20.2.3, §26.3

(Continued)

Term	Definition	Refer to:
Senior debt	Loans provided by the senior lenders; *see* senior lenders; *cf.* mezzanine debt, subordinated debt	
Senior lenders	Lenders whose debt service comes before debt service on mezzanine or subordinated debt, or distributions, and who are repaid first in a liquidation of the project company; *see* lenders, which refers to senior lenders unless otherwise stated	§22.6, §25.5
Sensitivities	Variations on the expected performance of a project as a result of using different assumptions	§8.7, §23.9.7
Separability	The question whether the various components of the PPP project can be separately bid or paid for	§2.4.7, §22.6.1 §27.1
Service area	A specific part of the facility defined for the purposes of measuring availability	§15.6.1
Service availability date	The date on which construction of the facility is complete and it meets the requirements to begin providing the services under the PPP contract	§5.3.7, §12.3.5, §15.4, §17.2, §25.4
Service commencement date	*See* service availability date	
Service concession	The term used in European Union law for a franchise	§2.4.2
Service fees	Payments under a PPP contract, *i.e.* tolls or other user payments (for a concession), payments by the contracting authority (for an availability PPP or shadow tolls); *cf.* tariff	§2.4.1
Service-fee mechanism	The PPP contract provisions that set out service-fee payments, deductions or penalties	Chapter 15
Settlement dates	The six-monthly dates on which payments are made or received under an interest-rate or inflation swap	§24.2.2
Shadow tolls	Tolls based on usage of the facility, but payable by the contracting authority rather than by users (*cf.* real tolls)	§2.4.7, §9.2.2, §15.5.4
Shareholder agreement	An agreement between sponsors relating to their investment in and management of the project company	§20.6.2

(Continued)

(Continued)

Term	Definition	Refer to:
Shareholder distribution account	The project company's bank account in which funds are held prior to being paid to its shareholders as distributions	§25.2.5
Site risks	Risks related to the acquisition or condition of the project site	§12.2, §16.2.5
Site-legacy risk	The risk of pre-existing contamination on the project site	§12.2.4
Social infrastructure	Public infrastructure required to sustain society, such as schools, hospitals, government accommodation and prisons; *cf.* economic infrastructure	§2.2
Soft FM	Services connected with the facility such as cleaning, catering and security	§2.4.7, §13.6, §15.6.7, §19.4.2, §23.9.3, §28.8
Soft mini-perm	A loan whose cost increases sharply after a period of several years from completion of the facility, usually accompanied by a cash sweep from that time, to encourage a refinancing; *cf.* hard mini-perm, mini-perm	§23.2.7-§23.2.8
Spens clause	The British term for a make-whole clause	§24.2.12
Sponsors	The investors that bid for, develop and lead the project through their participation in a consortium and subsequent investment in the project company	§2.3, §10.6.1, §20.2.1
SPV	Special-purpose vehicle, a legal entity with no activity other than those connected with its borrowing; *cf.* project company	§2.3, §20.6.1, §21.4
Stapled debt	A debt instrument with guaranteed and unguaranteed components that cannot be split and sold off separately	§18.9
State Aid	A public subsidy in any form that is considered to distort competition as it affects trade between EU member states and thus is incompatible with the internal market under EU rules	§18.13

(*Continued*)

(Continued)

Term	Definition	Refer to:
Step-in rights	• The right, under the direct agreement (*q.v.*) with the contracting authority, for the lenders to take over management of the project company to protect their security; • Rights that both the lenders and the contracting authority have to take over subcontracts *cf.* emergency step-in, substitution	§25.3.3 §17.6.1
STPR	Social time preference rate, the rate that consumers expect to receive for foregoing present consumption in favour of future consumption, which may be used as the PSDR	§8.6.2
Subcontract	A contract between the project company and a third party, providing for performance of part of project company's obligations under the PPP contract; *cf.* construction subcontract; FM subcontracts; O&M subcontract	§2.4.5-§2.4.7
Subcontractor	The party signing a subcontract with the project company	§2.4
Subordinated debt	Debt provided by investors whose debt service is paid after amounts due to senior lenders or on mezzanine debt, but before payment of dividends	§2.4.5, §20.3.5, §23.6.4
Subrogation	Right of an insurer or guarantor to take over an asset on which an insurance claim or guarantee has been paid	§14.6, §14.7
Sub-sovereign risk	Risk specific to a contracting authority other than the central government	§13.4
Substitution	The right, under the direct agreement with the contracting authority, for the lenders to substitute a new entity to take over the project company's rights and obligations under the PPP contract	§17.2.5, §25.3.3
Sunset date	A point where completion of the facility has been delayed so long that the contracting authority has the right to terminate the PPP contract (normally also the date when LDs from the construction subcontractor run out); *cf.* backstop date	§15.4.3

(Continued)

Term	Definition	Refer to:
Swap provider	A bank providing an interest-rate or inflation swap to the project company	§24.2.2–§24.2.4, §25.5.1
Syndication	The process by which the lead arrangers reduce their underwriting by placing part of the loan with other banks	§22.2.9
Tail	The period between the scheduled final repayment of the debt and the end of the PPP contract	§23.2.4, §23.2.8, §23.3.4, §26.2
Target repayments	A flexible repayment structure to allow for temporary cash-flow deficiencies	§23.2.5
Tariff	Payments under a PPA, or similar contract, consisting of an availability charge and a usage charge; *cf.* service fee	§2.4.3
Technical adviser	The lenders' technical adviser	§22.2.7, §25.2.1
Temporary *force majeure*	*See* relief event; *cf.* permanent *force majeure*	
Tenor	Duration of a loan or a contract	
Term sheet	Heads of terms for the senior debt	§22.2.8
Termination sum	The compensation payable by the contracting authority on early termination of the PPP contract	§17.2–§17.5
Third-party liability insurance	Insurance against damage or injury caused to third parties by construction or operation of the facility	§14.3, §14.4, §14.8, §14.6, §16.2.5
Third-party revenues	The ability for the project company to generate revenues other than those from users or the authority	§15.8, §28.9.6
Tolls	User charges payable on a toll-road concession	§2.4.1
Tripartite deed	*See* direct agreement	
Turnkey contract	A contract with single-point responsibility for design, engineering, procurement of any equipment, and construction	§2.4.5, §12.3.1, §28.6.1, §28.9.3
Unavailability	A period when the facility is not available; *cf.* availability	§13.6

(Continued)

(Continued)

Term	Definition	Refer to:
Unitary charge	A term for service fees under an availability PPP contract	§2.4.7, §15.6.5
Unitary payment	*See* Unitary Charge	
Unwind cost	*See* breakage cost	
Usage charge	The variable-charge element of a tariff, payable when a process plant is used, *e.g.* for power generation, intended to cover costs that vary with usage such as fuel; not normally a separate element in service fees; *cf.* availability charge, unitary charge	§2.4.3
User charge	A term for service fees under a concession; *cf.* tariff, tolls	§2.4.1
USP	Unsolicited proposals for a PPP project made without any initial bid request from the contracting authority	§10.7.5
Value testing	A regular review and testing or adjusting of the costs of the soft FM services in line with current market costs involving benchmarking or market-testing	§15.6.7, §19.4.2, §24.3.12
Variable charge	*See* usage charge	
Variable costs	The project company's costs subject to inflation (primarily opex); *cf.* fixed costs	§24.3
Variation bonds	Additional bonds which can be issued after financial close, to finance future capex, subject to certain conditions	§22.5, §16.2.1
VAT	Value-added tax	§23.9.2
Verifier	*See* independent checker	
VfM	Value for money, the combination of risk transfer, whole-life cost and quality of service provided by the project and/or procurement approach, as a basis for deciding what offers the best value to the contracting authority and/or taxpayer	Chapter 8, §28.6
vpd	Vehicles per day	§15.5, §15.5.4

(Continued)

(Continued)

Term	Definition	Refer to:
WACC	Weighted average cost of capital, the weighted average of the costs of a company's equity and debt financing	§20.3.1
Warranty period	The period after the service availability date during which the construction subcontractor continues to be liable for defects in construction	§2.4.7, §12.4.3
Waterfall	*See* cascade	
Willingness to pay	The willingness of users of a concession to pay the user charges or tolls required by the concessionaire; *cf.* affordability	§7.4.1, §9.2.3, §15.5, §23.9.5
Windfall gains	Politically-sensitive profits made by investors in PPPs from high returns on investment, debt refinancing or sale of their investment	Chapter 26, §28.13
Winner's curse	The winning bidder taking too optimistic a view of traffic or other demand risks for a concession	§13.2
Withholding tax	Taxes deducted before paying interest or dividends to overseas investors or lenders	§20.6.1, §23.4.2
Working capital	The amount of funding required for operating and financing costs incurred before receipt of revenues	§23.9.2
Works concession	The term used in EU law for a concession	§2.4.2
Wrapped bonds	Bonds guaranteed by a monoline-insurance company	§18.11, §22.4.4
WTO	World Trade Organisation	§10.5

Index

Note: Page numbers followed by "*f*" and "*t*" refer to figures and tables, respectively.

Printed in the United States
By Bookmasters